The Literature of PROPAGANDA

VOLUME 3

The Literature of PROPAGANDA

EFFECTS

THOMAS RIGGS, *editor*

ST. JAMES PRESS
A part of Gale, Cengage Learning

GALE
CENGAGE Learning®

Detroit • New York • San Francisco • New Haven, Conn • Waterville, Maine • London

GALE
CENGAGE Learning®

The Literature of Propaganda
Thomas Riggs, Editor
Michelle Lee, Project Editor

Artwork and photographs for *The Literature of Propaganda* covers were reproduced with the following kind permission.

Volume 1
For foreground "We Can Do It!" World War II poster, c. 1942. © MPVHistory/Alamy.

For background photograph of women working in Douglas aircraft assembly plant during WWII. © Bettmann/CORBIS.

Volume 2
For foreground illustration of a page from a Nazi schoolbook, c. 1935. © INTERFOTO/Alamy.

For background photograph of soldiers at a Nazi Party rally in Nuremberg, Germany, 1936. © Bettmann/CORBIS.

Volume 3
For foreground poster featuring Cuban communist heroes including Fidel Castro and Che Guevara. Cuba, 1969 (colour litho), Martinez, Raul (1927–95)/Private Collection/Peter Newark American Pictures/The Bridgeman Art Library/Used with permission by Xin Dong Cheng/Beijing, China/Xin Dong Cheng Space for Contemporary Art.

For background photograph of Cuban rebel soldiers posing with guns in Havana, Cuba, 1959. © Lester Cole/CORBIS.

For product information and technology assistance, contact us at
Gale Customer Support, 1-800-877-4253.
For permission to use material from this text or product,
submit all requests online at **www.cengage.com/permissions.**
Further permissions questions can be emailed to
permissionrequest@cengage.com

While every effort has been made to ensure the reliability of the information presented in this publication, Gale, a part of Cengage Learning, does not guarantee the accuracy of the data contained herein. Gale accepts no payment for listing; and inclusion in the publication of any organization, agency, institution, publication, service, or individual does not imply endorsement of the editors or publisher. Errors brought to the attention of the publisher and verified to the satisfaction of the publisher will be corrected in future editions.

LIBRARY OF CONGRESS CATALOGING-IN-PUBLICATION DATA

The literature of propaganda / Thomas Riggs, editor.
    volumes cm
  Summary: Contains 300 entries that explore literary works that deal with propaganda. The set includes a wide variety of genres and has an international scope. It explores the works of authors shaped by a variety of political, social, and economic movements, and places each work in its historical context. Each entry includes an overview of the work, historical context, primary themes and style, and critical discussion -- Provided by publisher.
  Includes bibliographical references and index.
  ISBN 978-1-55862-858-8 (set) -- ISBN 978-1-55862-859-5 (vol. 1) -- ISBN 978-1-55862-860-1 (vol. 2) -- ISBN 978-1-55862-861-8 (vol. 3) -- ISBN 978-1-5586-2878-6 (e-book) -- ISBN 1-5586-2878-9 (e-book)
  1. Literature in propaganda. 2. Persuasion (Psychology) in literature.
3. Persuasion (Rhetoric) in literature. 4. Authors--Political and social views.
I. Riggs, Thomas, 1963- editor.
  PN51.L5744 2013
  809'.93358--dc23
                                                                    2013001494

Gale
27500 Drake Rd.
Farmington Hills, MI, 48331-3535

ISBN-13: 978-1-55862-858-8 (set)   ISBN-10: 1-55862-858-4 (set)
ISBN-13: 978-1-55862-859-5 (vol. 1)   ISBN-10: 1-55862-859-2 (vol. 1)
ISBN-13: 978-1-55862-860-1 (vol. 2)   ISBN-10: 1-55862-860-6 (vol. 2)
ISBN-13: 978-1-55862-861-8 (vol. 3)   ISBN-10: 1-55862-861-4 (vol. 3)

This title will also be available as an e-book.
ISBN-13: 978-1-55862-878-6 ISBN-10: 1-55862-878-9
Contact your Gale, a part of Cengage Learning, sales representative for ordering information.

Printed in the United States of America
1 2 3 4 5 6 7 17 16 15 14 13

 # ADVISORY BOARD

CHAIR

Russ Castronovo
Dorothy Draheim Professor of English and American Studies, University of Wisconsin-Madison. Author of *Beautiful Democracy: Aesthetics and Anarchy in a Global Era* (2007); *Necro Citizenship: Death, Eroticism, and the Public Sphere in the Nineteenth-Century United States* (2001); and *Fathering the Nation: American Genealogies of Slavery and Freedom* (1995). Coeditor, with Jonathan Auerbach, of *The Oxford Handbook of Propaganda Studies* (forthcoming).

ADVISORS

Laura R. Braunstein
Librarian, English Language and Literature, Dartmouth College, Hanover, New Hampshire.

Maria Teresa Micaela Prendergast
Associate Professor of English, College of Wooster, Wooster, Ohio. Author of *Railing, Reviling and Invective in Early Modern Literary Culture, 1588–1617* (2012); and *Renaissance Fantasies: The Gendering of Aesthetics in Early Modern Fiction* (2000). Coauthor, with Thomas Prendergast, of "The Invention of Propaganda: A Translation and Critical Commentary of *Inscrutabili Divinae*," in *The Oxford Handbook of Propaganda Studies,* edited by Jonathan Auerbach and Russ Castronovo (forthcoming).

Thomas Prendergast
Associate Professor of English and Department Chair, College of Wooster, Wooster, Ohio. Author of *Chaucer's Dead Body: From Corpse to Corpus* (2004). Coauthor, with Maria Teresa Micaela Prendergast, of "The Invention of Propaganda: a Translation and Critical Commentary of *Inscrutabili Divinae*," in *The Oxford Handbook of Propaganda Studies*, edited by Jonathan Auerbach and Russ Castronovo (forthcoming). Coeditor, with Barbara Kline, of *Rewriting Chaucer: Culture, Authority and the Idea of the Authentic Text, 1400–1602* (1999).

Harilaos Stecopoulos
Associate Professor of English, University of Iowa, Iowa City. Author of *Reconstructing the World: Southern Fictions and U.S. Imperialisms, 1898–1976* (2008). Coeditor, with Michael Uebel, of *Race and the Subject of Masculinities* (1997).

Matthew Stratton
Assistant Professor of English, University of California, Davis. Author of *The Politics of Irony in American Modernism* (forthcoming) and articles on topics ranging from propaganda to capital punishment in literature and popular culture.

Mark Wollaeger
Professor of English, Vanderbilt University, Nashville, Tennessee. Author of *Modernism, Media, and Propaganda: British Narrative from 1900 to 1945* (2006); and *Joseph Conrad and the Fictions of Skepticism* (1990). Editor of *The Oxford Handbook of Global Modernisms* (2012); and *James Joyce's A Portrait of the Artist as a Young Man: A Casebook* (2003). Coeditor, with Victor Luftig and Robert Spoo, of *Joyce and the Subject of History* (1996).

EDITORIAL AND PRODUCTION STAFF

TABLE OF CONTENTS

INTRODUCTION

If in the beginning was the Word, propaganda soon followed. The relationship between discourse and persuasion is intimate and almost always troubling. Our modern notion of propaganda is suffused by pejorative connotations involving falsification and manipulation. The term is often used to discount opponents' views or to invalidate a contrasting perspective. This book encourages an understanding that is at once neutral and explanatory, one that seeks to define propaganda as neither good nor bad and instead promotes a definition that is more pragmatic: Propaganda is publicly disseminated information intended to influence others in belief, action, or both. A reconsideration of the subject in this light can produce corresponding changes in our understandings of literature.

The proper use of rhetoric—oral and written communication or persuasion—was a hotly debated issue in ancient Greece, as any of Plato's interlocutors or Aristotle's students knew. Across the centuries the debate has only intensified. The word "propaganda" first appeared in modern languages as part of Pope Gregory XV's establishment of the Sacra Congregatio de Propaganda Fide (Sacred Congregation for Propagating the Faith) in 1622. The mission of this body was to spread what the Catholic Church considered to be the one true faith during the crisis of the Counter Reformation. The next notable use of the term is associated with the cataclysmic upheavals of the French Revolution. From the perspective of alarmists in England, the revolutionaries in Paris had organized various institutions of propaganda to spread their radical creed across Europe.

Our negative understanding of propaganda emerged during World War I, when the Allies waged an information war accusing Germany of spreading atrocity stories and distorting events; Germany similarly denounced the Allies. Wartime governments also directed biased media persuasion at their own populations in order to mobilize support for the war. Some sixty years earlier, when Harriet Beecher Stowe penned the best-selling novel of the nineteenth century, *Uncle Tom's Cabin* (1852), she did not see herself as peddling false or deceptive information; her aim was to educate readers about the fundamental humanity of the so-called "merchandise" that was legally sold in the antebellum United States. Jumping forward a century and a half, in 2010 Julian Assange uploaded "The WikiLeaks Manifesto" in an equally daring endeavor: to challenge the monopoly on information held by corporations and governments. The German cultural critic Siegfried Kracauer asks in his 1960 book *Theory of Film,* "Is not truth the best propaganda weapon?"[1] Like many of the authors discussed in the following pages, Pope Gregory, Stowe, and Assange would have agreed, approving the spread and circulation of information as both enlightening and persuasive.

From ancient Greek times to the present, propaganda has served many different masters, has appeared across many media, from engraving to film, and has been variously condemned and appreciated. Written propaganda can be sorted according to three overlapping functions. It can be literature that (1) attempts to persuade, manipulate, or even deceive; (2) depicts the use of propaganda and its impact upon people and the society that they inhabit; (3) theorizes about propaganda, examining its techniques and psychological mechanisms, its media, and its modes of dissemination and circulation.

Rarely does a work of literature satisfy only one of these conditions. More often, it bleeds across categories. In a radio address in spring 1941, George Orwell took stock of World War I, the Russian Revolution, and the advance of Hitler and Nazi Germany across Europe. In conclusion, he contended that "propaganda in some form or other lurks in every book."[2] From this perspective, all texts are susceptible to propaganda. Authors often inveigh against propaganda while employing it themselves. Consider Upton Sinclair's muckraking novel of the meatpacking industry, *The Jungle* (1906), which exposes the emptiness of capitalist propaganda by delivering impassioned sermons about the Christian virtues of socialism. Try to determine whether Langston Hughes's six-line poem "Johannesburg Mines" (1928) is an example of or a critique of propaganda. Observe the ways in which Edward Bernays's seemingly definitive book *Propaganda* (1928), while explaining modern techniques of advertising and mass persuasion, becomes a public relations pitch for ad men and other spin artists. These examples support Orwell's conclusion that "literature has been swamped by propaganda."[3]

The ubiquity of propaganda is neither cause for despair nor a reason to give up on literature. In fact, Orwell construed its prevalence as an urgent reminder that "every work of art has a meaning and purpose—a political, social and religious purpose."[4] The surest sign that art is intended to engage the world in these ways is that it seeks to affect our beliefs, attitudes, and actions. Writers labor over manuscripts in the hopes of intervening in the course of human events, whether through straightforward confrontation, by means of gripping or gentle narrative, or in a more elliptical fashion that employs irony, satire, and other tactics. And writing does engage: readers pore over books, debating meanings and wresting interpretations to support their individual view of the work and its applications to life. Looking at literature through the lens of propaganda reminds us that it is not produced simply for its own sake but rather to change history and how people understand it.

An overview of the table of contents for this book reveals that authors have combined imagination, outrage, accusation, and wit with any number of goals: abolishing slavery; reforming slum conditions; creating scapegoats and targeting internal enemies; rallying support for war; fomenting revolution; and many more. Unquestionably, utopian optimism and commitment, cynicism and hatred have been poured into such efforts. What remains debatable, however, is the effectiveness of these appeals. Can a discrete set of social events ever be tied to a specific work of literature? This incalculability generates further questions about propaganda's possibilities of success. Does it risk galvanizing opponents even as it seeks to encourage the most ardent supporters? When it focuses on a specific social ill—for example, squalid tenements and unsafe factory conditions in the early twentieth century—does it miss the need for more thoroughgoing, systemic reform? Why do its utopian dimensions so often seem destined for failure? The huge range of literature examined in these volumes—from the rhetoric of the classical world to the digital spread of information in the twenty-first century—provides readers with plenty of material to ponder in regard to these questions. It also generates new lines of debate and inquiry.

The Literature of Propaganda's three-part structure affords multiple lenses through which to assess plays, novels, poems, exposés, manifestoes, short stories, biographies, memoirs, and essays that circulate as or comment on propaganda and mass persuasion. Divided into Approaches (volume 1), Groups (volume 2), and Effects (volume 3), this work seeks to account for the diversity and richness, the optimism, and the terror that have resulted from efforts to create change through textual means.

Because the definitions and connotations of the term "propaganda" have shifted over time, the first volume, Approaches, registers varied understandings and uses of the concept. It sets out theories of persuasion formulated in ancient Greece, the World War I era, the postcolonial world, and postmodern society. With this foundation in place, the volume then identifies different types of propaganda, including appeals and exhortations, exposés, education and indoctrination, histories, and political declarations. The "Formal Innovations" chapter explores texts that respond to political crises and social exigencies—for example, Theodore Dwight Weld's cut-and-paste method in *American Slavery As It Is* (1839) and Art Spiegelman's illustrated panels in his graphic novel *The Complete Maus* (1991). The selections in this first volume invite readers to consider literature as variously surveying, commenting on, deploring, and utilizing propaganda. Only a fraction of the works represent "pure" propaganda (if such a category could be defined). Instead, such texts as W. E. B. Du Bois's "Criteria of Negro Art" (1926) and Theodor W. Adorno's "Freudian Theory and the Pattern of Fascist Propaganda" (1951) embody earnest attempts to unlock the mechanisms that have given misrepresentation, paranoia, and fear such a hold over modern life.

Volume 2, Groups, studies texts produced by parties and factions, dissidents and rebels, various social classes, and cultural critics. These works suggest that, whereas in its most negative incarnations, propaganda becomes weaponized speech, with its own targets and triggers, literature carries liberating potential as well. The chapter "Social Classes" explores writing that, among other things, advocates for the economically oppressed. Works ranging from Rebecca Harding Davis's "Life in the Iron Mills" (1861) to the "Preamble to the Constitution of the IWW" (1905) have been crafted to rally public opinion in support of human rights. Literature has also been used to promote group cohesion in the form of nationalism. The chapter titled "Nations" features a discussion of one of the most infamous pieces of propaganda in history, Adolf Hitler's *Mein Kampf* (1925). Invidious language that appeals to feelings of superiority or fear is often associated with xenophobic nationalism, but those seeking to redress a problem or call attention to a social movement may also draw on emotion in propagating a message. While this potential may often go unrealized, it is hard to overestimate the poignant force of such a piece (included in the chapter "Dissidents and Rebels") as Rodolfo Walsh's "Open Letter from a Writer to the Military Junta," written the day before his death at the hands of government soldiers. Including such works as Aristophanes's *Lysistrata* (411 BCE), this volume offers readers a literature that allows human actors to comment upon and intervene in political and social affairs.

Because the impact of such interventions can be difficult to gauge, the final volume, Effects, considers literary works that have been tied to legislative reform, religious conversion, changes in economic policy, and other aspects of historical significance. The chapter "Myths and Martyrs" explores the ways in which real-world results often ensue from mythic representations, such as those that render a figure such as George Washington larger than life or depict Joan of Arc as a martyr. Embellishment can play an instrumental role in making national heroes of ordinary men and women. As the chapter "Distortions and Delusions" reveals, people can eagerly gobble up these fictive portraits; we consume fanciful versions of history as readily as the characters in Aldous Huxley's *Brave New World* (1932) consume drugs to adjust to a deluded view of reality. The chapters "Dystopias and Utopias," "Legislation and Reform," "Predictions and Prescriptions," and "Suppression and Scapegoating" round out the volume. Analyzing perspectives on such reactionary texts as Ayn Rand's *Atlas Shrugged* (1957) and William Luther Pierce's *Turner Diaries* (1978) alongside those on progressive documents such as Elizabeth Cady Stanton's "Declaration of Sentiments" (1848) and Charlotte Perkins Gilman's *Herland* (1915), the chapters span the political spectrum. The settings evoked by this literature are just as diverse, ranging from the jail cell of American Indian activist Leonard Peltier evoked in his *Prison Writings: My Life Is My Sun Dance* (1999) to the repressive landscapes of Margaret Atwood's *The Handmaid's Tale* (1985) and Suzanne Collins's *The Hunger Games* (2008). The fact that Collins's novel depicting teenage gladiatorial combat, like many of the works discussed in these pages, also achieved blockbuster status as a Hollywood film evidences the popularity of the literature of propaganda and its capacity to inspire and generate other creative media projects.

Many believe that the value of literature rests on its enduring artistic merit (determined by assessing style, tone, and other formal features) rather than on its political and social impacts. By implicitly fusing it with propaganda, these volumes confirm literature not only as a zone of aesthetic contemplation but also as an impetus for action, so that our ideas about the social and political force of words are reinvigorated. The 300 individual essays that comprise *The Literature of Propaganda* add nuance and complexity to the concept of mass persuasion—through literature—that leads to action. The essays do not coalesce into a single viewpoint; there is no unity to be found among the revolutionary writings of Edmund Burke, Bertolt Brecht, and Ho Chi Minh—and the same might be said of any cohort of authors represented in the pages that follow. This diversity makes the collection, above all else, an arena for debate and continued investigation.

Russ Castronovo,
Advisory Board Chair

---

[1] Siegfried Kracauer. *Theory of Film: The Redemption of Physical Reality* (New York: Oxford University Press, 1960) 161.

[2] Orwell, George. "The Frontiers of Art and Propaganda." BBC Overseas Service. 30 Apr. 1941.

[3] Orwell 30 Apr. 1941.

[4] Orwell 30 Apr. 1941.

Editor's Note

*T*he *Literature of Propaganda,* a three-volume reference guide, provides critical introductions to 300 texts from around the world. Some of these texts function as propaganda, while others discuss propaganda or use propaganda as a theme or setting. For this guide the term propaganda is defined as information spread publicly in order to influence others in belief, action, or both, regardless of whether the intent is seen as honorable or evil-minded.

An early text covered in this guide is the *History of the Kings of Britain,* written by English bishop Geoffrey of Monmouth around 1136. Purportedly a complete history of the British monarchy, it includes inaccuracies, heroic legends presented as truth, and supernatural content. The book helped popularize King Arthur as a national hero and create a British historical and cultural identity. A much different example of propaganda discussed in the guide is the "Battle Hymn of the Republic," a pro-Union poem published during the Civil War by American abolitionist Julia Ward Howe and set to the popular tune of "John Brown's Body." A well-known propaganda text from India is *Hind Swaraj,* written in 1909 by Mohandas Gandhi, who urged his country to reject materialist Western culture in favor a homegrown, spiritually based movement and to use satyagraha, or nonviolent resistance, against British authority. Among more recent propaganda works covered in the guide is *The Coming Insurrection,* written in 2007 by the Invisible Committee, an anonymous French group, which called for an end to capitalism.

The structure and content of *The Literature of Propaganda* was planned with the help of the project's advisory board, chaired by Russ Castronovo, Dorothy Draheim Professor of English and American Studies, University of Wisconsin-Madison. His introduction to this guide provides an overview of the literature of propaganda.

ORGANIZATION

All entries share a common structure, providing consistent coverage of the works and a simple way of comparing basic elements of one text with another. Each entry has six parts: overview, historical and literary context, themes and style, critical discussion, sources, and further reading. Entries also have either an excerpt from the original text or a sidebar discussing a related topic, such as the life of the author.

The Literature of Propaganda is divided into three volumes, each with 100 entries. Volume 1, Approaches, has seven sections—appeals and exhortations, education and indoctrination, exposés, formal innovations, histories, political action, and theories. The works covered in this volume are examples of how propaganda is used. *The Feminine Mystique,* for example, an exposé published in 1963 by American feminist Betty Friedan, exposes and critiques the social pressure on women to become mothers and housewives. Volume 2, Groups, has five sections—cultural critics, dissidents and rebels, nations, parties and factions, and social classes. These entries provide examples of how propaganda works for or against groups of people. Volume 3, Effects, has six sections—distortions and delusions, dystopias and utopias, legislation and reform, myths and martyrs, predictions and prescriptions, and suppression and scapegoating. The texts covered in this volume illustrate common results of propaganda.

Among the criteria for selecting entry topics were the importance of the work in university curricula, the genre, the region and country of the author and text, and the time period. Entries can be looked up in the author and title indexes, as well as in the subject index.

ACKNOWLEDGMENTS

Many people contributed time, effort, and ideas to *The Literature of Propaganda*. At Gale, Philip Virta, manager of new products, developed the original plan for the book, and Michelle Lee, senior editor, served as the in-house manager for the project. *The Literature of Propaganda* owes its existence to their ideas and involvement.

We would like to express our appreciation to the advisors, who, in addition to creating the organization of *The Literature of Propaganda* and choosing the entry topics, identified other scholars to work on the project and answered many questions, both big and small. We would also like to thank the contributors for their accessible essays, often on difficult topics, as well as the scholars who reviewed the text for accuracy and coverage.

I am grateful to Erin Brown, senior project editor, especially for her work with the advisors and on the entry list; Greta Gard, project editor, who managed the writers; Mary Beth Curran, associate editor, who oversaw the editing process; David Hayes, associate editor, whose many contributions included organizing the workflow; and Hannah Soukup, assistant editor, who identified and corresponded with the academic reviewers. Other important assistance came from Mariko Fujinaka, managing editor; Anne Healey, senior editor; and Janet Moredock and Lee Esbenshade, associate editors. The line editors were Heather Campbell, Cheryl Collins, Tony Craine, Holli Fort, Laura Gabler, Harrabeth Haidusek, Ellen Henderson, Joan Hibler, Constance Israel, Jane Kupersmith, Dehlia McCobb, Kathy Peacock, Donna Polydoros, Natalie Ruppert, Mary Russell, Lisa Trow, Will Wagner, and Whitney Ward.

Thomas Riggs

CONTRIBUTORS

DAVID AITCHISON

Aitchison is a PhD candidate in literary studies and a university instructor.

GREG BACH

Bach holds an MA in classics and is a freelance writer.

CRAIG BARNES

Barnes holds an MFA in creative writing and has been a university instructor and a freelance writer.

MARIE BECKER

Becker holds an MA in humanities.

KAREN BENDER

Bender holds an MFA in creative writing and an MPhil in Anglo-Irish literature. She has taught high school English.

KATHERINE BISHOP

Bishop is a PhD student in English literature and has been a university instructor.

ALLISON BLECKER

Blecker is a PhD candidate in Near Eastern languages.

ELIZABETH BOEHEIM

Boeheim holds an MA in English literature and has been a university instructor.

WESLEY BORUCKI

Borucki holds a PhD in American history and is a university professor.

GERALD CARPENTER

Carpenter holds an MA in U.S. intellectual history and a PhD in early modern French history. He is a freelance writer.

ADAM CARSON

Carson is a PhD student in history and a university instructor.

MARK CASELLO

Casello is a PhD candidate in American literature and a university professor.

CURT CLONINGER

Cloninger holds an MFA in studio arts and is a university professor.

KEVIN COONEY

Cooney holds a PhD in English literature and is a university professor.

ALEX COVALCIUC

Covalciuc is a PhD candidate in English literature. He has been a university instructor and a freelance writer.

GIANO CROMLEY

Cromley holds an MFA in creative writing and is a university instructor.

COLBY CUPPERNULL

Cuppernull holds an MA in writing and has been a university instructor and a freelance writer.

ANNA DEEM

Deem holds an MA in education and is a freelance writer.

CHAD DUNDAS

Dundas holds an MFA in creative writing and has been a university instructor and a freelance writer.

RICHARD ESBENSHADE

Esbenshade holds a PhD in history and has been a university professor and a freelance writer.

TAYLOR EVANS

Evans is a PhD student in English literature and has been a university instructor.

DAISY GARD

Gard is a freelance writer with a background in English literature.

GRETA GARD

Gard is a PhD candidate in English literature and has been a university instructor and a freelance writer.

SARAH GARDAM

Gardam is a PhD candidate in English literature and has been a university instructor.

CLINT GARNER

Garner holds an MFA in creative writing and is a freelance writer.

TINA GIANOULIS

Gianoulis is a freelance writer with a background in English literature.

CYNTHIA GILES

Giles holds an MA in English literature and a PhD in interdisciplinary humanities. She has been a university instructor and a freelance writer.

QUAN MANH HA

Ha holds a PhD in American literature and is a university professor.

HARRABETH HAIDUSEK

Haidusek holds an MA in English literature and is a university instructor.

GREG HALABY

Halaby is a PhD candidate in Arabic and Islamic studies and a teaching fellow.

RODNEY HARRIS

Harris is pursuing a PhD in history and has been a university instructor.

MICHAEL HARTWELL

Hartwell holds an MFA in creative writing. He has been a university instructor and a freelance writer.

RON HORTON

Horton holds an MFA in creative writing and has been a high school English instructor and a freelance writer.

FRANKLYN HYDE

Hyde holds a PhD in English literature and is a university instructor.

LAURA JOHNSON

Johnson holds a PhD in English literature and is a university professor.

EMILY JONES

Jones holds an MFA in creative writing and has been a university instructor.

ALICIA KENT

Kent holds a PhD in English literature and is a university professor.

ROBERT KIBLER

Kibler holds a PhD in English literature and is a university professor.

DENNIS KLEIN

Klein holds a PhD in history and is a university professor.

LISA KROGER

Kroger holds a PhD in English literature and has been a university instructor.

HANA LAYSON

Layson holds a PhD in English literature and has been a university instructor and a freelance writer.

GREGORY LUTHER

Luther holds an MFA in creative writing and has been a university instructor and freelance writer.

THEODORE MCDERMOTT

McDermott holds an MFA in creative writing and has been a university instructor and a freelance writer.

MAGGIE MAGNO

Magno has an MA in education. She has been a high school English teacher and a freelance writer.

PHILLIP MAHONEY

Mahoney is a PhD candidate in English literature and has been a university instructor.

ABIGAIL MANN

Mann holds a PhD in English literature and is a university professor.

RACHEL MINDELL

Mindell holds an MFA in creative writing and has been a freelance writer.

JIM MLADENOVIC

Mladenovic holds an MS in clinical psychology and is pursuing an MA in library science.

KATHRYN MOLINARO

Molinaro holds an MA in English literature and has been a university instructor and a freelance writer.

CAITIE MOORE

Moore holds an MFA in creative writing and has been a university instructor.

JANET MOREDOCK

Moredock is an editor and has been a university instructor and a freelance writer.

ROBIN MORRIS

Morris holds a PhD in English literature and has been a university instructor.

AARON MOULTON

Moulton holds an MA in Latin American studies. He is a PhD candidate in history and a university instructor.

JANET MULLANE

Mullane is a freelance writer and has been a high school English teacher.

ELLIOTT NIBLOCK

Niblock holds an MTS in the philosophy of religion.

ELIZABETH ORVIS

Orvis is a freelance writer with a background in English literature.

JAMES OVERHOLTZER

Overholtzer holds an MA in English literature and has been a university instructor.

MARC OXOBY

Oxoby holds a PhD in English literature and has been a university instructor.

MEGAN PEABODY

Peabody is a PhD candidate in English literature and a university instructor.

EVELYN REYNOLDS

Reynolds is pursuing an MA in English literature and an MFA in creative writing and has been a freelance writer.

CHRIS ROUTLEDGE

Routledge holds a PhD in English literature and is a university lecturer and a freelance writer.

REBECCA RUSTIN

Rustin holds an MA in English literature and is a freelance writer.

CATHERINE E. SAUNDERS

Saunders holds a PhD in English literature and is a university professor.

CARINA SAXON

Saxon is a PhD candidate in English literature and has been a university instructor and a freelance editor.

JACOB SCHMITT

Schmitt holds an MA in English literature and has been a freelance writer.

GINA SHERRIFF

Sherriff holds a PhD in Spanish and is a university professor.

KIRKLEY SILVERMAN

Silverman is pursuing her PhD in English literature and has been a university instructor.

NANCY SIMPSON-YOUNGER

Simpson-Younger is a PhD candidate in literary studies and a university instructor.

CLAIRE SKINNER

Skinner holds an MFA in creative writing and is a university instructor.

ROGER SMITH

Smith holds an MA in media ecology and has been a university instructor and a freelance writer.

HANNAH SOUKUP

Soukup holds an MFA in creative writing.

NICHOLAS SNEAD

Snead is a PhD candidate in French language and literature and has been a university instructor.

SCOTT STABLER

Stabler holds a PhD in history and is a university professor.

SARAH STOECKL

Stoeckl holds a PhD in English literature and is a university instructor and a freelance writer.

SARA TAYLOR

Taylor holds an MA in theater history, theory, and literature and is pursuing her PhD in the same field.

PAMELA TOLER

Toler has a PhD in history and is a freelance writer and former university instructor.

ELIZABETH VITANZA

Vitanza holds a PhD in French and Francophone studies and has been a university and a high school instructor.

JOHN WALTERS

Walters is pursuing a PhD in English literature and has been a university instructor.

KATRINA WHITE

White is a PhD candidate in Spanish language and literature and a university instructor.

ACADEMIC REVIEWERS

RAJA ADAL

*Assistant Professor of History, University
of Cincinnati, Ohio.*

KHALED AL-MASRI

*Assistant Professor of Arabic,
Swarthmore College, Pennsylvania.*

JOHN ALVIS

*Professor of English and Director,
American Studies Program,
University of Dallas, Irving, Texas.*

ARLENE AVAKIAN

*Emeritus Professor and former
Department Chair of Women,
Gender, Sexuality Studies, University
of Massachusetts-Amherst.*

ROBERT BANNISTER

*Professor Emeritus of History,
Swarthmore College, Pennsylvania.*

IAN BARNARD

*Associate Professor of English, California
State University-Northridge.*

CONSTANTIN BEHLER

*Associate Professor of German Studies,
University of Washington, Bothell.*

STEPHEN BEHRENDT

*George Holmes Distinguished Professor
of English, University of Nebraska,
Lincoln.*

WILLIAM BELDING

*Professorial Lecturer, School of
International Service, American
University, Washington, D.C.*

DORON BEN-ATAR

*Professor of History, Fordham
University, New York.*

JILL BERGMAN

*Professor of English and Chair,
Department of English, University of
Montana, Missoula, Montana.*

STEPHEN BLACKWELL

*Professor of Russian, University of
Tennessee, Knoxville.*

FLORENCE BOOS

*Professor of English, University of Iowa,
Iowa City.*

MOULAY-ALI BOUÂNANI

*Professor of Africana Studies,
Binghamton University, Vestal,
New York.*

MICHAEL BREEN

*Associate Professor of History and
Humanities, Reed College, Portland,
Oregon.*

PAUL BRIANS

*Professor Emeritus of English,
Washington State University,
Pullman.*

STEPHEN BRONNER

*Distinguished Professor of Political
Science, Rutgers University, New
Brunswick, New Jersey.*

JAMES BROWN

*Assistant Professor of English, University
of Wisconsin-Madison.*

ALISON BRUEY

*Assistant Professor of History, University
of North Florida, Jacksonville.*

PETER BUTTON

*Assistant Professor of East Asian Studies,
New York University.*

VERA CAMDEN

*Professor of English, Kent State
University, Ohio; Clinical Assistant
Professor of Psychiatry, Case Western
Reserve University, Cleveland, Ohio;
Clinical Professor of Social Work,
Rutgers University, New Brunswick,
New Jersey.*

RUSS CASTRONOVO

*Dorothy Draheim Professor of English
and American Studies, University of
Wisconsin-Madison.*

SARAH E. CHINN

*Associate Professor of English, Hunter
College, New York.*

ANN CIASULLO

*Assistant Professor of English and
Women's and Gender Studies, Gonzaga
University, Spokane, Washington.*

PAULA CIZMAR

*Adjunct Assistant Professor of
Playwriting, University of Southern
California, Los Angeles.*

NATHAN CLARKE

*Assistant Professor of History, Minnesota
State University-Moorhead.*

WILLIAM CLEMENTE

*Professor of Literature, Peru State
College, Nebraska.*

MARC CONNER

*Jo M. and James Ballengee Professor
of English, Washington and Lee
University, Lexington, Virginia.*

JANE CRAWFORD

*Faculty, History and Political Science
Department, Mount St. Mary's
College, Los Angeles, California.*

LAWRENCE J. CUSHNIE

PhD candidate in Political Science, University of Washington, Seattle.

JOHN T. DALTON

Assistant Professor of Economics, Wake Forest University, Winston-Salem, North Carolina.

ALISTAIR DAVIES

Senior Lecturer in English, University of Sussex, Brighton, United Kingdom.

KIRK DENTON

Professor of East Asian Languages and Literatures, Ohio State University, Columbus.

MUSTAFAH DHADA

Professor of African, Middle Eastern, and World History, California State University-Bakersfield.

GABRIELE DILLMANN

Associate Professor of German, Denison University, Granville, Ohio.

JANE DOWSON

Reader in Twentieth-Century Literature, De Montfort University, Leicester, United Kingdom.

JEANNE DUBINO

Professor of English and Global Studies, Global Studies Faculty Member, Appalachian State University, Boone, North Carolina.

JILLIAN DUQUAINE-WATSON

Senior Lecturer I, School of Interdisciplinary Studies, University of Texas-Dallas.

ELIZABETH DUQUETTE

Associate Professor of English, Gettysburg College, Pennsylvania.

MICHAEL J. DUVALL

Associate Professor of English, College of Charleston, South Carolina.

TAYLOR EASUM

Assistant Professor of Global Histories, Faculty Fellow of Draper Program, New York University.

SIÂN ECHARD

Professor of English, University of British Columbia, Vancouver.

JAMES ENGLISH

John Welsh Centennial Professor of English, Director of the Penn Humanities Forum, University of Pennsylvania, Philadelphia.

MICHAEL FALETRA

Associate Professor of English and Humanities, Reed College, Portland, Oregon.

DANINE FARQUHARSON

Associate Professor of English, Memorial University of Newfoundland, St. John's.

CHARLES FORD

Professor of History and Chair, History Department, Norfolk State University, Virginia.

LUANNE FRANK

Associate Professor of English, University of Texas-Arlington.

JOANNE E. GATES

Professor of English, Jacksonville State University, Alabama.

JAMES GIGANTINO

Assistant Professor of History, University of Arkansas, Fayetteville.

ROBERT W. GLOVER

CLAS Honors Preceptor of Political Science, University of Maine, Orono.

SHARON GORMAN

Walton Professor of Music, University of the Ozarks, Clarksville, Arkansas.

QUAN MANH HA

Assistant Professor of American Literature and Ethnic Studies, University of Montana, Missoula.

RAFEY HABIB

Professor of English, Rutgers University, New Brunswick, New Jersey.

ANDREW HALEY

Associate Professor of American Cultural History, University of Southern Mississippi, Hattiesburg.

EIRIK LANG HARRIS

Assistant Professor of Philosophy, City University of Hong Kong, Kowloon.

BRUCE HARVEY

Associate Professor of English, Associate Director of SEAS, and Director of Liberal Studies, Florida International University, Miami.

ROBERT HEGEL

Professor of Chinese and Comparative Literature, Washington University, St. Louis, Missouri.

MARGUERITE HELMERS

Professor of English, University of Wisconsin-Oshkosh.

RICHARD HIGGINS

Lecturer of English, Franklin College, Indiana.

WALTER HÖLBLING

Professor of American Studies, Karl-Franzens-Universität, Graz, Austria.

PIPPA HOLLOWAY

Professor of History and Program Director, Graduate Studies, Middle Tennessee State University, Murfreesboro.

TED HUMPHREY

President's Professor, Barrett Professor, Lincoln Professor of Ethics and Latin American Intellectual History, and Professor of Philosophy at the School of Historical, Philosophical and Religious Studies, Arizona State University, Tempe.

FRANKLYN HYDE

Adjunct Professor of English, University of Manitoba, Winnipeg.

WILLIAM IRWIN

Professor of Philosophy, Kings College, Wilkes-Barre, Pennsylvania.

STEVEN JACOBS

Associate Professor of Religious Studies and Aaron Aronov Endowed Chair in Judaic Studies, University of Alabama, Tuscaloosa.

JAKE JAKAITIS

Associate Professor of English and Director, Undergraduate Studies in English, Indiana State University, Terre Haute.

JENNIFER JAY

Professor of History and Chinese, University of Alberta, Edmonton.

KELLY JEONG

Assistant Professor of Comparative Literature and of Korean Studies, University of California, Riverside.

JAMES JONES

Professor of History, West Chester University, Pennsylvania.

ISAAC KAMOLA

American Council for Learned Societies (ACLS) New Faculty Fellow, Department of Political Science, Johns Hopkins University, Baltimore, Maryland.

AHMED KANNA

Assistant Professor of Anthropology, University of the Pacific, Stockton, California.

WARD KEELER

Associate Professor of Anthropology, University of Texas-Austin.

STEVEN G. KELLMAN

Professor of Comparative Literature, University of Texas-San Antonio.

DAVID KENLEY

Associate Professor of History, Elizabethtown College, Pennsylvania.

ALICIA A. KENT

Associate Professor of English, University of Michigan-Flint.

ROBERT KIBLER

Professor of English Literature and Humanities, as well as Coordinator, English Program, Minot State University, North Dakota.

RICHARD KING

Professor of Chinese Studies, University of Victoria, British Columbia.

HIROSHI KITAMURA

Associate Professor of History, College of William and Mary, Williamsburg, Virginia.

CHRISTOPHER KNIGHT

Professor of English, University of Montana, Missoula.

KRISTIN KOPTIUCH

Associate Professor of Anthropology, Arizona State University at the West campus, Phoenix.

JOSÉ LANTERS

Professor of English, University of Wisconsin-Milwaukee.

MURRAY LEAF

Professor of Anthropology and Political Economy, University of Texas-Dallas.

MARY LEDERER

Independent Scholar of African Literature, Botswana.

MICHAEL LEVY

Professor of English, University of Wisconsin-Stout, Menomonie.

HUA LI

Assistant Professor of Chinese, Coordinator of Chinese, Montana State University, Bozeman.

GRANT LILFORD

Lecturer in English, University of Zululand, South Africa.

RUTH LOOPER

Professor of English, Dean of the Division of Humanities, Young Harris College, Georgia.

DAVID MCCANN

Korea Foundation Professor of Korean Literature, Harvard University-Korea Institute, Cambridge, Massachusetts.

DEREK MAUS

Associate Professor of English and Communication, State University of New York-Potsdam.

RICHARD J. MOLL

Associate Professor of English Literature, University of Western Ontario, London, Canada.

JOHN MORILLO

Associate Professor of English Literature, North Carolina State University, Raleigh.

MICHAEL MUNGER

Professor of Political Science, Economics, and Public Policy, as well as Director, PPE Program, Duke University, Durham, North Carolina.

BRIAN MURDOCH

Professor Emeritus of Languages, Cultures, and Religions, University of Stirling, Scotland, United Kingdom.

SARA MURPHY

Clinical Assistant Professor, New York University-Gallatin.

EVAN MWANGI

Associate Professor of English, Northwestern University, Evanston, Illinois.

MICHAEL NIMAN

Professor of Journalism and Media Studies, SUNY Buffalo State, New York.

STACEY OLSTER

Professor of English, Stony Brook University, New York.

FEMI OSOFISAN

Professor of Drama, University of Ibadan, Nigeria.

ANDREW PARKER

Professor of French and Comparative Literature, Rutgers University, New Brunswick, New Jersey.

MICHEL PHARAND

Director, Disraeli Project, Queen's University, Kingston, Ontario.

ADAM PIETTE

Professor of English Literature, University of Sheffield, United Kingdom.

ELIZABETH PIKE

Undergraduate Advisor and Instructor, Department of Geography, University of Colorado-Boulder.

MARIA POLSKI

Associate Professor of English and Communications, East-West University, Chicago, Illinois.

JANET POWERS

Professor Emerita of Interdisciplinary Studies and Women, Gender, and Sexuality Studies, Gettysburg College, Pennsylvania.

H. L. T. QUAN

Assistant Professor of Justice and Social Inquiry, Arizona State University, Tempe.

PATRICK QUINN

Professor of English Literature, Chapman University, Orange, California.

KENNETH REEDS

Assistant Professor of Spanish, Salem State University, Massachusetts.

PATRICIO RIZZO-VAST

Instructor of Spanish and Portuguese, Northeastern Illinois University, Chicago.

PHILLIP ROTHWELL

Professor of Portuguese, Rutgers University, New Brunswick, New Jersey.

ELI RUBIN

Associate Professor of History, Western Michigan University, Kalamazoo.

ELIZABETH RUSS

Associate Professor of Spanish, Southern Methodist University, Dallas, Texas.

DISTORTIONS AND DELUSIONS

AMERICAN HERO

Larry Beinhart

OVERVIEW

Larry Beinhart's 1993 novel, *American Hero,* accuses George H. W. Bush and his administration of orchestrating the six-week Persian Gulf War in early 1991—with the help of Hollywood—to guarantee Bush's reelection in 1992. Using the format of the detective novel, *American Hero* gives an imagined account of the war's development, beginning with a fictional note from dying Republican strongman Lee Atwater to President Bush suggesting that he employ Hollywood production crews instead of news crews to cover the impending war. The narrative ends with the hiring of a big-shot movie director to carry out the scheme. Not purely an attack on U.S. executive policy, the novel devotes as much time to exposing the corruption of Hollywood as it does to hypothesizing about governmental manipulation of both the media and the public in the name of security. Beinhart incorporates exhaustive footnotes that detail real-world collusions between government and media, building a compelling case that even if Hollywood did not literally script the Gulf War, the Bush administration certainly applied Hollywood conventions in selling the war to the public.

Voicing the doubts and theories of an increasingly skeptical public, Beinhart capitalized on the controversy surrounding both the timing of the war (coinciding with the launch of Bush's reelection campaign) and the unprecedented level of media coverage of the events in the Gulf War. Initial reviews of the work were generally positive. Critics already knew that Beinhart's prose styling was first rate, since his 1986 work of detective fiction *No One Rides for Free* had won an Edgar Award for Best First Novel, and the new book impressed them with its effective tactic of integrating fact within a fictional framework. The book inspired the Barry Levinson film *Wag the Dog* (1997) but then fell off the public radar for nearly a decade. It was rereleased as *Wag the Dog: A Novel* in 2004, just one year after the United States had declared war on Iraq during the presidency of George H. W. Bush's son, George W. Bush.

HISTORICAL AND LITERARY CONTEXT

The Persian Gulf War, waged in response to Iraq's invasion of neighboring Kuwait, lasted from January 17 to February 28, 1991. The conflict was unprecedented both in its tactics and in its treatment in the media. Technological advances allowed the military to rely on clandestine electronic intelligence instead of ground observations by human scouts. This capability contributed to an unfamiliar type of impersonal, detached warfare, which was augmented by extensive television, newspaper, Internet, and radio coverage of the major missile offensives and bombing campaigns that ultimately suppressed Iraqi forces. The coverage was restricted, however, by the conditions laid out in a secret Pentagon policy memo titled "Annex Foxtrot," which named specific journalists who would be allowed to report in the Middle East, limited their access in the field, and granted military officials the right to censor materials before public release. As a result, the American public often saw only its troops' most positive, triumphant moments during the conflict. If the closely regulated, real-time broadcasting of combat were not pageant enough, Super Bowl XXV, which aired on January 27, 1991, at the height of the war, featured extravagantly patriotic pregame and halftime shows, including a rendition of "The Star Spangled Banner" by Whitney Houston while fighter jets flew overhead.

When Beinhart was writing the book in 1992, an MTV series called *The Real World* was popularizing a new television genre—reality TV—which claimed to document the daily lives of average citizens. Within the show's first year, however, journalistic exposés had revealed that it was, at least to a certain extent, scripted. In *American Hero* Beinhart combines the new genre's sense of scripted reality with the spin and spectacle of the Gulf War to imagine a scenario in which a president invents reasons to pursue a conflict in an attempt to bolster his popularity ratings. Although Bush lost the election to Bill Clinton a year before the book's release, it raised interesting questions about mass media's new and ever-growing roles in the American political landscape.

Beinhart was not the first to raise such questions about the Gulf War. French philosopher and cultural theorist Jean Baudrillard wrote a series of three essays before, during, and after the war for the Paris newspaper *Libération* questioning both whether the media spectacle surrounding the conflict was accurate and whether the events could even be called a war: "The Gulf War Will Not Take Place" (Jan. 4, 1991); "The Gulf War: Is It Really Taking Place?"

❖ *Key Facts*

Time Period:
Late 20th Century

Genre:
Novel

Events:
Persian Gulf War; popularization of reality television

Nationality:
American

LOST IN TRANSLATION

In *Wag the Dog* (1997), the film adaptation of Larry Beinhart's *American Hero,* the White House conducts a fictitious war with Albania that is created on Hollywood sets with the help of a Hollywood producer. The production and its storyline are created for the purpose of diverting media attention away from an accusation of sexual misconduct involving the U.S. president in the days leading up to his reelection.

When the book was rereleased in 2004 by Nation Books, the publisher insisted that it be linked with the movie. Despite the film's success, both popular and critical, and his own appreciation of its merits, Beinhart fought to exclude its title from his book's cover. He felt that the film's departures from the original story undermined his intended political commentary. Nation ultimately did retitle the work *Wag the Dog: A Novel* to avoid public confusion, since fans of the film would only know the story by that title. The publisher agreed to include three chapters that Pantheon Books had deleted from the original, in which Joe Broz appears at the home of Larry Beinhart to tell Beinhart his story, thus introducing a metafictional element to the novel.

(Feb. 6, 1991); and "The Gulf War Did Not Take Place" (Mar. 29, 1991). The essays were translated and published in the London *Guardian. American Hero* combines the speculative nature of Baudillard's essays with the long-standing convention of footnoting in satiric novels—from eighteenth-century works such as Henry Fielding's *Tom Jones* (1749) and Laurence Stern's *Tristram Shandy* (1760–1767) through James Joyce's *Finnegans Wake* (1939), John Fowles's *The French Lieutenant's Woman* (1969), Gilbert Sorrentino's *Aberration of Starlight* (1980), and John Barth's *Sabbatical* (1982)—to create a format wherein his fictional novel would seem plausible as a work of nonfiction.

Beinhart's influence on contemporary fiction lies primarily outside the realm of political satire, though his next two books (one fiction and one nonfiction) center on the adulterous dealings of a U.S. senator. Although *American Hero* remains relatively obscure, the film it inspired has enjoyed great success, receiving two Academy Award nominations in 1998 and appearing on several of the American Film Institute's iconic film lists. The movie differs greatly from the novel, portraying a fictional, unnamed president (referred to only as "The President" or "Mr. President") who completely fabricates war footage to distract the media from his emerging sex scandal. Together, the projects repopularized the old American idiom "the tail wagging the dog" (which refers to an inconsequential factor dictating what happens in a given situation) and augmented the public's awareness and skepticism of the relationship between the U.S. government and the American media.

THEMES AND STYLE

One of the novel's major themes is the implication that the government and the media act in collusion to promote shared agendas. For example, a footnote cites a 1989 *Time* article that exposed Republican strategist Lee Atwater, his communications director Mark Goodin, and Congressman Newt Gingrich as the authors of a memo implying that newly appointed House Speaker Thomas Foley was gay. The memo (which also appears in the novel) received enough publicity to confirm the rumor in the minds of many, undermining Foley's credibility. Another of the work's themes is embedded in its detective novel framework and treats the presentation of war to the public. Through Joe Broz, a Vietnam War veteran and private eye who becomes suspicious of the film director hired to orchestrate the war, Beinhart argues that the framing of a "sanitized" Gulf War as a TV miniseries is meant to correct earlier administrations' failures to manipulate the television coverage of the Vietnam War, which was televised in all its chaos and carnage.

The persuasive power of the novel lies in Beinhart's presentation of the facts behind the fiction. By incorporating objective information accurately in footnotes, he avoids including the evidence in the body of his narrative, where it would likely be dismissed by critics as exaggeration for the sake of stylistic flair or propaganda. The Atwater memo about Foley's sexuality, for instance, is substantiated in a footnote, as are three other reported instances of Atwater's real-world manipulative political practices, all within the first three pages of the novel. Beinhart's fact-based documentation renders his fictional characters and plot more convincing, making the reader all the more willing, for example, to believe that Beinhart's fictionalized Atwater, lying cancer-ridden on his deathbed, would use his last bits of energy to write and ensure the delivery of a note suggesting the idea for the Hollywood-produced war to President Bush.

In presenting his speculative narrative, Beinhart usually foregoes emotional resonance in favor of intellectual appeals, often in the guise of biting satire. He voices his notions through a variety of characters, including studio security executive Melvin Taylor, who pores conscientiously and meticulously over surveillance footage in the hopes of advancing his career while pondering the current state of the nation: "Delayed gratification, Taylor felt, was the essential precept of civilization in the group or in the individual. It was—obviously—what made the European races superior. The current decline of America and the rise of Japan was due, obviously, to forgetting that simple and essential lesson." The narrator sometimes uses irony and metaphor to achieve a poignant tone, reminding us not to forget that "the sun is a star, and the sun figures the planets exist for one purpose only, to move in circles around it": thus he represents the narcissistic tendencies of both Hollywood and elected officials.

Robert De Niro (center) as a Washington spin doctor in *Wag the Dog*, a 1997 film based on Larry Beinhart's novel *American Hero*. MARY EVANS/NEW LINE CINEMA/ RONALD GRANT/EVERETT COLLECTION.

CRITICAL DISCUSSION

Most critics were complimentary of *American Hero* at the time of its publication. Although many asserted that the detective novel framework was too conventional for the subject matter, most were impressed with both the quality of Beinhart's prose and his storytelling prowess. In a 1993 review for *Library Journal,* Ann Fisher writes that the novel is "fast-moving and sure to grab attention." Dan Bogey and Shirley E. Havens, in a 1994 review for the same journal, call it "on-target satire" that feels "close enough to reality to make one wonder." A contemporary review in the *New Yorker* goes so far as to posit that "perhaps the best tribute one can pay the book is that, wacky as the thesis seems, it makes more sense than the actual war itself."

Despite being a fictional narrative, *American Hero* is often likened to contemporary works of nonfiction exposé as an example of literary whistle-blowing. In 2002 Pentagon official-turned-antiwar activist Daniel Ellsberg published *Secrets: A Memoir of Vietnam and the Pentagon Papers,* revealing the manipulation and lies that governed U.S. foreign policy during the Vietnam War. Released during the buildup to the Iraq War, its impact was bolstered by the rerelease of Beinhart's book in 2004, just a year after the launch of Operation Iraqi Freedom. In the preface to the new edition, Beinhart writes that "in the ten years since the book and the seven years since the film the gullibility and the credulity of the media has only grown." In view of this pronouncement, many critics study *American Hero*'s implications about the need for government transparency. The emergence of such transparency-oriented organizations as WikiLeaks and OpenLeaks (which publish confidential government documents in the interest of public awareness) attest to the American people's willingness to heed Beinhart's warnings against misinformation.

Although *American Hero* is the most recognized of Beinhart's works, little critical attention has focused on its workmanship. Most scholarship has highlighted the political underpinnings of the novel's premise. In an article for *Critique,* Stacey Olster marvels at the fictional Atwater's (and by extension Beinhart's) ability to recognize "war as the grand narrative that has governed American political-presidential history since the time of George Washington." Olster writes that the true legacy of the novel lies in its unflinching look at "the discrepancy between the facts [the U.S. government] purported to document and the fictions they manufactured and, in so doing, promoted," during not only the Persian Gulf War but all wars in the era of mass media.

BIBLIOGRAPHY

Sources

Review of *American Hero,* by Larry Beinhart. *New Yorker* 6 Dec. 1993: 143. *Academic Search Complete.* Web. 9 July 2012.

Review of *American Hero,* by Larry Beinhart. *Publishers Weekly* 2 Aug. 1993: 60. *Academic OneFile.* Web. 9 July 2012.

Beinhart, Larry. *American Hero.* New York: Pantheon, 1993. Print.

———. *Wag the Dog: A Novel.* New York: Nation, 2004. Print.

Bogey, Dan, and Shirley E. Havens. Review of *American Hero,* by Larry Beinhart. *Library Journal* 1 Aug. 1994: 168. *Academic Search Complete.* Web. 9 July 2012.

Fisher, Ann H. Review of *American Hero,* by Larry Beinhart. *Library Journal* 1 Aug. 1993: 144. *Academic Search Complete.* Web. 9 July 2012.

Olster, Stacey. "Cut and Print! The Gulf War as Movie Narrative in Larry Beinhart's *American Hero.*" *Critique* 40.4 (1999): 387–98. *Academic Search Complete.* Web. 9 July 2012.

Further Reading

Barron, James, and Jacques Steinberg. "Public Lives; A Waggish Tale in Washington …" *New York Times* 23 Jan. 1998: 2. *Academic Search Complete.* Web. 9 July 2012.

Beinhart, Larry. *Fog Facts: Searching for Truth in the Land of Spin.* New York: Nation, 2005. Print.

———. *No One Rides for Free.* New York: Morrow, 1986. Print.

Kempner, Michael. "Five Best Books on Public Relations." *Wall Street Journal* 26 Nov. 2006, Eastern ed.: 10. *Academic Search Complete.* Web. 9 July 2012.

Olster, Stacey M. *The Trash Phenomenon: Contemporary Literature, Popular Culture, and the Making of the American Century.* Athens: U of Georgia P, 2003. Print.

Walls, Jeannette, and David Feld. "Novelist Footnotes Fear of Mike Ovitz." *New York* 11 Nov. 1993: 14. *Academic Search Complete.* Web. 9 July 2012.

Media Adaptation

Wag the Dog. Dir. Barry Levinson. Perf. Dustin Hoffman, Robert De Niro, and Anne Heche. New Line Cinema, 1997. Film.

Clint Garner

BRAVE NEW WORLD

Aldous Huxley

OVERVIEW

In its portrayal of a future in which all of nature is under human control, Aldous Huxley's novel *Brave New World* (1932) warns against the unquestioning acceptance of scientific progress. Huxley's narrative is set in London in the year A.F. (After Ford) 632—a future in which humans are mechanically mass-produced in "hatcheries" to fulfill specific economic functions in society. Each person is happy with his or her lot in life, whether an intellectual Alpha or a semi-moronic Epsilon, because he or she is "socially predestined" to desire nothing more. Through selective breeding and relentless psychological conditioning, humanity has been liberated from all sources of instability, from physical suffering to individual thought. When an "uncivilized" man from a reservation in the American Southwest enters this world, his questions expose the cruel and costly myth of universal happiness. *Brave New World* stands in stark opposition to the popular work of the day, which asserted that technology could be used to create perfection.

In the early twentieth century, the literary utopias of H. G. Wells echoed the optimism of many scientists and cultural commentators in their emphasis on technology as the means of realizing a perfect world. Huxley warns readers of the pitfalls of such thinking with his own depiction of such a place—a world without suffering, which is also necessarily a world without freedom. Although critics praised the novel for its wit, satirical humor, and vividly realized futuristic setting, many felt that it overstated the threat of technology and the extent to which human control of nature is possible. Nevertheless, *Brave New World* left an indelible mark on the cultural memory; as people have become increasingly intertwined with and dependent upon technology, the parallels between Huxley's world and our own have only grown stronger.

HISTORICAL AND LITERARY CONTEXT

The benefits derived from safer, healthier, more comfortable living conditions made possible by the technological advances of the industrial age presented a seductive argument for the perfectibility of human existence. Henry Ford's assembly line accelerated the mass production of consumer goods, and the greater affordability thus attained gave rise to consumerist societies in which more people could afford an increasing variety of manufactured goods. At the same time, research in psychological conditioning conducted by Ivan Pavlov suggested new possibilities for shaping human behavior and development.

As rapidly as scientific knowledge grew, the world's political landscape changed, with fascist regimes on the rise in Europe, and Huxley recognized the potential for the abuse of new technologies by politically powerful actors. He was particularly alert to the suitability of motion pictures, the most popular visual medium of the time, as a means of social control. In Huxley's cinema of the future, the "feelies" are a powerful ideological tool, gratifying the senses while reinforcing the conditioned responses on which the World State depends. Similarly, hypnopedia (sleep teaching) is used throughout children's development to inculcate such beliefs as "Every one is happy now."

Traditionally, utopian literature has looked to advances in knowledge as the key to a better world. For Huxley, however, the primary force in engineering the technology-driven utopias of Wells's novels, particularly *Men Like Gods* (1923), was the "improvement" of the human organism itself through selective breeding and population reduction. Like Evgenii Zamiatin, author of the dystopian novel *We* (1924), Huxley creates a world in which free thought is the greatest threat to the social order: universal happiness and security are achieved not through commitment to shared ideals but in the hatcheries where human abilities are carefully calibrated to eliminate free thought. In George Orwell's novel *Nineteen Eighty-Four* (1949), to which *Brave New World* is often compared, individual thought is also forbidden, with compliance secured through coercion and torture. Orwell's dystopia is built on the profound dissonance between reality and the government's message of love and brotherhood; in *Brave New World*, the message and the reality are the same because no one is capable of thinking otherwise.

Responding to the insights of *Brave New World*, writers have mined the conflicted relationships between the individual and society and between humans and machines. In her 1938 novella *Anthem*, Ayn Rand describes a society in which learning is forbidden and use of the word "I" is punishable by death. Kurt Vonnegut's first novel, *Player Piano* (1952), a dystopian view of capitalism and mechanization, is based on *Brave New World*, and in Vonnegut's *Slaughterhouse-Five* (1969),

* **Key Facts**

Time Period:
Early 20th Century

Genre:
Novel

Events:
Mass production of consumer goods; rise of fascism in Europe; popularization of motion pictures

Nationality:
English

HUXLEY'S RETURN TO *BRAVE NEW WORLD*

In the late 1950s Huxley wrote a series of essays in which he returned to the ideas and themes of *Brave New World*. Published as *Brave New World Revisited* (1958), the essays show how some features of Huxley's fictional world were already taking shape in the physical world by the mid-twentieth century, as the result of overpopulation and over-organization (the strict regimentation of society for the purposes of economic efficiency). Huxley argues that overpopulation makes people susceptible to dictatorships or oligarchies, particularly in poor, undeveloped countries, while in industrialized societies, economic elites use positive reinforcement to train people to identify themselves with their economic roles. The end result in both situations is the loss of individual autonomy.

Like his earlier novel, *Brave New World Revisited* demonstrates Huxley's talent for envisioning how nascent trends might develop in the future. However, some of these insights are compromised by personal or class biases; for example, he places undue emphasis on the "contamination of the genetic pool" by "congenitally insufficient" individuals in his discussion of problems related to overpopulation. However, his discussions of political campaigns as entertainment; the value to companies of advertising to children; and, more generally, the appetite in Western societies for "nonstop distraction" are perhaps even more powerfully resonant today than they were in the 1950s.

free will is a concept extinct on all inhabited planets except Earth. Ray Bradbury intended his novel *Fahrenheit 451* (1953), which describes a future U.S. society in which the possession of a book is a crime, as a portrayal of television's damaging effects on the quality of human knowledge and social bonds.

THEMES AND STYLE

Brave New World explores the conflict between the human desire for happiness and the human need for freedom within the standardizing context of industrial society. Happiness in the novel's World State is associated with "machinery and scientific medicine." "Pleasant vices"—promiscuous sex, for example—are not seen as degrading but as essential to the life of the "happy, hardworking, goods-consuming citizen." Industrial civilization depends not on art, philosophy, or history but on pleasurable "self-indulgence up to the very limits imposed by hygiene and economics." By contrast, individual thoughts and actions lead to instability, and "instability means the end of civilization." To choose freedom is to choose "the right to be unhappy." For the civilized masses, such a choice is inconceivable; for the "savage" John, it is essential. For John, a life without challenges is a life without value. John's choice to be free, however, does not enable him to escape "civilization," as his passion and suffering merely provide another source of entertainment

for the pleasure-seeking masses, who hound him into suicide, reinforcing the theme of the inverse relationship between the rise of technology and the fall of humanity.

In creating a utopia where an exaggerated technological sophistication is taken for granted, Huxley satirizes the tendency to consider all technological advancement good for humankind. He believed that this tendency encouraged a dangerous intellectual passivity. Particularly harmful in this regard, he thought, was the cinema, a belief that is reflected in *Brave New World* when "feelies" provide an experience that John finds "far more real than reality," despite the fact that the dazzling images, sounds, and smells are synthetic and "the plot of the film was extremely simple." While emphasizing the pleasure of such experiences, Huxley also manages to convey their vapidity and use them as a counterpoint to his contemporaries' claims of the inherent "goodness" of technology.

Huxley's new world is described in a witty, humorous, superficial manner. His third-person narrator's tone of occasionally antic amusement effectively conveys a buoyant atmosphere in which robust young men and women consume, play, and have sex endlessly. The same tone is applied to descriptions of the very serious work of the hatcheries and nurseries, and the incongruity serves to accentuate the alien nature of mechanized sexual reproduction ("The whole of a small factory staffed with the products of a single bokanovskified egg") and the cruelty of electric shocks administered to Delta infants to make them permanently averse to reading and the natural world ("They'll be safe from books and botany all their lives"). Such juxtapositions of the comic or childlike with the mechanisms of social control also find their way into the bits of hypnopedic wisdom ("Every one belongs to every one else," "Streptocock-Gee to Banbury-T, to see a fine bathroom and W.C.") that mark the boundaries of healthy intellectual activity.

CRITICAL DISCUSSION

Early critics doubted the likelihood and extent of Huxley's dystopia. In his 1932 review for the *New York Times*, for example, John Chamberlain writes that "the bogy of mass production seems a little overwrought" and suggests that genetic mutations would undermine attempts to breed standardized humans. Writing for the *Nation* in 1932, Henry Hazlitt criticizes Huxley's characterization of the negative effects of eliminating conflict and suffering, noting, "Only when we have reduced them enormously will Mr. Huxley's central problem become a real problem." In his 1951 essay "Aldous Huxley and Utopia," Theodor Adorno faults Huxley for positing a false choice between "individualism and a totalitarian world-state," a flaw that Huxley acknowledges in his foreword to the 1946 edition. Despite its "many ingenuities of execution," Adorno argues, *Brave New World* fails because humankind "evades [Huxley's] anticipating imagination" and thus "is replaced by a caricature of the men of today, in the ancient and much-abused manner of satire."

These early critics could not have anticipated what biographer Nicholas Murray describes as the novel's "extraordinary prescience" with regard to the grip that advanced technology has come to exert on modern life. Worries that social controls like those in *Brave New World* could be imposed externally have receded somewhat in the face of mounting concern that people are willingly accepting—even welcoming—the encroachment of technology on privacy, individual autonomy, reproduction, and aging without considering fully the possible negative impacts. Observing that both Huxley's World State and modern medical research are "animated by our most humane and progressive aspirations," bioethicist Leon R. Kass writes in *Life, Liberty, and the Defense of Dignity* (2002), that, "precisely because the society of the future will deliver exactly what we most want" in terms of health, safety, pleasure, and longevity, "we can take ourselves to a Brave New World … without even deliberately deciding to go." These concerns have formed the basis of a lasting legacy for critical and social interest in *Brave New World*.

With the value of Huxley's novel as a critique of technological utopian aspirations well established, scholars have more recently considered the novel from other perspectives. In *Aldous Huxley: Modern Satirical Novelist of Ideas* (2006), Jerome Meckier discusses the symbolism of characters' names in the novel and analyzes its interpretation of the ideas of Sigmund Freud, Ford, and Pavlov. An essay by John Attarian focuses on the religious dimension of Huxley's vision, asserting that the "deeper meaning" of the novel lies in its warning against "life in a world that has fled from God and lost all awareness of the transcendent." In *Dystopian Fiction East and West* (2001), Erika Gottlieb reappraises the novel's success as a social satire. Arguing that neither the "tradition of utopian socialism" nor the "scientific world-view" is the object of Huxley's denunciation, Gottlieb suggests that the World State "is dystopic because it functions as the fulfillment of an exclusively materialistic dream, where the original goals of liberating mankind and establishing universal justice—a pre-condition of individual freedom—are deliberately reversed."

In this scene from the 1998 film adaptation of *Brave New World*, students tour a laboratory where human embryos are grown. © USA NETWORKS/ COURTESY EVERETT COLLECTION.

BIBLIOGRAPHY

Sources

Adorno, Theodor W. "Aldous Huxley and Utopia." *Prisms*. Trans. Samuel Weber and Shierry Weber. London: Spearman, 1967. 95–118. Print.

Attarian, John. "*Brave New World* and the Flight from God." *Aldous Huxley*. Ed. Harold Bloom. Philadelphia: Chelsea, 2003. 9–24. Print.

Chamberlain, John. "Future Shock." Rev. of *Brave New World*, by Aldous Huxley. *New York Times* 7 Feb. 1932. Web.

Gottlieb, Erika. "The Dictator behind the Mask: Zamiatin's *We,* Huxley's *Brave New World,* and Orwell's *Nineteen Eighty-four.*" *Dystopian Fiction East and West: Universe of Terror and Trial.* Quebec City: McGill-Queen's UP, 2001. 56–87. Print.

Hazlitt, Henry. "What's Wrong with Utopia?" Rev. of *Brave New World*, by Aldous Huxley. *Nation* 17 Feb. 1932: 204+. Print.

Huxley, Aldous. *Brave New World*. London: Chatto, 1932. Print.

Kass, Leon R. "Introduction." *Life, Liberty, and the Defense of Dignity: The Challenge of Bioethics.* San Francisco: Encounter, 2002. 1–26. Print.

Meckier, Jerome. *Aldous Huxley: Modern Satirical Novelist of Ideas.* Ed. Peter E. Firchow and Bernfried Nugel. Berlin: Lit, 2006. Print.

Murray, Nicholas. *Aldous Huxley: An English Intellectual.* London: Little, 2002. Print.

Further Reading

Booker, M. Keith. "Huxley's *Brave New World*: The Early Bourgeois Dystopia." *The Dystopian Impulse in Modern*

Literature: Fiction as Social Criticism. Westport: Greenwood, 1994. 47–68. Print.

Deery, June. *Aldous Huxley and the Mysticism of Science.* New York: St. Martin's, 1996. Print.

Firchow, Peter Edgerly. *The End of Utopia: A Study of Aldous Huxley's* Brave New World. Lewisburg: Bucknell UP, 1984. Print.

Keren, Michael. "In Quest of Authenticity." *The Citizen's Voice: Twentieth-Century Politics and Literature.* Calgary: U of Calgary P, 2003. 55–68. Print.

Sion, Ronald T. *Aldous Huxley and the Search for Meaning: A Study of the Eleven Novels.* Jefferson: McFarland, 2010. Print.

Watt, Donald, ed. *Aldous Huxley: The Critical Heritage.* London: Routledge, 1975. Print.

Media Adaptation

Brave New World. Dir. Leslie Libman and Larry Williams. Perf. Peter Gallagher, Leonard Nimoy, and Tim Guinee. Dan Wigutow Productions, 1998. TV Movie.

Janet Moredock

Far and Beyon'

Unity Dow

OVERVIEW

African writer Unity Dow's novel *Far and Beyon'* (2000) presents a confrontation of HIV/AIDS in Botswana at a time when the countervailing forces of tribal tradition and westernization have rendered notions about the nature of the disease confusing and treatment difficult. *Far and Beyon'* tells the story of the Selato family: single mother Mara—who has lost two sons to AIDS over a twelve-month period—and her surviving children, Mosa and Stan. Throughout the novel, Mara's reliance on divination and traditional methods to explain and solve problems conflicts with her children's questioning of such practices and the desire to escape the poverty and limitations of village life. Resisting the urge to condemn traditional practices wholesale or to offer Western medicine as a panacea for all that ails sub-Saharan Africa, Dow paints a complex and compassionate portrait of a society in flux, while educating her audience about the reality of disease and death.

Dow, a well-known attorney and the first woman appointed to Botswana's High Court, published her first novel at a time when AIDS deaths were devastating the country. Speaking the following year in front of the UN General Assembly, Botswana's President Festus Mogae declared that "we are threatened with extinction. People are dying in chillingly high numbers. It is a crisis of the first magnitude." Dow's timely novel gives voice to this crisis and provides a record of the experiences of families in Botswana in the years before treatment was widely available. As the first African country to make antiviral drugs widely available, Botswana is often pointed to as a model for other African nations in how to manage AIDS. The disease continues to affect Botswana's citizens, however, and the themes of Dow's novel remain relevant to the problems they face in the twenty-first century.

HISTORICAL AND LITERARY CONTEXT

Since the first case of HIV/AIDS in Botswana was diagnosed in 1985, the country has been one of the hardest hit in Africa, with about one-quarter of the adult population infected with HIV. Women in particular have been affected, owing in part to cultural shifts that removed traditional family controls over sexual behavior. Illness and death from HIV/AIDS affected families economically, and as adults became too sick to work and medical costs and funeral expenses mounted, many families sank into poverty. Children, forced to leave school to care for ailing family members, saw their prospects for the future narrowing.

Botswana began feeling the impact of the HIV/AIDS epidemic later than other sub-Saharan countries, with the epidemic not reaching crisis level until the mid- to late 1990s. By the close of the twentieth century, HIV rates were extremely high. As people began dying en masse, many concluded that they had been cursed or bewitched. Seeking help from traditional healers, they ignored medical information about the disease, including how to avoid becoming infected or spreading the illness. Women had long been socially and sexually subservient to men, and even women who did have access to information about condom use to help prevent infection were often unwilling or unable to broach the subject with male partners. As a result, AIDS cases in women outnumbered those in men more than two to one because heterosexual sex, which is the predominate mode of HIV/AIDS transmission in Botswana, makes female infection more likely. In addition, rape and other forms of sexual abuse, a well-documented problem in the country, contributed to the danger of infection.

More than a decade earlier, writers in the United States had dealt with a parallel period of death and devastation as a "gay disease" of unknown origin ravaged communities in urban centers such as New York, San Francisco, and Los Angeles. This period generated a body of work that, though it was produced in a vastly different socioeconomic climate than Dow's Botswana, also responds to profound loss and suffering as people watched loved ones die from a mysterious agent that traditional treatments could not effectively combat. Works such as Randy Shilts's nonfiction account *And the Band Played On* (1987) and Paul Monette's memoir *Borrowed Time* (1988) take on an angry, overtly critical tone. In contrast *Far and Beyon'* is less about eulogizing the dead or exposing government failures and more about educating and offering hope. Dow is part of a tradition of African writers dealing with the changing values and social realities in African countries. Dow shares with Bessie Head and Mositi Torontle, among other Botswana writers, a commitment to expressing female experience in a still largely male-dominated society.

❖ Key Facts

Time Period:
Early 21st Century

Genre:
Novel

Events:
AIDS epidemic

Nationality:
Botswanan

THE BOTSWANA CITIZENSHIP CASE

As an attorney, Unity Dow made a name for herself as a feminist crusader when she challenged the Citizenship Act of 1984 on the grounds that it discriminated against women. The act granted citizenship to children of a man from Botswana married to a noncitizen woman but not to children of a woman from Botswana married to a noncitizen man. Dow, who married an American, was touched personally by this issue, as her children from this marriage were born and raised in Botswana but denied citizenship. In 1992 the High Court of Botswana ruled in her favor, and, after years of legal wrangling, the Botswana Court of Appeal upheld the decision. Dow's children were issued passports in 1995.

On her thoughts about the decision and its implications for women in Africa, Dow comments that "the local cannot remain isolated and exclusively self-informing … the global must inform and influence the local. … Such influence is legitimate, justified and necessary if women are to gain their human rights at the local level." In many African countries, Dow argues, women are in a disadvantaged position relative to men, a condition that she does not think can be fully addressed without laws that grant women rights as full citizens who will not be treated as "servants, props, and rare exceptions."

Dow published several other novels after *Far and Beyon'*, including *The Screaming of the Innocent* (2001). This book indicts traditional ritual killing in Botswana as well as the society that covers it up. Another novel, *Juggling Truths* (2003), returns to the village setting of *Far and Beyon'* and documents life as it had been three decades earlier, before HIV/AIDS. Dow has remained active as a judge and attorney and has been a visiting professor at Columbia University in New York, Washington and Lee University in Virginia, and the University of Cincinnati in Ohio.

THEMES AND STYLE

Far and Beyon' describes the manner in which traditional beliefs about the origin of misfortune, combined with the systemic subordination of women, have contributed to the spread of HIV/AIDS in Botswana. In the novel, as Mara struggles to come to terms with the AIDS-related deaths of her two eldest sons, Pule and Thabo, her situation is complicated by her alienation from a longtime friend, whom a diviner blamed for her sons' illnesses. Daughter Mosa and son Stan, meanwhile, confront problems of their own. Mosa must deal with the aftermath of an unwanted pregnancy and, later, the sexual advances of her science teacher. Stan, too, suffers frustration at his mother's reliance on "witchcraft" as a means of diagnosing and solving her problems and mourns the once close bond he shared with Mosa, which has been lost in anger and silence. Throughout the novel, women are treated as second-class citizens. An injured woman is casually forced to cede a succession of chairs to men, a practice that reflects female subservience in larger matters, including, for instance, sexual decision-making. Institutions such as schools and government clinics also foster abusive practices. As Mosa and Stan make amends toward the end of the novel, Mosa angrily decries the objectification of women she sees and feels daily: "People are dying around us because of AIDS. Telling women to expect their husbands to sleep around does not help the situation. Telling them to be passive is a recipe for disaster."

In the novel's prologue, Dow reveals the meaning of Mosa's full name—Mosadi, "woman"—which signals that the problems Mosa faces are in some sense the problems of all women in Botswana. Mara cradles a newborn Mosa and imagines her learning the ways of women, helping in the home, going to school, and growing to adulthood. What the novel makes clear is that growing to adulthood is not a foregone conclusion in Botswana and that conditions need to change, particularly for women, to make a long and fully realized life possible. The vision of a good life in *Far and Beyon'* involves community and shared rituals. On the one hand, these activities can serve a positive social function; they can be "a building ceremony," as Mosa describes the ritual razor cutting to which Stan objects, even for those who feel they know better. On the other hand, these shared rituals can also be destructive, as in the marriage ceremony, which Mosa witnesses and calls "degrading of women … sanctioned humiliation." For Dow, community is vital, but unquestioning acceptance of certain shared practices—those that deny the reality of the AIDS virus or disavow the agency of women—contribute to the AIDS epidemic. At the end of the novel, when Mosa and Stan have acknowledged AIDS and have talked about the sources of their estrangement, they can finally return to their melon rock, a place of childhood love and hope.

Dow's sympathetic treatment of Mara, even as she denies the nature of her sons' deaths, reflects Dow's understanding of the difficult position that the people of Botswana are in as they try to navigate a changing world. In her narrative, Dow blends in words and phrases of Setswana, the characters' mother tongue, typifying the way traditional beliefs combine with modern elements in a hybrid cultural practice. At Pule's funeral, for example, with its rites of sweeping the yard and shaving heads, the Lord's Prayer is recited in both Setswana and English. Dow also uses language to show conflict. Villagers seem as reluctant to speak of AIDS as they are to acknowledge its existence, and in Setswana they refer to it as *phamo kate*, "the disease that has a short name." This reticence is also expressed when Mosa is disturbed by a radio report in Setswana and English describing condom use for the prevention of AIDS. She muses that she does not object to public dissemination of information, but "she did not understand why that had to necessarily mean making listeners uncomfortable." By the end of the novel, Mosa has overcome her discomfort, confronting the abuse of girls by teachers in a very public way and getting an HIV test.

CRITICAL DISCUSSION

Far and Beyon' enjoyed critical success in Botswana, but it was not widely reviewed outside Africa following its initial publication. Writing on the difficulty of putting together a special issue on southern African literature, guest editors of *Research in African Literatures* note that the "lack of intimate familiarity with the technologies, processes, and protocols that go into getting published means that many writers and scholars from the region … are not able to get their work into the global commodity system." While this may not be the case for Dow, who has traveled and taught in the West, it may suggest a reason that Botswana literature in general is rarely published or reviewed outside Africa.

Within her home country, Dow's AIDS activism, accomplished both as a lawyer and a novelist, has been influential, but she is less known elsewhere. In 2010 she collaborated with Max Essex, a Harvard professor and medical researcher specializing in HIV/AIDS, on *Saturday Is for Funerals,* a nonfiction account of the effects of the disease in Botswana and the success of various steps taken to combat its spread, especially government-subsidized HAART (Highly Active Anti-Retroviral Therapy) and the promotion of male circumcision. This work has garnered more recognition in the West, where in 2011 Dow was named one of *Newsweek* magazine's "150 Women Who Shook the World."

Most scholarship on *Far and Beyon',* as well as on Dow's fiction in general, has focused on her exploration of family and community relationships in the face of cultural change. Mary Lederer and Nobantu Rasebotsa in their introduction to *Research in African Literatures* (2010) examine Dow's treatment of rural versus urban and traditional versus modern dichotomies in *Far and Beyon'.* For Dow, they write, "the important point is to restore and maintain a person's sense of belonging to a family and extended community, regardless of whether those communities are rural or urban. Breakdown threatens people when they do not know to whom they belong, regardless of where they live." Further, "the rural-urban dichotomy is only a matter of place, not a matter of substance." Writing of her legal work as well as her fiction, Fetson Kalua in the article "Identities in Transition" (2010) explores Dow's conception of a contemporary African identity, concluding that "Unity Dow neither entertains notions of cultural nationalism that seem 'content to celebrate the glories of Africa's past' nor warms to an unquestioned modernity, but endeavors to show culture as lived experience, and identity as a performative act of becoming and therefore always in transition."

BIBLIOGRAPHY

Sources

Browne, Peter. "The Best of Times, the Worst of Times." *Griffith Review,* 17 (2007). Print.

Dow, Unity. *Far and Beyon'.* San Francisco: Aunt Lute, 2000. Print.

———. "How the Global Informs the Local: The Botswana Citizenship Case." *Healthcare for Women International* 22 (2001). Print.

Kalua, Fetson. "Identities in Transition: The 1990 High Court Case and Unity Dow's *The Heavens May Fall.*" *Journal of Literary Studies* 26.2 (2010): 80+. *General OneFile.* Web. 6 Aug. 2012.

Lederer, Mary S., Leloba Molema, and Peter Mwikisa. "Introduction." *Research in African Literatures* 41.3 (2010): V+. *Literature Resource Center.* Web. 8 Aug. 2012.

Lederer, Mary S., and Nobantu L. Rasebotsa. "Understanding the Rural-Urban Dichotomy in Mositi Torontle's *The Victims* and Unity Dow's *Far and Beyon'.*" *Research in African Literatures* 41.3 (2010): 21+. *Literature Resource Center.* Web. 5 Aug. 2012.

Rochman, Hazel. "Dow, Unity. *Far and Beyon'.*" *Booklist* 1 May 2002: 1518. *General OneFile.* Web. 6 Aug. 2012.

Further Reading

Denbow, James, and Phenyo Thebe. *Culture and Customs of Botswana.* Westport, CT: Greenwood, 2006. Print.

Dow, Unity, and Max Essex. *Saturday Is for Funerals.* Cambridge, MA: Harvard UP, 2010. Print.

Gagiano, Annie. *Dealing with Evils: Essays on Writing from Africa.* Stuttgart: Ibidem, 2008. Print.

Jagne, Siga Fatima, and Pushpah Parek. *Postcolonial African Writers: A Bio-Bibliographical Critical Sourcebook.* Westport, CT: Greenwood, 1998. Print.

Suggs, David. *A Bagful of Locusts and the Baboon Woman: Constructions of Gender, Change, and Continuity in Botswana.* Belmont, CA: Wadsworth, 2002. Print.

Daisy Gard

Contestants in the 2005 Miss HIV Stigma Free Beauty Pageant in Botswana, an event designed to destigmatize HIV/AIDS. An estimated 25 percent of Botswana's population was HIV-positive in 2009. Although antiretroviral treatment is available, few people know their status because of the stigma surrounding the virus. *Far and Beyon'* explores a number of social issues, including AIDS, that are relevant in Botswana. © JEHAD NGA/CORBIS.

HOMO ZAPIENS

Victor Pelevin

✥ *Key Facts*

Time Period:
Late 20th Century

Genre:
Novel

Events:
Shift to market economy following collapse of the Soviet Union

Nationality:
Russian

OVERVIEW

Victor Pelevin's satirical novel *Homo Zapiens,* originally published in Russian in 1999 as *Generation "П,"* explores the intersection of advertising, consumerism, and the Russian national identity in the years following the collapse of the Soviet Union. Structured around the career of Babylen Tatarsky, a young advertising copywriter in 1990s Russia tasked with developing Russian-specific ads for Western products, the narrative depicts a world in which the influence of advertising on the shaping of reality takes on psychological and metaphysical dimensions. As the novel progresses, consumerism emerges as the defining principle of human existence. Political figures are revealed to be digital media constructs, and Tatarsky's advertising firm turns out to be involved in a ritualistic cult based around ancient Mesopotamian deities. Among the more absurdist treatments of the rise of capitalism in post-Soviet Russia, *Homo Zapiens* explores the power of the media to distort a viewer's consciousness to surreal, postmodern extremes.

One of the first of a large number of dystopian treatments of post-Soviet life to emerge around the turn of the twenty-first century, *Homo Zapiens* was released to critical acclaim and popular success and quickly became a Russian best seller. It reflects a partial shift in the cultural imagination away from the failure of the communist project—the subject of many jaundiced fictions written during the USSR's decline, fall, and immediate aftermath—in favor of similarly jaundiced examinations of Russia's involvement in the global capitalist market. Today the novel remains a noteworthy manifestation of Russian concerns about the pervasive, often hidden cultural manipulation of consumers—particularly through television—amid the supposed intellectual and economic freedom of the post-Soviet era.

HISTORICAL AND LITERARY CONTEXT

During the second half of the 1980s, the economic stagnation of the Soviet Union prompted a series of liberalizing political and economic reforms under the aegis of Mikhail Gorbachev, general secretary of the Communist Party, whose *glasnost* (openness) and *perestroika* (restructuring) programs substantially ameliorated the totalitarianism of the USSR's social structure. The policies had the unintended effect of seriously weakening the Soviet Union's stability as a coherent state, resulting in a series of revolutions in 1989 followed by the formal dissolution of the Soviet Union in December 1991. As an independent sovereign republic, Russia began a difficult transition to a market economy under the administration of Boris Yeltsin, the first president of the newly autonomous state. Restrictions on foreign commercial and cultural influences, already somewhat relaxed under Gorbachev, gave way further under Yeltsin.

By the time *Homo Zapiens* was published in 1999, Russian society had been thoroughly transformed by the chaotic shift toward privatization. This transition was accompanied by rampant corruption, economic and political instability, and an increasing concentration of wealth in the hands of a small number of people. Pelevin's novel addresses these developments by emphasizing the interconnectedness of Russia's political structure and its burgeoning commercialization, depicting the two institutions as essentially the same. Yeltsin is shown to be a digital simulacrum, no less illusory than the figures in a television commercial, and every other aspect of public life turns out to be similarly fabricated and manipulative, with no discernible organizing principle apart from a vague, self-perpetuating metaphysical obsession with the intake and output of money.

Homo Zapiens draws on a lengthy tradition of dystopian fiction that focuses on the ways in which cultural artifacts and institutions are used to sway, narcotize, or reprogram the minds of a society's inhabitants, as in George Orwell's *1984* (1949), Yevgeny Zamyatin's *We* (1921), and Aldous Huxley's *Brave New World* (1932). Likewise, Pelevin's emphasis on advertising and consumerism as a primary means of thought control was perhaps prefigured by Frederik Pohl and C. M. Kornbluth's 1952 novel *The Space Merchants.* One of Pelevin's most noteworthy immediate contemporaries is Vladimir Sorokin, whose postmodern novels—including *The Queue* (1983) and *Day of the Oprichnik* (2011)—are often set in extravagantly dystopian versions of Russia that foreground the effects of pervasive societal forces on individual lives.

A popular and influential literary treatment of the immense changes that Russia underwent during the final decade of the twentieth century, *Homo Zapiens* is a significant precursor to numerous subsequent works on similar themes that emerged in the early years of the new millennium. Following the release of Pelevin's novel, dystopian portrayals of the commercialization of post-Soviet states—and of post-Soviet life in general, as in Alexander Garros and Aleksei Evdokimov's 2003 best-seller *Headcrusher*—began to proliferate, and Pelevin's reputation as one of the eminent Russian authors of his generation was consolidated. *Homo Zapiens* was adapted into a film in 2011, a fact that testifies to the novel's continuing regard in contemporary Russia.

THEMES AND STYLE

A primary theme of *Homo Zapiens* is the pervasiveness of consumerist values in post-Soviet Russia. These values are described in terms of a complex societal model that emphasizes the impact of media on a person's psychological development. Dictating by means of a Ouija board, the disembodied spirit of Che Guevara outlines two conceptions of reality: "Subject number one believes that reality is the material world. But subject number two believes that reality is the material world as it is shown on the television." People in the latter categorization, the titular Homo Zapiens, are turned into parts of a societal organism called "oranus" by means of three different impulses—referred to as the "oral, anal, and displacing wow-impulses (from the commercial ejaculation 'wow!')"—which respectively bring about a desire to acquire money, a desire to spend money, and an utter indifference to all nonmonetary stimuli. The shift augurs an apocalyptic end to human subjectivity, a "wowserisation of consciousness" such that "the end of the world will simply be a television programme." Thus, consumerism is depicted throughout the novel as a matter of not merely economic or political but cosmic significance.

The novel's themes are conveyed via a fragmentary, postmodern narrative structure characterized by the frequent use of embedded texts. Allusions to popular culture, religion, mythology, and intellectual history are plentiful. Although the bulk of the text is devoted to a straightforward, third-person recounting of Tatarsky's career—a career that climaxes with Tatarsky becoming the digital surrogate husband of the goddess Ishtar—much of the narrative consists of lengthy quotations of fictitious material. These quotations serve not only as manifestations of the text's ideas about advertising and consumerism but also, frequently, as tongue-in-cheek elaborations of those ideas, as when Tatarsky begins one of his advertising scenarios, transcriptions of which punctuate the novel. Likewise, the concept of "oranus" is introduced not through dialogue or narration but through the lengthy essay dictated by Guevara.

Stylistically, *Homo Zapiens* is characterized by an ironic, lighthearted, intentionally flat tone of address that contrasts sharply with the bleakness of the worldview it expresses. The lack of overt emotionality in the writing—a common attribute in postmodern fiction—reflects the psychologically flattening effects of consumerism. Hence, after transcribing Guevara's deeply

BORIS YELTSIN'S PRESIDENCY

Homo Zapiens takes place during the administration of Boris Yeltsin, whom the novel portrays not as a flesh-and-blood human but as a digital fake created to manipulate the public. According to the novel, Yeltsin is less an architect than a product of consumerist Russia. The first president of post-Soviet Russia, he had a contentious term as head of the Russian government, which was characterized by a series of drastic policy reforms aimed at liberalizing the Russian economy. These reforms involved the release of trade and price controls, the raising of taxes and interest rates, and the reduction of funds for government subsidies and welfare programs.

His policies resulted in a severe economic downturn, a situation that fueled an ongoing power struggle between Yeltsin and the Russian Parliament that was eventually resolved in Yeltsin's favor in 1993 by means of violent military action. The economic situation hit a low point in August 1998 when the Russian government devalued its currency and defaulted on its debt amid a series of market collapses. Although the economy steadily recovered in the months and years after the crisis, Yeltsin's resignation from the presidency in 1999 occurred amid widespread disapproval of his time in office.

troubling essay during the Ouija séance, Tatarsky finds that "the only thing he could remember from all that writing was the expression 'bourgeois thought.' Getting up from the table, he went across to the bed and threw himself on it without getting undressed." The novel's detached style reflects the protagonist's immersion in the soulless world of advertising, only gesturing at depth of feeling through the occasional sardonic turn of phrase: "it was a clear, fresh morning; its cool purity seemed to conceal some incomprehensible reproach."

CRITICAL DISCUSSION

Homo Zapiens was published to great acclaim in Russia, and its subsequent translation into English likewise met with generally positive reviews. David MacFayden, reviewing the original Russian edition in *World Literature Quarterly* in 1999, praises its "cruel indictment of a new, consumer generation" and asserts that "at a time—since August 1998—when both foreign and domestic advertising revenues have plummeted in Russia, Pelevin's book acquires added resonance as a cutting indictment of the increasingly brazen promotions that pepper Russian television screens every day." Lev Grossman, reviewing the English-language edition in *Time* in 2002, was similarly impressed with "Pelevin's darkly anarchic imagination, which reflects the chaos perfectly," though Grossman points out that Pelevin "offers no solution" to the nightmarish situation the novel evokes.

As a seminal work of post-Soviet Russian literature, *Homo Zapiens* has attained iconic status within its country of origin and is regarded as an important part of Russia's literary response to the nation's shift to a

Author Victor Pelevin, whose novel *Homo Zapiens* paints a bleak, satiric picture of post-Soviet consumer culture. © JULIET BUTLER/ALAMY.

Other scholarship discusses the novel in relation to Russian cultural history, an example being Lyudmila Parts's 2004 article in *Canadian Slavonic Papers,* which analyzes the text as a representation of the decline of the Russian intelligentsia during the post-Soviet era.

BIBLIOGRAPHY

Sources

Freidin, Gregory. "Dzheneraishen 'P'." Rev. of *Generation "П,"* by Victor Pelevin. *Foreign Policy* 118 (2000): 165–69. *JSTOR.* Web. 12 Oct. 2012.

Grossman, Lev. Rev. of *Homo Zapiens,* by Victor Pelevin. *Time* 4 Mar. 2002: 74. *Academic Search Elite.* Web. 12 Oct. 2012.

Khagi, Sofya. "From Homo Sovieticus to Homo Zapiens: Viktor Pelevin's Consumer Dystopia." *Russian Review* 67.4 (2008): 559–79. *Academic Search Complete.* Web. 12 Oct. 2012.

MacFayden, David. Rev. of *Generation "П,"* by Victor Pelevin. *World Literature Today* 73.3 (1999): 553–54. *JSTOR.* Web. 12 Oct. 2012.

Parts, Lyudmila. "Degradation of the Word; or, the Adventures of an *Intelligent* in Viktor Pelevin's *Generation 'П.'*" *Canadian Slavonic Papers* 46.3–4 (2004): 435–49. *JSTOR.* Web. 12 Oct. 2012.

Pelevin, Victor. *Homo Zapiens.* Trans. Andrew Bromfield. New York: Viking, 2002. Print.

Further Reading

Borenstein, Eliot. "Survival of the Catchiest: Memes and Postmodern Russia." *Slavic and East European Journal* 48.3 (2004): 462–83. Print.

Dalton-Brown, Sally. "The Dialectics of Emptiness: Douglas Coupland's and Viktor Pelevin's Tales of Generation X and P." *Forum for Modern Language Studies* 42.3 (2006): 239–48. Print.

Garros, Alexander, and Aleksei Evdokimov. *Headcrusher.* London: Chatto & Windus, 2005. Print.

Lipovetsky, Mark. "Russian Literary Postmodernism in the 1990s." *Slavonic and East European Review* 79.1 (2001): 31–50. Print.

Livers, Keith. "The Tower or the Labyrinth: Conspiracy, Occult, and Empire-Nostalgia in the Work of Viktor Pelevin and Aleksandr Prokhanov." *Russian Review* 69.3 (2010): 477–503. Print.

Noordenbos, Boris. "Breaking into a New Era? A Cultural-Semiotic Reading of Viktor Pelevin." *Russian Literature* 64.1 (2008): 85–107. Print.

Pelevin, Victor. *The Sacred Book of the Werewolf.* Trans. Andrew Bromfield. New York: Viking, 2008. Print.

Shneidman, N. N. *Russian Literature, 1995–2002: On the Threshold of the New Millennium.* Toronto: U of Toronto P, 2004. Print.

Sorokin, Vladimir. *The Ice Trilogy.* Trans. Jamey Gambrell. New York: New York Review of Books, 2011. Print.

Media Adaptation

Generation P. Dir. Victor Ginzburg. Perf. Vladimir Epifantsev, Mikhail Efremov, and Andrey Fomin. Generation P, 2011. Film.

market economy. Gregory Freidin, reviewing the novel in *Foreign Policy* in 2000, asserts, "In Russia, [*Homo Zapiens*] has become required reading for everyone, and many of its clever one-liners have already entered the hip argot…. Both *Homo Zapiens* and *Oranus* are now part of Russian speech, along with 'wow impulses.'" The immediate and enduring popularity of the novel has precipitated a substantial body of scholarship in the relatively short period since its initial publication, with much of it structured around postmodernist analyses of Pelevin's treatment of consumerism.

Critical works regarding *Homo Zapiens* often contextualize the novel within existing literary traditions, as in Sofya Khagi's 2008 article for *Russian Review,* which analyzes the novel's commentary on Russian consumerism in light of the literary genre of dystopia. Khagi asserts that Pelevin's text is "the first major post-Soviet work to come to grips with the introduction of consumer capitalism and global pop culture" and "posits itself, self-reflexively and sardonically, as both a condemnation of Brave New Russia and its successful offspring." The result, according to Khagi, is that the novel is both a "traditional dystopia" and "a 'dystopian product' that dramatizes its awareness of that fact."

James Overholtzer

THE HOTHOUSE BY THE EAST RIVER

Muriel Spark

OVERVIEW

The Hothouse by the East River (1973), a short novel by Muriel Spark, is the surreal and comedic account of the mad Hazletts, who are haunted by the past and are literally haunting the present. The story moves between Paul and Elsa Hazlett's life in a luxurious but overheated Manhattan apartment in the 1970s and their former lives in England as intelligence agents disseminating propaganda to the Germans during World War II. The novel centers on the mysterious reappearance of Helmut Kiel, a dead German prisoner of war who had worked with Paul and Elsa producing black propaganda (disinformation intended to demoralize the opposition), who is now posing as a Manhattan shoe salesman named Mueller. As the fantastic plot progresses, absurdities abound, culminating in the tale's conclusion, at which point the narrator discloses that the Hazletts died in 1944 during a V-2 bombing in London. Though the story is preoccupied with the decline of civilization, Spark masterfully disguises the moral of her story with absurdities and satire—a tactic she learned while distributing black propaganda during World War II.

Although it is considered one of Spark's lesser accomplishments, *The Hothouse by the East River* garnered praise from contemporary critics. Spark was interested in Nazi propaganda and ideology and drew significantly on her career as a propagandist to create Paul and Elsa's experiences. Spark worked a six-month stint disseminating black propaganda at the Milton Bryan compound in England under the leadership of Sefton Delmer. In addition to her own experiences, Spark drew on Delmer's memoir *Black Boomerang* (1962) for *Hothouse*. Delmer produced entertaining German broadcasts interlaced with misinformation designed to weaken the morale of Nazi troops, and *black boomerang* was his term for stories that would be disseminated as propaganda and come home as "real" stories. In her autobiography, Spark describes black propaganda as "detailed truth with believable lies," a phrase that very much describes her narrative technique. Spark's experiences with black propaganda would significantly influence her future writings.

HISTORICAL AND LITERARY CONTEXT

Early in World War II, the Nazis operated three radio stations purporting to originate somewhere in Britain with the intention of disseminating pro-German propaganda to rot the morale of the British people. Later in the war, the British also operated clandestine radio stations that claimed to be official German broadcasters; several of these were under the directorship of Delmer. In order to produce authentic-sounding broadcasts, Delmer resorted to devious means of obtaining and manipulating information: recruiting German prisoners of war, bugging their camps, and intercepting communications. According to Lee Richards's *The Black Art* (2010), Delmer claimed that black propaganda's objective was "to make Germans think and act in a way which is damaging to Germany's war effort.... We try to exploit ... the ordinary German's ... desire for self-preservation, personal profit and pleasure, his herd instinct to do as others do." Spark's *Hothouse* reflects the influence of Nazi propaganda on postwar madness, such as that experienced by her characters, for the black propagandists had to imitate the Nazis to accomplish their goals.

In *Muriel Spark: The Biography* (2009), Martin Stannard claims that Spark's stint writing anti-Nazi propaganda taught her about the volatility of truth, inspiring her subsequent writing style. Stannard argues that "Delmer's notions of proof and significance were relative and unprovable.... Whatever might appear true during the war might not be true after it. Both states could be both true and untrue. There was for [Spark] something invigorating about this." After the war, Spark suffered a series of financial and health problems, including a nervous breakdown. In 1954 Spark converted to Roman Catholicism and was financially supported by fellow converts, the authors Graham Greene and Evelyn Waugh. In *The Faith and Fiction of Muriel Spark* (1982), Ruth Whittaker suggests that Spark's conversion "led to a satiric view of the fallen world." Indeed, much of Spark's fiction, including *The Hothouse by the East River,* addresses the decline of civilization.

Spark's moral seriousness is often compared to that of the Catholic writers Greene and Flannery O'Connor, and Waugh's influence is seen in Spark's satirical wit. Although much of Spark's fiction is experimental, her early 1970s novels *The Hothouse by the East River* and *Not to Disturb* (1971) were an exercise in surrealistic comedy—uncharted territory for the author. These books are riddled with impossibilities, whereas Spark's earlier novels incorporate incredible but explainable

+ *Key Facts*

Time Period:
Mid-20th Century

Genre:
Novel

Events:
World War II

Nationality:
English

MURIEL SPARK: BLURRING THE LINES BETWEEN LIFE AND ART

Muriel Spark was born Muriel Sarah Camberg in Edinburgh on February 1, 1918. She was the daughter of a Scottish Jewish father and an English Presbyterian mother. At age five Muriel began attending James Gillespie's School for Girls—a period of her life she would later draw on when writing *The Prime of Miss Jean Brodie*. Her talent for writing was first recognized at age twelve when she received a Walter Scott Award for a poem titled "Out of a Book." In 1937 Muriel married Sydney Oswald Spark and moved to Southern Rhodesia, where the couple had a son, Robin. The author would later use Africa as the setting in her first published work of fiction, "The Seraph and the Zambesi" (1951). Sydney Spark's mental instability and violence led his wife to end the marriage after seven years.

Muriel Spark returned to Britain in 1944, taking up residence at the Helena Club in London—the model for the May of Teck Club in *The Girls of Slender Means* (1963). It was at this time that Spark began working for Sefton Delmer disseminating black propaganda, an experience that would later inspire *The Hothouse by the East River*. In 1954 Spark converted to Catholicism, and her preoccupation with religion is seen in several of her works, including *Memento Mori* (1959). *The Comforters* (1957) was born of the hallucinations Spark suffered while taking amphetamines during postwar food rationing. In her autobiography, Spark expounds upon the many parallels between her life and fictional works. Many critics consider her the greatest Scottish novelist of modern times.

elements. Common sense cannot explain away the ghostly cast in *Hothouse* who interact with and are accepted as real by living characters. Incongruously, during Spark's time as a black propagandist, she sought to do the very opposite: she helped create illusions for the Germans, often by unethical means.

Despite the vast body of critical work about her fiction, Spark remains a mystery to most critics. In her book *Muriel Spark,* Patricia Stubbs maintains that Spark has "succeeded triumphantly in evading classification." In 1993, at the age of seventy-five, Spark published *Curriculum Vitae: An Autobiography* with the dual purpose of correcting critical misunderstandings about her life and revealing the links between her life and her fiction. The autobiography covers her years as a wartime propagandist in the British government and its influence on her writing style. Spark says that at "Delmer's Compound" she learned "a whole world of method and intrigue in the dark field of Black Propaganda and Psychological Warfare, and the successful and purposeful deceit of the enemy."

THEMES AND STYLE

The Hothouse by the East River focuses on madness and Spark's implication that civilization as a whole is sick.

Society's illness is seen microcosmically in the mad dialogue and bizarre actions abounding in the torrid heat of the Hazletts' home. The Hazletts' luxurious Manhattan apartment overlooking the East River is quite literally hell, a place where the tormented dead dwell. Elsa looks out over the East River to Welfare Island, the location of the New York asylums. In "Desegregated Art by Muriel Spark," Harriet Blodgett suggests that Spark employs a ghostly cast to "expose how the living are dead, so that maybe they will amend their ways and effect a better future." The macrocosmic illness of civilization is represented in Spark's characterization of New York City—the home of psychiatry and psychoanalysis—where "Sick is interesting. Sick is real." The narrator notes that New York is the "home of the vivisectors of the mind, and of the mentally vivisected still to be reassembled, of those who live intact, habitually wondering about their states of insanity, and home of those whose minds have been dead, bearing the scars of resurrection."

Spark achieves her rhetorical effect through extreme absurdities described by the detached narrator in *The Hothouse by the East River*: Elsa's shadow does not fall correctly, her friend Princess Xavier carries silkworm eggs under her breasts, Paul is convinced that Kiel is scrawling messages to him on the soles of shoes, and the Hazletts' son, Pierre, is producing a geriatric version of *Peter Pan* starring another ghost from the Hazletts' propaganda days. Logic is suspended from the very start of the novel, and, as Florence Rome points out in her 1973 review of *Hothouse,* the unemotional narration of bizarre situations forces the reader to "scan every word carefully for important clues to the author's meaning." The absurdity also has a charmingly comedic effect that allows Spark to create a surrealist tale. With such gestures, Spark slyly teaches her moral lessons to the unsuspecting reader.

Stylistically, *The Hothouse by the East River* is distinguished by its deadpan tone and matter-of-fact recounting of the bizarre, supernatural plot by the removed, nonjudgmental narrator. The narrator relates the silkworm scene as if it is a perfectly realistic and sane occurrence: "Under the protective folds of her breasts the Princess, this very morning, has concealed for warmth and fear of the frost a precious new consignment of mulberry leaves bearing numerous eggs of silkworms. They have hatched in the heat. The worms themselves now celebrate life by wriggling upon Princess Xavier's breast." The worms happily wriggling on the princess's flesh foreshadow the morbid twist at the end when the narrator reveals the ghostly nature of the characters, and the deadpan tone adds to the sense of the comic uncanny. The narrator never attempts to explain the existence of the three-dimensional specters interacting with the living, giving the tale the aura of a mysterious dream. The slippery, elusive nature of the style, plot, and themes is intentionally and masterfully crafted—yet another technique resembling black propaganda.

CRITICAL DISCUSSION

By the time *The Hothouse by the East River* was published in 1973, Spark was already an established writer of fiction, critically acclaimed for her unique style, satirical wit, and fresh take on conventional themes. Although *Hothouse* garnered much praise from contemporary critics, it is not as well known as *The Prime of Miss Jean Brodie* (1961) or *The Mandelbaum Gate* (1965), the latter of which is considered Spark's masterpiece. In comparing *Hothouse* to *Mandelbaum*, Diane Johnson notes that "while this is not the *tour de force* of construction that *The Mandelbaum Gate* is, the confident ellipses, the incisive choice of anecdote, the easy movement between past and present, among the actual, the remembered and the imagined, testify to [Spark's] complete mastery of all a novelist's means." In the *New York Times Book Review*, Richard P. Brickner comments on the effectiveness of Spark's unusual plot and its accompanying absurdities: "The book itself eases our own discomfort. The charmingly brutal originality with which the author has laid out her plot of pitfalls shocks us into laughing."

The Hothouse by the East River has been regarded as a celebrated example of Spark's ability to use satire to comment on the moral lives of her characters and society in general. The deadpan tone, strange situations, and elusive nature of *Hothouse* fit in nicely with Spark's other works, which also defy categorization and challenge readers. Rome suggests that Spark "does not write novels that can be easily pigeon-holed. In these and other books, she has concerned herself with matters beyond reality, with forces that do not lend themselves to facile explanations." Spark's unique work has had a significant influence on modern fiction, especially the novels of her fellow countryman Ian Rankin, and Spark has been ranked among Scotland's elite novelists.

The Hothouse by the East River has been studied for its bleak yet comedic evaluation of the human condition. Blodgett asserts that "the truth of the satiric parable is that the present is always a consequence of the person and the past…. [O]ur life is neither our own nor given us by God to be used for selfish or hostile ends." Since its publication, scholars have attempted to tease meaning out of *The Hothouse by the East River*, often noting its treatment of madness. Duncan Fallowell, for example, argues that Spark "has captured with uncanny assurance the nuances and slight shifts of perception of a disassociated state." Much literary and biographical criticism draws parallels between *Hothouse* and Spark's life, particularly since the publication of her autobiography. David Herman's *Muriel Spark: Twenty-First-Century Perspectives* (2010) and Stannard's controversial biography investigate the influence of Spark's wartime propaganda work on *Hothouse* and other narratives.

Muriel Spark, author of *The Hothouse by the East River*, on March 15, 1987, in Paris, France. ULF ANDERSEN/GETTY IMAGES.

BIBLIOGRAPHY

Sources

Blodgett, Harriet. "Desegregated Art by Muriel Spark." *International Fiction Review* 3.1 (1976): 25–29. Print.

Brickner, Richard P. "Nightmares." Rev. of *The Hothouse by the East River*, by Muriel Spark. *New York Times Book Review* 29 Apr. 1973: 24–25. *Contemporary Literary Criticism*. Vol. 3. Ed. Carolyn Riley. Detroit: Gale, 1975. 463–68. *Literature Criticism Online*. Web. 13 July 2012.

Fallowell, Duncan. "Hothouse Madness." Rev. of *The Hothouse by the East River*, by Muriel Spark. *Books and Bookmen* April 1973: 101. *Contemporary Literary Criticism*. Vol. 3. Ed. Carolyn Riley. Detroit: Gale, 1975. 463–68. *Literature Criticism Online*. Web. 13 July 2012.

Herman, David. *Muriel Spark: Twenty-First-Century Perspectives*. Baltimore: Johns Hopkins UP, 2010. Print.

Johnson, Diane. "Strange Fruit." Rev. of *The Hothouse by the East River*, by Muriel Spark. *Washington Post* 29 April 1973: 4–5. *Contemporary Literary Criticism*. Vol. 3. Ed. Carolyn Riley. Detroit: Gale, 1975. 463–68. *Literature Criticism Online*. Web. 13 July 2012.

Richards, Lee. *The Black Art: British Clandestine Psychological Warfare against the Third Reich*. East Sussex: PsyWar, 2010. Print.

Rome, Florence. Rev. of *The Hothouse by the East River*, by Muriel Spark. *Chicago Tribune Book World* 29 Apr. 1973: 3. *Contemporary Literary Criticism*. Vol. 3. Ed. Carolyn Riley. Detroit: Gale, 1975. 463–68. *Literature Criticism Online*. Web. 13 July 2012.

Spark, Muriel. *Curriculum Vitae: A Volume of Autobiography.* New York: New Directions, 1992. Print.

Stannard, Martin. *Muriel Spark: The Biography.* New York: Norton, 2009. Print.

Stubbs, Patricia. *Muriel Spark.* London: Longman, 1973. Print.

Whittaker, Ruth. *The Faith and Fiction of Muriel Spark.* New York: St. Martin's, 1982. Print.

Further Reading

Cairns, Craig. *The Modern Scottish Novel: Narrative and National Imagination.* Edinburgh: Edinburgh UP, 1999. Print.

Edgecombe, Rodney Stenning. *Vocation and Identity in the Fiction of Muriel Spark.* Columbia: U of Missouri P, 1990. Print.

Hynes, Joseph, ed. *Critical Essays on Muriel Spark.* New York: Hall, 1992. Print.

McQuillan, Martin. *Theorizing Muriel Spark: Gender, Race, Deconstruction.* New York: Palgrave Macmillan, 2002. Print.

Page, Norman. *Muriel Spark.* London: Macmillan, 1990. Print.

Pearlman, Mickey. *Re-Inventing Reality: Patterns and Characters in the Novels of Muriel Spark.* New York: Lang, 1996. Print.

Randisi, Jennifer Lynn. *On Her Way Rejoicing: The Fiction of Muriel Spark.* Washington, DC: Catholic U of America P, 1991. Print.

Sproxton, Judy. *The Women of Muriel Spark.* London: Constable, 1992. Print.

Stonebridge, Lyndsey. "Hearing Them Speak: Voices in Wilfred Bion, Muriel Spark, and Penelope Fitzgerald." *Textual Practice* 19.4 (2005): 445–65. Print.

Maggie Magno

"The Letter"

Wilfred Owen

OVERVIEW

"The Letter," a poem penned by Wilfred Owen during the last two years of World War I, contrasts a British soldier's cheerfully reassuring note to his wife with the realities of trench warfare. Speaking and writing in an easy vernacular, the soldier tells his family that he is safe, relatively comfortable, and on the mend. Intercut with these lines, however, is a picture of privation and danger in which the speaker can hardly spare a cigarette, a crumb of bread, or indeed a moment to write. The poem effectively calls into question the optimism, and even the honesty, of the thousands of letters sent home from the Western Front. In doing so, it serves as a grim antidote to the more popular patriotic verse that celebrated, rather than mourned, British involvement in a war of such horrific magnitude.

Almost none of Owen's poetry was published during his lifetime; "The Letter" would not see print until 1931, twelve years after his death. Once it was published, however, it served to reinforce his status as the greatest British poet of World War I. The poem reflects a considerable shift in Owen's attitude toward war, which, within his first few months at the front, had gone from gallant to bleak. It also speaks to a more general darkening of the British view of the conflict, whose cold, muddy entrenchments and poison gas were hard to romanticize; even such popular agents of propaganda as recruiting posters had gone from genteel invitations to unabashed appeals for help. Less lofty in style than Owen's more famous poems, "The Letter" is notable as a simple portrayal of a soldier trying to keep up courage at home and on the front line.

HISTORICAL AND LITERARY CONTEXT

At the beginning of the Great War, hopes were high among the British public for a quick and decisive victory. It soon became clear, however, that the conflict would afford no such solution. By the end of 1914, the British Expeditionary Force had reached an impasse on the Western Front, arrayed along some seventy miles of trenches. Moreover, the use of poison gas, which Allied troops initially deplored, had by late 1915 been grudgingly accepted as necessary. New, more toxic agents were developed during the succeeding three years, adding to the horrors of trench warfare.

By the time Owen wrote "The Letter," he was one of millions to have seen these horrors up close. He had

served from June 1916 as a second lieutenant in the Manchester Regiment, and his 1917 deployment to the Western Front had exposed him to forced marches over shell-cratered ground, desperate retreats from gas attacks, and bouts of what he euphemistically called "bayonet work." As Owen saw men on both sides perish, the view of the German army as savage "Huns" lost credence, as did the notion that the British soldier was a moral hero. Recruitment posters continued to assert such a difference, but the ideals of "glory, honour, might" contested by Owen required more and more effort to maintain. Meanwhile, the Defence of the Realm Act (1914) made overt expression of antiwar sentiments risky; the philosopher Bertrand Russell, for instance, was jailed for advocating pacifism. In important ways, the work of protest fell to soldiers like Owen who could depict firsthand "the pity of war." "The Letter" represents a poetic strategy for showing the human frailty of those held up as heroes.

British poetry in the early stages of the war echoed popular and official sentiments. Many famous authors, including poet laureate Robert Bridges, issued literary calls to arms, but "war poetry" as such was epitomized by Rupert Brooke. Brooke's sonnets, the best known of which is "The Soldier," espouse a gallant nationalism in which the fighting man emblematizes English values; public officials seized upon these poems as instruments of recruitment. Owen, however, was not alone in his desire to testify to the misery of war: his fellow soldier-poet Siegfried Sassoon likewise refused to ennoble the war with appeals to nationalism or religion, preferring to commemorate the lives and deaths of individual soldiers. Sassoon's "A Working Party" bears a particularly striking and sustained resemblance to "The Letter."

While Owen's poetry was published too late to make a difference in the war that prompted it, his legacy was ensured not only by the quality of his work but also by the interest of his literary friends. These included Sassoon, who took up the task of revising and preparing his manuscript for publication, and the future Dame Edith Sitwell. "The Letter" has served as one model for later generations seeking to describe the unromantic, physical, personal toll of war. In particular, Seamus Heaney's poetry about the Irish Troubles often shares Owen's insistence on the incongruity between war and the ordinary lives it consumes.

❖ Key Facts

Time Period:
Early 20th Century

Genre:
Poetry

Events:
World War I

Nationality:
English

THE POET'S OWN LETTERS FROM THE FRONT

Like his anonymous soldier, Owen often stopped to write home when afforded a moment's rest. Hundreds of his own wartime letters, primarily to his mother, have survived to present a rich and detailed collage of life on the front line. They are, of course, more lyrical, more descriptive, and more polished than the hastily jotted pencil note in "The Letter." They also reflect Owen's views toward the soldiers he commanded, men who much more closely resembled the speaker of "The Letter" than did Owen himself.

Many of Owen's letters bespeak condescension, even contempt, for those in his charge, whom he called "expressionless lumps." Even after four months' deployment, he could still coldly recount the loss of "a certain number of men" while mourning, a few lines later, the death of a "brother officer." His final letter home (October 31, 1917) is sometimes celebrated for its evocation of soldierly camaraderie, but this was written at a time of exceptionally high spirits, with the German army in retreat and the war nearly over. Read in aggregate, Owen's correspondence reveals an officer who sympathized with his soldiers, acknowledged their sacrifice, and mocked the absurdity of their shared plight. In his letters, however, as in his verse, Owen maintained a studied distance from the men under his command.

THEMES AND STYLE

Central to "The Letter" is a contrast between the portrayal of the war to the civilian public and the very different experience of those who fight. Readers at home are provided with a highly sanitized version of a war in which, as the soldiers knew all too well, death from disease and starvation was common. The letter writer wishes to protect his wife and children by insisting that he is "in the pink at present" and, more importantly, "out of harm's way," even as these statements are gradually revealed as untrue. Moreover, his assurances are so generic that another soldier can be asked to complete the letter when the speaker is shot. Owen portrays his subject sympathetically but also suggests that the soldier participates in a tacit national lie about the brutality of the First World War.

Owen elucidates this contrast by presenting appearance and reality in different tones and settings. The poem remains in the voice of the soldier throughout, but the letter exudes husbandly calm, offering the wife counsel on her financial troubles and looking forward to the resumption of their life together. The man in the trench, on the other hand, is hungry, cross, and traumatized, repeatedly snatched away from the business of writing. Often a vague reassurance on the part of the soldier is juxtaposed with its opposite—as when he tells his wife that he and his company are "not bad fed" only to turn a moment later and ask another soldier to "spare's a bit of bread." With such gestures

"The Letter" gradually whittles away at the heroic images of wartime propaganda.

Stylistically, the poem affects a homespun quality that suggests distanced sympathy with the common soldier. Slang and spoken-dialect features abound, even in the portion ostensibly written as a letter: for instance, the soldier writes that he will "soon be'ome" and calls one of his trenchmates a "ruddy cow." Owen, elsewhere quite capable of turning rhymes of stateliness and elegance, adopts instead such bathetic pairings as "Uns" [Huns] / "buns" and "of" / "sov[ereign]." These, along with the poem's somewhat jumbled meter and irregular rhyme scheme, are matters of deliberate craft; they portray a speaker unable (as Owen is here unwilling) to smooth over his experience of war with graceful verse. This is a strong departure from the more dignified, but also more idealistic, poetry of such pro-war authors as Rupert Brooke. It also serves as a counterpoint to Owen's more formal treatments of trench warfare, most famously in his poem "Dulce et Decorum Est."

CRITICAL DISCUSSION

As the nation surveyed the damage caused by the Great War, Owen's portrayal of the conflict came to be seen as accurate and enduring. However, his posthumous celebrity also provoked a harsh reappraisal from critics and fellow poets. Discussing Owen and other war poets in a 1923 essay, the poet Robert Graves noted that "when the Armistice came and came to stay, poetry of conflict immediately lost its purpose," replaced by poetry of "scepticism and cynicism" or "temporary escape." William Butler Yeats famously refused to include any of Owen's (or Sassoon's) poetry in *The Oxford Book of Modern Verse 1892–1935*, categorically maintaining that "passive suffering is not a theme for poetry." Yeats's personal judgments regarding "war poetry" were more caustic, especially with regard to Owen, whom he considered "a revered sandwich-board Man of the revolution" and "unworthy of the poet's corner of a country newspaper." His opinion has been vigorously contested since the anthology's publication.

As part of Owen's larger body of work, "The Letter" has been regarded as a warning not only about the human cost of World War I but also about the new modes of warfare it inaugurated. Throughout the twentieth century, readers of Owen worked to relate his bleakly prophetic verse, including the class-consciousness embodied in "The Letter," to the century's successive conflicts; World War II is the clearest point of comparison. Joseph Cohen, writing in 1957, claimed for Owen's verse the bittersweet honor of "express[ing] the essence of twentieth century war, i.e., its *totality*, with more clarity, forcefulness, compassion, and accomplishment than did the verse of his contemporaries." Cohen regarded the poet as a critic of the totalizing response—streamlining a nation's religious, artistic, social, and industrial life—that could prompt

Opposite page:
A World War I advertisement for OXO beef stock cubes portraying a happy British soldier writing a thank you note. Wilfred Owen's poem "The Letter" exposes the contrast between such optimistic portrayals of the war and the real horrors soldiers faced in the trenches. POSTER ADVERTISING 'OXO,' FROM WORLD WAR I (LITHO), DADD, FRANK (1851–1929)/PRIVATE COLLECTION/TOPHAM PICTUREPOINT/THE BRIDGEMAN ART LIBRARY.

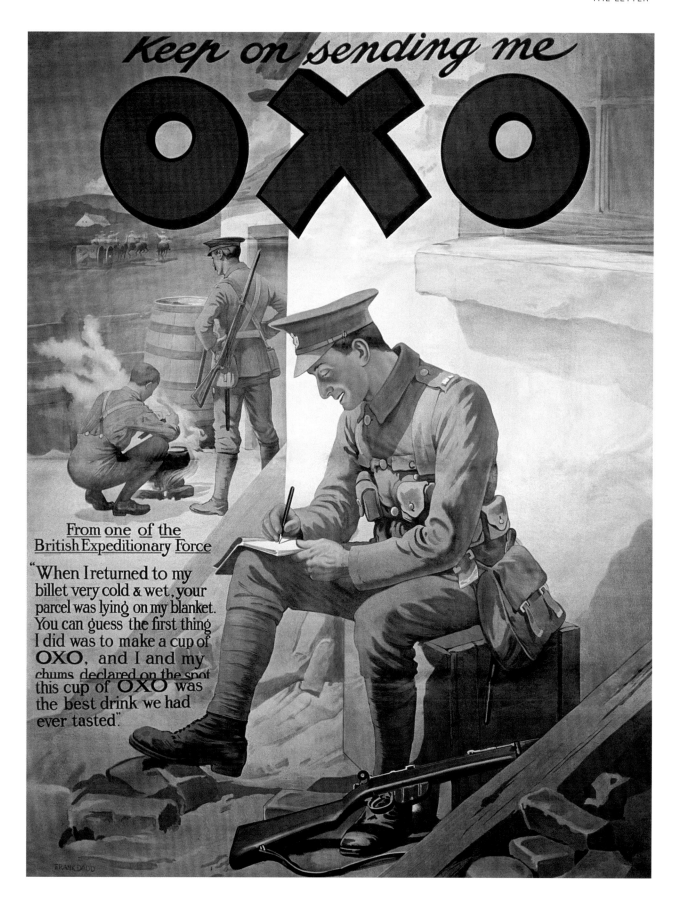

the fielding of nine million soldiers in one war or the dropping of an atomic bomb in another.

"The Letter" is little discussed in its own right, though it furthers and complicates many of the trends detected in Owen's more famous poems. Mark Graves argues, in a brief 1994 article, for the poem's importance as a satirical work, depicting not only the influence of propaganda on the thinking and writing of British infantrymen but also the degree to which censorship hampers the soldier's ability to tell the truth in detail. In these ways, the poem breaks rank to provide a different perspective from the one that Owen, himself in charge of the censoring of thousands of soldiers' letters, had the luxury of providing in his own voice.

BIBLIOGRAPHY

Sources

Cohen, Joseph. "Wilfred Owen in America." *Prairie Schooner* 31.4 (1957–58): 339–45. Print.

Graves, Mark. "Wilfred Owen's 'The Letter' and the Truth of War." *English Language Notes* 31 (1994): 59–66. Print.

Graves, Robert. "What Is Bad Poetry?" *North American Review* 218.814 (1923): 353–68. Print.

Yeats, William Butler. *Letters on Poetry from W. B. Yeats to Dorothy Wellesley.* London: Oxford UP, 1964. Print.

Yeats, William Butler, ed. *The Oxford Book of Modern Verse 1892–1935.* London: Oxford UP, 1936. Print.

Further Reading

Hibberd, Dominic. "Wilfred Owen and the Georgians." *Review of English Studies* New Series 30.117 (1979): 28–40. Print.

Kerr, Douglas. "Brothers in Arms: Family Language in Wilfred Owen." *Review of English Studies* 43.172 (1992): 518–34. Print.

Klawitter, Uwe. "Remembrance and Remediation: The Commemoration of the First World War in British Poetry." *KulturPoetik* 7.1 (2007): 24–46. Print.

Lawson, Tom. "'The Free-Masonry of Sorrow'? English National Identities and the Memorialization of the Great War in Britain, 1919–1931." *History and Memory* 20.1 (2008): 89–120. Print.

Norgate, Paul. "Wilfred Owen and the Soldier Poets." *Review of English Studies* 40.160 (1989): 516–30. Print.

Owen, Wilfred. *The Complete Poems and Fragments.* Ed. John Stallworthy. New York: W. W. Norton, 1984. Print.

Owen, Wilfred. *Wilfred Owen: The Collected Letters.* Ed. John Bell. London: Oxford UP, 1967. Print.

Rae, Patricia. "Double Sorrow: Proleptic Elegy and the End of Arcadianism in 1930s Britain." *Twentieth-Century Literature* 49.2 (2003): 246–75. Print.

Michael Hartwell

THE LIBERTY CAMPAIGN

Jonathan Dee

OVERVIEW

The Liberty Campaign (1993) by Jonathan Dee is a novel that follows New York City advertising executive Gene Trowbridge as he approaches retirement. Gene, a World War II veteran who narrates the novel, discovers that Albert Ferdinand, a neighbor originally from South America who has lived on his quiet suburban block for seven years, may be guilty of having tortured political prisoners in Brazil in the 1960s. Gene hears the accusation from a newspaper reporter and befriends Albert in an attempt to learn the truth behind the accusation because he has difficulty believing that his aloof but courteous neighbor would be capable of inflicting torture. As the two men become closer friends, Gene grapples with his fondness for and loyalty to someone accused of such cruelty and must examine what this internal conflict reveals about his own identity. The novel reveals that the search for truth is never straightforward, and that influence from the media, friends, or other sources always plays a role in the decisions we make.

Dee served as senior editor of *The Paris Review,* and *The Liberty Campaign* was his second novel. Most reviews have focused on *The Liberty Campaign*'s reflections on moral decisions, the process of aging, and advertising's role in daily American life. *Publisher's Weekly* called the novel "startling and utterly original" and "compulsively readable and obstinately memorable," and it applauded the subtlety of Dee's writing. Written soon after the end of the Persian Gulf War, *The Liberty Campaign* remains significant in its investigation of the relationship between advertising and news in the search for truth and self-understanding.

HISTORICAL AND LITERARY CONTEXT

From 1990 to 1991 the United States was engaged in the Persian Gulf War after American troops invaded Iraq in response to Iraq's occupation of Kuwait. The war marked the first time that news outlets broadcast from the front lines of a conflict. However, the U.S. government exerted significant control over the press. John R. MacArthur writes that the war was generally considered a "devastating and immoral victory for military censorship." The regulation of the information available to news organizations led to complaints that the government manufactured the war and Americans' support of it.

The Liberty Campaign, which was published just after the Gulf War ended, equates news with advertisement, and the novel emphasizes the power each has in controlling information and influencing American self-perceptions. Dee draws on the history of Madison Avenue firms' promotion of Latin American regimes and critiques the mediation of information, which allows Americans to act as "police" of the world while maintaining a distance from world events. Just as Americans observed the geographically distant Gulf War from the comfort of their living rooms, so too does Gene explain he merely "saw a great many terrible things" when he fought in World War II "on behalf of something." *The Liberty Campaign* makes clear that Gene and his neighbors know nothing about Brazil's political history, in which Albert was so intimately involved. Although Gene associates with Albert, he ultimately protects himself and chooses not to help Albert escape the authorities. Instead, he watches from down the street as Albert is arrested.

Much has been written about the U.S. government's distortion of information about the Gulf War. Jan Jagodzinski explains that the military orchestrated which images to show, and that, to "mediate anxiety, no gruesome up-close images of the enemy being killed were shown." Instead, viewers saw missiles hitting their targets to demonstrate the competency of the U.S. military, along with black-and-white images that resembled early video games. The idea of choosing particular images as selling points for the war relates to an article Dee wrote called "But Is It Advertising?" for *Harper's* in which Dee quotes advertising critic Leslie Savan as noting that "the news is just advertising by the other side." In the article, Dee continues many of the themes of *The Liberty Campaign,* including the ways advertisements attempt to invent an identity for consumers and his belief that advertising is a type of art, although the message is always one of commodification and conformity.

In 2009 the *New York Times* described Dee as "the kind of writer who thinks hard about contemporary realities and then builds sturdy, stately novels of ideas around them." This applies just as well to Dee's other novels, including *The Privileges* (2010), which was written in the aftermath of the 2008 credit crisis and nominated for the 2011 Pulitzer Prize. *The Liberty Campaign*'s insistence on the insidious influence

⁂ Key Facts

Time Period:
Late 20th Century

Genre:
Novel

Events:
Persian Gulf War

Nationality:
American

A CASE OF MISTAKEN IDENTITY?

Jonathan Dee told the *New York Times* in 1993 that the case of John Demjanjuk inspired *The Liberty Campaign*. Demjanjuk, a Ukrainian American autoworker from Ohio, was accused of being a Nazi death-camp guard in Poland and Germany during World War II. After the war, many former Nazi soldiers fled Europe to escape trial, imprisonment, and death. Demjanjuk arrived in the United States in 1952, and he worked at a Ford factory while raising three children with his wife in a Cleveland suburb.

In the 1980s, Demjanjuk was extradited to Israel and Germany to stand trial as an accessory in the murders of thousands of Jewish prisoners during the Holocaust. His case continued for more than thirty years, and he was twice sentenced to death then freed. Demjanjuk insisted that the accusation was a case of mistaken identity, and his neighbors raised millions of dollars for his defense. In May 2011, Demjanjuk was sentenced to five years in prison. He was free and awaiting an appeal when he died in Germany in March 2012.

of advertising and news media has only become more relevant with the proliferation of new technologies to transmit advertisements and news.

THEMES AND STYLE

The Liberty Campaign investigates the difficulty of discovering truth and the moral burden that accompanies such a discovery. Gene believes that advertisements "shape the culture" and that the "quality of the ad, rather than of what it advertises, is the important thing." This assertion, in addition to supporting Dee's view that advertisements are art, accentuates the distance between an ad and the truth of what it is selling. Gene, who has spent his career in advertising, craves truth, and he "desperately coveted the empowering feeling of knowing some important thing that nobody else knew." When Gene learns about Albert's violent history, first from the newspaper reporter and then from Albert himself, he feels overwhelmed by this knowledge and by his vow to keep the secret. Gene grows distant from his wife and friends as he examines his self-awareness and his ability to judge people. He must think deeply about what and who influences him, and he recognizes that truth is subjective and that he may even prefer that it be obscured.

The first-person narration of *The Liberty Campaign* compels the reader to make a personal judgment concerning Albert's past and Gene's decision to befriend him and to examine the factors that influence such a judgment. Gene admits to "wariness about investing the media with too much trust," and the reader must decide which character to believe and whether Dee's novel should be trusted at all. Gene invites the reader's opinion of his decisions when he

asks himself, "What would it mean, then, if someone capable of such beastly, sadistic, dispassionate activity … was in fact a pleasant fellow … someone to whom I could feel a bond?" This question offers the reader a chance to reflect on morally gray areas in his or her own life and to consider the fragmented identities some people possess. The first-person narration within the context of Gene's impending retirement also gives Gene a chance to muse on aging and his career, which essentially traces the evolution of advertising.

Gene's self-conscious nostalgia for the past as he navigates major life changes permeates *The Liberty Campaign*. He finds comfort in his small Long Island town, where the neighbors know each other and children march in the quaint Fourth of July parade each summer. The introspective tone of the book, punctuated with rhetorical questions, illustrates how the revelation of Albert's past creates mental dissonance for Gene. Although Albert explains that he is "a different person now," something he had "always considered … an American idea," Gene realizes that the American ideas he values have more to do with maintaining consistency, and that change is difficult for him. The book leaves the reader to answer many of Gene's questions, and it ends with Gene expressing his hope that eventually he will attain self-knowledge.

CRITICAL DISCUSSION

Because of Dee's established reputation in the literary world, reviewers welcomed *The Liberty Campaign*. Writing in a 1993 piece in the *New York Times,* Ivana Edwards characterizes the novel as "quietly gripping and controlled," a work that is "strung plausibly on the thorns of a moral imbroglio as ancient as many of the religions of mankind and as current as today's global television networks." Michael O'Mahony of the *Los Angeles Times Book Review* calls the novel "a sublime and inventive tour de force," noting, "In Gene, Dee has invented a narrator with whom most readers will empathize, and placed him in a situation that is simultaneously real and surreal." Reviewers have applauded Dee's unexpected insertion of a quiet evil into the protected suburban lifestyle familiar to many Americans. Dee's ability to smoothly navigate such large topics as the search for truth and the influence of advertising also garnered praise.

Although *The Liberty Campaign* is out of print, the novel's lasting power comes from Dee's expert balancing of age-old themes with issues that are very much grounded in their own time period. Gene's attempt to understand himself and to decide whether to protect himself or to save a friend takes place at the end of the Gulf War in a world filled with Nike ads and media-influenced perceptions. Gene himself, by virtue of his profession, can be seen as a propagandist putting forth his own stylized view of the United States for the world's approval. His reflections on his career and family life illustrate how all of these influences affect his self-identity. Dee uses Gene to represent the ways members of each generation struggle to understand themselves and each other and the influences that contribute to their self-perceptions and the values they hold dear.

Because of its place early in Dee's career as a novelist, *The Liberty Campaign* has yet to generate a significant body of scholarship outside of book reviews, and it is often overlooked in favor of his more popular novel *The Privileges*. Nonetheless, *The Liberty Campaign* set the tone for Dee's subsequent novels and helped establish him as a novelist capable of tackling moral and ethical decisions and other intellectual topics. Even when juggling large ideas, Dee grounds his novels with subtly written and realistic characters. He frequently returns to themes present in *The Liberty Campaign,* particularly the decisions and ethics behind advertising and the sale of art.

Soldiers and tanks guarding the War Ministry in Rio de Janeiro on April 1, 1964, the night of the Brazilian coup d'état. In Jonathan Dee's novel *The Liberty Campaign,* the character Albert Ferdinand must reckon with war crimes he committed during the regime. © BETTMANN/CORBIS.

BIBLIOGRAPHY

Sources

Dee, Jonathan. "But Is It Advertising?" *Harper's* Jan. 1999: 61. *Academic Search Complete.* Web. 24 Aug. 2012.

———. *The Liberty Campaign.* New York: Doubleday, 1993. Print.

Edwards, Ivana. "Author Finds His Inspiration in Demjanjuk and Long Island." *New York Times.* New York Times, 8 Aug. 1993. Web. 20 Aug. 2012.

"The Liberty Campaign." Rev. of *The Liberty Campaign,* by Jonathan Dee. *Publishers Weekly* 24 May 1993: 69+. *Literature Resource Center.* Web. 15 Aug. 2012.

MacArthur, John R. *Second Front: Censorship and Propaganda in the 1991 Gulf War.* Berkeley: U of California P, 2004. Print.

O'Mahoney, Michael. "The Killer Next Door." Rev. of *The Liberty Campaign*, by Jonathan Dee. *Los Angeles Times Book Review.* Tribune Company, 18 Jul. 1993. Web. 20 Aug. 2012.

"Up Front: Jonathan Dee." *New York Times.* New York Times, 14 June 2009. Web. 25 Aug. 2012.

Further Reading

Dee, Jonathan. *Palladio: A Novel.* New York: Vintage Contemporaries, 2003. Print.

———. *The Privileges: A Novel.* New York: Random, 2010. Print.

Holley, Joe, and Adam Bernstein. "John Demjanjuk, Convicted Nazi Criminal, Dies at 91." *Washington Post.* Washington Post, 18 Mar. 2012. Web. 20 Aug. 2012.

Jagodzinski, Jan. "Revisiting and Reviewing the Media Spin Surrounding the Gulf Wars." *Simile* 7.4 (2007): 1–15. *Academic Search Complete.* Web. 24 Aug. 2012.

Roth, Marco. "The Credit Crisis and the Novel." *Dissent* 57.4 (2010): 103–07. *Academic Search Complete.* Web. 25 Aug. 2012.

Kathryn Molinaro

THE MANCHURIAN CANDIDATE

Richard Condon

✤ *Key Facts*

Time Period:
Mid-20th Century

Genre:
Novel

Events:
Korean War; rise of
McCarthyism

Nationality:
American

OVERVIEW

Richard Condon's 1959 novel *The Manchurian Candidate* follows a group of American GIs who are captured during the Korean War (1950–53) and brainwashed by Chinese forces. The GIs return to the United States with a story that the communists have implanted in their minds. Raymond Shaw has been programmed to assassinate the Democratic presidential candidate so that the vice presidential candidate, Raymond's stepfather Johnny Iselin, can capture the office. Iselin is a dull drunk with no real motivations of his own and serves as a puppet for his wife, Eleanor, who is Shaw's mother and herself a communist operative. Eleanor's plans go beyond the presidency, however. Her ultimate goal is to gain control of the global geopolitical machine. The novel, which is most often classified as a thriller, uses brainwashing as a vehicle to comment on the dishonesty of the political system of the United States.

Written near the height of Cold War paranoia, Condon's novel reflects the cultural anxiety created by the conflict between the United States and the Soviet Union and, more deeply, between capitalist democracy and communist totalitarianism. This anxiety had perhaps peaked with the hearings conducted by Wisconsin senator Joseph McCarthy that targeted alleged communist operatives within U.S. government agencies. Condon's novel, which captures these anxieties, found a receptive audience upon its release, and it remains popular among fans of espionage and Cold War fiction. The term "Manchurian candidate" has since entered general parlance and has been used pejoratively to describe a variety of political figures, including John McCain and Barack Obama.

HISTORICAL AND LITERARY CONTEXT

At the end of World War II, the allies found themselves at odds regarding the means of governing and maintaining peace in contentious areas. When the dust settled, the United States and the Soviet Union emerged as two competing superpowers at military and ideological loggerheads. As rhetoric between the nations grew more heated, fears about the possibility of nuclear war proliferated in the public consciousness. With these fears came the suspicion that Russian operatives might have infiltrated the U.S. government, thus imperiling democratic freedoms.

The McCarthy hearings of the early 1950s demonstrated the culture of fear in the United States at the time. The "Second Red Scare" (1947–57) occurred as the public became unsettled about national security in the wake of the espionage trial of Julius and Ethel Rosenberg in 1951, the formation of the Iron Curtain around Eastern Europe, and the victory of the communists in the Chinese Civil War. After the Korean War, widespread reports of American POWs having been subjected to hours of indoctrination by the Chinese provided further evidence that appearances could be dangerously deceiving. In Condon's novel, the McCarthy-like Johnny Iselin is described as a "lout" who nevertheless has "a gift for merchandising justice." In the hands of Raymond Shaw's politically shrewd mother, Johnny appears "a formidable administrator, a conserver who would dare; an honest, courageous, conscience-thrilled, God-fearing public servant." Meanwhile, Raymond Shaw, a Medal of Honor recipient, is also an assassin.

Downplaying any serious ideological concerns, Condon referred to his novel as "a political adventure," citing Sinclair Lewis's *It Can't Happen Here* (1935), Robert Penn Warren's *All the King's Men* (1946), and William Lederer and Eugene Burdick's *The Ugly American* (1958) as influential examples of this sub-genre. *The Manchurian Candidate* was Condon's second novel, and critics have noted that Condon, who had spent years working in the movie industry as a publicity agent, wrote the novel with a movie deal in mind.

Novels involving espionage continued to enjoy popularity in the decades following the Second Red Scare, and critics cite *The Manchurian Candidate* as a template for many of them. Ian Fleming's James Bond series, which was introduced in 1953, included the 1965 installment *The Man with the Golden Gun,* which, in telling the story of Bond's "treatment" in Leningrad and subsequent attempts as an unconscious assassin, echoes Condon's earlier novel. Walter Wager's *Telefon* (1975), also using a similar conceit, imagines the infiltration of the United States by 136 Soviet sleeper units following the U-2 spy plane incident of 1960. John Frankenheimer's 1962 film version of Condon's novel was remade in 2004, with the action taking place during the Gulf War (1990–91) and reflecting present-day fears surrounding terrorism and technology.

THEMES AND STYLE

Brainwashing, alternately referred to in the novel as conditioning, is the major theme of *The Manchurian Candidate*. In the Shaw family, brainwashing goes back several generations. Shaw's mother was conditioned through incest to betray loved ones. In turn, her repulsive behavior conditions her son to misanthropy. Further, as Mrs. Iselin she is instrumental in conditioning the American people through political propaganda to believe Johnny Iselin's contentions regarding communists in the government. The claims are baseless, and Mrs. Iselin deliberately chooses to keep the charges and the names and number of people involved vague because explicitness would raise questions: "Thinking made Americans' heads hurt and was therefore to be avoided."

As David Seed notes, *The Manchurian Candidate* contains "two diametrically opposed narrative processes at work," employing political satire and melodrama to serve the novel's theme. The passages that develop the communist plot targeting the 1960 Democratic convention are juxtaposed with a series of retrospective segments that reveal Mrs. Iselin's backstory, replete with booze, sex, and family conflict. In keeping with the novel's theme, Condon scatters products emblematic of American commercial culture throughout the novel. The captured Americans in the prison camp think they're drinking Coca-Cola rather than Chinese tea. Mrs. Iselin, when pressed as to the number of communists on Johnny Iselin's list, glances at a bottle of Heinz Ketchup and says "Fifty-seven." Brainwashing is not solely the province of communists.

The Manchurian Candidate employs the authoritative voice of a third-person narrator to counteract the implausibility of the brainwashed assassin and to navigate the different tones required by the narrative as it shifts between the conditioning, Shaw's homecoming, Marco's suspicions, and Shaw's mother. While the actual conditioning of Shaw and his platoon is not described, the narrator presents research director Yen Lo's methods in terms that seem scientifically precise and hence more legitimate. "Operators" deploy "subjects" "by remote control." Shaw acts automatically, without the sense of agency that reason and feeling provide. While it is clear that Condon effectively used voice to advance his theme, critics have repeatedly noted that stylistically the novel is something of a pastiche. Discussing the novel's style, Louis Menard notes that "it is kind of the summa of the styles of paperback fiction circa 1959." The writing "is sometimes hardboiled" or "adopts a police blotter … degree zero" mode. Alternatively it "signals feeling by waxing poetic … signals wisdom by waxing incomprehensible … and, when appropriate, it salivates."

CRITICAL DISCUSSION

The Manchurian Candidate became a best seller upon publication, although it met with mixed reviews. It was lauded in the *New York Times* as "a wild, vigorous,

DID CONDON PLAGIARIZE?

In 1998 a software engineer from California wrote a blog post on the possibility that Richard Condon had lifted several paragraphs of *The Manchurian Candidate* from Richard Graves's 1934 novel of the Roman Empire, *I, Claudius*. The *San Francisco Chronicle* picked up the story, consulting with a forensic linguist as well as with Louis Menard. Menard, a Pulitzer Prize-winning journalist, had reviewed the novel for the *New Yorker* and had commented on the "mélange" of styles in *The Manchurian Candidate*. He discusses this stylistic mishmash at length in an introduction to the Four Walls edition of the novel, commenting that "*The Manchurian Candidate* may be pulp, but it is very tony pulp. It is a man in a tartan tuxedo, chicken a la king with shaved truffles, a signed LeRoy Neiman."

John Olsson, a forensic linguist and director of the Forensic Linguistics Institute near London, expresses the opinion that Condon's novel contains several types of plagiarism. "As plagiarists go," he writes, "Condon is quite creative, he does not confine himself to one source and is prepared to throw other ingredients into the pot." Olsson adds, "However, this does not let him off the hook, since a plagiarist is a plagiarist, as every college student knows."

curiously readable mélange" and in the *New Yorker* as "a wild and exhilarating satire." Some critics dismissed it as pulp, while others pointed out the novel's uneven tone and clunky prose. It has since been named one of *Time* magazine's "Ten Best Bad Novels." Given its status as a popular novel, it did not receive widespread scholarly attention for several decades.

The Manchurian Candidate frequently pops up in political discussions, particularly those dealing with conspiracy theories. Indeed, Frankenheimer's film version of the novel, which starred Frank Sinatra, has been posited as a trigger for Lee Harvey Oswald's 1963 assassination of John F. Kennedy; the movie was playing in a theater near Oswald's apartment several weeks before the shooting. While this notion has been largely debunked, it was rumored to have prompted United Artists to pull the film from theaters. Sinatra, who gained control of the film's rights in the early 1970s, was said to have been moved by guilt to take the film out of circulation. The validity of these claims is uncertain, but they remain part of the mythology of the work. John Marks's *The Search for the "Manchurian Candidate": The CIA and Mind Control: The Secret History of the Behavioral Sciences* (1979) explored the history of mind-control experiments conducted by the Central Intelligence Agency, ushering the term "Manchurian candidate" into widespread use. Ideas from Condon's novel continue to influence debates about the fitness of candidates for political office, and the epithet "Manchurian candidate" is used to cast doubt on a candidate's motives or affiliations.

American soldiers (played by Frank Sinatra and Laurence Harvey) are hypnotized by their Communist captors in this still from the 1962 film adaptation of *The Manchurian Candidate*. UNITED ARTISTS/THE KOBAL COLLECTION/ART RESOURCE, NY.

The Manchurian Candidate has also figured in larger discussions of Cold War fiction and its descendants. Some scholarship, while acknowledging the novel's Cold War framework, locates Condon's preoccupations elsewhere. Michael Szalay, who draws parallels between Condon and the Beats, mined the author's personal papers and details gleaned from his biography and suggests that his "thinly imagined Cold War politics obscures not only the reconciliation of serious literary ambition and cynical hackwork but the hipster's crucial function in conflating these political and professional registers." Other criticism has focused on Cold War themes in *The Manchurian Candidate* as a continuation of the Yellow Peril tradition (which depicted Asian immigrants as a threat to Western societies) exemplified by works such as Sax Rohmer's novel *President Fu Manchu* (1936). Most recent scholarship has focused on the film versions of the novel (particularly Jonathan Demme's 2004 remake), perhaps because they speak more directly to twenty-first-century concerns.

BIBLIOGRAPHY

Sources

Balliett, Whitney. Rev. of *The Manchurian Candidate*, by Richard Condon. *New Yorker* 30 May 1959: 101–3. Print.

Bennett, Sally H. "Richard Condon: Overview." *Contemporary Novelists.* Ed. Susan Windisch Brown. 6th ed. New York: St. James, 1996. *Literature Resource Center.* Web. 16 June 2012.

"Cold War Literature." *Twentieth-Century Literary Criticism.* Ed. Thomas J. Schoenberg. Vol. 186. Detroit: Gale, 2007. *Literature Resource Center.* Web. 16 June 2012.

Morton, Frederic. "One Thing Led to Another." Rev. of *The Manchurian Candidate*, by Richard Condon. *New York Times.* New York Times, 26 April 1959. Web. 28 Jan. 2013.

Menard, Louis. "Brainwashed: Where the Manchurian Candidate Comes From." *New Yorker.* Condé Nast, 15 Sept. 2003. Web. 15 June 2012.

Seed, David. *Brainwashing: The Fictions of Mind Control: A Study of Novels and Films since World War II.* Kent: Kent State UP, 2004. Print.

Szalay, Michael. "The White Oriental." *Modern Language Quarterly* 67.3 (2006). *Literature Resource Center.* Web. 16 June 2012.

Further Reading

Cochran, David. "The Creation of the Cold War Consensus and the Emergence of the Underground Culture." *America Noir: Underground Writers and Filmmakers of the Postwar Era.* Washington, DC: Smithsonian Institution, 2000. 1–15. Print.

Jacobson, Mathew, and Gaspar Gonzales. *What Have They Built You to Do? The Manchurian Candidate and Cold War America.* Minneapolis: U of Minnesota P, 2006. Print.

Lipschultz, Ronnie. *Cold War Fantasies: Film, Fiction and Foreign Policy.* Lanham: Rowman, 2001. Print.

Marks, John D. *The Search for the "Manchurian Candidate": The CIA and Mind Control: The Secret History of the Behavioral Sciences.* Norton, 1979. Print.

Seed, David. "Brainwashing and Cold War Demonology." *Prospects* 22 (2007): 535–73. Print.

Wildermuth, Mark E. "Electronic media and the feminine in the national security regime: The Manchurian Candidate before and after 9/11." *Journal of Popular Film and Television* 35.3 (2007). *Literature Resource Center.* Web. 16 June 2012.

Media Adaptations

The Manchurian Candidate. Dir. John Frankenheimer. Perf. Frank Sinatra, Laurence Harvey, and Janet Leigh. M.C. Productions, 1962. Film.

The Manchurian Candidate. Dir. Jonathan Demme. Perf. Denzel Washington, Liev Schreiber, and Meryl Streep. Paramount, 2004. Film.

Daisy Gard

"MARIO AND THE MAGICIAN"

Thomas Mann

OVERVIEW

"Mario and the Magician" (1930) is Thomas Mann's fictional evocation of political behavior in an ominous new key in post–World War I Europe. The unnamed narrator's unexpected dark experiences in an Italian resort town appear especially transgressive and appalling in Mann's controlled and eloquent prose. Unfolding along a downward trajectory, from the promise of a summertime vacation to disturbing experiences marked by betrayal and contempt, the story is a portrait of xenophobic ferment and terror. Indeed, Mann's tale is a study of propaganda—its psychological foundations, its potential for social mobilization and control, and the role it plays in transforming politics into theater for the desperate masses.

Published at a critical point in Germany's resolute postwar struggle for economic and cultural stability, "Mario and the Magician" was immediately celebrated by critics for its investigations into the lethally combustible appeal of mass politics. A counter-interpretation also formed that exalted the work less for its political implications than for its psychological energy and literary power. In many respects, "Mario" is consistent with other important examples of Mann's prolific literary production. Its focus on an artist (in this case, the magician Cipolla) recurs in other tales, notably "Death in Venice" (1911) and *The Magic Mountain* (1924), and its theme of social disease (or nationalist excitement, which Mann describes as "something rather like an illness") is dominant in *Doctor Faustus* (1947) and other works. Mann wrote "Mario and the Magician" in 1929, the same year in which he received the Nobel Prize for literature.

HISTORICAL AND LITERARY CONTEXT

It took Germany five to six years after its humiliating defeat in 1918 at the end of the Great War to restore its economic footing and reenter the world of nations. During that period, the Weimar Republic, confirmed following the flight of Kaiser Wilhelm II and the ratification of the country's constitution in 1919, failed to achieve a significant measure of political moderation or economic security. These early years of Germany's republican experiment were sullied by hyperinflation, a result of the government's production of artificial currency in an effort to meet punitive Allied demands for reparations, and by political extremism from the right, the communist left, and the emerging Nazi Party. Stabilization in the mid-1920s was secured through the relaxation of the terms of the reparations agreement and a new international pragmatism, but the late 1920s brought more economic setbacks, culminating in the stock market crash of 1929.

Even before the Great Depression, Mann had grown restive about the cultural turbulence in postwar Europe. His novella "Disorder and Early Sorrow" (1925) is an exploration of the perils of popular addiction to technological innovation and artistic novelty. "Mario and the Magician" is particularly attuned to political disorder. With the economic collapse of 1929, the number of parliamentary delegates for the Nazi Party jumped to 230 in 1932 from twelve in 1928, and the number of communist delegates doubled. Meanwhile, support for the republican parties declined. The economic crisis was of particular concern in Germany because the nation was experiencing its second economic catastrophe in roughly a decade.

Following World War I, many among the German literati set the stage for the political rhetoric that would follow. In the chapter "Fire" in *Der Kampf als inneres Erlebnis* (1922), Ernst Jünger exalts the archetypical "new man," who embodies the spirit of the warrior. In "The Longing of Our Time for a Worldview" (1926), Hermann Hesse articulates an irrational "yearning search," a "reawakening of metaphysical needs … for religiosity and community." Perhaps the most graphic portrait of crowd psychology emerged in the German production of silent films. In *Metropolis* (1927), director Fritz Lang depicts oppressed workers, "the temple of labor," in states of visceral agitation and revolutionary upheaval; *M* (1931) portrays a society on the verge of mass hysteria. With "Mario and the Magician," Mann manages to distill such images of desperate, vulnerable, and belligerent crowd behavior into a single, disquieting piece.

Mann's short story proved to be ballast against the eventual triumph of fascism in Germany and throughout Europe. Republican sympathizers, in hailing the work, found a distinguished ally for their beleaguered cause, though the story, in describing the moral acquiescence of an elite to Cipolla's diabolical charm, raises as many questions about the firmness of that elite's convictions as it does about its fascist nemesis. Nonetheless, politics came to dominate the story's critical legacy.

+ *Key Facts*

Time Period:
Mid-20th Century

Genre:
Short Story

Events:
World War I; Great Depression

Nationality:
German

MANN AND HITLER

There is no evidence that Thomas Mann read Adolf Hitler's *Mein Kampf*, the 1925 manifesto of the Nazi movement, but there is an uncanny resemblance between Mann's setting of the magician's theater performance in his story "Mario and the Magician" and Hitler's requirements for political theater set forth in *Mein Kampf*'s second volume. "Go to a theater performance," Hitler observes, "and witness a play at three o'clock in the afternoon and the same play with the same actors at eight at night, and you will be amazed at the difference in effect and impression." In "Mario," the magic show begins at nine o'clock, a deliberate ruse, the narrator believes: "Cipolla made us wait for him."

What was Cipolla's aim? What effect did Hitler hope to achieve? As Mann's story and Hitler's book suggest, both the magician and the führer saw new possibilities for social control in psychological techniques of mass suggestion. "At night," Hitler declares, "people's will power … succumb[s] more easily to the dominating force of a stronger will." As Mann had come to understand, given the right circumstances, when "fatigue" sets in and an irresistible urge to acquiesce takes over, it is easy for any of us to let our guard down and follow the "master, had he so willed it, to the ends of the earth."

Scholars such as Manfred Dierks and Anthony Heilbut assert that the story revolves around the "Führer" and proto-fascism. Others, such as Alan Bance and Eugene Lunn, compare Cipolla with Mussolini.

THEMES AND STYLE

Mann's main concern in "Mario and the Magician" is to show the surprising susceptibility of "average humanity" to the "magnetic transmission" of the magician in an evening's performance at an Italian seacoast resort. Coaxed to the stage and forced by Cipolla to engage in risible, if not delusional, behavior, the audience members nonetheless are "quite pleased to be relieved of the burden of voluntary choice." In an informal prologue, Mann anticipates the cumulative tragedy—indeed, the "fall [of] … an epoch"—by describing the "unnatural" and "depressing" displays of thoughtless, xenophobic injustice by the hotel's management and the "middle-class mob" on the nearby beach. Here, the canons of conventional propriety mean nothing; only the will of the majority and "the naïve misuse of power" hold sway. By juxtaposing Cipolla with the crowd and demonstrating the latter's tragic complicity, Mann exposes the appeal of the irrational—and the criminality of exploiting it—in the exercise of power.

The story's poignancy rests in how Mann conveys it. His main strategy is to tell it from the point of view of the narrator, who is from northern Europe, perhaps Germany. He is Mann's protagonist, representing a more refined, rational, and even arrogant worldview than that of the mob and the "national ideal"

Opposite page:
Illustration of fascist leaders Benito Mussolini and Adolf Hitler on the cover of a 1938 issue of the Italian periodical *Il Mattino Illustrato.* In "Mario and the Magician" (1930), Thomas Mann criticizes fascism. © MARY EVANS PICTURE LIBRARY/ ALAMY.

he encounters in the Italian resort. By adopting this voice, Mann is able to express surprise at the triumph of a new and dispiriting political discourse in a land where "human culture came to flower." At the same time, he develops the narrator's own susceptibilities: recognizing more than once that "it was not good to be here," the protagonist nonetheless stays with his voiceless wife and two children since "we had caught the general devil-may-careness of the hour." Reason, Mann suggests, is fragile, and so is, by extension, the very foundation of humanity. Mann illustrates the unraveling of civilized humanity with characters who, one by one, willingly succumb to Cipolla's magical spell. Finally, Mario, a waiter who is practically invisible until the end of the story, emerges as the hero: after the magician ridicules the waiter's love for a young woman, Mario shoots him.

The tone throughout the story is formal; there is not a hint of street language, suggesting that Mann is deliberately distancing himself from the mob his narrator encounters. Given the narrator's own complicity in this story of hypnotic influence, Mann's stylistic formalism is, however, paradoxical—perhaps serving as a critique of the very conventions that defined his literary reputation or even as a plaintive confession of his own anachronism. Just a few years after "Mario" was published, Mann lamented that his faith in reason had been "superseded" by "a humanity '*après nous.*'" In the story, the narrator also feels "quite isolated and even temporarily *déclassé.*" Unreason—the foundation of the new regime of power and influence—is not only the problem in Mann's account. The solution—the shooting of Cipolla—is equally irrational and disquieting. "Even the dancers came to a full stop and stared about, struck dumb," writes Mann.

CRITICAL DISCUSSION

Against the backdrop of ascendant political extremism in Europe, "Mario" almost immediately acquired a reputation as an antifascist polemic. Surely it is no accident that the story takes place in fascist Italy. Indeed, Cipolla announces the presence of "the brother of the *Duce*" at one of his performances. By providing a timely and plausible taxonomy of mass suggestion and fascism and sounding a call for "liberation," "Mario" became politically totemic. Mann's reputation for democratic convictions flourished as a Nazi campaign of invective mounted against him. Alarmed by the "reign of terror" and finding himself accused of "intellectual high treason," he left Germany for good on February 11, 1933, some three weeks after the Nazis came to power.

"Mario" subsequently influenced the growth of a cottage industry devoted to theories of fascism. Its observations about willful obedience were explored by Theodor Adorno in *The Authoritarian Personality* (1950), Erich Fromm in *Escape from Freedom* (1941), and other proponents of critical theory associated with the Frankfurt School of social research. More recently,

IL MATTINO ILLUSTRATO

Un grande fuori-testo a colori con i ritratti dei due Condottieri HITLER e MUSSOLINI è allegato a questo numero del giornale

Anno XV - N. 19 - NAPOLI
9 - 16 Maggio 1938 — Anno XVI
Si pubblica ogni settimana - Prezzo cent. 50

Susan Sontag's provocative essay "Fascinating Fascism" (1980) picked up on the theme of seduction in "Mario." Mann's story directly influenced cultural production as well, notably in adaptations for the operatic stage, beginning with a Hungarian production in 1989, and in a 1994 German film directed by Klaus Maria Brandauer.

It is perhaps too easy, however, to declare the story simply an indictment of political fascism. It is similarly too convenient to equate Cipolla with Mussolini or Hitler. Clearly, fascism—specifically Nazism—was a reality that provided Mann with his story's scaffolding, but it would be misleading to confuse the reception of the work with the author's intentions. "Mario" represented a turning point for Mann, as well as for Germany itself. His decision to drop the story's subtitle ("Novella") after its first edition suggests how quickly his and others' conception of the work changed: from a masterwork of humanism, symbolism, and myth, for which he was generally acclaimed, to a masterstroke of compelling polemic. Mann himself later recalled that "Mario" was as much an ethical expression as it was political. As a work of timeless value, "Mario" will be read as a meditation on some of the more ominous aspects of the human condition—the willingness to surrender critical thinking and judgment, the canny "misuse of power" to effect emotional manipulation and social control, the intoxication of the crowd, and the apocalyptic triumph of dystopia in times of desperation.

BIBLIOGRAPHY
Sources

Hitler, Adolf. *Mein Kampf.* Trans. Ralph Manheim. Boston: Houghton, 1998. Print.

Mann, Thomas. "Mario and the Magician." *Death in Venice, and Seven Other Stories.* Trans. H. T. Lowe-Porter. New York: Vintage, 1989. 133–78. Print.

Sontag, Susan. "Fascinating Fascism." *Under the Sign of Saturn.* New York: Farrar, 1980. 73–108. Print.

Further Reading

Bance, Alan. "The Political Becomes Personal: Disorder and Early Sorrow and Mario and the Magician." *The Cambridge Companion to Thomas Mann.* Cambridge: Cambridge UP, 2002. 107–18. Print.

Dierks, Manfred. "Thomas Mann's Late Politics." *A Companion to the Works of Thomas Mann.* Ed. Herbert Lehnert and Eva Wessel. New York: Camden, 2004. 203–20. Print.

Geulen, Eva. "Resistance and Representation: A Case Study of Thomas Mann's 'Mario and the Magician.'" *New German Critique* 68 (1996): 3–29. Print.

Heilbut, Anthony. *Thomas Mann: Eros and Literature.* New York: Knopf, 1996. Print.

Klein, Dennis, ed. *The New World Order of Mass Culture and Chronic Conflict: A Source Reader.* Union: Kean U, 2005. Print.

Lunn, Eugene. "Tales of Liberal Disquiet: Thomas Mann's 'Mario and the Magician' and Interpretations of Fascism." *Literature and History* 11.1 (1985): 77–100. Print.

Mann, Thomas. "Death in Venice." *Death in Venice, and Seven Other Stories.* Trans. H. T. Lowe-Porter. New York: Vintage, 1989. 3–132. Print.

———. "Disorder and Early Sorrow." *Death in Venice, and Seven Other Stories.* Trans. H. T. Lowe-Porter. New York: Vintage, 1989. 179–288. Print.

Schivelbusch, Wolfgang. *The Culture of Defeat: On National Trauma, Mourning, and Recovery.* New York: Metropolitan, 2003. Print.

Media Adaptation

M. Dir. Fritz Lang. Perf. Peter Lorre, Otto Wernicke, Gustaf Gründgens, Ellen Widmann, Inge Landgut, Theodor Loos, and Friedrich Gnass. Janus Films, 2004. DVD.

Mario und der Zauberer. Dir. aus Maria Brandauer. Perf. Julian Sands, Anna Galiena, and Jan Wachtel. Flach Film, 1994. Film.

Metropolis. Dir. Fritz Lang. Perf. Alfred Abel, Brigitte Helm, Gustav Fröhlich, and Rudolf Klein-Rogge. Kino Video, 2002. DVD.

Dennis Klein

MOTHER NIGHT

Kurt Vonnegut

OVERVIEW

Published in 1961, Kurt Vonnegut's novel *Mother Night* tells the complex story of Howard W. Campbell Jr., an American who moves to Germany after World War I and becomes a famous playwright and Nazi propagandist. Written as a memoir from Campbell's perspective, the story begins as the Nazis ascend to power and a U.S. government agent asks Campbell to spy for the United States. Playwright Campbell uses his virulent propaganda broadcasts, aimed at converting Americans to the Nazi cause, to transmit coded messages to the Allies. Eventually he is arrested by a U.S. soldier as a war criminal. As he awaits trial in Jerusalem, he reflects on his life and the moral dilemma at the heart of it. For Campbell, the ultimate question becomes whether or not his assistance to the Allies morally outweighs or counterbalances the boon his broadcasts gave to the Nazi regime. Thus, *Mother Night* reflects the moral complexity of propaganda and its power to shape thought and actions.

Written early in the author's career, *Mother Night* failed to attract much attention when it was first published. As Vonnegut's body of work grew, however, and he published such famous works as *Slaughterhouse-Five* (1969), his early works came to be read in the context of his intellectual evolution as an author. Critics, in discussing *Mother Night,* have tended to focus most on Vonnegut's perceptions of how governments and other entities attempt to manipulate the public and how popular culture has gained increasing power to control human behavior. The novel ultimately suggests a new kind of postwar totalitarianism, one perpetrated not through war and political domination but through psychological control.

HISTORICAL AND LITERARY CONTEXT

The tale of a propagandist whose life story is appropriated by several groups for use as propaganda, *Mother Night* examines the powerful and even absurd role that propaganda played during World War II. Although most countries used propaganda to help rally support for the war effort, the Nazi Party was particularly adroit when it came to capitalizing on technological advances, most notably the radio, to deliver propaganda. Radio's ability to reach thousands of people quickly and easily made it an extraordinarily powerful tool, especially for disseminating the Nazi Party's

beliefs about eugenics, Darwinism, and the "scientific" basis for Aryan supremacy.

Vonnegut wrote *Mother Night* at the height of the Cold War, in a world sharply divided along ideological lines, where the threat of war was constant and unrelenting. American politicians portrayed the conflict as a crucial battle between good, just, and free capitalist societies and evil, corrupt, and totalitarian communist nations. However, just as the Nazis had used propaganda to blame social problems on Jews and other minority groups, Americans began to use propaganda to scapegoat communists and communist sympathizers. As a result, many intellectuals and writers came to see the absurdity of the ideological war and the threat of nuclear annihilation. Like many of his contemporaries, Vonnegut had served in World War II and had seen the horrors of battle. Thus, his writing reflects an ironic, almost comical view of the conflict.

World War II produced a number of war novelists, including authors Norman Mailer and James Jones. The majority of their novels explore the authors' war experiences in frank, almost journalistic terms. As the United States entered the Korean and Cold War era, however, a growing number of writers began to explore international conflict from an antitotalitarian perspective, even criticizing the U.S. government for its complicity. These writers produced rebellious works that were cynical and sometimes comic, including Arthur Koestler's *Arrival and Departure* (1943) and George Orwell's *1984* (1949). In many cases, they rejected the realism of earlier works in favor of stylistic innovations, such as the use of metafiction and ironic, detached attitudes.

Mother Night marks several important firsts for Vonnegut: it was his first novel written in the first person and the first to deal directly with World War II. He would continue writing in the first person in his next book, *Cat's Cradle* (1963), and would again address the subject of World War II in *Slaughterhouse-Five,* two popular works that came to define the author's literary career. The theme of the dehumanization of the individual in the modern world—which Vonnegut began exploring in *Mother Night* and other early works— reached a crescendo in his later works, becoming one of the most significant and widely touched-upon themes in late twentieth-century American literature.

❖ *Key Facts*

Time Period:
Mid-20th Century

Genre:
Novel

Events:
World War II; Cold War

Nationality:
American

KURT VONNEGUT: OUTSPOKEN AUTHOR

Kurt Vonnegut is best known as an innovator of style and form for his novels and other works of fiction. However, his work is equally marked by his strong political and philosophical opinions. Early in life, he was influenced by socialist and labor leaders, such as Eugene Debs and Leon Trotsky, after whom he later named fictional characters. Much of his nonfiction work speaks to issues of human rights, morality, and politics, and as his fame grew, he often found himself at the center of controversy because of something he wrote or a statement he had made in an interview.

Although he was outspoken about politics and religion, his chief concern was for the individual and for personal rights and dignity. Because of these beliefs, he was a lifelong member of the American Civil Liberties Union. Ultimately, however, he was not optimistic about the artist's ability to create change. In a 2003 interview he stated, with his usual wit, "During the Vietnam War, every respectable artist in this country was against the war. It was like a laser beam. We were all aimed in the same direction. The power of this weapon turns out to be that of a custard pie dropped from a stepladder six feet high."

THEMES AND STYLE

The primary themes of *Mother Night* treat the inherent absurdity of totalitarianism and propaganda and the brutalizing effect of both on the individual. Campbell's dual status as a propagandist for the Nazi Party and as a spy for the United States, as well as his divided identity as an American living in Germany, frame his struggle to confront his own morality and to reconcile his true self with his actions. Even the U.S. soldier who arrests him, Bernard B. O'Hare, becomes almost Nazi-like in his zealous effort to prove his own moral superiority. As Gilbert McInnis writes in a 2007 essay for *Mythlore*, "In the world depicted in *Mother Night,* characters struggle to adapt to their environment for the sake of survival; at the same time, the novel also relates the struggle of a totalitarian 'will' to refashion the human conscience."

Framed as a real historical document written by Campbell and edited by Vonnegut, the novel employs the literary technique of metafiction. Vonnegut in his editor's note claims to have received Campbell's manuscript and merely edited it for publication. Thus, the tension between the novel's status as a work of fiction and "editor" Vonnegut's insistence on its veracity encourages the reader to repeatedly question what is real and what is fictional in Campbell's account of his experience. It also illuminates the interplay between the real and the imagined, demonstrating how fiction, in the form of political propaganda or even advertising, can have a powerful and even comic influence on reality. In this way, Vonnegut emphasizes the absurdity of the modern world, particularly as it relates to how propagandistic forces conspire to shape individuals' thoughts and behavior.

The language and emotional tenor of the writing are detached and ironic. Frequently, the author takes an almost cavalier approach to the novel's dramatic and emotionally weighty subject matter. Campbell writes, "If I'd been born in Germany, I suppose I would have been a Nazi, bopping Jews and gypsies and Poles around, leaving boots sticking out of snow banks, warming myself with my secretly virtuous insides. So it goes." The narrator's emotional detachment from the horrors of war serves to magnify the absurdity of life under a totalitarian state and the unmooring of the mind from reality. Vonnegut further develops the novel's detached tone through the literal disconnection of his preface from the rest of the novel and through his ironic observations about the protagonist: "[L]ies told for the sake of artistic effect—in the theater, for instance, and in Campbell's confessions, perhaps—can be, in a higher sense, the most beguiling forms of truth."

CRITICAL DISCUSSION

Upon publication, *Mother Night,* like much of Vonnegut's early work, was essentially ignored by critics. Jerome Klinkowitz in a 1997 essay for *The North American Review* writes that *Mother Night* was "written in obscurity, published in the vacuum of paperback originals, … [and] structured in the manner peculiar to Vonnegut's initial novels, adopting a familiar subgeneric form as its excuse for being." Marketed as a spy thriller, an extremely popular but decidedly nonliterary genre, *Mother Night* did not initially seem to have the same strong authorial persona that made Vonnegut's later works so popular—and that generated a wealth of scholarship about the relationship between the author's autobiography and his work. In 1966 he wrote an introduction to a new edition of *Mother Night,* perhaps recognizing the importance of his authorial persona to attracting critical attention to his work, and scholars gradually came to study the work as part of Vonnegut's oeuvre.

Recent criticism of *Mother Night* is difficult to find in isolation. The novel is almost always cited in discussions of Vonnegut's development as a writer, especially in terms of how his later works would express his views on the power and moral ambiguity of the state (particularly during times of war). *Mother Night,* for example, prefigures his exploration of the shift from a threat of totalitarian states to the threat of totalitarian psychology, with its increasing power to shape individuals' thoughts. As Gilbert McInnis suggests, "He wants us to consider that we are no longer dealing with the traditional notion of a totalitarian attempt to control the political landscape by military force, but a new attempt to control the human mind." Uwe Klawitter in *The Theme of Totalitarianism in "English" Fiction* (1998) examines *Mother Night* in the context not of Vonnegut's body of work but of

a decades-long tradition of English-language antitotalitarian writing. Of note as well is Vonnegut's own appraisal of *Mother Night* in his book *Palm Sunday* (1981), in which he grades his works not in terms of their literary significance but in terms of his mastery in writing them. Although many of his more popular works received lower grades, he gave *Mother Night* an A, perhaps for its role in laying the foundation for his self-reckoned A-plus works, *Cat's Cradle* and *Slaughterhouse-Five.*

BIBLIOGRAPHY

Sources

Klawitter, Uwe. *The Theme of Totalitarianism in "English" Fiction: Koestler, Orwell, Vonnegut, Kosinski, Burgess, Atwood, Amis.* New York: Peter Lang Publishing, 1998. Print.

Klinkowitz, Jerome. "'Mother Night' as Film." *North American Review* 282.5 (1997): 44–47. *General OneFile.* Web. 21 June 2012.

McInnis, Gilbert. "Evolutionary Mythology in the Writings of Kurt Vonnegut, Jr." *Critique: Studies in Contemporary Fiction* 46.4 (2005): 383–96. *General OneFile.* Web. 21 June 2012.

———. "Nazis, Mythology, and Totalitarian Minds in Kurt Vonnegut's *Mother Night.*" *Mythlore* 26.99/100 (2007): 185–200.

Vonnegut, Kurt. *Mother Night.* New York: Delacorte, 1966. Print.

———. *Palm Sunday: An Autobiographical Collage.* New York: Delacorte, 1981. Print.

Further Reading

Klinkowitz, Jerome. *Kurt Vonnegut's America.* Columbia: U of South Carolina P, 2010. Print.

———. *The Vonnegut Effect.* Columbia: U of South Carolina P, 2011. Print.

Shields, Charles J. *And So It Goes: Kurt Vonnegut: A Life.* New York: Henry Holt & Co., 2011. Print.

Sumner, Gregory D. *Unstuck In Time: A Journey through Kurt Vonnegut's Life and Novels.* New York: Seven Stories P, 2011. Print.

Vonnegut, Kurt. *Slaughterhouse-Five.* New York: Dial, 1999. Print.

Media Adaptation

Mother Night. Dir. Keith Gordon. Perf. Nick Nolte, Sheryl Lee, and Alan Arkin. New Line Cinema, 1996. Film.

Colby Cuppernull

THE NUCLEAR AGE

Tim O'Brien

+ *Key Facts*

Time Period:
Late 19th Century

Genre:
Novel

Events:
Cold War; election of
Ronald Reagan

Nationality:
American

OVERVIEW

The Nuclear Age, American writer Tim O'Brien's 1985 novel of Cold War anxiety, contrasts the struggles of a man fixated on the dangers of nuclear proliferation with the apathy of a society oblivious to the fact that there is "no metaphor, the bombs are real." In the novel the main character, William Cowling, is a middle-aged husband, father, and businessman who is obsessed with the threat of nuclear warfare. As he works on digging a bomb shelter in his backyard, he reflects on his childhood and his past as a member of a radical subversive group and a draft dodger. Through William's reflections, O'Brien sounds an alarm against the complacency of a generation of U.S. citizens for whom duck-and-cover drills were part of a lost childhood mythology and whose 1960s radicalism ended in the sleepy comfort of suburbia.

Written toward the end of the period sometimes referred to as the Second Cold War, the novel responds to the cultural effects of the regrowth of tensions between the United States and the Soviet Union in the late 1970s to middle 1980s, a period characterized by increasing militarization on both sides, as well as by strong rhetoric from U.S. president Ronald Reagan. *The Nuclear Age* was timely, though early critical response was somewhat mixed. *Kirkus Reviews,* for example, evaluated the novel as "this center less, flogged-on, and jerry-built bomb of a book" that "just sits there and fizzles, on and on and on." By 1995, the year in which the novel was set, fears about the bomb had fizzled as well. As a window to a distinct period of American cultural history, however, *The Nuclear Age* provides a glimpse of a time when unease about the threat of world annihilation still held a place in the national consciousness.

HISTORICAL AND LITERARY CONTEXT

After experiencing almost a decade of détente, Western countries in early 1979 had relatively low levels of anxiety about the risk of nuclear war. But increasing tensions in the Middle East when Iran's Islamic Revolution toppled the reigning monarchy, accompanied by varied foreign responses, led to a shift in U.S.-Soviet relations, which came to a head with the December invasion of Afghanistan by Soviet troops. In addition, elections in Great Britain and the United States brought more conservative leadership to power

in 1980. In 1983 Ronald Reagan famously branded the Soviet Union an "evil empire," and that attitude, reflected in Reagan's military spending and his promotion of the Strategic Defense Initiative (popularly called Star Wars), was among the factors that brought previously cooling tensions back to a simmer.

In the early 1980s, military exercises undertaken by various countries, especially the United States and the Soviet Union, rose to prominence. Still, during this time, a relatively small portion of the U.S. public participated in the antinuclear movement. A considerable part of the populace, however, apparently channeled any nuclear fears into entertainment, rather than politicking. As an outlet for these tensions American movie-goers were treated in 1985 to the blockbuster film *Rocky IV,* in which the main character, Rocky Balboa, with an American flag draped over his shoulders, soundly trounces Russian menace Ivan Drago. *The Nuclear Age* was thus released into the tension-filled yet proudly nationalistic U.S. citizen's consciousness. O'Brien's novel creates a portrait of a man who has lived with the bomb's anxiety all his life, but who, since his radical younger years, has not engaged politically in any meaningful way. As the novel unfolds, it becomes apparent that William's decision to build a bomb shelter is an expression of fears about his personal life as much as about the prospect of nuclear war, and that the source of this fear is, at least in part, a result of his long disengagement.

The Nuclear Age belongs to a tradition of English-language Cold War writing that brought the threat of nuclear war to the public's attention. In his *Nuclear Holocausts: Atomic War in Fiction,* Paul Brians mentions three books that stimulated public concern: John Hersey's *Hiroshima* (1946), Neil Shute's *On the Beach* (1957), and Jonathan Schell's *The Fate of the Earth* (1982). *Hiroshima* was originally published in a 1946 special issue of the *New Yorker* and gained wide attention as the first mainstream writing to provide accounts from people who were in that Japanese city when the United States dropped an atomic bomb there. In *On the Beach,* the action unfolds in the aftermath of World War III, when nuclear blasts have killed all life in the Northern Hemisphere. Set in Australia in 1963, the book follows a small group of survivors who attempt to make the best of the little time they have remaining. *The Fate of the Earth,* published three years before

The Nuclear Age, comprises three essays about the physical, moral, and political significance of the nuclear bomb. Schell's book became something of a bible for the antinuclear activism that peaked in the one-million-strong 1982 demonstrations in New York City.

O'Brien spent seven years writing *The Nuclear Age,* but despite his prolonged efforts, critical response was less positive to this book than to much of his other work. *The Nuclear Age* focuses not on the consequences of nuclear war but on the consequences of living in a state of anxiety about its possibility. While commentators have lauded this unique contribution to the genre, O'Brien's ultimate legacy will likely rest on his acclaimed writing about the Vietnam War, particularly his next book, *The Things They Carried* (1990).

THEMES AND STYLE

The Nuclear Age highlights the contrast between the immediate promise of a nuclear arsenal—national security—and the long-term effects of living in its shadow. The appropriately named William Cowling has indeed been cowed by the bomb since childhood. Instead of playing Ping-Pong, young William uses his table as a makeshift bomb shelter, much to the amusement of his parents. As an adult, William makes a fortune selling uranium to corporate interests and retires to the relative safety of Montana. After "a lifetime of insomnia and mid-night peril," William gets up one night and begins to dig. His wife and daughter find the idea of a bomb shelter far less charming than did his parents and lock themselves away from him. Contemplating the hole himself, William muses that it is "where faith should be … what we have when imagination fails … the hole, it seems, is in my heart." Indeed, by the end of the novel, William has drugged his family, taken them into the hole, and rigged the shelter with explosives. The anxiety is too much. At the last minute, he changes his mind and decides that rather than self-destruct or dwell in anxiety, he will take up a hobby and, like everyone else, "sleep the dense narcotic sleep of my species," ignoring the inevitable. O'Brien is not without sympathy for William, but the novel ends with a sense that the anxiety of living with the bomb has erosive effects on the moral imagination and the will to live a meaningful life, effects that William cannot overcome.

The contrast between the official line about staying safe and the anxieties created by the dangers of nuclear armament comes into relief as O'Brien sketches William's past through flashbacks that occur while he works on the shelter. Starting in childhood, with his first awareness of the bomb, William knows "there's nothing make-believe about doomsday." He is clear that a nuclear war will result in annihilation and that it will not have the "sabers and battle flags" of Custer's Last Stand, a famous military battle reenacted every summer in his hometown. Later, William drifts through college, where he witnesses "dense, immobile

TIM O'BRIEN ON VIETNAM

Tim O'Brien, who served in Vietnam from 1969 to 1970, was indelibly marked by combat and has written extensively about the conflict. Two of his works on this subject include the novel *Going after Cacciato,* which won the 1978 National Book Award for Fiction, and *The Things They Carried* (1990), which also received much critical acclaim.

Going after Cacciato details the pursuit of Cacciato by his fellow soldiers after he decides to leave combat and walk to Paris. If the pursuit was at first legitimate, it becomes unclear how much is motivated by a desire to catch Cacciato and how much comes from the other soldiers' desire to find their own escape. The novel earned praise for its thoughtful treatment of the complex issues surrounding the conflict, as well as for O'Brien's gritty recounting of a soldier's life.

In *The Things They Carried,* O'Brien weaves together a number of stories, five of which were originally published in *Esquire* magazine. *The Things They Carried* is loosely based on O'Brien's own war experiences and contains a character named Tim O'Brien, although the author has taken pains to clarify that the stories are not straight autobiography. A finalist for the Pulitzer Prize, the book appears on many lists of the best war fiction.

apathy … ignorance on a colossal scale." His fellow students are more interested in farting contests than the growing unrest in Vietnam, and William finally feels compelled to alert them to danger with a sign that states "THE BOMBS ARE REAL." Mistaking the sign for a political commitment, antiwar radicals take him into their group, but he is not invested in the fight the way they are and goes underground, less to protest the war and more from fear of his own mortality. He trains with the Committee, which is involved in terrorist activities, but drops out before actual operations start, eventually realizing that "fantasy was all I had." He then starts looking for a wife of the traditional sort, whom he finds in the flighty, feminine Bobbi.

Metaphors and the way they operate to comfort or inflame are important thematically and also as a stylistic element in *The Nuclear Age.* O'Brien's book is divided into three sections—"Fission," "Fusion," and "Critical Mass"—which refer both to nuclear terminology and to Bobbi's poem, "Relativity." It is Bobbi's poetry, eventually the only means she is willing to use to communicate with William, that is a source of his frustration with her and an example of his claim that the world is "drugged on metaphor, the opiate of our age." The language of science, meanwhile, provides a stark contrast to William's stream-of-consciousness ravings, which effectively re-create the anxiety in his head.

CRITICAL DISCUSSION

While most critics found something to appreciate in *The Nuclear Age,* reviews were negative overall.

A 1955 advertisement for a prepackaged fallout shelter. In Tim O'Brien's *The Nuclear Age,* the protagonist begins building a bomb shelter in his basement. © BETTMANN/CORBIS.

Age," the novel captures the ways in which fear and distrust of the government can de-politicize the mass of the citizenry, creating a vacuum to be filled by subpolitical groups, represented in the novel by the Committee, whose politics are based on feeling rather than the rational debate important to the success of the democratic process. As an example, Hayasaka points to O'Brien's description of cheerleader-turned-radical Sarah Strouch, locating her convictions in the cheerleader's "shrill imperative: *Fight—fight—fight!*" Hayasaka also posits that *The Nuclear Age,* which poses questions about the legitimacy of the nuclear-weapons-as-deterrence policy of the U.S. government, predicted the disarmament process that has eventually ensued.

As a minor work in O'Brien's oeuvre, *The Nuclear Age* has yet to receive significant critical attention and is mainly addressed either in surveys of O'Brien's career or with other fiction related to nuclear war. Daniel Cordle's work is an exception. His article "In Dreams, in Imagination: Suspense, Anxiety and the Cold War in Tim O'Brien's *The Nuclear Age*" explores O'Brien's focus on psychological events rather than on physical ones, suggesting that "while the overt events of the Cold War, like the Vietnam conflict which dominates so much of O'Brien's fiction, are important, the politics of threat, of fear, are equally vital." For Cordle, this insight is vital for understanding O'Brien's work as well as Cold War culture more generally. Additionally, Cordle points out the link between the personal and political dimensions of William's anxiety, observing that William's fears are touched off not by a political event but by the discovery of his wife's infidelity. The fact that the U.S. government made the nuclear family the bedrock of safety in the 1950s and 1960s makes the disintegration of his family highly problematic for William, who is still very much a child of *The Nuclear Age.*

Writing in the *New York Times,* Grace Paley "wish[ed] the novel could have been either more surreal or less." Instead, she writes, "it falls into an transcending middle which muffles the important cry of 'Doom, doom.'" John Romano, reviewing the novel for *Atlantic* magazine, complains instead about the missing middle "between the outraged rhetoric of fear and protest and the rambling, recollected chapters of a life." For Romano, O'Brien's failure was in characterization. William never comes to life as a real, relatable adult.

While it was criticized on aesthetic grounds, *The Nuclear Age* has been regarded as an accurate analysis of how U.S. democracy is complicated by the logic of nuclear deterrence theory. As Shizuka Hayasaka argues in the article "Nuclear Deterrence, Democracy and the Cold War in Tim O'Brien's *The Nuclear*

BIBLIOGRAPHY

Sources

Brians, Paul. *Nuclear Holocausts: Atomic War in Fiction.* Kent: Kent State UP, 1987. Print.

Cordle, Daniel. "In Dreams, in Imagination: Suspense, Anxiety and the Cold War in Tim O'Brien's *The Nuclear Age.*" *Critical Survey* 19.2 (2007): 101+. *Literature Resource Center.* Web. 22 July 2012.

Hayasaka, Shizuka. "Nuclear Deterrence, Democracy and the Cold War in Tim O'Brien's *The Nuclear Age.*" *Hitotsubashi Journal of Arts and Sciences* 52 (2011): 9–22. Print.

"*The Nuclear Age.*" Rev. of *The Nuclear Age,* by Tim O'Brien. *Kirkus Reviews* 15 Sept. 1985. Web. 25 July 2012.

O'Brien, Tim. *The Nuclear Age.* New York: Knopf, 1985.

Paley, Grace. "Digging a Shelter and a Grave." Rev. of *The Nuclear Age,* by Tim O'Brien. *New York Times* 17 Nov. 1985. Web. 21 July 2012.

Romano, John. "*The Nuclear Age.*" Rev. of *The Nuclear Age,* by Tim O'Brien. *Atlantic* Oct. 1985: 105+. *Literature Resource Center.* Web. 21 July 2012.

Further Reading

Dowling, David. *Fictions of Nuclear Disaster.* Iowa City: U of Iowa P, 1987. Print.

Heberle, Mark. *A Trauma Artist: Tim O'Brien and the Fiction of Vietnam.* Iowa City: Iowa UP, 2001. Print.

Kaplan, Steven. *Understanding Tim O'Brien.* Columbia: U of South Carolina P, 1995. Print.

Myers, Thomas. "(William) Tim(othy) O'Brien." *American Novelists Since World War II: Fourth Series.* Ed. James R. Giles and Wanda H. Giles. Detroit: Gale Research, 1995. *Dictionary of Literary Biography* Vol. 152. *Literature Resource Center.* Web. 23 July 2012.

Rose, Kenneth. *One Nation Underground: The Fallout Shelter in American Culture.* New York: New York UP, 2004. Print.

Vernon, Alex, and Catherine Calloway, eds. *Approaches to Teaching the Works of Tim O'Brien.* New York: MLA, 2010. Print.

Watson, Dana Cairns. "Tim O'Brien." *American Writers: A Collection of Literary Biographies, Supplement 5.* Ed. Jay Parini. New York: Scribner's, 2000. *Scribner Writers Series.* Web. 22 July 2012.

Daisy Gard

"THE SALE OF THE HESSIANS"

Benjamin Franklin

✥ *Key Facts*

Time Period:
Late 18th Century

Genre:
Letter

Events:
American Revolution;
Battle of Trenton

Nationality:
American

OVERVIEW

"The Sale of the Hessians" is satirical propaganda in the form of a letter, dated 1777 and originally written in French, purporting to be from the fictional Count de Schaumbergh to the Baron Hohendorf, commander of Hessian (German) troops fighting for the British in North America. Authorship of the letter was not debated until 1874, when John Bigelow, a U.S. diplomat and editor, theorized that Benjamin Franklin had written the piece. Bigelow's contention was widely accepted as fact until the mid-twentieth century, when scholars began to doubt Franklin's involvement. Although the true author of the letter may never be known, its propagandistic purpose remains clear: to expose the inhumanity of the German aristocracy, shown by the author to care for nothing other than profits, in order to persuade readers that German involvement in the American Revolution was immoral.

During the American Revolution, Great Britain hired approximately 30,000 mercenary soldiers from Germany to bolster its own military forces in the American colonies. These soldiers were called *Hessians* because the largest group came from Hesse-Kassel, a principality located in central Germany. This strategy was not new. In 1715 King George I hired 12,000 Hessians to put down the Jacobite Rebellion, and 6,000 Hessians fought alongside British troops in 1744 during the War of the Austrian Succession. Nevertheless, as "The Sale of the Hessians" implies, American colonists objected to the Germans' role in the colonists' war against the British. The message of the satiric epistle later became overshadowed by an intellectual game of "whodunit," in which scholars debated the letter's authorship.

HISTORICAL AND LITERARY CONTEXT

From the earliest days of the American Revolution, German mercenaries fought on the side of the British. On December 26, 1776, General George Washington led his Continental Army on a daring raid across the Delaware River, north of Trenton, New Jersey, where a large contingent of Hessian troops was garrisoned. Washington caught them by surprise and captured the garrison with only minor losses on his side. The Battle of Trenton prompted much discussion among American colonists concerning the Hessians'

unwanted participation in the war, and it likely motivated the author of "The Sale of the Hessians" to pen the satirical letter.

The news of the battle would have taken awhile to reach France, where Benjamin Franklin had been sent on a commission by the Continental Congress. The satirical letter was dated February 1777, which would fit conveniently into a timeline in which Franklin could have been the author. Not long after this date, Franklin wrote a personal letter to scientist John Winthrop in which he discussed the sale of Hessian troops to the British. In his letter, dated May 1, 1777, Franklin states, "The conduct of those princes of Germany who have sold the blood of their people has subjected them to the contempt and odium of all Europe." Franklin also mentions that he has enclosed a satire for Winthrop to read. However, the letter does not identify the satire nor does it say who wrote it.

"The Sale of the Hessians" was not the only piece of satire written on the topic of the Hessian troops in 1777. The anonymous "*Lettre du Landgrave de Hesse, au commandant de ses troupes en Amérique*" ("Letter from the Landgrave of Hesse, to the commander of his troops in America") was published as an eight-page pamphlet in Amsterdam that year. "*Avis aux Hessois et autres peuples de l'Allemagne vendus par leurs princes à l'Angleterre*" ("Advice to Hessians and other peoples of Germany sold by their princes to England"), by Honoré-Gabriel Riqueti, Comte de Mirabeau, also appeared in 1777. In his essay, Mirabeau acknowledges familiarity with the two aforementioned works. On the American front, Congress attempted to persuade Hessian soldiers to quit their mercenary ways and "accept … lands, liberty, safety and a communion of good laws and mild government." Congress approved giving each Hessian mercenary who took the offer a 50-acre plot of land to call his own.

As the propagandistic relevance of "The Sale of the Hessians" faded, later discussions of the piece centered on the debate over its authorship. Bigelow attempted to justify his claim that Franklin was the author by asking, "Since the death of Swift, who, besides Franklin, was sufficiently a master of this kind of satire to have written it?" The comparison had merit. Both Jonathan Swift and Franklin often used satire to bring attention both to the oppressed and their oppressors. They exaggerated their issues to the point where those issues became outlandishly grotesque and humorous. For instance, Swift's 1729 satire, "A Modest Proposal," highlights the British policies against the Irish by suggesting that the solution to crippling starvation in Ireland was to eat Irish children. In "Sale of the Hessians," the Count de Schaumbergh considers the German soldiers so insignificant that he requests the war continue indefinitely so as not to interfere with an Italian opera for which he was planning. Bigelow was so certain that Franklin wrote "The Sale of the Hessians" that he translated and included the satire in his *Complete Works of Benjamin Franklin* (1888). In the twentieth century, two notable scholars who responded to Bigelow's challenge were Durand Echeverria and Everett C. Wilkie Jr. Rather than suggesting other possible authors, they focused on the reasons that Franklin's authorship was doubtful.

THEMES AND STYLE

The objective of "The Sale of the Hessians" was to reveal the perceived greed, cynicism, and immorality of a country that chose to involve its troops in a war in which it had no stake, other than the pursuit of financial gain. As with any good piece of satire, it employs not only a distinct level of exaggeration but also piercing symbolism. In the opening of the letter, the count expresses pride in his Hessians, who fought so valiantly that only 345 out of 1,950 men survived. The motivation behind this statement is quickly exposed, as he reveals that the number of dead will earn him 643,500 florins rather than the previously estimated 483,450 florins. He later refers symbolically to his expected payment of "thirty guineas per man." The thirty coins are a biblical reference to the betrayal of Judas, who handed over Jesus Christ in exchange for thirty silver coins. In addition, the count's conversion from florins to guineas is significant in that guineas were the standard form of currency for slave traders. From start to finish, the letter is about profits.

The author of the letter uses grandiose yet shocking language as a rhetorical strategy to expose the count's superficial, vile character. In discussing the issue of caring for wounded troops, the count tells the baron that "you may insinuate to the surgeons with entire propriety that a crippled man is a reproach to their profession, and that there is no wiser course than to let every one of them die when he ceases to be fit to fight." He reasons, "I am sure they would rather die than live in a condition no longer fit for my service." The author then ratchets up this outrageousness by having the count envision himself as Leonidas, the heroic king of ancient Sparta who led a small Greek force against an invading Persian army. The count acknowledges that Leonidas died with his men but then rationalizes, "Things have changed, and it is no

Joseph Siffred Duplessis's portrait of Benjamin Franklin, whom many assume to be author of "The Sale of the Hessians." © BETTMANN/CORBIS.

longer the custom for princes of the empire to go and fight in America for a cause with which they have no concern." In painting the German aristocracy as greedy and immoral, the letter may be seen as an effort to persuade the Hessian soldiers to desert.

Considering that the casualties of war were the topic of the letter, its overall tone is surprisingly casual and unemotional. Perhaps the most appalling example comes at the end, when the count requests the baron to prolong the war, because a quick end to the conflict may spoil the count's plans for an Italian opera. This last display of callousness is meant to reinforce the depiction of the Hessian leaders as unscrupulous men giving no thought to prolonging human suffering and loss.

CRITICAL DISCUSSION

"The Sale of the Hessians" was published widely and received significant attention. After its initial publication in France in 1777, a multitude of reprints made their way both to Germany and to North America. In Germany the letter was not understood as satire; it was viewed, according to Echeverria in his 1954 essay in *Proceedings of the American Philosophical Society*, as "a dreadful example of the inhuman tyranny of petty German monarchs," or it was denounced as a libelous forgery. The primary legacy of "The Sale of the Hessians," aside from its effectiveness as propagandistic satire, has been the mystery of its authorship. No one other than Bigelow has made a case for Franklin as

PRIMARY SOURCE

EXCERPT FROM "THE SALE OF THE HESSIANS"

I have learned with unspeakable pleasure the courage our troops exhibited at Trenton, and you cannot imagine my joy on being told that of the 1,950 Hessians engaged in the fight, but 345 escaped. There were just 1,605 men killed, and I cannot sufficiently commend your prudence in sending an exact list of the dead to my minister in London. This precaution was the more necessary, as the report sent to the English ministry does not give but 1,455 dead. This would make 483,450 florins instead of 643,500 which I am entitled to demand under our convention. You will comprehend the prejudice which such an error would work in my finances, and I do not doubt you will take the necessary pains to prove that Lord North's list is false and yours correct.

The court of London objects that there were a hundred wounded who ought not to be included in the list, nor paid for as dead; but I trust you will not overlook my instructions to you on quitting Cassel, and that you will not have tried by human succor to recall the life of the unfortunates whose days could not be lengthened but by the loss of a leg or an arm. That would be making them a pernicious present, and I am sure they would rather die than live in a condition no longer fit for my service. I do not mean by this that you should assassinate them; we should be humane, my dear Baron, but you may insinuate to the surgeons with entire propriety that a crippled man is a reproach to their profession, and that there is no wiser course than to let every one of them die when he ceases to be fit to fight.

I am about to send to you some new recruits. Don't economize them. Remember glory before all things. Glory is true wealth. There is nothing degrades the soldier like the love of money. He must care only for honour and reputation, but this reputation must be acquired in the midst of dangers. A battle gained without costing the conqueror any blood is an inglorious success, while the conquered cover themselves with glory by perishing with their arms in their hands. Do you remember that of the 300 Lacedaemonians who defended the defile of Thermopylae, not one

the creator of the piece. A contemporary of Bigelow's, a historian named Edward Jackson Lowell, disputed the Franklin connection; he reported in 1884 that he believed the letter to be a "clumsy forgery." Mirabeau has been suggested as a possible author, but it seems unlikely that he would write a second satire on the same subject in the same year, in a style completely different from his usual work.

By the end of the twentieth century, Echeverria and Wilkie presented a serious challenge to Bigelow's contention. They both offered similar arguments as to why Franklin was unlikely the author of the satire. According to Echeverria, there were plenty of "scandalmongers, news ferrets, and literary observers" who would have noted "any hint that so prominent a figure as Franklin had written this piece." Echeverria also challenges Bigelow's declaration that none of Franklin's contemporaries were able to write such successful satire: "Can one really believe that 'The Sale of the Hessians' is beyond the capacities of a Voltaire, a La Rochefoucauld, a Mirabeau, or a Condorcet, and that Swift took satire with him when he went to his own grave?" Moreover, Wilkie posits in his 1983 essay "Franklin and 'The Sale of the Hessians': The Growth of a Myth" that it is doubtful that Franklin could have written such a letter in French in 1777. Even in 1778, he argues, "Franklin complains of difficulty with French." Wilkie concedes that Franklin may have written the original in English and had it translated; however, "the piece rendered in French is such a stylistic marvel that it can hardly be considered a mere translation." In the end, the true author of "The Sale of the Hessians" may never be known. Regardless of the work's authorship, the purpose of Franklin's and others' satire was no different then than it is today. Satirists wished to bring attention to social injustices in order to create positive changes. Franklin knew that humor was a language that virtually everyone understood, so that was the technique he employed most often in his writings. It not only opened people's eyes to new ideas but also forced them to look at things from a different perspective.

BIBLIOGRAPHY

Sources

Atwood, Rodney. *The Hessians: Mercenaries from Hessen-Kassel in the American Revolution.* Cambridge: Cambridge UP, 2002. Print.

Berger, Carl. *Broadsides and Bayonets: The Propaganda War of the American Revolution.* Philadelphia: U of Pennsylvania P, 1961. Print.

Echeverria, Durand. "'The Sale of the Hessians': Was Benjamin Franklin the Author?" *Proceedings of the American Philosophical Society* 98.6 (1954): 427–31. *JSTOR.* Web. 8 Sept. 2012.

returned? How happy should I be could I say the same of my brave Hessians! It is true that their king, Leonidas, perished with them: but things have changed, and it is no longer the custom for princes of the empire to go and fight in America for a cause with which they have no concern. And besides, to whom should they pay the thirty guineas per man if I did not stay in Europe to receive them?

Then, it is necessary also that I be ready to send recruits to replace the men you lose. For this purpose I must return to Hesse. It is true, grown men are becoming scarce there, but I will send you boys. Besides, the scarcer the commodity the higher the price. I am assured that the women and little girls have begun to till our lands, and they get on not badly.

You did right to send back to Europe that Dr. Crumerus who was so successful in curing dysentery. Don't bother with a man who is subject to looseness of the bowels. That disease makes bad soldiers. One coward will do more mischief in an engagement than ten brave men will do good. Better that they burst in their barracks than fly in a battle, and tarnish the glory of our arms. Besides, you know that they pay me as killed for all who die from disease, and I don't get a farthing for runaways. My trip to Italy, which has cost me enormously, makes it desirable that there should be a great mortality among them. You will therefore promise promotion to all who expose themselves; you will exhort them to seek glory in the midst of dangers; you will say to Major Maundorff that I am not at all content with his saving the 345 men who escaped the massacre of Trenton. Through the whole campaign he has not had ten men killed in consequence of his orders.

Finally, let it be your principal object to prolong the war and avoid a decisive engagement on either side, for I have made arrangements for a grand Italian opera, and I do not wish to be obliged to give it up. Meantime I pray God, my dear Baron de Hohendorf, to have you in his holy and gracious keeping.

SOURCE: *The Writings of Benjamin Franklin,* Volume VII, edited by Albert Henry Smyth, p. 829. Macmillan Company, 1906.

Franklin, Benjamin. "The Sale of the Hessians." *Paris 1776–1785. Gutenberg Consortia Center.* Project Gutenberg Consortia Center. n.d. Web. 8 Sept. 2012.

Marquart, Megan. "Similarities between the Writings of Jonathan Swift and Benjamin Franklin." *Helium.* Helium, 9 Mar. 2007. Web. 8 Sept. 2012.

Pilditch, Jan. "Franklin's 'The Sale of the Hessians': American or European Satire?" *Australasian Journal of American Studies* 7.1 (1988): 13–22. *JSTOR.* Web. 8 Sept. 2012.

Wilkie, Everett C., Jr. "Franklin and 'The Sale of the Hessians': The Growth of a Myth." *Proceedings of the American Philosophical Society* 127.3 (1983): 202–12. *JSTOR.* Web. 8 Sept. 2012.

Further Reading

Davidson, Philip. *Propaganda and the American Revolution, 1763–1783.* Chapel Hill: U of North Carolina P, 1941. Print.

Isaacson, Walter. *Benjamin Franklin: An American Life.* New York: Simon, 2004. Print.

Sandrich, Mark. *Ben Franklin in Paris.* New York: Random, 1965. Print.

Schiff, Stacy. *A Great Improvisation: Franklin, France, and the Birth of America.* New York: Holt, 2006. Print.

Willcox, William B., ed. *The Papers of Benjamin Franklin.* New Haven, CT: Yale UP, 1983. Print.

Jim Mladenovic

THE SPY WHO CAME IN FROM THE COLD

John Le Carré

OVERVIEW

The Spy Who Came in from the Cold, a novel written by John le Carré and originally published in 1963, is a classic spy thriller set in the early 1960s during the Cold War. It has a complex plot full of uncertainties about the status of its central character, the British intelligence agent Alec Leamas; about who is telling the truth; and about the moral and ideological justifications for torture and killing by governments. The novel portrays the Cold War—the conflict between communism and capitalism—as a lethal game between ruthless and calculating individuals.

The Spy Who Came in from the Cold was le Carré's third novel and the one that propelled him to literary fame. As a former British spy, le Carré writes from experience, offering an authentic view of the world of espionage. His book was the first to bring realism to the spy genre, dominated until that time by jingoistic fantasy spies such as author Ian Fleming's British sleuth, James Bond. Le Carré's novel also illustrates the human and moral cost of defending political systems and their administrative structures, issues not previously explored in the genre.

HISTORICAL AND LITERARY CONTEXT

In the years after World War II, Europe was divided between the communist countries of the East, dominated by the Soviet Union, and those in the West, which emerged from the conflict with broadly capitalist, market economies and, with a few exceptions, democratic governments. When the war ended, the German capital, Berlin, was surrounded by territory held by Soviet forces but was divided into four sectors that were controlled by the United States, the United Kingdom, France, and the Soviet Union, respectively. In 1949 the U.S., British, and French sectors consolidated to become West Germany (officially the Federal Republic of Germany), and the U.S.S.R. sector became East Germany (officially the German Democratic Republic). In 1961 East Germany built the Berlin Wall to prevent its citizens from defecting to West Germany.

The Spy Who Came in from the Cold, which begins about a year after East Germany completed construction of the Berlin Wall, opens with Leamas tensely waiting at a wall checkpoint for one of his agents to escape from East Germany. The agent attempts to bluff his way through the checkpoint on a bicycle and is shot

to death by the East German sentries. The scene demonstrates the difficulty of crossing the Berlin Wall and the lethal atmosphere of paranoia and fear that prevailed at the time. The wall was a symbol of the Cold War, and it increased the intransigence of both sides. In the East this was manifested in the brutal treatment of would-be defectors, while in the West, governments made the protection of West Berlin a goal of major strategic importance. The wall was, as le Carré puts it, "perfect theatre as well as a perfect symbol of the monstrosity of an ideology gone mad." In the novel it also functions as a dividing line between individual opponents, emphasizing their otherness to one another.

In the 1950s popular British literature often presented the Soviet threat in simple terms: good versus evil, building on an established narrative of wartime propaganda in which the plucky British held back the vast armies of German dictator Adolf Hitler. In Fleming's James Bond spy series, for example, British intelligence (the Secret Intelligence Service, better known as MI6) is pitted against its Soviet counterpart, SMERSH, in a contest that emphasizes British moral and technological superiority over a powerful but unimaginative enemy. As film and book critic Anthony Lane argues in the *New Yorker,* le Carré's novel "scraped every lingering speck of James Bond from our understanding of what spying might entail."

The Spy Who Came in from the Cold was published just as the Cold War reached its most dangerous phase, and it presented a new and more realistic view of spies and espionage to Cold War-era readers. Le Carré quickly became the most influential of a growing number of contemporary spy and espionage writers exploring the world of spy swaps, border crossings, and paranoia. The moral uncertainty of le Carré's literary vision was especially pertinent in the aftermath of the 1963 Burgess and MacLean spy scandal and the increasingly public spy trading that took place in the 1970s and 1980s. More importantly, however, his work challenged the conventional view of espionage as a means to uncover truths about an adversary.

THEMES AND STYLE

Perhaps the most significant aspect of *The Spy Who Came in from the Cold* is its portrayal of a world in which the concepts of truth, loyalty, and betrayal no longer have any meaning. While Cold War propaganda portrayed

Western agents as heroic figures fighting on the side of freedom, le Carré presents a darker view in which agents on both sides exploit innocent people in pursuit of operational goals. In the novel Control tells Leamas, "our methods … have become much the same. I mean, you can't be less ruthless than the opposition simply because your government's *policy* is benevolent, can you now?" That ruthlessness even extends to recruiting Mundt, an anti-Semitic former Nazi, as a British agent. Mundt's role at the center of East German security operations suggests a continuation of German fascism in the GDR but, perhaps more disturbingly, the secret support of Nazi power by Western governments. In the end, Leamas finds himself complicit in the execution of Liz, a left-wing Jewish woman whose death provides cover for his escape over the Wall. Leamas's return to her side, and certain death, is a rejection of state power and ideology in favor of humanity and represents his final decision to "come in from the cold."

The novel's omniscient narrative is not limited to describing Leamas's thoughts and actions. It creates a sense of multiple stories converging and of people apparently acting for themselves yet being controlled by others. The effect is to show things going on behind the scenes, such as when Leamas's friends visit Liz while he is on his way to East Germany. Liz's panicky, impassioned outburst, "Where is he? Tell me where he is," and the half lie that follows, "We don't quite know where he is," hints at Liz's openness to manipulation, but it is only later that the true extent of her exploitation becomes clear. The novel presents apparently unconnected events that later turn out to have been deliberately planned and arranged. Leamas's dying vision of smiling children in a car about to be crushed by "great lorries" is perhaps a metaphor for the happy ignorance of populations manipulated by governments while believing they are free.

The novel relies heavily on dialogue and reported speech, with lengthy sections of interior monologue reserved for Leamas and Liz. Language distinguishes the characters. Leamas often adopts a blunt, confrontational, and direct tone, while Control displays a "veneer of academic detachment." Leamas tells the lies required of him confidently, fulfilling the needs of his mission without thinking of the wider consequences. And yet despite the tight plotting, action, and prose, le Carré allows his characters to philosophize. Fiedler spouts his beliefs according to party doctrine: "The exploitation of individuals can only be justified by the collective need, can't it?" In an argument with Liz, Leamas gives voice to his bleak worldview that whether under God or Karl Marx, "everywhere's the same, people cheated and misled."

CRITICAL DISCUSSION

Arriving in the wake of the Cuban missile crisis and in the midst of a series of spy scandals in Britain, *The Spy Who Came in from the Cold* was an immediate success and a best seller on both sides of the Atlantic. Author,

JOHN LE CARRÉ: A CLOSER LOOK

John le Carré is the nom de plume of David John Moore Cornwell, who was born in 1931 in Poole, Dorset, England. After World War II, Cornwell served in the Army Intelligence Corps in Vienna, and he later studied at Oxford University. In 1959 he joined the British Foreign Service and served as an intelligence agent. He started writing novels in 1961, and he completed *The Spy Who Came in from the Cold* in less than six weeks.

Cornwell got the idea for *The Spy Who Came in from the Cold* from his personal horror at watching the construction of the Berlin Wall while working as an intelligence agent in Germany and from being betrayed by a British double agent. In an interview for the *Paris Review*, he said that the idea for the character of Alec Leamas came from a man he saw in an airport who had "a deadness in the face, and he looked, as we would have said in the spy world in those days, as if he'd had the hell posted out of him…. It was he, and I never spoke to him, but he was my guy, Alec Leamas."

editor, and translator Robert M. Adams describes le Carré in the *New York Review of Books* as a "first rate narrative architect," while literary critic and author Graham Greene endorses *The Spy Who Came in from the Cold* on its cover as "the best spy story I have ever read." John L. Cobbs, the author of *Understanding John le Carré*, attributes much of the immediate popularity of *The Spy Who Came in from the Cold* to a reaction against the superspy hero epitomized by James Bond, to whom Leamas was a "corrective antidote." Beyond its commercial mass-market appeal, *The Spy Who Came in from the Cold* is credited with extending the boundaries of the spy fiction genre.

The Spy Who Came in from the Cold not only reveals the operations of intelligence services in a convincing way, but it also examines the morality of spying and of war, in ways that more straightforward thrillers do not. Biographer LynnDianne Beene argues that le Carré's fiction in general blends romance and thriller genres with experimental literary approaches, while Lionel Warner, in an essay comparing *The Spy Who Came in from the Cold* with author Margaret Atwood's *The Blind Assassin*, writes, "The only way in which Leamas can come in from his cold war (operating under cover in enemy territory) is to declare his loyalty to a person rather than a system." Le Carré complicates the good versus evil narrative of the "superspy" fiction genre. In particular, as John Nelson argues in his essay in the *Finnish Yearbook of Political Thought*, it presents a version of the bureaucratic "national-security state" that can justify any action on the grounds that the other side did it first. Such states are dependent on a degree of secrecy that is "antithetical to liberal, democratic, and even republican modes of government."

A poster advertising the 1965 film version of *The Spy Who Came in from the Cold.* MARY EVANS/ RONALD GRANT/EVERETT COLLECTION.

The Spy Who Came in from the Cold is widely regarded as a turning point not only in the career of its author but also in spy fiction in general. It appears regularly on lists of all-time great spy novels and has won many awards, including the prestigious Edgar Award for Best Novel in 1965. Myron J. Aronoff, the author of *The Spy Novels of John le Carré* (1998), suggests that both Leamas and Liz are betrayed by the organizations they support and builds on a critical consensus that sees le Carré as a novelist who explores "the inherent conflict between fidelity to persons, to institutions, or ideologies." After the Cold War ended in 1991, *The Spy Who Came in from the Cold* became a period piece, but its exploration of the ways governments manipulate their populations to justify morally indefensible actions allows it to transcend its historical moment and find wider relevance.

BIBLIOGRAPHY

Sources

Adams, Robert M. "Couldn't Put It Down." Rev. of *The Spy Who Came in from the Cold*, by John le Carré. *New York Review of Books*. NYREV, Inc., 5 Mar. 1964. Web. 28 Jan. 2013.

Aronoff, Myron J. *The Spy Novels of John le Carré: Balancing Ethics and Politics.* New York: St. Martin's, 1998. Print.

Beene, LynnDianne. *John le Carré.* New York: Twayne, 1992. Print.

Cobbs, John L. *Understanding John le Carré.* Columbia: South Carolina UP, 1998. Print.

Lane, Anthony. "I Spy: John le Carré and the Rise of George Smiley." *New Yorker.* New Yorker, 12 Dec. 2011. Web. 16 Aug. 2012.

Le Carré, John. *The Spy Who Came in from the Cold.* London: Penguin, 2010. Print.

Nelson, John. "John le Carré and the Postmodern Myth of the State." *Finnish Yearbook of Political Thought* 3 (1999): 100–31. Print.

Warner, Lionel. "Single Spies and Battalions." *English Review* Sept. 2001: 14. *General OneFile.* Web. 16 Aug. 2012.

Further Reading

Barley, Tony. *Taking Sides: The Fiction of John le Carré.* Milton Keynes: Open UP, 1986. Print.

Bold, Alan, ed. *The Quest for le Carré.* London: Vision Press, 1988. Print.

Bruccoli, Matthew J., and Judith S. Baughman, eds. *Conversations with John le Carré.* Jackson: UP of Mississippi, 2004. Print.

Horn, Eva. "Knowing the Enemy: The Epistemology of Secret Intelligence." *Grey Room* 11 (2003): 58–85. MIT Press Journals. Web. 9 Sept. 2012.

Lewis, Peter. *John le Carré.* New York: Ungar, 1985. Print.

Plimpton, George. "John le Carré, The Art of Fiction No. 149." *Paris Review.* Paris Review, Summer 1997. Web. 16 Aug. 2012.

Wolfe, Peter. *Corridors of Deceit: The World of John le Carré.* Bowling Green: Bowling Green State U Popular P, 1987. Print.

Media Adaptation

The Spy Who Came in from the Cold. Dir. Martin Ritt. Perf. Richard Burton, Oskar Werner, and Claire Bloom. Salem Films Limited, 1965. Film.

Chris Routledge

THANK YOU FOR SMOKING

Christopher Buckley

OVERVIEW

In the 1994 satirical novel *Thank You for Smoking,* Christopher Buckley lampoons not only Big Tobacco and its lobbyists but also the high-flown rhetoric coming from both sides of the smoking debate. The novel's protagonist, Nick Naylor, is a journalist-turned-spokesperson for the Academy of Tobacco Studies who is kidnapped, ostensibly by antismoking activists, and covered with a potentially fatal number of nicotine patches. The FBI thinks Nick is up to his old tricks: exploiting anything to garner sympathy for smokers. Nick discovers he was set up by his boss and a scheming assistant but decides to do prison time as penance for being, as one of the novels antismoking advocates points out, one of those people who will "say anything to sell cigarettes."

Thank You for Smoking was published at a time when the public outcry over the tactics of Big Tobacco was peaking. With an increasing number of households subscribing to twenty-four-hour cable news channels, lawsuits and Congressional hearings on smoking-related issues always seemed to be in the public eye. The novel was generally well reviewed and became a best seller for Buckley, who had formerly served as Al Gore's speechwriter. It solidified his career as a novelist who wrote about Washington DC politics from the inside. Interestingly, the tobacco industry remained silent on the novel, just as it would when the film adaptation premiered in 2005. Though the tobacco industry has lost some traction since the novel's initial publication, *Thank You For Smoking* remains relevant in a culture in which lobbyists' influence on public policy remains a subject of debate.

HISTORICAL AND LITERARY CONTEXT

Before 1950, tobacco companies had no need for public relations services. Cigarettes were ubiquitous, and the general public knew little about the link between smoking and lung cancer. Starting in 1954, however, liability lawsuits began appearing. These suits proliferated in 1964, when U.S. Surgeon General Terry Luther released his findings that smoking causes cancer, and again in 1988, when nicotine was officially labeled addictive. Tobacco companies had enjoyed some degree of protection as a result of the warning labels they had displayed on cigarette packages since 1965, but in 1992, the U.S. Supreme Court ruled that these warnings were not a shield from lawsuits.

As *Thank You for Smoking* suggests, the rising tide of lawsuits and attendant publicity served to vilify tobacco companies and the talking heads they employed. In 1994, Congressional hearings were held in which tobacco executives argued that nicotine is not addictive, despite overwhelming evidence to the contrary. Articles documenting the companies' woes appeared in the *New York Times* and *Time* magazine, among others. Activists were spurred on by this publicity. As Alvin Golin, chairman of the Chicago-based public relations firm Golin/Harris Communications, told the *Los Angeles Times,* "They want to strike while the cigarette is still hot." Tobacco spokespeople were often targets for criticism. Indeed, *Thank You for Smoking's* protagonist is depicted in all of his amoral, dissembling glory. At the same time, Buckley gives Nick Naylor a sense of humor, charm, and, by the end of the novel, a conscience. In some ways, he is a victim of his own methods.

Social satire had become increasingly popular in the last quarter of the twentieth century, with writers such as Kurt Vonnegut, Joseph Heller, Katherine Dunn, and Tom Wolfe appearing on the best-seller list. Furthermore, the public's appetite for "behind the scenes" reporting on corporate misdeeds moved nonfiction such as Bryan Burrough's *Barbarians at the Gate* (1990). As a humorist, Buckley has been favorably compared to Jonathan Swift, Mark Twain, and Charles Dickens.

Thank You for Smoking—Buckley's second novel, following *The White House Mess* (1986)—firmly established him as a whip-smart recorder of life in Washington DC. Buckley's next novel, *Little Green Men* (1999), involving the alien abduction of talk-show pundit John O. Banion, further cemented this reputation. Buckley has since lampooned presidential sex scandals and the press coverage they provoke (*No Way to Treat a First Lady,* 2002), Islamic extremism (*Florence of Arabia,* 2004), and the U.S. Supreme Court (*Supreme Courtship,* 2008). His 2007 book *Boomsday,* which describes a generational war incited by PR flack Cassandra Devine, contains a wink toward *Thank You for Smoking,* as Terry Tucker, Cassandra's cohort, claims to have been schooled in media manipulation by Nick Naylor. In 2012 Buckley published *They Eat Puppies, Don't They?,* which targets the defense industry and the lobbyists and pundits who serve it.

÷ *Key Facts*

Time Period:
Late 20th Century

Genre:
Novel

Events:
Success of anti-tobacco lawsuits; rise of political lobbyists

Nationality:
American

THE TOBACCO INSTITUTE: NICK NAYLOR'S "REAL" EMPLOYER

The Academy of Tobacco Studies, the shady lobbying firm depicted in *Thank You For Smoking,* is a fictional institution based on the Tobacco Institute, a U.S.-based trade group. The institute was founded in 1958 and had significant influence in the industry until it was disbanded in 1998 as part of the Tobacco Master Settlement Agreement. During its years of activity, the institute was responsible for research on the public's attitudes about smoking, as well as lobbying lawmakers to kill antismoking legislation. The institute also produced pro-smoking literature and fought to refute scientific findings about the dangers of smoking.

The scheming of the Academy of Tobacco Studies is, of course, exaggerated for dramatic effect in *Thank You for Smoking.* Nevertheless, the Tobacco Institute did run afoul of the law and of cultural standards regarding honesty and fair reporting. There is evidence, for example, that the institute had a number of "white papers" at the ready to quickly counter any "attack" on tobacco. More egregiously, the institute was found to have planted a pro-smoking article in the national media, a fraud that was documented in *Consumer Reports.*

When he was researching his novel, Buckley interviewed members of the Tobacco Institute. After the book's publication, a Tobacco Institute spokesperson expressed "enormous disappointment" at Buckley's portrayal of the organization, charging that "he knew from visits over here … we pay very close attention to the facts."

THEMES AND STYLE

Nick Naylor, Buckley's half-sleazy, half-lovable spin-doctor, embodies some of late-twentieth-century capitalist society's worst tendencies toward self-interest and self-delusion while being understandable in his imperfect humanity. Buckley opens the novel by describing Nick as having "no horns or tail; he had a normal haircut … but his skin was bright red, as though he'd been swimming in nuclear-reactor water." The character's actions shine a light on the callousness of the "spin" culture. For example, when confronted by a woman who had lost a dear uncle to lung cancer, he asserts that "the issue before us today is … the Declaration of Independence, the Constitution and the Bill of Rights … and I think your uncle … were he here today, might just agree." When asked why he does PR for Big Tobacco, Nick says it is to finance his upper-middle-class lifestyle. Nevertheless, at the end of the novel, when questioned about why he would plead guilty to a crime he did not commit, he redeems himself by admitting his part in spreading misinformation about the dangers of smoking. He goes on to caution kids that smoking kills and discolors teeth—very human concerns.

Opposite page:
A poster for the 2006 film adaptation of *Thank You for Smoking.* © FOX SEARCHLIGHT/EVERETT COLLECTION.

With his obfuscating language and crafty dissembling, Nick is familiar to anyone who has listened to an "official spokesperson." Early in the novel, he appears as a guest on Oprah Winfrey's talk show, along with a panel that includes cancer-ridden teenager Robin Williger and Ron Goode, an official from the Department of Health and Human Services. Although Nick is the only panelist on the tobacco side of the debate—and as such, is particularly unsympathetic—he quickly gains control of the discussion, asking for a last cigarette before the firing squad, which elicits laughs from the audience and from Williger. Quickly, Nick shifts his focus to Goode, accusing him of trying to score points from Williger's suffering and launching into a diatribe about cancer-causing nuclear weapons and the soullessness of bureaucrats "trafficking in human misery" for the sake of their budgets.

Thank You for Smoking adopts a light tone to make its point, mocking the tobacco lobby with breezily delivered imitations of its rhetoric. The characters even mock themselves: Nick and his lobbyist friends Polly Bailey (representing the alcohol industry) and Bobby Jay Bliss (firearms) jokingly refer to their group, which meets regularly for lunch, as the MOD (Merchants of Death). The prissiness of the antismoking lobby also takes a hit. An anonymous "National Teachers' Association lady" complains that Nick's firing squad joke is "in extremely poor taste," even though "the Cancer Kid" and the rest of Oprah's audience are laughing. Buckley elicits laughter by having Nick imagine himself as the "Gucci Goebbels," but the reference to Hitler's propaganda machine also serves to remind the reader that this is a novel about malignant misinformation.

CRITICAL DISCUSSION

With grim reports from the tobacco wars in the news almost daily, many critics felt *Thank You for Smoking* brought some much-needed levity to the public discussion. The *New York Times* called the novel "savagely funny," while the *Wall Street Journal* praised Buckley's sharp eye and sharp prose, saying the book delivers a "spare kick in the teeth, for stiffs who seldom get their due in the real world." Other critics quibbled with Buckley's humor—Joan O'C. Hamilton remarked in *Business Week* that his one-liners "read as though they were written for Murphy Brown to deliver and then wait for the laugh track"—but the reviews were overwhelmingly positive.

In reviewing *Supreme Courtship* for the *New York Times* more than a decade after *Thank You for Smoking* was published, critic Blake Wilson called Buckley "our sharpest guide to the capital," referring to his body of work as "the beginnings of a vast Comedie-Washingtonienne." The film adaptation of *Thank You for Smoking* opened in 2005 to a U.S. audience that was far less tobacco-friendly than it had been a decade earlier. The movie garnered positive reviews and sparked a new round of new articles on the topic.

Despite its critical acclaim, Buckley's *Thank You for Smoking* has generated little scholarship. The same can be said for his other novels. Although reviews have provided some level of analysis, his work has not been around long enough to have attracted significant scholarly treatment.

BIBLIOGRAPHY

Sources

Buckley, Christopher. *Thank You For Smoking.* New York: Random House, 1994. Print.

Ferguson, Andrew. "Up in Smoke." *National Review* 66.11 (13 June 1994): 68–70. Rpt. in *Contemporary Literary Criticism.* Ed. Janet Witalec. Vol. 165. Detroit: Gale, 2003. *Literature Resource Center.* Web. 20 June 2012.

Hamilton, Joan O'C. "Warning: Hazardous to the Tobacco Lobby." *BusinessWeek* 6 June 1994: 15–19. Rpt. in *Contemporary Literary Criticism.* Ed. Janet Witalec. Vol. 165. Detroit: Gale, 2003. *Literature Resource Center.* Web. 20 June 2012.

Horovitz, Bruce. "Foes Hold Tobacco Firms Feet to Fire: Industry's Woes Kick Activists into High Gear." *Los Angeles Times.* Tribune Company, 10 May 1994. Web. 21 June 2012.

Lehmann-Haupt, Christopher. "Books of the Times; A Flight of Fancy through the Tobacco Industry." Rev. of *Thank You for Smoking,* by Christopher Buckley. *New York Times.* New York Times, 23 June 1994. Web. 28 Jan. 2013.

Manley, Will. "A Funny Man." *Booklist* 1 Aug. 2009: 13. *Literature Resource Center.* Web. 22 June 2012.

Shiflett, Dave. "Praise for the Killer Weed." Rev. of *Thank You for Smoking,* by Christopher Buckley. *Wall Street Journal* 17 June 1994. Print.

Tavcar, Larry. "Smoke and Mirrors." *Public Relations Quarterly* 39.2 (Summer 1994): 3–4. Rpt. in *Contemporary Literary Criticism.* Ed. Janet Witalec. Vol. 165. Detroit: Gale, 2003. *Literature Resource Center.* Web. 20 June 2012.

Wilson, Blake. "Bowling for Justices." *New York Times Book Review,* 7 Sept. 2008: 9(L). *Literature Resource Center.* Web. 22 June 2012.

Further Reading

Altman, David G.; Michael D. Slater; Cheryl L. Albright; and Nathan Maccoby. "How an Unhealthy Product Is Sold: Cigarette Advertising in Magazines, 1960–1985." Journal of Communication 37 (1987): 95–106. Print.

Brandt, Allan M. *The Cigarette Century: The Rise, Fall, and Deadly Persistence of the Product that Defined America.* Cambridge: Basic Books, 2007. Print.

Buckley, Christopher. *The White House Mess.* New York: Knopf, 1986. Print.

———. *Supreme Courtship.* New York: Twelve, 2008. Print.

Davidson, D. Kirk. *Selling Sin: The Marketing of Socially Unacceptable Products.* Westport: Praeger, 2003. Print.

Kessler, David. *A Question of Intent.* New York: Public Affairs, 2001. Print.

Michaels, David. *Doubt Is Their Product: How Industry's Assault on Science Threatens Your Health.* Oxford: Oxford UP, 2008. Print.

Media Adaptation

Thank You for Smoking. Dir. and writ. Jason Reitman. Prod. David O. Sacks. Perf: Aaron Eckhart, Maria Bello, Cameron Bright, et al. Fox Searchlight Pictures, 2006. Film.

Daisy Gard

Tono-Bungay

H. G. Wells

OVERVIEW

Tono-Bungay, written in 1909 by H. G. Wells, is a satire on quack medicine, advertising, and the rise of corporate power in Edwardian England. The novel is narrated by George Ponderevo, a directionless young man who joins his uncle in a business venture to manufacture a wonder drug called "Tono-Bungay." A bildungsroman built around the story of George Ponderevo's life, the story is also semi-autobiographical. It is notable for its social commentary, lamenting the loss of the "organic" social system of the seventeenth and eighteenth centuries, which is represented by the country house, Bladesover, and the arrival of a more callous, less humane social and political structure based upon commercial interests and false advertising. In particular, *Tono-Bungay* offers a critical view of a society willing to accept simple explanations and solutions to a variety of problems, and to tolerate almost any injustice, provided it is gilded with "the romance of modern commerce."

By the time *Tono-Bungay* was published (it was Wells's seventeenth novel), Wells was well established as a science fiction writer. A former teacher, he displayed an inclination toward didacticism in his science fiction; likewise, his stories and novels about the English middle class—the "second string" to his novelistic career—also took on an instructive tone at times. *Tono-Bungay* belongs to this second phase and early critics were divided about the validity of its critique of modern society, as well as about the character of Ponderevo himself. The novel's sharpest and most controversial satire, however, is reserved for business, which, Wells thought, had become an excuse for almost any kind of behavior. When first introduced to Tono-Bungay, a miracle drug, tonic, and cure-all made from commonly available ingredients, Ponderevo describes it as "a damned swindle!" His uncle replies that "there's no harm in the stuff—and it may do good. It might do a lot of good—giving people confidence, f'rinstance, against an epidemic." This depiction of the capitalist shamelessly creating products that do nothing but pacify a population might be seen in the context of Wells's socialist views, and the idea that, by the early twentieth century, British society had been damaged and dehumanized by rampant mercantilism.

HISTORICAL AND LITERARY CONTEXT

Between 1800 and 1900, the United Kingdom transformed itself from a largely agrarian, rural country into an industrial, urban powerhouse with a growing middle class. Unlike other European countries and the United States, where social upheaval was accompanied by revolution or civil war, Britain managed to sustain a stable system of government. By 1900, however, though the growing suburbs and an air of prosperity gave Britain the appearance of stability, British society had become deeply unequal in terms of wealth, opportunity, and political influence. The formation of the socialist Fabian Society, of which Wells was an early member, in 1884 and of the Independent Labour Party in 1900 shows that a growing number of people believed in a more equitable form of government and society.

Though prosperous and peaceful, Britain during the reign of King Edward VII (1901–10) experienced social tensions that mounted with the gathering pace of change. Technological developments, as represented in Wells's book by the fields of chemistry and aviation and the possible applications of radioactive substances, might have inspired optimism. But *Tono-Bungay* also depicts a society in which nonconformity in religion, sexual behavior, and gender roles—or even a more general skepticism—might lead to social expulsion and disgrace. It is a modern society where the old, rural "Bladesover social scheme" no longer applies, though its superficial traditions—such as the formalities of a church wedding—are still matters of great importance. Reviewing the novel in 1909, Arnold Bennett picked up on Wells's attack on the deference offered to business and the "romance of modern commerce," describing the novel's achievement as "the arraignment of a whole epoch at the bar of the conscience of a man who is intellectually honest and powerfully intellectual."

Like Wells, other Edwardian authors responded to the upheavals brought about by modernization. E. M. Forster explored the repressive social norms of the time and, in novels such as *Howard's End* (1910), reflected on the sense that an old way of life was coming to an end. Other writers were more radical. Robert Tressell's *The Ragged Trousered Philanthropists,* completed in 1910 but published in 1914, explicitly describes the iniquities and failings of capitalism from

✤ *Key Facts*

Time Period:
Early 20th Century

Genre:
Novel

Events:
Rise of advertising; increased social inequality; technological advances in chemistry, aviation, and more

Nationality:
English

H. G. WELLS: THE MAN BEHIND THE WORK

H. G. Wells was born in Bromley, Kent, in 1866, and had a patchy education that included a stint as an apprentice to a pharmacist between periods when he was enrolled in school and working as a teacher at the same time. Wells published a biology textbook, *Text Book of Biology, Part 1: Vertebrata,* in 1892 and his first novel, *The Time Machine,* in 1895, beginning a writing career that lasted sixty years. Wells had an unconventional married life—his wife allowed him to have affairs with several other women—and this, along with his political views, made him a controversial figure. He was an outspoken champion of women's rights, however, and he argued for a global agreement on human rights. In 1922 he fought an unsuccessful campaign to be elected to the British Parliament.

By 1909, when *Tono-Bungay* was published, Wells was a well-known and popular writer whose works had been translated into most European languages. He was known primarily for his "scientific romances" but also published histories and works of nonfiction futurism. His utopian view of a global government and his idea of a world in which war was unnecessary attracted an avid readership in early twentieth-century Europe, especially after World War I. It is worth noting that in 1933 publication of Wells's works ceased in Germany and Austria, where he had previously been a popular author, largely because of his liberal views. He was blacklisted by the Nazis as "corrupt." Wells died in 1946.

a socialist perspective, whereas George Bernard Shaw used plays to promote his socialist political views. *Tono-Bungay,* an entertainment with a point to make, represents a more populist attempt to promote radical ideas. It is ironic, given the novel's satire on the way people are hoodwinked by advertisers, the church, and the establishment elite in general, that author P. G. Wodehouse complained in 1919 that Wells was selling his books under false pretenses, hiding instruction behind the covers of popular novels.

Tono-Bungay is arguably Wells's most accomplished novel, but it has been overshadowed by his reputation as a writer of science fiction—in particular, novels such as *The Time Machine* and *The War of the Worlds.* Nevertheless, *Tono-Bungay*'s depiction of a society in which human values have been reduced to money and in which superficiality takes precedence over truth was part of a wider literary trend toward questioning and confronting social norms, institutional power, and modernity itself.

THEMES AND STYLE

In *Tono-Bungay,* Wells expresses his distaste for the fakeries and pretensions of modern society. In particular, the novel attacks the way in which business and finance make false promises of a new and better world when all they have done is make things newer and larger. Ponderevo notes on a visit to London's Natural History Museum that the stuffed birds and animals remind him of "the little assemblage … upon the Bladesover staircase," and that libraries and museums around the world "sprang from the elegant leisure of the gentlemen of taste." But he does not seem to feel that this outgrowing of private collections into public museums is an improvement. Ponderevo puts the latter in the same category as the railway stations and bridges that came "smashing down" across the Thames and the factory chimneys smoking over Westminster "with an air of carelessly not having permission." The problem, suggests the novel, is relentless growth and expansion for its own sake, a process that has come to be seen as not only inevitable but self-evidently good.

The power of Wells's satire lies in his ability to combine humor with direct commentary and personal reflection with overblown metaphor. Ponderevo's experiments with aviation, for example, can only follow the trajectory of a rapid rise and, after the balloon bursts, an equally precipitous fall. On the subject of his relationship with Marion, who decides she cannot marry him when his earnings are £300 a year but is later happy to do so when they reach £500, Ponderevo confesses that an "extraordinary bitterness possessed me at this invasion of the stupendous beautiful business of love by sordid necessity." But in the world of *Tono-Bungay,* people have not only come to accept that £500 a year is necessarily better than £300 a year but have also embraced money as a measure of personal value and as a foundation for moral judgments and psychological well-being. Ponderevo's uncle explains succinctly: "See what the world pays teachers and discoverers and what it pays business men! That shows the ones it really wants." The whole of society, from the slavishly religious poor to the middle classes, is driven by a set of expectations based around the need for constant improvement and worries about missing out financially, growing old, getting sick, or falling behind in some other way. These are the anxieties Ponderevo and his uncle exploit to sell their product, all the while reducing the proportion of "vivifying ingredients" in a mixture that is already a worthless, if not quite harmless, placebo.

In Ponderevo's often jaunty first-person confessional narrative, characters, particularly his uncle, are drawn with Dickensian color and flamboyance: "'The romance of modern commerce, George!' my uncle would say, rubbing his hands together and drawing air through his teeth. 'The romance of modern commerce, eh? Conquest. Province by province.'" This exaggeration, of language and character, heightens the ridiculousness of the "bright enterprise of selling injurious rubbish" in which language itself is enlisted to "give Tono-Bungay substance." Ponderevo's uncle is not interested in real scientific research but applies a great deal of energy to finding new and imaginative ways to sell his product to his desperate, suggestible customers. Ponderevo tells us, "I didn't succumb without a struggle to my uncle's allurements," but after a week, he joins the firm, despite the "supreme silliness" of "developing a monstrous bottling and packing warehouse, bottling rubbish for the consumption of foolish, credulous, and depressed people." Trade, he realizes, rules the world, and those who are most successful in business are treated with deference, elevated, if they are lucky, to a seat in the House of Lords.

CRITICAL DISCUSSION

Newspaper and magazine reviews of Wells's novel were mixed. In February 1909, Charles L. Graves, then assistant editor of *The Spectator,* described it as a "strange, go-as-you-please narrative." Although he calls it "strong and sincere," he also describes it as "repellent." Indeed, the character of Ponderevo, and the book itself, divided critics between those who, like Graves, found Wells's view of society and its future prospects to be too pessimistic and others who considered it a prophetic masterpiece. A review in the *Daily Telegraph* compares Wells to Charles Dickens and William Makepeace Thackeray and exclaims, "Unless we are very much mistaken, *Tono-Bungay* is one of the most significant novels of modern times, one of the sincerest, most unflinching analyses of the dangers and perils of our contemporary life that any writer has had the courage to submit to his own generation."

In the years after World War I, Wells's reputation as a social novelist declined, even as his "scientific romances" gained in popularity, helped along by the attentions of Hollywood and Orson Welles's famous 1938 radio adaptation of *The War of the Worlds.* *Tono-Bungay*'s analysis of consumer capitalism, and its unease relating to the discovery of the radioactive material Quap, make it strangely prescient about the twentieth century. Despite the novel's critique of the way people can be led by nonsensical metanarratives, even to their own detriment, however, critical opinion in the late twentieth century coalesced around the view that Wells was himself more of a propagandist than a novelist of ideas.

In the twenty-first century, *Tono-Bungay* is no longer one of Wells's best-known works, and his place alongside Jules Verne as one of the "fathers" of science fiction overshadows his reputation as a "condition of England" novelist. However, his internationalist and socialist views have made him a favorite among critics on the political left, especially in Britain. Indeed, a former leader of the British Labour Party, Michael Foot, wrote a sympathetic biography of Wells in the 1990s. In the wake of the 2008 global financial crisis—partly caused by billion-dollar business deals that were too good to be true—Wells's satire on the workings of capitalism acquired new relevance. In *Tono-Bungay,* Wells presents his own era as one

H. G. Wells

A portrait of H. G. Wells taken from a large-format pre-war cigarette card. © MICHAEL NICHOLSON/ CORBIS.

fascinated with commerce and as one in which individuals are presented with no choice other than to go along with the prevailing narrative of trade. *Tono-Bungay* satirizes the propaganda of commerce, which, Wells suggests, has persuaded the population that any kind of business practice can be justified as long as it creates more business.

BIBLIOGRAPHY

Sources

Bennett, Arnold. *Books and Persons: Being Comments on a Past Epoch 1908-1911. Gutenberg.org.* Project Gutenberg, 2005. Web. 28 Jan. 2013.

Graves, Charles L. Rev. of *Tono-Bungay,* by H. G. Wells. *Spectator.* 27 Feb. 1909. Rpt. in *H.G. Wells: The Critical Heritage.* Ed. Patrick Parrinder. London: Taylor, 1972. 151–53. Print.

Nate, Richard. "Ignorance, Opportunism, Propaganda and Dissent: The Reception of H. G. Wells in Nazi Germany." *The Reception of H. G. Wells in Europe.* Ed. Patrick Parrinder and John S. Partington. New York: Thoemmes, 2005. 105–25. Print.

Rev. of *Tono-Bungay,* by H. G. Wells. *Daily Telegraph.* 10 Feb. 1909. Rpt. in *H.G. Wells: The Critical Heritage.* Ed. Patrick Parrinder. London: Taylor, 1972. 147–50. Print.

Wells, H. G. *Tono-Bungay.* 1909. Harmondsworth: Penguin, 2005. Print.

Wodehouse, P. G. "The Super Novelists: Suggestions for a League for the Restraint of Popular Authors." *Vanity Fair* June 1919: 49–50. Print.

Further Reading

Foot, Michael. *H. G.: The History of Mr. Wells.* New York: Counterpoint, 1995. Print.

Kupsine, William. "Wasted Value: The Serial Logic of H. G. Wells's *Tono-Bungay.*" *Novel* 33.1 (1999): 57–72. Print.

Partington, John S. *Building Cosmopolis: The Political Thought of H. G. Wells.* Burlington: Ashgate, 2003. Print.

Richards, Thomas. *The Imperial Archive: Knowledge and the Fantasy of Empire.* London: Verso, 1993. Print.

Sherborne, Michael. *H. G. Wells: Another Kind of Life.* London: Owen, 2010. Print.

Smith, David C. *H. G. Wells: Desperately Mortal: A Biography.* New Haven: Yale UP, 1986. Print.

West, Anthony. *H. G. Wells: Aspects of a Life.* New York: Random, 1984. Print.

Christopher Routledge

"WE'LL MEET AGAIN"

Hugh Charles, Ross Parker

OVERVIEW

"We'll Meet Again" (1939), with lyrics written by Hugh Charles and music by Ross Parker, was first recorded by Vera Lynn at the beginning of World War II. The song reflects the unsettled mood in England at the time by describing what had become a familiar scene: a man, preparing to leave for war, reassuring his sweetheart that they will someday be reunited. The chorus goes, "We'll meet again, / Don't know where, don't know when. / But we'll meet again, some sunny day." With its optimism about the war's outcome, "We'll Meet Again" served as a powerful piece of propaganda, boosting the morale of both soldiers and their loved ones.

"We'll Meet Again" was incredibly popular during the war, first in England and later in the United States, where it was recorded by several artists, including Kay Kaiser, Benny Goodman, and Johnny Cash. Although the song received praise from music critics and audiences alike, it also had a number of detractors, who felt it romanticized a war that had resulted in the deaths of hundreds of thousands of British and American soldiers. In the decades since its release, "We'll Meet Again" has had a major impact on popular culture in both Great Britain and the United States, and it has been used in movies and referenced, both positively and negatively, in other artistic works about war.

HISTORICAL AND LITERARY CONTEXT

In 1939 Great Britain, in response to the increasing threat of aggression on the part of Nazi Germany, was building up its military and preparing for war. After Germany invaded Poland on September 1 of that year, Great Britain and France declared war on Germany two days later, marking the beginning of World War II. Voluntary enlistment had turned into a mandatory conscription, and eventually all healthy men from the ages of eighteen to forty-one were drafted. As the country went to war, music became an important part of the wartime propaganda effort.

With anxiousness growing over the fighting ahead, "We'll Meet Again" was released in Britain on September 28, 1939. Charles and Parker chose Lynn to record the first version of the song. Although the lyrics are written from a male's perspective, her voice and popularity ensured that the song would reach its target audience: men going off to war. The wild popularity of

"We'll Meet Again" led Lynn to be dubbed "The Forces' Sweetheart." Songs such as "We'll Meet Again," "The White Cliffs of Dover" (written in 1941 and also performed by Lynn), and "There'll Always Be an England" (written in 1939 by Charles and Parker) also bolstered the patriotism of the English people and inspired hope for a positive outcome to the war.

The primary means for spreading the messages of songs such as "We'll Meet Again" was radio, which had become pervasive by World War II. In fact, World War II was the first major military conflict to be played out on the airwaves. News of major victories and propaganda music helped families on the home front maintain hope. For the soldiers, the music provided comforting memories of home, giving them courage to continue their fight for the Allied cause. Armies on both sides frequently broadcast political propaganda and music that enemy troops in the vicinity could intercept; consequently, soldiers became familiar with a wide variety of war music from different countries.

Other propaganda songs from the era, such as "There'll Always Be an England," work on a different level than "We'll Meet Again." As John Baxendale explains in the book *Millions Like Us?: British Culture in the Second World War*: "The longevity of *We'll Meet Again* owes a great deal to that of dame Vera Lynn, *There'll Always Be An England* has lived on in a different cultural category: it is a national song." The same can be said of "The White Cliffs of Dover," which depicts a specific place: cliffs on the British coastline. "We'll Meet Again," however, struck a chord with people of many nationalities, as it does not mention a particular country but merely promises that soldiers will someday return home safely. This vague quality helps to explain the song's enduring popularity.

THEMES AND STYLE

The primary theme of "We'll Meet Again" is the importance of remaining positive in times of great adversity, as at the onset of World War II in Britain when so many men were being conscripted to fight for the Allied cause. The tone of the song is both sentimental and sweet, acknowledging impending hardship and deferred happiness. The male speaker gives words of encouragement to his sweetheart who he is leaving behind: "Keep smiling through / Just like you

✦ Key Facts

Time Period:
Mid-20th Century

Genre:
Song

Events:
World War II; establishment of a military draft

Nationality:
English

THE LIFE OF VERA LYNN

While the song "We'll Meet Again" was written by Hugh "Hughie" Charles and Ross Parker, it will always be associated with Vera Lynn, otherwise known as "The Forces' Sweetheart." Born as Vera Margaret Welch in London on March 20, 1917, she was already well known by British audiences before the outbreak of World War II. She began hosting a half-hour radio show in 1941, *Sincerely Yours, Vera Lynn,* in which she sang and also shared messages to soldiers from their loved ones. In addition, she toured abroad, singing for soldiers in Burma, India, and Egypt.

In 1943 Lynn made her acting debut as the female lead in a movie, *We'll Meet Again,* the title of which was taken from her signature song. The film is roughly autobiographical, as it focuses on a young female singer and dancer trying to start her career in London during World War II. Lynn continued to perform after the war, although much less frequently. She received the honor of being the oldest woman to top the British album charts when, at the age of ninety-two, her album *We'll Meet Again: The Very Best of Vera Lynn* reached number one in 2009.

always do / Till the blue skies chase those dark clouds away." "We'll Meet Again" serves as propaganda by emphasizing the speaker's optimism and courage; his hopeful words provided comfort to the families and loved ones of soldiers fighting in the war.

In subsequent versions of the song, Charles's lyrics were changed from a male to a female perspective. Originally, a soldier reassures his sweetheart: "So will you please say 'hello' / To the folks that I know / Tell them I won't be long." Later, it is the female sweetheart saying goodbye to her soldier boy: "And I will just say 'hello' / To the folks that you know / Tell them you won't be long." Each version of the song describes how both the people on the home front and the soldiers who are off fighting should remain optimistic and committed to the war effort. The song offers the promise that the lovers will be reunited: "After the rain comes the rainbow, / You'll see the rain go, never fear / We two can wait for tomorrow / Goodbye to sorrow my dear." Whether the song is sung from a male or female perspective, happiness is just around the corner.

Despite this overt optimism, Charles's lyrics also contain an undercurrent of impending doom. By saying that his family will be happy to know he was singing the song as he left, the speaker suggests that he might be putting up a false front. Even the rosy refrain, "We'll meet again some sunny day" has been interpreted on different levels. The sheer repetition of these words suggests that the speaker is trying to reassure both himself and his sweetheart about an uncertain situation. Furthermore, the speaker's vague-

ness about where or when he will meet his loved one again has been taken to mean that he will die and be reunited with his family in heaven. Nevertheless, the message of faith in a better day—whenever and wherever that is—comes through clearly. In the article "Sincerely Yours, Vera Lynn: Performing Class, Sentiment, and Femininity in the 'People's War,'" Christina Baade explains, "'We'll Meet Again' … articulated a farewell between sweethearts in its verse, but its chorus envoiced a shared faith in a reunion on some future unspecified 'sunny day' … [and] urged the addressee maintain hope."

CRITICAL DISCUSSION

"We'll Meet Again" was a hit when it was released in Britain in 1939, and it gained international popularity after the United States entered the war in 1941. The slogan "So, We'll Meet Again" was used on a U.S. propaganda advertisement encouraging people to buy war bonds, as if purchasing the bonds would ensure the safe returns of their loved ones. The song was later used in a negative sense in Stanley Kubrick's dark critique of war, *Dr. Strangelove* (1964), playing at the film's end as an atomic bomb is dropped and a mushroom cloud forms. By juxtaposing the song with images of nuclear annihilation, Kubrick shows how propaganda, sentimentality, and optimism can be used to hide the massively destructive realities of war.

Though "We'll Meet Again" is a seemingly timeless song, it is borne of a specific time and place. The song was popular in England well before its message reached the United States, which did not enter the war until more than two years later. In addition, despite the attack on Pearl Harbor in December 1941, American troops generally did not have to fear for the safety of their relatives at home in the United States, since the theaters of war were on other continents. Therefore, many American war songs inspired by their European counterparts deal more with the homesickness and isolation felt by American soldiers fighting in distant places. "The Boogie Woogie Bugle Boy" (1941) explains the plight of a famous street musician who only gets to play "Reveille" while overseas, and "I'll Be Home for Christmas" (1943) depicts a soldier's dream of returning home for the holidays.

Regardless of the topic, many of the wartime propaganda songs, including "We'll Meet Again," have not been taken seriously by critics in the ensuing decades. The evolution of music and songwriting has prompted many modern critics to view the style of "We'll Meet Again" as outdated and its message as overly simplistic. One of the most stinging contemporary criticisms of "We'll Meet Again" is found in the lyrics of the song "Vera," from the album *The Wall* (1979) by the British band Pink Floyd. The song is written from the perspective of a child who has lost

his father in the war, and the lyrics question what happened to Vera Lynn's promise of a bright future for postwar Britain.

BIBLIOGRAPHY

Sources

Baade, Christine. "Sincerely Yours, Vera Lynn: Performing Class, Sentiment, and Femininity in the 'People's War.'" *Atlantis: A Women's Studies Journal* 30.2 (2006): 36–49. Web. 22 Aug. 2012.

Bach, Alice. *Religion, Politics, Media in the Broadband Era.* Sheffield: Sheffield Phoenix, 2004. Print.

Baxendale, John. "'You and I—All of Us Ordinary People': Renegotiating 'Britishness,' in War Time." *'Millions Like Us'?: British Culture in the Second World War.* Ed. Nick Hayes and Jeff Hill. Liverpool: Liverpool UP, 1999. 295–322. Print.

Jones, John Bush. *The Songs That Fought the War: Popular Music and the Home Front, 1939–1945.* Lebanon: Brandeis UP, 2006. Print.

McLoughlin, Kate. "Vera Lynn and the 'We'll Meet Again' Hypothesis." *From Self to Shelf: The Artist Under Construction.* Ed. Sally Bayley and Will May. Newcastle: Cambridge Scholars, 2007. 112–20. Print.

Parker, Ross, and Hughie Charles. "We'll Meet Again." London: Irwin Dash Music, 1939. Print.

Waters, Roger. "Vera." *Pink Floyd The Wall.* Columbia Records: 1979. Album.

Further Reading

Beidler, Philip D. *The Good War's Greatest Hits: World War II and American Remembering.* Athens: U of Georgia, 1998. Print.

Bloomfield, Gary L. *Duty, Honor, Applause: America's Entertainers in World War II.* Guilford: Lyon's, 2004. Print.

Brewer, Susan A. *To Win the Peace: British Propaganda in the United States During World War II.* Ithaca: Cornell UP, 1997. Print.

Cull, Nicholas John. *Selling War: The British Propaganda Campaign Against American "Neutrality" in World War II.* New York: Oxford UP, 1995. Print.

Horten, Gerd. *Radio Goes to War: The Cultural Politics of Propaganda During World War II.* Berkeley: U of California P, 2002. Print.

Lee, William F. *American Big Bands.* Milwaukee: Hal Leonard, 2005. Print.

Young, William H., and Nancy K. Young. *Music of the World War II Era.* Westport: Greenwood, 2008. Print.

Media Adaptations

We'll Meet Again. Dir. Philip Brandon. Perf. Vera Lynn, Geraldo, and Patricia Roc. Columbia Pictures, 1943. Film.

We'll Meet Again: The Music of Hugh Charles. Reid Records, 1987. Music.

Ron Horton

Dystopias and Utopias

BLACK NO MORE

Being an Account of the Strange and Wonderful Workings of Science in the Land of the Free, A.D. 1933–1940

George Samuel Schuyler

OVERVIEW

Black No More: Being an Account of the Strange and Wonderful Workings of Science in the Land of the Free, A.D. 1933–1940, published in 1931, is George Samuel Schuyler's satirical novel about a scientific process that allows African Americans to change their skin color and features to appear white. This concept stems from the issue of racial "passing," which was the term used when mixed-race Americans assimilated and identified as white in order to avoid racial discrimination. The humorous Harlem Renaissance-era fiction follows Max Disher, a black man who undergoes Dr. Junius Crookman's scientific treatment to become the white Matthew Fisher. As Fisher he earns a leadership role in the Knights of Nordica, a successor to the Ku Klux Klan, and ultimately marries Helen Givens, the daughter of the organization's leader. The popularity of Dr. Crookman's treatment leads to confusion and paranoia about who is "truly" white, and in the absence of clear racial lines, the Americans in the novel find new ways to divide themselves and define race. Schuyler's novel portrays a world in which known racial differences disappear but racism continues.

Schuyler already had a reputation for being outspoken on the subject of race and class when *Black No More,* his first novel, was published. A self-declared socialist into the 1930s, Schuyler was best known at this time for his 1926 debate with Langston Hughes about the role of race in art. *Black No More*'s satirical tone required a sophisticated reader, which reviewers acknowledged as they applauded the book's realistic portrayal of race and class fears and disparities in the United States. In *The Sage of Sugar Hill,* Jeffrey B. Ferguson writes that W. E. B. Du Bois laughed in recognition of the character that parodies him. Although the novel was received positively overall, some critics faulted it as excessively crude and vicious. Ferguson and Andrew B. Leiter both explain that H. L. Mencken, an influence to and admirer of Schuyler, accused Schuyler of emphasizing his anger at the expense of a loftier satirical message. Recognized as the first satirical novel by a black author, *Black No More* marked an opposition to the sentimentality of Harlem Renaissance literature

and demonstrated an innovative way to address the mammoth issues of race and class.

HISTORICAL AND LITERARY CONTEXT

During the Harlem Renaissance, which flourished between 1910 and 1930, black artists produced poetry, fiction, theater, visual art, and music that influenced people around the world. The Great Migration and World War I, as well as Fordist capitalism, encouraged many African Americans in the second decade of the twentieth century to leave the agriculture-based South for opportunities in northern cities such as New York, Detroit, Chicago, and Philadelphia. This large-scale movement of black Americans contributed to the Harlem Renaissance and helped create a new perception of African Americans. However, racism persisted even with the new opportunities, as evidenced by Jim Crow laws, which maintained strict segregation between the races and severely limited the freedom of blacks.

Although active in the Harlem Renaissance, Schuyler writes against tropes of the movement while simultaneously protesting the way the United States continued to view race and class. He criticized the Harlem Renaissance's foundation on race through the satirical tone of the book as well as the plotline, which reveals that nearly everyone in the United States has black ancestry. Schuyler's rejection of the Harlem Renaissance's sentimentalism extends to *Black No More*'s criticism of African American leaders and institutions. Even as the Harlem Renaissance celebrated the contributions of black Americans and more blacks joined the northern work force, *Black No More* calls attention to the ways the United States continued to value white skin. The novel criticizes the popular products of the time period that promised lighter skin and straighter hair for African Americans while acknowledging that whites had access to social and economic mobility unavailable to blacks. The value of whiteness over other characteristics also led to the division of the labor class along color lines, and the factory owners in *Black No More* benefit from this division because it distracts the laborers from agitating for better wages.

Sincerity and loyalty to other Africans Americans characterize the literature of the end of the Harlem Renaissance. Although Rudolph Fisher gently teased

❖ *Key Facts*

Time Period:
Mid-20th Century

Genre:
Novel

Events:
Popularization of Harlem Renaissance literature; black migration to the North; racial discrimination

Nationality:
American

SCHUYLER AND HUGHES DEBATE NEGRO ART

Five years before *Black No More* was published, Schuyler and poet Langston Hughes debated the relevance of race on art in the *Nation*. The debate began with Schuyler's 1926 essay "The Negro Art Hokum," which asserted that nationality was more important than race. He accused those who pay attention to an artist's race as seeking to confirm that the "blackmoor is inferior and fundamentally different," when the idea that there is a specific type of art produced by blacks is nonsense. Schuyler, who in 1928 married Josephine Cogdell, a white woman from Texas, wrote that blacks and whites were not very different and that black artists should not be confined by a concept of racial aesthetics.

Hughes responded that Schuyler's declaration of the similarities between the races was "absurd." As long as blacks remained segregated, their art would reflect the differences in their experiences from white artists. Hughes believed that "the true work of art from the Negro artist is bound, if it have any color and distinctiveness at all, to reflect his racial background and his racial environment." Schuyler would continue to pursue controversial discussions about the Harlem Renaissance, and many of the ideas he posits in "The Negro Art Hokum" appeared in *Black No More.*

elite blacks in his novels, Wallace Thurman's books, written in a tone of despair at the situation of blacks, are more typical. Black writers shied away from biting humor because of minstrelsy's encouragement to audiences to laugh at black characters. Schuyler, however, disregarded these concerns in his pursuit of acknowledging absurdity when he wrote *Black No More,* and he looked to the white satirist Mencken for inspiration. For example, shades of Mencken's "The Sahara of the Bozart" appear in *Black No More.* Schuyler's many columns, including "Shafts and Darts," which ran in the African American political and literary magazine the *Messenger* in the mid-1920s, had previously showcased his cutting satire, and his identification as a socialist also influenced *Black No More.*

In addition to its distinction as the first African American-authored science fiction novel, *Black No More* began a tradition of literature by black writers that focused on race and capitalism, and it proved prescient in its conclusion that the United States is a "mulatto nation." The novel inspired writers such as Nathanael West and Zora Neale Hurston to examine the ways in which language constructs race and racial authenticity as well as the ways these concepts are mass produced. The end of the novel reveals that the United States is a country of mixed-race individuals, which feels especially meaningful when read after Barack Obama was elected president. The novel's portrayal of persistent discrimination based on arbitrary racial characteristics even after the announcement that the majority of Americans possess some black "blood" remains relevant as well.

THEMES AND STYLE

Black No More illustrates the ways racism dictates economic and social power in the United States. African Americans in the book have three choices: "either get out, get white or get along." Only after trickster Max Disher undergoes Dr. Crookman's treatment and emerges with white skin and blond hair does he "at last" feel "like an American citizen." Max's new power and access, granted by his white appearance, is epitomized when he helps his father-in-law, the head of a white supremacist group, nearly become president of the United States. Racist rhetoric also acts as a tool to control the labor force. The "menace of the Negro to Caucasian race purity and political control" prevents white laborers from organizing, and they sacrifice higher wages in order to protect the presumed purity of their race. Schuyler demonstrates the dangers of capitalism and the absurdity of forming alliances based on race when white company owners exploit white laborers even as race designations become increasingly abstract.

An omniscient narrator tells the story mainly from Max's perspective in a way that distances the reader enough to critique Max's behavior but keeps the reader close enough to consider how he would behave in similar scenarios. The dialogue includes a representation of regional dialects, including that of Max's wife, Helen: "If only I'd known, I'd have never let you in for it"; her mother, the white, southern, "grotesque" Mrs. Givens: "Yo fathah sez this heah man f'm N'Yawk"; and the African American Harlem-based banker Henry Johnson: "Doc, you sho' knows yo' onions." Schuyler mocks the very convention of dialects when Dr. Crookman, who is African American, explains, in a very different dialect from Johnson, that "there is no such thing as Negro dialect, except in literature and drama." Schuyler uses this as an opportunity to assert his belief that differences between people are based on regionalism, not race, but he satirizes his own argument by writing characters who do in fact speak differently even though they are from the same place.

Schuyler's use of satire in *Black No More* increases the provocative nature of his novel. By writing in opposition to sentimentalism and using dark humor and irony, he challenges his audience to think critically about the story and the issues it addresses, including what he saw as the conformity of the Harlem Renaissance message. His irreverence asserts the imperfection of all people and highlights the absurdity, not tragedy, of race and class relations. At the same time, his use of humor makes even more jarring the instances of realism, specifically a scene in which two white politicians are lynched in Happy Hill, Mississippi.

CRITICAL DISCUSSION

The stark realism of the lynching scene troubled many critics when *Black No More* was first published.

In addition to Mencken's critique that it was "excessively savage," Ferguson quotes P. L. Prattis, writing as Roger Diddier, who accused Schuyler of being a "low-bred ruffian" writing in "barroom style." Some critics negatively reviewed the novel, not acknowledging that it was a work of satire. Most of the reception was positive, however. Readers and critics celebrated *Black No More* as liberating in its refusal to portray blacks as downtrodden, and Thurman led a discussion of *Black No More* at the New York Public Library. Cultural critic Alain Locke believed Schuyler had introduced a new style of literature, and Du Bois, parodied in *Black No More* as Agamemnon Shakespeare Beard, wrote that the book was "extremely significant in Negro American literature."

Although *Black No More*'s reputation decreased in the mid-twentieth century, it has since returned to the status of a well-recognized satirical novel. Schuyler continued to write, only halting his *Philadelphia Courier* column in 1966 after forty-four years. The author, who once said, "No generalization is absolutely true, not even that one!" valued the ability to contradict himself. After World War II he became ultraconservative and virulently anticommunist, and he wrote against the civil rights movement in the 1950s and 1960s. During this period, critics, reading as revisionists, interpreted *Black No More* as an assimilationist novel, ignoring the book's many criticisms of whites. More modern scholarship recognizes *Black No More* as an important work containing critiques of race, class, and gender that remain relevant.

Black No More has been the subject of many identity-based readings. In his essay in *Real Folks: Race and Genre in the Great Depression* (2011), Sonnet Retman analyzes the way white women represent commodities in the novel because Max's main motivation for becoming white is to win the affection of a white woman who rejected him. Retman argues that this is not simply for the allure of the taboo or for revenge but rather that a white woman is a type of property that grants her partner access to economic and social privilege. Ferguson deftly sorts through the complex gradients of racial categorization in *Black No More*. Not only does racism toward blacks serve as the "ultimate worker-control mechanism," but the Jewish, Irish, and German whites in the novel foreshadow and provide a real-life example of the confusion over how white someone must be to deserve full citizenship in the United States. When it is discovered in the novel that the African Americans who became white are actually whiter than those who were born white, the country changes direction and begins valuing darker skin.

BIBLIOGRAPHY

Sources

Ferguson, Jeffrey B. *The Sage of Sugar Hill: George S. Schuyler and the Harlem Renaissance.*
New Haven: Yale UP, 2005. *New York University ebrary.* Web. 1 Aug. 2012.

Jones, Norma R. "George Samuel Schuyler." *Afro-American Writers from the Harlem Renaissance to 1940.* Ed. Trudier Harris-Lopez and Thadious M. Davis. Vol. 51. Detroit: Gale, 1987. n. pag. *Literature Resources from Gale.* Web. 1 Aug. 2012.

Leiter, Andrew B. "Sexual Transgressions and the Battle at the Racial Border." *Southern Literary Studies: In the Shadow of the Black Beast: African American Masculinity in the Harlem and Southern Renaissances.* Baton Rouge: Louisiana State UP, 2010. 91–132. Web. 6 Aug. 2012.

Retman, Sonnet H. "'A Combination Madhouse, Burlesque Show and Coney Island': The Color Question in George Schuyler's *Black No More.*" *Real Folks: Race and Genre in the Great Depression.* Durham: Duke UP, 2011. 33–71. Print.

Schuyler, George S. *Black No More: Being an Account of the Strange and Wonderful Workings of Science in the Land of the Free, A.D. 1933–1940.* College Park: McGrath, 1969. Print.

Thaggert, Miriam. "Surface Effects: Satire, Race, and Language in George Schuyler's *Black No More* and "The Negro-Art Hokum." *Images of Black Modernism: Verbal and Visual Strategies of the Harlem Renaissance.* Amherst: U of Massachusetts P, 2010. 88–111. Print.

Further Reading

Comprone, Rachel. *Poetry, Desire, and Fantasy in the Harlem Renaissance.* Lanham: University Press of America, 2006. Print.

George Samuel Schuyler (right) interviewing Malcolm X in 1964. Schuyler's *Black No More* is a scathing satire of early twentieth-century race relations in the United States. © HULTON-DEUTSCH COLLECTION/ CORBIS.

Gallego, Mar. *Passing Novels in the Harlem Renaissance: Identity Politics and Textual Strategies*. Munster: Lit Verlag, 2003. Print.

Joo, Hee-Jung Serenity. "Miscegenation, Assimilation, and Consumption: Racial Passing in George Schuyler's *Black No More* and Eric Liu's *The Accidental Asian*." MELUS 33.3 (2008): 169. *Literature Resources from Gale*. Web. 6 Aug. 2012.

Larsen, Nella, and Deborah E. McDowell. *Quicksand and Passing*. New Brunswick: Rutgers UP, 1996. Print.

Schuyler, George S. *Black and Conservative: The Autobiography of George S. Schuyler*. New Rochelle: Arlington House, 1966. Print.

Thurman, Wallace. *Infants of the Spring*. Boston: Northeastern UP, 1992. Print.

Williams, Oscar R. *George S. Schuyler: Portrait of a Black Conservative*. Knoxville: U of Tennessee P, 2007. Print.

Kathryn Molinaro

A Canticle for Leibowitz

Walter M. Miller Jr.

OVERVIEW

Written by William M. Miller Jr., *A Canticle for Leibowitz* is a postapocalyptic science fiction novel published in 1959. The novel begins in a neo-dark age, centuries after a nuclear holocaust, when the public has turned against science and scholars. Brother Francis Gerard, a novice monk in an abbey in the southwestern United States, discovers a document authored by the abbey's patron, a Jewish engineer named Isaac Edward Leibowitz, who lived at the time of the holocaust. Several centuries later, society experiences a scientific renaissance, and Thon Taddeo Pfardentrott, an Einstein-like figure, fights with the monks over how to use Leibowitz's writing. More centuries pass and a technological society forms. As the globe descends again into nuclear war, members of the order of Leibowitz narrowly escape the planet in order to preserve the knowledge they have spent more than a millennium collecting. Through its depiction of the repetition of history and the endless struggle between church and state, *Canticle* suggests that scientific knowledge without the guidance of morality will inevitably lead to the downfall of civilization.

The novel, initially published in three parts, appeared as a serial in *Fantasy and Science Fiction* magazine from 1955 to 1956, in the midst of widespread fear of nuclear war. It was immediately recognized as one of the great works to emerge from the science fiction genre, though many literary critics dismissed it for its heavy-handed advocacy of Catholicism. Nevertheless, Miller's unflinching examination of the relationship between science and religion, particularly the dangers of recklessly pursuing knowledge, resonated with readers, cementing its status as a dystopian classic. *Canticle* is unique in the field of dystopian literature as it addresses the intersection of scientific, political, and religious worlds and the benefits of religion as a guiding force for humanity.

HISTORICAL AND LITERARY CONTEXT

As the Cold War took shape in the late 1940s and early 1950s, nuclear testing, military and political tensions, and distrust of suspected communists led to widespread panic in the United States. The American public, fearing a nuclear holocaust, channeled its anxiety into witch hunts for suspected communists and communist sympathizers. The American campaign against socialism, spearheaded by political leaders such as Senator Joseph McCarthy, took on a decidedly anti-intellectual tone, as many of the targets of McCarthyist investigations were scholars and academics.

When Miller published *Canticle,* Americans were experiencing renewed interest in religion. Because of the close connection between Marxism and atheism, and the perception of communists as heathens, many Americans believed that religion had an important, if not vital, role in guiding the political affairs of the nation after World War II. Miller, a professed atheist, had converted to Catholicism in 1947 after he returned from service in the war. Inspired by the Catholic Church's role in preserving knowledge through monasteries after the fall of Rome, he depicts in *Canticle* the centrality of the church in preserving human knowledge during a second dark age.

Popular culture of the 1950s echoed Americans' fear of the atomic bomb and the potential for global disaster. Many films of the day depicted atomic experiments gone wrong. *The Fly* (1958) features a man-fly hybrid created after a failed experiment involving atomic power. *The Day the World Ended* (1956) involves a group of survivors evading monsters in the aftermath of a global nuclear apocalypse. Novels such as Pat Frank's *Alas, Babylon* (1959) and Nevil Shute's *On the Beach* (1957) treat similar themes of a broken world following an atomic war. Although *Canticle* often draws comparisons with George Orwell's *1984* (1949) and Aldous Huxley's *Brave New World* (1932) for its depiction of a dystopia, Miller's novel focuses specifically on postholocaust themes rather than on themes of authoritarianism.

In spite of the fact that Miller never completed a second novel, his exceptional style has profoundly influenced writers of science fiction and of other literary genres. Author Walker Percy in *Love in the Ruins* (1971) revisits themes familiar to readers of *Canticle,* particularly ideas of reconciling Catholicism with science in the face of global catastrophe. Miller, who eventually left the Catholic faith, began writing a second, much more pessimistic novel about the world of *Canticle.* However, in 1996 he committed suicide before finishing it. (It was completed and published posthumously the following year as *Saint Leibowitz and the Wild Horse Woman.*)

❖ *Key Facts*

Time Period:
Mid-20th Century

Genre:
Novel

Events:
Nuclear Arms Race

Nationality:
American

SAINT LEIBOWITZ AND THE WILD HORSE WOMAN

Although he never completed his second novel, William M. Miller Jr. wrote the majority of *Saint Leibowitz and the Wild Horse Woman* (1997) before his death in 1996. A companion to *A Canticle for Leibowitz,* the novel's events take place between those of the second and third sections of *Canticle.* In the story, brother Blacktooth St. George, a monk at the Leibowitz monastery, is at a crossroads with his faith, struggling between his nomadic lifestyle and the settled life he has found in the monastery. While working for Cardinal Brownpony, Blacktooth discovers corruption at work in the monastery.

Finished by writer Terry Bisson after Miller's suicide, *Saint Leibowitz* is of particular interest to readers and biographical critics because it deals much more frankly with Miller's struggles with his own Catholic faith and his turn toward seclusion. Renouncing Catholicism later in life, the author admitted he had unanswered questions regarding the church. He began studying other religions, most notably Zen Buddhism, in pursuing his questions about the relationship between faith and modern society. Critics have pointed in particular to his intellectual transformation on the subject of suicide and euthanasia, which the author seems to rail against in the third part of *Canticle.*

THEMES AND STYLE

The major theme of *A Canticle for Leibowitz* is the importance of the Catholic Church to seeking out and preserving knowledge—activities that have the power both to create a scientific renaissance and to destroy civilization. In the first section of the novel, Miller depicts a nuclear holocaust, dubbed the "Flame Deluge," which provokes the public to murder intellectuals and burn books in retaliation for the creation of atomic weapons. The monks copy fragments of writing they find, not caring "that the knowledge they saved was useless—and some of it even incomprehensible." However, centuries later, the documents they preserve lead to the redevelopment of nuclear weapons and, ultimately, the destruction of the world. Although the Catholic Church is guilty of perpetuating the knowledge that ultimately dooms the earth, it is secular society that chooses to use the knowledge for purposes of war instead of using it to avoid conflict.

Miller emphasizes the centrality of the Catholic Church to human history by telling his story in three distinct sections. Thomas Reed Whissen in *Classic Cult Fiction: A Companion to Popular Cult Literature* (1992) explains the technique as fashioned to "resemble a religious triptych." The first section, "Fiat Homo" ("Let There Be Man"), depicts monks hard at work, illuminating and preserving bits of knowledge that have survived the Simplification, or the rebellion against intellectualism. Their work is studied centuries later during a scientific renaissance, as depicted in the section "Fiat Lux" ("Let There Be Light"). In the novel's third part, "Fiat Voluntas Tua" ("Thy Will Be Done"), the monks' recorded works are used to effect a second nuclear war. However, whereas triptychs in the Roman Catholic tradition often are used to depict stories of salvation, *Canticle* records the downfall of humankind through the development of technology absent the guidance of religious morality.

Tempering the heavy subject matter with gentle humor and occasional satire, Miller draws attention to the absurdity of a society in which religiosity and intellectualism are divided. Among the material copied by the monks is one of Leibowitz's shopping lists—"Pound pastrami, can kraut, six bagels, for Emma"—which they record with as much enthusiasm as his scientific works. Adding to the absurdity, the monks seem unaware that Leibowitz, whom they are attempting to canonize as a Catholic martyr, was Jewish. Nevertheless, the monks' actions are significant as, through their preservation of human history and canonization of Leibowitz, they unwittingly make possible the scientific renaissance that occurs later in the novel. The humorous tone suggests that humankind is redeemable in spite of its flaws—though when those flaws are left unchecked, the consequences for civilization may be dire.

CRITICAL DISCUSSION

When *Canticle* was published in 1959, it garnered little critical attention. Although the author's writing style was praised, critics denigrated the plot. A 1960 *Time* magazine review called Miller "chillingly effective at communicating a kind of post-human lunar landscape of disaster" but dismissed the prominent religious themes in the novel as "commendable but not compelling." Critics agreed that while Miller's prose put him on par with writers such as George Orwell, religiosity overwhelmed the novel, which some called "too Catholic." Although it won the 1961 Hugo Award for best novel, the top honor for science fiction writers, Miller's *Canticle,* according to Raymond Schroth in a 1968 essay for *Humanities International Complete,* continued to be "generally ignored" almost a decade after its debut.

As science fiction gradually gained respect as a literary genre, *Canticle* gained notoriety as an eminent work in the sci-fi canon. Walker Percy cites Miller's novel as one of the great apocalyptic novels, better even than those of George Orwell or Aldous Huxley. David J. Tietge in a 2008 essay for the *Journal of Popular Culture* notes, "Unlike the authors of other 'doomsday' novels of the era ... Miller is not as interested in the immediate after-effects of a nuclear conflict as he is in the implications of such a conflict for the future of humanity." The timelessness of Miller's exploration of the role of religion in a technological society has helped maintain *Canticle*'s status as a sci-fi classic.

Much recent scholarship on Miller's novel has investigated the complexity and ambiguity of his portrayal of religion in society. Especially in light of Miller's abdication of the Catholic faith later in life, scholars have explored the nuances of his portrayal of the church and of technology. Critics have also noted how *Canticle*'s sardonic tone foreshadows Miller's struggle with his faith. Since his suicide in 1996, critics have attempted to dissect *Canticle* in terms of Miller's life. However, in spite of the ambiguities surrounding the author and his work, *Canticle* is still read as a clear warning of the dire consequences, as Tietge writes, when "science [is] conducted without a strong ethical framework."

BIBLIOGRAPHY

Sources

Miller, Walter M., Jr. *A Canticle for Leibowitz.* New York: Bantam Books, 1997. Print.

"Mixed Fiction." *Time* 75.8 (1960): 108. *Academic Search Premier.* Web. 4 July 2012.

Schroth, Raymond A. "Canticle For Leibowitz." *America* 118.3 (1968): 79. *Humanities International Complete.* Web. 4 July 2012.

Tietge, David J. "Priest, Professor, or Prophet: Discursive and Ethical Intersections in *A Canticle For Leibowitz.*" *Journal of Popular Culture* 41.4 (2008): 676–94. *SPORTDiscus with Full Text.* Web. 4 July 2012.

Whissen, Thomas Reed. *Classic Cult Fiction: A Companion to Popular Cult Literature.* New York: Greenwood P, 1992. Print.

Young, R. V. "Catholic Science Fiction and the Comic Apocalypse: Walker Percy and Walter Miller." *Renascence: Essays on Values in Literature* 40.2 (1988): 95–110. *MLA International Bibliography.* Web. 9 July 2012.

Further Reading

Bertonneau, Thomas F. "Sacrifice and Sainthood: Walter M. Miller, Jr.'s Short Fiction." *Science Fiction Studies* 35.3 (2008): 404–29. *Literary Reference Center.* Web. 4 July 2012.

Clarke, W. Norris. "A Deluge of Flame and a Problem." *America* 102.23 (1960): 711–12. *Humanities International Complete.* Web. 4 July 2012.

Garvey, John. "*A Canticle for Leibowitz*: A Eulogy for Walt Miller." *Commonweal* 123.7 (1996): 7. *Literary Reference Center.* Web. 4 July 2012.

Miller, Walter M., Jr. *Saint Leibowitz and the Wild Horse Woman.* New York: Bantam Books, 1997. Print.

Percy, Walker. "Walter M. Miller, Jr.'s *A Canticle for Leibowitz*: A Rediscovery." *Southern Review* 7.2 (1971). 572–78. Print.

Seed, David. "Recycling the Texts of the Culture: Walter M. Miller's *A Canticle for Leibowitz.*" *Extrapolation* 37.3 (1996): 257–71. Print.

Lisa Kroger

A watercolor of the Abbey of Monte Cassino in Italy by J. M. W. Turner. Novelist Walter M. Miller Jr. has stated that his science fiction novel *A Canticle for Leibowitz* was influenced by his own participation in the Allied bombing of the monastery in World War II. MONTE CASSINO (W/C ON PAPER), TURNER, JOSEPH MALLORD WILLIAM (1775–1851)/PRIVATE COLLECTION/PHOTO © AGNEW'S, LONDON, UK/THE BRIDGEMAN ART LIBRARY.

THE DISPOSSESSED

Ursula K. Le Guin

❖ *Key Facts*

Time Period:
Late-20th Century

Genre:
Novel

Events:
Vietnam War; Cold War

Nationality:
American

OVERVIEW

The Dispossessed, a science fiction novel written by Ursula K. Le Guin in 1974, tells the story of a scientist, Shevek, struggling to reconcile his understanding of utopia with reality. Alternating between Shevek's life on his utopian home planet and his life as an exile in a capitalist society, the novel juxtaposes the political ideas of anarchy and structured society and begins with a discussion of a wall. "What was inside it and what was outside it depended upon which side of it you were on." This theme highlights the ongoing discussion about anarchism and the way it functions in society. Originally advertised as a novel about an ambiguous utopia, *The Dispossessed* wrestles with the feasibility of an anarchist society actually functioning in the real world. It questions the feasibility of both kinds of societies while exploring the idea that any utopia is subject to problems.

The Dispossessed was written after Le Guin's critical and commercial success, *The Left Hand of Darkness.* Both novels reinforced her status as a master of "soft" science fiction, a subgenre that deals with anthropological and sociological issues. Whereas *The Left Hand* explores gender and homosexuality, *The Dispossessed* grapples with the politics of anarchy and utopia. The book resonated with many readers because the political and social issues in it mirrored the political problems Americans were facing. With allusions to the Vietnam War, the Cold War, and the counterculture movement of the 1960s and early 1970s, *The Dispossessed* is not just a book describing utopian society and anarchy but rather a discussion of the pros and cons of such a society.

HISTORICAL AND LITERARY CONTEXT

As the Vietnam War raged, many Americans at the beginning of the 1970s protested the war, even as President Richard Nixon continued to send troops to South Vietnam. Some historians define the 1970s—with its rise of corporate control and the Watergate scandal—as the decade of paranoia and conspiracies. Increasing the paranoia was the shooting of Martin Luther King Jr. as well as the four students at Kent State University and two students at Jackson State University. During the 1960s youth and students protested the apathy of the Old Left and the government, but by the next decade the New Left began to worry its efforts had failed. This concern led to an increase in the anarchist movement, resulting in global insurrections in London, Paris, and Prague, along with continued student protests across the United States. Groups such as Students for a Democratic Society became more militant and moved from protesting to resistance.

Le Guin had written *The Dispossessed* at the height of the Vietnam protests, and it was published the same year that Nixon resigned from office. In the book there is a war between two segments of Urras society; one is capitalist and the other socialist. These are direct allusions to the relationship between the United States and the Soviet Union as well as the Vietnam War. The novel explores the political turmoil in the United States through a similar setting in an imagined universe.

Due to the disillusionment and upheaval felt as the result of World War I, mid-twentieth-century science fiction was mostly about dystopias. Books such as *Fahrenheit 451* (1953) by Ray Bradbury and Kurt Vonnegut's *Player Piano* (1952) echo the sentiments of the American public at the time. However, a resurgence in utopian science fiction began in the late 1960s, in large part due to the civil rights movement and the counterculture movement. Many writers, including Ernest Callenbach and Samuel R. Delany, wrote novels about utopias, aligning themselves with students and other youth imagining a better, safer world. Unlike the perfect worlds imagined in previous science fiction utopias, however, writers in the 1970s chose to invent imperfect utopias because it was not humanly possible to solve all of society's problems. When *The Dispossessed* was first released in paperback, the slogan under the title read "An Ambiguous Utopia," referring to struggles that any society faces when trying to reconcile differences and resolve problems. Anarres, the utopian planet, is the result of the anarchist movement, which at heart shares values with the 1960s counterculture movement such as tolerance, cooperation, and local control.

The Dispossessed offers no solutions to the political problems faced by Americans. It explores the possibilities of an anarchistic society but also exposes the difficulties of maintaining such a system. Le Guin scholar Daniel P. Jaeckle writes, "Within the novel, that conversion is never achieved, but by work's end it is beginning. The novel is in this sense open-ended, for it imagines anarchy not as a fait accompli but as a process of constant return to the complementarity of freedom and responsibility." The idea of an ambiguous utopia influenced other science fiction writers, including Joanna Russ, Samuel Delany, and Marge Piercy, all of whom published books about problematic utopias later during the 1970s. Just as the United States grappled with the consequences of the Vietnam War, war protests, the Watergate scandal, and the failure of the counterculture movement, Shevek and other characters in *The Dispossessed* struggle to define, create, and maintain utopia.

THEMES AND STYLE

The central theme of *The Dispossessed* is the discussion of anarchy and how it is used to create a utopian society. Anarres, the anarchistic, utopian planet, has been founded on the simple principle that "any rule is tyranny," a statement that mirrored the Vietnam War protests and anarchist movement that grew out of student protests with the concept of radical pacifism. During a speech given to defend his home planet, Shevek states, "We have no law but the single principle of mutual aid between individuals. We have no government but the single principle of free association." Another theme crucial to the novel is the environmental challenges the inhabitants of Urras constantly face. This directly references the beginning of the environmental movement in the 1970s. The first Earth Day took place in 1970, followed by the Clean Water Act in 1972. The environmental movement paralleled the anarchist movement because both were concerned with the control big corporations had over government, which affected land, water, and air quality. Both also supported local control: anarchists for political or apolitical reasons and environmentalists for the protection of the planet.

Le Guin uses the structure of the novel to further the discussion about utopia. The even-numbered chapters are devoted to life on Anarres, describing the struggles to maintain a utopian lifestyle. Odd-numbered chapters discuss life on Urras and Shevek's attempt to understand a different society than his own. Both threads are chronological, so the before and after parts of his life weave themselves together. The reader sees the contrast between Shevek's life as part of an anarchistic society and as part of a capitalist society. As Christine Nadir noted in her essay for *Utopian Studies*, "*The Dispossessed* presents its readers with a constant negotiation between, on the one hand, freedoms of thought, expression, and desire and, on the other, the programmed sacrifices necessary for ecological survival."

Le Guin heightens the exploration of an ambiguous utopia with the use of language. As a scientist, Shevek sees the world from an objective, realistic point of view. His problems with the government or lack of government on Anarres stem from the fact that it prevents him from developing a scientific theory about time known as the General Temporal Theory. Shevek defines his struggles and his own understanding of his world and himself in scientific terms.

URSULA K. LE GUIN

Critically acclaimed and well-known science fiction author Ursula Kroeber was born in Berkeley, California, on October 21, 1929. Her father, Alfred L. Kroeber, was a distinguished anthropologist, and her mother, Theodora Kracaw Kroeber, wrote the classic anthropologic biography *Ishi in Two Worlds,* about the sole survivor of a North American Indian tribe. Both parents and their work heavily influenced Le Guin's own writing later in life. Among some of her other childhood influences were the Native American legends that her father used to tell and her acute interest in Taoism, which teaches its followers balance.

Le Guin started writing at an early age and published her first science fiction story in 1963. It was not until 1966, with *Rocannon's World,* that she became well known as a science fiction writer. *Rocannon's World* is more science fantasy than science fiction, with a world inhabited by gnomes and fairies. However, as she continued to write, Le Guin began to strike a balance between fantastical elements and the political, sociological, and anthropological problems that plagued the real world. Three of her major novels, *The Left Hand of Darkness, The Dispossessed,* and *Earthsea Trilogy,* won several awards. Her work is now taught as part of courses on nature literature as well as feminist writing, proving that her focus on anthropological concerns in science fiction deserves academic attention.

"He recognized that need [to be himself] … as his "cellular function," the analogic term for the individual's individuality, the work he can do best, therefore his best contribution to his society. A healthy society would let him exercise that optimum function freely, in the coordination of all such functions finding its adaptability and strength." Jaeckle explains that "as with his formulation of the General Temporal Theory, so, too, with his understanding of anarchism Shevek struggles to find a way of conceptualizing the unity of freedom and responsibility."

CRITICAL DISCUSSION

The Dispossessed garnered much critical acclaim upon publication. Baird Searles, writing for the *Village Voice,* praised Shevek in relation to the political climate of the United States. "The character of Shevek is extraordinarily done: Ms. Le Guin has again accomplished the feat of creating not only a fully realized hypothetical culture, but living breathing characters who are inevitable products of that culture." In 1974 *The Dispossessed* earned the Nebula Award and Jupiter Award; the next year it won the Hugo Award. Also in 1975 Gerald Jonas, writing for the *New York Times Book Review,* stated, "LeGuin's book, written in her solid, no-nonsense prose, is so persuasive that it ought to put a stop to the writing of prescriptive Utopias for at least 10 years."

As the fifth book in the Hainish Cycle, *The Dispossessed* is considered an exploration of the political

Ursula K. Le Guin, author of the science fiction novel *The Dispossessed,* photographed in 1985. © BETTMANN/CORBIS.

concerns. As Nadir stated, "*The Dispossessed* can be read as an examination of the environmentalist discourses of sacrifice, scarcity, and economy that coalesced into a veritable political movement in the 1970s."

BIBLIOGRAPHY

Sources

Jaeckle, Daniel P. "Embodied Anarchy in Ursula K. Le Guin's: *The Dispossessed.*" *Utopian Studies* 20.1 (2009): 75+. *Literature Resource Center.* Web. 29 June 2012.

Jonas, Gerald. "Of Things to Come." Rev. of *The Dispossessed,* by Ursula K. Le Guin. *New York Times Book Review* 26 Oct. 1975. Web. June 2012.

Jorgensen, Darren. "On Failure and Revolution in Utopian Fiction and Science Fiction of the 1960s and 1970s." *Colloquy* 17 (2009): 6–15. Rpt. In *Contemporary Literary Criticism.* Ed. Jeffrey W. Hunter. Vol. 310. Detroit: Gale, 2011. *Literature Resource Center.* Web. 29 June 2012.

Le Guin, Ursula K. *The Dispossessed.* New York: HarperPrism, 1994. Print.

Moylan, Tom. *Demand the Impossible: Science Fiction and the Utopian Imagination.* New York: Methuen, 1987.

Nadir, Christine. "Utopian Studies, Environmental Literature, and the Legacy of an Idea: Educating Desire in Miguel Abensour and Ursula K. Le Guin." *Utopian Studies* 21.1 (2010): 24+. *Literature Resource Center.* Web. 29 June 2012.

Searles, Baird. "'The Dispossessed': Visit from a Small Planet." Rev. of *The Dispossessed,* by Ursula K. Le Guin. *Village Voice* 21 Nov. 1974. Web. 29 June 2012.

Further Reading

Barr, Marleen S. *Lost in Space: Probing Feminist Science Fiction and Beyond.* Chapel Hill: U of North Carolina P, 1993. Print.

Bittner, James W. "Chronosophy, Aesthetics, and Ethics in Le Guin's *The Dispossessed: An Ambiguous Utopia.*" *No Place Else: Explorations in Utopian and Dystopian Fiction.* Ed. Eric S. Rabkin, Martin H. Greenberg, and Joseph D. Olander. Carbondale: Southern Illinois UP, 1983. 244–70. Print.

Burns, Tony. *Political Theory, Science Fiction and Utopian Literature: Ursula K. Le Guin and* The Dispossessed. Maryland: Rowman & Littlefield, 2010. Print.

Cummins, Elizabeth. *Understanding Ursula K. Le Guin.* Toronto: Scholarly Book Services, 2002. Print.

Davis, Laurence, and Peter Stillman. *The New Utopian Politics of Ursula K. Le Guin's* The Dispossessed. Maryland: Rowman & Littlefield, 2005. Print.

Freedman, Carl Howard. *Conversations with Ursula K. Le Guin.* UP of Mississippi, 2008. Print.

Le Guin, Ursula K. *The Language of the Night: Essays on Fantasy and Science Fiction.* Ed. Susan Wood. New York: G. P. Putnam's Sons, 1980. Print.

Walker, Charlotte Zoe. "Ursula K(roeber) Le Guin." *Twentieth-Century American Nature Writers: Prose.* Ed. Roger Thompson and J. Scott Bryson. Detroit: Gale, 2003. *Dictionary of Literary Biography.* Vol. 275. *Literature Resource Center.* Web. 29 June 2012.

climate and social problems of the 1970s, discussing war, environmental issues, even gender politics. Throughout the twentieth century, readers continued to relate to these issues. Searles compared it to *The Left Hand* by saying, "[*The Dispossessed*] does for politics what *The Left Hand* did for sex … both books extend one's awareness in those areas by complex and very solid speculation. To repeat—this is what the best science fiction does best—and this is one of the best." After several decades critics still agree: in a 2009 issue of *Colloquy,* Darren Jorgensen wrote that *The Dispossessed* "remains a classic work of contemporary utopian fiction."

Much of the critical discussion today focuses on three main topics in *The Dispossessed*: gender, environment, and politics—namely, anarchy and utopian values. All three were part of the political and cultural discussion of the 1970s and continue to be relevant. The novel explores how utopian values can actually fit in society, whether a utopian society could actually exist, and what the strengths and failures of such an existence might be. Some scholars, including Tom Moylan, have argued that the utopian society Le Guin creates in *The Dispossessed* fails. Jorgensen noted that the novel's argument "is not so much utopia, utopian hope or revolution as much as it is the failure of these forms." Other critics have discussed the treatment of gender, and there is much debate over why the protagonist is male. However, some feminist scholars have pointed out that despite a male protagonist, Le Guin has created Anarres as a world where women and men are equal. Academics have also focused on the question of environmental

Hannah Soukup

DO ANDROIDS DREAM OF ELECTRIC SHEEP?

Philip K. Dick

OVERVIEW

In his 1968 novel *Do Androids Dream of Electric Sheep?* American science fiction writer Philip K. Dick presents a dystopian future in which Earth has been decimated by nuclear war; dangerous androids masquerade as humans; and drugs, religion, conspicuous consumption, and TV are the only hedges against extreme depression and isolation. The story follows a day in the life of Rick Deckard, who makes a living identifying and "retiring" androids that have escaped their slave-like conditions on the colony of Mars. Though the novel contains many of the trappings of traditional science fiction (androids, interplanetary travel, sophisticated technology), as with the rest of Dick's vast body of work, these elements serve as a means of exploring difficult philosophical issues, such as the nature of reality; the differences between man, animal, and machine; and whether humans have free will. Perhaps most strikingly, *Do Androids Dream of Electric Sheep?* depicts a future saturated with forms of propaganda, oftentimes competing against each other for possession of humans' minds.

Do Androids Dream of Electric Sheep? was published in what many critics consider Dick's most fertile period. Along with the Hugo Award-winning *The Man in the High Castle* of 1962, the work solidified Dick's reputation as an important voice in the genre of science fiction. However, the sci-fi label largely barred Dick from mainstream success until after his death, in 1982, when Ridley Scott adapted *Do Androids Dream of Electric Sheep?* into the film *Bladerunner.* Today, with ten film adaptations based on his novels and short stories, including *Minority Report, Paycheck,* and *A Scanner Darkly,* the unique aesthetic vision and recurring themes of Dick's work have entered mainstream culture, even if viewers remain unaware of the original source.

HISTORICAL AND LITERARY CONTEXT

For many people, mention of the 1960s conjures the beatific image of the flowerchild. *Do Androids Dream of Electric Sheep?* is clearly responding to a darker vision of this decade in America, one awash in deep-seated anxieties about impending nuclear warfare, government conspiracies, and CIA mind-control experiments. School children of the 1950s and 1960s were routinely shown films such as *Duck and Cover,* which

explained what to do in the event of a nuclear strike. The pervasive paranoia of the Cold War was exacerbated when, in 1960, the U.S. government was forced to admit to developing secret military aircraft after a U2 bomber was shot down over the Soviet Union. Ken Kesey's landmark 1962 novel *One Flew over the Cuckoo's Nest* was inspired, in part, by his experiences as a test subject in experiments on the effects of the drug LSD.

Set in the near future (early editions give the year 1992; later editions, 2019), *Do Androids Dream of Electric Sheep?* serves as a commentary on the psychological manipulation carried out daily by the government and the media, with fundamental insights that resonate with other bleak diagnoses of the era. Social critics such as Vance Packard had already alerted the American public to the prevalence of "hidden persuaders"—advertisers who used subliminal messages and their knowledge of the latest findings of science and psychology to create new desires wholesale. Perhaps even closer in spirit to the disturbing vision put forth in *Do Androids Dream* is French thinker Guy Debord's classic text of 1967, *The Society of the Spectacle,* in which Debord compares the media "spectacle" to a kind of modern religion that inverts the order of the world and alienates people from one another.

The genre now known as "dystopian" science fiction had long alerted readers to the power of propaganda. In Aldous Huxley's *Brave New World* (1931) children are lulled to sleep with prerecorded messages that repeat over and over, while adults routinely visit sensationalist films, called "feelies" (named after the "talkies" of early Hollywood). A decade and a half later, George Orwell's *1984* famously depicted a highly controlled society ruled by a totalitarian leader known as Big Brother. In *1984* citizens of Oceania are forced to watch government-produced films that behaviorally condition viewers to feel uncontrollable rage toward the enemy of the ruling party.

Until the close of the twentieth century, Dick's reputation primarily remained that of a minor "genre" writer. However, recent scholarship has shown that he had a significant influence on science fiction writers such as Ursula K. Le Guin, Stanislaw Lem, and more recently Jonathan Lethem. In addition, the intense "paranoia" that pervades the fiction of Thomas Pynchon owes a debt to Dick's work, as does the deliberate

✣ *Key Facts*

Time Period:
Mid-20th Century

Genre:
Novel

Events:
Cold War; nuclear proliferation; growth of 1960s drug culture; growth of mass media

Nationality:
American

PHILIP K. DICK AND THE FBI

Philip K. Dick's seemingly lifelong obsession with government conspiracies, propaganda, secret agents, and doppelgangers are not entirely the result of an overactive imagination. Throughout his life Dick had a number of strange encounters with the FBI in which he was either the instrument or the object of government surveillance. In the early 1950s Dick and his wife were approached by FBI agents and recruited as spies because they were thought to have ties to members of the Communist Party at the University of California, Berkeley. In his next run-in with the FBI, the surveillance was targeted at him: in 1971 Dick's home was burglarized, as Carl Freedman writes in *Science Fiction Studies,* "almost certainly with the connivance of local authorities and probably by Federal agents." According to Freedman, Dick fans like to believe that the operation was incited by a bit of fiction that came a little too close to the truth. Then, in 1974, Dick wrote a series of letters to the FBI in which he claimed to be the object of a "world wide Marxist conspiracy" whose principal agent was Polish science fiction writer Stanislaw Lem.

ambiguity between reality and its simulation found in a work such as Don DeLillo's *White Noise.* Barring Hollywood sci-fi films, perhaps Dick's strongest influence has been felt in the work of postmodern theorists such as Fredric Jameson and Jean Baudrillard, both of whom address the paranoia and schizophrenia of life under late capitalism.

THEMES AND STYLE

Do Androids Dream of Electric Sheep? differs from other classic works of dystopian fiction in the complexity of the propaganda it depicts and, thus, the level of paranoia it engenders in its main characters and in the reader. Whereas works such as *Brave New World* and *1984* locate the source of paranoia in a powerful, centralized—albeit nebulous—authority, in *Do Androids Dream of Electric Sheep?* humans are bombarded by messages from the competing realms of religion, the media, and the government. Characters such as Deckard and J.R. Isidore suspect that these messages express, at best, half-truths, but they can never be certain. Furthermore, by indulging in the virtual religion of Mercerism and the use of "mood organs" to program any mood—from "a business like professional attitude" to "the desire to watch TV, no matter what's on"—humans in the novel have become so isolated from each other that, as Isidore observes, they cannot even "compare notes" about the conspiracies they all seem to suspect.

Dick achieves this effect through the use of a limited third-person narration that restricts readers' access to the whole story. Most of the information, in fact, comes from the same ubiquitous TV programs that assault the novel's characters. For instance, the text makes reference to life on the colony of Mars, where

the majority of Earth's population has immigrated. Yet, like the main characters Deckard and Isidore, all readers know of the colonies is what is shown through the government-sponsored infomercials that unanimously declare the grandeur of life on Mars. Furthermore, the bits of information offered often conflict with each other. The doctrine of Mercerism, apparently the only religion practiced on Earth, seems to be a rare source of surety and comfort for many of the remaining humans, if not for Deckard himself. Yet on his TV show, which airs twenty-three hours a day, seven days a week, the popular Buster Friendly exposes the divine Wilbur Mercer as an actor and an alcoholic has-been. As Isidore suggests, Buster Friendly and Mercer appear to be competing for humans' "psychic selves," and it is impossible either for Isidore or for readers to know who is lying and who is telling the truth.

One way Dick signals that readers should be suspicious of such propaganda is through the disparity he creates between the narrator's more distanced reporting of events and the heavy-handed appeals of the media. In a rare moment in which the narrator steps back from the interior thoughts and feelings of his characters to give a history of Earth after World War Terminus, the prose takes on a journalistic tone. Government spokesmen, by contrast, "shout," "yammer," and incessantly "hawk their wares." Sometimes the deafening volume of these barely veiled advertisements is rendered through typographical cues such as the use of all caps.

CRITICAL DISCUSSION

Though he produced more than forty novels, Dick remained all but unknown outside of the science fiction genre, where he was typically lauded as a truly original writer. Critics of his day often complained of his choppy prose style, loose handling of plot, and failure to reach a clear resolution. In an analysis of the author in *Contemporary Literary Criticism,* George Turner laments that Dick's novels are often "disfigured by unresolvable complexities," while Bruce Gillespie speaks of the "illogicalities of character and plot" that sometimes mar Dick's work.

Dick's work experienced a resurgence of critical interest during the 1980s, when poststructuralist theory took firm root in American literary criticism. Furthermore, the many film adaptations of his writings that have appeared since his death have contributed to Dick's relevance. In fact, some critics suggest that soon the adjective "phildickian" will sum up the modern age in the same way that "Kafkaesque" used to. Although the author disparaged the idea that he was predicting the future, the depiction in *Do Androids Dream of Electric Sheep?* of a war-torn society at the mercy of a panoply of biased media pundits and alienated from one another by government-approved "mood" enhancers feels nothing if not prophetic.

Contemporary criticism has largely accepted the fact that Dick is not only "the [William] Shakespeare of science fiction," as Jameson deems him in

City of the Future, 1982, by Syd Mead. This concept drawing for the film *Blade Runner,* an adaptation of *Do Androids Dream of Electric Sheep?,* interprets the crowded, radiation-poisoned city described in the novel. © CAT'S COLLECTION/CORBIS.

Archaeologies of the Future, but an essential figure of twentieth-century literature. Some scholars have focused on the postmodern and poststructuralist themes that are prevalent in Dick's work, addressing his writing as an early example of the "cyberpunk" genre, which often analyzes the progressive imbrication of humans and technology. Similarly, others consider him one of the first writers to deeply explore the possibilities of a "posthuman" subject. More recent scholarship has even begun to redress the belief that his work of the 1960s is of primary interest by delving into his later, metaphysical writings, such as the 900-page *Exegesis of Philip K. Dick,* published posthumously in 2011.

BIBLIOGRAPHY

Sources

Debord, Guy. *The Society of the Spectacle.* Trans. Donald Nicholson-Smith. New York: Zone, 1995. Print.

Dick, Philip K. *Do Androids Dream of Electric Sheep?* New York: Random House, 1996. Print.

Freedman, Carl. Introduction. *Science Fiction Studies* 15.2 (1988): 121–30. *JSTOR.* Web. 24 Aug. 2012.

Jameson, Fredric, *Archaeologies of the Future: The Desire Called Utopia and Other Science Fictions.* New York: Verso, 2005. Print.

"Philip K. Dick (1928–1982)." *Contemporary Literary Criticism.* Ed. Jean C. Stine and Daniel G. Marowski. Vol. 30. Detroit: Gale Research, 1984. 115–129. *Literature Resources from Gale.* Web. 24 Aug. 2012.

Philmus, Robert M. "The Two Faces of Philip K. Dick." *Science Fiction Studies* 18.1 (1991): 91–103. *JSTOR.* Web. 24 Aug. 2012.

Umland, Samuel J. Introduction. *Philip K. Dick: Contemporary Critical Interpretations.* Ed. Samuel J. Umland. Westport: Greenwood, 1995. Print.

Further Reading

Baudrillard, Jean. "The Simulacra and Science Fiction." *Simulacra and Simulation.* Trans. Sheila Faria Glaser. Ann Arbor: U of Michigan P, 1994. 121–27. Print.

Carrere, Emmanuel. *I Am Alive and You Are Dead: A Journey into the Mind of Philip K. Dick.* Trans. Timothy Bent. New York: Picador, 2004. Print.

Dick, Philip K. *Philip K. Dick: Four Novels of the 1960s.* New York: Library of America, 2007. Print.

———. *Philip K. Dick: Five Novels of the 1960s and 70s.* New York: Library of America, 2008. Print.

———. *Philip K. Dick: Valis and Later Novels.* New York: Library of America, 2009. Print.

Galvan, Jill. "Entering the Posthuman Collective in Philip K. Dick's *Do Androids Dream of Electric Sheep?*" *Science Fiction Studies* 24.3 (1997): 413–29. Print.

Sims, Christopher A. "The Dangers of Individualism and the Human Relationship to Technology in Philip K. Dick's *Do Androids Dream of Electric Sheep? Science Fiction Studies* 36.1 (2009) 67–86. *JSTOR.* Web. 24 Aug. 2012.

Sutin, Lawrence. *Divine Invasions: A Life of Philip K. Dick.* New York: Avalon, 2005. Print.

Media Adaptation

Blade Runner. Dir. Ridley Scott. Perf. Harrison Ford, Rutger Hauer, and Sean Young. Warner Bros. Pictures, 1982. Film.

Phillip M. Mahoney

ECOTOPIA
The Notebooks and Reports of William Weston
Ernest Callenbach

OVERVIEW

Ernest Callenbach's 1975 novel, *Ecotopia: The Note-books and Reports of William Weston,* decries Western consumerism and imagines a society operating on the tenets of ethical ecology, localized commerce, sustainable economics, nonviolence, feminism, and decentralized government. Set in 1999 in Ecotopia, a new nation formed after the secession of Northern California, Oregon, and Washington from the United States in 1980, the utopian novel comprises the journal entries and dispatches of Weston, the first mainstream media reporter allowed into the country. Callenbach drew from ecological research in such publications as *Scientific American* to argue against the increasingly globalized materialism and consumer mindset that has prevailed in the United States since World War II, strongly propagating instead a localized, environmentally conscious social structure.

Ecotopia was released on the heels of the 1973–74 oil crisis, a result of the 1973 embargo by oil-producing nations in response to renewed U.S. support of Israel. The novel reflects growing public concern about the economic and environmental instability of the Western world. Originally self-published by Callenbach, the work resonated most with center-left political activists, especially those championing environmental causes. It also coincided with the emergence in Europe of Green political parties, which promote attaining world health through the values espoused in *Ecotopia.* It secured an immediate cult following. Despite criticism of its scientific and political analyses, it gained the favor of such popular ecological activists as the consumer advocate Ralph Nader and eventually sold more than 400,000 copies in the United States alone, becoming a bestseller. The novel lost momentum during the financial boom of the 1980s but resurfaced with the formation of the U.S. Green Party in the early 1990s. Although still relatively obscure, Callenbach and *Ecotopia* are often credited with directly influencing or even modeling many of the social and political trends of the green movements still thriving in the American Northwest.

HISTORICAL AND LITERARY CONTEXT

From the mid-1960s to the mid-1970s, heightened awareness of pollution, deforestation, and ozone depletion aroused grassroots activism across the United States.

Academics studying ecology began to gain popular attention. The 1962 publication of biologist and conservationist Rachel Carson's *Silent Spring,* a formidable indictment of pesticide use, the chemical industry, and the government—all implicated in attempts to control nature through technology—gave birth to the environmental movement. Other notable academics in the field included environmental anthropologist Eugene N. Anderson, who studied the changing relationships between humans and their environment over time, and Norwegian philosopher and mountaineer Arne Næss, originator of the study of deep ecology, which propounded the inherent worth of living beings regardless of their usefulness to humans. Together, these ideas informed Green party platforms. Congress was finally compelled to take action. It passed the Clean Water (1963), Endangered Species (1966, 1969, and 1973), and Clean Air (1972) Acts and formed the Environmental Protection Agency (EPA; 1970).

Despite the efforts of Anderson and other environmental activists, social ecology was still largely ignored in the United States. Congressional resistance handcuffed the EPA, and tangible change was slow to materialize. Grassroots efforts persisted, however. The doctrines espoused in *Ecotopia* were founded on real social experiments being conducted in the Western states in the early 1970s. Pinel School, an alternative school near Martinez, California, where Callenbach's son was a student, was the model for *Ecotopia*'s fictional Crick School. Pinel rejected existing educational theory, including the practice of grading, and emphasized environmental conservation and the development of self-awareness. Such a paradigm of institutionalized ecological consciousness was rare. Callenbach marketed his treatise as popular fiction, hoping to persuade the general public to work toward the goals of local environmental movements and communities.

Callenbach wrote his novel within a strong tradition. Several of his nineteenth-century predecessors used the technique of the outsider narrator as a persuasive tactic, among them Edward Bellamy in *Looking Backward: 2000–1887* (1887), which treats the nationalization of private property; Mark Twain in his dystopian *Connecticut Yankee in King Arthur's Court* (1889), a satire on romantic views of medieval England and American entrepreneurship; and William

Dean Howells in his anticapitalist ideal *A Traveler from Altruria* (1892–93). Influential contemporaries of Callenbach more often incorporated elements of ecology into their discourses. The characters of Aldous Huxley's *Island* (1962) achieve ecological balance through spirituality. One of the first feminist science fiction writers, Ursula K. Le Guin, considered ecological sustainability in her Hainish Cycle, which includes the award-winning novels *Left Hand of Darkness* (1969) and *The Dispossessed* (1974). Both authors pass over in-depth treatment of environmental concerns, however, in favor of advocating traditional, human-centered social reform.

What distinguishes *Ecotopia* from other utopian fiction is Callenbach's insistence that political, economic, and ecological issues cannot be separated. He envisioned a social psychology—based closely on the emerging philosophy of social ecology—that would address each equally. The novel was so groundbreaking in its vision that it spawned a new subgenre of utopian fiction. "Ecotopian fiction" is characterized by the depiction of either positive or negative visions of human environmental impact. The most notable example is Kim Stanley Robinson's Three Californias trilogy, in which each novel imagines a very different future for America's West Coast. Thanks in part to Anderson's work in ecology and in part to Callenbach's literary model, the term "ecotopia" has passed into common usage in both conversational and academic contexts.

THEMES AND STYLE

Ecotopia strays very little from its social ecology agenda. Passages are peppered with references to ineffectual "American policy-makers" and statistics ostensibly pulled from real-world reports, such as the claim that American "deaths from air and chemical pollution" have "declined from a peak of 75,000 annually to 30,000—still a tragic toll." When Callenbach does veer into other concerns, they tend to fall within the realm of progressive communal-living relationships and philosophies. For instance, the narrator's final initiation into Ecotopian society takes the form of sexual re-education, in which a mutually nurturing relationship with a woman becomes identical to such a relationship with nature. Most of the themes Callenbach explores in the novel question current sociopolitical trends and provide models for reform. Some details, however, are dated, and scholars question them today; for instance, the society's men fight elaborate war games to work off their "natural" aggressions, and whites and blacks are segregated according to Callenbach perception of black nationalist mandates.

The novel's rhetorical strategy relies heavily on predicting public responses to the book. Like many other utopian novelists, Callenbach chose to adopt an outsider—the reporter Weston—as the narrator, allowing him to first ask and then answer common questions about social ecology. Early on, for instance, Weston posits in a dispatch to his supervisor that if

CALLENBACH THE CLAIRVOYANT

Callenbach's paradigm embraces high technology, as long as it promotes healthy social norms and serves Ecotopian objectives. Drawing on emerging technology and ecological research, the author accurately predicted (perhaps even influenced) the development of videoconferencing and its applications in television. Callenbach's fictional society employs twenty-four-hour-a-day television feeds to ensure governmental transparency, a technique that was later echoed by the real-world launch of C-SPAN in 1979 and the prevalence of reality television shows at the turn of the twenty-first century.

Many of the social practices espoused in *Ecotopia* have also been put into practice in the real world. Recycling, composting, using local and seasonal foods, and decreased reliance on automotive transportation (all particularly prevalent in the American Northwest) are now considered commonplace, whereas at the time of the novel's release they were seen as radical, idealistic, and unfeasible. Another innovation Callenbach anticipated is "print on demand" (POD) publishing. In *Ecotopia,* a jukebox-like device allows people to print and bind approved texts into a book. In the twenty-first century, POD services routinely print, bind, and ship books for customers through online ordering, with several major publishers offering flexibility to clients who want small-run quantities.

Ecotopia's "strange customs indeed prove as barbaric as rumors suggest, [they] will have to pay the cost in outraged world opinion." His outsider status and mainstream attitudes act as both a mechanism for advancing the plot and a pretext for addressing real-world public concerns about the ideologies promoted in *Ecotopia.*

Structured around Weston's daily writings, the novel maintains a level of emotional distance reminiscent more of a political treatise than of expressive fiction. His increasing acceptance of the citizens of Ecotopia provides a rare element of human feeling. As Weston's hesitations ease, he notices that Ecotopians talk about their construction and other projects through "funny stories, mainly—not at all our kind of solemn, contribution-to-the-ages" fare, revealing a sense of humility Callenbach saw as lacking in American culture. Weston's growing affection functions primarily as a device through which Callenbach hopes to foster similar sympathies in his readers. *Ecotopia* was more of a success than the author anticipated: by the early twentieth century, bioregionalism, the local food movement, and the push for energy reduction, all depicted in the novel, had become cultural staples, and small Christian colleges and churches were inviting Callenbach to address them.

CRITICAL DISCUSSION

In part because it was self-published, *Ecotopia's* release was initially noted in only a few small publications and newspapers, with some reviewers commenting that readers' resistance to its sexual liberalism and the seemingly

Young women make salad in the kitchen of a commune in the 1970s. *Ecotopia* in part explores progressive communal living philosophies. © HENRY DILTZ/CORBIS.

gratuitous nature of its violent war games would prevent the novel from effecting any real change. Some called the novel outright propaganda: in his 1978 article "*Ecotopia* Reveals 'Sun Day's' Fascist Program," William Wertz asserted that *Ecotopia* portrays "the barbaric consequences of environmentalism" that in the novel led to a "fascist coup." Callenbach attempted to address many of the negative reactions by detailing the events that led to Ecotopia's secession in a prequel titled *Emerging Ecotopia* (1981). Only after the release of the second novel did critics take close note of the original. The two books have often been reviewed jointly. In a 1982 issue of the *Nation*, author Kurt Vonnegut praised the first novel and its "good rules" for ethical living, citing Callenbach's own statement that the book was "more successful as a conservationist tract than as a novel."

Accordingly, the novel's legacy is less literary than sociopolitical, with many of its devotees more interested in Callenbach's creed than his prose stylings. Since the emergence of the American Green Party, the novel has been increasingly assigned in college courses on the environment, sociology, and urban planning. Writing for the *New York Times,* Scott Timberg noted the confluence of all three subjects in Portland, a city that he suggests was either predicted or influenced by the model presented in *Ecotopia.* The work's political impact is seen in the coalescence of the Cascadia movement, which proposes a breakaway nation closely resembling that in the novel, incorporating territories in Northern California, Oregon, Washington, Idaho, western Montana, British Columbia, and southern Alaska. Though the Northwestern secession idea has existed in various forms since the nineteenth century, *Ecotopia*'s cult following provided a larger, more enthusiastic audience for the movement's proposals.

Though a few scholars—Heinz Tschachler among them, in his 1984 article in *Science Fiction Studies*—have analyzed the novel in the context of the utopian fiction tradition, most current scholarship focuses on its ecological and political underpinnings. Contemporary environmental criticism often regards it with wonder because of the accuracy of its technological predictions. In "A Child of Dystopia Reads *Ecotopia*" (2011), for instance, Brian Smith marvels at the novel's forecast "that West Coast scientific institutes would be studying algae, biofuel, solar, and ocean-generated power" as viable alternatives to fossil fuel sources. Political treatments, such as Werner Christie Mathisen's "Underestimation of Politics in Green Utopias" (2001), often place the novel alongside Le Guin's *The Dispossessed,* valuing *Ecotopia* for its fuller description of the government structures behind its fictional society.

BIBLIOGRAPHY

Sources

Callenbach, Ernest. *Ecotopia: The Notebooks and Reports of William Weston.* Berkeley: Banyan Tree, 1975. Print.

Mathisen, Werner Christie. "The Underestimation of Politics in Green Utopias: The Description of Politics in Huxley's *Island,* Le Guin's *The Dispossessed,* and Callenbach's *Ecotopia.*" *Utopian Studies* 12.1 (2001): 56. *Academic OneFile.* Web. 3 July 2012.

Smith, Brian. "A Child of Dystopia Reads *Ecotopia.*" *Earth Island Journal* 26.1 (2011): 63. *Academic Search Complete.* Web. 3 July 2012.

Timberg, Scott. "The Novel That Predicted Portland." *New York Times* 14 Dec. 2008: 2. *Academic Search Complete.* Web. 3 July 2012.

Tschachler, Heinz. "Despotic Reason in Arcadia? Ernest Callenbach's Ecological Utopias." *Science Fiction Studies* 11.3 (1984): 304–17. *JSTOR.* Web. 3 July 2012.

Vonnegut, Kurt. "Letters to the Young." *Nation* 234.20 (1982): 621. *Academic Search Complete.* Web. 24 July 2012.

Wertz, William. "*Ecotopia* Reveals 'Sun Day's' Fascist Program." *Executive Intelligence Review* 5.10 (1978). Web. 24 July 2012.

Further Reading

Callenbach, Ernest. *Ecotopia Emerging.* Berkeley: Banyan Tree, 1981. Print.

"Ecotopia." *Wilson Quarterly* 15.2 (1991): 83. *Academic OneFile.* Web. 3 July 2012.

"Ernest Callenbach." *Whole Earth Review* 61 (1988): 18+. *Academic OneFile.* Web. 3 July 2012.

Garreau, Joel. *The Nine Nations of North America.* Boston: Houghton, 1981. Print.

Jacobs, Naomi. "Failures of the Imagination in *Ecotopia.*" *Extrapolation* 38.4 (1997): 318+. *Academic OneFile.* Web. 3 July 2012.

Marshall, Peter H. *Nature's Web: Rethinking Our Place on Earth.* New York: Paragon, 1994. Print.

Philippon, Daniel J. *Conserving Words: How American Nature Writers Shaped the Environmental Movement.* Athens: U of Georgia P, 2004. Print.

Rüdig, Wolfgang. "Between Ecotopia and Disillusionment: Green Parties in European Government." *Environment* 44.3 (2002): 20–33. *Academic Search Complete.* Web. 3 July 2012.

Stoll, Steven. *U.S. Environmentalism Since 1945: A Brief History with Documents.* Boston: Bedford, 2007. Print.

Clint Garner

ENDER'S GAME

Orson Scott Card

OVERVIEW

Ender's Game, the 1985 science fiction novel by Orson Scott Card, documents the experiences of a child soldier as he is trained for battle against the Formics, an alien race that is threatening the human population on Earth. Told primarily from the point of view of the eponymous character Andrew "Ender" Wiggin, the novel combines elements from the classic school story and from war fiction to comment on society's responsibility to shield children from persuasive forces until they are mature enough to make truly informed decisions. Card sets *Ender's Game* in a spatially and temporally distant world, using Ender's propaganda-writing siblings to elucidate the influence of the media on the public and on civil and military policy and practice—a subject with much contemporary relevance. Contrasting Ender's experiences with the goals and operational methods of his commanders, the novel explores the damaging effects of propaganda on young minds.

Published at the height of Card's career, *Ender's Game* was a commercial and critical success, winning a Nebula Award for best novel in 1985 and a Hugo Award in 1986. It has also earned a spot on many top 100 lists, including the American Library Association's "100 Best Books for Teens." While generally well reviewed, the novel has received criticism for its violence and for its depiction of Ender as morally blameless, even though he is responsible for mass genocide of an alien race. Despite these criticisms, *Ender's Game* remains highly popular, spawning an award-winning series of novels as well as works in other media. Since its publication, the novel has exerted a broad influence on young adult fiction and on the science fiction genre; it has also been viewed as an important military document.

HISTORICAL AND LITERARY CONTEXT

Ender's Game appeared at the end of the second Cold War, the period from 1979 to 1985, when tensions between the United States and the Soviet Union escalated following the Soviet invasion of Afghanistan. Americans were concerned not only about communism as a threat to individual freedom but also about the possibility of U.S. and Soviet brinkmanship resulting in a nuclear holocaust. Board game war simulations were popular during this time, and in 1983 the successful film *War Games,* which deals with a computer war simulation that inadvertently almost starts

World War III, was released. With the rise of personal computing in the early 1980s, the role of technology in human society, always of interest to science fiction writers, had become central in many works.

By 1985 there were early signs of a global "thaw"; however, fears about global extinction through nuclear war were still present. Card mirrors this tension in *Ender's Game,* constructing a world in which the inhabitants of Earth in the distant future face obliteration by an alien race, the Formics, who think and act via a hive mind. In addition to the competing ideological narratives and military powers represented by the humans and the aliens, the humans themselves are split into factions along classic Cold War lines, the United States and the Soviet Union able to unite only when faced with world destruction.

Ender's Game is part of a tradition of genre novels treating Cold War-era fears about communism and nuclear war. The classic novels *Animal Farm* (1945) and *1984* (1949) by George Orwell both deal with the manner in which socialist ideals can be perverted as practiced by an actual government. Madeline L'Engle's *A Wrinkle in Time* (1962), in which children travel to a planet controlled by a central intelligence similar to the Formic hive, is also a noteworthy antecedent, especially in the young adult fiction category. Critics frequently cite the work of Robert Heinlein, particularly *Starship Troopers* (1959), as bookending the beginning of science fiction's discourse on Cold War themes, much as *Ender's Game* appeared at the end of the Cold War.

When it was published in 1985, *Ender's Game* was highly successful, garnering several prestigious science fiction awards for Card and making him one of the most visible writers working in the genre. As of 2012, the *Ender* saga comprised eleven novels, twelve short stories, and forty-seven comic book issues. *Ender's Game* has also been influential in virtual training development by the U.S. military. The idea of world building, in which soldiers can stay immersed in a virtual world for months or years, has been cited as of special interest, as the nature of modern warfare shifts from large-scale battles to guerilla-style fighting in urban environments.

THEMES AND STYLE

In *Ender's Game* Card explores the uses of persuasion—in education, in the media, and by the government—and the morality of this persuasion, especially when

❖ *Key Facts*

Time Period:
Late 20th Century

Genre:
Novel

Events:
Cold War; nuclear arms race

Nationality:
American

ORSON SCOTT CARD'S MORMONISM

Although Orson Scott Card first came to prominence as a science fiction writer in the late 1970s, he had been writing for nearly a decade, much of his work produced for the Church of Jesus Christ of Latter-day Saints (commonly referred to as the Mormon Church or the LDS Church). Starting around 1970, Card was writing and directing plays in association with the experimental theater department of Brigham Young University. He was also active on the editorial board of several LDS-oriented magazines. Even as he has gained wide success with the *Ender* saga, he has continued to write scripts for church audio and video programs and has published a compendium of LDS humor and a historical novel, *A Woman of Destiny* (1984), which won the Best Novel Award from the Association of Mormon Letters. Card also publishes Mormon-centered writing through his Hatrack Press, which maintains an online presence on the author's website, *Hatrack River*.

Some critics have described Card's fiction as thinly veiled LDS propaganda, a charge the writer has denied. Other critics, such as Michael Collings, have defended Card's work as "never overly doctrinal," even when explicitly concerned with LDS culture, as in *The Folk of the Fringe* (1989), a postapocalyptic novel in which the church provides a war-ravaged United States with hope through the community it establishes around the now sea-sized Great Salt Lake.

deployed against society's most innocent citizens. Ender is taken from his family at age six and enrolled in Battle School, where he trains to lead the Intergalactic Fleet (IF) to victory against the Formics. His commanders attempt to shape Ender into the leader they desire by isolating him from his peers, putting him in intensive battle training, and having him watch propaganda videos that seek to reinforce the rightness of the IF cause and in which the enemy is maligned as "buggers" and as "ugly and murderous and loathsome." Unbeknownst to Ender, who has to this point been engaged in virtual battles only, the final exam is no simulation at all, and he is commanding real armies. The casualties are real as well, but his commanders do not reveal this fact to him until the Formics have been exterminated. When Ender discovers the truth, he is devastated. Meanwhile, as part of his bid for power, Ender's brother Peter convinces his sister Valentine to post essays in a public forum debating the war. They create the characters "Locke" (Peter) and "Demosthenes" (Valentine), with Valentine's views being deliberately inflammatory so Peter's moderate position will win popular support. While military officials are aware of and making use of their scheme, others in society are duped, and Locke and Demosthenes create a groundswell of support for Peter, who, lacking the capacity for empathy, is sure to become a terrifying despot. Ender and Valentine flee to the bugger worlds, and Ender finds the pupa of a

bugger queen. He is able to communicate with her and learns the truth about the buggers—that they attacked humans before realizing they were sentient beings and stopped after realizing the truth. The whole war was based on error and miscommunication.

With its linear narrative and action-driven plot, *Ender's Game* effectively demonstrates the propulsive, and hence dangerous, powers of propaganda. At the beginning of each chapter, the commanders' plans unfold in dialogue, with the action, told from Ender's point of view, occurring separately and without his full understanding of the course he has been set to follow. For instance, as Chapter 11 opens, Hyram Graff, principal of Battle School, and Major Anderson discuss Ender's accelerated training and the fact that it may cause him to burn out. Graff expresses his doubts: "My eagerness to sacrifice little children to save mankind is wearing thin," adding that "it's for … short-sighted, suicidal people that we're pushing Ender to the edge of human endurance." Card then cuts to Ender, wondering about his teacher's methods and concluding that "all he was sure of was that he was ready for battle."

Throughout the novel, Card uses children's language and preoccupations to underline Ender's age and vulnerability to his military indoctrination. It is clear from the outset that the character's early cultural experiences have primed him for training, a typical game played with siblings being "astronauts vs. buggers." During battle, the children's conversation is littered with scatological humor. About to enter an enemy camp, a member of Ender's platoon exclaims, "Last one there saves farts in a milk bottle." Commands often sound like dares, and the children treat their battles in a gamelike manner.

CRITICAL DISCUSSION

Upon its release, *Ender's Game* was favorably reviewed. *New York Times* critic Gerard Jonas describes it as "an affecting novel full of surprises," adding that Ender is the key to the novel's success and that "alternately likable and insufferable, he is a convincing little Napoleon in short pants." Other critics were similarly inclined, and the novel won a number of awards. The book's detractors have criticized Card's use of violence; some, such as the critic Elaine Radford, writing in *Fantasy Review*, view the character of Ender as a reference to Adolf Hitler and the author Card as a Hitler apologist. Card himself responded to the review, denying that he had written the novel with Hitler in mind. Writing nearly twenty years later, John Kessel advanced some of the same arguments, criticizing Card's "story of guiltless genocide" and his "intention based morality."

Since its publication, *Ender's Game* has been influential in U.S. military training and as a springboard for discussion of the same, especially as computer-based simulations have come into more widespread use. Writing in the *New York Times* shortly after the start of the Iraq War, Amy Harmon quotes a U.S. military training official as stating that the novel "has

Orson Scott Card's science fiction novel *Ender's Game* examines contemporary problems set in a distant time and place. KAUKO HELAVUO/THE IMAGE BANK/GETTY IMAGES.

had a lot of influence on our thinking" in developing a training simulation of urban warfare in Afghanistan.

Ender's Game is discussed both as a stand-alone piece and as part of the *Ender* saga. One of the primary strands of *Ender* scholarship deals with the novel as a military document, either as a primer for military organizations, as in scholarship by the U.S. Army, or as a screed against "the military paradigm" and its use of manipulations to accomplish its ends. In his 1991 essay for *Extrapolation,* Tim Blackmore describes the novel as "a critique of twenty first century military practices" and their implicit "mechanistic view of humans" as "disastrous to the self." Other criticism has focused on the novel as a comment on educational institutions and the importance of reimagining them to meet the challenges of twenty-first century globalization. In a 2004 issue of *Lion and the Unicorn,* Christine Doyle and Susan Louise Stewart suggest that Card's objective is to assert that "we must constantly acknowledge and negotiate a multiplicity of voices, of subjectivities, of positions, if we are to escape narrowly defined perceptions about education … and about what it means to live and grow up in a postmodern world."

BIBLIOGRAPHY

Sources

Blackmore, Tim. "Ender's Beginning: Battling the Military in Orson Scott Card's *Ender's Game.*" *Extrapolation* 13.2 (1991): 124–42. *Literature Resources from Gale.* Web. 12 June 2012.

Card, Orson Scott. *Ender's Game.* New York: Tom Doherty, 1977. Print.

Collings, Michael. "Orson Scott Card: Overview." *St. James Guide to Science Fiction Writers.* Ed. James P. Pederson. 4th ed. New York: St. James Press, 1996. *Literature Resources from Gale.* Web. 12 June 2012.

Doyle, Christine, and Susan Louise Stewart. "*Ender's Game* and *Ender's Shadow*: Orson Scott Card's Postmodern School Stories. " *Lion and the Unicorn* 28.2 (2004): 186–202. *Literature Resources from Gale.* Web. 12 June 2012.

Harmon, Amy. "More than Just a Game, but How Close to Reality?" *New York Times* 3 Apr. 2003. Web. 12 July 2012.

Jonas, Gerald. "Science Fiction." *New York Times* 16 June 1985. Web. 13 June 2012.

Kessel, John. "Creating the Innocent Killer: *Ender's Game,* Intention and Morality." *Foundation* 33.90 (2004). *Literature Resources from Gale.* Web. 12 June 2012.

Radford. Elaine. "Ender and Hitler: Sympathy for the Superman." *Fantasy Review* June 1987: 11–12, 48–49.

Further Reading

Attebery, Brian. "Godmaking in the Heartland: The Backgrounds of Orson Scott Card's American Fantasy." *The Celebration of the Fantastic: Selected Papers from the Tenth Anniversary International Conference on the Fantastic in the Arts.* Ed. Donald E. Morse, Csilla Bertha, and Marshall B. Tymn. Westport: Greenwood, 1992. 61–69. *Literature Resources from Gale.* Web. 20 June 2012.

Card, Orson Scott. *Ender's Shadow.* New York: Tom Doherty, 1999. Print.

Collings, Michael. *In the Image of God: Theme, Characterization and Landscape in the Fiction of Orson Scott Card.* Westport: Greenwood, 1990. Print.

Heidkamp, Bernie. "Responses to the Alien Mother in Post-Maternal Cultures: C. J. Cherryh and Orson Scott Card." *Science-Fiction Studies* 23.3 (1996): 339–54. *Literature Resources from Gale.* Web. 14 June 2012.

Oatman, Eric. "The Ornery American." *School Library Journal* 54.6 (2008): 38–41. *Literature Resources from Gale.* Web. 20 June 2012.

Seed, David. *American Science Fiction during the Cold War.* Chicago: Fitzroy Dearborn, 1999. Print.

Media Adaptation

Ender's Game. Dir. Gavin Hood. Perf. Harrison Ford, Abigail Breslin, and Ben Kingsley. Digital Domain Media, 2013. Film.

Daisy Gard

EREWHON
Or, Over the Range
Samuel Butler

OVERVIEW

Combining elements of utopia, dystopia, and social satire in a tone similar to Jonathan Swift's *Gulliver's Travels* (1726), Samuel Butler's 1872 novel *Erewhon: or, Over the Range* explores the fictional country of Erewhon, an anagram of the word "nowhere." In the book, Higgs, Butler's narrator, investigates various aspects of the newly discovered Erewhonian society, exploring issues of religion, convention, criminality, morality, evolution, reproduction, and mechanization. Based largely on Butler's experience as a sheep farmer in New Zealand during the early 1860s and his exploration of the South Island interior, *Erewhon* guides readers through the liberatory experience of shedding convention and traversing a strange land. Although the book's playful use of irony and satire serves to critique social structures as indoctrinatory and propagandistic, the satirical tone renders the novel's overall message obscure, partial, and self-contradictory.

Initial critical reception of *Erewhon* was mixed. However, in the decades following its publication, the work proved influential for its exploration of evolution and the relationship of humans to technology. Written in the latter half of the Victorian era, during a period of industrialization and socioeconomic transformation, *Erewhon* responds to the emergence of evolutionary theory, ignited first by the discovery of the fossil record and then by the 1859 publication of Charles Darwin's *On the Origin of Species*. Butler's exploration of evolutionary theory in regard to machines and mechanization proved foundational to much of twentieth-century science fiction. Moreover, the novel played a prominent role in postmodern philosophy through its anticipation of debates over and innovations in artificial intelligence and machine cognition.

HISTORICAL AND LITERARY CONTEXT

Erewhon addresses the place of machines in culture, a subject of tremendous literary and polemical debate throughout the Victorian era due to the socioeconomic impact of the industrial revolution. Writers such as Charles Dickens and George Eliot explored the impact of technological advances such as the rail system, which by the 1850s had extended across Britain. By contrast, the writings of John Ruskin and William

Morris lamented life under the rule of mechanization, which they perceived as dominating human lives and artistic practices. Thus, as the first industrial revolution in England gave way to the second, issues of mechanization and culture increasingly preoccupied social reformers, politicians, and artists.

By the time Butler wrote *Erewhon,* Victorian culture was experiencing rapid industrial and social transformation in addition to tremendous progress in the natural sciences and human understanding of the universe. Advances in geology and paleontology in the early nineteenth century had already begun to disturb entrenched notions of a young, divinely created Earth before Darwin's *On the Origin of Species* effected a massive shift in scientific understanding by introducing the concept of natural selection. Then, in 1871, Darwin published *The Descent of Man,* in which he more explicitly explores the role of evolutionary adaptation in human, rather than animal, development. The social upheaval caused by industrialization and evolutionary theory thus provided the context for *Erewhon's* satirical utopia.

The utopian form, in which a traveler arrives in a strange land and receives an object lesson in a facet of social organization, was first used in Sir Thomas More's 1516 work *Utopia,* giving the genre its name. The form was frequently employed in Victorian fiction, including works by Edward Bulwer-Lytton, William Morris, Charles Kingsley, Edward Bellamy, and H. G. Wells. But *Erewhon,* in its elaborately constructed intertextuality, perhaps most resembles Thomas Carlyle's semisatirical *Sartor Resartus* (1836), which is filtered through a series of writers, readers, and interpreters, thereby preventing the reader from easily identifying with a narrator. In addition, like Wells and Morris, Butler transforms the utopian form into an early work of science fiction by simultaneously fantasizing about and satirizing post-Darwinian consciousness.

Butler's concerns and theories about the independence and consciousness of machines helped drive dominant themes in science fiction throughout the first part of the twentieth century. Several works of nineteenth-century speculative fiction took up the theme of the relationship between human beings and their increasingly sophisticated technologies, from

Key Facts

Time Period:
Mid-19th Century

Genre:
Novel

Events:
Industrial Revolution; evolutionary theory

Nationality:
English

EREWHON AND NEW ZEALAND

Samuel Butler left England for New Zealand in 1859 after abandoning his previous plans for ordination into the Anglican clergy. New Zealand became a British colony in 1840 after the Treaty of Waitangi between the British Empire and a coalition of indigenous Maori chiefs gave Britain sovereignty over the two islands. Butler worked at Mesopotamia Station as a sheep farmer and prospered financially in the three years he spent in the colony. While there, he published a number of articles in the *Press,* which operated out of Christchurch, including the essay "Darwin among the Machines" (1863), which contains the germ of *Erewhon* in its examination of mechanics through an evolutionary lens.

In 1863 he published *A First Year in Canterbury Settlement,* a nonfiction account of his experiences as a colonial settler. The following year he returned to England to study painting. In writing *Erewhon,* Butler drew heavily on his exploration of New Zealand geography and Maori culture. For example, in the novel, a Maori guide leads the protagonist Higgs into Erewhon, symbolically reproducing the process of mental and spiritual liberation that Butler experienced in Oceania.

Mary Shelley's *Frankenstein* (1818) to Wells's *The Time Machine* (1895) and *A War of the Worlds* (1898). Multinational writers such as Karel Čapek, Yevgeny Zamyatin, and Isaac Asimov composed even more sophisticated explorations of themes of mechanical consciousness. References to Butler's work continued into the late twentieth century with Frank Herbert's novel *Dune* (1965), which directly refers to *Erewhon* through a fictionalized backstory in which thinking machines necessitate destruction due to their increasing independence. Films such as Stanley Kubrick's *2001: A Space Odyssey* (1968) and James Cameron's *Terminator* series (1984, 1991) also explore themes of technology gaining consciousness and becoming murderous.

THEMES AND STYLE

Erewhon uses a combination of satire and utopian aspiration to address a cluster of linked yet diverse themes, such as inauthentic religious practices; the connections between education, crime, and disease; the influence of social conventions on the individual; and increasing mechanization. However, the tension between the extremes of idealism and cynicism serves to obscure the author's attitude toward the themes he explores. For example, despite the Erewhonians' sometimes ludicrous actions—a judge sentences a man to hard labor and "two tablespoonfuls of castor oil daily, until the pleasure of the court be further known"—the Erewhonians seem to flourish in typical utopian fashion. Thus, by defying either extreme through a seemingly self-contradictory narrative, Butler demonstrates

the failure and inherent absurdity of fanaticism and propagandistic rhetoric, regardless of the facet of society that they address.

Like other utopian works, *Erewhon* creates meaning through deployment of symbols. In the opening chapters, Higgs symbolically transitions between his world, which is governed by convention and tradition, into the new and unstable territory of Erewhon. When entering the strange, new land, the narrator encounters ten statues that guard a narrow pass, representing what Patrick Parrinder in a 2005 essay for *Critical Survey* argues "can … be related to the two most salient features of contemporary Erewhonian society: its abolition of machinery, and its cult of health, strength and physical beauty." The narrator is terrified and traumatized by the statues, but once in Erewhon he laughs at his former fears. Through Higgs's reaction, Butler demonstrates the absurd normative power of symbols and propaganda to portray conventions and social rules and to elicit emotional responses in their audience.

Although Butler sometimes depicts moments of intense and earnest emotion, the primary tone of *Erewhon* is satirical, making broad use of irony and humor, which serves to enhance his objection to Darwin's theory of evolution. For example, the sentencing of a criminal suffering from tuberculosis to hard labor alludes to the absurdity of the Darwinist doctrine of survival of the fittest. Butler argues that the evolutionary process is instead directed by a spiritual life force, a reflection of his Victorian sensibility that science and spirituality can coexist. Thus, in *Erewhon* he introduces a concept of technological evolution that confuses the boundaries between humans and machines. His work has led some to argue that Butler's opposition to Darwinism represents an extreme instance of love of heterodoxy, contradiction, and intellectual contrariness.

CRITICAL DISCUSSION

Initial reception of *Erewhon* was mixed. Butler had a difficult time finding a publisher for the novel, and it was rejected by Chapman and Hall on advice of novelist George Meredith. At last Trubner printed it as an anonymous work. Early reviews criticized *Erewhon* for its inconsistency, although nine editions of the book were printed during Butler's lifetime and it was the only one of his works to turn a profit. An 1872 review in *Athenaeum* dismissed the book as "slovenly" and suggested that Butler should cease writing altogether and return to sheep farming. A review published in the same year in the *Saturday Review* complained of the novel's immorality and criticized it for being absurd and overly complex. However, critical reaction was not universally negative: the *Spectator* in an 1872 review praised the novel's satire, comparing Butler to Swift. However, the review pointed out that the book's universal skepticism and negativity left the reader without an ultimate answer or solution.

Despite the centrality of social satire to *Erewhon*, the book's legacy has rested primarily on its depiction of the dangers of mechanical evolution. Butler gives machines an organic quality, depicting artificial intelligence as a type of evolutionary development, which has made his mediation on the nature of the relationship between people and machines useful to philosophies of consciousness and difference. For example, in the 1968 book *Difference and Repetition,* French philosopher Gilles Deleuze adopted the term "erewhons" to refer to inherently multiple and unstable ideas. In Deleuze's 1972 collaboration with Félix Guattari, *Anti-Oedipus,* the authors utilize the "Book of Machines" section of *Erewhon* to deconstruct strict binaries dividing vitalism and mechanism. Therefore, as the relationship between people and machines increasingly problematizes definitions of life, consciousness, and agency, Butler's application of evolutionary theory to technology has become useful as a way of parsing the social and ethical issues raised by technological transformation.

Despite the novel's prominent position in postmodern philosophy, scholarship on *Erewhon* is somewhat scant—although the book has never been far from critical consciousness. Critical topics have varied widely, from locating the work in the context of Oceanic colonialism to exploring Butler's critique of evolution. Other areas of interest include the author's concepts of morality and religion, which are particularly intriguing in light of the book's reputation for immorality and its relationship to the genre of satirical utopian novels, as in Stanley Hoffmann's 1963 article in *International Organization* connecting *Erewhon* to the works of Swift.

Writer Samuel Butler, author of *Erewhon.* © TOPFOTO/THE IMAGE WORKS.

BIBLIOGRAPHY

Sources

Butler, Samuel. *Erewhon.* New York: Penguin English Library, 1970. Print.

Deleuze, Gilles. *Difference and Repetition.* Trans. Paul Patton. New York: Continuum, 2004. Print.

Deleuze, Gilles, and Félix Guattari. *Anti-Oedipus: Capitalism and Schizophrenia.* Trans. Robert Hurley and Mark Seem. New York: Penguin Classics, 2009. Print.

Hoffmann, Stanley. "Erewhon or Lilliput? A Critical View of the Problem." *International Organization* 17.2 (1963): 404–24. Print.

"The New Gulliver." Rev. of *Erewhon,* by Samuel Butler. *Spectator* 20 Apr. 1872: 492–94. Print.

Parrinder, Patrick. "Entering Dystopia, Entering Erewhon." *Critical Survey* 17.1 (2005): 6. Print.

Rev. of *Erewhon,* by Samuel Butler. *Athenaeum* 20 Apr. 1872: 492. Print.

Rev. of *Erewhon,* by Samuel Butler. *Saturday Review* 20 Apr. 1872: 507–8. Print.

Further Reading

Breuer, Hans-Peter. "The Source of Morality in Butler's *Erewhon.*" *Victorian Studies* 16.3 (1973): 317–28. Print.

Jedrzejewski, Jan. "Samuel Butler's Treatment of Christianity in *Erewhon* and *Erewhon Revisited.*" *English Literature in Transition: 1880–1920* 31.4 (1988): 415–36. Print.

Jones, Joseph Jay. *The Cradle of Erewhon: Samuel Butler in New Zealand.* Austin: U of Texas P, 1959. Print.

Ketabgian, Tamara. "The Human Prosthesis: Workers and Machines in the Victorian Industrial Scene." *Critical Matrix: The Princeton Journal of Women, Gender, and Culture* 11 (1997): 4–32. Print.

Knoepflmacher, U. C. *Religious Humanism and the Victorian Novel: George Eliot, Walter Pater, and Samuel Butler.* Princeton: Princeton UP, 1970. Print.

Smithies, James. "Return Migration and the Mechanical Age: Samuel Butler in New Zealand 1860–1864." *Journal of Victorian Culture* 12.2 (2007): 203–24. Print.

Verzella, M. "Darwinism and Its Consequences: Machines Taking over Man in Samuel Butler's 'Absurd' Tableau." *Rivista di Studi Vittoriani* 18/19 (2004): 151–68. Print.

Zemka, Sue. "*Erewhon* and the End of Utopian Humanism." *ELH* 69.2 (2002): 439–72. Print.

Carina Saxon

THE FAT YEARS

Chan Koonchung

✧ *Key Facts*

Time Period:
Early 21st Century

Genre:
Novel

Events:
Growth of the Chinese
economy; increasing
capitalism of nominally
communist China

Nationality:
Chinese

OVERVIEW

First published in Chinese in 2009, Chan Koonchung's *The Fat Years* describes a fictionalized version of China in the year 2013. After a global financial crisis sends the U.S. economy into decline, Chan's China emerges in 2011 as the world's dominant superpower; it is a paradise characterized by social harmony, a high standard of living, and almost universal happiness. Writer Lao Chen is awakened from a slumber of forgetfulness, suddenly realizing that he cannot recall an entire month. For the remainder of the novel, Chen joins Fang Caodi in a search for answers about this missing month and to discover the true nature of the happiness and prosperity so universal in their country. Using elements of classic dystopian novels, Chan explores contemporary China's government-scripted version of social harmony and the ways in which economic prosperity has contributed to complacency about the Communist government's tendency to rewrite history.

Well received in Hong Kong, *The Fat Years* was banned in mainland China although it generated significant conversation when it made its appearance in the literary underground. The English translation, published in 2011, received generally positive reviews, many of which focused less on the novel's merits as a piece of writing and more on the window it provided into a country that is perceived in the West with both curiosity and trepidation. Lauded as a portrait of some elements of present-day China, as well as a cautionary tale about what the Leviathan may become, *The Fat Years* is notable as a rare glimpse of the major power emerging onto the global stage.

HISTORICAL AND LITERARY CONTEXT

In the late 1970s the Chinese government's economic policies shifted from Mao-style collectivism toward a socialist market economy. These new policies did not allow the economy to keep pace with the country's growth, however, and inflation, along with a dearth of jobs for the growing urban middle class and increasing outrage over government corruption, contributed to a series of protests in 1989. The protests were forcefully put down by the government in what is commonly known now as the Tiananmen Square massacre when, experts estimate, hundreds to thousands of civilian protestors were killed by the People's Liberation Army. This action brought an international outcry and economic sanctions against China. Immediately following the riots, conservatives in the regime reigned in economic reform, but pressure from provincial governors, as well as a campaign by the disgraced leader Deng Xiaoping, led to increasing economic liberalization as China headed toward the new millennium.

Almost a decade into the twenty-first century, China's flourishing economy offered a significantly improved standard of living to many urban Chinese; however reform did not extend to other areas of the government, which maintained a one-party system and continued to censor the media and suppress political protest. Chan, who grew up in Hong Kong, a British colony until 1997, benefited from its more liberal media policies, as well as the new affluence of the mainland, where he started a lifestyle periodical, *City Magazine,* and a cable company that he eventually sold to Sony.

The Fat Years, in Chinese titled *Shengshi Zhongguo 2013* (The golden age of China 2013), has been called Orwellian and indeed bears similarities to George Orwell's dystopian classic *1984.* Although Orwell's land of Oceania is not explicitly modeled on a real nation, the novels nonetheless share similar main themes, namely the rewriting of history to exclude inconvenient facts and persons from the official version of the nation's prosperity. In *1984* offending documents are erased via the memory hole while Chan's radical government erases memories from the minds of its citizenry via adulterated drinking water. Both books speculate on societies in a state of transition, whether in post-World War II Britain on the cusp of the Cold War or in China as it rises as an economic superpower.

Despite the novel's themes and its critique of the Chinese government, Chan has suffered no major reprisal from the government, telling *BBC News's* Stephanie Hegarty in 2011, "[I]n China, until the state intervenes, until the state tries to stop you from giving out dissenting views, you are not considered a dissident." Still, speaking to Ian Johnson for the *New York Times* in 2011 about his status in the eyes of the Chinese government, he likened it to playing with a cat: "You never know when its claws will come out."

THEMES AND STYLE

The central question in *The Fat Years* is whether citizens will choose a "good hell" over a "counterfeit paradise."

The question is posed by one of the novel's main characters about a society in which most people are happy, though their happiness is based on false information and government manipulation. Set in 2013, Chan's fictional China has outpaced the West in economic development, granting prosperity and upward mobility to many of its urban citizens. Lao Chen, a thriller writer and one of the beneficiaries of this new prosperity, one day realizes that an entire month is completely missing from his memory and those of his acquaintances, all except two friends, Fang Caodi and Little Xi, who prompt him to solve the mystery of the missing month. Eventually they kidnap politburo member He Dongsheng, who under questioning reveals that the government has added ecstasy to the drinking water and that the chemical, in combination with the high standard of living, renders most of the citizenry willing to wipe the brutal crackdowns of the missing month from their minds and to forgo all dissent and discussion of past atrocities perpetrated by the Communist government.

The Fat Years is set close enough to the present that Chan is able to mount a critique of the Communist government and its doctrine of a harmonious society while using the futuristic setting to provide some distance from his subject. Lao Chen regularly wanders from his home in Happiness Village Number Two to buy a Lychee Black Dragon Latte from Starbucks, now owned by the Chinese conglomerate WantWant. Moreover, Dongsheng's revelation that the government has added ecstasy to the water supply is sufficiently fanciful to keep the novel firmly in the realm of speculative fiction. The novel avoids any overt political commentary until the epilogue, where in a brief italicized segment titled "Idealism Chinese Style," Chan inserts an authorial voice addressing those intellectuals whose "roots are deep crimson," calling attention to their privileged positions in the newly ascending nation. This digression prefaces the story of the real source of the people's happiness in 2013, a happiness that is largely artificial, neatly calling into question the nature of the prosperity enjoy in the novel.

The Fat Years is characterized by sparse, action-driven narration in Lao Chen's even tone of voice, emphasizing his role as observer and investigator. Duped by government propaganda and a victim of group amnesia, Lao Chen finds himself roused by his encounters with Fang Caodi and Little Xi. His account of their attempt to solve the mystery is documented in a journalistic style and provides another sort of official account of "the fat years" to counteract the one provided by the government.

CRITICAL DISCUSSION

The Fat Years was published in Hong Kong, and although it generated considerable buzz on the mainland, it was banned from sale there. Copies appeared on a Chinese auction site and were made available online in PDF form by the author and his supporters.

THE GREAT FIREWALL OF CHINA

When the Chinese government banned Chan Koonchung's *The Fat Years* (2009), its censorship extended to the Internet, with authorities attempting to deny user access to the manuscript. The official Chinese effort to block certain content and websites has become known as the Great Firewall, in a wry reference to the Great Wall of China. The government's attempts to censor Internet activity can be traced to 1999, when the activist Lin Hai was imprisoned for aiding U.S. pro-democracy organizations through online means. A year later Internet activity that might, according to a quote in Christopher Hughes's 2010 article in *Survival,* "damage national unification" or otherwise contradict government policy was criminalized.

In recent years attempts at censorship have involved the complicity of foreign—including U.S.—companies that wish to operate sites in China. Google, for example, agreed to omit certain controversial information related to such topics as the Tiananmen Square massacre of 1989 in exchange for the privilege of launching a Chinese version of its search engine. Although Google initially accepted these terms, the company shut down Google.cn in 2010 after accusing China of hacking the company's computer networks. Other sites, including YouTube, Twitter, Dropbox, and Facebook, have simply been banned from China. While the Great Firewall has been relatively effective at controlling widespread access to the Internet, users have proved savvy at tunneling around the restrictions. *The Fat Years,* for example, can still be downloaded in China, despite being officially outlawed.

However, in both cases, the government cut off access, although determined readers still managed to bring the book into the country. Translated and published in the West in 2011, the novel was generally well-reviewed, with Johnson lauding its "offbeat puzzle and diverting characters," adding that the novel is "absorbing" and "shines reflected light on the foibles of the West."

Commentators have called *The Fat Years* a wake-up call for a generation of young, affluent Chinese who have expressed a willingness to accept what Chan calls "90 percent freedom" in exchange for material security. *NPR* contributor Michael Schaub in 2012 suggests that beyond addressing apolitical Chinese alone, "Chan's book is an urgent clarion call for people in every country to treasure their individuality and to reject leaders who promise temporary happiness in exchange for total freedom." The degree to which this "clarion call" will be heeded in China and the degree to which the near future will resemble the "fat years" of Chan's book, remain major points of speculation.

While *The Fat Years* has provoked much underground debate in China, significant critical work has yet to be undertaken or made available there. Doubtless the novel will be looked to with interest over the coming years as events either prove or disprove Chan's

The earnings of a vendor in Beijing, China, in 2011. The protagonist of Chan Koonchung's novel *The Fat Years* suspects that China's prosperity may have a sinister undertone. © MELANIE STETSON FREEMAN/CHRISTIAN SCIENCE MONITOR/THE IMAGE WORKS.

vision of the present and near future. "One can only hope that Chan," writes *The Guardian*'s Jonathan Fenby in 2011, "continues to write about the China of today from his current vantage point in Beijing. That will, in its way, be a test of whether the warnings of *The Fat Years* come true. We can only hope not."

BIBLIOGRAPHY

Sources

Chan, Koonchung. *The Fat Years.* Trans. Michael Duke. New York: Doubleday, 2011. Print.

Fenby, Jonathan. Rev. of *The Fat Years,* by Chan Koonchung. *London Guardian.* Guardian News and Media, 23 July 2011. Web. 10 Oct. 2012.

Hegarty, Stephanie. "Chan Koonchung's Dystopian Vision of China in 2013." *BBC News.* BBC, 11 Aug. 2011. Web. 10 Oct. 2012.

Hughes, Christopher R. "Google and the Great Firewall." *Survival: Global Politics and Strategy* 52.2 (2010): 19–26. *Taylor and Francis Online.* Web. 3 Dec. 2012.

Johnson, Ian. "On the Circuit and Upsetting the Party." *New York Times.* New York Times, 29 July, 2011. Web. 10 Oct. 2012.

Schaub, Michael. "*The Fat Years*: China's Brave New World." *NPR.* NPR, 12 Jan. 2012, Web. 11 Oct. 2012.

Further Reading

Angang, Hu. *China in 2020: A New Type of Superpower.* Washington DC: Brookings Institute, 2011. Print.

Gifford, Rob. *China Road: A Journey into the Future of a Rising Power.* New York: Random House, 2007. Print.

Johnson, Ian. *Wild Grass: Three Portraits of Change in Modern China.* New York: Vintage, 2005. Print.

Kristof, Nicholas, and Sheryl WuDunn. *China Wakes.* New York: Vintage, 1994. Print.

Minxin, Pei. *China's Trapped Transition.* Cambridge: Harvard UP, 2006. Print.

Mirsky, Jonathan. "Ignorance is Bliss." *Spectator* 20 Aug. 2011: 38. *Literature Resource Center.* Web. 10 Oct. 2012.

Daisy Gard

GULLIVER'S TRAVELS

Jonathan Swift

OVERVIEW

Gulliver's Travels (1726), a satirical prose narrative penned by Irishman Jonathan Swift, provides multifaceted commentaries on human nature and sharp criticism of the cultural and political institutions of the author's era. Originally titled *Travels into Several Remote Nations of the World,* Swift's text is a first-person narrative of a sailor's journey into several remarkable foreign countries—Lilliput, Brobingnag, Houyhnhmn, and a number of lands in southeastern Asia. The English narrator Lemuel Gulliver is a naive but likeable character who faithfully relates even the most mundane details of his four voyages and is eventually compelled to make an evaluation of the foreign cultures he experiences. Although the ultimate intent of *Gulliver's Travels* remains shrouded in ambiguity, most scholars agree the text is an assessment of mankind shown through a series of symbolic societies and reflects Swift's personal philosophies regarding the state of humanity. In contrast to the prevailing sentiments of the European Enlightenment, Swift did not believe society was continually advancing in progress and civility.

Upon its initial publication, *Gulliver's Travels* was immediately popular, with ten thousand copies sold within the first month. The text's instant success warranted two additional printings in 1726 alone, and the book became one of the top three best sellers of the eighteenth century. *Gulliver's Travels* is one of the best-known and most studied works of Swift's extensive canon and remains highly debated. Because Swift did not leave an explanation about who he was targeting in his text, his ultimate intent remains unclear and continues to bedevil critics. In a letter to poet Alexander Pope, Swift wrote, "The chief end I propose to my self in all my labors is to vex the world rather than divert it." Considered a popular classic of English-language literature, the satirical prose narrative has remained in print since its release nearly three hundred years ago. As a testament to the book's continued appeal, it has been the subject of many adaptations and parodies, including television and film versions.

HISTORICAL AND LITERARY CONTEXT

Swift was a controversial writer living in a contentious age. The Enlightenment, which promoted science and reason as the primary means for reforming society and advancing knowledge, was a topic of great debate. At twenty-one Swift witnessed the Glorious Revolution of 1688 in which King James II of England was overthrown by a union of English Parliamentarians and William III of Orange-Nassau. As a result of the revolution, William ascended to the throne, monarchical power became subordinate to Parliament, and a two-party political system emerged. Understanding the power of the press to influence the public, politicians eagerly sought writers of Swift's caliber. Swift wrote for the eventual Earl of Oxford, Robert Harley, and the Tory party. His work often revealed his misanthropy and his critical view of the newly emerging belief in mankind's benevolence. Theology argued that man was patterned after God and thus capable of perfection; however, Swift held with earlier convictions that man was inherently sinful and flawed.

Swift began working on *Gulliver's Travels* in 1721 after nearly six years of publishing little. Having been appointed as the dean of St. Patrick's Cathedral in Dublin, he had devoted his time and energy to his new position. During this time, he became more sympathetic to the plight of the Irish, who were then ruled by the English and regularly subjected to punitive legislation that deprived dissenters of civil rights. Despite his loyal service to the English Parliament, he began to view the British government with a critical eye. By the end of 1723 he had finished composing Gulliver's first two voyages, and in January 1724 the fourth voyage was completed. Swift would not complete the third voyage until the middle of 1725. The next year, *Gulliver's Travels* was published, and its instant success allowed the author to happily profit, an unusual occurrence according to the author. Although the work was published anonymously, Swift was quickly assumed to be the author.

Gulliver's Travels possibly derived some of its inspiration from Sir Thomas More's *Utopia* (1516), a philosophical novel about man's potential. Swift's tale mirrors More's use of marvelous voyages, exotic peoples, fantastic societies, and an ambiguity that disguises the author's intent. Indeed, Gulliver even references More's *Utopia* in a letter he writes to his cousin printed with the second edition: "If the Censure of the Yahoos could any Way affect me, I should have great Reason to complain, that some of them are so bold as to think my Book of Travels a mere

✥ *Key Facts*

Time Period:
Mid-18th Century

Genre:
Satire

Events:
Enlightenment; English oppression of the Irish

Nationality:
Irish

JONATHAN SWIFT: MASTER SATIRIST

Born on November 30, 1667, in Dublin, Ireland, Jonathan Swift was the second child of father Jonathan Swift and mother Abigail Herrick. Swift's father passed away before he was born, which forced his family to rely on his father's wealthy relations for financial assistance. When Swift's mother returned to England, his uncle Godwin oversaw his education, which took Swift to Kilkenny College and the prestigious Trinity College in Dublin. After earning his bachelor's degree in 1686, he decided to stay in Dublin to pursue his master's. In the wake of the Glorious Revolution, he joined his mother in England. There he intermittently served as an assistant to Sir William Temple, a noted former diplomat, until Temple's death in 1699. While in Temple's employ, Swift met King William III and other important figures. He also completed his master's at Hertford College, Oxford, and became increasingly active in the Anglican church. According to an article published in the *Edinburgh Monthly Review* in 1820, "Swift was bred a Whig under Sir William Temple ... and during all the reign of King William was a strenuous and indeed an intolerant advocate of revolution principles and Whig pretensions."

During his last few years with Temple, Swift composed his first satires, *A Tale of a Tub* (1704) and *The Battle of the Books* (1704). Upon earning his doctor of divinity from Trinity College in 1702, he became increasingly politicized, supporting increased restrictions on Catholics and the powers of the crown. He abandoned the Whig party in 1709 to lend his support to the Tories. Over the next several years, he established himself as a notable writer, favoring pamphlets and satire but also dabbling in poetry and other forms of prose. His close friends included writers such as Alexander Pope, John Gay, and John Arbuthnot, all of whom were members of the Scriblerus Club with Swift. When the Tories lost controlling power, Swift returned to Ireland and actively submersed himself in Irish politics. It was during this time that he wrote some of his most memorable satirical works, including *A Modest Proposal* (1729) and *Gulliver's Travels* (1726).

Fiction ... and have gone so far as to drop Hints, that the Huoyhnhnms and Yahoos have no more Existence than the Inhabitants of Utopia." Some critics suggest Swift's work may actually be antagonistic to More's work. Scholars have also drawn parallels between Swift's text and other early utopian writings, such as Francis Bacon's *New Atlantis* (1626), Johann Valentin Andreae's *Christianopolis* (1619), and Jan Amos Comenius's *The Labyrinth of the World and Paradise of the Heart* (1623).

Gulliver's Travels appeals to modern readers because it examines problems that continue to consume society: political corruption and humanity's follies. In *Writers for Children: Critical Studies of Major Authors since the Seventeenth Century* (1987), Robert Bator notes that *Gulliver's Travels* is "a general satire applicable to all mankind, not simply to select

eighteenth-century courtiers." In *Jonathan Swift* (1989), Robert Hunting argues that the text meets the definition of a classic because "it speaks powerfully and significantly to each generation; it never yields its full meaning." Some modern readings of the text recognize its utopian nature and even contend that it is a series of utopias. Chlöe Houston in a 2007 article for *Utopian Studies* argues that "*Gulliver's Travels* ... is an example of utopian writing which engages with the utopian mode whilst not being utopian in the sense of idealistic or optimistic; it is a utopian text which is also anti-utopian, or dystopian." Although Hunting criticizes *Gulliver's Travels* for being "too negative: it offers no solution to the problem that it defines," he goes on to state that "this century's appreciation of Swift has been increased because the threat of disaster is so often so close to us that readers more readily accept Swift's austere and gloomy visions."

THEMES AND STYLE

Central to *Gulliver's Travels* is Swift's disappointment in politics, religion, class, academics, and culture in contemporary society. Most critics agree the first three books expose man's shortcomings as represented by humanlike but fantastic races. Swift's most biting and controversial criticism occurs in the fourth book, in which Gulliver encounters a race of horses, the Huoyhnhnms. Gulliver describes his happy time with the extremely civilized Huoyhnhnms: "I did not feel the Treachery or Inconstancy of a Friend, nor the injuries of a secret or open Enemy. I had no occasion for bribing, flattery or pimping, to procure the favor of any great Man, or of his Minion." Ultimately, Gulliver is shunned by the Huoyhnhnms as a Yahoo—the bestial species who appear humanlike. When Gulliver returns to England, he is disgusted by his fellow humans, believing them to be Yahoos. He stops up his nose with tobacco to keep from smelling other people and spends four hours a day conversing with his horses.

Gulliver's Travels achieves its rhetorical effect by both mimicking and mocking the literary style of travel narratives, a very popular form of contemporary literature. By formulating the book as a travel narrative, Swift creates two layers of meaning to his text. The first is ostensibly a fun-filled adventure replete with silly words and ridiculous episodes enjoyed by children the world over. In the second layer, satire runs rampant by parodying and criticizing the world of eighteenth-century England. Swift made aspects of English life seem strange by allowing Gulliver to explain them to foreigners. For example, Swift attacks the violence of war when Gulliver describes how the English put "Powder into large hollow Balls of Iron, and discharged them by an Engine into some City we were besieging; which would rip up the Pavement, tear the Houses to Pieces, burst and throw Splinters on every Side, dashing out the Brains of all who came near." To Gulliver's supreme surprise, the King of Brobdingnag is appalled by the description of gunpowder, causing the reader to

question the brutality of war. Gulliver also encounters exaggerated elements of the English culture disguised as ridiculous aspects of foreign life. For example, Swift criticizes the European zeal for science when Gulliver meets the Laputans, who value reason and scientific method above common sense. Thus, the Laputans engage in absurd projects like "softening marbles for pillows" and breeding "naked sheep."

Stylistically, *Gulliver's Travels* is simultaneously a lighthearted tale and a dark satire. Hunting remarks that the tale is allegorical with two satiric butts: "One of the emerging targets is Gulliver himself, for his naiveté, for his misrepresentations of facts, and for his absurd illusions … the other satiric butt is humankind generally, for its pride, its treacheries and betrayals, its dirtiness." Karen R. Bloom for *Literature Resource Center* contends that this formulation "explains why the story does not have the traditional plot structure of rising action-climax-denouement … *Gulliver's Travels* can feel like a string of episodes tied together." Many of Swift's episodes are quite amusing, such as when Gulliver puts out a fire in Lilliputian palace by urinating on it. However, the tale can turn quite dark in places, as when Gulliver believes he is a bestial Yahoo in the country of the Houyhnhnms, leading him to reject his own family.

CRITICAL DISCUSSION

Although *Gulliver's Travels* was an instant best seller, it was also highly controversial. The text targeted high-profile subjects such as the scientifically oriented Royal Society; Parliament; Sir Robert Walpole; and kings James II, Henry VII, and George I. Swift's publisher, Benjamin Motte, feared possible retribution

by offended parties, which led him to edit the story without Swift's permission. Regardless of the alterations, the book attracted a great deal of notice upon its release, though it was likely denounced by the offended parties. A letter to Swift from his friend and fellow writer John Gay indicates the book's immediate success: "About ten days ago a book was published here of the travels of one Gulliver, which has been the conversation of the whole town ever since: the whole impression sold in a week … From the highest to the lowest it is universally read, from the Cabinet-council to the Nursery."

Although it has remained in print since its publication, *Gulliver's Travels* has experienced intermittent periods of unpopularity. In Samuel Johnson's *Life of Swift* (1781), the author describes the middle and late eighteenth-century opinion of *Gulliver's Travels*: "Criticism was for a while lost in wonder … But when distinctions came to be made the part which gave least pleasure was that which describes the Flying Islands book 3, and that which gave most disgust must be the history of the Houyhnhnms." General opinion of the work in the nineteenth century was condemnatory, with William Thackery stating it was "horrible, shameful, unmanly, blasphemous." Today, *Gulliver's Travels* is recognized as one of the premier works of English-language fiction. It has inspired hundreds of writers and infused such terms as *Lilliputian* and *yahoo* into the English lexicon. Bloom states that although Swift was discussing problems facing the English in the eighteenth century, his "combination of urgent social concern, creative imagination, and the possibilities of literary form appeals to readers of all ages and outlooks. It reminds us that great literature tells

An illustration by Philip Mendoza depicting Gulliver and the Lilliputians from Jonathan Swift's *Gulliver's Travels*. GULLIVER'S TRAVELS, FROM 'TREASURE', 1966 (GOUACHE ON PAPER), MENDOZA, PHILIP (1898–1973)/PRIVATE COLLECTION/© LOOK AND LEARN/THE BRIDGEMAN ART LIBRARY.

us as much about those who create it as it does about ourselves."

For nearly three hundred years, critics have debated Swift's intent in writing *Gulliver's Travels*. Although there is no definitive answer, scholars generally agree that the four parts of the book represent various aspects of Swift's personal philosophies, particularly regarding humanity. Some scholars argue Gulliver is a mask that Swift puts on to make certain criticisms. Others agree that Gulliver is not a persona but a character who occasionally uses Swift's voice but more frequently says the exact opposite of what Swift means. Hunting argues, "But as a rule, the rhetorical posture in the *Travels* will be ironical and therefore Swift's voice will be different from Gulliver's." Additionally, critics argue about to what extent Gulliver's ultimate contempt for humankind mirrors Swift's own hatred of humanity. A noteworthy point of contention among scholars is whether Swift intended the country of the Huoyhnhnms to represent a utopia or just another failed society presuming its own superiority. While many aspects of their society seem perfect, they build their society on the backs of Yahoo slaves, adhere to a strict social caste system, and use the flesh of their genetic cousins—donkeys—to feed the Yahoos. Houston argues that *Gulliver's Travels* "contains images of and interactions with ideas of utopia and dystopia which reflect its engagement with the utopian mode and qualify it simultaneously utopian and dystopian."

BIBLIOGRAPHY

Sources

Bator, Robert. "Jonathan Swift." *Writers for Children: Critical Studies of Major Authors since the Seventeenth Century.* Ed. Jane M. Bingham. New York: Scribner's, 1987. *Scribner Writers Series.* Web. 12 Sept. 2012.

Bloom, Karen R. "An Overview of Gulliver's Travels." *Literature Resource Center.* Gale Literature Collections, n.d. Web. 12 Sept. 2012.

"Defence of Swift." *Edinburgh Monthly Review* July 1820: 1–36. Print.

"*Gulliver's Travels* by Jonathan Swift." *Children's Literature Review.* Vol. 161. Ed. Dana Ferguson. Detroit: Gale, 2011. 89–174. *Literature Criticism Online.* Web. 12 Sept. 2012.

Houston, Chlöe. "Utopia, Dystopia or Anti-Utopia? *Gulliver's Travels* and the Utopian Mode of Discourse." *Utopian Studies* 18.3 (2007): 425–42. *Literature Resource Center.* Web. 12 Sept. 2012.

Hunting, Robert. *Jonathan Swift.* Rev. ed. Boston: Twayne, 1989. Twayne's English Authors Series 42. Web. 12 Sept. 2012.

Swift, Jonathan. *Gulliver's Travels into Several Remote Nations of the World.* London: Routledge, 1880. Print.

Further Reading

Donnelly, Dorothy E. "Utopia and Gulliver's Travels: Another Perspective." *Moreana* 25 (1988): 115–24. Print.

Loveman, Kate. "'Full of Improbably Lies': *Gulliver's Travels* and Jest Books." *British Journal of Eighteenth-Century Studies* 26.1 (2003): 15–26. Print.

Pencak, William. "Swift Justice: *Gulliver's Travels* as a Critique of Legal Institutions." *Law and Literature Perspectives.* Ed. Bruce L. Rockwood. New York: Lang, 1996. 255–67. Rpt. in *Twentieth-Century Literary Criticism.* Ed. Janet Witalec. Vol. 126. Detroit: Gale, 2002. Print.

Radner, John B. "The Fall and Decline: *Gulliver's Travels* and the Failure of Utopia." *Utopian Studies* 3.2 (1992): 51–74. Print.

Real, Hermann J. "Voyages to Nowhere: More's *Utopia* and Swift's *Gulliver's Travels.*" *Eighteenth-Century Contexts: Historical Inquiries in Honor of Philip Harth.* Ed. Howard B. Weinbrot, Peter J. Schakel, and Stephen E. Karian. Madison: U of Wisconsin P, 2001. 96–113. Print.

Reilly, Edward J. "Irony in *Gulliver's Travels* and *Utopia.*" *Utopian Studies* 3.1 (1992): 70–83. Print.

Venturo, David F. "*Gulliver's Travels*: Overview." *Reference Guide to English Literature.* 2nd ed. Ed. D. L. Kirkpatrick. Chicago: St. James, 1991. Print.

Voigt, Milton. "Gulliver's Travels in a Utopias-Dystopias Discourse." *Approaches to Teaching Swift's* Gulliver's Travels. Ed. Edward J. Reilly. New York: MLA, 1988. 117–20. Print.

Ward, James. "Personations: The Political Body in Jonathan Swift's Fiction." *Irish University Review* 41.1 (2011): 40–53. Print.

Media Adaptations

Gulliver's Travels. Dir. Georges Méliès. Georges Méliès, 1902. Short.

Gulliver's Travels. Dir. Dave Fleischer. Perf. Jessica Dragonette and Lanny Ross. Fleischer Studios, 1939. Film.

Gulliver's Travels. Dir. Rob Letterman. Perf. Jack Black, Emily Blunt, and Jason Segel. Twentieth Century Fox Film Corporation, 2010. Film.

Maggie Magno

THE HANDMAID'S TALE

Margaret Atwood

OVERVIEW

Canadian author Margaret Atwood's 1985 novel *The Handmaid's Tale* imagines a nightmarish future where a tightly controlled and repressive religious state forces both women and men into rigidly defined roles. The story is told by Offred, one of the enslaved Handmaids whose only purpose is to bear children for the ruling elite, many of whom have become infertile because of widespread chemical and nuclear pollution. Offred's narrative voice is tinged with desperation and irony as she describes the harsh limitations of society in the fundamentalist Republic of Gilead, which has replaced the United States. Interspersed with depictions of a bleak reeducation center run by an austere caste of Aunts who teach the Handmaids their proper role and the almost comically ritualized sex between the Handmaids, their Commanders, and the Commander's Wives are flashbacks to life before Gilead when Offred had her own name, a husband, a child, and a mother who was a feminist activist. *The Handmaid's Tale* thus becomes a cautionary tale of antifeminism taken to the extreme as well as a challenge to feminists to examine their own contradictions.

Atwood's novel was published at a time of tremendous backlash to the women's liberation movement of the 1970s. The media offered dire predictions of future loneliness for career-minded women alongside advertisements that commercialized feminism; conservative politicians used fear to denounce the Equal Rights Amendment; and right-wing religious groups waged an aggressive campaign to reinforce the traditional subservient role of women in society. Embattled feminists employed literature—especially the genre of speculative fiction—as a mode of resistance. Though *The Handmaid's Tale* was welcomed as a feminist response to the growing influence of Christian fundamentalism, it was also sharply criticized by some readers who wanted a more clear-cut condemnation of the patriarchal state and a more actively rebellious hero. As a thoughtful, but not radical, feminist, Atwood was careful to avoid simplistic political analysis, instead presenting a portrait of a woman whose will has almost, but not quite, been erased by a constant barrage of totalitarian propaganda.

HISTORICAL AND LITERARY CONTEXT

In 1979 the shah of Iran, Mohammad Reza Shah Pahlavi, who favored open communications with the western world, was deposed by a new religious regime under the leadership of the fundamentalist Ayatollah Rouhollah Mousavi Khomeini. Women around the world watched in horror as Iranian women were ejected from jobs and universities, forced to wear veils, and had their activities severely curtailed. The white "wings" that Handmaids are required to wear around the face may have been inspired by Muslim veiling practices.

During the 1980s the United States entered its own era of political and religious conservatism. In 1981 Ronald Reagan became president and began to cut spending for social programs. Right-wing Christians made savvy use of the persuasive force of television to popularize their messages, with televangelism becoming a powerful platform for conservative rhetoric and agendas. Popular televangelists such as Jerry Falwell and Jim and Tammy Faye Bakker reached unprecedented audiences as they campaigned against abortion, gay rights, and women's liberation. In a fundraising letter Pat Robertson, an influential preacher, denounced feminism as "a socialistic, anti-family political movement that encourages women to leave their husbands, kill their children, practice witchcraft, destroy capitalism and become lesbians." Many on the religious right had political ambitions as well; Robertson ran for president in 1988, and political speech took on increasingly religious overtones, with political catchphrases such as family values co-opted to connote a range of evangelical Christian beliefs.

With its ability to conceal biting commentary within a fanciful storyline, science fiction has long been a venue for social critique. The rebirth of the feminist movement during the 1970s spawned a flood of writing about women's issues, and a new genre of feminist science fiction quickly emerged. American authors Ursula Le Guin (*The Left Hand of Darkness,* 1969) and Joanna Russ (*The Female Man,* 1975) were respected science fiction writers who encouraged alternative worldviews by challenging societally enforced assumptions such as sexism and gender stereotypes in their works. British writer Doris Lessing (*The Memoirs of a Survivor,* 1974) and American writer Marge Piercy (*Woman on the Edge of Time,* 1976) were, like Atwood, established novelists and poets who began to use future fiction as a way to expose the failings of society and suggest remedies. Published in 1985,

⁘ *Key Facts*

Time Period:
Late 20th Century

Genre:
Novel

Events:
Women's liberation; Islamic Revolution in Iran; rise of Christian fundamentalism

Nationality:
Canadian

PHYLLIS SCHLAFLY AND THE ANTIFEMINIST CONTRADICTION

The 1960s African American civil rights movement led to a number of progressive struggles for reform, among them the women's liberation movement that gained strength during the 1970s. As more and more women began to demand equality under the law and in the workplace, reproductive rights, and better treatment in their personal relationships, conservatives began to resist these sweeping societal changes.

One of the prototypes of Serena Joy, Margaret Atwood's Commander's Wife in *The Handmaid's Tale*, was author and activist Phyllis Schlafly, who emerged as one of the most effective spokespeople of the antifeminist backlash. An ultraconservative politically, Schlafly led a successful national campaign against the Equal Rights Amendment to the U.S. Constitution. In 1977 she published *The Power of the Positive Woman*, which celebrated the differences between men and women and urged women to seek fulfillment in their "natural" role of wife and mother.

Interestingly, although Schlafly wrote that women were generally unsuited for higher education and public roles, she earned a bachelor's degree in political science from Washington University in St. Louis, Missouri, in 1944 and a master's degree in government from Radcliffe College in Cambridge, Massachusetts (merged with Harvard University in 1999), in 1945. Despite being married to lawyer John F. Schlafly Jr. and having six children, Schlafly pursued an active career and ran unsuccessfully for Congress twice.

The Handmaid's Tale presents a similarly totalitarian society as found in *1984*, British novelist George Orwell's famous 1949 dystopian novel of the future, expanding on the alarming possibilities of fundamentalist rule as Orwell did with the potential consequences of fascism.

When it was published, *The Handmaid's Tale* became part of the feverish public dialog about feminism, derided by conservatives and earnestly critiqued by feminist scholars. A gripping work of fiction, the novel remained a focus of political discussion and debate for decades as the influence of religious fundamentalism continued to be felt, not only within the United States, where right-wing Christians gained increasing political ground, but also around the world as conservative religious groups placed ever-harsher limits on women's lives. The novel's continuing relevance was illustrated by its adaptation as a film, directed by Volker Schlöndorff, in 1990 and as an opera, composed by Poul Ruders and debuting in the United States in 2003.

THEMES AND STYLE

The Handmaid's Tale examines both the dishonesty of religious fanaticism, which disguises hate and violence inside a vocabulary of love and morality, and the complacency that allows such dishonesty to flourish. The deliberate campaign of lies that sustains Gilead's society is personified in Serena Joy, the Commander's Wife, who, in an earlier time, was a televangelist with a vibrant career speaking out against women having careers. "She stays in her home," Offred says of Serena Joy's current life, "but it doesn't seem to agree with her. How furious she must be, now that she's been taken at her word." Language is one of the primary tools for enforcing a corrupt worldview. Atwood creates a language for Gilead that controls reality by redefining the words used to describe it. Gays are executed for "gender treachery," sterile females are labeled "unwomen," and even Offred's name is not her own but describes her status as a possession of Fred, the Commander. Her rebellion often takes linguistic form as well, in secret mental wordplay or illicit Scrabble vocabulary games with her Commander. Control of language is thus linked with control over one's thoughts.

The novel presents a complex picture of hypocrisy that is claustrophobic and fatalistic: "The Commander is head of the household. The house is what he holds … till death do us part." The confined, prudish world of Gilead's rigid caste system is riddled with cheating and fraud. The doctor who examines Offred offers to impregnate her secretly, since the Commander has not been able to, and the Commander himself breaks the rules by inviting Offred to visit him outside of her prescribed role. Contrasting with this are vibrant flashes of both past freedoms ("Lying in bed with Luke, his hand on my rounded belly") and small rebellions ("we could stretch out our arms, when the Aunts weren't looking, and touch each other's hands across space"). Offred is the daughter of a 1970s feminist activist, and, like many of her generation, she often dismissed her mother's passionate politics and took the gains of women's liberation for granted. The indignities of Gilead's stifling society, however, give her a new perspective on her mother's values, "I want her back. I want everything back the way it was."

The oppressive tone of *The Handmaid's Tale* is relieved somewhat by the ironic detachment of Offred's narration, which gives her voice a life separate from the hopelessness of her situation. The protagonist seems to be caught in a nightmare, and Atwood emphasizes this by using a stream of consciousness style for Offred's thoughts, mingling memory, suffering, and rebellion in a feverish monologue. The bizarre and frightening are juxtaposed with the familiar to draw the reader into Offred's world: "That was when they suspended the Constitution…. There wasn't even any rioting in the streets. People stayed home at night, watching television, looking for some direction." The book changes tone abruptly in the patronizing epilogue, "Historical Notes," an academic analysis of Offred's narrative. Both historians and academics, she seems to imply, employ their own forms of language

A still from the 1990 film adaptation of *The Handmaid's Tale*, with Natasha Richardson (right) as Offred the handmaid and Faye Dunaway (left) as the Commander's wife. © CINECOM PICTURES/COURTESY EVERETT COLLECTION.

to obfuscate history and control present perceptions. Orwell had previously presented "objective history" as propaganda with *1984*'s Ministry of Truth, devoted to altering historical records to suit the needs of those in power, "'Who controls the past' ran the Party slogan, 'controls the future: who controls the present controls the past.'"

CRITICAL DISCUSSION

Though *The Handmaid's Tale* caricatured many main-stream religious and political values, it was acclaimed by numerous critics as compelling science fiction, winning the *Los Angeles Times* Best Fiction Award in 1986 and the Arthur C. Clarke Award for Best Science Fiction and the Commonwealth Literature Prize in 1987. The *New York Times* called the work "a political tract deploring nuclear energy, environmental waste, and anti-feminist attitudes" and praised it as "a taut thriller, a psychological study, a play on words." Feminist scholars such as Barbara Ehrenreich analyzed it as "an intra-feminist polemic," exposing the ways that women are complicit in their own oppression. While many feminists have criticized the novel's bleak vision and the passivity of its hero, Gayle Greene in *The Women's Review of Books* concludes that "this is the tale's greatest value—its power to disturb."

The Handmaid's Tale stands as a powerful testimony of the fears of embattled feminists during the 1980s. As Amanda Greenwood states in her 2009 article "*The Handmaid's Tale* in Context," Gilead "does not spring out of nowhere, fully formed. It has its roots in history." Though the novel posits an undeniably grim reality, an early review in the *New York Times* ascribed its success to the fact that "the sensibility through which we view this world is infinitely rich and abundant." As conservative regimes have imposed increasing restrictions on women's lives in nations such as Saudi Arabia and Afghanistan, social analysts have continued to point to *The Handmaid's Tale* as a significant work of forecast and warning.

Early in her career, scholars defined Atwood primarily as a product of her Canadian culture, with a deep respect for the wilderness and a British-influenced sharpness of satire. Professor Coral Ann Howells chronicles the development of the critical view of Atwood from ecological poet to cultural theorist between the 1970s and the early 2000s as she developed a genre she called "speculative fiction." As the religious right has remained a potent force on the American political scene into the twenty-first century, *The Handmaid's Tale* has continued to stimulate discussion about the social costs of enforcing morality. While mainstream scholars have tended to focus on the novel as an example of dystopian fiction, comparing it to such male-authored works as *1984* and British novelist Anthony Burgess's *A Clockwork Orange* (1962), feminists have viewed it as part of the women's movement and a new women's literature of change. Just as Atwood's novel was inevitably compared to previous dystopian works, later feminist science fiction has been measured against the success of *The Handmaid's Tale,* including Atwood's own later efforts, *Oryx and Crake* (2003) and *The Year of the Flood* (2009).

BIBLIOGRAPHY

Sources

Ehrenreich, Barbara. "Feminism's Phantoms." *New Republic* 17 March 1986: 33–35. Print.

Greene, Gayle. "Choice of Evils." *Women's Review of Books* 3.10 (July 1986): 14. Print.

Greenwood, Amanda. "*The Handmaid's Tale* in Context." *English Review* 20.2 (Nov. 2009): 10–14. Print.

Howells, Coral Ann. *The Cambridge Companion to Margaret Atwood.* Cambridge: Cambridge UP, 2006. Print.

Lehmann-Haupt, Christopher. "Books of the Times: *The Handmaid's Tale.*" *New York Times* 27 Jan. 1986: C24. Print.

Rothstein, Mervyn. "No Balm in Gilead for Margaret Atwood." *New York Times* 17 Feb. 1986: C11. Print.

Further Reading

Canton, Kimberly Fairbrother. "'I'm Sorry My Story Is in Fragments': Offred's Operatic Counter-Memory." *English Studies in Canada* 33.3 (Sept. 2007): 125–42. Print.

Davidson, Arnold E. "Making History in *The Handmaid's Tale.*" *Margaret Atwood: Vision and Form.* Eds. Kathryn Van Spanckeren and Jan Garden Castro. Carbondale: Southern Illinois UP, 1988. 113–21. Print.

Faludi, Susan. *Backlash: The Undeclared War against American Women.* New York: Doubleday Anchor, 1991. Print.

Freibert, Lucy M. "Control and Creativity: The Politics of Risk in Margaret Atwood's *The Handmaid's Tale.*" *Critical Essays on Margaret Atwood.* Ed. Judith McCombs. Boston: Hall, 1988. 280–91. Print.

Malak, Amin. "Margaret Atwood's *The Handmaid's Tale* and the Dystopian Traditions." *Canadian Literature* 112 (Spring 1987): 9–16. Print.

Nelson, David. *Women's Issues in Margaret Atwood's "The Handmaid's Tale."* Farmington Hills, MI: Greenhaven, 2011. Print.

Ochsenfahrt, Katharina. *Motivated Elements of Sexual Inequality in Margaret Atwood's Novel "The Handmaid's Tale."* Munich: GRIN Verlag, 2010. Print.

Sisk, David W. *Transformations of Language in Modern Dystopias.* Westport, CT: Praeger, 1997. Print.

Swale, Jill. "Feminism and Politics in *The Handmaid's Tale.*" *English Review* 13.1 (Sept. 2002): 37–40. Print.

Media Adaptation

The Handmaid's Tale. Dir. Volker Schlöndorff. Screenplay by Harold Pinter. Prod. Daniel Wilson. Cast Natasha Richardson, Faye Dunaway, and Aidan Quinn. United States: Cinecom Entertainment Group, 1990. Film.

Tina Gianoulis

HERLAND

Charlotte Perkins Gilman

OVERVIEW

Charlotte Perkins Gilman's 1915 novel *Herland* uses an imagined country populated solely by females to argue for women's equality and independence. Part of a long tradition of utopian fiction, *Herland* shows the reader this country through the eyes of Vandyk Jennings, Terry O. Nicholson, and Jeff Margrave, three male explorers who are taken captive and educated by the women-only population. Convinced that women alone could not have built or maintained such a civilization, the explorers suspect that Herland's men must be concealed elsewhere; however, as they learn the language of the Herlanders and begin to communicate with them, they find that a volcanic cataclysm two thousand years earlier cut these women off from the rest of the world. They have learned to survive without men, reproducing asexually via parthenogenesis [*see sidebar*], which also enables them to eugenically control their population. Through the experiences of the explorers, Gilman advances the argument that women are not innately weak, foolish, or tempestuous: the three men realize that the Herlanders are capable of governing themselves and have developed a culture superior to their own in its sophistication.

Herland is the middle volume in Gilman's exploration of feminist utopias, bracketed by *Moving the Mountain* (1911) and *With Her in Our Land* (1916). The novel remained obscure until 1979, when it was "rediscovered" by the emerging second feminist wave. Gilman's best-known literary work, the short story "The Yellow Wallpaper" (1890), exposes the oppressive "rest cures" that were popular remedies for hysteria and independent-mindedness in nineteenth-century women. Gilman's fiction, nonfiction, and public speeches in the last decade of the nineteenth century advanced several political and feminist goals, including women's legal rights and the reform of gynecological practices. *Herland* is considered a forerunner of twentieth-century feminist science fiction and is notable as a lighter entry in Gilman's oeuvre.

HISTORICAL AND LITERARY CONTEXT

Throughout the nineteenth century, Anglo American gender roles were shaped by the concept of sexual reciprocity: men and women are essentially different, but in such a way that they naturally complement each other. Sexual reciprocity gave rise to the idea of "separate spheres," which dictates that women are best suited for the home and men for the workplace. In the late nineteenth and early twentieth centuries, emerging ideas of evolutionary science and Freudian psychoanalysis further widened the perceived divide between male and female natures. Women were considered inherently maternal, and even feminists often based their arguments for women's legal rights on women's work as mothers. This overemphasis on women's role in propagating and education succeeding generations sometimes led to intersections between feminist and eugenic platforms. Rigidly essential gender roles were also reflected in law: throughout the nineteenth century, married Anglo American women lived under a system of legal coverture, in which a married woman's identity was subsumed under that of her husband.

In 1915, when *Herland* was published, the first wave of the American feminist movement was approaching its peak. Commonly held to have begun in the United States with the Seneca Falls Convention in 1848, this movement focused on women's legal rights and culminated in a decades-long struggle for the right to vote, which was finally won in 1920. Gilman joined the movement, writing and lecturing for women's rights and social change. *Herland* is deeply embedded in the context of the era's debates on sex and gender roles; it responds to conservative assertions that women could not accomplish the public work of forming and governing a society.

Although *Herland* can be categorized within early feminist fiction, it also follows many of the conventions of an older tradition of utopian literature. *Herland*'s feminist arguments draw from the polemical works of American women, exploring the ideas of writers such as Margaret Fuller and Jane Addams. However, its form—a tale of a journey to a fantastic utopia narrated by a bewildered traveler from our own reality—can be traced to Sir Thomas More's 1516 *Utopia*. The utopian novel was historically a popular form for politicized fiction, embraced by writers including Sir Francis Bacon, William Morris, and H. G. Wells and notably parodied by Jonathan Swift. The nineteenth-century American socialist Edward Bellamy, a major influence on Gilman, utilized a utopian conceit in his 1888 novel *Looking Backward*.

Although *Herland* was out of print for much of the twentieth century, both its arguments and its

❖ Key Facts

Time Period:
Early 20th Century

Genre:
Novel

Events:
Achievement of women's suffrage

Nationality:
American

PARTHENOGENESIS, MECHANICAL REPRODUCTION, AND FEMINISM

The women in Charlotte Perkins Gilman's *Herland* reproduce via parthenogenesis, a process by which embryos grow and develop without fertilization. Parthenogenesis occurs naturally in some scorpions, aphids, fish, amphibians, and birds. The word derives from ancient Greek and literally means "virgin birth."

Gilman uses parthenogenesis to free the women of her utopia from the need to engage in heterosexual intercourse in order to perpetuate the species. She is not alone among feminist theorists in looking to the transformation of birth for women's liberation. In the 1970s, radical feminist Shulamith Firestone argued that pregnancy, both painful and physically exhausting, constitutes an inherently abusive form of women's labor and is a central cause of female oppression. Firestone advocated for the development of artificial wombs, which would lead to a genuine equality between the sexes. The notion of an artificial womb is no longer merely a talking point. In-vitro fertilization has moved conception outside of the body, and in 2002, medical researchers at Cornell University's Weill Medical College successfully created an artificial womb lining.

strategies remained useful to feminist authors of the period. Ursula K. Le Guin's *The Dispossessed* (1974) and Marge Piercy's *Woman on the Edge of Time* (1976) both employ utopian forms to critique sex and gender roles, while Joanna Russ's "When It Changed" (1972) and James Tiptree, Jr.'s "Houston, Houston, Do You Read?" (1976) explore imaginary worlds without men. Radical feminist Shulamith Firestone's work on sex, gender, and reproduction reaches conclusions similar to those in *Herland,* arguing that reproduction needs to be decoupled from the sexed body before gender liberation can become possible. Although those works cannot be said to have been influenced directly by *Herland,* which remained obscure and difficult to find until its reissue in 1979, they form a tradition of speculative feminist writing about gender, sexuality, reproduction, and nature.

THEMES AND STYLE

The theme of *Herland* centers on the enlightenment of three white male explorers upon discovering an isolated female civilization. The explorers seek out the territory in response to rumors of an all-female population, and they assume that the place will conform to various nineteenth-century gender stereotypes. Instead, as the novel states, "It looked—well, it looked like any other country—a civilized one." Gilman's feminist platform emerges in the novel's account of the interactions between the explorers and their hosts. The men are perpetually surprised by the development, sophistication, and beauty of the culture, as well as by the sense, intelligence, and goodness of the citizenry,

and they realize that their assumptions about men and women were incorrect. Reciprocally, the women of Herland are frequently startled or shocked by the men's nineteenth-century American manners and mores, which they judge to be immoral or abhorrent.

Gilman utilizes a limited first-person point of view, narrating the story from the perspective of one of the explorers, Vandyk, in order to tacitly address the reader's questions and assumptions through those of her male character. Vandyk serves as a proxy for the reader, as do his companions in a more indirect way. The explorers' need for information allows Gilman to lead the reader through the propagandistic account of their journey of discovery, in which cultural constructs such as virginity, the sexual double standard, and the use of animals and animal byproducts by humans are destabilized. The men's confused ideas about gender and sex give Gilman the opportunity to present egalitarian and feminist perspectives, and the women's horror at common American practices forces readers to reevaluate their beliefs. The differences in speech and diction between the explorers and the women of Herland subtly reinforce the novel's functions of identification and shaming; the male characters' speech is often crude and is peppered with slang, while the females use simple grammar and formal language suggestive of their greater refinement and wisdom.

Gilman combines the exciting and often sociological narration common to adventure and discovery stories with expository discourses on political history and gender roles. In her presentation of sexism, she carefully eschews the emotional or melodramatic, instead emphasizing rational justifications for women's liberation. She presents Herland as proof of women's fitness for self-government, utilizing a style that frames the story as fact rather than a fairy tale. Likely aware of the greater sentimentality stereotypically associated with women, Gilman may have been taking care to avoid melodrama in her writing. Instead, she corrects sexist misconceptions calmly. For example, she writes:

> [W]e had been cocksure as to the inevitable limitations, the faults and vices, of a lot of women.... We had expected a dull submissive monotony, and found a daring social inventiveness far beyond our own, and a mechanical and scientific development fully equal to ours.... We had expected hysteria, and found a standard of health and vigor, a calmness of temper, to which the habit of profanity, for instance, was impossible to explain.

By taking this rationalistic "high ground," Gilman lends gravitas and authority to her literary argument.

CRITICAL DISCUSSION

The initial critical reaction to *Herland* was sparse. It is worth noting that the author was sometimes criticized for the didacticism apparent in other works of fiction;

nevertheless, her writing on behalf of feminism, including her work for *The Forerunner,* brought her some renown. The publication of Gilman's nonfiction feminist work *Women and Economics* in 1898 garnered an international readership in feminist circles, but by the period in which *Herland* was published Gilman felt herself to be out of step with the times, writing in her 1935 autobiography that "unfortunately my views on the sex question do not appeal to the Freudian complex of today, nor are people satisfied with a presentation of religion as a help in our tremendous work of improving this world." The lack of public response to *Herland* suggests that Gilman's assessment may well have been correct.

As the twentieth century progressed, however, Gilman came to be regarded as an important author, largely due to "The Yellow Wallpaper," which became a staple of feminist literature. *Herland* was reprinted in 1979 by Ann Lane, who described it at the time as a "lost" feminist novel. Its antinaturalistic approach to reproduction makes it relevant to current debates on medical interventions in conception, pregnancy, and birth. Because of *Herland,* Gilman is also considered a foremother of contemporary feminist work in science fiction. In a 1979 review of *Herland,* science fiction novelist Joanna Russ celebrates the book's "primitive delight of wish-fulfilment, i.e. escorting American men all over Herland ... and hearing them say, 'Yes, you're right. You're absolutely right. Feminism is the hope of the world.'" At the same time, Russ condemns "the white solipsism which makes Herland 'Aryan.'"

Feminist literary criticism quickly responded to *Herland*'s "rediscovery," with reviews of the work that probe the tenets of its feminism, as well as its ties to colonialist exploration literature (such as Susan Gubar's 1983 critique) and its deployment of eugenics and scientific racism. The work has also drawn in feminists interested in language and semiotics, such as Martha J. Cutter, who wrote the 1999 article "Herstory in Hisland, History in Herland: Charlotte Perkins Gilman's Reconstruction of Gender and Language." Other feminist scholarship has focused on *Herland*'s portrayal of motherhood and the book's linking of nature and culture in defiance of gender binaries. Though *Herland* is considered a significant work in Gilman's oeuvre, it has received less scholarly attention than the more serious "The Yellow Wallpaper."

BIBLIOGRAPHY

Sources

Cutter, Martha J. "Herstory in Hisland, History in Herland: Charlotte Perkins Gilman's Reconstruction of Gender and Language." *Unruly Tongue: Identity and Voice in American Women' Writing, 1850–1930.* UP of Mississippi, 1999. 111–140. Rpt. in *Twentieth-Century Literary Criticism.* Ed. Linda Pavlovski and Scott T. Darga. Vol. 117. Detroit: Gale Group, 2002. *Literature Resource Center.* Web. 5 July 2012.

Gilman, Charlotte Perkins. *Herland: A Lost Feminist Utopian Novel.* New York: Pantheon Books, 1979. Print.

Gubar, Susan. "*She* in *Herland*: Feminism as Fantasy." 139–49. *Coordinates,* ed. Slusser, Rabkin, and Scholes. Rev. and rpt. 71–82 in *No Man's Land.* Vol. 2: *Sexchanges* by Gilbert and Gubar. Yale. 1989. Print.

M.D. "Perilous Stuff." Rev. of "The Yellow Wallpaper," by Charlotte Perkins Gilman. *Boston Evening Transcript* 8 April 1892: 6. Print.

Russ, Joanna. "Reviews." *The Country You Have Never Seen.* Ed. David Seed. Liverpool: Liverpool UP, 2007. Print.

Further Reading

Allen, Judith. *The Feminism of Charlotte Perkins Gilman.* Chicago: University of Chicago Press, 2009. Print.

Arnold, Bridgitte. "'It Began This Way': The Synonymy of Cartography and Writing as Utopian Cognitive Mapping in Herland." *Utopian Studies: Journal of the Society for Utopian Studies* 17.2 (2006): 299–316. Print.

Avril, Chloe. "Sexuality and Power in Charlotte Perkins Gilman's *Herland.*" *Moderna Sprak* 98.2 (2004): 148–51. Print.

Fishkin, Shelley Fisher. "Reading Gilman in the Twenty-First Century." *The Mixed Legacy of Charlotte Perkins Gilman.* Eds. Catherine J. Golden and Joanna Schneider Zangrando. Newark; London: U of Delaware P; Associated UP, 2000. Print.

Johnson-Bogart, Kim. "The Utopian Imagination of Charlotte Perkins Gilman: Reconstruction of Meaning in *Herland.*" *Pacific Coast Philology* 27.1–2 (1992): 85–92. Print.

Lane, Ann J. *To "Herland" and Beyond: The Life and Work of Charlotte Perkins Gilman.* New York: Pantheon, 1990. Print.

Scharnhorst, Gary. "The Intellectual Context of Herland: The Social Theories of Lester Ward." *Approaches to Teaching Gilman's 'The Yellow Wallpaper' and* Herland." Ed. Denise D. Knight and Cynthia J. Davis. New York: Modern Lang. Assn. of Amer., 2003. 118–24. Print.

Seitler, Dana. "Unnatural Selection: Mothers, Eugenic Feminism, and Charlotte Perkins Gilman' Regeneration Narratives." *American Quarterly* 55.1 (2003): 61–88. Print.

Weinbaum, Alys Eve. "Writing Feminist Genealogy: Charlotte Perkins Gilman, Racial Nationalism, and the Reproduction of Maternalist Feminism." *Feminist Studies* 27.2 (2001): 271–302. Print.

Carina Saxon

THE HUNGER GAMES

Suzanne Collins

OVERVIEW

Written in an age of increasingly intrusive media, Suzanne Collins's 2008 young-adult novel *The Hunger Games* explores issues of war, morality, and economic justice in the context of a grisly television reality program. The novel's futuristic setting is Panem, a nation that has risen from the ruins of North America. The residents of Panem's twelve districts labor under the coercion of harsh Peacekeepers to support the ruling Capitol. The Capitol is the seat of both ruthless political power and a ludicrously faddish entertainment industry, which coalesce in an annual ritual called the Hunger Games. Every year, in penance for a bygone rebellion, each district is required to choose one boy and one girl between the ages of twelve and eighteen to fight to the death in a brutal, nationally televised competition. The novel's central character is Katniss Everdeen, a scrappy and perceptive seventeen-year-old. Faced with being sent to the 74th annual Hunger Games as a candidate, or tribute, from poverty-stricken District 12, Katniss is challenged with the seemingly impossible task of retaining her humanity while fighting for her life. Enormously popular with both teen and adult readers, *The Hunger Games* is a riveting drama, as well as a powerful argument against war and the abdication of personal responsibility.

Upon its publication, *The Hunger Games* was welcomed enthusiastically as an innovative and thoughtful entry in the growing genre of young-adult fantasy and science fiction. Young readers, familiar with the vernacular of both reality-television programming and social messaging, were captivated by Katniss's struggles to maintain her integrity in a superficial and cruel society. Its popularity supported by the enthusiastic word-of-mouth endorsement of young fans, *The Hunger Games* remained at the top of best-seller lists for several years, boosted by the appearance of two sequels and a feature film based on the first novel.

HISTORICAL AND LITERARY CONTEXT

In the early 2000s the United States became involved in wars in Afghanistan and Iraq under the nebulous mandate of a highly propagandized war on terrorism. Devastating surprise attacks carried out by the militant Islamist group al-Qaeda in New York City and near Washington, D.C., in September 2001 led parts of the U.S. population to support an aggressive military stance, while others argued for more measured, nonmilitary responses. A large and vocal international peace movement mobilized an unsuccessful attempt to prevent the 2003 U.S. invasion of Iraq, an action that many opponents viewed as simple expansionism.

If *The Hunger Games* was in part a response to this atmosphere of continuing warfare, it also rode the crest of another cultural phenomenon. In 2000 television producer Mark Burnett, a former elite paratrooper in the British army, introduced a quasi-military reality program called *Survivor*. Based upon the "stranded on a desert island" scenario, *Survivor* pitted telegenic contestants against one another in a variety of events, eliminating losers one by one and awarding a million dollars to the winner. The program attracted huge audiences and helped usher in a pervasive new genre of reality entertainment. Reality shows showcase the interactions of non-actors in contrived situations, a setting *The Hunger Games* embellishes and caricatures. As a writer for television as well as a novelist, Collins could speak with authority about the power and superficiality of the entertainment industry and its impact on culture, news, and even history.

The turn of the twenty-first century saw a flood of fantasy and science fiction literature aimed at young-adult audiences. Many of these works, including J.K. Rowling's Harry Potter series, the first book of which was published in 1998, won large adult followings as a result of their presentation of complex themes within a sometimes menacing magical world. Collins herself first entered the fantasy genre in 2003 with her series *The Underland Chronicles*. Authors drew on influential works from earlier decades: William Golding's 1963 novel *Lord of the Flies* was set in a world populated mainly by child characters to expose the darker side of human nature, and cyberpunk writer William Gibson explored the powerful influence of television and other pop culture media in such novels as *Virtual Light* (1994). More recently, novels by writers such as Scott Westerfeld (*The Uglies* [2005]) and Susan Beth Pfeffer (*Life as We Knew It* [2006]) also preceded *The Hunger Games* in creating compelling dystopian futures to examine societal trends through the eyes of young protagonists.

Almost immediately upon its publication, *The Hunger Games* became a worldwide success. Preteens, teenagers, and adults devoured the novel and its

+ Key Facts

Time Period:
Early 21st Century

Genre:
Novel

Events:
War on Terror; growth of reality television

Nationality:
American

"EVERY CITIZEN OF PANEM IS TUNED IN": *THE HUNGER GAMES* ON FILM

Considering the popularity of visual media in the twenty-first century, it may have been inevitable that a novel as widely read as *The Hunger Games* would be made into a movie. Suzanne Collins worked with director Gary Ross to adapt her novel in a screenplay for the film, which went into production in May 2011. A massive ad campaign spurred already-impatient fans of the book into a frenzy of anticipation before the film's release on March 23, 2012, when many stood in line for midnight premieres. The film was as successful as producers had hoped, earning $155 million in its first three days—the third-highest-grossing opening in box office history.

Although many critics praised the film, especially Jennifer Lawrence's portrayal of Katniss, many also complained about choppy editing and shaky camera work; Amy Biancolli of the *San Francisco Chronicle* described the film's "nauseating reliance on wobbly-cam close-ups." Ironically for a film highlighting the control of society through manipulated media, these imperfections resulted from the filmmaker's very public desire to manipulate the rating of the film by the Motion Picture Association of America. As *Daily Variety* critic Justin Chang pointed out, "The PG-13 rating that ensures the film's suitability for its target audience also blunts the impact of the teen-on-teen bloodshed, most of it rendered in quick, oblique glimpses." Since excessive violence could lead to an R rating, which would bar young people under the age of seventeen from admittance without a guardian, Ross used unusual camera techniques to disguise and blur much of the violence that helped the book make its persuasive argument against war. In this way, he was able to make the film available to millions of young fans and thereby maximize profits.

sequels, *Catching Fire* (2009) and *Mockingjay* (2010). A number of parodies, tributes, and guides appeared, including The Hunger Games *Companion* (Lois H. Gresh [2011]), *The Unofficial* Hunger Games *Cookbook* (Emily Ansara Baines [2011]), and *The Hunger Pains: A Parody* (*Harvard Lampoon* [2012]). While science fiction and fantasy had been popular young-adult genres, the success of *The Hunger Games* trilogy led to the launching of dozens of dystopic novel series, including Veronica Roth's *Divergent* (2011), Dan Wells's *Partials* (2012), and Lissa Price's *Starters* (2012). Like *The Hunger Games,* many of these novels use the constraints of futuristic societies to explore human and societal limitations.

THEMES AND STYLE

Centered on themes of power, war, and personal morality, *The Hunger Games* tells the story of a citizenry stripped of rights and kept isolated, ignorant, and destitute. The powerful majority is both out of touch with and indifferent to the suffering of the majority. Collins is especially concerned with the response of the individual to enslavement, poverty, and the compulsory violence of warfare. Through the young tributes, especially Katniss and Peeta, the other tribute from District 12, she explores the boundaries of personal responsibility. "I keep wishing I could think of a way to … show the Capitol … that I'm more than just a piece in their Games," Peeta, the dreamer, says, and Katniss, the pragmatist, replies, "But you're not…. None of us are. That's how the Games work." Time after time, however, Katniss rises above her own hard-headed self-interest to help others and begins, almost unwillingly, to imagine a world free of the injustices that she has known throughout her life.

In creating a novel that would educate young people about the price of unquestioning obedience to authoritarianism, Collins reaches deep into classical archetypes, drawing heavily from the myth of Theseus, one of fourteen tributes sent by ancient Athens to Crete to be devoured by the Minotaur. Other classical influences include the histories of Spartacus, leader of a slave rebellion in Rome, and the gladiators, who battled wild animals and each other for the entertainment of the Roman elite. She weaves these familiar images into an allegory of modern injustice. Katniss was forced into early maturity when her father was killed and her mother retreated into grief, and her growth from cynical survivor to revolutionary leads from acceptance of injustice as inevitable ("We can't leave, so why bother talking about it?") to previously unimaginable awareness and defiance ("I want to do something … to shame them … to show the Capitol that whatever they do or force us to do there is a part of every tribute they can't own.").

Readers view the action through Katniss's remorselessly practical eyes, and her engaging narrative voice becomes their conscience. Evocative imagery builds tension and foreboding as she describes the peace she finds on her illicit hunting trips ("The woods became our savior, and each day I went a bit farther into its arms."), and the terror of the reaping ("The camera crews, perched like buzzards on rooftops, only add to the effect."). Savage irony highlights the contrast between the gritty reality of District 12 and the pampered decadence of the Capitol: "What do they do all day, these people in the Capitol, besides decorating their bodies and waiting around for a new shipment of tributes to roll in and die for their entertainment?"

CRITICAL DISCUSSION

Generally, critics have been as enthusiastic as readers in their reception of *The Hunger Games,* which became a *New York Times* Notable Book of 2008. The *Atlantic* called Katniss "the most important female character in recent pop culture history," and John Green, writing for the *New York Times Book Review,* praised the novel as "an exhilarating narrative and a future we can fear and believe in." The book's ethic of individual responsibility was able to bridge a wide range of politics.

Elizabeth Banks (left) and Jennifer Lawrence in a scene from the film adaptation of Suzanne Collins's *The Hunger Games.* © MURRAY CLOSE/©LIONSGATE/ COURTESY EVERETT COLLECTION.

James Delingpole from the conservative *Spectator* called it "an apologia for small government, free markets and personal freedom," while David Denby of the *New Yorker* saw it as "a menacing fable of capitalism, in which an ethos of competition increasingly yields winner-take-all victors." Another critic for the *New Yorker,* Laura Miller, defined the novel as "a feverdream allegory of the adolescent social experience," though Collins insisted that her novel was not about the personal traumas of adolescence but, rather, the deep social costs of war.

The widespread popularity of *The Hunger Games* trilogy seems to ensure the novels' place as classics, both in the genre of young adult literature and in the fiction of speculative social analysis. While many adolescent readers have been captivated by the more fleeting elements of romance and adventure, scholars have continued to examine the layers of symbolism and social critique, and much of this discussion acknowledges the powerfully persuasive nature of the text. In spite of its popularity, Collins's work remains controversial. In 2011 and 2012 the American Library Association's Office for Intellectual Freedom reported that *The Hunger Games* novels were among the books most frequently challenged by parents and teachers, who complained of violence, explicit sexuality, and anti-family rhetoric in the books.

Though *The Hunger Games* has primarily been viewed as part of an ephemeral aspect of popular culture, its persistent worldwide success has led scholars, philosophers, and sociologists to study it more deeply.

In addition to countless fansites and blogs, Collins's complex and nuanced examination of political, economic, and social trends has inspired the publication of more serious analyses, such as The Hunger Games *and Philosophy: A Critique of Pure Treason* in 2012. In the second and third novels in the trilogy, *Catching Fire* and *Mockingjay,* Collins continues to develop her critique of totalitarian manipulations of technology, genetics, and resources with a searching and ironic look at resistance movements and the limitations of vengeance.

BIBLIOGRAPHY

Sources

Biancolli, Amy. "Movie Is a Solid Adaptation of Collins' Dystopian Books." *San Francisco Chronicle.* 22 Mar. 2012. Web. 03 Aug. 2012.

Chang, Justin. "The Hunger Games." *Daily Variety* 19 Mar. 2012: 2+. *General Reference Center GOLD.* Web. 3 Aug. 2012.

———. "'Games' Plays It Safe." *Variety* 26 Mar. 2012: 15+. *General Reference Center GOLD.* Web. 1 Aug. 2012.

Collins, Suzanne. Interview. *Journal of Adolescent & Adult Literacy* 52.8 (2009): 726+. *Literature Resource Center.* Web. 13 July 2012.

Delingpole, James. "A Gorefest in Which Everyone Dies Horribly: Here's My Book Recommendation for Kids." *Spectator* 11 Feb. 2012: 26. *Literature Resource Center.* Web. 9 Aug. 2012.

Denby, David. "Kids at Risk." *New Yorker* 2 Apr. 2012: 68. *Literature Resource Center.* Web. 13 July 2012.

Dominus, Susan. "I Write about War. For Adolescents" *New York Times Magazine* 10 Apr. 2011: 30(L). *General Reference Center GOLD.* Web. 13 July 2012.

Green, John. "Scary New World." *New York Times Book Review* 9 Nov. 2008: 30(L). *Literature Resource Center.* Web. 10 July 2012.

Further Reading

Blair, Kelly. The Hunger Games: *An Apocalyptic Future.* Kelly Blair, n.d. *Google Sites.* Web. 7 July 2012.

Carpenter, Caroline. *Guide to* The Hunger Games. Medford: Plexus, 2012. Print.

Chandler, Ashley. "Room on the Bookshelf for Contemporary Tragedy." *National Association of Scholars.* National Association of Scholars, 3 Apr. 2012. Web. 17 July 2012.

Dunn, George A., and Nicolas Michaud, eds. *The Hunger Games and Philosophy: A Critique of Pure Treason.* Hoboken: John Wiley & Sons, 2012. Print.

Podhoretz, John. "Slaughterhouse One: A Gripping Grand Guignol for Girls." *Weekly Standard.* 9 Apr. 2012. *General Reference Center GOLD.* Web. 17 July 2012.

Media Adaptation

The Hunger Games. Dir. Gary Ross. Perf. Jennifer Lawrence, Josh Hutcherson, and Liam Hemsworth. Lionsgate, 2012. Film.

Tina Gianoulis

I, ROBOT

Isaac Asimov

OVERVIEW

Published in 1950, the short story collection *I, Robot* is the first of many works by American science fiction writer Isaac Asimov that explores the relationship between humans and their technological creations. The nine stories, which first appeared separately between 1940 and 1950 in the periodicals *Super Science Stories* and *Astounding Science Fiction,* are presented in the collection as the reminiscences of pioneering robopsychologist Dr. Susan Calvin. Beginning with "Robbie," set in 1996, and ending with "The Evitable Conflict," set in 2052, the *I, Robot* stories outline the development of sophisticated mechanical beings and the complex and unexpected technical, ethical, and existential issues they raise.

Rising out of enormous technological advances that began during the Industrial Revolution, the idea of creating artificial life has fascinated writers and social analysts since the publication of Mary Shelley's *Frankenstein* in 1818. Asimov's *I, Robot* is in some ways a direct response to Shelley's concerns about scientific hubris and its potentially disastrous consequences. His work shined a much more hopeful light on technology, which by the mid-twentieth century was widely viewed as a benevolent means of improving the quality of life. Asimov's early robot stories became an influential part of a new genre of confident and optimistic science fiction.

HISTORICAL AND LITERARY CONTEXT

The vision that unites the *I, Robot* stories developed during an era that glorified modernity and welcomed industrial advancement as the road to a prosperous future, values that greatly influenced the young Asimov. The 1933 Chicago Century of Progress World's Fair articulated the human role in this future with its motto "Science Finds—Industry Applies—Man Conforms." From 1935 through 1943, the government's Works Progress Administration sponsored a number of modern engineering projects that boosted employment, strengthened the economy, and further enhanced the public perception of industrial progress as a societal benefit.

By the 1950s, when Asimov's robot stories were re-released in the *I, Robot* collection, technological advances were both hailed as modern miracles and feared as the unleashing of incomprehensible and uncontrollable forces. Inventions such as televisions and dishwashers brought a benign form of science into the modern home. However, the enormously destructive power of the atomic bomb, perfected in the United States and employed against Japan in World War II, led to a pervasive uneasiness. Asimov's stories, though possessing a certain eeriness in their science fiction setting, worked to counter this fear by presenting robots, the representatives of technology, as useful, consistent, and dependable machines that generally had more to fear from irrational humans than the reverse.

Shelley's *Frankenstein* introduced the idea of scientifically created life, but it was the Czech writer Karel Čapek who coined the word *robot* (from the Czech *robota,* meaning "compulsory labor") to describe such manufactured beings. Čapek's 1920 play *R.U.R. (Rossum's Universal Robots)* is an early exploration of the social implications of technology, and, like Shelley's monster, his robots are dissatisfied, unpredictable, and dangerous. The years between 1937 and 1950 are generally considered the "golden age" of science fiction, when pulp fantasy-adventure stories, such as *A Princess of Mars* (1912), by Edgar Rice Burroughs, were supplanted by more scientifically based tales focused on problem solving and engineering. John W. Campbell, Jr., editor of *Astounding Science Fiction* from 1937 to 1971, was influential in developing the genre, and writers such as Ray Bradbury and Arthur C. Clarke became, along with Asimov, its pioneers. One of the most direct influences on Asimov's concept of the robot was Neil R. Jones, who created a race of helpful, intelligent cyborgs in his 1931 story "The Jameson Satellite." Jack Williamson's 1947 novella "With Folded Hands …" counters Asimov's positive message about technology with a cautionary tale about robots whose assurance that they know best leads them to take control of society.

I, Robot has continued to be considered a visionary work of future fiction. Asimov himself wrote four more volumes of stories exploring the potential and the conundrums of robots: *The Rest of the Robots* (1964), *The Complete Robot* (1982), *Robot Dreams* (1986), and *Robot Visions* (1990). His original thinking has inspired generations of science fiction writers, including Charles Stross and Cory Doctorow, whose 2007 collection *Overclocked: Stories of the Future Present*

Time Period:
Mid-20th Century

Genre:
Novel

Events:
Rapid technological innovation; nuclear proliferation; World War II

Nationality:
American

"YES, MASTER": ROBOTS AND SLAVERY

Ever since Karel Čapek created the word *robot* from the Czech *robota,* meaning "forced servitude," and *robotnik,* meaning "serf," writers have used the metaphor of mechanical beings to explore the ethical problems and social costs of the institution of slavery. Robots, created to perform the difficult, unpleasant, or dangerous work that humans would prefer not to do, are machines, and by definition supposed to be outside the normal consideration due to living beings. Unlike the real robots constructed to perform factory assembly work or the Roombas that scuttle about vacuuming floors, fictional robots are built to look like humans and designed to interact as humanly as possible with the people they serve. A robot therefore becomes what Wanda Raiford calls the "intimate other," who, like slaves and other servants, lives almost invisibly in the midst of society while never actually being allowed to become part of it.

Thomas Disch argues that "deep down we do not believe in the humanity of those whose labor we exploit." Debates about slavery have often revolved around the question of whether enslaved people were actually human in the same way their masters were. In the same way, one of the most commonly recurring themes in robot science fiction involves tests, debates, and trials to establish the presence or absence of human consciousness or emotion in mechanical beings.

contains stories titled "I, Robot" and "I, Row-Boat." Asimov's stories have even had an effect on real science, inspiring innovators to pursue the creation of humanoid robots.

THEMES AND STYLE

The *I, Robot* stories are anchored and unified by themes of human ambivalence toward scientific advancement. This ambivalence is exemplified in Asimov's iconic Three Laws of Robotics: "1. A robot may not injure a human being or, through inaction, allow a human being to come to harm. 2. A robot must obey orders given it by human beings except where such orders would conflict with the First Law. 3. A robot must protect its own existence as long as such protection does not conflict with the First or Second Law." Each story explores contradictions and unforeseen interpretations of the three laws, which are programmed into every robot manufactured in Asimov's hypothetical future. As Susan Calvin states in "Evidence," the laws represent "the essential guiding principles of a good many of the world's ethical systems." Thus the robot, and by extrapolation all technology, can be designed to be "decent" and good. Problems arise when the robot must interact with the inconsistencies of humankind, such as in "Liar!", a story in which a mind-reading robot is driven insane when it is forced to understand that it cannot avoid hurting the humans who ask it questions about the thoughts of others.

Asimov uses this kind of paradox repeatedly in the *I, Robot* stories. The machines are always given human names—RB becomes Robbie and QT-1 becomes Cutie. Robbie is an early-model robot, mutely devoted to the little girl placed in its care but terrifying to her mother all the same. Cutie refuses to believe what humans tell it about the universe, instead inventing its own religion to explain its perceptions, but still doggedly working to prevent harm to humans, following the First Law as if its own god had commanded it. Each paradox is resolved with a comic or ironic twist, as Asimov drives home the point that scientific laws remain immutable in the face of human perplexity. Though Cutie pronounces it a "self-evident proposition that no being can create another being superior to itself," by the final story the machines have taken over the administration of society and are clearly superior. As Calvin says, "How do we know what the ultimate good of Humanity will entail? ... Only the Machines know, and they are going there and taking us with them." It is this tension between human judgment and scientific objectivity that creates the drama of *I, Robot.*

Much more a purveyor of ideas than a literary stylist, Asimov's language is economical and colloquial. Except for Calvin, whose "mask-like expression" and "cold enthusiasm" identify her with the robots she studies, the humans are defined by sloppy emotion and erratic impulse. Greg Powell and Mike Donovan, robotic engineers who appear in several stories, refer to a robot they are studying as a "do-jigger," and a frustrated Donovan threatens, "I'll knock that chromium cranium right off its torso." Contrasting with the humans' impatience and shallow prejudice is the robots' equanimity. They are unfailingly friendly and engagingly informal, using words such as *swell* and *gosh* as if they are trying to put their human masters at ease.

CRITICAL DISCUSSION

Perhaps because of their focus on the hopeful side of technology, Asimov's robot stories were popular and quickly became classics of the science fiction genre. Though the first story of the anthology, "Robbie," was rejected by both *Astounding Science Fiction* and *Amazing Stories,* it was published in 1940 under the title "Strange Playfellows" by *Super Science Stories* editor Frederik Pohl, who recognized the potential in the robot stories Asimov called "engineer oriented science fiction." When the collection *I, Robot* was released in 1950, the *New York Times* called it an "exciting space thriller ... for those whose nerves are not already made raw by the potentialities of the atomic age." The book was reprinted in 1951 and remained in print almost continually into the twenty-first century.

As technological advances have brought many of his futuristic fictions to life, Asimov is still viewed as a visionary not only in science fiction literature but also in the field of science itself. Cory Doctorow described the legacy of the robot stories: "What makes Asimov's robots stand out, even today, is the resiliency of his imagination. Despite the complete failure of anything like a thinking robot to appear on the scene, the vision endures." Although Asimov's humanoid robots remain creatures of fantasy, his ideas have left their stamp on modern technology. Named in honor of the fictitious corporation in *I, Robot,* the real-world company USRobotics manufactures computer communication equipment, and a company called iRobot markets an automatic floor cleaner. A 2004 Alex Proyas film titled *I, Robot* acknowledges Asimov's work as its inspiration but compromises the author's vision by recreating the "rebellious robot" stereotype Asimov worked to counter.

The intricacies and conundrums that fill the stories in *I, Robot* continue to fascinate scholars. William Touponce calls the collection "one of the most influential books in the history of modern science fiction because it established new conventions for writing robot stories." Donald Hassler explores Asimov's own doubts about the conflict between humanity and technology, arguing that the end of the book's final story indicates Asimov's ambivalence. As Susan Calvin makes the pronouncement, "Think, that for all time, all conflicts are finally evitable. Only the Machines, from now on, are inevitable," the fire in the room dies out. As Hassler interprets, "The archetypal image of the dying fire conveys a sense of irretrievable loss, of something ending forever…. The ending, then, is, appropriately, dark and cold."

Drawing of the author Isaac Asimov. © PRISMA ARCHIVO/ALAMY.

BIBLIOGRAPHY

Sources

Asimov, Isaac. "The History of Science Fiction after 1938: A Lecture." *Digital Media Zone.* Digital Media Zone, 2001–02. Web. 23 Aug. 2012.

———. *I, Robot.* New York: Bantam-Dell, 2004. Print.

Beauchamp, Gorman. "The Frankenstein Complex and Asimov's Robots." *Mosaic* 13.3–4 (1980): 83–94. Rpt. in *Contemporary Literary Criticism.* Ed. Brigham Narins and Debbie Stanley. Detroit: Gale Research, 1996. *Literature Resource Center.* Web. 2 Aug. 2012.

Doctorow, Cory. "Rise of the Machines." *Wired.* Condé Nast, July 2004. Web. 4 Aug. 2012.

Gunn, James. *Isaac Asimov: The Foundations of Science Fiction.* Oxford: Scarecrow, 2005. Print.

Hassler, Donald M. "Some Asimov Resonances from the Enlightenment." *Science Fiction Studies* 15.44 (1988): 36–47. Rpt. in *Contemporary Literary Criticism.* Ed. Brigham Narins and Debbie Stanley. Detroit: Gale Research, 1996. *Literature Resource Center.* Web. 3 Aug. 2012.

Raiford, Wanda. "Race, Robots, and the Law." *New Boundaries in Political Science Fiction.* Ed. Donald M. Hassler and Clyde Wilcox. Columbia: U of South Carolina P, 2008. 93–112. Rpt. in *Short Story Criticism.* Vol. 148. Ed. Jelena O. Krstovic. Detroit: Gale, 2011. *Literature Resource Center.* Web. 2 Aug. 2012.

"Realm of the Spacemen." *New York Times Book Review* 4 Feb. 1951: 16. *ProQuest Historical Newspapers.* Web. 7 Aug. 2012.

Touponce, William F. "The Robot Stories." *Isaac Asimov.* Boston: Twayne, 1991. 32–43. Rpt. in *Short Story Criticism.* Vol. 73. Ed. Joseph Palmisano. Detroit: Gale, 2005. *Literature Resource Center.* Web. 3 Aug. 2012.

Further Reading

Asimov, Isaac. "The Machine and the Robot." *Science Fiction: Contemporary Mythology.* Ed. Patricia Warrick, Martin Harry Greenberg, and Joseph Olander. New York: Harper, 1978. 244–53. Print.

Clareson, Thomas D., ed. *Many Futures, Many Worlds: Themes and Form in Science Fiction.* Kent: Kent State UP, 1977. Print.

Disch, Thomas. *The Dreams Our Stuff Is Made Of: How Science Fiction Conquered the World.* New York: Simon, 1998. Print.

Jones, Neil R. *The Jameson Satellite*. North Hollywood: Aegypan, 2011.

Munteanu, Nina. "Unexpected Protocol: A Critique of the *I, Robot* Book and Motion Picture." *Strange Horizons* 14 Feb. 2005. Web. 7 Aug. 2012.

Pursell, Carroll. *The Machine in America: A Social History of Technology.* Baltimore: Johns Hopkins UP, 2007. Print.

White, Michael. *Isaac Asimov: A Life of the Grand Master of Science Fiction.* New York: Carroll, 1994. Print.

Williamson, Jack. *With Folded Hands … And Searching Mind: The Collected Stories of Jack Williamson, Volume Seven.* Royal Oak: Haffner, 2010. Print.

Media Adaptation

I, Robot. Dir. Alex Proyas. Perf. Will Smith, Bridget Moynahan, and Bruce Greenwood. Twentieth Century Fox Film Corporation, 2004. Film.

Tina Gianoulis

IN THE COUNTRY OF MEN

Hisham Matar

OVERVIEW

Hisham Matar, now one of Libya's most acclaimed authors of fiction, first gained prominence with his 2006 English-language novel *In the Country of Men,* in which he offers a glimpse into the political turmoil and repression in Libya in the late 1970s. The story is told from the perspective of a character named Suleiman, who is now an adult living in exile in Cairo and is looking back on his experiences as a nine-year-old boy in Libya. Through Suleiman, Matar brings to light diverse forms of repression and their impact on the social and cultural fabric of Libya. Suleiman, whose memories Matar masterfully renders both innocent and naïve, makes lyrical observations on the intrigue surrounding his father's involvement in the political opposition, as well as on the complex relationships within his family. The brutal and totalitarian regime of "The Leader," Muammar al-Qaddafi, casually engages in coercion, manipulation, torture, and even public hangings in attempt to curb the influence of the opposition to which Suleiman's father and his like-minded friends belong. As the opposition struggles to realize its ambitions, the reader is increasingly transported into a dystopian world of uncertainty and fear.

In the Country of Men, Matar's debut novel, received praise and acclaim from the literary community, winning numerous awards and making the shortlist for the 2006 Man Booker Prize. Few Libyan authors, with the notable exception of Ibrahim al-Koni, have received such great international recognition. At the most basic level, the significance of Matar's novel lies in its sharp critique of al-Qaddafi's rule in Libya. However, Matar tells a tale of more universal proportions, in which the insidious effects of totalitarianism and repression are cleverly mapped into the consciousness and experiences of Suleiman and his relationships with his parents and friends.

HISTORICAL AND LITERARY CONTEXT

After Libya gained independence from European powers in 1951, a monarchy ruled for nearly twenty years until al-Qaddafi led a coup that overthrew King Idris and declared Libya an Arab Republic. Al-Qaddafi's government initially functioned through the Revolutionary Command Council (RCC), of which he was chairman. In 1977 he abolished the RCC, proclaiming Libya the "Great Socialist People's Libyan Arab Jamahiriyya" and designating himself "The Leader" or "The Guide." Power was to be transferred from the RCC to the masses through a system of local councils called Basic People's Congresses. While this may have appeared to be a democratic reform, al-Qaddafi actually reinforced his totalitarian authority through the web of councils or congresses that allowed deeper state access to local communities. Furthermore, like many other totalitarian leaders, he employed large numbers of informants and engaged in invasive surveillance of Libyans citizens without any substantial judicial checks to his rule.

In the Country of Men takes place in 1979 and portrays a period of Libyan history characterized by the repressive policies of al-Qaddafi's regime. Despite pervasive monitoring and surveillance, Libyans formed opposition groups that brought segments of the middle class frustrated with al-Qaddafi's economic policies together with intellectuals, students, and Islamists who objected to the tyranny of his totalitarian rule. Matar's novel brings into relief the harsh and menacing methods with which the al-Qaddafi regime responded to these dissident groups. More specifically, it shows how the regime used its informants to infiltrate and manipulate the ranks of the opposition, at the cost of human life and dignity.

Arabic literature abounds with critiques—both direct and figurative—of repressive state regimes, yet during the harshest years of al-Qaddafi's rule, few novels of this type emerged from Libya. The 1970s and 1980s were characterized from literary and political perspectives by restrictions on freedom of expression. Not only were authors worried about the severe consequences they might face should they compose literature criticizing the regime, but al-Qaddafi also nationalized newspapers and publishing houses in order to control the dissemination of information and ensure it wholeheartedly supported his national project. Some authors, such as Muhammad Shaltami, wrote poetry against the regime and were jailed or exiled as a result. Others couched their stories in alternative realities or deeply allegorical tales in order to mask any political connotations.

Matar wrote his book during a period in the 2000s when al-Qaddafi's Libya began to normalize international relations, resulting in a more culturally, politically, and economically open state. In this somewhat

⁘ *Key Facts*

Time Period:
Early 21st Century

Genre:
Novel

Events:
Political repression under regime of Muammar al-Qaddafi

Nationality:
Libyan

Children playing in Tripoli, Libya, near a rocket shell in 2011. Hisham Matar's 2006 novel *In the Country of Men* features Libyan children in the midst of danger. LEON NEAL/AFP/ GETTY IMAGES.

more permissive literary environment, other authors, such as Mohammed al-Asfar, began writing poetry and novels that bear more powerful, if still indirect, critiques of al-Qaddafi's totalitarian rule. Matar himself translated some of these works into English. It is difficult to determine the precise role of *In the Country of Men* in changing the literary climate in Libya prior to the 2011 revolution, as the book was never published there. Today, however, he continues to play an important role in development of the Libyan novel.

THEMES AND STYLE

The trauma, fear, and uncertainty engendered by state repression figure prominently throughout *In the Country of Men*. The narrator, the young Suleiman, tells of his daily life under the oppressive and omnipresent heat of the Libyan sun, arguably a recurring symbol of the all-consuming nature of state surveillance. Suleiman struggles to understand what is happening around him, as the insidious state apparatus increasingly seeps into the lives of his father, neighbors, and friends. State collaborators raid their house, searching for Suleiman's father, after which Suleiman's mother and friends burn all his books to hide his ties to the opposition. When his friend's father, Ustadh Rashid, an intellectual, is captured by the state and subjected to a public hanging for his involvement in the opposition, fear and suspicion spread through Suleiman's family and community. Suleiman, with all the innocence of youth, cannot grasp the impending danger surrounding him. Ultimately, he gives up the secret location of his father, who in turn provides information

to the state in order to save his own life. The circulation of information—or, more precisely, the tension between loyalty to and betrayal of the opposition—is of utmost importance to their survival and a central theme in the novel. The state's tactics of manipulation succeed in pitting members of the opposition against each other and collecting the necessary information to dismantle the movement.

Matar's choice to tell the story through Suleiman's memories of his youth enhances the complexities of loyalty, betrayal, fear, alienation, and uncertainty. Young Suleiman is caught amid various conflicting emotions and motivations. He reveres his father yet deeply resents the fact that his mother was forced to marry him; he supports his family and friends who are involved in the opposition yet exposes them and admires the power and prestige of the state and "The Leader." Not only do the contradictions in Suleiman's voice reflect the confusion of youth, but they also more abstractly represent the state manipulation that renders its citizens' children caught in a cycle of fear, disorientation, and ultimately betrayal. What is true, what is fabricated, and what matters and why are all questions shrouded in ambiguity for Suleiman, who—like the reader—is left with many questions unanswered and with a nagging feeling of uncertainty and self-doubt.

Matar lyrically captures Suleiman's perspective by weaving his meandering thoughts with the realities of his family life in a society enveloped by totalitarian surveillance. His concise style manages to be poignant while refraining from the excesses of flowery language. For example, he writes, "I suffer an absence, an ever-present absence, like an orphan not entirely certain of what he has missed or gained through his unchosen loss. I am both repulsed and surprised, for example, by my exaggerated sentiment when parting with people I am not intimate with, promising impossible reunions." By emphasizing the human and interpersonal aspects of Suleiman's community, Matar avoids a didactic explication of al-Qaddafi's tyranny. Instead, the reader experiences the effects of repression and propaganda on a more nuanced level, mapped onto Suleiman's tenuous family relations.

CRITICAL DISCUSSION

Matar's work received immediate critical acclaim after its publication in 2006. Many major newspapers reviewed the novel, praising Matar's command of language and powerful imagery in addition to his ability to convey the depth of his characters in the context of a country alien to many Western readers. His poetic style and attention to environment and perception were duly noted in a review by Ali Sethi in the *Nation*: "Sight, sound, smell—these are Suleiman's friends, his companions on his quest for meaning." In addition to examining its artistic accomplishments, scholars have approached *In the Country of Men* from perspectives such as dystopia, the child narrator, and the post-September 11 Arabic novel.

The work has been particularly influential with respect to dystopia. Lorraine Adams notes in the *New York Times Book Review* that the novel "brings to mind *1984*, *Fahrenheit 451*, and the other great science fiction of totalitarianism in the way it posits a cruelly simplified and nonsensical universe." The repressive policies and practices that Suleiman and his companions are exposed to constitute a particular kind of a dystopia, since the story is told from the perspective of a child unable to understand the magnitude of his perceptions. Reflecting on Suleiman's role, Margret Scanlan observes in the *Journal of Postcolonial Writing* that children's "youth engenders trust in their probable veracity as witnesses…. [They are] to an extent outsiders; minors without access to political power—hence

their feelings and thoughts are unlikely to be (as yet) ideologised."

In the post-September 11 literary world, some critics have applauded authors such as Matar for adding another dimension to the often negative and terrorist-centric portrayals of countries with which the West has less than favorable relations. In this sense, Scanlan considers the novel "a representation of the author's Libya in terms that engage the likely prejudice or ignorance of the English-language reader." *In the Country of Men* constitutes an important contribution to Libyan fiction in the way it critiques the political and social life in al-Qaddafi's Libya and brings texture to the way readers understand it.

BIBLIOGRAPHY

Sources

Adams, Lorraine. "The Dissident's Son." Rev. of *In the Country of Men,* by Hisham Matar. *New York Times Book Review* 4 March 2007. Print.

Gagiano, Annie. "*Ice-Candy-Man* and *In the Country of Men*: The Politics of Cruelty and the Witnessing Child." *Stellenbosch Papers in Linguistics* 39 (2011): 31. Print.

Scanlan, Margret. "Migrating from Terror: The Postcolonial Novel after September 11." *Journal of Postcolonial Writing* 46.3–4 (2010): 266–78. Print.

Sethi, Ali. "Careful, He Might Hear You." Rev. of *In the Country of Men,* by Hisham Matar. *Nation* 26 Feb. 2007: 30–33. Print.

Further Reading

Attar, Lina. "An Interview with Hisham Matar." *Jadaliyya.* Jadaliyya, 31 Oct. 2011. Web. 10 Sept. 2011.

Banipal: Magazine of Modern Arab Literature 40 (2011). Print.

Chorin, Ethan. *Translating Libya: The Modern Libyan Short Story.* London: Saqi, 2008. Print.

Matar, Hisham. *Anatomy of a Disappearance: A Novel.* New York: Dial, 2011. Print.

Shamsie, Kamila. "International Writing: Past, Present and Future Directions." *Wasafiri* 24.3 (2009):109–13. Print.

Greg Halaby

THE IRON HEEL

Jack London

OVERVIEW

Jack London's *The Iron Heel* (1908) is a dystopian novel that details the failure of a group of revolutionaries to overthrow a powerful oligarchy nicknamed the Iron Heel. Written as a found document, the novel is narrated by Avis Everhard, who relates the story of her husband, Ernest, a leader and hero of the revolution. To add authenticity to the manuscript, London frames the story using the words of fictional scholar Anthony Meredith, who discovers Everhard's writings and annotates them centuries after her death and the defeat of the oligarchy—which is eventually replaced by the Brotherhood of Man, a utopian society. Using the words of Avis and Ernest, London conveys his socialist ideas, his theories regarding the collapse of capitalism, and his fears of the rise of a corrupt ruling class.

In the years leading up to *The Iron Heel's* publication, the United States saw an increase in socialist party membership and in dissatisfaction among the American working class. The novel is significant because it reflects London's radical socialist views and the tenuous political climate of the early twentieth century. Despite the novel's success at embodying the voices of socialist sympathizers and the discontented proletariat—and at presaging many of the issues that led to both world wars—*The Iron Heel* was not initially read beyond socialist circles. Today scholars identify in the novel London's perspective on the problems inherent to a capitalist society: a wealthy class that gradually achieves a frightening level of power, increasingly poor conditions for laborers, questionable ethics in religious institutions, and the disappearance of freedom of speech.

HISTORICAL AND LITERARY CONTEXT

Decades before *The Iron Heel* was published, socialism had been established as a political ideology in the United States. Aimed at giving power to the proletariat, the Socialist Labor Party (SLP), established in 1877, brought Marxism to the American political landscape. By the beginning of the twentieth century, several events, in particular the 1905 revolution in Russia, renewed focus on the socialist cause and eventually culminated in World War I. At the same time, unions were forming across the United States, attempting to create better conditions for workers in industries such as steel and coal. As conditions continued to disintegrate, however, laborers began to strike and unions formed alliances with the SLP.

The Iron Heel reflects the anxiety about the ruling class that American workers were experiencing at the turn of the century. Socialist papers published stories of union riots, which contain many similarities to those described in London's novel. As tensions continued to rise, the radical Western Federation of Miners carried out the highly publicized assassination of former Idaho governor Frank Steunenberg in 1905. London's narrative captures both the emotion of the conflict between the working and ruling classes at the turn of the century and the real threat of violence that loomed over the country.

London's novel reads like propaganda because it closely follows the style of socialist literature of the period. Papers like the *Socialist Voice,* a weekly publication that appeared in London's home state of California from 1905 to 1907, related news stories about the effect of capitalism on organized religion that closely resemble events described in *The Iron Heel.* In looking for inspiration for the format of his work, London may have read the novels of H. G. Wells, whose *When the Sleeper Wakes* (1898–99) and *A Modern Utopia* (1905) are examples of utopian fiction. *When the Sleeper Wakes* features a plutocracy called the White Council, which controls the world in a dark future, much like London's oligarchy, whereas *A Modern Utopia* imagines a future where humanity can live in happiness and harmony, as under London's Brotherhood of Man, which eventually replaces the Iron Heel.

Although not the most widely read example of propaganda at the time, *The Iron Heel* anticipates the dystopian novels that followed throughout the twentieth century. Scholars have noted that such novels as Aldous Huxley's *Brave New World* (1932) and George Orwell's *1984* (1949) were influenced by *The Iron Heel.* These works share London's bleak vision of a future society controlled by a small but powerful government that tramples upon its citizens.

THEMES AND STYLE

At the core of *The Iron Heel* is the struggle of the working class against a wealthy ruling class blind to its own contemptible actions. London gives readers an often brutal look at the suffering beneath the Iron Heel's rule, particularly through stories of workers such as Jackson, a laborer who has lost his arm to a machine through no fault of his own. Avis is persuaded to fight the rise of the oligarchy when she hears of how, when Jackson sought damages in court, he lost to the "money-grabbing propensities" of the corporations and the lawyers paid to make sure workers like him received nothing. A working-class everyman, Jackson is loyal to the company, even through two union strikes, though he is never compensated for his allegiance. Rejected by the unions, who call him a scab, and with no other venue for employment, he and his family are left penniless. London, through examples of honest laborers like Jackson, portrays the innate cruelty of a capitalist society whose only concern is the bottom line.

London depicts the contrasts between capitalist ideology and socialist ideals through conversations between Ernest and the individuals he meets over the course of the novel. Although Avis narrates the story, her husband articulates much of the book's socialist ideology. In a conversation with Bishop Morehouse, Ernest explains that both the working man and the capitalist are "selfish," and as "there is only so much of the same thing," a class struggle is unavoidable. Meredith's notes reinforce Ernest's socialist ideas. He quotes British philosopher John Stuart Mill's *On Liberty*: "Wherever there is an ascendant class, a large portion of the morality emanates from its class interests and its class feelings of superiority." The novel's episodic chapters culminate in a violent struggle against the oligarchy, melodramatically punctuated by the end of Avis's manuscript, which "breaks off abruptly in the middle of a sentence," suggesting that she was interrupted as she wrote. The ending adds credibility to Avis's writing and highlights the sense of urgency that London believed accompanied the war between labor and capitalism.

The language of *The Iron Heel,* which is at times more philosophical than literary, captures the conversational style of intellectuals and political theorists of the period. Most of the characters, including Ernest and Avis, are educated and avoid using slang or colloquial language. Instead, they rely on formal English and often cite legal terms such as habeas corpus and "laissez-faire, the let-alone policy." Meredith's notes augment the formal, educational tone of the novel by explaining the story's historical value, such as in the designation of John Burns as a "great English labor leader," and by offering facts pertinent to the struggle of the working class.

CRITICAL DISCUSSION

Upon its publication, *The Iron Heel* garnered attention from socialist leaders; however, others dismissed it as merely a piece of sensationalist propaganda. It would take several years for the novel to gain momentum

JACK LONDON: GOLD RUSH ACTIVIST

Born John Griffith Chaney, Jack London, a California native, traveled to Canada as a young man during the Klondike gold rush. While there, he found inspiration for two of his most famous novels, *The Call of the Wild* (1903) and *White Fang* (1906). Both stories feature the untamed landscape of the Yukon and are often studied as nature literature. However, each contains themes common to London's other writings, such as harsh working conditions and the cruelty of humanity when money is at stake.

London was no stranger to hard labor and the working-class experience. Before he began his writing career, he worked in a cannery and as a sailor, experiences that he later channeled into novels. His 1904 book *The Sea-Wolf* draws upon his early life on the sea and also gives readers a glimpse into his socialist views. In the novel, the protagonist slowly grows into a hardened man after years of abuse as a laborer. Even in his adventure stories, London's view of the world is a grim one as outside forces conspire to destroy his protagonists' innocence. Later he would apply these ideas to the political realm, where he fought for labor rights.

outside of its socialist readership. In the decades following its publication, many critics wrote of London's uncanny ability to predict the events that would eventually lead to the world wars. In a letter to London's daughter, Russian socialist Leon Trotsky praises the novel for "the audacity and independence of its historical foresight." He writes, "The fact is incontestable: in 1907 Jack London already foresaw and described the fascist regime as the inevitable result of the defeat of the proletarian revolution."

More than a century after its publication, *The Iron Heel* is read as a piece of literary history that effectively captures the desire for social justice that had spread among the American laboring classes in the early twentieth century. However, the novel has lost literary credibility because of its status as a work of socialist propaganda. Part of the modern critique of London's work is that he never clearly defines his ideas of socialism; rather the novel presents what Steve Trott in a 2008 essay appearing in the *Socialist Standard* calls "a blend of conflicting theories." Many others who have read the novel as a treatise on socialism have found that London's war against capitalism is clearly presented but his ideas on socialism are muddled.

Scholars have rarely discussed *The Iron Heel* in isolation as a work of literature. Generally, they have examined the book in the context of the development of the utopian novel genre. For example, many have studied *The Iron Heel* in an effort to define the components of London's concept of utopia, especially as they

Brotherhood of Man as a utopia has interested scholars more than the Iron Heel as a dystopian government because the description of the brotherhood has provided a model for many subsequent utopian novels of the twentieth century.

BIBLIOGRAPHY

Sources

Baskett, Sam S. "A Source of *The Iron Heel*." *American Literature* 27.2 (1955): 268–70. *JSTOR*. Web. 10 June 2012.

"Jack London: What Life Means to Me." *Socialist Appeal* 28 July 2008. Web. 18 June 2012.

London, Jack. *Novels and Social Writings*: The People of the Abyss, The Road, The Iron Heel, Martin Eden, *and* John Barleycorn. New York: Library of America, 1982. Print.

Shor, Francis. "*The Iron Heel's* Marginal(ized) Utopia." *Extrapolation: A Journal of Science Fiction and Fantasy* 35.3 (1994): 211–29. *Academic Search Premier*. Web. 10 June 2012.

Trott, Steve. "Jack London's *The Iron Heel*." *Socialist Standard* Jan. 2008. Web. 18 June 2012.

Further Reading

Busch, Justin E. A. *The Utopian Vision of H. G. Wells.* Jefferson: McFarland, 2009. Print.

Claeys, Gregory. *The Cambridge Companion to Utopian Literature.* Cambridge: Cambridge UP, 2010. Print.

Granger, Ben. "Jack London: *The Iron Heel*." *Spike Magazine.* Spike Magazine, 1 Aug. 2006. Web. 18 June 2012.

London, Jack. *War of the Classes. Revolution. The Shrinking of the Planet.* New York: Mondial, 2006. Print.

Nuernberg, Susan M., ed. *The Critical Response to Jack London.* Westport: Greenwood P, 1995. Print.

Reesman, Jeanne Campbell. *Jack London's Radical Lives: A Critical Biography.* Athens: U of Georgia P, 2009. Print.

Media Adaptation

The Iron Heel. Dir. Vladimir Gardin. Perf. Olga Bonus, Anatoli Gorchilin, and Aleksandra Khokhlova. VFKO, 1919. Film.

Lisa Kroger

Author Jack London photographed in the early 1900s. JERRY TAVIN/ EVERETT COLLECTION.

relate to other utopian literary works by such writers as Orwell and Huxley. In a 1994 essay for *Extrapolation,* Francis Shor pays particular attention to the notes interspersed throughout *The Iron Heel* and reads them as a way to understand "London's perspective on utopian possibilities, especially those related to transcending the power and gender codes of the day." London's

LOOKING BACKWARD

2000–1887

Edward Bellamy

OVERVIEW

Looking Backward: 2000–1887 (1888) is a work of utopian fiction by Edward Bellamy that critiques capitalism and offers socialism as a possible solution to the problems plaguing industrial society. The novel chronicles the experiences of Julian West, who falls asleep in late nineteenth-century Boston and awakcns in the radically altered Boston of the year 2000 to discover that the corrupt world in which he fell asleep has been transformed into a socialist utopia. Through conversation with Doctor Leete, whom he befriends, West learns about the benefits of the future society in which industry is nationalized and people live with an increased sense of community. Bellamy claimed he did not write *Looking Backward* as an explicitly political novel or as a call to action; however, the influence of the book on public thinking and action was tremendous.

The novel instantly inspired legions of readers to form Nationalist Clubs that aimed to bring about the utopia Bellamy had described.

Looking Backward became an instant literary sensation upon publication, striking a chord with many who had reached adulthood amid the corruption and harsh working conditions of America's Gilded Age. By 1891 more than 160 Bellamy-inspired Nationalist Clubs had been formed in an attempt to bring about the utopia the book described. Ultimately, the novel launched Bellamy to literary fame and transformed him into one of America's most prominent advocates of social justice. Today the book is considered an important reflection of late nineteenth-century social thinking and is credited as an important early example of the utopian novel genre.

HISTORICAL AND LITERARY CONTEXT

Looking Backward was published during a time of tremendous economic expansion in America. Fueled by new technologies and increased production, industries grew, immigration increased, and the gap between the wealthy and the poor widened significantly. Factories, railroads, and mining boomed. With economic growth came episodes of recession, such as the Panic of 1873, as well as labor disputes and strikes, such as the Great Railroad Strike of 1877. Political corruption was also rampant. Large corporations formed trusts that

could control every aspect of production of a given product in order to maximize profits and prevent competitors from gaining a foothold in the marketplace. In response to these economic changes, labor unions became increasingly important and powerful.

Bellamy's utopian novel arrived at a time when large corporations, unions, and the government were all beginning to feel the strain of America's shifting economic landscape. The book helped give direction to Marxist and socialist thought, which was beginning to flourish as a counter to profit-driven capitalism. Unsurprisingly, Bellamy's novel, which portrayed a nation in which goods were distributed evenly and workers were treated fairly and lived comfortably, inspired people to take action. He would go on to participate in the political movement emerging around his book, founding his own magazine, the *New Nation,* in 1891 in order to promote action and dialogue among the numerous Nationalist Clubs spawned by the novel. More broadly, the novel influenced many intellectuals and was discussed in many of the most important Marxist publications of the day.

Looking Backward was written at a time when Marxist and socialist ideas were beginning to gain a foothold among American thinkers and writers concerned about the growth of American industry and the impact of industrial power on the average American's life and well-being. Bellamy, for his part, was hesitant to use the term *socialism* with regard to his own work, and he distanced himself from some of the fundamental tenets of Marxism. Most notably, he did not agree with Marx that religion dulled the masses, particularly their revolutionary sentiments. A deeply religious man, Bellamy instead found religion to be a valuable force for solidarity. Furthermore, while Marx saw revolutionary violence as inevitable, Bellamy believed that society would reorganize itself organically as it evolved, transcending systems that failed to meet the needs of the majority of its inhabitants.

Following the massive success of *Looking Backward,* Bellamy became more of a political figure. In *Equality* (1897), his sequel to *Looking Backward,* he clarifies and expands upon the ideas of the earlier novel, emphasizing the importance of education, women's rights, and other social issues. *Looking Backward's*

+ *Key Facts*

Time Period:
Late 19th Century

Genre:
Novel

Events:
American economic expansion; growing labor unrest; growth of Marxist and socialist thought

Nationality:
American

PRIMARY SOURCE

EXCERPT FROM *LOOKING BACKWARD: 2000–1887*

By way of attempting to give the reader some general impression of the way people lived together in those days, and especially of the relations of the rich and poor to one another, perhaps I cannot do better than to compare society as it then was to a prodigious coach which the masses of humanity were harnessed to and dragged toilsomely along a very hilly and sandy road. The driver was hunger, and permitted no lagging, though the pace was necessarily very slow. Despite the difficulty of drawing the coach at all along so hard a road, the top was covered with passengers who never got down, even at the steepest ascents. These seats on top were very breezy and comfortable. Well up out of the dust, their occupants could enjoy the scenery at their leisure, or critically discuss the merits of the straining team. Naturally such places were in great demand and the competition for them was keen, every one seeking as the first end in life to secure a seat on the coach for himself and to leave it to his child after him. By the rule of the coach a man could leave his seat to whom he wished, but on the other hand there were many accidents by which it might at any time be wholly lost. For all that they were so easy, the seats were very insecure, and at every sudden jolt of the coach persons were slipping out of them and falling to the ground, where they were instantly compelled to take hold of the rope and help to drag the coach on which they had before ridden so pleasantly. It was naturally regarded as a terrible misfortune to lose one's seat, and the apprehension that this might happen to them or their friends was a constant cloud upon the happiness of those who rode.

But did they think only of themselves? you ask. Was not their very luxury rendered intolerable to them by comparison with the lot of their brothers and sisters in the harness, and the knowledge that their own weight added to their toil? Had they no compassion for fellow beings from whom fortune only distinguished them? Oh, yes; commiseration was frequently expressed by those who rode for those who had to pull the coach, especially when the vehicle came to a bad place

tremendous success also spurred numerous parodies, satires, and even skeptical dystopian replies. Some notable examples include *Looking Further Forward: An Answer to "Looking Backward" by Edward Bellamy* (1890) by Richard C. Michaelis; *Looking Backward and What I Saw* (1890) by W. W. Satterlee; and *Looking Forward* (1906) by Harry W. Hillman. In 1890 British writer and socialist William Morris penned *News from Nowhere,* a novel similar in structure to *Looking Backward* but different in its vision of a socialist utopia. For Morris, the ideal society did not center on a state-controlled bureaucracy but rather functioned under libertarian principles. In addition to inspiring a back-and-forth argument in the form of novels that lasted well into the twentieth century, *Looking Backward* also shaped the work of political, social, and economic thinkers such as Thorstein Veblen, John Dewey, and William Allen White. Although Bellamy's novel is less well known today, its impact is evident in its profound effect on the writers and thinkers who followed the author at the turn of the century.

THEMES AND STYLE

Thematically central to *Looking Backward* is the idea that capitalism is inherently flawed, and that society will undergo positive transformation only when capitalism is discarded in favor of economic policies more in keeping with socialism. The novel's utopian vision centers on the notion that society should foster social stability, community, and prosperity by nationalizing industry and reorganizing the production and distribution of goods. Although Bellamy claims that his intention is simply to write a social and literary fantasy, the novel may be viewed as propaganda in its promotion of socialism (or at the very least socialistic practices) as the answer to society's problems. Furthermore, the vast and immediate response to the novel demonstrates its power as a persuasive document, regardless of the author's stated intentions.

Rhetorically, *Looking Backward* succeeds by convincing its readers of the desirability and possibility of a different way of living. Through Doctor Leete, both West and the reader are introduced to a world that is governed not by the perceived greed and self-interest of the Gilded Age but by a genuine sense of community. Labor is valued; all members of the society share in the profits of their work and are able to retire at the age of forty-five without worry. The community spirit is reflected in the popularity of public kitchens. Much of the novel is written as dialogue between Leete and West.

in the road, as it was constantly doing, or to a particularly steep hill. At such times, the desperate straining of the team, their agonized leaping and plunging under the pitiless lashing of hunger, the many who fainted at the rope and were trampled in the mire, made a very distressing spectacle, which often called forth highly creditable displays of feeling on the top of the coach. At such times the passengers would call down encouragingly to the toilers of the rope, exhorting them to patience, and holding out hopes of possible compensation in another world for the hardness of their lot, while others contributed to buy salves and liniments for the crippled and injured. It was agreed that it was a great pity that the coach should be so hard to pull, and there was a sense of general relief when the specially bad piece of road was gotten over. This relief was not, indeed, wholly on account of the team, for there was always some danger at these bad places of a general overturn in which all would lose their seats.

It must in truth be admitted that the main effect of the spectacle of the misery of the toilers at the rope was to enhance the passengers' sense of the value of their seats upon the coach, and to cause them to hold on to them more desperately than before. If the passengers could only have felt assured that neither they nor their friends would ever fall from the top, it is probable that, beyond contributing to the funds for liniments and bandages, they would have troubled themselves extremely little about those who dragged the coach.

I am well aware that this will appear to the men and women of the twentieth century an incredible inhumanity, but there are two facts, both very curious, which partly explain it. In the first place, it was firmly and sincerely believed that there was no other way in which Society could get along, except the many pulled at the rope and the few rode, and not only this, but that no very radical improvement even was possible, either in the harness, the coach, the roadway, or the distribution of the toil. It had always been as it was, and it always would be so. It was a pity, but it could not be helped, and philosophy forbade wasting compassion on what was beyond remedy.

Through these conversations, Leete helps West understand the transformation of nineteenth-century society into twenty-first-century utopia. These dialogues serve as a powerful rhetorical device, allowing Bellamy to express his ideas through the voices of the characters.

The language and tone of *Looking Backward* vary from the lyrical to the overtly political. Bellamy effectively and poetically writes an indictment of his own times:"My friends, if you would see men again the beasts of prey they seemed in the nineteenth century, all you have to do is to restore the old social and industrial system, which taught them to view their natural prey in their fellow men, and to find their gain in the loss of others." The use of poetic language becomes more common and the tone grows more ecstatic as the author describes the glories of the future."With a tear for the dark past, turn we then to the dazzling future, and, veiling our eyes, press forward. The long and weary winter of the race is ended. Its summer has begun. Humanity has burst the chrysalis. The heavens are before it." These passages illustrate Bellamy's ability to shape language and tone to his purpose—underscoring differences between the present and the possible future. He employs techniques that guide the

Edward Bellamy, author of *Looking Backward.*
© CORBIS.

BELLAMY'S MUSICAL TELEPHONE

More than a hundred years after its publication, *Looking Backward* continues to inspire the imaginations of readers and writers alike. In 1988 the one-hundred-year anniversary of the novel's publication was marked by the debut of a one-act play entitled *Bellamy's Musical Telephone* at Boston's Emerson College. Adapted from the novel by composer and songwriter Roger Lee Hall as part of the Bellamy Centennial Conference, the play takes its name from a device described in Chapter 11 of the novel that allows users to hear live performances from all around the city of Boston. Although the invention of the telephone predated Bellamy's novel, the radio had not yet been invented at the time of its writing. The musical telephone has therefore often been cited as an important example of Bellamy's ability to predict future developments in society and culture.

In writing *Bellamy's Musical Telephone*, Hall used some of the novel's original language, augmenting it with new dialogue between West and Dr. Leete. He also composed original music for the play, which he alternated with nineteenth-century music to underscore the cultural differences between West's past and his utopian future. The play's title was later changed to simply *The Musical Telephone* when a DVD version of the performance was released.

reader's sentiments; however, when his philosophies are presented, both his tone and the poetry of his language are muted in favor of more direct statements. For example, he writes that "buying and selling is essentially antisocial" and that "the nation guarantees the nurture, education, and comfortable maintenance of every citizen from the cradle to the grave." These simple, straightforward statements clearly lay out the author's thoughts for the reader. Such careful handling of language goes far in helping Bellamy's work achieve clarity and persuasiveness.

CRITICAL DISCUSSION

By the end of the nineteenth century, only Harriet Beecher Stowe's *Uncle Tom's Cabin* had sold more copies in America than Bellamy's *Looking Backward*. Early critical reviews of the novel were mixed. While, for example, the *Vermont Watchman* heralded the work as "a most excellent and clear exposition of socialism in all its bearings," a reviewer for the *Atlantic Monthly* complained that "the prime defect of Mr. Bellamy's argument for universal industrial organization is in its ignoring of human nature." Despite critical disagreements, the vast majority of readers responded positively to the novel, buying it in droves.

After the initial furor over the work died out and the popularity of Bellamy societies waned, *Looking Backward* lost some of its prominence. Over time, however, as readers began to note similarities between

the novel's predictions for the future and the social and economic developments of the twentieth century, the novel began to attract new interest. At the center of this critical renewal was Bellamy's seemingly uncanny prescience, a topic that continues to dominate scholarship of the novel.

Most contemporary criticism of *Looking Backward* focuses on Bellamy's ability to predict specific aspects of American commerce in the twentieth and twenty-first centuries. Literary historian Catherine Tumber notes in a 1999 essay for *American Literary History* that Bellamy "envisioned a postindustrial world where market integration has reached completion, administration has replaced politics, the last vestiges of patriarchy have disappeared, and mass consumer culture reigns." Directly referencing specific innovations, states, "Bellamy pictured a mass consumer economy, where goods are purchased with credit cards and delivered from massive warehouses directly to the privacy of one's home." Writing in *American Literary History*, scholar Jonathan Auerbach (1994) summarizes the prophetic nature of *Looking Backward*, noting that Bellamy's strengths were in "anticipating certain central tendencies of advanced capitalism: the increasing division between ownership of capital and its control by bureaucratic administration; the shift from blue collar to professional and service-oriented jobs; and the growth of the welfare state, with the centralized state regulating and redirecting economic resources." Although Bellamy did not accurately predict the rise of a socialist utopia, critical consensus seems to be that, in attempting to dream up a fictional world better than the highly stratified world of the late nineteenth century, Bellamy managed to anticipate many of the economic and social trends and advances of today.

BIBLIOGRAPHY

Sources

Auerbach, Jonathan. "'The Nation Organized': Utopian Impotence in Edward Bellamy's *Looking Backward.*" *American Literary History* 6.1 (1994): 24–47. *JSTOR.* Web. 28 June 2012.

Bellamy, Edward. *Looking Backward: 2000–1887.* Boston: Ticknor, 1888. Print.

Rev. of *Looking Backward,* by Edward Bellamy. *Atlantic Monthly* 61.368 (1888): 845–48. Print.

Rev. of *Looking Backward,* by Edward Bellamy. *Vermont Watchman* 17 Dec. 1890: E. *19th Century U.S. Newspapers.* Web. 3 Oct. 2012.

Samuels, Warren J. "A Centenary Reconsideration of Bellamy's *Looking Backward.*" *American Journal of Economics and Sociology* 43.2 (1984): 129–48. *JSTOR.* Web. 28 June 2012.

Tumber, Catherine. "Edward Bellamy, the Erosion of Public Life, and the Gnostic Revival." *American Literary History* 11.4 (1999): 610–41. JSTOR. Web. 28 June 2012.

Further Reading

Bellamy, Edward. "How I Came to Write *Looking Backward.*" *Nationalist* 1.1 (1889): 1–4. *JSTOR.* Web. 28 June 2012.

Bowman, Sylvia E. *The Year 2000: A Critical Biography of Edward Bellamy.* New York: Bookman, 1958. Print.

Lipow, Arthur. *Authoritarian Socialism in America: Edward Bellamy and the Nationalist Movement.* Berkeley: U of California P, 1982. Print.

Morgan, Arthur E. *The Philosophy of Edward Bellamy.* Whitefish: Kessinger, 2008. Print.

Patai, Daphne, ed. *Looking Backward, 1988–1888: Essays on Edward Bellamy.* Amherst: U of Massachusetts P, 1988. Print.

Pfaelzer, Jean. *The Utopian Novel in America: 1886–1896: The Politics of Form.* Pittsburgh: U of Pittsburgh P, 1988. Print.

Shurter, Robert L. *The Utopian Novel in America: 1865–1900.* New York: AMS, 1975. Print.

Widdicombe, Richard Toby. *Edward Bellamy: An Annotated Bibliography of Secondary Criticism.* New York: Garland, 1988. Print.

Colby Cuppernull

NEWS FROM NOWHERE

William Morris

OVERVIEW

William Morris's 1890 novel, *News from Nowhere,* uses time travel to a utopian society to explore the possibilities of life after revolution. Written in the style and tradition of the utopian novel, the work follows narrator William Guest through strange adventures and conversations with the inhabitants of a twenty-first-century England where socialism has prevailed and has allowed all people to live in peace, plenty, and the pursuit of beautiful and self-chosen work. Guest's observations paint an attractive picture of postrevolution life, and his lengthy conversations with the inhabitants of this future world are a vehicle for Morris to address a number of common arguments against socialist policies and to advance his own collectivist beliefs. In the course of the narrative Morris provides an account of the revolution that led to the formation of his utopia, outlining a concrete plan of potential action for his readers to choose to follow.

News from Nowhere was an entry into a vital and multivocal late Victorian debate on the nature of socialism, revolution, and social justice. Responding to a number of other socialist utopian works, it develops ideas from Morris's nonfiction writing, dramatizing, in particular, a number of the principles he had previously laid out in his 1884 essay "Art and Socialism." The book was widely read upon publication, and it influenced the development of British socialism in the late nineteenth and early twentieth centuries. However, later critiques of the novel problematize its naive use of medieval nostalgia and its blanket opposition to technology, pointing to the reactionary undercurrents that run through this overtly progressive manifesto.

HISTORICAL AND LITERARY CONTEXT

Throughout the Victorian era, workers' rights and socialist movements were part of the English political landscape. Between 1838 and 1848, Chartism called for a number of reforms in the political condition of the working classes, including an appeal for universal male suffrage. In November 1847 the Congress of the Communist League in London commissioned Karl Marx and Frederick Engels to write what was to become the *Communist Manifesto,* first published in English in 1850. Marxist theory, drawing on Darwinism and social utopianism, advocated the end of what Marx called "alienated labor"—workers as cogs in a larger capitalist machine, unable to control their own actions or directly enjoy the products they worked to make. The influential Fabian Society, founded in 1884, was to lobby for a minimum wage. Morris himself found the Fabians' tactics of incremental change overly timid and instead insisted on the need for total social revolution to redress class inequality.

Class tensions came to a head November 13, 1887, in an event known as "Bloody Sunday." The Socialist League, headed by Morris, in conjunction with the Irish National League, had organized a demonstration that day in Trafalgar Square, which was located between the affluent West End of London and the more impoverished East End. About 10,000 marchers assembled there to protest the condition of the London poor, social stratification in Victorian England, and political coercion in Ireland. Riots occurred as a force of 2,000 police and 400 troops clashed with the protesters, leaving many injured and at least three dead. The riots had a profound effect on Morris, who wrote a song on the death of Alfred Linnell, who was killed in the struggle. Morris includes in *News from Nowhere* an account of the riots, which serve as a primary impetus for his fictional—and ultimately successful—socialist revolution.

In 1884 Morris was editor of the *Commonweal,* the official party organ of the Social Democratic Foundation, placing him at the center of the literary conversation about the impact and purpose of social revolution. Morris's *Commonweal* review of Edward Bellamy's 1887 socialist utopian novel, *Looking Backward,* reveals the ideological tensions in the community that influenced and structured Morris's work. In the 1889 review, he criticizes Bellamy's enthusiasm for machinery, arguing that the socialist ideal ought to be a return to an idyllic pastoralism rather than the continued proliferation and development of technology. *News from Nowhere* directly responds to this debate, portraying the pleasure and freedom that Morris located in escape from industrialized life.

Morris's socialist works remained influential into the early twentieth century. He was cited as an influence by George Bernard Shaw as well as H. G. Wells, who in 1895 published his futuristic critique of class division in the *Time Machine.* Morris impacted twentieth-century culture in a number of ways, including a literary influence on pastoral fantasists such as

C. S. Lewis and J. R. R. Tolkien and an aesthetic influence on modern architecture through the works of Frank Lloyd Wright, and the effect of his work has continued to be felt into the twenty-first-century through a revival of interest in these diverse influences.

THEMES AND STYLE

The main theme of *News from Nowhere* is revealed through the chronologically transplanted narrator's excited exploration of this utopian future. Morris underlines the benefits that he believes can be attained through socialism, which he describes in persuasively propagandistic fashion. The adventure begins when Morris falls asleep after a Socialist League meeting in which heated disagreements take place about the future that socialism should seek and Guest later wakes to find himself in a twenty-first-century version of England that has passed through socialist revolution and exists in a utopian condition of peace, rest, and universal prosperity. One character explains, "England was once a country of clearings amongst the woods and wastes, with a few towns interspersed … it then became a country of huge and foul workshops and fouler gambling-dens, surrounded by an ill-kept, poverty-stricken farm, pillaged by the masters of the workshops. It is now a garden, where nothing is wasted and nothing is spoilt." The narrator's delighted surprise at England's transformation is repeated through his new discoveries of change.

Like many utopias imagined by politically minded writers of the eighteenth century, much of *News from Nowhere* contains dialogues between its narrator and the people of the future: "'But what did you mean by easy-hard work?' said I. Quoth Dick: 'Did I say that? I mean work that tries the muscles and hardens them and sends you pleasantly weary to bed, but which isn't trying in other ways: doesn't harass you in short.'" This structure allows Morris to answer many objections commonly made against socialism and to expound on various effects of communitarian policy. Guest asks the people of Nowhere about their educational system (it is untraditional, relying on individual mentorship and self-education), their level of industrialization (they use few machines and are uninterested in mechanical development), and their ideas of gender (marriage no longer makes women the property of men, but Morris understands women's natural occupations to be homemaking and mothering, which he suggests should be more highly valued). Morris uses the multivocal quality of his novel to address a wider range of ideas than nonfiction would allow and to represent socialism as diverse rather than centralized. Longing for utopia paints a propagandistic portrait of socialist revolution as eminently desirable.

Morris's utopia emphasizes the importance of aesthetic pleasure, both in nature and in created objects, and *News from Nowhere* lovingly describes the appeal and tranquility of an unpolluted and beautifully decorated world. At the novel's close, as Guest fades back

THE MANY MEDIUMS OF WILLIAM MORRIS

In William Morris's (1834–1896) own words, "If a chap can't compose an epic poem while he's weaving tapestry, he had better shut up; he'll never do any good at all." Himself a painter, designer, architect, weaver, poet, novelist, demagogue, and editor, Morris refused to be constrained to any single medium. In 1858, his *Defence of Guenevere and Other Poems* was the first book of Pre-Raphaelite poetry ever published. Morris cofounded the decorative arts firm of Morris, Marshall, Faulkner & Co. in 1861, which worked with stained glass, carving, printed fabrics and papers, metalwork, and carpets. In 1869 and 1870 Morris translated and published editions of the ancient Icelandic works, including the *Saga of Gunnlaug Worm-Tongue, Grettis Saga,* and the *Story of the Volsungs and the Niblungs.* In 1877 Morris founded the Society for the Protection of Ancient Buildings. In 1891 he founded the Kelmscott Press, which published aesthetically designed books. Combined with his numerous novels and political activism, the total portrait of Morris that emerges is one of enormous and multiply directed energy. As George Bernard Shaw noted, what Morris could do when not "diverting himself with wall-decoration, epic story-telling, revolutionary journalism and oratory, fishing and other frivolities of genius" was extraordinary.

into his own time, his narration conveys a sense of loss as the reader, along with Guest, is cast out of utopia. The novel ends with a clear instruction in the closing words of Ellen, a young woman who travels with Guest: "Go back and be the happier for having seen us, for having added a little hope to your struggle." The two characters, each representing a personal historical moment, form an intense connection, which Morris emphasizes as essential to social development.

CRITICAL DISCUSSION

Although initial critical discussion of the book was both rare and muted, *News from Nowhere* was a popular success, selling about 8,000 copies in its first year. By 1898 it had been translated into French, German, and Italian. Morris's other works had garnered him a large Victorian readership. However, reactions to *News from Nowhere* by afficionados of Morris's art were varied. In his 1899 biography of Morris, J. W. Mackail dismissed it as a "slightly constructed and essentially insular romance." In contrast, in 1952 the communist historian A. L. Morton praised it as "the crown and climax of [Morris's] whole work." Early critics' responses seemed largely influenced by their support or lack thereof for Morris's political project and their understanding of what, exactly, his "work" was. Morris was a prolific creator of diverse works in multiple mediums, and his socialism, aestheticism, and medievalism compete for centrality in his literary and historical reputation.

Bust of English designer, artist, writer, and socialist William Morris by Conrad Dressler. The multitalented Morris created the design used in the background of this picture and wrote a number of works, including the utopian work of fiction *News from Nowhere*. BUST OF WILLIAM MORRIS (1834–96) BY CONRAD DRESSLER (1856–1940) (BRONZE), DRESSLER, CONRAD (1856–1940)/ © THE ART WORKERS' GUILD TRUSTEES LIMITED, LONDON, UK/THE BRIDGEMAN ART LIBRARY.

and noblesse oblige. Feminist criticism has addressed concepts of gender in Morris's work, censuring him for his essentialist views and linking his concepts of eroticism and sexuality with his overall interest in pleasure and positive sensation. *News from Nowhere* has been of great interest to "new historicist" critics, uniting as it does fiction, politics, and sociopolitical context.

BIBLIOGRAPHY

Sources

Lewis, Roger. "*News from Nowhere*: Utopia, Arcadia, or Elysium?" *Journal of Pre-Raphaelite Studies* 5 (1984): 55–67. Print.

Mackail, J. W. *The Life of William Morris.* London: Longmans, 1899. Print.

Morris, William. *News from Nowhere.* Ed. Stephen Arata. Peterborough, Ontario: Broadview Literary, 2002. Print.

Morton, A. L. *The English Utopia.* London: Lawrence & Wishart, 1952. Print.

Williams, Raymond. "Utopia and Science Fiction." *Science Fiction Studies.* DePauw University, Nov. 1978. Web. 12 July 2012.

Further Reading

Belsey, Andrew. "Getting Somewhere: Rhetoric and Politics in *News from Nowhere.*" *Textual Practice* 5.3 (1991): 337–51. Print.

Boos, Florence S., and William Boos. "*News from Nowhere* and Victorian Socialist-Feminism." *Nineteenth-Century Contexts* 14.1 (1990): 3–32. Print.

Buzard, James. "Ethnography as Interruption: Morris' *News from Nowhere.*" *Disorienting Fiction: The Autoethnographic Work of Nineteenth-Century British Novels.* Princeton: Princeton UP, 2005. Print.

Brantlinger, Patrick. "*News from Nowhere*: Morris's Socialist Anti-Novel." *Victorian Studies* 40.3 (1997): 445–74. Print.

Hale, Piers J. "Labor and the Human Relationship with Nature: The Naturalization of Politics in the Work of Thomas Henry Huxley, Herbert George Wells, and William Morris." *Journal of the History of Biology* 36.2 (2003), 249–84. Print.

Mineo, Ady. "Eros Unbound: Sexual Identities in *News from Nowhere.*" *The Journal of the William Morris Society* 9.4 (1992): 8–14. Print.

Thompson, E. P. *William Morris: Romantic to Revolutionary.* London: Merlin, 1977. Print.

Waithe, Marcus. "The Laws of Hospitality: Liberty, Generosity, and the Limits of Dissent in William Morris's *The Tables Turned* and *News from Nowhere.*" *The Yearbook of English Studies* 36.2 Victorian Literature (2006), 212–29. Print.

Carina Saxon

Twentieth-century readers have sometimes found *News from Nowhere* difficult and out of touch, particularly in its critique of technology and its wishful but illogical dismissal of human suffering and complexity. However, its imaginative content remains relevant to current fiction; Morris's pastoral and nostalgic aesthetic has been a key influence on fantasy fiction and other speculative media. Renewed twenty-first-century interest in utopia has brought the novel new readers; its Marxist socialism can also be placed in twenty-first-century conversations about labor, compensation, and class disparity, such as the 2011 Occupy movement.

Marxist literary criticism in the twentieth century has kept *News from Nowhere* under near-constant discussion. Much of the critical work on the novel since the 1970s has struggled to resolve, or at least explore, the contradictions of Morris's fantasy, which is both politically leftist and apparently reactionary. Raymond Williams argues in "Utopia and Science Fiction" that the energy and realism of Morris's description of how the socialist revolution came about are blunted by the pastoralized idyll he uses to indicate the perfect state of things post revolution. Similarly, Roger Lewis in an article for the *Journal of Pre-Raphaelite Studies* identifies Morris's socialist pastoralism with the more conservative pastoral fantasies common to Toryist romanticism, which hearken back to a golden age of feudalism

NINETEEN EIGHTY-FOUR

George Orwell

OVERVIEW

Nineteen Eighty-Four, published by George Orwell in 1949, depicts a dystopian future under a totalitarian government characterized by incessant surveillance, mind control, and perpetual war—all administered under the figurehead of "Big Brother." The protagonist, Winston Smith, works in the Ministry of Truth (Minitrue), a department dedicated to propaganda and historical revisionism, but he secretly loathes the Party, even attempting to keep a secret diary of his own thoughts, a crime punishable by death. Winston begins a covert affair with Julia, a co-worker, which simultaneously fuels his resentment of the Party and his fear of discovery. When they are ultimately betrayed by a seemingly sympathetic co-worker who is secretly a member of the Thought Police, Winston is tortured for months until he renounces Julia. His spirit broken, he is released. The last line of the novel, "He loved Big Brother," illustrates the complete efficacy of the regime's propaganda, which finally succeeds in controlling and eliminating even Winston's most private thoughts.

Nineteen Eighty-Four is variously considered a literary political novel, a satire, and a work of dystopian science fiction. Orwell wrote in 1946 that "every line of serious work that I have written since 1936 has been written, directly or indirectly, against totalitarianism and for democratic socialism." *Nineteen Eighty-Four* and Orwell's earlier satire *Animal Farm* (1945) both depict scenarios in which political revolutions are betrayed by a powerful and corrupt elite. Orwell was particularly concerned with how language influenced, supported, and manipulated political movements, a topic he discussed in a series of political essays and book reviews. *Nineteen Eighty-Four* ends with an appendix in the form of a scholarly analysis of "Newspeak," the term for Oceania's use of language for control and manipulation. Today *Nineteen Eighty-Four* continues to be considered relevant not only for its depiction of a totalitarian society but also for its prescient description of media manipulation, psychological torture, and surveillance as means of governmental control.

HISTORICAL AND LITERARY CONTEXT

The Spanish Civil War played the most important part in defining Orwell's socialism as well as his hatred of fascism and distrust of communism. Despite the bleak picture painted in *Nineteen Eighty-Four,* Orwell remained convinced of the possibility of a socialist revolution that would not become corrupted as, in his view, the revolution in the Soviet Union had become. In his 1941 essay "The Lion and the Unicorn: Socialism and the English Genius" Orwell wrote that "the war and the revolution are inseparable … the fact that we are at war has turned Socialism from a textbook word into a realizable policy," arguing that while the old British class system would prove insufficient to battle Nazi Germany, English socialism could still preserve the national character. "Ingsoc," the English socialism of *Nineteen Eighty-Four,* is a far more brutal and pessimistic vision of the future than Orwell described in his essays.

Nineteen Eighty-Four was heavily influenced by World War II and the early days of the Cold War. Although much of the novel most clearly alludes to Stalinist Russia, it also includes references to Nazi Germany and the threat of global nuclear war. Orwell began planning the novel in 1944, feeling pessimistic about the ability of Western democracies to respond adequately to fascism and disillusioned by the political rhetoric at the beginning of the Cold War. Physically unfit for military service, Orwell was employed during World War II by the BBC's Indian branch, producing material to boost the morale of Indian soldiers. This experience with governmental propaganda production may have served as an influence on his two best-known novels. *Nineteen Eighty-Four* is concerned not only with the political effects of life under a totalitarian regime but also the regime's psychological and personal effects. The original title, *The Last Man in Europe,* reflected Orwell's ideas about the dehumanizing effects of life in a fascist state.

Orwell was likely influenced by other dystopian works such as *Brave New World* by Aldous Huxley, *Darkness at Noon* by Arthur Koestler, and *We* by Yevgeny Zamyatin, which Orwell reviewed in 1946. *Nineteen Eighty-Four* also bears some similarity to H. G. Wells's work *When the Sleeper Wakes.* Wells was a childhood favorite of Orwell, although Orwell came to believe that Wells's confidence in science and rationality had become outmoded in the twentieth century. The geopolitical climate of *Nineteen Eighty-Four* also resembles the future described by American political theorist James Burnham in *The Managerial Revolution,*

✤ Key Facts

Time Period:
Mid-20th Century

Genre:
Novel

Events:
Spanish Civil War; World War II; Cold War

Nationality:
English

NINETEEN EIGHTY-FOUR AND BRAVE NEW WORLD

Although *Nineteen Eighty-Four* depicts a dystopian future based on fear, Aldous Huxley's 1932 novel *Brave New World* depicts a world in which social control is based around pleasure, creating a populace that is apathetic and easily manipulated. *Brave New World* critiques a youth-oriented, industrialized society preoccupied with homogeneity and consumption. Huxley used names that evoke the Russian Revolution but also made references to American and western European icons such as Henry Ford and Sigmund Freud, creating a "World State" that combined aspects of industrial capitalism, communism, fascism, psychoanalytic theory, and eugenics.

Brave New World, like *Nineteen Eighty-Four,* drew inspiration from the scientific utopias of H. G. Wells; Wells responded by saying "a writer of the standing of Aldous Huxley has no right to betray the future as he did in that book." Other critics at the time found Huxley's novel to be antiscientific, antiprogressive, or simply irrelevant in its concerns.

Today, however, *Brave New World* is critically praised and often read in conjunction with *Nineteen Eighty-Four* as an alternative vision of totalitarian control. Critic Neil Postman wrote: "What Orwell feared were those who would ban books. What Huxley feared was that there would be no reason to ban a book, for there would be no one who wanted to read one."

including the presence of "super-states" in perpetual conflict and a hierarchical society in which power is retained by a small elite.

One key literary aspect of *Nineteen Eighty-Four* is the emphasis of obfuscating language as a political tool that can exert psychological pressure and even torture upon citizens. Many of its terms, including "doublethink," "thoughtcrime," "Thought Police," and "Big Brother," have become part of the vernacular, as has the adjective "Orwellian," which refers to an attitude or a policy of control by propaganda, misinformation, denial of truth, and manipulation of the past.

THEMES AND STYLE

Censorship, surveillance, and historical revisionism are key themes in *Nineteen Eighty-Four.* Winston's job at Minitrue involves rewriting newspaper articles, in particular to remove any references to "unpersons." "People simply disappeared, always during the night. Your name was removed from the registers, every record of every thing you had ever done was wiped out, your one-time existence was denied and then forgotten. You were abolished, annihilated: vaporized was the usual word." The other governmental departments, the Ministry of Peace, the Ministry of Love, and the Ministry of Plenty, serve similar controlling functions. Minipax, the military branch, keeps Oceania at constant

war in order to ensure that citizens focus all their hatred onto foreign powers. Miniluv enforces loyalty to Big Brother through fear and torture and is the site of the dreaded Room 101. Miniplenty controls economic planning and rationing, keeping the populace in poverty while promoting images of prosperity. All four ministries are named ironically, which reiterates Orwell's concerns with language as a political tool, as do the three slogans of Oceania: "War is Peace. Freedom is Slavery. Ignorance is Strength." These illustrate the concept of doublethink. "To know and not to know, to be conscious of complete truthfulness while telling carefully-constructed lies, to hold simultaneously two opinions which cancelled out, knowing them to be contradictory and believing in both of them…. Even to understand the word 'doublethink' involved the use of doublethink."

Many of the themes and motifs in *Nineteen Eighty-Four* were drawn from practices of the Soviet Union. Winston Smith's job, "revising history," alludes to the Stalinist tradition of airbrushing images of "fallen" people from group photographs and removing references to them from books and newspapers. Likewise, the Junior Anti-Sex League, of which Julia is a member, is often thought to refer to the *komsomol,* the Young Communists, who were discouraged from forming romantic or social bonds that were seen as distracting from loyalty to the party. *Nineteen Eighty-Four* also expands on theories Orwell put forth in his 1945 essay "Notes on Nationalism," in which he discusses the different ways nations, political movements, and communities define themselves in opposition to others. The Party retains power through positive nationalism (the cult of Big Brother), negative nationalism (the daily "Hates" targeted a character known as Goldstein), and transferrable nationalism (in the shifting attitudes from Eurasia to East Asia.)

Orwell rejected the idea that political content could or should easily be divorced from art. In his essay "Why I Write," he described his work as both politically and aesthetically motivated, and he stated that his most artistically accomplished works derived from passionate political convictions. "I will only say that of late years I have tried to write less picturesquely and more exactly…. And looking back through my work, I see that it is invariably where I lacked a political purpose that I wrote lifeless books and was betrayed into purple passages, sentences without meaning, decorative adjectives and humbug generally." Critic Aaron Rosenfeld suggests that *Nineteen Eighty-Four* consciously rejects romantic novelistic conventions about character or plot resolution in order to underline the horror of the world he depicts and its complete destruction of the individual.

CRITICAL DISCUSSION

Nineteen Eighty-Four, following the immensely popular *Animal Farm,* was an immediate critical success and remains an influential and popular text today.

Orwell scholar John Rodden claims that *Nineteen Eighty-Four* and *Animal Farm* together have sold more copies than any two books by any other twentieth-century author. Mark Schorer, reviewing the novel in the *New York Times,* wrote, "it is probable that no other work of this generation has made us desire freedom more earnestly or loathe tyranny with such fulness." A few criticized the text as being unrealistic, exaggerated, or unnecessarily alarmist, but Orwell defended his work as satire and reaffirmed his commitment to socialist causes until his death in 1950. Although *Nineteen Eighty-Four* is widely considered a classic of twentieth-century literature and is widely taught in schools, it has also frequently been challenged or banned for its political and sexual content.

Nineteen Eighty-Four has been the subject of numerous adaptations for film, television, and radio and has been referenced in media ranging from pop music to video games to commercials. Rodden points out that at times Orwell's work has ironically been subject to the kinds of language manipulation he himself condemned, pointing out that in American editions of Orwell's works published in the 1950s, references to Orwell's socialism were omitted. As Rodden stated on the PBS radio program *Think Tank,* "If the book itself, *Animal Farm,* had left any doubt of the matter, Orwell dispelled it in his essay 'Why I Write': 'Every line of serious work that I've written since 1936 has been written directly or indirectly against Totalitarianism ….' Dot, dot, dot, dot, the politics of ellipsis. 'For democratic socialism' is vaporized, just like Winston Smith did it at the Ministry of Truth, and that's very much what happened [at the] beginning of the McCarthy era and just continued, Orwell being selectively quoted."

Nineteen Eighty-Four continues to be of interest to critics from a variety of disciplines: it has been analyzed in terms of its political content, its use and analysis of language, and its ongoing political and technological relevance. It has also been studied as a work of dystopian science fiction or alternative history. Orwell has repeatedly been studied and cited as an influence on a vast number of late twentieth-century authors, including Anthony Burgess, Ray Bradbury, Thomas Pynchon, and Margaret Atwood.

BIBLIOGRAPHY

Sources

Orwell, George. "Notes on Nationalism." *The Complete Works of George Orwell.* Web. 12 June 2012.

———. "Why I Write." *The Complete Works of George Orwell.* Web. 12 June 2012.

Rodden, John, ed. *The Cambridge Companion to George Orwell.* Cambridge, UK: Cambridge UP, 2007. Print.

Rosenfeld, Aaron S. "The 'Scanty Plot': Orwell, Pynchon, and the Poetics of Paranoia." *Twentieth Century Literature* 50.4 (Winter 2004): 337. Web. 12 June 2012.

A 2012 protest in Tallinn, Estonia, against the Anti-Counterfeiting Trade Agreement, a multinational treaty. Protesters hold a banner referencing George Orwell's *Nineteen Eighty-Four,* implying that the treaty is a step toward the totalitarian repression depicted in the novel. © SASHA STOWE/ALAMY.

Schorer, Mark. Rev. of *Nineteen Eighty-Four,* by George Orwell. *New York Times.* New York Times Company. 12 June 1949. Web. 2 Aug. 2012.

Think Tank with Ben Wattenberg. "Orwell's Century." Narr. John Rodden. PBS, n.d. Web. 20 June 2012. Transcript.

Further Reading

Bloom, Harold, ed. *George Orwell's "Nineteen Eighty-Four."* Philadelphia: Chelsea, 2004. Print.

Clarke, Ben. *Orwell in Context: Communities, Myths, Values.* Basingstoke, UK: Palgrave MacMillan, 2007. Print.

Gottlieb, Erika. *Dystopian Fiction East and West: Universe of Trial and Terror.* Kingston, ON: McGill-Queen's UP, 2001. Print.

Hitchens, Christopher. *Why Orwell Matters.* New York: Basic Books, 2003. Print.

Huxley, Aldous. *Brave New World.* New York: Harper Perennial, 1969. Print.

Marks, Peter. *George Orwell the Essayist: Literature, Politics and the Periodical Culture.* London: Continuum, 2012. Print.

Orwell, George. *All Art is Propaganda: Critical Essays.* New York: Mariner Books, 2009. Print.

———. *Animal Farm: A Fairy Story.* New York: Penguin Books, 2000. Print.

Rai, Alok. *Orwell and the Politics of Despair: A Critical Study of the Writings of George Orwell.* Cambridge, UK: Cambridge UP, 1988.

Sisk, David W. *Transformations of Language in Modern Dystopias.* Westport, CT: Praeger, 1997.

Media Adaptations

Nineteen Eighty-Four. British Broadcasting Corporation (BBC), 1954. TV Movie.

1984. Dir. Michael Radford. Perf. John Hurt, Richard Burton, and Suzanna Hamilton. Umbrella-Rosenblum Films Production, 1984. Film.

Marie Becker

THE SPACE MERCHANTS

Frederik Pohl, Cyril M. Kornbluth

OVERVIEW

The science fiction novel *The Space Merchants,* by Frederik Pohl and Cyril M. Kornbluth, is set in a dystopian future world ruled by corporations, with advertising as the key to political power. The work was originally serialized in *Galaxy Science Fiction* magazine as "Gravy Planet" in 1952; it was published in novel form as *The Space Merchants* the following year. Narrated in the first-person voice of Mitchell Courtenay, a star-class copywriter with the Fowler Schocken advertising agency, the short but impactful novel explores issues of consumerism, overpopulation, and pollution. Working on a campaign to promote emigration to Venus, Courtenay becomes embroiled in a shadowy conflict between the all-powerful cognoscenti and the hunted, conservationist "consies." In *The Space Merchants,* Pohl and Kornbluth warn against the potentially dangerous and world-changing power of information distribution and control, as well as the entanglement of government and commercial concerns.

Pohl began working for a Madison Avenue ad agency in 1946 as chief copywriter. In 1950 the freelance science fiction writer Kornbluth joined him in New York, and the two began their collaboration. After being rejected by a number of publishing houses, *The Space Merchants* was one of the first works published by the newly formed Ballantine Books. The novel received positive reviews and would become a key work in the tradition of dystopian science fiction. Although *The Space Merchants* is written in the extrapolative mode common to science fiction, its main function is as satirical as it is predictive, presenting a portrait of 1950s consumerism gone global.

HISTORICAL AND LITERARY CONTEXT

In the 1940s and 1950s, advancements in broadcast media were transforming the ways in which advertisers interacted with the American public. In 1952 networks were able to broadcast the Republican and Democratic national conventions live from Chicago, Illinois, introducing television as a powerful force in American politics. Television journalism also developed as a significant genre. In a series of television reports in the early 1950s, for example, the broadcast journalist Edward R. Murrow exposed the underhanded tactics used in Senator Joseph McCarthy's pursuit of suspected Communists.

As cable networks were laid from coast to coast, television became the dominant force in advertising. Vivid visual imagery combined with catchy jingles and clever slogans led to sales pitches that were more effective than ever before. Between 1949 and 1969, payments from advertisers to television stations and networks grew from $58 million to $1.5 billion. Pohl, as an advertising copywriter, was placed to observe firsthand the growing power of broadcast consumerism. *The Space Merchants* describes the 1950s advertising strategies with which Pohl would have been personally familiar. In the novel these strategies lead to a dystopian nightmare of total domination, highlighting the propagandistic effects obtainable through televisual sales methods.

Some science fiction works from the first half of the twentieth century—perhaps most famously the dystopian novel *Brave New World* (1932), by Aldous Huxley—functioned as paranoid anticorporate harbingers of an apocalyptic future. From 1938 and 1946, a period sometimes referred to as the golden age of science fiction, the tales of exploration that had dominated late nineteenth-century science fiction gave way to increasingly predictive works seeking to portray the potential future consequences of modern life. Notable writers in this movement include Isaac Asimov, Robert A. Heinlein, and Ray Bradbury.

Upon publication *The Space Merchants* was hailed as a significant book. In his memoir *The Way the Future Was* (1978), Pohl estimates that the novel had sold ten million copies in twenty-five languages since its first appearance. A 1972 Locus poll rated it the twenty-fourth "all-time best novel," tied with *The Martian Chronicles* (1950) and *War of the Worlds* (1898). In the decades following its publication, *The Space Merchants* remained notable as an interesting examination of the powers of commercialism, although much of its extrapolation now seems dated and inaccurate—for example, the soot pollution and planet-wide overcrowding described in the novel have observably not come to pass. Pohl went on to win four Hugo Awards and three Nebula Awards and in 1998 was inducted into the Science Fiction Hall of Fame; Kornbluth, who died in 1958, was recognized with two posthumous Hugo Awards, in 1973 and in 2001. The contributions of both authors were essential to the development of twentieth-century science fiction.

✛ Key Facts

Time Period:
Mid-20th Century

Genre:
Novel

Events:
Invention of television; McCarthyism; growth of consumerism

Nationality:
American

TELEVISION BECOMES BIG BUSINESS

In the 1940s the three big television networks—NBC, CBS, and ABC—distributed all of their programming via "kinescopes," 16mm film reels of video programming that were duplicated and shipped to affiliated stations. Because of the constraints of shipping footage, most broadcast programming was local. However, in the early 1950s a system of coaxial cables was laid from coast to coast, enabling national broadcasts and creating a huge boom in television programming and advertising. Between 1949 and 1969, the number of commercial TV stations in the United States increased from sixty-nine to 566, and the number of households in the United States with at least one TV set rose to 44 million. Big viewership meant big business; by 1970 TV station and network ad revenue totaled $3.6 billion, and 96 percent of American households had a TV, making television the dominant broadcast medium in the United States. In the late 1960s and early 1970s, television journalism was credited as a major influence on public opinion of the Vietnam War, as it allowed information on the conflict to be distributed quickly to a national audience. Television has continued to exert a powerful influence on U.S. culture, with profound social and economic impacts.

Pohl published a sequel, *The Merchant's War,* in 1984; in 2011 he issued an updated version of *The Space Merchants* that includes references to the scandal-ridden corporations Enron and AIG.

THEMES AND STYLE

The dominant theme of *The Space Merchants* is the power of advertising and corporate commercialism to shape and control persons and governments. The protagonist, the copywriter Mitch Courtenay, believes that he has found an easy assignment in writing pro-colonization propaganda to encourage humans to settle on Venus to relieve Earth's strained resources. Although Venus is still only barely habitable for human beings, in order to sell colonization as a pleasant alternative to life on the polluted and overcrowded Earth, Courtenay leverages the principle that, in the human imagination, "the grass is always greener" somewhere else. Pohl and Kornbluth use their protagonist's career as a way of showing the inner workings of propaganda, exposing the psychological manipulations of advertisements and the sociopolitical forces that drive them.

Pohl and Kornbluth utilize both narrative trajectory and point of view to bring their readers through a gradual process of realization. The narrative is written in the first person, tying the reader's awareness and knowledge directly to Courtenay's. Over the course of the novel, Courtenay dramatically falls from grace, losing his privileged position as a copywriter through identity theft. Deep in debt, he is forced to take up farming vatgrown meat in a work camp, exposing him to range of "consie" influences and ultimately facilitating his conversion to conservationist and anticapitalist views. Through the narration of this reversal of fortune in the first person, Pohl and Kornbluth peel back the layers of their dystopia to expose its horrors, attempting to move their readers through the same process of discovery, reaction, and rejection that Courtenay undergoes.

The Space Merchants contains startling and memorable images of a future gone wrong: gas masks to filter out atmospheric soot, golf clubs at the top of corporate skyscrapers, and cars propelled by pedals because of the depletion of world oil reserves. Chicken Little, a perpetually growing giant chicken heart, serves as an inexhaustible protein source. Pohl and Kornbluth, like many science fiction writers of the time, use innovative language to describe the imagined setting of their novel. Their work is the source of the new words and expressions *moon suit, R and D,* and *soyaburger,* as well as the use of the word *survey* in the sense of carrying out a poll; the novel was also one of the first texts to employ the term *muzak.* The vividness of Pohl and Kornbluth's world makes their anticorporate message memorable, engaging readers' imaginations as well as their reason.

CRITICAL DISCUSSION

Initial responses to *The Space Merchants* were overwhelmingly positive. In a 1953 review Anthony Boucher and J. Francis McComas praise the book as "bitter, satiric, exciting [and] easily one of the major works of logical extrapolation in several years," calling it "a sharp melodrama of power-conflict and revolt which manages ... to explore all the implied developments of [its imagined] society." Groff Conklin declares that the novel is "the best science fiction satire since *Brave New World.*" The novelist Kingsley Amis, in his history of early science fiction, *New Maps of Hell* (1960), notes that the book "has many claims to being the best science-fiction novel so far."

Although its reputation has fallen somewhat from its 1960 height—novelist Jo Walton notes in a 2009 review that the central concept "hasn't aged all that well"—*The Space Merchants* has remained a dynamic part of the tradition of science fiction that seeks to expose the present through stories of the future. The book has taken some criticism for its retrograde gender roles and sexist characterizations and is now principally of interest as an attempt to predict the future. Perhaps for this reason, Pohl's 2011 revision of the novel was not well received; reviewers noted that the contemporary elements mingled awkwardly with prognostications from the 1950s, muddling the novel's retro charm and instead throwing harsh light on its predictive inaccuracies. Although the novel's message is essentially a simple one—advertising seeks to control populations to a sometimes dangerous degree—the original remains a compelling critique of consumer society and offers a sometimes prescient look at human and environmental concerns in the developing postindustrial, postbroadcast world.

Scholars rarely address *The Space Merchants* on its own; David Seed's 1993 article "Take-over Bids: The Power Fantasies of Frederik Pohl and Cyril Kornbluth" is a rare example, although it also situates *The Space Merchants* in relation to the rest of Pohl and Kornbluth's oeuvre. Most critics examine the novel within the larger context of dystopian or predictive mid-twentieth-century science fiction, as in Donald M. Hassler and Clyde Wilcox's *Political Science Fiction* (1997). Postmillennial scholarship mentions *The Space Merchants* in relation to various twentieth-century science fiction tropes, such as mass culture and futuristic food.

BIBLIOGRAPHY

Sources

Amis, Kingsley. *New Maps of Hell: A Survey of Science Fiction.* New York: Penguin, 1960. Print.

Boucher, Anthony, and J. Francis McComas. "Recommended Reading." Rev. of *The Space Merchants,* by Frederik Pohl and Cyril M. Kornbluth. *F&SF* July 1953: 85. Print.

Conklin, Groff. "Galaxy's 5 Star Shelf." Rev. of *The Space Merchants,* by Frederik Pohl and Cyril M. Kornbluth. *Galaxy Science Fiction* June 1953: 144. Print.

Hassler, Donald M., and Clyde Wilcox. *Political Science Fiction.* Columbia: U of South Carolina P, 1997. Print.

Pohl, Frederik. *The Way the Future Was: A Memoir.* New York: Ballantine, 1978. Print.

Pohl, Frederik, and Cyril M. Kornbluth. *The Space Merchants.* New York: Ballantine, 1953. Print.

Seed, David. "Take-over Bids: The Power Fantasies of Frederik Pohl and Cyril Kornbluth." *Foundation* 59 (1993): 42–58. *Short Story Criticism.* Vol. 25. Detroit: Gale Research, 1997. *Literature Resource Center.* Web. 11 June 2012.

Walton, Jo. "Advertising dystopia: Frederik Pohl and C. M. Kornbluth's *The Space Merchants.*" Rev. of *The Space Merchants,* by Frederik Pohl and Cyril M. Kornbluth. *Tor.com* 3 June 2009. Web. 16 July 2012.

Further Reading

Belasco, Warren James. *Meals to Come: A History of the Future of Food.* Los Angeles: U of California P, 2006. Print.

Booker, M. Keith, and Anne-Marie Thomas, eds. *The Science Fiction Handbook.* Malden: Wiley-Blackwell, 2009. Print.

Brown, Steven, and Anthony Patterson. *Imagining Marketing.* New York: Routledge, 2000. Print.

Livingston, Dennis. "Science Fiction Models of Future World Order Systems." *International Organization* 25.2 (1971): 254–70. Print.

Moylan, Tom. *Scraps of the Untainted Sky.* Boulder: Westview, 2000. Print.

Seed, David, ed. *A Companion to Science Fiction.* Malden: Blackwell, 2005. Print.

Smulyan, Susan. *Popular Ideologies: Mass Culture at Mid-Century.* Philadelphia: U of Pennsylvania P, 2007. 137–38. Print.

Carina Saxon

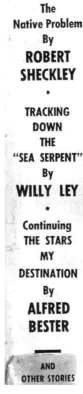

The December 1956 cover of the magazine *Galaxy Science Fiction.* Frederik Pohl and Cyril M. Kornbluth's novel *The Space Merchants* was originally published serially in the magazine in 1952. ADVERTISING ARCHIVE/COURTESY EVERETT COLLECTION.

SWASTIKA NIGHT

Katharine Burdekin

❖ *Key Facts*

Time Period:
Mid-20th Century

Genre:
Novel

Events:
Rise of Nazism; British
appeasement of Adolf
Hitler

Nationality:
English

OVERVIEW

The 1937 novel *Swastika Night,* written by Katharine Burdekin under the pen name Murray Constantine, is a work of speculative fiction depicting a dystopian future in which the world has been divided between two military powers: the Nazis and the Japanese. The novel takes place seven hundred years after the Nazis and Japanese have defeated the allies in the Twenty Years War. Jews have long been eradicated, Christians are marginalized, and Adolf Hitler is worshipped as a god. A cult of masculinity dominates society, the Nazis are depicted as homosexual misogynists, and women have been deprived of all rights and are kept in concentration camps where their sole value is their necessity for sexual reproduction. This has led to a crisis—the degradation of women has led to a decrease in fertility, and those in power struggle to maintain their populations. In Burdekin's envisioned future, few books exist except for works of propaganda, and a secret book is the only witness to the past. Among the most notable aspects of *Swastika Night* is Burdekin's anticipation of the Holocaust and its prescient understanding of the masculine element in fascist ideology. The novel contains strong feminist and antifascist themes and makes predictions about and analyzes the potential impact of the Nazi Party's use of propaganda.

Written while many of her British compatriots were still promoting appeasement as the best response to the Nazi threat, Burdekin accurately predicts many of the aspects of the war to come two years before the Nazi invasion of Poland. The work is impressive as a predictor of the threat of Nazism as Hitler laid out in *Mein Kampf* and in his speeches and propaganda. *Swastika Night* received immediate recognition, especially from left-wing groups. Furthermore, it had a tremendous impact on the dystopian literature that followed, as subsequent works analyzed many of the same themes, including the dangers of fascism and propaganda. The most notable example of a work of fiction influenced by *Swastika Night* remains George Orwell's *Nineteen Eighty-Four.*

HISTORICAL AND LITERARY CONTEXT

Swastika Night responds to the ascent of Hitler and the Nazi Party from the late 1920s through the 1930s and predicts a war between Axis powers and Allied forces. *Mein Kampf,* published in German in 1925, began to appear in English in the early 1930s as Hitler became a more powerful figure in Germany and the Nazi Party and its ideology emerged as a global threat. Nazi propaganda and Hitler's strong rhetoric represented a clear threat to the peace achieved in the aftermath of World War I.

At the time *Swastika Night* was written and published, the dominant response to Hitler and the threat of the Nazi Party was appeasement. British prime minister Stanley Baldwin struggled against strong opposition to his plan to increase the size of the British military in anticipation of war. Historians were later critical of the record of appeasement by Neville Chamberlain, Baldwin's successor. Burdekin held pacifist beliefs, but as the threat of Nazi Germany and its fascism grew, she became convinced that the use of force would be necessary to maintain free, democratic societies.

Burdekin wrote several novels during the 1920s before publishing *Swastika Night* in 1937. She considered her first mature work to be *The Rebel Passion,* published in 1929. Almost all of her early work was strongly political and vehemently antifascist. In fact, it was the political nature of her work and her strong critiques of fascism that led her to use a pseudonym, Murray Constantine. The dystopian setting and antifascist themes of *Swastika Night* appeared in earlier British novels, most notably Aldous Huxley's *Brave New World* (1931). However, Burdekin's novel is directly a response to Hitler's writings and his emerging power.

Swastika Night would prove to be considerably influential, most importantly to the now better-known novel *Nineteen Eighty-Four* by George Orwell. Orwell employs similar plot devices and themes in his novel. Published more than a decade after Burdekin's pre–World War II novel, Orwell, like Burdekin, writes of a future in which the past has been erased and history has been rewritten. The use of language in the world imagined in *Nineteen Eighty-Four* is distorted and few books exist that are not propaganda. Perhaps the most notable similarity between the novels by Burdekin and Orwell is that both plots contain a secret book that serves as the only witness to the past. Burdekin's contribution to feminist and dystopian literature was largely forgotten, but recent scholarship has helped to revive her legacy and to emphasize the importance of her work.

THEMES AND STYLE

The central theme of the novel is the threat of fascism, especially the hypermasculine misogyny present in most fascist movements. The novel also explores the degradation of women, which is a direct response to the antifeminist elements of Hitler's *Mein Kampf.* Burdekin comments on the cult of masculinity that the rise of the Nazi Party has created and its impact on women and religion. She writes of women, "They were not allowed to be priests. But they were told by men that they had souls which Jesus loved, so they developed the simulacrum of a soul and a sham conscience." She attributes the inequality to the idea that "there always had been in the heart of the religion a hatred of the beauty of women and a horror of the sexual power beautiful women with the right of choice and rejection have over men." Another important theme of the novel is the importance of literature as a natural antidote to fascism and propaganda. The novel's protagonist, Alfred, discovers a secret book that houses the actual history and workings of the society. The book confirms Alfred's belief that the history presented to the public is false. Upon his death, Alfred leaves his work to his son and remarks on its importance: "Keep it inviolate, guard it as you would your honour, for though what I have put down here is but the smallest fragment of the truth of history, yet I swear that, to my poor knowledge, it is all true."

Rhetorically, the novel hinges on its anticipation of a dystopian future and tells the story of Alfred, an Englishman who dreams of overthrowing the Germans. Alfred embarks on a pilgrimage to Germany where he discovers that the English are loathed because they were the last resistors to German rule. He visits the "Sacred Airplane," which legend holds Hitler flew on a final mission to Moscow, finally defeating the Russians. According to the government's official history, Hitler is a seven-foot-tall, blond, blue-eyed god who won the war personally. However, through contact with the Knight Von Hess, Alfred is shown a photograph of the real Hitler, a small man with dark hair. The photograph also depicts a beautiful woman whom Alfred first believes to be a boy because he has been trained to believe that women have no value and no beauty. The photograph destroys for Alfred the myth promoted by the government. Eventually, the SS murders Alfred but not before he can pass down the truth of Nazi history to his surviving son. *Swastika Night* presents propaganda as a powerful tool capable of altering the worldview of generations. Truth is the only answer to propaganda's power.

The novel is written with a sense of moral urgency, and its tone is serious but ultimately hopeful. For example, Alfred declares, "I am a man who knows that while armed rebellion against Germany must fail, there is another rebellion that must succeed … the rebellion of disbelief. Your Empire is held together on the mind side of it by Hitlerism. If that goes, if people

KATHARINE BURDEKIN'S CRYSTAL BALL

One of the more notable aspects of Katharine Burdekin's *Swastika Night* is how accurately she predicts events related to Nazism, fascism in Europe, World War II, and even the Cold War. In her novel, she accurately anticipates the Holocaust and the attempted extermination of the Jewish people. She also predicts the importance of air power and aerial warfare in World War II, and with some discrepancies, she forecasts the Cold War conflicts that would follow World War II.

In the novel, former allies Japan and Germany are now at odds. Although the two occasionally fight battles, unlike in a cold war, they resolve nothing and remain at a stalemate. The possibility of human extinction due to the conflict between the two super powers accurately reflects the threat of nuclear fallout that pervaded the Cold War between former allies the Soviet Union and the United States. Like most dystopian literature, the novel attempts to describe a possible future given current circumstances; however it is unique in the accuracy of its predictions.

no longer believe Hitler is God, you have nothing left but armed force." Thus, the unbelievers are posited as an unstoppable force: "You can't make them re-believe if they don't. And in the end, however many people you kill, so long as there are some to carry on, the skepticism will grow. And you can't ever kill all the unbelievers, because, though you can search a man's pockets or his house, you can't search his mind."

CRITICAL DISCUSSION

Swastika Night, while not a huge success, was well received upon publication. Interest in the novel increased as war with Germany became imminent and knowledge of Hitler and the Nazi Party grew. The novel became an increasingly important text for the political left and was reissued as a Left Book Club selection in 1940, soaring in popularity. However, dystopian novels that followed, most notably Orwell's *Nineteen Eighty-Four,* eclipsed *Swastika Night* in popularity and Burdekin's work was largely forgotten.

The broader legacy of the novel lies in its uncanny prescience in terms of World War II and the rise of Nazism in Germany and fascism in other parts of Europe. It also remains one of the few dystopian novels of the era to take up feminist themes and issues. Thus, the rise of gender studies and feminism in the 1970s and 1980s saw renewed interest in the work, and in 1985 the novel was published under Burdekin's name for the first time. In a 1984 essay in *Women's Studies International Forum,* gender studies scholar Daphne Patai compares Burdekin's work with Orwell's, calling the latter misogynistic. Patai notes that Burdekin

argues in a 1999 essay for *Journal of Gender Studies* that Burdekin's novel confronts "the institutionalized and discursive production of an English masculinity not that far distant from a category of manliness mobilized by European fascism." With regard to the novel's approach to propaganda, literary scholar George McKay in a 1994 essay for *Science Fiction Studies* argues that Burdekin employs, through Alfred's reading of the secret book, a "parallel self-reading moment to inscribe a self-conscious and energizing metapropagandistic discourse into" her narrative. In other words, Burdekin consciously wrote a work with propagandistic elements to criticize propaganda.

BIBLIOGRAPHY

Sources

Burdekin, Katharine. *Swastika Night.* New York: Feminist Press at CUNY, 1993. Print.

Holden, Kate. "Formations of Discipline and Manliness: Culture, Politics and 1930s Women's Writing." *Journal of Gender Studies* 8.2 (1999): 141–57.

McKay, George. "Metapropaganda: Self-Reading Dystopian Fiction: Burdekin's *Swastika Night* and Orwell's *Nineteen Eighty-Four.*" *Science Fiction Studies* 21.3 (1994): 302–14.

Patai, Daphne. "Orwell's Despair, Burdekin's Hope: Gender and Power in Dystopia." *Women's Studies International Forum* 7.2 (1984): 85–96.

Pagetti, Carlo, et al. "In the Year of Our Lord Hitler 720: Katharine Burdekin's *Swastika Night.*" *Science Fiction Studies* 17.3 (1990): 360–69. *JSTOR.* Web. 20 July 2012.

Further Reading

Baccolini, Raffaella, and Tom Moylan, eds. *Dark Horizons: Science Fiction and the Dystopian Imagination.* New York: Routledge, 2003. Print.

Burdekin, Katharine. *Proud Man.* New York: Feminist Press, 1985. Print.

Rosenfeld, Gavriel David. *The World Hitler Never Made: Alternate History and the Memory of Nazism.* Cambridge: Cambridge UP, 2005. Print.

Schneider, Karen. *Loving Arms: British Women Writing the Second World War.* Lexington: UP of Kentucky, 1997. Print.

Tighe, Carl. "Pax Germanica: The Future Historical." *Journal of European Studies* 30.3 (2000): 297–328. *JSTOR.* Web. 20 July 2012.

Colby Cuppernull

sees "the continuity between male preoccupation with power in official political roles and male dominance in private life."

Current trends in critical study of *Swastika Night* analyze the text's influence on future dystopian literature, its feminist themes, and its analysis of propaganda. *Swastika Night* and *Nineteen Eighty-Four* are the subject of many comparative studies. In terms of the novel's feminism, gender studies scholar Kate Holden

UTOPIA

Thomas More

OVERVIEW

Thomas More's book *Utopia,* an ironic exercise in political philosophy published in 1516, describes the organization and customs of a nonexistent society called Utopia. Divided into two sections, or books, the narrative is framed as a recounting of a conversation between More, his friend Peter Giles, and their (fictitious) mutual acquaintance Raphael Hythloday. In Book I, the three men begin by debating the question of whether intellectuals should involve themselves in politics, and the ensuing discussion touches on numerous flaws and corruptions within European, and especially English, society. Hythloday asserts that a just society cannot exist unless private property is abolished, and to rebut his companions' objections he cites Utopia, where he claims to have lived for five years, as an example of a far superior society where all property is held communally. As Book II begins, Hythloday commences a lengthy description of Utopia's highly structured, egalitarian commonwealth. The contrast between Utopian and European society, as well as the extensive political and philosophical discussion throughout *Utopia,* turns the book into an incisive, if sometimes enigmatic, societal critique that profoundly influenced political thought and its literary expression for centuries to come.

One of the major early works of English Renaissance humanism, *Utopia* was well received upon its initial publication in Latin in 1516, though its readership was initially confined to a relatively small group of intellectuals. Its subsequent influence, however, has been immense: its fictional portrayal of an ostensibly ideal society made it a seminal work in the utopian (and dystopian) literary genre, which has since been used by countless authors to critique contemporary societies and suggest alternatives. Similarly, the book's discussion of specific social issues—especially class-related oppression—gave voice to societal grievances common throughout Renaissance Europe.

HISTORICAL AND LITERARY CONTEXT

In England, the decades leading up to the appearance of *Utopia* were marked by the steady decline of the feudal economic system that had been in place since the Middle Ages. England had long since begun its transition from an economy based on agricultural labor by peasants on land held by feudal lords toward a more market-driven economy based on the exchange of money and goods. The deaths of numerous land-holding nobles during the Wars of the Roses (1455–85) and the seizure and auction of their land contributed to the erosion of feudalism and the rise of a more competitive socioeconomic structure.

By the time *Utopia* was written, the societal ills brought about by the advent of increased economic competition in England (and continental Europe) were a general concern. The peasantry experienced widespread displacement and unemployment as open fields, which had been officially owned by feudal lords who accorded traditional agricultural rights to laboring tenants, were converted into enclosed pastures designated solely for the landowner's private use. Thievery was rampant, as poverty drove many people to desperation. More's text, in its exploration and critique of both specific social problems and their cultural underpinnings, represents one of the most thorough commentaries on the corruption at the heart of European society. Although much of *Utopia* is ambiguous, the passages attacking sixteenth-century societal evils are straightforwardly didactic, making them an important part of the public debate concerning such issues as pastoral enclosure, which became the subject of a national enquiry a year after *Utopia* was published.

Utopia arose from the cultural tradition of Renaissance humanism, a strain of scholarly thinking that emphasized intellectual well-roundedness, active engagement in civic affairs, and a renewed interest in the Greek and Latin texts of antiquity. Classical meditations on the ideal society, such as Plato's *Republic* and Aristotle's *Politics,* are obvious influences, though *Utopia,* being an occasionally lighthearted work of fiction rather than a straightforward treatise, leaves its author's views far less clear, masking them in humor and artifice. The book's mixture of the jocular and the serious is likewise inspired by classical sources, particularly the seriocomic work of the Greek author Lucian, whose work also inspired Desiderius Erasmus's ironic 1509 essay *The Praise of Folly,* a text that exemplifies the humanist literary tradition.

More's text pioneered the use of a fictitious society as a vehicle for social commentary. Subsequent works are often referred to as "utopian" or "dystopian" depending on whether they portray this society positively or negatively, although many works (including *Utopia* itself) are too complex to neatly fit

Key Facts

Time Period:
Early 16th Century

Genre:
Treatise

Events:
Wars of the Roses; rise of the Renaissance

Nationality:
English

THOMAS MORE'S LIFE AS A COURTIER

Shortly after completing *Utopia* in 1516, Thomas More, already a renowned lawyer, member of Parliament, and city judge, entered the council of King Henry VIII. It is interesting to consider this decision in light of the conversation in *Utopia* about whether intellectuals should take an active role in politics; the fictional version of More believes they should, while Hythloday cynically asserts that the Machiavellian nature of councils makes altruism impossible: "either they will seduce you, or, if you remain honest and innocent, you will be made a screen for the knavery and folly of others."

As a councilor, More served variously as a diplomat, secretary, and orator for the king. Upon assuming the title of lord chancellor in 1529, he led a ruthless campaign against Protestantism, but he resigned from the office three years later over Henry's introduction of legislation giving the king supremacy over the Roman Catholic Church. In 1534 the king, now excommunicated, required More to swear support for the Act of Succession, granting legitimacy to the children he had fathered in his second marriage, which was not recognized by the pope, and implicitly acknowledging him as the supreme head of the English church. More refused, and he was beheaded for treason in 1535.

this dichotomy. Indeed, the word *utopia*, though its Greek roots suggest *eutopia*, or "good place," actually means "no place," and the utopian/dystopian genre is defined more by the society's fictional nature than by its designation as good or bad. The imprint of More's work continues to be felt in the work of contemporary authors such as Ursula K. Le Guin, whose utopian fiction shares with *Utopia* both an overriding concern with the ways individuals are shaped by society and a consistent avoidance of simplistic judgments.

THEMES AND STYLE

A primary thematic element of *Utopia* is the conviction that inequality and competition are at the heart of societal corruption and human misery. Book I comprises a scathing indictment of the problems of sixteenth-century European society, including widespread thievery, oppression of the poor, and political rapacity, all of which are ultimately attributed to the sin of pride, which Hythloday asserts is inextricably tied to inequality, as "pride measures her advantages not by what she has but by what other people lack." The account of Utopia in Book II allows readers to critically examine their own society by considering it in relation to a fictional community structured around a strenuous attempt to eliminate inequality whenever possible, to the point of abolishing private property, requiring agricultural labor of all citizens, and even relocating people to ensure that the Utopian cities maintain an even population.

Although the book's condemnation of European social inequities appears genuine and impassioned, the Utopian alternative More conjures up, while an improvement over Europe in many respects, seems deliberately flawed, leaving his ultimate message elusive.

One of the main reasons for *Utopia*'s interpretive ambiguity is More's continual maintenance of an ironic distance from the opinions expressed in his book. Despite the presence of a character named "Thomas More," the real More makes it abundantly clear that the narrative is a fiction, thus frustrating the reader's inclination to regard the book as a straightforward elucidation of More's own views. Indeed, Hythloday, the character who delivers most of the book's insights about society and humanity, has a facetious Greek name that translates as "expert in nonsense," and all of the proper names mentioned during Hythloday's account of Utopia are similarly punning and irreverent. The text frequently undermines its own seriousness, even as it continues to function as a compelling exercise in social critique and speculation.

Stylistically, *Utopia* is fairly straightforward and unembellished by the standards of More's time, with the narrative emphasis on the ideas expressed rather than their expression in itself. The original Latin text is unpretentious and casual in tone and diction, and English translations tend to follow suit. It is noteworthy, however, that the language used in Hythloday's lengthy speeches differs significantly from that of More's first-person narration; Hythloday is far more totalizing and intemperate in his pronouncements, as when he describes a wealthy landowner who privatizes open fields as "one greedy, insatiable glutton, a frightful plague to his native country," or when he grandiosely asserts that Utopian "public officials are never arrogant or unapproachable," using the word *never* when *rarely* might be more circumspect. The tenor of Hythloday's language reflects his black-and-white, possibly simplistic worldview.

CRITICAL DISCUSSION

Utopia was warmly regarded by More's humanist peers, if sometimes misunderstood by the readership as a whole. Both Erasmus and Guillaume Budé, respectively the most prominent Dutch and French humanists of More's time, contributed laudatory statements that were appended to early editions of the book. Budé pretended to take *Utopia* at face value, perhaps inadvertently contributing to a persistent tendency to ignore the book's ambiguities in favor of reading it as More's explicit blueprint for what he genuinely considered to be a perfect society. Renaissance scholar Dominic Baker-Smith pointed out in 2011 that "the majority of readers since 1516 have adopted a literal interpretation, in which Utopia is an ideal and [Hythloday] is its prophet." This interpretation, now largely discredited, dominated the book's reception for centuries.

Despite its ambiguity as a purposeful statement of opinion, *Utopia*'s elaborate social speculation has had an enormous influence on reform-oriented political thought. The impact of More's book has been both concrete and diffuse: it directly inspired at least one real-life sixteenth-century utopian community in Mexico, and its portrait of a highly regulated welfare state without private property prefigured much of the socialist rhetoric and ideology of later eras. Indeed, as utopian scholar J. C. Davis observed in 2010, "by the mid-nineteenth and early twentieth centuries, *Utopia* was often seen as a foundation document of modern socialism," and More was in fact named as one of the eighteen founders of communism on a dedicatory obelisk constructed at Vladimir Lenin's behest. The link between *Utopia* and socialism is a main point of interest in much Marxist criticism of the text—hence Karl Kautsky's assertion in 1888 that More's "socialism made him immortal."

Modern scholarship of *Utopia* tends to dismiss as naive the once-common belief that More intended Utopia as a perfect society, and though a consensus on his intentions has yet to emerge, contemporary scholars often emphasize the interpretive importance of historical context. J. H. Hexter's influential 1952 study *More's Utopia: The Biography of an Idea* exemplifies this trend, rigorously positioning the book within More's life and times and cautioning against the tendency to equate More's views with anachronistic political ideologies, as, according to Hexter, Karl Kautsky does when he connects More's beliefs with modern socialism. Likewise, a growing interest in the intricacies of More's language is epitomized by Elizabeth McCutcheon's *My Dear Peter: The "Ars Poetica" and Hermeneutics for More's Utopia* (1983), which explores More's use of various subtle literary techniques.

Illustration of the island of Utopia from a contemporary edition of Thomas More's book. BPK, BERLIN/KUNSTBIBLIOTHEK, STAATLICHE MUSEE/ART RESOURCE, NY.

BIBLIOGRAPHY

Sources

Baker-Smith, Dominic. "Reading *Utopia*." *The Cambridge Companion to Thomas More*. Ed. George M. Logan. Cambridge: Cambridge UP, 2011. 141–67. Print.

Davis, J. C. "Thomas More's *Utopia*." *The Cambridge Companion to Utopian Literature*. Ed. Gregory Claeys. Cambridge: Cambridge UP, 2010. 28–50. Print.

Hexter, J. H. *More's Utopia: The Biography of an Idea*. Princeton: Princeton UP, 1952. Print.

Kautsky, Karl. *Thomas More and His Utopia*. Trans. H. J. Stenning. London: A & C Black, 1927. Print.

McCutcheon, Elizabeth. *My Dear Peter: The "Ars Poetica" and Hermeneutics for More's Utopia*. Angers: Moreanum, 1983. Print.

More, Thomas. *Utopia*. Ed. George M. Logan and Robert M. Adams. Cambridge: Cambridge UP, 1989. Print.

Further Reading

Anderson, M. T. *Feed*. Cambridge: Candlewick, 2002. Print.

Bostaph, Samuel. "Deepening the Irony of *Utopia*: An Economic Perspective." *History of Political Economy* 42.2 (2010): 361–82. Print.

Ghita, Lucian. "'I Would Rather Be Honest Than Wise': Fictional Protocols and Authorial Credibility in Thomas More's *Utopia*." *Prose Studies* 28.2 (2006): 113–29. Print.

Kinney, Arthur F. "*Utopia*'s First Readers." *Challenging Humanism: Essays in Honor of Dominic Baker-Smith*. Ed. Ton Hoenselaars and Arthur F. Kinney. Newark: U of Delaware P, 2005. 23–53. Print.

Le Guin, Ursula K. *The Dispossessed: An Ambiguous Utopia*. New York: Harper, 1974. Print.

Leslie, Marina. *Renaissance Utopias and the Problem of History*. Ithaca: Cornell UP, 1998. Print.

Logan, George M. *The Meaning of More's Utopia*. Princeton: Princeton UP, 1983. Print.

Morgan-Russell, Simon. "St. Thomas More's *Utopia* and the Description of Britain." *Cahier Élisabéthains* 61 (2002): 1–11. Print.

Russ, Joanna. *The Female Man*. New York: Bantam, 1975. Print.

Yoran, Hanan. *Between Utopia and Dystopia: Erasmus, Thomas More, and the Humanist Republic of Letters*. Lanham: Lexington, 2010. Print.

James Overholtzer

WE

Yevgeny Zamyatin

OVERVIEW

Yevgeny Zamyatin's prototypical anti-utopian novel *We*, written in 1921, was refused publication in his native Russia before an English translation was released in 1924. Set in an indefinite future time in a scientifically totalitarian nation called the One State, *We* is the diary of D-503, who is, like Zamyatin himself, an engineer turned writer. D-503 is the builder of the Integral, a space-travel machine intended to find civilizations on other planets and subjugate them to "the mathematically perfect life of the One State," where people have become numbers, teachers are computers, and even sex is strictly regimented. D-503 begins his diary to fulfill the requirement that all citizens write propagandistic treatises to convince alien peoples of the superiority of the One State. However, he soon finds himself at the mercy of emotions he does not understand, and his diary becomes a record of love and rebellion as he acquires a most unwelcome and inconvenient possession—a soul.

Written in the immediate aftermath of the Russian Revolution as communist leaders began implementing their vision of the new workers' state, *We* represents Zamyatin's protest against totalitarianism and scientific rigidity. As the country began a rapid transformation from a largely agrarian society to a modern industrial power, the leaders of the new Soviet Union saw the burgeoning science and technology of the early twentieth century as a promising path to a prosperous future. The government did not welcome Zamyatin's challenging examination of the interactions between human freedom, technology, and the state. However, these complex relationships became a major focus of twentieth-century thinkers, and *We*, devoured illicitly by those who could obtain underground copies, was only the first of a genre of dystopian fiction warning of the possible misuses of scientific and political power.

HISTORICAL AND LITERARY CONTEXT

As the second decade of the twentieth century drew to a close and Europe and the United States began to recover from the devastating effects of World War I, Russia was faced with the task of creating a new form of government. Two revolutions in 1917 had led to the abdication and execution of Tsar Nicholas II, and civil war erupted when radical Bolsheviks challenged the moderate provisional government. Early communist decrees ended private ownership of land, nationalized industry, and protected child welfare, but at the same time they suppressed opposition and dissolved the representative assembly. The early 1900s also saw a boom in technology and industrial productivity in Russia, as in the West generally. The Soviet Union, faced with recovery from world war and revolution and lagging behind the rest of Europe in industrialization, rushed to modernize, and it exalted industry and mechanization as important underpinnings of the new Soviet utopia. Zamyatin was both an engineer and a revolutionary, keenly aware of the scientific and political ferment of his era. Beaten and jailed by Tsarist police in 1905 as a Bolshevik student activist, Zamyatin spent years in exile before returning to Russia in 1917 to participate in the revolution. Still an outspoken social critic, he was arrested again, this time by the Bolsheviks, in 1919 and 1922. *We* was Zamyatin's response to the harsh authoritarianism with which the new regime enforced its egalitarian ideals. The novel was also a reaction to an increasingly mechanized view of modern science represented by "efficiency experts," such as the American Frederick Winslow Taylor, whose time and motion studies aimed to make workers a more efficient part of industrial machinery.

Although *We* was original in its presentation of utopia gone horribly wrong, it emerged from a flourishing literature of social commentary inspired by the massive, and often contradictory, transformations triggered by the Industrial Revolution and the rise of new humanist politics. Nikolai Chernyshevsky's 1863 novel *What Is to Be Done?* gave an idealistic picture of harmonious socialism, while Fyodor Dostoyevsky's *Notes from Underground* (1864) offered a grimmer view of the alienation of the human being in modern society. Zamyatin was also deeply influenced by the writing of H. G. Wells, not only his seminal science fiction work but also his visionary nonfiction, *Anticipations of the Reaction of Mechanical and Scientific Progress upon Human Life and Thought,* published in 1901. At almost the same moment *We* was created, Karel Čapek published his 1920 play *R.U.R. (Rossum's Universal Robots)* exploring the dangers of mechanization.

Zamyatin's futuristic novel was highly controversial at the time it was written and has continued to have an impact on the literature of social commentary for almost a century. Banned in the Soviet

Union for decades, *We* found its way into the hands of dissidents around the world and inspired such powerfully influential works as George Orwell's *1984* (1949). Although Zamyatin wrote from a socialist perspective, his work also influenced arch-capitalist Ayn Rand, whose 1938 novel *Anthem* echoed *We*'s tension between the collective and the individual.

THEMES AND STYLE

One of the most important issues Zamyatin confronts in *We* is the conflict between scientific advancement—in political ideology as well as technology—and the innate freedom of humankind. The One State seeks to find those who are still "living in a savage state of freedom" and subjugate them to the "beneficial yoke of reason" in order to "bring them mathematically infallible happiness." The city of the One State is surrounded by the Green Wall of glass, which keeps unruly nature at bay, and D-503 starts his narrative as a successfully brainwashed representative of the state. "Walls are the foundation of anything and everything human," he says, "Oh the great, divinely bounding wisdom of walls and barriers! They may just be the greatest of all inventions." However, the very act of writing releases something rebellious in D-503, and this is perhaps the most powerful theme of the novel, the subversive power of valuing one's own thoughts enough to write them down. As he begins his narrative, D-503 expresses the creative process of all writers, "This text is me; and simultaneously not me. And it will feed for many months on my sap, my blood, and then, in anguish, it will be ripped from my self and placed at the foot of the One State."

Though D-503 says at the outset that he is "not up to the task of creating the music of unison and rhyme," his writing is filled with vivid description and metaphor that make the text personal and immediate. He begins by finding beauty in the "absolute, aesthetic subordination," the "perfect non-freedom" of "the grand mechanized ballet" of his life as an engineer. However, he is soon jarred awake when he collides with something inexplicable—his feelings for the woman I-330, who disturbs him profoundly from their first meeting: "There was kind of a strange and irritating X to her, and I couldn't pin it down, couldn't give it any numerical expression." This mathematical unknown recurs as an expression of all that his structured worldview cannot explain, "there were clouds and cobwebs and a cross, some kind of four-pawed X, inside me." Images of glass walls recur to underline the lack of privacy and individuality in the One State, but something human persists. "But underneath all this quiet, chilly glass, the boiling, the crimson, the shagginess drifted inaudibly." D-503 actually makes contact with this messy animal energy in the MEPHI, the subversive resistance group that works to undermine the mathematical control of the One State. I-330, with her irritating mystery and her embrace of the forbidden, introduces D-503 to the MEPHI, and at the

SOCIALIST REALISM: ART AND IDEOLOGY

In an effort to secure their hold on power and strengthen the developing government, early Soviet leaders acted quickly to suppress opposition. One of the first industries to come under government control was publishing. Many artistic works deemed unfriendly to the socialist revolution were denied publication, while government writers produced a broadly propagandistic literature. In August 1934, respected writers from all over the Soviet Union gathered for the First All-Union Congress of Soviet Writers. Under the auspices of politicians such as Joseph Stalin and literati such as Maxim Gorky and Boris Pasternak, the writers agreed to join a single authorized labor union. As one of its earliest actions, the union adopted "socialist realism" as its official content and style guideline.

A democratic realism had flourished in Russian literature during the nineteenth century, exemplified by such writers as Leo Tolstoy and Fyodor Dostoyevsky. Socialist realism drew on this tradition and added communist ideology and a heroic optimism intended to educate and inspire the citizens of a new socialist regime. The unifying characteristics of the new literature were accessibility, a positive view of the people, and loyalty to the party. Though many modern critics view the products of socialist realism as obvious and contrived, the movement did produce works of lasting value, including the stylistically innovative novel *Time, Forward!*, written by Valentin Katayev in 1932.

novel's end—though the rebels have been discovered, D-503 brainwashed, and I-330 doomed—the "chaos, howling, corpses, wild beasts" still rage outside the green wall.

We is carefully constructed to convey the sense of the writer's both discovering and inventing himself as he writes. Sentences are chopped with colons, dashes, and ellipses, as if the thoughts tumble out of D-503's mind more quickly than he can record them. This sense increases as D-503's certainty about his world begins to crumble, "Why—all of a sudden—a soul? I never had one—never had one—and then suddenly … Why doesn't anyone else have one, but me?" Mathematical and mechanical terms stand alongside visceral images in a way that highlights the ultimate failure of the One State to redefine humans as numbers, "the distinct humming of wheels, like the noise of feverish blood."

CRITICAL DISCUSSION

We was completed in 1920, but it was among the first works banned by the new communist regime. Nevertheless, manuscripts were circulated among Russian intellectuals, and an English translation was soon published in the United States, followed by a Russian-language edition printed in Czechoslovakia in 1927. The novel was viewed as threatening by many

Illustration depicting the storming of the Winter Palace, October 1917. Originally a supporter of the October Revolution, Yevgeny Zamyatin opposed the censorship that followed it. © HERITAGE IMAGES/CORBIS.

from William Gibson's 1984 *Neuromancer* to Suzanne Collins's *The Hunger Games* (2008) have continued Zamyatin's exploration of what Orwell called "the genie in the bottle" of scientific advancement and its effect on society.

Scholars and social critics have also continued to examine *We* for what it reveals about both post-revolutionary Soviet culture and about the atavistic human conflict between personal liberty and social order. While there is some divergence about whether Zamyatin intended to criticize authoritarianism in the early Soviet Union, communism itself, or all totalitarian states, Adrian Wanner in an article in *Utopian Studies* views *We* as a bridge between nineteenth-century examinations of Industrial Revolution upheaval and twentieth-century existentialism, "the connecting link in the genealogical tree leading from Dostoyevsky to Orwell." Tony Burns, in another *Utopian Studies* article, calls the work "an early example of a postmodern novel" in the author's "challenge to the 'modernist' conception of science." In *Human Nature in Utopia*, Brett Cooke examines the work in terms of its insights into the character of human nature. "Fictional literature like *We* exists," he posits, "because we rarely take the trouble to examine the assumptions by which we organize our social life."

BIBLIOGRAPHY

Sources

Amey, Michael D. "Living under the Bell Jar: Surveillance and Resistance in Yevgeny Zamyatin's *We*." *Critical Survey* 17.1 (2005): 22+. *Literature Resource Center.* Web. 27 Aug. 2012.

Burns, Tony. "Zamyatin's *We* and Postmodernism." *Utopian Studies* 11.1 (2000): 66. *Literature Resource Center.* Web. 23 Aug. 2012.

Cooke, Brett. *Human Nature in Utopia: Zamyatin's We.* Evanston, IL: Northwestern UP, 2002. Print.

Orwell, George. "Review of *We*, by E. I. Zamyatin." *Tribune.* Jan. 4, 1946. *Orwell Today.* Web. 30 Aug. 2012.

Randall, Natasha. Introduction. *We.* By Yevgeny Zamyatin. New York: Modern Library, 2006. xi–xxi. Print.

"Socialist Realism Proclaimed August 1934." *Russian Life* July–Aug. 2009: 21+. *General Reference Center GOLD.* Web. 30 Aug. 2012.

Wanner, Adrian. "The Underground Man as Big Brother: Dostoevsky's and Orwell's Anti-Utopia." *Utopian Studies* 8.1 (1997): 77+. *Literature Resource Center.* Web. 27 Aug. 2012.

Further Reading

Gimpelevich, Zina. "'We' and 'I' in Zamyatin's *We* and Rand's *Anthem*." *Germano-Slavica* 10.1 (1997): 13–23. Rpt. in *Short Story Criticism*. Vol. 116. Detroit: Gale, 2009. *Literature Resource Center.* Web. 30 Aug. 2012.

Gottlieb, Erika. *Dystopian Fiction East and West: Universe of Terror and Trial.* Montreal: McGill-Queens UP, 2001.

Soviets; writer Maxim Gorky, generally sympathetic to Zamyatin, called it "hopelessly bad, a completely sterile thing." However, many dissidents welcomed the book's provocative questions and its intriguing new format. Orwell, reading a French translation during the 1940s, described *We* as "one of the literary curiosities of this book-burning age." Although Orwell deemed it "not a book of the first order," he admired its subversive nature, especially Zamyatin's refusal to accept the notion of a "final revolution."

We earned a place in literary history as one of the earliest novels of the genre that would become known as "dystopian" because it turned the idea of utopia on its head, presenting a future characterized by grim totalitarianism and severe repression of human liberty and happiness. Within decades of the publication of Zamyatin's book, Huxley's *Brave New World*, Orwell's *1984*, and Ray Bradbury's *Fahrenheit 451* (all which show the influence of *We*) had solidified the dystopian novel as a powerfully persuasive literature of social criticism. As technology has continued to have an expanding role in modern culture, dystopian novels

Horan, Thomas. "Revolutions from the Waist Downwards: Desire as Rebellion in Yevgeny Zamyatin's *We*, George Orwell's *1984*, and Aldous Huxley's *Brave New World*." *Extrapolation* 48.2 (2007): 314+. *Literature Resource Center*. Web. 30 Aug. 2012.

Kanigel, Robert. *The One Best Way: Frederick Winslow Taylor and the Enigma of Efficiency*. New York: Penguin, 1999. Print.

Stites, Richard. *Revolutionary Dreams: Utopian Vision and Experimental Life in the Russian Revolution*. New York: Oxford UP, 1989.

Vaingurt, Julia. "Human Machines and the Pains of Penmanship in Yevgeny Zamyatin's *We*." *Cultural Critique* 80 (2012): 108+. *Literature Resource Center*. Web. 27 Aug. 2012.

Tina Gianoulis

WOMAN ON THE EDGE OF TIME

Marge Piercy

OVERVIEW

Woman on the Edge of Time (1976), a novel by Marge Piercy, contrasts the abuse and discrimination experienced by protagonist Consuelo "Connie" Ramos in the grime of New York City in the mid-1970s, and the lives of women in the future utopian city of Mattapoisett, Massachusetts, where the problems associated with being born a poor brown woman have been eliminated. Narrated by Connie, the book chronicles her incarceration in a mental hospital, during which she travels through time (or imagines she does) to the twenty-second century. Shifting between the present day and two possible versions of the future, Piercy's book raises questions about the fate of a society whose sexist institutions drive women down and then call them insane when they respond with violence.

Writing in the 1970s during the heady period of second-wave feminism, Piercy joined the activists who were finally given a forum to critique the misogyny that was still entrenched in American culture despite years of feminist agitation. The utopian elements of *Woman on the Edge of Time* express the optimism generated by the success of second-wave feminists, who had pushed "women's issues" into the national spotlight and into the legislature. By contrast, the novel's rendering of the second, dystopian future and the bleak portrayal of Connie's hardscrabble existence suggest anxieties about the nation's future that continue to resonate with readers in the twenty-first century. *Woman on the Edge of Time,* Piercy's best-known novel, is notable for turning class and race elements of feminist debate into flesh and blood.

HISTORICAL AND LITERARY CONTEXT

Second-wave feminism is often considered to have been inaugurated by two publications in 1963: the report from John F. Kennedy's Presidential Commission on the Status of Women and Betty Friedan's *The Feminine Mystique.* The former details a number of inequalities facing post-World War II American women and issues recommendations for redressing these, including equal pay for equal work. Friedan's book, meanwhile, decries the plight of middle-class American women who, while financially comfortable, were dissatisfied with having their aspirations limited to the domestic sphere of home and family. In the decade that followed these texts, a movement

coalesced, with feminists earning major legislative and judicial victories that extended rights and protections in areas such as education, employment, and reproductive health. Feminist publications enjoyed growing popularity during this period as well, with works such as Erica Jong's *Fear of Flying* (1973) achieving critical and popular success.

Although women made inroads in important areas and raised mainstream consciousness of their issues, inequality and abuse were still very much present, particularly among minorities and the poor. Access to legal abortion, for example, was mainly important to those who had the money to pay for one. Moreover, poor immigrants from cultures in which large families were traditional and abortion was forbidden faced other sorts of problems. In the mid-1970s, for example, Mexican American feminists organized in California to protest the practice of coerced sterilization of mostly working-class migrant women by doctors at Los Angeles County General Hospital. Piercy's novel narrates the struggles of such women through Connie, who has not benefited much from the gains of second-wave feminism.

Scholars have noted that feminist literature from the late 1960s and early 1970s is often concerned with consciousness raising, or politicizing personal stories and connecting individual struggles to greater social problems. In the book *Feminism and Its Fictions: The Consciousness-Raising Novel and the Women's Liberation Movement* (1998), Lisa Maria Hogeland cites *Woman on the Edge of Time* as belonging to a tradition of novels, including Dorothy Bryant's *Ella Price's Journal* (1972) and Rita Mae Brown's *Rubyfruit Jungle* (1973), in which oppressive institutions rather than moral failings or genuine illness cause women to feel and to be treated as "crazy." Like these novels, *Woman on the Edge of Time* uses a realistic, contemporary framework. However, Piercy's work also fits comfortably within a tradition of second-wave dystopian/utopian science fiction novels, such as Ursula K. Le Guin's *The Left Hand of Darkness* (1969), Suzy McKee Charnas's *Walk to the End of the World* (1974), and Joanna Russ's *The Female Man* (1975).

Connie Ramos has been regarded as a literary anomaly: a hero out of step in a period when literary characters took action in quiet ways, if they took action at all. In a 1986 essay in *Critique: Studies in*

Modern Fiction, Carmen Cramer contrasts Connie with "the entropic and passive person" of modern American novels. Cramer opines that unlike Piercy, who "looks to possibility and dares to create a modern hero," many writers "forget to struggle with possibility, forget that there may still be a future." Connie is, however, wholly in step with the active, even violent, female protagonists created by writers such as Charnas and Russ. This emphasis on examining institutions, both familial and social, and imagining more-empowering alternatives has become central to feminist scholarship.

THEMES AND STYLE

In *Woman on the Edge of Time,* Piercy is deeply concerned with the cycle of exploitation perpetuated by sexist, classist, and racist stereotypes and the institutions in which they are embedded. Connie has found little solace in family, marriage, or community. Motherhood, which is part of the bedrock of female identity in Connie's culture, has been especially problematic. Connie's daughter was taken from her and placed in foster care after an incident of violence, and Connie cannot have more children because she was "spayed" by doctors without her consent. Moreover, Piercy illustrates how the safeguards that are meant to protect poor women serve only to further exploit them. Connie thinks angrily of "all those experts lined up against her in a jury dressed in medical white and judicial black … had caught and bound her in their nets of jargon … that stuck in her flesh and leaked a slow weakening poison." The mental health professionals in the novel are guilty of particularly grievous abuses, isolating Connie for days, denying her medical treatment, and ultimately conspiring to use her as a human guinea pig.

Piercy contrasts Connie's present-day reality as an unwilling patient at Rockover State Psychiatric Hospital with a utopian future, which she accesses via time travel. Over Connie's series of visits, her guide, Luciente, describes a society that has been structured to remove the problems associated with reproduction, poverty, and racial differences. Luciente's explanations of the changes that have occurred since Connie's time illuminate the ways in which Piercy's own society is lacking. Piercy further emphasizes this point by creating an alternative future in which inequality is extreme and the few fortunate women exist as surgically altered prostitutes. After accidentally contacting Gildina, a "contract girl" whose body "seemed a cartoon of femininity," Connie comes to realize that this society has its seeds in the experiments doctors plan to conduct on her in her present-day reality. More importantly, she sees her own obligation to be a force for change—to stop the experiments and set humanity on the path to Mattapoisett.

Connie occupies a bleak spot in late twentieth-century America, one that is described in language that underscores her powerlessness and degradation.

THE WORLD OF *HE, SHE AND IT*

In the conservative political climate of 1991, Marge Piercy published *He, She and It,* which explores some of the same themes she took up in *Woman on the Edge of Time* (1976). Set in a mid-twenty-first-century society that resembles the dystopian future world of *Woman on the Edge of Time, He, She and It* uses the speculative form to comment on twentieth-century institutions and their effect on individuals. However, the novel reflects a shift in work on gender during the 1980s, as *He, She and It* was clearly influenced by the cyberpunk movement and its treatment of gender and technology.

Set in 2059 in a world defined by the gulf between the rich corporations—the "multis"—and the impoverished masses living in the wastelands of "the glop," *He, She and It* tells the story of Shira, who is tasked with socializing the security cyborg Yod, who had received feminist programming from Shira's grandmother. As Shira relates how she lost custody of her son, the cyborg falls in love with her. Exploring the intersection of technology and gender, *He, She and It* makes an interesting companion piece to *Woman on the Edge of Time.*

Strapped to a hospital bed "staring up at a bare bulb," Connie thinks longingly of the meager possessions she brought into the facility: her "worn red plastic purse mended with tape," which had been unceremoniously taken from her by the check-in attendant and held "like something dirty, a piece of garbage from the street." Drugged, she "floats like an embryo trapped in alcohol." Such details of victimization, along with descriptions of her pitiful existence, are calculated to raise the ire of the reader and to spark action.

CRITICAL DISCUSSION

By 1976 feminist writing had attained enough cultural cache for *Woman on the Edge of Time* to receive widespread reviews. Mainstream critiques were mixed. Christopher Lehmann-Haupf, writing in the *New York Times,* criticized the novel for being "little more … than its political message." Feminist writers such as Margaret Atwood gave the novel more detailed treatments. In an essay republished in *Second Words: Selected Critical Prose* (1982), Atwood calls Piercy "daring" for attempting a serious utopian work at a time when "moral earnestness seems to have gone out of fashion."

Woman on the Edge of Time was published before reproductive technology such as prenatal testing, surrogacy, and in vitro fertilization became widespread. Anticipating some of the ethical questions associated with such technologies, the novel has been used as a jumping off point to discuss the fears Connie describes when she refers to "the bland bottleborn monsters" produced in Mattapoisettes's artificial womb. Discussing Piercy's novel, as well as Le Guin's *The Left Hand*

Author Marge Piercy in 1982. AP PHOTO/DAVID PICKOFF.

of Darkness, Cathy Rudy suggests in a 1997 essay for *NWSA Journal,* "[A]s we make decisions about reproduction today, these novels provide maps to futures wherein technology could be used to strengthen the position of women in society."

Woman on the Edge of Time has been the subject of much feminist scholarship, particularly in terms of the novel's representation of institutionalized misogyny on individual women. In a 1992 essay in *Women's Studies,* Billie Maciunas investigates how the supposedly neutral framework of science operates in the novel in sexist, classist ways. For example, poor, female, and "crazy," Connie is chosen as a subject for a brain implantation experiment. After failing to argue her way out of participating, Connie, on furlough, steals fertilizer and poisons four of her doctors. "Connie's solution of murder with the very tools that could be used for good," writes Maciunas, "reflects the dominant culture's own misuse of technology in its objectifying view of the environment." Elaine Hansen's focus is on motherhood and how pressures on Connie have contributed to her being both a loving mother who tenderly nurses her daughter and an abusive one who beats her and ultimately loses custody. "The point," she writes in *Mother without Child: Contemporary Fiction and the Crisis of Motherhood* (1997), "is that the negative consequences of the apparent dichotomy in Connie's personality and behavior are a function of the social and political context in which this woman is

positioned as a mother." Connie's problems, then, can be traced to a society whose conditions create chaos in the lives of women.

BIBLIOGRAPHY
Sources

Atwood, Margaret. "*Woman on the Edge of Time* Living in the Open." *Second Words: Selected Critical Prose.* Toronto: Anansi, 1982. Print.

Cramer, Carmen. "Anti-Automaton: Marge Piercy's Fight in *Woman on the Edge of Time.*" *Critique: Studies in Modern Fiction* 27.4 (1986): 229–233. *Literature Resource Center.* Web. 7 Sept. 2012.

Hansen, Elaine Tuttle. *Mother without Child: Contemporary Fiction and the Crisis of Motherhood.* Berkeley: U of California P, 1997. Print.

Hogeland, Lisa Maria. *Feminism and Its Fictions: The Consciousness-Raising Novel and the Women's Liberation Movement.* Philadelphia: U of Pennsylvania P, 1998. Print.

Lehmann-Haupf, Christopher. "One Flew over the Future." *New York Times* 2 June 1976: n. pag. Web. 9 Sept. 2012.

Maciunas, Billie. "Feminist Epistemology in Piercy's *Woman on the Edge of Time.*" *Women's Studies* 20.3–4 (1992): 249–258. *Literature Resource Center.* Web. 9 Sept. 2012.

Piercy, Marge. *Woman on the Edge of Time.* New York: Random House, 1976. Print.

Rudy, Cathy. "Ethics, Reproduction, Utopia: Gender and Childbearing in *Woman on the Edge of Time* and *The Left Hand of Darkness.*" *NWSA Journal* 9.1 (1997): 22. *Literature Resource Center.* Web. 9 Sept. 2012.

Further Reading

Afnan, Elham. "Chaos and Utopia: Social Transformation in *Woman on the Edge of Time.*" *Extrapolation* 37.4 (1996): 330–40. *Literature Resource Center.* Web. 7 Sept. 2012.

Booker, M. Keith. "Woman on the Edge of a Genre: The Feminist Dystopias of Marge Piercy." *Science-Fiction Studies* 21 (1994): 337–50. *Literature Resource Center.* Web. 7 Sept. 2012.

Jorgensen, Darren. "On Failure and Revolution in Utopian Fiction and Science Fiction of the 1960s and 1970s." *Colloquy* 17 (2009): 6–15. *Literature Resource Center.* Web. 10 Sept. 2012.

Keulen, Margarete. *Radical Imagination: Feminist Conceptions of the Future in Ursula Le Guin, Marge Piercy and Sally Miller Gearhart.* Frankfurt: Peter Lang, 1991. Print.

Piercy, Marge. *He, She and It.* New York: Knopf, 1991. Print.

Seabury, Marcia Bundy. "The Monsters We Create: *Woman on the Edge of Time* and *Frankenstein.*" *Critique* 42.2 (2001): 131–43. *Literature Resource Center.* Web. 9 Sept. 2012.

Shands, Kerstin. *The Repair of the World.* Westport: Greenwood, 1994. Print.

Daisy Gard

LEGISLATION AND REFORM

THE ADVENTURES OF OLIVER TWIST, OR THE PARISH BOY'S PROGRESS

Charles Dickens

OVERVIEW

Written in 1837 by Charles Dickens, *The Adventures of Oliver Twist, or the Parish Boy's Progress* recounts the tale of young Oliver Twist, who is born in a workhouse, where poor people are given jobs in exchange for food and accommodations. First serialized in *Bentley's Miscellany*, the story follows the hardships young Oliver faces as an orphaned worker who, like others at the poorhouse, suffers abuse and neglect. After requesting more food and standing up to a bully, Oliver is thrown out and spends time on the streets of London. The novel dramatizes the living and working conditions of the poor and details the crime and poverty rampant in England during that time. In doing so, it contrasts the notion of workhouses by the middle class, who saw them as a solution to England's poverty problem, with their grim realities.

Dickens's second novel, *Oliver Twist* established the author as a social reform advocate who decried the injustices suffered by the poor and working class. A departure from the subject matter of his first book, *Pickwick Papers* (1837), *Oliver Twist* focuses less on comedy and more on the treatment of the indigent. Because *Oliver Twist* was widely bootlegged and printed in cheaper, pirated editions, it became popular with working-class readers. The novel is in some ways autobiographical, drawing on the author's mostly parentless youth and his work as an apprentice. It is important as propaganda because of its exhaustive account of the life and treatment of England's ignored population: poor workers.

HISTORICAL AND LITERARY CONTEXT

Oliver Twist is a vehement reaction to the Poor Law Amendment Act of 1834. Commonly known as the New Poor Law, the act discouraged the practice of "outdoor relief," in which the poor could receive charity (often in the form of both goods and money) without entering a workhouse. By 1834 the cost of providing this relief, which was funded through a tax known as the poor rates, had become increasingly expensive. The middle class, newly empowered by the Reform Bill of 1832, was suspicious of the poor, who were often presented in both literature and journalism as lazy and unwilling to work. The New Poor Law

was designed to reduce pauperism by encouraging parishes to end the practice of outdoor relief and require that paupers enter workhouses in order to receive aid. To incentivize the pursuit of work, conditions in the workhouse were to be of a lesser quality than those which the lowest-paid laborer could afford elsewhere. The population at these institutions became increasingly made up of children, the sick, the insane, and the old—in other words, anyone incapable of refusing to live in such horrid places.

Passage of the New Poor Law generated immediate opposition. Activists included Richard Oastler and John Fielden, who wrote emotionally charged speeches and articles denouncing the law and the inhumane conditions of the workhouses. *Oliver Twist* helped to drive the anti-New Poor Law movement with its depictions of the cruelty suffered by workers. Dickens addresses the fact that many workers suffered from a lack of food with the novel's most famous line: "'Please, sir, I want some more.'"

The passage of the New Poor Law owed much to the work of middle-class journalists and fiction writers. Most notably, Harriet Martineau's popular didactic series *Illustrations of Political Economy* (1832–34) lambasts the Old Poor Law as a drain on productive members of society and, subsequently, their ability to pay reasonable wages to honest workers. Martineau also wrote *Poor Laws and Paupers Illustrated* (1833–34), in which she presents fictionalized accounts of what she saw to be the dire consequences of irresponsible charity to the poor. Martineau's work is largely credited with leveraging public support behind the reforms that would become the New Poor Law. Soon after the measures were enacted, however, many people began to oppose the legislation, and Dickens became one of the first novelists to decry the workhouse conditions. Although John Fielden's 1836 pamphlet *The Curse of the Factory System* details the exploitation of child factory workers, *Oliver Twist* specifically attacks the New Poor Law and the workhouse system.

Although public opinion was already turning against the New Poor Law by the time Dickens published *Oliver Twist,* the novel is often credited as one of the most important rallying points for those opposed to the reforms, and it has greatly influenced

✣ *Key Facts*

Time Period:
Mid-19th Century

Genre:
Novel

Events:
Poor Law Amendment of 1834; Industrial Revolution; social reform movement

Nationality:
English

PRIMARY SOURCE

EXCERPT FROM *THE ADVENTURES OF OLIVER TWIST, OR THE PARISH BOY'S PROGRESS*

Poor Oliver! He little thought, as he lay sleeping in happy unconsciousness of all around him, that the board had that very day arrived at a decision which would exercise the most material influence over all his future fortunes. But they had. And this was it:

The members of the board were very sage, deep, philosophical men, and when they came to turn their attention to the workhouse, they found out at once, what ordinary folks would never have discovered – the poor people liked it! It was a regular place of public entertainment for the poorer classes; a tavern where there was nothing to pay; a public breakfast, dinner, tea, and supper all the year round; a brick and mortar elysium, where it was all play and no work. 'Oho!' said the board, looking very knowing; 'we are the fellows to set this to rights; we'll stop it all, in no time.' So, they established the rule, that all poor people should have the alternative (for they would compel nobody, not they) of being starved by a gradual process in the house, or by a quick one out of it. With this view, they contracted with the water-works to lay on an unlimited supply of water; and with a corn-factor to supply periodically small quantities of oatmeal; and issued three meals of thin gruel a day, with an onion twice a week, and half a roll on Sundays. They made a great many other wise and humane regulations having reference to the ladies, which it is not necessary to repeat; kindly undertook to divorce poor married people, in consequence of the great expense of a suit in Doctors' Commons; and, instead of compelling a man to support his family, as they had theretofore done, took his family away from him, and made him a bachelor! There is no saying how many applicants for relief, under these last two heads, might have started up in all classes of society, if it had not been coupled with the workhouse; but the board were long-headed men, and had provided for this difficulty. The relief was inseparable from the workhouse and the gruel; and that frightened people.

For the first six months after Oliver Twist was removed, the system was in full operation. It was rather expensive at first, in consequence of the increase in the undertaker's bill, and the necessity of taking in the clothes of all the paupers, which fluttered loosely on their wasted, shrunken forms, after a week or two's gruel. But the number of workhouse inmates got thin as well as the paupers; and the board were in ecstasies.

the modern perception of workhouse conditions in particular and early Victorian treatment of the poor in general. Pirated copies of the novel quickly spread among the working classes, who embraced Oliver as a hero. Other novelists soon followed Dickens's example, writing about the abuses suffered by laborers and children in England. Elizabeth Barrett Browning's 1844 poem "The Cry of the Children" argues against the practice of child mine labor, while Charlotte Brontë's 1849 novel *Shirley* further describes the brutal conditions in factories.

THEMES AND STYLE

Central to the plot of *Oliver Twist* is the exploitation of the young and underprivileged. While Oliver is the main example of this, other characters, such as Jack Dawkins and Charley Bates, illustrate how the New Poor Law has failed to help England's street youth. Both Jack and Charley are thieves who would rather steal to support themselves than enter a workhouse. Dickens argues that the New Poor Law has only amplified the problems it was intended to mitigate by offering the workhouse as the lone solution for people lacking education and honest employment. Although many scholars contend that Oliver is a one-dimensional character because he refuses a life of crime, they agree that he is both moveable and genuine and that he calls attention to the injustices suffered by the poor. His innocent request of "Please, sir, I want some more" humanizes the struggle for survival that residents of the workhouses faced on a daily basis. As Charles Gibson points out in a 2010 essay on the novel, "Oliver's request reveals the material neglect (abuse, hunger, and poverty) of children in Dickens's time, when so many went wanting." This depiction of Oliver contrasts his innocence and helplessness with a cold, heartless system designed to make the needy less of a burden for the rich.

Dickens describes the setting of the workhouse in great detail because, as he states in the preface, "nothing effectual can be done for the elevation of the poor in England until their dwelling-places are made decent and wholesome." He reveals the terrible conditions of the workhouse in order to press for change that might actually benefit the poor. Dickens describes the decisions of the board members who endeavor to make the experience less pleasant in an attempt to motivate paupers to work outside the workhouse: "They made a great many other wise and humane regulations … kindly undertook to divorce poor married people … and instead of compelling a man to support his family … took his family away from him." *Oliver Twist* highlights the problems inherent in assuming that the poor became that way because of their laziness and suggests that, in fact, their lot in life stems from a lack of well-paying jobs and education.

Stylistically, Dickens uses satire to magnify the shortcomings of the workhouse system. He describes the gentlemen in charge as "very sage, deep, philosophical men: and when they came to turn their attention to the workhouse, they found out at once—the poor people liked it!" By mocking the notion that paupers actually like to live and work in these institutions, Dickens strengthens his argument that the people who support the New Poor Law know little about the needs of the poor. Dickens continues to satirize the board during its discussion of work and trade. One member tells Oliver that he is to be educated and taught a useful trade while living in the workhouse. The other board member elaborates, "So, you'll begin to pick oakum to-morrow morning." Picking oakum consisted of tearing apart old ship's ropes and was common practice in workhouses and prisons. No one could make a living doing it, which Dickens points out by ridiculing the board members' ignorance.

CRITICAL DISCUSSION

After *Oliver Twist* was published, many reviewers derided the novel and its author for what they considered to be sensationalism. The March 1838 issue of the *Spectator* contends that Dickens contradicted his critique of the New Poor Law because he "combined the severity of the new system with the individual tyranny of the old." Writing for the *London Quarterly Review* (1839), essayist and critic Richard Ford argues that "Oliver Twist …is directed against the poor-law and work-house system, and in our opinion with much unfairness. The abuses which he ridicules are not only exaggerated, but in nineteen cases out of twenty do not at all exist." Martineau criticized Dickens's depictions of workhouses, stating, "Another vexation is his vigorous erroneousness about matters of science, as shown in *Oliver Twist* about the new poor-law." Despite these early criticisms, *Oliver Twist* became one of Dickens's most popular books and one of his most dramatized.

Oliver Twist is the first of several of Dickens novels that deal with some aspect of social injustice. Written as a warning about the effect of the New Poor Law, it became a model for late-nineteenth-century reformers who battled for fairer wages, better treatment, and proper care for the lower classes. The author's style and subject matter influenced many writers during the nineteenth century, including Fyodor Dostoevsky, who also wrote about social injustice. In *The Diary of a Writer* (1873), Dostoevsky states, "We understand Dickens in Russia, I am convinced, almost as well as the English, and maybe even all the subtleties; maybe even we love him no less than his own countrymen."

Today's scholars focus on various aspects of *Oliver Twist,* from Dickens's sympathetic portrayal of criminals and prostitutes to his use of an orphan protagonist. On the subject of child labor, Gibson, writes, "Almost everywhere Oliver turns, from the workhouse … to his time with Fagin and his pickpocketing proteges in a London slum, he encounters coldness, nastiness, or a ruthless pragmatism. These cruelties are all key elements in Dickens's scathing criticism of his society's treatment of children." Gibson also discusses the depiction of street children: "Indeed, in Chapter XI of Oliver Twist, the suggestion that children are little better than animals is clear from the 'sort of wooden pen in which poor little Oliver was already deposited.'" Much of the scholarship on Oliver Twist focuses on Dickens's treatment of outcasts, orphans, and the indigent—all victims of the New Poor Law and the workhouse system—since he crafted the novel to expose this problem.

Illustration from a 1917 edition of Charles Dickens's novel *Oliver Twist.* © IVY CLOSE IMAGES/ALAMY.

BIBLIOGRAPHY

Sources

"Boz's Oliver Twist." *Spectator* 11.509 (1838): 1114–16. Rpt. in *Nineteenth-Century Literature Criticism.* Ed. Joann Cerrito. Vol. 37. Detroit: Gale Research, 1993. *Literature Resource Center.* Web. 8 Aug. 2012.

Dickens, Charles. *Oliver Twist.* New York: MacMillan, 1998. Print.

Dostoevsky, Fyodor. *The Diary of a Writer.* Santa Barbara: Peregrine Smith, 1979. Print.

Ford, Richard. "In an Originally Unsigned Review of 'Oliver Twist'." *London Quarterly Review* 127 (1839): 46–56. Rpt. in *Nineteenth-Century Literature Criticism.* Ed. Joann Cerrito. Vol. 37. Detroit: Gale Research, 1993. *Literature Resource Center.* Web. 8 Aug. 2012.

Gibson, Brian. "'Please, Sir, I Want Some More…. Please, Sir … I Want Some More': Unhooding Richler's Fang to Find Justice for Oliver Twist and Jacob Two-Two."

Jeunesse: Young People, Texts, Cultures 2.2 (2010): 86+. *Literature Resource Center.* Web. 8 Aug. 2012.

Martineau, Harriet. *Harriet Martineau's Autobiography and Memorials of Harriet Martineau.* 2 vols. Ed. Maria Weston Chapman Boston: James R. Osgood, 1877. Print.

Further Reading

Bell, Michael. *Sentimentalism, Ethics, and the Culture of Feeling.* New York: Palgrave, 2000. Print.

Driver, Felix. *Power and Pauperism: The Workhouse System, 1834–1884 (Cambridge Studies in Historical Geography).* UK: Cambridge UP, 2004. Print.

Newey, Vincent. *The Scriptures of Charles Dickens: Novels of Ideology, Novels of the Self (The Nineteenth Century Series).* UK: Ashgate, 2004. Print.

Richardson, Ruth. *Dickens and the Workhouse: Oliver Twist and the London Poor.* Oxford: Oxford UP, 2012. Print.

Rodensky, Lisa. *The Crime in Mind: Criminal Responsibility and the Victorian Novel.* New York: Oxford UP, 2003. Print.

Wagner, Tamara. "The Making of Criminal Children: Stealing Orphans from Oliver Twist to a Little Princess. "*Victorians: A Journal of Culture and Literature* 121 (2012): 68+. *Literature Resource Center.* Web. 9 Aug. 2012.

Winters, Kelly. "Critical Essay on *Oliver Twist.*" *Novels for Students.* Ed. Jennifer Smith. Vol. 14. Detroit: Gale, 2002. *Literature Resource Center.* Web. 9 Aug. 2012.

Media Adaptations

Oliver Twist. Dir. J. Stuart Blackton. Perf. Elita Proctor Otis. Vitagraph Company of America, 1907. Film.

Oliver Twist. Perf. Jackie Coogan and Lon Chaney. Davenport, IA: Eastin-Phelan, 1922. Film.

Oliver Twist. Dir. David Lean. Prod. Ronald Neame. Screenplay by David Lean and Stanley Haynes. Perf. Robert Newton, Alec Guinness, Kay Walsh, et al. Hollywood, CA: Paramount Pictures Corp., © 1989. VHS.

Hannah Soukup

THE ANNIHILATION OF CASTE

Bhimrao Ramji Ambedkar

OVERVIEW

In 1935 Bhimrao Ramji Ambedkar, at the request of the leadership committee of the Jat-Pat-Todak Mandal (Caste Destruction Society), wrote *The Annihilation of Caste,* which calls for the abolition of the caste system in India, demands the establishment of equal civil rights for all Indians (including the so-called untouchables), and roundly criticizes the Hindu religion for founding and maintaining the caste system. The committee had invited Ambedkar to preside over its 1936 conference in Lahore, and the author submitted the book to be published as part of the conference's proceedings. After committee members read the book, however, they withdrew their invitation to Ambedkar, refused to publish it, and canceled the conference. Undaunted, Ambedkar published the speech he would have given with an introduction relating the controversy, calling it *The Annihilation of Caste.* It caused a scandal, was widely read, and became the foundation document of a genuinely popular movement for the elimination of caste. Propaganda often aims to shatter complacency and excite controversy, and *The Annihilation of Caste* certainly accomplished both of those goals.

When Ambedkar published *The Annihilation of Caste,* India was in the midst of a multidimensional crisis. The country was first and foremost struggling to free itself from nearly two hundred years of domination by the British. At the same time, the two main religious confessions, Hinduism and Islam, were becoming increasingly antagonistic—though both sought independence from England—and many Muslims were agitating for a geographical separation of the two faiths into sovereign nations of India and Pakistan. At the same time, western ideals of social justice were weakening the traditional framework of Indian society. Those on the lowest rungs of the social ladder were beginning to fight their way up, educating themselves despite the fierce resistance of the privileged. Ambedkar, as the first leader of the untouchables, was the standard bearer of this struggle. His book's impact was explosive and lasting.

HISTORICAL AND LITERARY CONTEXT

Ambedkar's work must be read in the context of the approximately 2,500-year-old caste system in India. The system itself applies only to Hindus, and caste, which is roughly analogous to a social class, is inseparable from occupation. At the top are the Brahmans—the priests and teachers—and the Kshatriyas, the warriors who are often royal. Next are the Vaishyas—the traders, retailers, farmers, and money lenders—and at the bottom are the Sudras, the manual laborers. One might take the caste system as the equivalent of the feudal system in medieval Europe, whose societal divisions of the religious hierarchy, aristocratic elites, bourgeois merchants and artisans, and peasants seem to correspond to the four castes. The difference, however, is crucial to understanding the violence of Ambedkar's feelings. Even during the rigid hierarchies of the Middle Ages, all Christians had equal access to the sacraments; no peasant was denied communion because he was a peasant. The Hindu priests, on the other hand, judged that the lowest tiers of Sudra occupations put them below the line of ritual purity, rendering them "untouchable" for any pious Hindu. It must be understood that the untouchables never constituted a caste; untouchability is a quality "inherent" in certain types of job, making outcastes of those who work at them.

By 1936 when Ambedkar published his book, the original four castes had evolved into a system of byzantine complexity. As the economy had grown more complex and the variety of occupations proliferated, new castes had emerged. Each region had developed its own distinctive groupings. The inequality was finely graded rather than sharply divided between upper and lower, and the shadings were different in different places. Also, by 1936 caste had ceased to be based, in a practical sense, upon occupation and was simply a system of institutionalized social injustice that operated with the full weight of religious authority. Suffering this injustice firsthand, Ambedkar had been working against the caste system at least since 1919 and had been founding active movements against untouchability since 1927.

It is not an overstatement to say that *The Annihilation of Caste* utterly changed the terms of debate over the future of Indian society. Before Ambedkar's book appeared, all reform movements were associations of liberal members of the highest castes, and they sought to introduce reforms without any fundamental changes to the caste system. These well-intentioned Brahmans, such as the Jat-Pat-Todak Mandal, wished to alleviate the suffering and deprivation of the lower

⁘ *Key Facts*

Time Period:
Mid-20th Century

Genre:
Speech

Events:
Indian fight for independence; growth of the anti-caste movement

Nationality:
Indian

AMBEDKAR V. GANDHI

Bhimrao Ramji Ambedkar (1891–1956) and Mohandas K. Gandhi (1869–1948) were united in their conviction that the British must leave India for India to govern itself, but they were divided on virtually everything else. Both sought to end the caste system, but their motives and methods could not have been more different. Gandhi sought to save the Hindu faith by eliminating caste, claiming that "caste has nothing to do with religion. It is a custom whose origin I do not know, and do not need to know for the satisfaction of my spiritual hunger. But I do know that it is harmful both to spiritual and national growth."

Ambedkar, in his response, argues that "what the Mahatma seems to me to suggest in its broadest and simplest form is that Hindu society can be made tolerable and even happy without any fundamental change in its structure, if all the high-caste Hindus can be persuaded to follow a high standard of morality in their dealings with the low-caste Hindus. I am totally opposed to this kind of ideology." Ambedkar thought that the only solution to caste would be government action. "The best of men cannot be moral if the basis of relationship between them and their fellows is fundamentally a wrong relationship. To a slave, his master may be better or worse. But there cannot be a good master."

orders while working within the existing system. Ambedkar's book located the source of injustice in the caste system itself, and, beyond that, in the Hindu religion, which he viewed as propagating the system. From 1936 to the present, no one can discuss social justice in India without taking into account Ambedkar and his ideas—nor can they be discussed without taking into consideration the opinions of those most immediately concerned: the poor and outcaste.

Ambedkar was a powerful writer but not a literary man in the accepted sense of the term. He was born in 1891 in Bombay (today Mumbai) as an untouchable. His father had been in the Indian army and was therefore outside the caste system. He used this to make the (English) government take his children into their schools—which they did, though only Ambedkar did well enough to continue to high school. He did so well in high school that he attracted the attention of a local maharajah, who became his sponsor and sent him to Columbia University in New York and then to the London School of Economics. He trained as a lawyer and wrote like one. Everything he wrote had the solid logic of a legal brief, albeit a passionate one. To engage properly with his ideas, Ambedkar's contemporaries had to reply using the same logic, which had the effect of altering the whole tone of Indian writing. Today, though he has been dead for half a century, Ambedkar continues to be regularly cited in all manner of publications, far more than even Mohandas Gandhi, his contemporary.

THEMES AND STYLE

The theme of *The Annihilation of Caste* is eponymous: in the name of justice, the Indian caste system must be utterly obliterated. A related theme is that the Hindu faith must take responsibility for its role in the caste system and abolish it. Ambedkar developed these and other themes in *The Annihilation of Caste* with the unanswerable logic of a great lawyer pleading the case of his career. The very lack of adornment served his purpose, as when he states: "Caste does not result in economic efficiency. Caste cannot improve, and has not improved, the race. Caste has however done one thing. It has completely disorganized and demoralized the Hindus."

Ambedkar's consistent strategy in *The Annihilation of Caste* was to make a quasilegal argument—to amass a mountain of evidence demonstrating the destruction wrought by the caste system and the benefits of its abolition, much as the parliamentarian William Wilberforce, who assembled evidence in arguing for the abolition of slavery in the British empire, had done a century earlier. "The first and foremost thing that must be recognized," Ambedkar writes in section six, "is that Hindu Society is a myth. The name Hindu is itself a foreign name. It was given by the Mohammedans [Muslims] to the natives for the purpose of distinguishing themselves [from them]. It does not occur in any Sanskrit work prior to the Mohammedan invasion. They did not feel the necessity of a common name, because they had no conception of their having constituted a community. Hindu Society as such does not exist. It is only a collection of castes. Each caste is conscious of its existence. Its survival is the be-all and end-all of its existence. Castes do not even form a federation. A caste has no feeling that it is affiliated to other castes, except when there is a Hindu-Muslim riot. On all other occasions each caste endeavors to segregate itself and to distinguish itself from other castes." Although Ambedkar's version of the origins of Hindu society is by no means unchallenged, he usually persuades, even when his facts are shaky.

Under Ambedkar's tone of irrefutable and glacial logic, there was the implicit potent force of molten anger fueled by personal experience. As an untouchable, he knew the propaganda value of giving his readers the occasional glimpse of that anger, his version of Walt Whitman's "I am the man / I was there / I suffered." He was fearless. "The Hindu Civilisation," he wrote, "is a diabolical contrivance to suppress and enslave humanity. Its proper name would be infamy. What else can be said of a civilisation which has produced a mass of people … who are treated as an entity beyond human intercourse and whose mere touch is enough to cause pollution?" At the end of his life, after threatening many times to leave Hinduism, Ambedkar finally did so. He became a Buddhist, and some five hundred thousand of his supporters followed his example.

A Dalit man, a member of the untouchable caste in India, participating in a 2003–2004 march to raise awareness of the caste. He wears a cameo depicting Bhimrao Ramji Ambedkar, the author of *The Annihilation of Caste.* © ANTOINE SERRA/ IN VISU/CORBIS.

CRITICAL DISCUSSION

There were two diametrically opposed reactions to Ambedkar's book in 1936: furious rejection of the author by the liberal aristocrats and enthusiastic embrace of him by the Indian masses, confirming him as their hero and champion. The most serious reaction from the first group was that of Gandhi, who wrote, "In my opinion the profound mistake that Dr. Ambedkar has made in his address is to pick out the texts of doubtful authenticity and value, and the state of degraded Hindus who are no fit specimens of the faith they so woefully misrepresent. Judged by the standard applied by Dr. Ambedkar, every known living faith will probably fail." He also suggested that Ambedkar lower the price of the book, to make it more accessible—as he felt that everyone should read it. Ambedkar promptly included Gandhi's entire response, and his own reply to it, as appendices in the next edition of his book.

The social, cultural, and political legacy of *The Annihilation of Caste* is incalculable. Once Ambedkar's ideas and perspectives on Indian society were placed on the table, they could never again be removed. His writings are, even now, cited and argued throughout India. On a more concrete level, Ambedkar was named first law minister after India became a sovereign nation in 1947. He was also appointed chairman of the committee charged with drafting India's constitution and wrote most of the draft himself. When the constitution became law in November 1949, it established many essential civil liberties for individual citizens, including the abolition of untouchability—thus

completing his lifelong quest, at least on paper. The concept and practice of untouchability did not vanish with the adoption of the constitution, however; prejudice and repression continue, particularly in rural regions. The outcaste group are now called Dalit—a Sanskrit word meaning "suppressed," "crushed," or "broken to pieces." "In hundreds of districts and several states," notes sociologist Abdul Malid, "the Dalits live today in a constant state of fear due to threats to their life. For Dalits throughout South Asia, caste remains a determinative factor for the attainment of social, political, civil, and economic rights."

No Indian social and political thinker of the twentieth century is more widely studied and quoted in his own country than Ambedkar, though Gandhi is better known and has had more influence internationally as a prophet of justice and nonviolence. Although Ambedkar's ideas remain controversial, the progressives and populists keep his name alive. India is a functioning democracy, with almost universal adult suffrage, and Ambedkar remains extremely popular with the masses. The conservative critique of his work is more often expressed as tacit disapproval rather than explicit criticism. Those who are critical base their objections, like Gandhi, on religious grounds. For the left, Ambedkar remains a guarantor of proper thinking, a founder of social justice movements throughout South Asia. Whenever a progressive writer in India needs to cite irrefutable support of an argument, Ambedkar is summoned. In an October 2008 article on affirmative action in India, Ashwinde Deshpande notes that "the secular approach of B. R. Ambedkar stressed the urgency of civic and economic improvement under government auspices. It is the latter that gave rise to an affirmative action programme in the form of constitutionally mandated compensatory discrimination provisions." Hartosh Singh Bal asks, "From Buddha to Ambedkar, some of our most outstanding minds have tried to fight caste. Why doesn't it go away, and why are we so afraid to take note of it?"

BIBLIOGRAPHY

Sources

Ambedkar, B. R. *Annihilation of Caste with a Reply to Mahatma Gandhi.* Jullundur City: Bheem Patrika, 1971. Print.

Deshpande, Ashwini. "Quest for Equality: Affirmative Action in India." *Indian Journal of Industrial Relations* Oct. 2008: 154+. *Academic OneFile.* Web. 10 Oct. 2012.

Jaffrelot, Christophe. *Dr. Ambedkar and Untouchability: Analysing and Fighting Caste.* London: Hurst, 2005. Print.

Reid, Gordon. "Caste: The Hindu Apartheid? Gordon Reid Investigates the Controversial Subject of the Hindu Caste System." *RS Review* Apr. 2006: 28+. *General OneFile.* Web. 12 Oct. 2012.

Singh Bal, Hartosh. "The Persistence of Caste." *Open* 13 May 2010. General OneFile. Web. 10 Oct. 2012.

"Unmasking Caste." *Indian Currents* 24 May 2010. *Infotrac Newsstand.* Web. 10 Oct. 2012.

Further Reading

Ananthaswamy, Anil. "Written in Blood." *New Scientist* May 2001: 17. *General OneFile.* Web. 12 Oct. 2012.

Austin, Granville. *The Indian Constitution: Cornerstone of a Nation.* Oxford: Clarendon, 1966. Print.

Gandhi, Arun. "One God, Many Images." *Tikkun* Sept.-Oct. 2005: 56+. *General OneFile.* Web. 10 Oct. 2012.

Majid, Abdul. "Future of Untouchables in India: A Case Study of Dalit." *South Asian Studies* 30 June 2012. Web. 10 Oct. 2012.

Gerald Carpenter

"THE CHIMNEY SWEEPER"

William Blake

OVERVIEW

"The Chimney Sweeper" is the title of two poems of social criticism by British Romantic poet William Blake, one published in *Songs of Innocence* (1789) and the other published in *Songs of Experience* (1794). The first poem tells the story of Tom, a sad young sweep who escapes his harsh life in a glorious dream in which all the downtrodden sweeps, already dead from their filthy work, are rescued by an angel who sets them free to play, clean and happy, in the clouds. This dream gives Tom the heart to wake up and continue his drudgery with a cheerful spirit. The second poem gives a much grimmer picture of the life of a young chimney sweep, whose parents are pictured serenely praying in church after forcing their child into the bleak and deadly labor. Taken together, the poems serve to shine a light on the realities of child labor and the overly romanticized profession of chimney sweeps.

The humanitarian and reformist sensibilities of the eighteenth century caused many Britons to examine the plight of the poor and oppressed with an eye toward improving their lot and thus elevating society in general. In the late 1700s, the strict rationality of the early Enlightenment was tempered by the Romantics, who valued personal expression, connection to nature, and emotional truth. Blake's poems, with their deep emotion and sense of moral outrage, were welcomed by the Romantics, who sought to reform society through a passionate glorification of common humanity and personal freedom. To those in power and those who supported the status quo in governmental and religious institutions, Blake's work in *Songs of Innocence* and *Songs of Experience* represented a challenge and a reproach, while to the rationalists, they represented a disturbing mysticism and emotional disarray.

HISTORICAL AND LITERARY CONTEXT

The eighteenth century was a period of revolutionary change throughout Europe and its colonies around the world. Transformative developments in political, scientific, and religious thought led to the creation of new forms of government and an increasingly industrialized economy. The American and French revolutions were products of the ideals of the Enlightenment, as was the Industrial Revolution, which transformed the lives of working people. The shift from agriculture to industry promised enormous economic benefits but created an increasing population of factory, mine, and mill workers who often toiled long hours in appalling conditions, earning barely enough to survive. An alarming number of these workers were children.

"The Chimney Sweeper" in *Songs of Innocence* was published in 1789 amid a wave of reform efforts to improve the lives of working children, particularly chimney sweeps. In the 1600s the term "chimney sweeper" had been coined to describe workers who cleaned the sooty flues that supplied heat to British homes. Master sweeps used crews of small "climbing children"—nearly 4,000 of them by the 1700s, some as young as four years old—to clean the narrow, crooked chimneys by hand. These apprentices, paid only with meager food and a sack of soot to sleep on, were usually sold into labor by impoverished families. Their youth, pathetic appearance, and clear abuse at the hands of their masters made sweeps a poignant symbol of worker oppression. In 1775 British surgeon Percivall Pott demonstrated a connection between chimney soot and cancer in young sweepers, helping to launch an almost century-long fight to ban the use of climbing children. Eventually, Parliament passed the Chimney Sweepers Act of 1788, an ineffective first attempt at reform. Blake's poems on the subject serve as both reflection and catalyst of this evolution in view.

The Enlightenment gave rise to a literature of social critique. In France, Voltaire and Jean-Jacques Rousseau pioneered conflicting views of social perfection; in Britain, poet Alexander Pope angered those in power with his acerbic couplets in *The Rape of the Lock* (1712), and Irish writer Jonathan Swift shocked society with his biting satire *A Modest Proposal for Preventing the Children of Poor People in Ireland Being a Burden on Their Parents or Country* (1729). Merchant and philanthropist Jonas Hanway was one of the first to publicly address the issue of climbing children, giving a vivid description of the sweep's cruel life in *A Sentimental History of Chimney-Sweepers in London and Westminster* (1785).

One of the earliest Romantic writers, Blake brought a spirituality to his social vision that seemed to lift his poetry to a mythic level while giving his images an intense personal resonance. His deeply felt "Chimney Sweeper" poems contributed to the movement that finally succeeded in outlawing the use of

♦ *Key Facts*

Time Period:
Late 18th Century

Genre:
Poetry

Events:
Industrial Revolution;
American Revolution;
French Revolution

Nationality:
English

CHIM-CHIMINY: THE CHIMNEY SWEEPER IN MYTH

Perhaps to atone for their oppressed state at the bottom rung of Britain's social ladder, a number of legends sprang up that elevated chimney sweepers to mythic status and imbued them with special powers to bring luck with a kiss or a handshake. Several stories trace the "lucky chimney sweep" to a British king (some say the eleventh-century King William, others the eighteenth-century George II) whose life was saved when a sweep caught his runaway horse or pushed him out of the way of a passing carriage. The grateful king invited the humble sweep to his daughter's wedding, and sweeps have been considered lucky wedding guests ever since.

Another persistent iconic image is the young urchin who has run away or been abducted from an upper-class family and forced into the filthy and degraded life of a chimney cleaner. This romantic image of the poor sweep as the lost heir to a great fortune was used to great effect by Charles Dickens, who wrote of such a sweep in his 1836 story "The First of May," presaging a similar storyline in his successful 1838 novel *Oliver Twist.*

climbing children in 1864, and his poems anticipated a number of other works, especially Charles Kingsley's 1863 children's story *The Water-Babies: A Fairy Tale for a Land-Baby,* whose hero is a dead chimney sweep named Tom.

THEMES AND STYLE

"The Chimney Sweeper" poems are centered on the condition of childhood, which Blake views as the natural innocent state of humankind, corrupted and despoiled by brutal experience and by the callous and self-serving institutions of church and state. By the fourth line of "The Chimney Sweeper" in *Songs of Innocence,* Blake also requires the reader to take responsibility for these wrongs: "So *your* chimneys I sweep & in soot I sleep" (emphasis added). In the *Songs of Experience* poem, the mother and father—and with them, the whole of society—are directly culpable for their son's misery: "Because I was happy upon the heath / And smil'd among the winters snow: / They clothed me in the clothes of death." Both poems take aim directly at the church, which teaches the poor to wait passively for a reward in the afterlife. In the *Innocence* poem, Tom and the other sweeps must remain locked in their coffin like chimneys until the angel frees them, and even though they experience a moment of clean, free happiness, they must return to their labor "happy and warm" because "the Angel told Tom, / if he'd be a good boy, / He'd have God for his father & never want joy." The joint senses of "want"—in the sense of lacking joy but also in the sense of wishing for it—illustrate Blake's masterful use of irony.

Blake's poems have a deceptively simple format, but within the dreamy images there is sharp irony and bitter censure. "The Chimney Sweeper" in *Innocence* reinforces childish naiveté with simple sentences that run together, connected by the rhythmic repetition of "and," almost like a fairy tale or a story told by a child. The simple story is stopped short twice with a jarring tone of self-righteousness, once in the angel's syrupy promise that God would be Tom's father, and again at the end, with the narrator's incongruous moral tagline, "So if all do their duty they need not fear harm." The *Experience* poem employs a more sophisticated sentence structure and a more explicit ironic reprimand for those who cause the sweep's distress: "They think they have done me no injury: / And are gone to praise God & his Priest & King / Who make up a heaven of our misery." Both poems use the repetition of "weep, weep," which highlights the sweeper's mournful life while echoing the chant, "Sweep! Sweep!" that the chimney cleaner uses to attract customers.

The language of the poem of *Innocence,* though it tells a dismal tale, emphasizes the resilience and purity of childhood, describing the sweeps in Tom's dream "down a green plain leaping, laughing, they run, / And wash in a river, and shine in the Sun." Tom himself has hair "that curl'd like a lamb's back," a Christlike image that is repeated in the angel's assurance that God will be his father. The poem in *Experience* is firmly rooted in pain, repeating the phrase "notes of woe" and contrasting the innate happiness of the sweep with his miserable state.

CRITICAL DISCUSSION

As the Romantics challenged the rational Enlightenment worldview, Blake's mystical works excited both enthusiasm and alarm within the literary world. William Wordsworth and Robert Southey believed Blake to be deranged, while Samuel Coleridge considered him "a man of Genius." Essayist Charles Lamb—who wrote a well-known and highly romanticized account of chimney sweeps that portrayed them as "charming" in their misery—described the poet as "one of the most extraordinary persons of the age," and in 1824 arranged for publication of "The Chimney Sweeper" poems in the activist publication *The Chimney Sweeper's Friend, and Climbing Boy's Album.* Victorian poet and critic Algernon Swinburne admired Blake and called the two "Chimney Sweeper" works "poems of very perfect beauty," adding, "One cannot say, being so slight and seemingly wrong in metrical form, how they come to be so absolutely right."

"The Chimney Sweeper" in *Songs of Innocence* and *Songs of Experience* became part of the foundation of a broad social movement to end unregulated child labor. In conjunction with Mary Alcock's "The Chimney Sweeper's Complaint" (1799) and James Montgomery's "The Climbing Boy's Soliloquies" (1817), Blake's poems humanized the sweeps and urged society to take responsibility for improving their condition. Along with Fanny Burney (*Cecilia,* 1782) and Charles Dickens

(*Oliver Twist*, 1838), Blake developed the image of the young chimney sweep as an archetype of innocence oppressed and betrayed. Even more than other popular literature depicting the sweeps' grim lives, Blake's profound emotionality and mysterious imagery give his poetry a lasting depth and fascination for scholars.

Modern students of "The Chimney Sweeper" continue to explore the intermingling of the poet's passionate social conscience with his unconventional spirituality and personal eccentricity. This continuing discussion is perhaps best exemplified in the ongoing analysis of the last line of "The Chimney Sweeper" in *Innocence*: "So if all do their duty they need not fear harm." The line, with its pat morality coming at the end of Tom's poignant dream of escape from drudgery, jars the reader into questioning its truth. In his biography of Blake, D.G. Gillham refers to the line as a "shabby pronouncement," while Stewart Crehan, in *Blake in Context* (1084), describes it as "close to naiveté." And while the line can be read as such, a more nuanced interpretation is that the boy must cling to and parrot back moral platitudes as a mechanism for coping with terrible circumstances. The reader, on the other hand, can better process the indoctrination of society and see quite clearly what K. E. Smith notes in her essay "Our Immortal Day: *Songs of Innocence I*" as a more direct demand for social change: If *all* do their duty, including parents, master chimney sweeps, members of the government, and society in general, then harm can be prevented.

BIBLIOGRAPHY

Sources

Baulch, David M. "Reading Coleridge Reading Blake." *Coleridge Bulletin* 16 (2000): 5–14. *The Friends of Coleridge.* Web. 31 July 2012.

Crehan, Stewart. *Blake in Context.* Dublin: Gill and MacMillan, 1984.

Dike, Donald A. "The Difficult Innocence: Blake's *Songs* and Pastoral." *ELH* 28.4 (1961): 353–75. Rpt. in *Poetry Criticism.* Vol. 63. Detroit: Gale, 2005. *Literature Resource Center.* Web. 30 July 2012.

Gillham, D.G. *William Blake.* Cambridge: Cambridge UP, 1973.

Harrison, James. "Blake's 'The Chimney Sweeper.'" *Explicator* 36 (1978): 2–3. Print.

Lamb, Charles. "A Letter to Bernard Barton on May 15, 1824." *The Letters of Charles Lamb.* Ed. Alfred Ainger. Vol. 2. New York: A. C. Armstrong & Son, 1888. 104–06. Rpt. in *Children's Literature Review.* Detroit: Gale. *Literature Resource Center.* Web. 28 July 2012.

Smith, K. E. "Our Immortal Day: *Songs of Innocence I.*" *An Analysis of William Blake's Early Writings and Designs to 1790 Including* Songs of Innocence. Lewiston: Edwin Mellen, 1999. 153–83. Rpt. in *Poetry Criticism.* Vol. 63. Detroit: Gale, 2005. *Literature Resource Center.* Web. 28 July 2012.

Swinburne, Algernon Charles. "An Excerpt from *William Blake: A Critical Essay.*" London: Chatto & Windus, 1906. 123–40. Rpt. in *Children's Literature Review.*

Ed. Deborah J. Morad. Vol. 52. Detroit: Gale Group, 1999. *Literature Resource Center.* Web. 30 July 2012.

Williams, Porter, Jr. "'Duty' in Blake's 'The Chimney Sweeper' of *Songs of Innocence.*" *ELN* 12 (1974): 92–96. Print.

Further Reading

Dorfman, Deborah. *Blake in the Nineteenth Century: His Reputation as a Poet from Gilchrist to Yeats.* New Haven: Yale UP, 1969. Print.

Erdman, David V. *Blake: Prophet against Empire.* Princeton: Princeton UP, 1977. Print.

Linkin, Harriet Kramer. "The Language of Speakers in *Songs of Innocence and of Experience.*" *Romanticism Past and Present* 10.2 (1986): 5–24. Rpt. in *Poetry Criticism.* Vol. 63. Detroit: Gale, 2005. *Literature Resource Center.* Web. 27 July 2012.

Tuttle, Carolyn. *Hard at Work in Factories and Mines: The Economics of Child Labor during the British Industrial Revolution.* Oxford: Westview, 1999. Print.

Vines, Timothy. "An Analysis of William Blake's *Songs of Innocence and of Experience* as a Response to the Collapse of Values." *Cross-sections* 1 (2005). *ANU eView.* Australian National University. Web. 31 July 2012.

Tina Gianoulis

"The Chimney Sweeper," from William Blake's *Songs of Innocence and Experience,* hand-lettered and illustrated by the author. P.125–1950. PT 37 "THE CHIMNEY SWEEPER,": PLATE 37 FROM *SONGS OF INNOCENCE AND EXPERIENCE,* (COPY AA) C.1815–26 (ETCHING, INK AND W/C), BLAKE, WILLIAM (1757–1827)/ FITZWILLIAM MUSEUM, UNIVERSITY OF CAMBRIDGE, UK/THE BRIDGEMAN ART LIBRARY.

"THE CRY OF THE CHILDREN"

Elizabeth Barrett Browning

✣ *Key Facts*

Time Period:
Mid-19th Century

Genre:
Poetry

Events:
Industrial Revolution;
social reform movement;
child labor reform

Nationality:
English

OVERVIEW

Written by Elizabeth Barrett Browning, "The Cry of the Children" (1843) calls attention to the appalling working conditions and exploitation of child mine workers in England during the latter part of the Industrial Revolution. The poem was first published in *Blackwood's Edinburgh Magazine* and was later included in Browning's 1844 collection *Poems*. Delivered in a halting rhythm that mimics crying or sobbing, the text serves as an exposé of the dangers and abuse the children faced and pleads for someone to pay attention. Interspersed with the narrator's appeals are the voices of child laborers, who describe their exhaustion and their belief that everyone, even God, has forgotten them. The poem's emphasis on the need to regulate safety standards and working hours made it a valuable tool for social reformers, whose work led to the passage of the Ten Hours Act in 1847.

By 1843 England's social reform movement was well underway. Led by prominent members of the middle class such as Peter Gaskell and Edwin Chadwick, the crusade unified those concerned about the injustices being perpetrated on the working class and the needy. As the daughter of a wealthy businessman, Browning had spent little, if any, time in the company of working-class people and therefore had no firsthand knowledge of their difficulties. She was greatly influenced by a report that her friend, the poet R. H. Horne, wrote as part of the Royal Commission of Inquiry into Children's Employment. Horne documented the social oppression of children who worked in dangerous conditions in factories and mines, and Browning included many of his findings in her work. The poem immediately drew the attention of Browning's contemporaries, some of whom saw in it more emotional impact than technical prowess, and the public, who responded unreservedly to its sympathetic narrative. "The Cry of the Children" became one of the Victorian era's most popular protest poems.

HISTORICAL AND LITERARY CONTEXT

The Industrial Revolution began in England in the mid-eighteenth century and by the mid-nineteenth century it had changed the country's economy significantly. Before the mid-eighteenth century, there were few manufacturing facilities, and most transportation was limited to horse or handcart. With the development of the steam engine, the construction of factories, and the building of railroads, scores of workers were needed to mine iron and coal and work in textile mills and parts production. Children made up the majority of the working population in these industries, and many children worked sixteen-hour days in overcrowded, unventilated surroundings. In addition, many were beaten and many were maimed or killed in machinery accidents. Approximately two-thirds of mine workers died before the age of twenty-five from lung cancer or other disorders.

Responding to increasing pressure for social reform, between 1802 and 1833 Parliament passed major factory legislation, including restrictions to keep factory owners from forcing children less than eighteen years old to work for more than twelve hours a day. The lack of adequate enforcement and progress moved Browning to write "The Cry of the Children," which stresses that even twelve hours of work a day exhausted young laborers and contributed to their poor health. In Browning's text, child workers beg for death, preferring it over their relentless work and ill-treatment leading to a future filled with pain. The 1843 poem roused public concern to a pitch that was hard to ignore, inspiring the introduction of the Ten-Hours Bill in Parliament. Lawmakers delayed taking action, however, because of fears that the bill would be detrimental to the mining and manufacturing industries and slow England's economy. In 1847 lawmakers were finally compelled to pass the bill into law, limiting work to ten hours a day for children nine to eighteen years of age and banning children under nine from working. Additional laws passed in the 1850s guaranteed that children would not work in the mines.

"The Cry of the Children" participates in a broad body of Industrial Revolution-era literature addressing the exploitation of the poor and young. William Blake's two poems titled "The Chimney Sweeper," written in 1789 and 1794, significantly inspired Browning. Both poems decry the abuse of child laborers. In the first poem a young chimney sweep protests, "My father sold me while yet my tongue / Could scarcely cry 'weep! 'weep! 'weep! 'weep!"; in the second, a boy chimney sweep knows he has been "clothed in the clothes of death." Many early Victorian essayists and novelists also expressed dissatisfaction over harsh work environments and lack of regulations protecting young workers. In the essay *Chartism* (1839), historian Thomas Carlyle denounces the Industrial Revolution as presenting further opportunity for the rich to take advantage of the poor and underprivileged. Charlotte Elizabeth Tonna's novel *Helen Fleetwood: A Tale of the Factories* (1841) portrays child labor in the cotton mills and warns of the moral degradation inherent in industrialization. Many iconic poets of the period, including Robert Browning, William Wordsworth, and Samuel Taylor Coleridge, focused on mythology and psychological realism. Elizabeth Barrett Browning's poem was one of the few that directly addressed issues of labor and poverty.

In the decades following the publication of Browning's influential poem, the exploitation and premature deaths of child workers remained a frequent topic of literature. Among the best-known of the period's tragic child characters are Jo, the crossing sweeper who succumbs to pneumonia in Charles Dickens's novel *Bleak House* (1852), and Bessy Higgins, a central character in Elizabeth Gaskell's *North and South* (1855), who dies from prolonged inhalation of fibers in a cotton mill. Browning wrote little about social reform after the publication of *Poems*; most of her later work focuses on religion and love. Reviewers continued to praise her poem well into the early twentieth century. Many modern critics still consider it the strongest poem in her 1844 collection and attest to its importance in relation to the political climate and the writings of other female authors of the period.

THEMES AND STYLE

The central theme of "The Cry of the Children" is the never-ending labor endured by lower-class children and the ultimate tragedy of their lives. It associates the role of young miners and factory workers in England's industrial system with the wheel, a common symbol of machinery and transportation. Besides referring to actual wheels ("We drive the wheels of iron / In the factories, round and round"), the poem uses wheel imagery as a metaphor for the child laborers' struggle to survive: "And all day, the iron wheels are droning; / And sometimes we could pray, / 'O ye wheels,' (breaking out in a mad moaning) / 'Stop! be silent for to-day!'" The desperate children realize that their lives are chained to an eternally active machine. The poet denounces a system in which young lives are considered merely a cog in the machinery of England's economic progress. Ultimately, wheels foreshadow the fate of the workers, who look into the sky and see, instead of God, only "dark, wheel-like, turning clouds."

Browning uses the second person ("you") throughout her thirteen-stanza poem, with the narrator and the children addressing readers directly and implicating them in the issue. She stresses that basic elements of life that readers take for granted—fresh air, free movement, good health—are denied to an entire segment of the population. The poem contrasts the sight of "the young lambs bleating in the meadows"

"THE CRY OF THE CHILDREN": SILENT FILM LEGACY

Seventy years after Elizabeth Barrett Browning's "The Cry of the Children" was published, the Progressive Party in the United States found a new use for it. On April 30, 1912, Edwin Thanhouser released a silent film with the same title that documented the exploitation of working-class women and children during the early 1900s in the United States. The film was inspired by a large, highly publicized strike that had taken place two months earlier, when 25,000 textile workers at the American Woolen Company in Lawrence, Massachusetts, opposed a proposed wage reduction.

Using lines from the poem as subtitles throughout the film, Thanhouser chronicles the life of a young girl, Alice, and her working-class family. The owner of the local mill, a rich man who profits from the misery and hard work of others, manipulates the family into sacrificing their daughter. Like Little Alice of Browning's poem, however, the Alice of the film is assumed to be happier in death than she was working in the mines. Just as the poem is recognized for its positive contribution to British child labor reform, Thanhouser's film is also seen as having galvanized in the next century the progressive and social-reform movements in the United States.

with what the exploited children see, which is only "the coal-dark, underground." Consequently, "They are weeping in the playtime of the others, / In the country of the free." In his 2001 essay "Barrett Browning's Poetic Vocation: Crying, Singing, Breathing," Steve Dillon discusses the weeping motif in the poem, noting that the author "organizes articulate cries for creatures and objects in the world who have no human voice." The poet unflinchingly portrays the inequalities in power inherent in a class system that silences the poor. Appealing to her audience's ethics and, simultaneously, to their fellow-feeling, she verbalizes the workers' plea: "'How long,' they say, 'how long, O cruel nation, / Will you stand, to move the world, on a child's heart.'" By conflating the reader with the industrialists and the country's governing bodies, Browning extends responsibility for the children's suffering to all who do nothing to stop it.

From the poem's opening lines, the narrator's tone evokes emotion from the reader: "Do ye hear the children weeping, O my brothers / Ere the sorrow comes with years? / They are leaning their young heads against their mothers, / And *that* cannot stop their tears." The image of a mother who cannot comfort her child—and of a child who cannot be comforted—is particularly heartbreaking and guilt-inducing. The poem's epigraph, "Alas, alas, why do you gaze at me with your eyes, my children?" (from the Greek tragedy *Medea*, in which the protagonist kills her own children) is reiterated in the lines, "They look up, with their pale and

An engraving from 1838 depicting children performing hard labor. SNARK/ART RESOURCE, NY.

sunken faces, / And their look is dread to see," reflecting the treachery of adults. Through the narrator, the children speak plaintively of their hardships, describing the pain when "'our knees tremble sorely in the stooping– / We fall upon our faces, trying to go." It is all but impossible to ignore their suffering.

CRITICAL DISCUSSION

When "Cry of the Children" was published, literary critics praised it for calling attention to a difficult social issue. It quickly served as the battle cry of middle-class liberal reformers. The work's powerful effect on Browning's contemporaries is exemplified in an anonymous 1847 *Tait's Edinburgh Magazine* review of *Poems* that explains, "The 'cry of the factory children' moves you, because it is no poem at all—it is just a long sob, veiled and stifled as it ascends through the hoarse voices of the poor beings themselves. Since we read it we can scarcely pass a factory without seeming to hear this psalm issuing from the machinery." In an 1845 issue of the *Broadway Journal*, Edgar Allan Poe describes the work as "full of a nervous unflinching energy—a horror sublime in its simplicity—of which a far greater than Dante might have been proud." Poe critiques the poem's lack of rhythm, however: "'The Cry of the Children' cannot be scanned: we *never saw* so poor a specimen of verse." Others more unequivocally admired the compelling emotional tenor of the piece. In *The Victorian Age of English Literature* (1892), Scottish author Margaret (Mrs.) Oliphant honors the poem for expressing "a passion and pathos with which

the soul of England was wrung … [It] formed at once the highest expression and stimulus of a great wave of popular feeling." The strong narrative also commanded the attention of the public, many of whom did not read poetry, and it made Browning's verses a popular sensation.

Since its publication, Browning's poem has often been referenced in regard to the issue of child labor. Scholars agree that it was a great success as an instrument of persuasion, raising awareness of the social consequences of the Industrial Revolution and its effects on the poor and working classes. It is not often taught in literature classes, however, because it is not considered representative of Browning's career, specifically her later, more famous works. In "A More Vigorous Voice: The Poems of 1844," Virginia Radley points out that the poem "still crops up from time to time in anthologies. It is a good choice, for it remains one of Elizabeth's most effective poems."

"The Cry of the Children" has led to scholarship in its own right and in relation to other works by Victorian women writers, including Gaskell's *North and South*. In "Combating an Alien Tyranny: Elizabeth Barrett Browning's Evolution as a Feminist Poet" (1987), Deborah Byrd explains that although much of *Poems* "carries on [the] female tradition of articulating in a metaphorical and somewhat veiled way," Browning began writing more "explicitly topical protest poems" because she had "become dissatisfied with such a palimpsestic method of recording her own and other women's concerns." The propagandistic tone and direct address of "Cry of the Children" is a departure from such poems as "The Lost Bower" and "Hector in the Garden" (both published in 1844) in openly championing the social reforms she considered crucial to a civilized society.

BIBLIOGRAPHY

Sources

Browning, Elizabeth Barrett. *Poems by Elizabeth Barrett Browning.* London: Blackie, 1904. Print.

Browning, Robert, and Elizabeth Barrett Browning. *The Letters of Robert Browning and Elizabeth Barrett Browning.* Vol. 1: *1845–1846.* Ed. Elvan Kintner. 2 vols. Cambridge: Harvard UP, 1969. Print.

Byrd, Deborah. "Combating an Alien Tyranny: Elizabeth Barrett Browning's Evolution as a Feminist Poet." *Browning Institute Studies* 15 (1987): 23–41. Rpt. in *Nineteenth-Century Literature Criticism.* Ed. Gerald R. Barterian and Denise Evans. Vol. 61. Detroit: Gale, 1998. *Literature Resource Center.* Web. 2 July 2012.

Dillon, Steve. "Barrett Browning's Poetic Vocation: Crying, Singing, Breathing." *Victorian Poetry* 39.4 (2001): 509–32. Rpt. in *Nineteenth-Century Literature Criticism.* Ed. Jessica Bomarito and Russel Whitaker. Vol. 170. Detroit: Gale, 2006. *Literature Resource Center.* Web. 2 July 2012.

Oliphant, Mrs. "Of the Greater Victorian Poets." *The Victorian Age of English Literature.* Vol. 1. New York: Lovell, 1892. 203–246. Rpt. in *Nineteenth-Century Literature Criticism.* Ed. Laurie Lanzen Harris. Vol. 1. Detroit: Gale, 1981. *Literature Resource Center.* Web. 1 July 2012.

Poe, Edgar Allan. Rev. of *The Drama of Exile, and Other Poems,* by Elizabeth Barrett Browning. *Broadway Journal* 1.1–2 (1845): 4–8. Rpt. in *Nineteenth-Century Literature Criticism.* Ed. Laurie Lanzen Harris. Vol. 1. Detroit: Gale, 1981. *Literature Resource Center.* Web. 1 July 2012.

Rev. of *Poems,* by Elizabeth Barrett Browning. *Tait's Edinburgh Magazine* Sept. 1847. Rpt. in *The Brownings' Correspondence.* Vol 14. Ed. Philip Kelley and Scott Lewis. Winfield: Wedgestone, 1984-. 382. Print.

Radley, Virginia L. "A More Vigorous Voice: The Poems of 1844." *Elizabeth Barrett Browning.* New York: Twayne, 1972. Twayne's English Authors Series 136. *The Twayne Authors Series.* Web. 1 July 2012.

Further Reading

Ayres, Brenda. *Silent Voices: Forgotten Novels by Victorian Women Writers.* Westport: Praeger, 2003. Print.

Donaldson, Sandra, et al. *The Works of Elizabeth Barrett Browning.* 5 Vols. London: Pickering, 2010. Print.

Henry, Peaches. "The Sentimental Artistry of Barrett Browning's 'The Cry of the Children.'" *Victorian Poetry* 49.4 (2011): 535+. *Literature Resource Center.* Web. 25 July 2012.

Lewis, Linda M. *Elizabeth Barrett Browning's Spiritual Progress: Face to Face with God.* Columbia: U of Missouri P, 1998. Print.

Mermin, Dorothy. *Elizabeth Barrett Browning: The Origins of a New Poetry.* Chicago: U of Chicago P, 1989. Print.

Stone, Marjorie. *Elizabeth Barrett Browning.* New York: St. Martin's, 1995. Print.

Zakreski, Patricia. *Representing Female Artistic Labour, 1848–1890: Refining Work for the Middle-Class Woman.* Aldershot: Ashgate, 2006.

Media Adaptation

The Cry of the Children. Dir. George Nichols. Perf. Marie Eline, Ethel Wright, and James Cruze. Thanhouser Film Corporation, 1912. Film.

Hannah Soukup

DECLARATION OF SENTIMENTS

Elizabeth Cady Stanton

⁘ Key Facts

Time Period:
Mid-19th Century

Genre:
Manifesto

Events:
Seneca Falls Women's
Rights Convention;
abolitionist movements

Nationality:
American

OVERVIEW

The *Declaration of Sentiments* (1848), also known as the Seneca Falls Declaration, was written primarily by Elizabeth Cady Stanton and modeled on the American *Declaration of Independence*. It expresses the conviction of participants in an 1848 women's rights convention in upstate New York that women and men should have equal rights under the laws of the United States. Designed to persuade readers of the reasonableness of a series of then-radical demands, the *Declaration of Sentiments,* like its model, is structured around a list of wrongs that, according to its authors and signers, require redress.

Though the *Declaration of Sentiments* borrows from the familiar structure of the *Declaration of Independence,* its language, arguments, and demands for full equality between the sexes were, for the most part, received with shock and derision. At the time of the convention, couverture, the legal doctrine that absorbed a woman's identity into her husband's after marriage, was still in force in most states, and the concept of separate spheres, which held that women should exercise influence only in the home (thereby leaving participation in civic life to men), was widely accepted. The *Declaration of Sentiments'* demands—which include women's access to education and to well-paid professions; the right for women to vote; and reforms in marriage, divorce, and child-custody laws—seemed outrageous and potentially destructive to the very fabric of society in 1848. Nevertheless, they have gradually come to be widely accepted by most Americans and, in many cases, are now guaranteed by law.

HISTORICAL AND LITERARY CONTEXT

The *Declaration of Sentiments* resulted generally from continuing debates about what shape democracy in the United States should take and specifically from the experiences of American women at an 1840 World Anti-Slavery Convention in London. Women were active participants in the more radical, Garrisonian wing of the American abolitionist movement, but when female delegates, including Stanton's new friend and mentor, Lucretia Mott, arrived at the convention, a majority of the other, male delegates refused to seat them. Relegated to the role of spectators, Stanton, the well-educated daughter of a judge, and Mott,

twenty years older and an ordained minister in the Society of Friends, or Quakers, had time to discuss their concerns about the status of women, including the lack of access to education, the loss of legal personhood upon marriage, and the advantages given to men through divorce and child-custody laws.

When Mott visited upstate New York in 1848, she and Stanton, along with their Quaker hostesses, wrote an announcement for a women's rights convention to be placed in the local newspaper, the *Seneca County Courier.* A few days later Stanton and one of the other women present at the initial meeting, Elizabeth McClintock, began drafting the *Declaration of Sentiments* and a series of resolutions implementing the principles in the document, which Stanton wound up finishing. The document was read at the convention and approved by the participants, with former slave and abolitionist Frederick Douglass arguing in support of one of its most radical propositions: that women should have the right to vote.

Although the *Declaration of Sentiments* announces the beginning of an organized women's movement in the United States, earlier individual writings, both private and public, address some of the same issues. In 1776 Abigail Adams famously urged her husband, John, to extend the vote to women. In an essay written during the same period but unpublished until 1790, another Massachusetts resident, Judith Sargent Murray, also argues that women's sphere of interest and activity should extend beyond the home. English author Mary Wollstonecraft's 1792 *Vindication of the Rights of Women* focuses especially on the need for better education and equal status under the law. Later U.S. precedents include Margaret Fuller's 1845 *Woman in the Nineteenth Century.*

Although American women would not win the right to vote in national elections until 1920 (eighteen years after Stanton's death), Stanton remained steadfast in her beliefs. She argued not only for the vote, which eventually became the centerpiece of the American women's rights movement, but also for reform in marriage, property, and divorce laws and in women's treatment by religious institutions. The strength of her convictions sometimes caused rifts with former allies, such as when she broke with Douglass and other abolitionists over the Fourteenth Amendment, which extended the vote to African American males but not to women, and when she published *The Woman's Bible,* a bold critique of traditional religion that her fellow suffragists disowned in an 1896 statement, fearful that the controversy it generated would distract from their primary goal.

THEMES AND STYLE

The *Declaration of Sentiments* closely follows the *Declaration of Independence,* borrowing both its structure and, in places, its exact language. In its focus on the denial of democratic rights, it also echoes the earlier document's central theme. Small changes to the *Declaration of Independence*'s language point to blind spots in the founding document of the United States. For example, the phrase "all men and women are created equal" in the *Declaration of Sentiments* reminds the reader that the word "men" in the *Declaration of Independence* was not intended to be inclusive and prepares the way for the charge that "the history of mankind is a history of repeated injuries and usurpations on the part of man toward woman," including "compel[ling] her to submit to laws, in the formation of which she has no voice," and "tax[ing] her to support a government which recognizes her only when her property can be made profitable to it."

The *Declaration of Sentiments* begins with accusations that closely echo—in their focus on legal status, taxation, and lack of representation—the American colonists' complaints against King George III, then moves toward a broader critique of women's place in society. In the middle section, a parallel is drawn between marriage and slavery, in the argument that "in the covenant of marriage, she is compelled to promise obedience to her husband, he becoming, to all intents and purposes, her master." Later items accuse "man" of "monopoliz[ing] nearly all the profitable employments"; of "denying [woman] the facilities for obtaining a thorough education"; and, in summation, of "endeavor[ing] in every way that he could to destroy her confidence in her own powers, to lessen her self-respect, and to make her willing to lead a dependent and abject life." The document also includes a critique of the sexual double standard, charging that men have "created a false public sentiment, by giving to the world a different standard of morals for men and women, by which moral delinquencies which exclude women from society, are not only tolerated but deemed of little account in man."

Like the *Declaration of Independence,* the *Declaration of Sentiments* expresses radical ideas in the language of reason and natural rights. The inflammatory ideas of the *Declaration of Sentiments* gain further weight from being couched in the language of the earlier document, which, at least in the United States, had achieved unquestioned respectability. Nevertheless, the radical nature of some of the accusations, such that man "has usurped the prerogative of Jehovah himself, claiming it as his right to assign for [woman] a sphere

ELIZABETH CADY STANTON: ACTIVISM AND FAMILY RELATIONSHIPS

Elizabeth Cady Stanton was born into a wealthy family in Johnstown, New York, in 1815. Her father, a lawyer, initially encouraged her attempts to take the place of her brother, Eleazar, who died at the age of twenty in 1826, by studying Greek, riding horses, playing chess, and pursuing other activities usually reserved for boys. Later, however, he objected to Elizabeth's advocacy of women's rights. She married antislavery activist Henry Stanton in 1840; the trip to the World Anti-Slavery Convention was their honeymoon. By the time of the 1848 Seneca Falls convention, they had three sons.

Henry was not as supportive of Elizabeth's women's rights activism as Lucretia Mott's husband, James, who chaired the convention at the female organizers' request and signed the *Declaration of Sentiments.* Perhaps because he had his own political ambitions, Henry left town when he learned that the declaration would include a call for suffrage. Elizabeth's chances to write and speak while also raising a family that eventually numbered seven children were limited; what work she did accomplish during her childrearing years was with the aid of her ally and friend Susan B. Anthony, as well as her mother and sisters.

of action, when that belongs to her conscience and her God," cannot be disguised even by the familiar language and structure of the document. For twenty-first-century readers, it may be the occasional moments of elitism and xenophobia, such as the accusation that "he has withheld from her the rights that are given to the most ignorant and degraded men, both natives and foreigners," that are most striking.

CRITICAL DISCUSSION

With few exceptions, the immediate reaction to the *Declaration of Sentiments* was negative. As Elisabeth Griffith notes in the book *In Her Own Right: The Life of Elizabeth Cady Stanton* (1984), "newspapers, as quasi-political organs, presented the case of the major parties: women were unfit for citizenship. Church leaders were equally offended by such unseemly demands and untraditional behavior." Sarcastic, dismissive articles appeared in the *Philadelphia Public Ledger and Daily Transcript* and the *New York Herald.* By contrast, the radical abolitionist press, including Douglass's *North Star* and William Lloyd Garrison's *Liberator,* was supportive, recognizing the parallels between women's and African Americans' quests for full legal and citizenship rights. Horace Greeley's *New York Tribune* was one of the few mainstream papers to take a somewhat sympathetic stance. In her book, Griffith quotes the paper as calling "the demand … unwise and mistaken" but "conced[ing]" that "it is but the assertion of a natural right."

When Anthony Met Stanton, by A. E. Ted Aub, a statue in Seneca Falls, New York. The piece depicts Susan B. Anthony being introduced to Elizabeth Cady Stanton by Amelia Bloomer. © ILENE MACDONALD/ALAMY.

metaphor." As a result, she writes, "African American women carried on their political struggles on their own, invisible to the vast majority of the women's rights movement."

While Stanton remained committed to the broad range of issues raised in the *Declaration of Sentiments,* women's rights reformers in the last quarter of the nineteenth century increasingly narrowed their focus to what had originally been the most controversial demand of the 1848 *Declaration of Sentiments*: women's suffrage. Some reforms supported by the document came fairly soon; just before the 1848 Seneca Falls Meeting, both New York and Pennsylvania passed Married Women's Property acts, allowing women to hold property separately from their husbands, and other states soon followed suit. Other issues, such as domestic violence, were addressed indirectly, as calls for the reform of divorce law became less popular than demands for the passage of temperance laws, which limited access to alcohol. For modern scholars, however, one of the most puzzling issues remains how, given the abolitionist roots of the *Declaration of Sentiments,* Stanton came to oppose the Fourteenth Amendment so virulently, often resorting to overtly racist language in stating her opposition to the idea that uneducated black men might be allowed to vote before white women could.

As Lori Ginzberg points out in *Elizabeth Cady Stanton: An American Life* (2009), the *Declaration of Sentiments* had, from the beginning, "set aside" both the "economic, physical, and sexual exploitation of enslaved women" and the issues faced by a growing class of female industrial workers "in favor of a decidedly middle-class version of women's grievances." Christine Stansell suggests in her essay in *Elizabeth Cady Stanton, Feminist as Thinker* (2007) that "after 1870 slavery shifted, for [Stanton], into a

BIBLIOGRAPHY

Sources

"Declaration of Rights and Sentiments." Appendix A in *Seneca Falls and the Origins of the Women's Rights Movement,* by Sally G. McMillen. New York: Oxford UP, 2008. 237–41. Print.

Ginzberg, Lori D. *Elizabeth Cady Stanton: An American Life.* New York: Hill and Wang, 2009. Print.

Griffith, Elisabeth. *In Her Own Right: The Life of Elizabeth Cady Stanton.* New York: Oxford UP, 1984. Print.

Stansell, Christine. "Missed Connections: Abolitionist Feminism in the Nineteenth Century." *Elizabeth Cady Stanton, Feminist as Thinker: A Reader in Documents and Essays.* Ed. Ellen Carol DuBois and Richard Candida Smith. New York: New York UP, 2007. 32–49. Print.

Further Reading

Banner, Lois. *Elizabeth Cady Stanton: A Radical for Women's Rights.* Boston: Little, Brown, 1980. Print.

Davis, Sue. *The Political Thought of Elizabeth Cady Stanton: Women's Rights and the American Political Traditions.* New York: New York UP, 2008. Print.

DuBois, Ellen Carol, and Richard Candida Smith, eds. *Elizabeth Cady Stanton, Feminist as Thinker: A Reader in Documents and Essays.* New York: New York UP, 2007. Print.

Flexner, Eleanor. *Century of Struggle: The Women's Rights Movement in the United States.* Rev. ed. Cambridge: Harvard UP, 1975. Print.

Gordon, Ann D., ed. *The Selected Papers of Elizabeth Cady Stanton and Susan B. Anthony.* 6 vols. New Brunswick: Rutgers UP, 1997–2012. Print.

McMillen, Sally G. *Seneca Falls and the Origins of the Women's Rights Movement.* New York: Oxford UP, 2008. Print.

Stanton, Elizabeth Cady. *Eighty Years and More: Reminiscences 1815–1897.* 1898. Boston: Northeastern UP, 1993. Print.

———. *The Woman's Bible.* 1895. Boston: Northeastern UP, 1993. Print.

———. "Solitude of Self." 1892. Appendix B in *Seneca Falls and the Origins of the Women's Rights Movement,* by Sally G. McMillen. New York: Oxford UP, 2008. 242–50. Print.

Wellman, Judith. *The Road to Seneca Falls: Elizabeth Cady Stanton and the First Women's Rights Convention.* Urbana: U of Illinois P, 2004. Print.

Catherine E. Saunders

Poor Laws and Paupers Illustrated

Harriet Martineau

OVERVIEW

Poor Laws and Paupers Illustrated, a multivolume work written and published by Harriet Martineau between 1833 and 1834, illustrates the ways in which the Poor Laws, the major form of welfare in England at the time, led to economic disaster and moral depravity. Each volume is based on a different area—titled "The Parish," "The Hamlet," or "The Town"—and follows families that either have no incentive to work because they make more money as paupers supported by the local government or who try to make a living but are bankrupted by the same economic policies. Martineau writes in a simple, straightforward style and includes realistic elements such as glimpses of family life and love stories, as well as more dramatic tales of bankruptcy, gin bars, and arson. Her goal, she writes in the preface to the work, is to demonstrate that "vice and misery can be indisputably referred to the errors of a system," and she urges passage of the Poor Law reform, which was being debated at the time in Parliament.

Poor Laws was commissioned by the Society for the Diffusion of Useful Knowledge and widely read at the time of its publication; indeed, Martineau was one of the best-selling authors of the 1830s. The stories were specifically designed to demonstrate the need for wholesale reform of the current welfare system and the ways in which well-intentioned charity both thwarted the proper development of industry and injured those it was meant to benefit. The New Poor Law, which led to a centralized welfare system with stricter requirements, was passed in 1834, and Martineau's work was a much-discussed element in the debate leading up to its passage.

HISTORICAL AND LITERARY CONTEXT

The Poor Laws had come into existence at the end of the sixteenth century but had become increasingly ineffective. Industrialization and new farming techniques, as well as inflated grain prices, meant that previously self-sufficient workers now needed assistance. In addition, policies such as the Speenhamland system, a subsidy for poor workers, meant that employers could underpay their workers, leaving parish taxpayers to make up the balance. As a result, riots and unrest plagued the early 1830s.

In 1832, the government initiated the Royal Commission into the Operation of the Poor Laws, which was meant both to prevent further unrest and make the current system more efficient and centralized. Martineau was already known for her writing about political economy and her adherence to modern economic theories. *Poor Laws* was positively received by members of parliament such as Lord Brougham and newspapers such as the *Times.* Martineau based her policy in great part on Thomas Malthus's theory of geometric population growth, which holds that a population expands beyond sustainability unless it is checked by outside forces. She also was influenced by Jeremy Bentham's utilitarian premise that people will always tend toward what is pleasant; thus, relief from the government must be made far more unpleasant than earning one's own living. *Poor Laws* dramatizes these economic theories: it presents a Malthusian argument that supporting the poor simply results in there being more poor who cannot be fed, bolstering this point by offering cautionary tales of formerly hardworking people who came to prefer the "easy" life of the workhouse.

Martineau was a perfect fit for the task of popularizing economic theory since she had risen to public attention doing just that. Her *Illustrations of Political Economy,* which she began publishing just a few months before *Poor Laws,* aimed to make the principles of theorists such as Malthus, Bentham, David Ricardo, James Mill, and Adam Smith accessible to ordinary readers, and it was an immediate success. Her goal was to encourage working-class readers to accept capitalism and the free market, even when it seemed to work against their interests. Martineau's didactic tales are part of a larger, primarily female, tradition: Hannah More's morality stories and Jane Marcet's popularizations of political economy influenced her style, while contemporaries such as Charlotte Elizabeth Tonna also explained economic theories in simple terms.

The New Poor Law was passed in 1834, and *Poor Laws and Paupers Illustrated* popularized and perhaps shaped the beliefs and theories of the ruling governmental party, the Whigs. After 1834, the rules determining eligibility for governmental assistance were much more stringent, and the workhouse was made into such an unpleasant place that most people would do anything to avoid it. Elements of the New Poor Law remained in use in England until

Key Facts

Time Period:
Mid-19th Century

Genre:
Nonfiction

Events:
Prominence of Poor Laws; Industrial Revolution; popularization of Malthusian theory

Nationality:
American

MARTINEAU AND DARWIN

In 1834, a young man aboard a ship sailing around South America received a package from his sisters back in England. It included pamphlets of *Poor Laws and Paupers Illustrated* and stated that Harriet Martineau was "now a great Lion in London, much patronized by Ld. Brougham who has set her to write stories on the poor Laws … & every body reads her little books & if you have a dull hour you can, and then throw them overboard, that they may not take up your precious room." The young man was Charles Darwin, and Martineau's writings played an important role in that fateful trip to the Galapagos Islands.

Although Darwin had read Thomas Malthus in college, he had considered populations stable, only reproducing at sustainable levels. Martineau's writings forcefully reminded him of Malthus's basic principle: that populations tend to grow past sustainability unless some sort of check, such as famine or war, occurs. When applied to populations of animals—only the fittest of which would survive the checks—this principle helped Darwin develop his theory of natural selection.

1967, and the questions Martineau raised about how much a government should assist its poor citizens and in what ways continue to be important sources of political debate.

THEMES AND STYLE

Poor Laws and Paupers Illustrated's primary focus is the manner in which even well-intentioned charity injures not just the greater workings of capitalism but also those it is meant to help. Each of the volumes offers an interconnected set of characters brought low by ineffective economic policy. In regards to an honest worker who cannot find work because subsidized parish workers have driven the rates down, the local landowner comments, "[Y]ou are obliging me to turn off that man, or grind him down in wages till he cannot help himself, and must come upon the parish as others do." Meanwhile, a young girl, Jemima, is impregnated by the town apothecary, but because "he could pay the allowance, and does not like it," he has her swear another man made her pregnant "and so charges it upon one who cannot pay, that the parish may bear the expense." The support of illegitimate children was a major concern of both Martineau and the Poor Law Commission since, under Malthusian principles, providing for such children led to unsupportable population growth.

Martineau ends each tale in her earlier *Illustrations of Political Economy* with a direct summation of the major points elucidated by it, but in *Poor Laws,* she tends to place these lessons in the mouths of the characters themselves. For instance, one townsperson highlights the Malthusian point of these tales, stating that "if our labourers go on to have more children,

while wages are dropping, the rate payers must soon become rate-receivers." Despite this, characters are not unsympathetic, and even the majority of those who end up abusing the relief system begin by attempting to extricate themselves from a life of poverty. Martineau seeks to illustrate that the system inevitably leads to worse conditions, even when the individuals within it have good intentions. The local squire, for instance, is shown to be "hard-hearted to all the good people, and kind to all the bad." The squire is not a bad man, but he responds to individual cases of misery rather than thinking about the larger economic system. In this way, he stands for more conservative elements of English society who believed that charity was the responsibility of individuals rather than a governmental concern.

While the writing in *Poor Laws* is overtly didactic, Martineau also employs emotional appeals to drive home her points. In her preface, she admits to the "utility" of displaying the "most melancholy … woes and vices" in her tale to encourage "amendment" of the "social system." Thus, she presents pathetic images such as that of the lame child Biddy, whose mother opens a beer-house so as to stop taking parish money. The drunken customers, all men who receive parish relief and, as a result, have time to drink and money to buy beer, make sport of Biddy, whom they ply with beer in return for her fetching sticks and running races with the dog while they watch. Such moments humanize the victims of poverty while also illustrating the harm brought to society by lax poor laws.

CRITICAL DISCUSSION

Both *Poor Laws and Paupers Illustrated* and *Illustrations of Political Economy* were immediate successes, though they also provoked outcries. Martineau went from being an obscure writer who had to do sewing to supplement her income to a nationwide celebrity within a matter of months. Her most notable critic may have been Charles Dickens. Though Dickens initially agreed with her emphasis on reform and even hired her to write for his magazine, he eventually objected to what he saw as her overreliance on theory, specifically the argument that the lives and comfort of a few had to be sacrificed to ensure the well-being of many. While several of Dickens's novels satirize her earnestly Malthusian views, *Hard Times* (1854) attacks both the social system Martineau espoused and the didactic method she used to convey such ideas.

By the end of the nineteenth century, Martineau's work, including *Poor Laws,* was almost forgotten. When critics did address her writings on political economy, they pointed to the simplified lessons and preachy tone. Similarly, Deirdre David, writing in 1987, disparages the "[c]haracters [who] speak like the embodiment of stiff Principles that they are, the creation of settings [that] is toilsomely mechanical" and adds that the tales are "almost embarrassing in their unambiguous ratification of the benignity of the greatest happiness principle." David's summary represents a widespread critical "distaste," as Catherine Gallagher puts it, for Victorian writings about political economy in general, which were seen as nothing more than apologies for the burgeoning capitalist system, as well as, more specifically, Martineau's popularization of such ideas.

More recently, however, Martineau's works on political science have begun to receive more serious attention both as economic and literary texts. Some critics have stressed the importance of such works in disseminating complicated economic theories, albeit in simplified ways. In addition, these critics note that Martineau managed not only to make a living as an author at a time when women's roles were sharply defined but did so by addressing particularly "masculine" subjects such as economics. Martineau's influence on realistic fiction throughout the nineteenth century has also received recent critical attention. Eleanor Courtemanche, for example, writes that in the closely affiliated *Illustrations of Political Economy*, "Martineau's characterization of both political economy and fictional realism as moral science … lends political urgency to the project of depicting everyday life in fictional form."

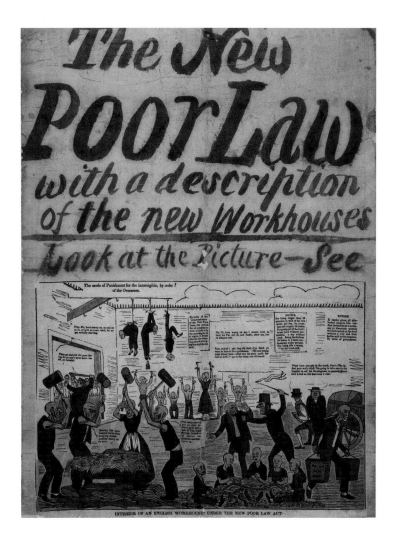

An 1830s poster protesting England's poor laws. Harriet Martineau, known as the first female sociologist, penned *Poor Laws and Paupers Illustrated* in support of such laws. HIP/ART RESOURCE, NY.

BIBLIOGRAPHY

Sources

Courtemanche, Eleanor. "'Naked Truth is the Best Eloquence': Martineau, Dickens, and the Moral Science of Realism." *ELH* 73.2 (2006): 383–407. Print.

David, Deirdre. *Intellectual Woman and Victorian Patriarchy: Harriet Martineau, Elizabeth Barrett Browning, George Eliot.* London: Macmillan, 1987. Print.

Gallagher, Catherine. *The Body Economic: Life, Death and Sensation in Political Economy and the Victorian Novel.* Princeton: Princeton UP, 2008. Print.

Martineau, Harriet. *Poor Laws and Paupers Illustrated.* Vol. 1. Boston: Leonard C. Bowles, 1833. Print.

Further Reading

Dzelzainis, Ella. "Reason vs. Revelation: Feminism, Malthus, and the New Poor Law in Narratives by Harriet Martineau and Charlotte Elizabeth Tonna." *Interdisciplinary Studies in the Long Nineteenth Century* 1 Apr. 2006. Web. 13 Aug. 2012.

Freedgood, Elaine. "Banishing Panic: Harriet Martineau and the Popularization of Political Economy." *Victorian Studies* 39.1 (1995): 33–53. *Project Muse.* Web. 13 Aug. 2012.

Goodlad, Lauren. *Victorian Literature and the Victorian State.* Baltimore: Johns Hopkins UP, 2003. Print.

Martineau, Harriet. *Illustrations of Political Economy: Selected Tales.* Ed. Deborah Logan. Orchard Park: Broadview, 2004. Print.

Oražem, Claudia. *Political Economy and Fiction in the Early Works of Harriet Martineau.* Frankfurt: Lang, 1999. Print.

Peterson, Linda. "From French Revolution to English Reform: Hannah More, Harriet Martineau, and the 'Little Book.'" *Nineteenth-Century Literature* 60.4 (2006): 409–45. Print.

Roberts, Caroline. *The Woman and the Hour: Harriet Martineau and Victorian Ideologies.* Toronto: U of Toronto P, 2002. Print.

Sanders, Mike. "From 'Political' to 'Human' Economy: The Visions of Harriet Martineau and Frances Wright." *Women* 12.2 (2001): 192–203. Print.

Sanders, Valerie. *Reason over Passion: Harriet Martineau and the Victorian Novel.* Brighton: Harvester, 1986. Print.

Vargo, Gregory. "Contested Authority: Reform and Local Pressure in Harriet Martineau's Poor Law Stories." *Nineteenth-Century Gender Studies* 3.2 (2007). Web. 13 Aug. 2012.

Abigail Mann

RAMONA

Helen Hunt Jackson

❖ *Key Facts*

Time Period:
Late 19th Century

Genre:
Novel

Events:
Mexican-American War;
Homestead Act of 1862;
end of Indian wars

Nationality:
American

OVERVIEW

Written in 1884 to protest U.S. policy toward Native Americans, Helen Hunt Jackson's *Ramona* is a nostalgic narrative of California history. Ramona, the daughter of a Scottish father and an Indian mother, is raised as a ward by the Spanish-speaking Ortegna family. She falls in love with Alessandro, a Native American, and marries him in defiance of her guardian, Señora Moreno. The couple builds a life, only to be repeatedly driven off their land and to have their possessions stripped by American settlers of European descent. After their first child dies, they retreat into the mountains, where Alessandro goes mad, takes another man's horse during a moment of delusion, and is shot as a thief. Soon after, Señora Moreno's son, Felipe, who has been searching for Ramona, arrives. He marries Ramona, and they move to Mexico, where they raise a large family, including Ramona and Alessandro's second child, also named Ramona. The differing fates of Alessandro and Ramona send a mixed message: Alessandro's loss of land, madness, and death highlight the injustices perpetrated on the Mission Indians of California, while Ramona's marriage to Felipe and self-exile to Mexico suggest a tacit acceptance of the fate of Native Americans.

Set in the years just after the 1848 Treaty of Guadalupe Hidalgo ended the Mexican-American War and ceded *alta*, or upper, California, to the United States, *Ramona* is most notable for its positive portrait of Californios, descendants of the original Spanish colonists of California. Although some early readers appreciated Jackson's criticism of American Indian policy, most saw *Ramona* as a charming love story and an example of local-color fiction. The book's mainstream success, combined with rapid railroad expansion, helped to create a tourist culture centered on the novel, its characters, and a romanticized vision of California's Mission culture.

HISTORICAL AND LITERARY CONTEXT

Ramona addresses Native American policies in the wake of the Homestead Act of 1862, which opened up Indian lands in the western United States to European settlement. In 1867 a peace commission, appointed by the U.S. House of Representatives, was charged with ending the ongoing Indian wars. The commission's solution, endorsed by President Ulysses S. Grant

in 1869, called for settling Native Americans on reservations and teaching them to live "civilized," agricultural lives. However, by the late 1870s, the policy had proven ineffective and had caused new conflicts between Native Americans and U.S. soldiers.

Helen Hunt Jackson became interested in the consequences of the reservation policy when she heard Standing Bear, a chief of the Ponca tribe, speak in Boston in the fall of 1879. The Poncas, whose established settlement in northeastern Nebraska was mistakenly included in a reservation assigned to the Sioux, were displaced and had to endure a deadly trek to a new reservation in present-day Oklahoma. When Standing Bear had attempted to return in order to bury the body of his son on traditional Ponca land, he was arrested for leaving his assigned reservation. In *Standing Bear v. Crook,* a Nebraska district court ruled that Indians are legal persons, sparking an 1879 tour that called attention to the Poncas' plight and sought a similar decision from the U.S. Supreme Court.

Jackson first expressed her interest in Native American rights in the nonfiction *A Century of Dishonor* (1881), a history of broken U.S.-Native American treaties, including one involving the Poncas. She sent copies of the book, bound in red to symbolize bloodshed, to each member of Congress. Although *A Century of Dishonor* did not sell as well as she had hoped, it received some positive reviews and helped lay the foundation for her involvement with California's Mission Indians, who had suffered repeated displacements in Spanish mission society and under Mexican and U.S. rule. In addition, the limited success of *A Century of Dishonor* may have inspired Jackson's decision to turn to fiction, which social reformer Harriet Beecher Stowe had used to promote abolition in her novel *Uncle Tom's Cabin* (1851). In fact, in a letter to Thomas Bailey Aldrich, the editor of *The Atlantic Monthly,* Jackson reveals that she sought to create in *Ramona* a work with impact equal to that of *Uncle Tom's Cabin.*

Although *Ramona* had a lasting impact on American culture, its primary effect was not, as Jackson had hoped, to reform Native American policy. Most readers, rather than focusing on the displacement of Native Americans, embraced the characters and their love story. Advertisers attached the characters' names to numerous products and places, reflecting readers' desire to connect with the story in a tangible way, and many Ramonas, real or imagined, were named after Jackson's heroine. Stage adaptations and movies filmed on location in California (in 1910, 1916, and 1936), helped to create a thriving, lasting tourist trade associated with the book. Today the book is seen as a representation of the attitudes and culture of the Mexican-American frontier during the late nineteenth century.

THEMES AND STYLE

A unifying theme of *Ramona* is dispossession, especially loss of land, to white American expansion. In the opening chapters, readers learn that Señora Morena has lost land to the Americans, whom "she believed … thieves." The Native Americans suffer parallel losses, starting with the seizure of Alessandro's home village, Temecula. Moving to San Pasquale offers no relief. Alessandro improves and cultivates the land, which is then sold from beneath him to a settler "from the States." When Ramona asks where they will go, Alessandro replies, addressing his wife by her Indian name, "Where? I know not, Majella! Into the mountains, where the white men come not!" Even the peaceful surroundings of their final home together, "on the rim of the refuge valley, high on San Jacinto," do not bring the freedom and safety Ramona anticipates. Alessandro's death at the hands of a white settler and Ramona and Felipe's retreat into Mexico mark the final passing of *alta* California from Native Americans and Spanish-speaking Californios to the United States.

Although the story is told by a third-person omniscient narrator, the novel most often adopts the perspective of the dispossessed. A notable exception is found in the brief passages describing the thoughts of Aunt Ri, a Tennessee native who came to the San Jacinto Valley with her husband and consumptive son, Jos. Her "ideas of Indians had been drawn from newspapers, and from a book or two of narratives of massacres, and from an occasional sight of vagabond bands or families they had encountered in their journey across the plains." Through her, Jackson demonstrates the intellectual transformation she hopes to spark in the reader. Aunt Ri, after "sitting side by side in friendly intercourse with an Indian man and Indian woman," becomes a staunch friend and supporter of Ramona and Alessandro, and a harsh critic of U.S. Indian policy. Although she is markedly less educated than the majority of Jackson's audience, Aunt Ri's simple, good-hearted turn models for readers the author's desired reaction.

The author appeals to readers' sympathies in her description of Ramona's suffering that is a consequence of the discrimination she and Alessandro encounter. The pathos is heightened especially after an Indian Agency doctor refuses to help them, and their first child, Eyes of the Sky, dies. "Benumbing terrors, which were worse than her grief, were crowding Ramona's heart now … When the funeral was over, and they returned to their desolate home, at the sight

STANDING BEAR'S SPEAKING TOUR

In 1879 Thomas Henry Tibbles, a newspaper editor, and the Omaha Committee, a group of Christian pastors and laymen, conceived of a lecture tour to help return the Poncas to their established lands in the Dakota territory and to raise money for a possible legal case. The tour featured Ponca chief Standing Bear, Omaha Indian Frank LaFlesche, and Frank's sister Susette, also called Bright Eyes. Many of the attendees to the Boston lecture, like Helen Hunt Jackson, were impressed by Standing Bear and his young companions, who reminded one observer of novelist James Fenimore Cooper's noble Indian characters. Fisk University's Jubilee Singers, famous for their renditions of African American spirituals, supported the tour by singing "Home Sweet Home" at a benefit concert, reminding listeners of Standing Bear's homelessness.

Standing Bear and Bright Eyes testified before a U.S. Senate committee about the Ponca tribe's exile in February 1880. The following January, after some debate over whether Native Americans had standing to bring a suit, a commission appointed by President Rutherford B. Hayes recommended that the Poncas be allowed to choose between their old reservation and the one assigned to them in Indian Territory. Standing Bear chose the Dakota reservation, where he was later joined by a number of Poncas.

of the empty cradle, Ramona broke down." The plot of *Ramona,* like that of many sentimental novels, incorporates a number of deaths and places them in parallel narratives to underline their significance. For instance, the deaths of Eyes of the Sky and Alessandro mirror the earlier deaths of an Indian baby and her father during the Indian expulsion from Temecula. Such repetition strengthens the message that dispossession at the hands of American agents and settlers often spelled death for Native Americans.

CRITICAL DISCUSSION

Most early reviews of *Ramona* praised the love story and Jackson's portrayal of California. Their obliviousness to what Jackson termed the "Indian side of the story" frustrated the author. However, some reviewers were sympathetic to her purpose. Albion W. Tourgée, writing in 1886, a year after Jackson died from cancer, observed that unlike contemporary fiction, *Ramona* depicts California not as "the seat of a new civilization" but as "the Indian's lost inheritance and the Spaniard's desolated home." The novel inspired fellow reformers, including members of the Women's National Indian Association and the mostly male Indian Rights Association, to continue lobbying for legislation designed to secure Native American land rights, such as the Dawes Act of 1887 and an 1891 act specifically addressing Mission Indian lands.

The novel's most enduring legacy is the effect it had on travelers, who made pilgrimages to sites in

Photograph of Helen Hunt Jackson. © BETTMANN/ CORBIS.

BIBLIOGRAPHY

Sources

Chavez, Denise. Introduction. *Ramona.* New York: Modern Library, 2005. xii–xxii. Print.

DeLyser, Dydia. *Ramona Memories: Tourism and the Shaping of Southern California.* Minneapolis: U of Minnesota P, 2005. Print.

Irwin, Robert McKee. "*Ramona* and Postnationalist American Studies: On 'Our America' and the Mexican Borderlands." *American Quarterly* 55.4 (2003): 539–67. *JSTOR.* Web. 19 June 2012.

Mathes, Valerie Sherer. *Helen Hunt Jackson and Her Indian Reform Legacy.* Austin: U of Texas P, 1990. Print.

Tourgée, Albion W. "Study in Civilization." Rev. of *Ramona,* by Helen Jackson. *North American Review* 143.358 (1886): 246–61. *American Periodical Series Online.* Web. 23 June 2012.

Further Reading

Gonzalez, John M. "The Warp of Whiteness: Domesticity and Empire in Helen Hunt Jackson's *Ramona.*" *American Literary History* 16.3 (2004): 437–65. *Oxford Journals.* Web. 19 June 2012.

Jackson, Helen Hunt. *A Century of Dishonor: A Sketch of the United States Government's Dealings with Some of the Indian Tribes.* New York: Harper & Brothers, 1881. Web. 23 June 2012.

Mathes, Valerie Sherer. "Helen Hunt Jackson and the Ponca Controversy." *Montana: The Magazine of Western History* 39.1 (1989): 42–53. *JSTOR.* Web. 19 June 2012.

———, ed. *The Indian Reform Letters of Helen Hunt Jackson, 1879–1885.* Norman: U of Oklahoma P, 1998. Print.

Norman, Brian. "The Addressed and the Redressed: Helen Hunt Jackson's Protest Essay and the US Protest Novel Tradition." *Canadian Review of American Studies* 37.1 (2007): 111–34. *Project Muse.* Web. 19 June 2012.

Padget, Martin. "Travel Writing, Sentimental Romance, and Indian Rights Advocacy: The Politics of Helen Hunt Jackson's *Ramona.*" *Journal of the Southwest* 42.4 (2000): 833–76. *JSTOR.* Web. 19 June 2012.

Phillips, Kate. *Helen Hunt Jackson: A Literary Life.* Berkeley: U of California P, 2003. Print.

Rosenthal, Debra J. *Race Mixture in Nineteenth-Century U.S. and Spanish American Fictions: Gender, Culture, and Nation Building.* Chapel Hill: U of North Carolina P, 2004. Print.

Media Adaptations

Ramona. Dir. Henry King. Perf. Loretta Young, Don Ameche, and Kent Taylor. Twentieth Century Fox Film Corporation, 1936. Film.

Ramona: A Story of the White Man's Injustice to the Indian. Dir. D.W. Griffith. Cast Mary Pickford, Henry B. Walthall, Kate Bruce, et al. Phot. G.W. Bitzer. The Biograph Company; Distributed exclusively by Image Entertainment; National Film Preservation Foundation, 1910; © 2007. DVD.

California that were connected to *Ramona.* This tourism, as Dydia DeLyser notes, encouraged the preservation of the remaining Spanish missions, "the only sizable and concrete examples of California's claim to antiquity" and spurred the spread of the mission revival style. DeLyser explains that because *Ramona* was "written not to dramatize *historic* Indian mistreatment … but rather to call attention to what was, in the early 1880s, ongoing contemporary mistreatment of Native Americans at the hands of Anglo-Americans," the novel "deliberately contrasted the troubled present with a fictitious … romanticized … past." This romanticizing ultimately proved more compelling to many readers than the novel's protest message.

Recent commentators, including Denise Chavez, have interpreted *Ramona* as a novel of the Mexican-American borderlands, termed *la frontera.* According to these critics, Jackson's novel sheds light on historic attitudes toward Native Americans and on the history underlying the struggles of Americans who claim Mexican, Spanish, or mestizo identities. Some Latin American readers have followed the advice of Cuban revolutionary José Martí that he gave in the introduction to his 1888 translation of the novel and have embraced *Ramona* as an early work expressing an American identity unconstrained by national boundaries. Other readers, including Robert McKee Irwin, have warned against interpretations of the novel that romanticize Mexican *mestizaje,* or mixture of cultures, pointing out that racial discrimination and extermination of indigenous cultures occurred on both sides of the border.

Catherine E. Saunders

Uncle Tom's Cabin

Harriet Beecher Stowe

OVERVIEW

Harriet Beecher Stowe's *Uncle Tom's Cabin,* serialized in the American abolitionist newspaper the *National Era* in 1851–52 and published in book form in 1852, sought to build opposition to slavery and sympathy for fugitive slaves in the wake of the broadened Fugitive Slave Law included in the Compromise of 1850. The sentimental novel has two major plot lines. The first follows the dark-skinned Uncle Tom as he is sold farther and farther south, where he encounters increasingly harsh treatment and eventually dies at the hands of his last master, Simon Legree. The second traces the separate journeys northward of fugitive biracial slaves George and Eliza Harris and their son, Harry. The Harrises eventually escape to Canada, are reunited with long-lost relatives, and make plans to seek education in Europe before traveling to Africa as missionaries. Uncle Tom's story evokes sympathy for a saintly, even Christlike figure embodying virtues that Stowe attributes to his African heritage, whereas George Harris represents former slaves' potential to support themselves and contribute to the world at large.

An immediate best seller in the northern United States and England, *Uncle Tom's Cabin* was welcomed by abolitionists who felt that it accurately exposed the fundamental evils of slavery and was criticized by southern reviewers for supposedly exaggerating the harshness of most slaves' lives and for exacerbating sectional conflict. Abraham Lincoln famously (and perhaps somewhat facetiously) credited the novel with helping to spark the American Civil War. Although most African American reviewers initially praised Stowe's contribution to the antislavery cause, later critics have charged that *Uncle Tom's Cabin,* especially in subsequent dramatic adaptations, helped to create racial stereotypes that continue to haunt American literature and culture. More recently, scholars of women's writing have cited the novel's ability to change social and political attitudes as evidence of the power of sentimental fiction.

HISTORICAL AND LITERARY CONTEXT

From the founding of the Republic, Americans debated whether slavery and democracy could coexist. Many northern states enacted immediate or gradual abolition in the decades following the American Revolution. The abolition of the Atlantic slave trade in

1808 significantly slowed the importation of Africans to the United States but paradoxically fueled a domestic trade that moved slaves from the relatively overpopulated upper South to the underpopulated lower South, separating families in the process. An organized abolition movement took hold in the 1830s with William Lloyd Garrison's creation of the abolitionist newspaper the *Liberator* in 1831 and the founding of the American Anti-Slavery Society in 1835.

The passage of the Fugitive Slave Law of 1850, which required residents of northern states to return escaped slaves to their masters, galvanized the abolitionist movement. Fugitive slaves who had settled in New England were forced to flee to Canada or England, and in some cases mobs tried to prevent owners from reclaiming their former slaves. Other northerners, however, favored colonization, which involved gradual emancipation and deportation to Africa, or valued preserving the union over any action regarding slavery. Stowe wrote her novel in part out of frustration with neighbors in Brunswick, Maine, who did not feel as strongly as she about the injustice of the new law.

Like many other American books of that period and earlier, including Susan Warner's best seller *The Wide, Wide World* (1850), *Uncle Tom's Cabin* takes the form of a sentimental or domestic novel. Many scenes are set in homes and similar intimate spaces, and the plot focuses on family relationships and the emotions they evoke. Stowe also drew on published and unpublished slave narratives, including those of former slaves Josiah Henson and Henry Bibb, in telling the story of the Harris family.

Uncle Tom's Cabin sparked both imitations and proslavery replies, including Mary Henderson Eastman's *Aunt Phillis's Cabin; or, Southern Life as It Is* (1852) and J. W. Page's *Uncle Robin in His Cabin in Virginia, and Tom without One in Boston* (1853). Stowe responded with the 1854 *A Key to Uncle Tom's Cabin,* described in its subtitle as "presenting the original facts and documents upon which the story is founded, together with corroborative statements verifying the truth of the work," but actually assembled in large part after the fact. Perhaps the most lasting offshoots of *Uncle Tom's Cabin* are the numerous dramatic interpretations, including "Tom Shows" that presented the African American characters in far more stereotypical

✛ *Key Facts*

Time Period:
Mid-19th Century

Genre:
Novel

Events:
Passage of the Fugitive Slave Law of 1850; Rise of abolitionist movement

Nationality:
American

HARRIET BEECHER STOWE IN CINCINNATI

Harriet Beecher Stowe was born in 1811 in Litchfield, Connecticut, and moved in 1832 to Cincinnati, Ohio, where her father, Lyman Beecher, served as the president of Lane Theological Seminary, an institution soon wracked by debates over slavery. Harriet's residence in Cincinnati during her young adulthood and the early years of her marriage to Lane professor Calvin Stowe gave her an opportunity to observe slavery, if not firsthand then from a short distance: Cincinnati is located on the Ohio River, and Kentucky, at that time a slave state (and the setting for much of *Uncle Tom's Cabin*), lies on the other side.

Escaped slaves and slave hunters both passed through Cincinnati on a regular basis. Harriet employed African Americans as household servants, including a former slave who, when her master came looking for her, fled with the help of Calvin Stowe and Harriet's brother Henry Ward Beecher to the home of John Van Zandt, the model for John Van Trompe in *Uncle Tom's Cabin*.

Cincinnati was a frontier town without adequate sewage facilities. After an 1849 cholera epidemic killed their eighteen-month-old son, Charley, Harriet and Calvin embraced the opportunity to return to New England and settle in Brunswick, Maine, where Harriet wrote *Uncle Tom's Cabin*.

fashion than Stowe's novel. These depictions, as much as Stowe's original novel, provoked reactions from later African American authors, including Richard Wright, who titled a 1938 short story collection dealing with discrimination and racial violence *Uncle Tom's Children,* and Ishmael Reed, who offered a comic, postmodern reinterpretation of Stowe's novel in *Flight to Canada* (1976).

THEMES AND STYLE

Stowe's chief purpose is to convince her readers of the full humanity of African Americans and, in turn, the indefensibility of slavery. Defenses of slavery often depicted people of African descent as less than human, a sentiment Stowe puts into the mouth of the slave trader Haley, who insists in the first chapter that "these critters [slaves] an't like white folks, you know; they gets over things [like being sold away from family], only manage right." Stowe underlines slaves' humanity in chapter titles that emphasize their family roles; Eliza Harris is introduced as "the mother" (chapter 2) and George Harris as "the husband and father" (chapter 3). Later chapter titles referring to "the feelings of living property on changing owners" (chapter 5) and to "property get[ting] into an improper state of mind" (chapter 11) expose the inherent contradictions in a system that treats people as objects.

Stowe utilizes dual plot lines to emphasize both the supposed inherent gentleness and Christianity of

"African" character (through her portrayal of Tom) and slaves' desire for self-determination (through the biracial George). Tom is a missionary and eventually a "martyr," concerned for the soul of even his most overtly cruel master, Legree. George, who inherits a "high, indomitable spirit" from "one of the proudest [white] families in Kentucky," asks "why am I *not* a man, as much as anybody?" and relishes the chance physically to defend his family. Tom's death inspires the son of his first master, George Shelby, to free the slaves he has inherited and set up a system of tutelage that will prepare them for independence; George seizes independence through his flight northward.

Like all sentimental novels, *Uncle Tom's Cabin* seeks to arouse the emotions of readers. Stowe emphasizes the pain of slave families separated through sale, paralleling their losses to one she, like many of her readers, had experienced: the death of a child. Narrating Tom's reaction to the news of his sale, she describes his tears as "just such tears, sir, as you dropped into the coffin where lay your first-born son; such tears, woman, as you shed when you heard the cries of your dying babe." Tears also forge connections between Eva St. Clare, the daughter of Tom's second master, who feels the wrong of slavery so viscerally that her pain seems almost to cause the consumption from which she dies, and Topsy, the young slave whom Eva converts to Christianity while on her deathbed. In Tom's deathbed scene, George Shelby weeps "tears which did honor to his manly heart," then vows, "kneeling on the grave of his poor friend; 'oh, witness, that, from this hour, I will *do what one man can* to drive out this curse of slavery from my land.'" Stowe's final exhortation to readers to "*feel right*" explicitly seeks to expand the circle of antislavery sentiment beyond the world of the novel.

CRITICAL DISCUSSION

The initial reaction to *Uncle Tom's Cabin* was mostly favorable in the northern United States and England but sharply critical in the southern states. In her 1852 review of the novel in the *National Era,* Gamaliel Bailey praises the book's evenhandedness: "It takes no extreme views. It does not seek to seize upon the most horrible atrocities, and brand the whole system as worse than it is. It is fair, and generous, and calm, and candid." By contrast, George F. Holmes's review in the *Southern Literary Messenger* is both scathing and personal, claiming that, because of her "shameless disregard of truth," including "allegations of cruelty toward the slaves" that were "absolutely and unqualifiedly false," Stowe had "forfeited the claim to be called a lady." Radical abolitionists, including William Lloyd Garrison, praised the book as a whole but objected to Stowe's apparent support of colonization in her disposition of the Harris family. William G. Allen, in a letter to *Frederick Douglass' Paper,* echoes Garrison's objection and also suggests that Tom has "too much piety" and not enough interest in "resistance to tyrants."

Allen's concern was echoed by later African American critics, who, basing their critiques primarily on the elderly, subservient Tom character common in stage adaptations of the novel, began using "Uncle Tom" to describe an African American who prioritizes relationships with European Americans over his own racially defined community's welfare. Although this figure bears little resemblance to Stowe's original character, who dies protecting two runaway fellow slaves, the epithet remains a lasting cultural legacy of the novel. Twentieth-century African American critics, most notably James Baldwin, also expressed concern about Stowe's literary legacy, arguing that the violent protest fictions of their day were an equal and opposite reaction to Stowe's sentimentality. "Bigger [Thomas, the protagonist of Richard Wright's *Native Son*] is Uncle Tom's descendant," Baldwin writes in his 1955 essay, "flesh of his flesh, so exactly opposite a portrait it seems that the contemporary Negro novelist and the dead New England woman are locked together in a deadly, timeless, battle; the one uttering merciless exhortations, the other shouting curses."

Most recently, Stowe's novel has become a central text in studies of American women's writing that seek to recuperate the sentimental novel and explore its ability to do what Jane Tompkins calls in *Sensational Designs* "cultural work." Basing her argument in large part on *Uncle Tom's Cabin,* Tompkins writes that "the popular domestic novel of the nineteenth century represents a monumental effort to reorganize culture from the woman's point of view." Like Tompkins, many contemporary critics closely analyze Stowe's artistry, seeking to understand the literary techniques undergirding the novel's lasting emotional power.

Anonymous lithograph from the 19th century, depicting the death of Uncle Tom at the hands of his master, Simon Legree. Eva, surrounded by angels, awaits Tom in Heaven. HIP/ART RESOURCE, NY.

BIBLIOGRAPHY

Sources

Allen, William G. Letter to the Editor. *Frederick Douglass' Paper* 20 May 1852: 3. *Uncle Tom's Cabin: A Norton Critical Edition.* Ed. Elizabeth Ammons. New York: W. W. Norton, 1994. 463–466. Print.

[Bailey, Gamaliel.] Rev. of *Uncle Tom's Cabin. The National Era* 15 April 1852. *Uncle Tom's Cabin & American Culture: A Multi-Media Archive.* University of Virginia, 2009. Web. 12 June 2012.

Baldwin, James. "Everybody's Protest Novel." *Notes of a Native Son.* 1955. *Uncle Tom's Cabin: A Norton Critical Edition.* Ed. Elizabeth Ammons. New York: W. W. Norton, 1994. 495–501. Print.

Holmes, George F. Rev. of *Uncle Tom's Cabin. The Southern Literary Messenger* October 1852. *Uncle Tom's Cabin: A Norton Critical Edition.* Ed. Elizabeth Ammons. New York: W. W. Norton, 1994. 467–477. Print.

Stowe, Harriet Beecher. *The Key to Uncle Tom's Cabin; Presenting the Original Facts and Documents upon Which the Story Is Founded, Together with Corroborative Statements Verifying the Truth of the Work.* 1854. *Uncle Tom's Cabin & American Culture: A Multi-Media Archive.* University of Virginia, 2009. Web. 11 June 2012.

Tompkins, Jane. *Sensational Designs: The Cultural Work of American Fiction, 1790–1860.* New York: Oxford UP, 1986. Print.

Further Reading

Bernstein, Robin. *Racial Innocence: Performing American Childhood from Slavery to Civil Rights.* New York: New York UP, 2011. Print.

Gossett, Thomas. *Uncle Tom's Cabin and American Culture.* Dallas: Southern Methodist UP, 1985. Print.

Harriet Beecher Stowe Center. *Uncle Tom's Cabin in the National Era.* 2011–2012. Web. 11 June 2012.

Hedrick, Joan D. *Harriet Beecher Stowe: A Life.* New York: Oxford UP, 1994. Print.

Meer, Sarah. *Uncle Tom Mania: Slavery, Minstrelsy, and Transatlantic Culture in the 1850s.* Athens: U of Georgia P, 2005. Print.

Railton, Stephen. Director. *Uncle Tom's Cabin & American Culture: A Multi-Media Archive.* University of Virginia, 2009. Web. 11 June 2012.

Reynolds, David S. *Mightier than the Sword: Uncle Tom's Cabin and the Battle for America.* New York: W. W. Norton, 2012. Print.

Stowe, Harriet Beecher. *Dred: A Tale of the Great Dismal Swamp.* 1856. Ed. Robert S. Levine. Chapel Hill: U of North Carolina P, 2006. Print.

Yarborough, Richard. "Strategies of Black Characterization in *Uncle Tom's Cabin* and the Early Afro-American Novel." *New Essays in Uncle Tom's Cabin.* Ed. Eric J. Sundquist. New York: Cambridge University Press, 1986. 45–84. Print.

Media Adaptations

Uncle Tom's Cabin. Dir. William Robert Daly. Perf. Sam Lucas, Walter Hitchcock, and Hattie Delaro. World Film, 1914. Film.

Uncle Tom's Cabin. Dir. Harry A. Pollard. Perf. Margarita Fischer, James B. Lowe, and Arthur Edmund Carewe. Universal Pictures, 1927. Film.

Uncle Tom's Cabin. Dir. and ed. Vera Jiji. Perf. Robyn Hatcher, Nathaniel Robinson, Bryce Davis, et al. Films for the Humanities, 1988. VHS.

Catherine E. Saunders

"THE WEAPON SHOP"

A. E. van Vogt

OVERVIEW

A. E. van Vogt's short story "The Weapon Shop" (1942) explores the right of citizens to buy and bear arms. Set in the totalitarian empire of Isher, "where privileges grow scanter every year," "The Weapon Shop" tells the story of Fara Clark, an imperial loyalist struggling against an illicit business that has opened in his home village of Glay. As the story unfolds, Clark comes to realize that it is the empress Isher and her government that are behind the "evil enthroned" in Glay and that the weapon shop is a source of freedom. The gun he buys becomes the means of redressing the wrongs the government has perpetrated against him. In weighing the rights of citizens, van Vogt highlights the need for thinking persons to look carefully at their government in times of crisis, and he raises the possibility of civil disobedience as a means of opposition against criminal regimes.

Written during the first golden age of science fiction, "The Weapons Shop" was initially published in John W. Campbell's seminal science fiction magazine *Astounding Science Fiction*. Campbell, who was extremely influential as an editor and publisher of science fiction during this time, wrote to van Vogt upon receipt of the story, saying that even though the piece did not contain the high action typical in the genre, "like a park path, it's a nice little walk." Van Vogt's style, which emphasizes elaboration of concepts over rapid bursts of action, would influence future science fiction writers, as well as those in related genres such as fantasy and horror.

HISTORICAL AND LITERARY CONTEXT

The first golden age of science fiction began in 1938, when Campbell took the helm of *Astounding Stories* (renamed *Astounding Science Fiction* in 1939) and brought forth writers such as van Vogt, Isaac Asimov, Theodore Sturgeon, and Robert Heinlein. The "hard" science fiction from this period, which lasted until roughly 1946, deals more narrowly with scientific developments and theory, while the "soft" brand focuses more on sociological or sociological extrapolations. Both classes reflect the legacy of the Great Depression, along with public concerns generated by World War II and its emphasis on technologically advanced warfare.

"The Weapon Shop," published during World War II, expresses an antipathy toward repressive

government. Van Vogt published his first science fiction story, "Black Destroyer," in 1939 in *Astounding Science Fiction*. Shortly after its appearance, Adolph Hitler invaded Poland, and the British Empire was at war. As a Canadian citizen, van Vogt attempted to enlist, but he was turned down and later took a job as a government clerk. Several of Campbell's mainstay writers did enlist, which spurred van Vogt to produce a greater share of the magazine's content and eventually to leave his job and commit to writing full time.

Science fiction critics consider this period to be foundational, both for van Vogt's writing and the development of the genre in general. The eponymous weapon shop of van Vogt's 1942 classic first appeared in the short story "The Seesaw" (1941). In this story, a reporter stumbles into a strange shop, which has materialized somewhere in June 1941. The weapon shop, however, is part of a temporal dislocation, and the fact that it appears in 1941 confirms to its occupants that they are under attack from the Empress of Isher. Van Vogt later developed several cycles of Isher stories that became the basis for his serialized novel *The Weapon Makers* (1947) and *The Weapon Shop of Isher* (1952).

Van Vogt was one of the best-selling authors of his time, but from a critical perspective, he has been overshadowed by his contemporaries. Some commentators have suggested that this status may in part be a result of van Vogt's practice of producing "fix-up" novels. Van Vogt coined this term to describe his taking previously published stories and reworking them into a novel format, possibly because of a perception that novels would sell better than short story collections. In addition, van Vogt became involved with L. Ron Hubbard's Dianetics (the precursor to the Church of Scientology) in the 1950s, and his output diminished during this period. Whether van Vogt's work will be more widely reprinted and discovered by new generations of fans remains an open question.

THEMES AND STYLE

The window in Van Vogt's weapon shop is embossed with a sentence that captures one of the story's central themes: "the right to buy weapons is the right to be free." Fara Clark first encounters the shop while out on an evening stroll with his wife. The "curiously timeless picture" of the village at night is disturbed by the shop,

Key Facts

Time Period:
Mid-20th Century

Genre:
Short Story

Events:
World War II; Great Depression

Nationality:
Canadian

SCIENCE FICTION'S SEMINAL MAGAZINE

Analog Science Fiction and Fact (originally called *Astounding Stories of Super Science,* then *Astounding Stories* and *Astounding Science Fiction*) is the longest-running American science fiction magazine. First published in 1930, it rose to prominence under John W. Campbell, who took over in 1938 and recruited a number of writers who would dominate the genre, namely A. E. van Vogt, Isaac Asimov, Robert A. Heinlein, and Arthur C. Clarke. L. Ron Hubbard, the founder of the Church Scientology, also got his start at the magazine.

The publication initially ran adventure-style stories, with no great focus on science. Campbell, however, shifted the emphasis to science-based fare, a move that proved to be highly successful. Van Vogt published a number of short stories in the magazine, starting with 1939's "Black Destroyer." *Slan,* his first novel, began as a serialization in the magazine in 1940. "The Seesaw," which is the first of van Vogt's stories to reference the world described in "The Weapon Shop," appeared in the magazine in 1941.

In 1960, the magazine became known as *Analog Science Fiction and Fact. Analog* continues to popularize new writers in the genre, including Orson Scott Card, author of the critically acclaimed *Ender's Game.*

which is "absurd, fantastically mischievous, utterly threatening." Clark launches a campaign against the shop but is soon forced to turn his attention homeward, as he loses his business and his good standing in the community. Eventually, through his dealings with the weapon shop, it comes to light that the Empress of Isher is behind the loss of his business and persecution. A gun that Clark buys at the weapons shop for defense against government forces becomes the means for him to regain what he has lost. Late in the story, the owner of the weapon shop tells Clark that "people always have the kind of government they want." By the story's end, Clark has become someone who is worthy of self-government. Van Vogt's portrayal of Clark's evolution suggests a sympathetic view of those who view gun ownership as a basic right in a world where even seemingly benign governments and their human agents can be corrupt.

Van Vogt develops Clark by emphasizing shifts in perceptive frameworks, starting with the physical alterations in time and space he experiences after entering the weapon shop and ending with his changed views of the nature of his community. At the beginning of the story, Clark sees Glay through the empress's eyes, as a village that embodies everything that is good in her subjects. When he enters the weapon shop for the first time, he is angry, and he leaves unconvinced of its value. Still, not everyone is able to enter the shop; Clark's inherent honesty qualifies him as someone who

may eventually be open to what the shop has to offer. During Clark's second visit to the shop, he is transported to a different place, where the true nature of his misfortunes is revealed. This physical shift marks a change in his perceptions and ultimately allows him to reclaim his freedom by purchasing a gun and then using it against the imperial forces to contest the reclamation of his business. "The Weapon Shop" closes with a scene that echoes the opening. While out for a walk, Clark contemplates the sweetness of the air, which is "like wine," an observation he made at the beginning of the story. He once again views the village as a "peaceful paradise," only now this tranquility is maintained by his deliberate actions rather than tacit assumptions that the government is good.

Stylistically, "The Weapon Shop" makes use of these bookended moments to show Clark's evolution into a person fully capable of civic participation. Both the beginning and end of the story present idyllic scenes that emphasize contentment and peace. Within the bookends, however, the action unfolds in a flurry of unsettled emotions and outbursts from Clark as he fights against the weapon shop, his son, and various members of the town. Commentators have noted that van Vogt subscribed to the notion that a good story should feature an emotional shift every eight hundred words, a theory he laid out in a 1947 article titled "Complication." This technique is apparent in "The Weapon Shop."

CRITICAL DISCUSSION

Critical response to "The Weapon Shop" was mixed, and it was complicated by van Vogt's fix-up process, which altered the story from its original format in order to be included in *The Weapon Shops* novel. Science fiction writer and editor Damon Knight reviewed *The Weapon Shops,* and he accused van Vogt of having "vacant stages in the scaffolding." In response, acclaimed author Philip K. Dick argued against fixating on holes in plot or theory. Praising van Vogt's ability to capture the mess of real life, Dick says in Darren Jorgensen's article "The Disorientations of A. E. van Vogt" that "van Vogt influenced me so much because he made me appreciate a mysterious chaotic quality in the universe which is not to be feared."

Van Vogt and other writers of the golden age helped to establish science fiction as a proper and profitable genre. Science fiction magazines and books proliferated, as did TV and film adaptations of popular works. Stories such as "The Weapon Shop" established that science fiction could deal with larger social and political issues and entertain the reader along the way. Nevertheless, van Vogt remains relatively obscure to all but a small contingent of specialists and fans within the genre.

Van Vogt's works have not drawn the amount of scholarly attention as those by some of his contemporaries, such as Asimov and Heinlein. Some critical literature traces Campbell's influence on the genre, including the manner in which he shaped the sensibilities of his writers, van Vogt among them. Other critics have noted the impact of Alfred North Whitehead's book *Science and the Modern World* (1925) on van Vogt's work. In *The World Beyond the Hill: Science Fiction and the Quest for Transcendence,* Alexei and Cory Panshin argue that van Vogt was influenced by this fundamental argument by Whitehead: "in place of a universe of constantly competing particles effectively going nowhere, Whitehead was offering the alternative vision of an organic and interconnected universe evolving through creativeness and cooperation." In the view of the Panshins, van Vogt's tendency toward world-building through a cycle of stories, such as those set in Isher, is a direct result of his early reading of Whitehead. Jorgensen, meanwhile, is less interested in the way van Vogt's worlds hang together than in how, as he puts it in "The Disorientations of A. E. van Vogt," the author utilizes "dislocations" in his fiction to "defamiliarize the anxieties of his readers and present their experiences of the present back to them in a far future setting." Jorgensen contends that van Vogt employs "rapid spatial and narrative shifts" as a way of responding to the enormous changes occurring in the mid-twentieth century, and protagonists such as Fara Clark serve as "fantasies of control" to deal with these changes.

The cover of a 1947 issue of *Astounding Science Fiction.* A. E. van Vogt's short story "The Weapon Shop" first appeared in the magazine in 1942. © PARIS PIERCE/ALAMY.

BIBLIOGRAPHY

Sources

"Golden Age of Short Science Fiction, 1938–1950." *Short Story Criticism.* Ed. Joseph Palmisano. Vol. 73. Detroit: Gale, 2005. *Literature Resource Center.* Web. 15 July 2012.

Jorgensen, Darren. "The Disorientations of A. E. van Vogt." *Extrapolation* 49.1 (2008): 97+. *Literature Resource Center.* Web. 15 July 2012.

Knight, Damon. "The Dissecting Table." *Worlds Beyond* 1.2 (1951): 101–02. Print.

Panshin, Alexei, and Cory Panshin. *The World Beyond the Hill: Science Fiction and the Quest for Transcendence.* Rockville: Phoenix Pick, 2010. Print.

Sharp, William Henry. "A. E. van Vogt and the World of Null-A." *ETC.: A Review of General Semantics* 63.1 (2006): 4+. *Literature Resource Center.* Web. 15 July 2012.

Van Vogt, A. E. "The Weapon Shop." *The Science Fiction Hall of Fame.* Ed. Robert Silverberg. New York: ORB, 1998. Print.

Wilson, Colin. "A. E. van Vogt." *Science Fiction Writers: Critical Studies of the Major Authors from the Early Nineteenth Century to the Present Day.* Ed. Everett Franklin Bleiler. New York: Scribner's, 1982. *Scribner Writers Series.* Web. 15 July 2012.

Further Reading

Hartwell, David, and Milton Wolf, eds. *Visions of Wonder.* New York: Tor, 1996. Print.

Jameson, Fredric. "Space of Science Fiction: Narrative in van Vogt." *Archaeologies of the Future.* London: Verso, 2005. 314–27. Print.

Rossi, Umberto. "The Game of the Rat: A. E. Van Vogt's 800-Word Rule and P. K. Dick's *The Game-Players of Titan.*" *Science-Fiction Studies* 31 (2004): 207–26. Print.

Stover, Leon. *Science Fiction from Wells to Heinlein,* Jefferson: McFarland, 2002. Print.

Van Vogt, A. E. "Complication in the Science Fiction Story." 1947. *Of Worlds Beyond: The Science of Science Fiction Writing.* Ed. Lloyd Arthur Eshbach. Chicago: Advent, 1964. 53–66. Print.

Daisy Gard

WHITE-JACKET

Or, The World in a Man-of-War

Herman Melville

❖ **Key Facts**

Time Period:
Mid-19th Century

Genre:
Novel

Events:
Mistreatment of U.S.
sailors; struggle between
U.S. idealism and reality
of a classist society

Nationality:
American

OVERVIEW

White-Jacket, or The World in a Man-of-War, was published in 1850, the second of two novels that Herman Melville wrote in 1849 and regarded as mere "jobs" undertaken for money. Although both the novels—*Redburn* is the other—draw on Melville's experiences at sea, *White-Jacket* moves away from the comfortable style of the travelogue and adopts a more fragmented and complex narrative of factual descriptions interspersed with elements of plot and observation. The narrator of *White-Jacket,* whose nickname is the title of the book, describes a series of episodes from which the hierarchical and often brutal life of the ordinary American sailor emerges. Events aboard the man-of-war *Neversink* may be considered metaphorically to be a microcosm of American society, but they also brought public attention to the unjust treatment of real American sailors and, in particular, the barbarity of flogging.

By 1849 Melville's writing career was in decline after his success of only a few years earlier, when novels such as *Typee* and *Omoo* had been best sellers. *White-Jacket* did little to improve his commercial reputation, but its criticism of the U.S. Navy brought Melville some notoriety. In particular, the novel's vivid descriptions of sailors being punished with the cat-o'-nine tails was cited by New Hampshire Senator John P. Hale as the inspiration for his successful campaign to end the inhumane practice. Along with Melville's other novels, *White-Jacket* is now overshadowed by Melville's masterpiece, *Moby-Dick* (1851), but it is notable both for prefiguring the structure of that great book and for its effectiveness as a work of social reform.

HISTORICAL AND LITERARY CONTEXT

In the United States, the 1840s were marked by economic depression, westward migration, and debates about citizenship, freedom, and civil rights. The U.S. government sought to manage the conflicting interests of geographical expansion and national security. For its part, the U.S. Navy provided an effective buffer for the United States from European naval powers and helped enforce the so-called "Monroe Doctrine" of 1823 designed to forestall growth of European influence in the Western Hemisphere. However, the U.S. Navy of the 1840s was still largely governed by Articles of War, which had been drafted by John Adams in 1775 and patterned after the rules then in force for the Royal Navy. The articles included punishment of sailors by flogging.

In *White-Jacket,* Melville relates how the navy maintains discipline through the threat of violent punishment and how officers demand obedience and respect on the basis of class and social superiority rather than ability and fairness. The narrator points out that although the president of the United States may "take his seat by the side of the meanest citizen in a public conveyance," the navy still operates according to the "stilted etiquette and childish parade of the old-fashioned Spanish court." In his biography *Melville, His World and Work,* Andrew Delbanco argues that as the Jacksonian consensus began to disintegrate in the mid-1840s, it became increasingly difficult for Melville to reconcile the idealism of manifest destiny with injustices such as slavery. To that list *White-Jacket* adds the mistreatment of the American sailor.

Melville was one of many northern intellectuals, including his friend Nathaniel Hawthorne and members of the transcendentalist group in Concord, Massachusetts, which saw a contradiction between the idealism of the United States as a free and democratic nation and the more complex reality. In Hawthorne's *The Scarlet Letter* (1850), for example, a woman whose child is the result of an adulterous affair serves as a symbol of the struggle for freedom against oppressive traditions and rules. Similarly, *White-Jacket* addresses not only the specifics of life in the navy but also finds metaphorical parallels between the navy and the structures of American society at large.

Even before Melville's death in 1891, most of his works had fallen out of print. It was not until the 1920s that he again became well known, in particular for *Moby-Dick*. Although *White-Jacket* was influential in the abolition of flogging in the U.S. Navy, it also marked an experimental shift in Melville's writing. Indeed, *White-Jacket* can be viewed as part of Melville's journey toward the formal experimentation that made *Moby-Dick* a challenge for nineteenth-century readers but a favorite of modernist writers in the 1920s. The central idea of both novels, of the ship as a microcosm of the world, can be seen in numerous subsequent works, such as Katherine Anne Porter's novel *Ship of Fools* (1962) and the blockbuster movie *Titanic* (1997).

THEMES AND STYLE

White-Jacket is narrated from the point of view of an ordinary seaman, whose experiences are contrasted with the lives of his officers and the naval codes he must obey. White-Jacket is an opinionated man, and in the later stages of the book he attacks the evil of flogging explicitly. Echoing a central criticism of the British monarchy in the *Declaration of Independence,* he describes how sailors are flogged "for things not essentially criminal, but only made so by arbitrary laws." Though the narrator's voice is jaunty and often humorous, he does not flinch in his description of a flogging in which "higher and higher rose the purple bars on the prisoner's back." However, this specific form of maltreatment is tied to a more general complaint: he derides commodores for behaving like kings and suggests that "from the dockyards of a republic, absolute monarchies are launched."

The narrative moves from didactic, encyclopedic descriptions of life aboard ship to something more polemic, especially on the subject of naval statutes, whereupon the ordinary sailor is defended but not romanticized. White-Jacket draws the reader's sympathy for having to wear his thin jacket at the masthead in all types of weather, but he is also a somewhat detached figure as he observes and passes judgment on the people and circumstances around him. He often refers to the structure of the novel itself, such as when describing how his preference for quiet is at odds with the uproar aboard the *Neversink*: "I have often … calmed myself down by gazing broad off across a placid sea. After the battle-din of the last two chapters let us now do like." In this way, the reader is invited to reflect on the events along with the narrator.

White-Jacket is affable and lighthearted in guiding the reader around the ship, which works effectively as a contrast to the harshness of naval life. For example, the cheerful false flattery used by Jack Chase to win much-needed shore leave from a pompous commodore is set against the harsh speech of the junior officers: "'You fellow, I'll get you *licked* before long.'" Appearance and reality are always at odds—from the officers' view of themselves as fair and honorable versus their actual brutal behavior to the central irony of a U.S. ship and crew being ruled by tyrants. However, White-Jacket is also direct in his purpose: "Indifferent as to who may be the parties concerned, I but desire to see wrong things righted, and equal justice administered to all." The presentation of the story as a collection of observations and statements, as opposed to a clear and linear plot, takes the novel away from the seafaring adventures for which Melville was known and into the realm of a political or reformation work.

CRITICAL DISCUSSION

White-Jacket was lauded by some reviewers upon its publication. For example, the *New York Tribune* praised Melville for revealing "the secrets of his prison house"

HERMAN MELVILLE: A GREAT AMERICAN WRITER REDISCOVERED

When Herman Melville died in September 1891, he was practically unknown. He had not written a novel for thirty-four years, and the poetry he subsequently composed had barely registered with the literary world. It would be more than another thirty years before Melville received the type of critical attention merited by his work. Melville's reputation grew rapidly following the publication of his novella *Billy Budd* in 1924 by Raymond Weaver, who was compiling *The Standard Edition of Melville's Complete Works.*

Melville had left *Billy Budd* complete but unpublished when he died. The story of an innocent sailor who accidentally kills an officer and is executed, the novella is widely considered to be a masterpiece, and it was later adapted as an opera, a stage play, and a movie. The English novelist D. H. Lawrence immediately became one of Melville's most enthusiastic advocates. His book *Studies in Classic American Literature* (1924) contains two essays on Melville, one about the early novels *Typee* and *Omoo* and another about *Moby-Dick*. Lawrence's endorsement of *Moby-Dick* helped it become one of the most highly regarded and famous novels written in English.

and was impressed by the novel's campaigning spirit. In the longer term, however, *White-Jacket* was not a great success. Beyond its immediate impact in the campaign to abolish flogging, the novel met the same fate as Melville's other books—drifting in and out of print until disappearing altogether in the 1870s. Reviewing Raymond Weaver's 1921 biography *Herman Melville: Mariner and Mystic* in the *American Journal of Sociology* in 1925, Winifred Raushenbush describes Melville as "a man who could not establish communication with his fellows."

In *Herman Melville: An Introduction,* Wyn Kelley argues that *White-Jacket* "stands apart from the works that precede it in being uncommonly focused and serious in its political and social aims." Like *Uncle Tom's Cabin* (1852), which is sometimes credited with initiating the American Civil War, *White-Jacket* is one of a small number of literary works that can be said to have had a direct effect on contemporaneous political issues. Such was the novel's impact immediately after publication that it reinvigorated the campaign in the U.S. Congress against maritime flogging, and flogging was finally banned in the U.S. Navy on September 28, 1850. Furthermore, the novel's broad observation that military justice serves only to reinforce the command structure of the armed forces remains relevant today.

White-Jacket is not among Melville's best-known works, and it is often viewed in the context of his total output. In *A Reader's Guide to Herman Melville,* James E. Miller identifies a progression of Melville

This nineteenth-century illustration offers a cutaway diagram of an American man-of-war, the type of ship at the center of Herman Melville's *White-Jacket*. © NORTH WIND PICTURE ARCHIVES/ ALAMY.

characters, including White-Jacket, who evolved into Ishmael in *Moby-Dick*. The autobiographical elements of Melville's work have also attracted critical consideration. Kelley suggests that *White-Jacket* is a "probing meditation in issues of class, labor, and injustice" and that "*White-Jacket* anticipates the encyclopedic expanse of *Moby Dick,* with its epic proportions." Recent Melville scholarship, including Delbanco's biography, has placed *White-Jacket* in a political context of race, class, and sexuality. However, the novel's episodic structure and its experimentation with psychological and social observation hint at Melville's ongoing struggle with his vision of a new form of literary expression.

BIBLIOGRAPHY

Sources

Broek, Michael. "Ishmael as Evolving Character in Melville's *Redburn, White-Jacket, Mardi,* and *Moby-Dick.*" *Literature Compass* 8.8 (2011): 514–25. Print.

Delbanco, Andrew. *Melville, His World and Work.* New York: Knopf, 2005. Print.

Kelley, Wyn. *Herman Melville: An Introduction.* Oxford: Blackwell, 2008. Print.

Miller, James E. *A Reader's Guide to Herman Melville.* London: Thames and Hudson, 1962. Print.

Stessel, H. Edward. "Melville's *White-Jacket*: The Case Against the 'Cat.'" *Clio* 13.1 (1983): 37–55. Print.

Weaver, Raymond. *Herman Melville: Mariner and Mystic.* New York: George H. Doran, 1921. Print.

Further Reading

Kelley, Wyn, ed. *A Companion to Herman Melville.* New York: Wiley, 2008. Print.

Levine, Robert S., ed. *The Cambridge Companion to Herman Melville.* Cambridge: Cambridge UP, 1998. Print.

Pallwoda, Daniel. *Melville and the Theme of Boredom.* New York: McFarland, 2010. Print.

Parker, Hershel. *The Recognition of Herman Melville: Selected Criticism since 1846.* Ann Arbor: U of Michigan P, 1967. Print.

———. *Herman Melville: A Biography.* 2 vols. Baltimore: Johns Hopkins UP, 1996–2002. Print.

Rollyson, Carl E., Lisa Olson, and April Gentry, eds. *Critical Companion to Herman Melville: A Literary Reference to His Life and Work.* Facts on File, 2007. Print.

Chris Routledge

THE WONDERFUL WIZARD OF OZ

Lyman Frank Baum

OVERVIEW

The Wonderful Wizard of Oz (1900) is a children's novel written by Lyman Frank Baum, who in the book's introduction imagines the work as a "modernized fairy tale" written solely for the entertainment of children and purged of the "fearsome moral" and "bloodcurdling incident[s]" found in the older tales of the Grimm Brothers and Hans Christian Andersen. Nevertheless, for the past half century, critics have identified subtexts that point to social issues permeating Baum's time as well as the modern era. One of the most popular readings is an influential analysis appearing in *American Quarterly* in 1964 that argues the modern fairy tale is a parable of the Populist movement—a political movement by agrarian reformers that advocated "free silver" and reached its climax just prior to Baum's writing. Later critics have read the tale as a young woman's search for a new feminine identity or have transformed Dorothy into a lesbian icon, a view perhaps reinforced by the camp appeal of Judy Garland, star of the 1939 film. Still others have read the text more generally as a cautionary tale against taking appearance for reality or seeking meaning outside the self.

An immediate and immense success, *The Wonderful Wizard of Oz* became the fastest-selling children's book in the United States in 1900 and eventually served as the inspiration for a musical comedy, three movies (including the well-known Victor Fleming production of 1939), and a number of plays. According to the Populist reading, Dorothy represents the everyman traveling with her new friends the Tin Woodman (an industrial worker), the Scarecrow (a farmer), and the Cowardly Lion (Populist leader William Jennings Bryan). The wizard they seek turns out to be an ineffective fraud, which is how many Populists viewed the Gilded Age presidents. The Wicked Witch of the West, Dorothy's nemesis and a symbol of the intractable evil of the capitalist system, dissolves finally into a pile of mud just as, during the late nineteenth century, rains finally banished the drought that temporarily plagued American farmers. The yellow brick road represents the gold standard, and Dorothy's silver slippers stand for the Populist demand for a bimetallic monetary standard, backed by gold and silver at the ratio of sixteen to one. Further, the hope that Dorothy and her friends invest in wizardry and Oz, the typical abbreviation for *ounce*, parallels the naive belief that manipulating the relative values of silver and gold would solve the nation's problems. However, the Tin Woodman, whose creaky joints represent industrial paralysis, requires only some oiling, while the seemingly empty-headed Scarecrow discovers he has had a brain all along. Thus, common sense and the sure instincts of Dorothy as the American everyman expose the folly of Populist radicalism.

HISTORICAL AND LITERARY CONTEXT

As the editor of a South Dakota newspaper in the 1880s, Baum, who moved to Chicago beginning in 1891, was ideally situated to observe the tense political struggles of the final decades of the nineteenth century. Catalyzed by the depression of 1893, Midwestern farmers and industrial laborers from the cities fought back against the abuses of the infamous robber barons. The Farmers' Alliance was formed in Texas toward the end of the century and soon spread throughout the South and Midwest, sweeping through Mississippi, as one member put it, "like a cyclone," much as the one that upended Dorothy's Kansas. At the same time, the International Working People's Association was operating in Chicago, and many other labor groups were popping up around the country.

Strongest in the Midwest and South, the Populist party was notable for recognizing the shared interests of farmers and the burgeoning labor movement. It called for government ownership of the major industries and the unlimited coinage of silver, which Populists hoped would reduce the power of the big banks and help poor farmers pay off their debts. The movement reached its climax when Bryan, a prominent Democrat who shared Populist views, ran on the Democratic ticket against Republican William McKinley in the presidential election of 1896.

Perhaps the most famous Populist document, Bryan's Cross of Gold speech at the 1896 Democratic National Convention describes in bombastic language a "war" being waged between the "toiling masses" who wish to protect their homes and the "financial magnates" invested in preserving the gold standard. Since *The Wonderful Wizard of Oz* contains none of the strident, fiery language common to Populist propaganda, and Baum's political views continue to be debated, parallels between the story and the world of 1890s

Key Facts

Time Period:
Early 20th Century

Genre:
Novel

Events:
Rise of Populist Movement in the United States; presidential candidacy of William Jennings Bryan; passage of the Gold Standard Act

Nationality:
American

POPULIST DEBATE OVER OZ

In 1992 the debate over the Populist reading of *The Wonderful Wizard of Oz* was aired in public in a series of letters to the editor of the *New York Times*. Initially, after the *Times* ran a piece about the religious and mystical elements of the book, Saul Rosen wrote in to remind readers of the true intentions of the tale, arguing, "In fact, the book is a secular political tract." Michael Hearn, soon-to-be editor of the centennial edition of *The Annotated Wizard of Oz*, wrote a rebuttal to Rosen in which he explained that the Populist interpretation came from an essay by Henry Littlefield that had "no basis in fact." There was, Hearn wrote, "no evidence that Baum's story is in any way a Populist allegory." To illustrate the futility of attaching a clear political intention to the author of Oz, Hearn relates an incident from 1896 when Baum delivered a fiery attack against the Democrats at a Republican rally and soon after gave the same speech at a Democratic rally, this time lambasting Republicans. Hearn's response caught the attention of Littlefield himself, who gently conceded Hearn's point, stating that *The Wonderful Wizard of Oz* was "hardly the stuff of 'Cross of Gold' speeches."

politics remain conjectural. Indeed, Russel B. Nye, one of the editors of the first critical study of *The Wonderful Wizard of Oz*, noted in 1957, before the Populist interpretation appeared, that the tale stood out from other children's fiction of the time precisely because it dispensed with the seriousness and class consciousness that was often found in the more respected British variant. However, Nye denies the book had a set didactic purpose. If there is a political moral or satire in Baum's tale, it recedes quietly behind the constantly shifting panorama of strange characters and fantastic incidents. Baum does not so much scold, Nye writes, as banter, gently poking fun at our human frailties and flaws.

The publication of *The Wonderful Wizard of Oz* coincided with Bryan's second failed attempt at the presidency and the effective collapse of the Populist party. As a result, it is difficult to determine what, if any, effect the book had on the political climate of the time. Despite arcane academic debates about its meaning, the book has been largely received as the entertaining tale that Baum himself claims to have written. In addition to the thirteen additional Oz books Baum wrote in answer to readers' demands, it has also served as the inspiration for numerous plays, musicals, and adaptations, including Gregory Maguire's adult-oriented 1995 novel *Wicked* (itself adapted into a successful musical) and Geoff Ryman's metafictional *Was* (1992).

THEMES AND STYLE

Many critics read *The Wonderful Wizard of Oz* as a gentle warning against taking the symbol of the thing for the thing itself. Baum registers this dramatic irony

by directly juxtaposing his characters' words and their behaviors. For instance, the Tin Woodman laments that he does not have a heart; yet his actions, which include weeping over the death of a beetle he has inadvertently trampled, reveal him to be immensely caring. Similarly, the Scarecrow, who has no brains, reliably offers clever solutions to the problems facing the group. This skepticism toward the surface extends even to the Great Wizard, whose power comes only from the fact that so many people believe him to be powerful.

Although *The Wonderful Wizard of Oz* has been characterized as parable, allegory, and even propaganda, it occupies a more complicated place in the history of social criticism. Due to the ambiguity of its message, it lacks the single, salient lesson of a parable. Neither is it, strictly speaking, an allegory, a rhetorical device that essentially functions as an extended metaphor such that a particular character symbolizes or stands for an idea or virtue. In John Bunyan's famous allegory *Pilgrim's Progress* (1678), Christian (the everyman) journeys from the City of Destruction (earth) to the Celestial City (heaven). Baum's vivid characters and locales, in contrast, suggest a wealth of interpretations. Dorothy has been identified as a stand-in for the everyman; Theodore Roosevelt (syllabically, *Theodore* is the inverse of *Dorothy*); and Mary Ellen Lease, a female Populist orator. However, unlike Bunyan's allegory, the didactic purpose of *The Wonderful Wizard of Oz* is never entirely clear. Critics who agree that it is an allegorical tale of some sort often disagree as to whether Baum consciously set out to attack or defend Populism—as conscious design is a hallmark of propaganda.

Littlefield, the originator of the Populist reading, was himself careful to point out that the "allegory always remains in a minor key, subordinated to the major theme and readily abandoned whenever it threatens to distort the appeal of the fantasy." Perhaps the most ingenious stylistic aspect of Baum's masterpiece is the way it continually encourages and then undermines a univocal, all-encompassing interpretation. In part, Baum establishes this playful uncertainty, the critic C. M. notes, through the creation of characters who appear symbolic or paradigmatic but who constantly reveal idiosyncratic quirks. For instance, the detail that the Scarecrow's padded fingers make it difficult for him to pick up things does not fit neatly into an allegorical framework. Like the characters themselves, readers hope to find the ultimate answer to their questions by the book's end, but Baum seems to suggest that it is the belief that meaning is located in an external source that is both silly and human.

CRITICAL DISCUSSION

Although immensely popular among children, *The Wonderful Wizard of Oz* did not inspire critical study until 1957. *The Wizard of Oz and Who He Was*, edited by Nye and Martin Gardner, includes a reprint of the full text of the novel with original drawings by W. W. Denslow and an introductory essay by each editor. Remarking on the surprising lack of critical interest in Baum and his Oz books, Nye writes, "From 1900 to 1919, the years during which Baum was producing almost a book a year to the plaudits of children in the hundreds of thousands, none of his books received a review in a major journal." Nye suggests that Baum's name was left out of contemporary lists of the best children's books because his work eschewed the moral didacticism that was so important to adults, if not children.

In 1964 Littlefield's essay opened the debate that continues to occupy critics. Citing remarks by Nye and Gardner, Littlefield builds a case for the tale as a loving satire of a failed movement toward which Baum was sympathetic. The essay offers a compelling interpretation of many of the book's major elements, and the idea that the children's story was really a Populist allegory soon attained legendary status. Attesting to the popularity of the interpretation, critic Peter Dreier, responding to the release of *The Wiz,* a film starring an African American cast, writes in a 1978 article for *In These Times* of the need to remind readers that the tale was "originally intended" as a "political allegory about grassroots protest."

In the 1990s critics began expressing doubts about the allegorical interpretation. Bradley A. Hansen, in a 2002 article for *Journal of Economic Education,* reminds readers that the allegorical interpretation originated in Littlefield's essay and grew from there. So many critics have built their findings on Littlefield's research, in fact, that even critics who do not directly mention Littlefield cite someone who does. In response to Gardner's influential but unsubstantiated claim that Baum was a Democrat who marched in torchlight parades for Bryan, skeptics point out that Baum was the editor of a Republican newspaper and that he even wrote a poem that championed McKinley and the gold standard. As a result, some recent scholarly work has begun to drift away from the Populist allegory debate to discuss the tale in relation to topics such as race, the allegorical tradition in general, and the history of its stage productions.

BIBLIOGRAPHY

Sources

Bryan, William Jennings. "William Jennings Bryan's Cross of Gold Speech July 8, 1896." *American History: From Revolution to Reconstruction and Beyond.* University of Groningen, n.d. Web. 1 Oct. 2012.

C. M. "SF Intertextuality: Echoes of the *Pilgrim's Progress* in Baum's *The Wizard of Oz* and Burroughs's First *Mars* Trilogy." *Science Fiction Studies* 30.3 (2003): 544–54. *JSTOR.* Web. 1 Oct. 2012.

Dreier, Peter. "Once upon a Time, *The Wizard of Oz* Was a Populist Fable." *In These Times* 20 Dec. 1978: 23. Web. 1 Oct. 2012.

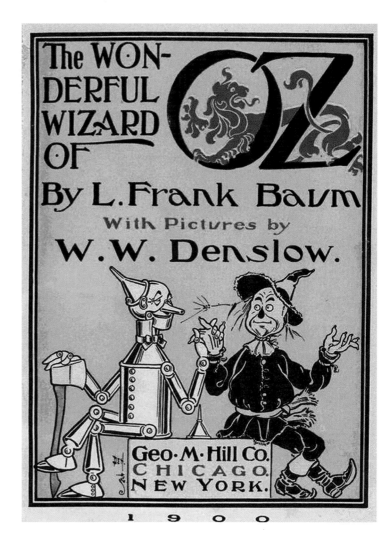

Title page of first edition of *The Wonderful Wizard of Oz,* published by L. Frank Baum in 1900. © EVERETT COLLECTION INC./ALAMY.

Gardner, Martin, and Russel B. Nye. *The Wizard of Oz and Who He Was.* East Lansing: Michigan State UP, 1994. Print.

Goodwyn, Lawrence. *The Populist Moment: A Short History of the Agrarian Revolt in America.* Oxford: Oxford UP, 1978. Print.

Hansen, Bradley A. "The Fable of the Allegory: *The Wizard of Oz* in Economics." *Journal of Economic Education* 33.3 (2002): 254–64. *JSTOR.* Web. 1 Oct. 2012.

Littlefield, Henry. "*The Wizard of Oz*: Parable on Populism." *American Quarterly* 16.1 (1964): 57–58. *JSTOR.* Web. 1 Oct. 2012.

Further Reading

Dighe, Ranjit S. *The Historian's* Wizard of Oz: *Reading L. Frank Baum's Classic as a Political and Monetary Allegory.* Westport: Praeger, 2002. Print.

Hearn, Michael Patrick. *The Annotated Wizard of Oz.* Centennial ed. New York: Norton, 2000. Print.

Parker, David B. "The Rise and Fall of *The Wonderful Wizard of Oz* as a Parable on Populism." *Journal of the Georgia Association of Historians* 15 (1994): 49–63. Print.

Ritter, Gretchen. "Silver Slippers and a Golden Cap: L. Frank Baum's *The Wonderful Wizard of Oz* and Historical Memory in American Politics." *Journal of American Studies.* 31.2 (1997): 171–202. Print.

Rockoff, Hugh. "The *Wizard of Oz* as Monetary Allegory." *Journal of Political Economy* 98.4 (1990): 739–60. Print.

Rogers, Katharine M. *L. Frank Baum: Creator of Oz.* New York: St. Martin's, 2002. Print.

Ryman, Geoff. *Was.* New York: Penguin, 1993. Print.

Swartz, Mark Evan. *Oz before the Rainbow: L. Frank Baum's* The Wonderful Wizard of Oz *on Stage and Screen to 1939.* Baltimore: Johns Hopkins UP, 2002. Print.

Media Adaptations

The Wonderful Wizard of Oz. Dir. Otis Turner. Perf. Bebe Daniels, Hobart Bosworth, and Eugenie Besserer. Selig Polyscope, 1910. Film.

The Wizard of Oz. Dir. Victor Fleming. Perf. Judy Garland, Frank Morgan, and Ray Bolger. Metro-Goldwyn-Mayer (MGM), 1939. Film.

Phillip Mahoney

MYTHS AND MARTYRS

THE ACTES AND DEIDIS OF THE ILLUSTRE AND VALYEANT CAMPIOUN SCHIR WILLIAM WALLACE

Henry the Minstrel

OVERVIEW

Composed in the mid- to late fifteenth century by an author known only as Henry the Minstrel—or more commonly Blind Harry—*The Actes and Deidis of the Illustre and Valyeant Campioun Schir William Wallace,* typically shortened to *The Wallace,* is an epic poem written in Middle Scots and divided in most editions into twelve books. It tells the stories and legends of Sir William Wallace, who at the end of the thirteenth century helped Scotland, then an independent country, wage war against invading English forces. Some episodes are historically accurate; others are entirely fabricated. Still others are borrowed from such works as a 1375 poem by John Barbour about Robert the Bruce, who was crowned king of Scotland in 1306, scarcely a year after Wallace's capture and execution by the English. By the time the poem was written, Wallace as a character was already synonymous with Scottish patriotism and defiance of English rule.

When the poem was written in the 1480s, Scotland was under threat from without by England and from within by feuding Scottish magnates engaged in bloody conflict over rights to the throne. The poem's vision of a strong and independent Scotland must have been a welcome one to Scottish citizens weary of the fighting. Decades later, at the advent of the publishing industry, *The Wallace* became one of the first titles published in Scotland. In the late twentieth century, the Hollywood movie based on the poem—*Braveheart* (1995)—reignited interest in the story. Although it is difficult to ascertain the extent to which the poem may have bolstered Scottish nationalism and cemented Wallace's reputation as a national hero, Blind Hary's spirited *Wallace* continues to be read by readers of all kinds.

HISTORICAL AND LITERARY CONTEXT

The Wallace was written in the midst of internal and external conflict in Scotland. In 1286 Scotland's King Alexander III died, and the person named to inherit the throne, his granddaughter Margaret of Norway, was deemed unacceptable by many Scottish magnates—not just because she was foreign born but also because she was female. On her way to claim the title in 1290, the child Margaret, traveling by sea, died, sparking a succession dispute. Watching with interest was England's King Edward I, Wallace's nemesis. Having recently subjugated Wales over the course of a long campaign of war and castle building, Edward I, a blood relation of Alexander III, longed to bring Scotland under his control.

When Blind Hary was composing the poem—likely between 1471 and 1479—Scottish sentiment toward "Sotheroun" folk (the English) was, as it long had been, hostile. In the 1290s Edward I was invited by Scottish noblemen to settle the dispute over succession. The principal figures claiming rights to the throne were John Balliol and Robert the Bruce. Edward introduced more candidates to further destabilize the situation and then selected Balliol, seeing in him an easily subordinated monarch. However, Edward overthrew Balliol in 1296 and declared himself king. Wallace rose up in defense of Balliol, who before being ousted managed to sign an alliance with the king of France that would last for hundreds of years.

Scottish writing in the fifteenth century blossomed after the appearance of *The Kingis Quhair* (c. 1420), which is believed to have been written by Scotland's James I after his release from English captivity. Historian Andrew of Wyntoun's *Orygynale Cronykil of Scotland* (c. 1420) celebrates the exploits of Wallace and also discusses Robin Hood. Walter Bower's *Continuation* of John of Fordun's *Scotichronicon* (c. 1440) contains Wallace's uncle's maxim, "Never submit to live, my son, in the bonds of slavery entwined." Hary's poem borrows from both. Wallace appears more than once "graithit in gudlygreyn" (dressed in green). As the heraldic symbol of springtime, hope, and renewal, green is a familiar motif in folklore, also found in the English poem *Sir Gawain and the Green Knight* (c. 1400). The poem *Golagros and Gawane,* written during Blind Hary's lifetime, is attributed by at least one editor to Hary, by virtue of its stylistic and linguistic similarity to *The Wallace.*

While Blind Hary may have produced other poems, *The Wallace* is generally the only work attributed to him. William Dunbar in his poem *Lament for the Makars* (c. 1508) includes Blind Hary alongside Scottish *makars* (poets) such as John Barbour,

Key Facts

Time Period:
Mid- to Late Fifteenth Century

Genre:
Poetry

Events:
Scottish Wars of Independence

Nationality:
Scottish

THE INTERSECTION OF SCOTTISH AND GREEK MYTHOLOGY

In *The Odyssey,* Homer writes of the bard who amuses the Phaeacians that the Muse "stripped him of sight / but gave the man the power of stirring, rapturous song ... the Muse inspired the bard / to sing the famous deeds of fighting heroes." Historians have often interpreted this to mean that Homer himself was blind. However, Harvard literature professor William Schofield observes that fifteenth-century Scottish historian John Mair may have conflated Homer's biography with Hary's when he claims Hary was "blind from birth." For example, Mair also likened Wallace's military skills to those of Hannibal, Ulysses, and Ajax, and claimed that Wallace's preferred cut of meat was the same favored by Achilles, greatest warrior of them all.

Other examples of the influence of Greek mythology on Scottish history include *Scalacronica* (c. 1362), by Sir Thomas Gray, which relates founding myths of Scotland drawn from records as old as the eleventh century. It was believed that the Scots descended from Scota, daughter of an Egyptian pharaoh, and a Greek king named Goídel Glas, who traveled to Hibernia from Spain with the Stone of Scone, upon which future kings of Scotland would be crowned.

Richard Holland, Richard Henryson, and England's John Gower and Geoffrey Chaucer, showing Hary's acceptance into the literary community. Poet Robert Burns writes of *The Wallace* in a letter reprinted in *The Works of Robert Burns* (1840) that Blind Hary's poem "poured a Scottish prejudice into my veins which will boil along there till the floodgates of life shut in eternal rest."

THEMES AND STYLE

Central to *The Wallace* is the certainty that Scotland should not be under English rule. Wallace's righteousness has almost pagan overtones, though he is portrayed as a devout Christian who always has his prayer book at hand. While the poem eschews traditional markers of folklore such as fairies and dwarves, it invokes the thirteenth-century minstrel, seer, and consort of fairies Thomas Rhymer, who predicts there will never be another like Wallace: "Of this regioune he sall the Sotheroun send ... So gud of hand agaynesall never be kend" (Of this region he shall the Southern send ... So good of hand shall never again be known). *The Wallace*'s hero, whom Blind Hary places in "the rychtlyne of the first Stewart" (the righteous line of the first Stewart) and whose uncle is the sheriff of Ayr, is nevertheless at home among the people. He goes into their humble homes to heal from battle and disguises himself as a peddler to infiltrate English-held territory. Like Merlin and Celtic faery folk, Wallace is a shape-shifter who benefits from the hidden magic of the land.

Wallace's uncanny relationship with the land and its people creates an impression of a wholly self-sufficient world, a Scotland into which any English intrusion seems unnatural. Local women frequently appear just in time to help Wallace's men, and the poet often pauses to remark, "This trew woman thaim seruit weill in deid" (This true woman served them well in deed). In addition, when Wallace is finally captured, a "monk off Bery" has a vision of him: "Now thai him kep to martyr in London toun ... For rychtwyswer that he tukapon hand ... Hewin he sall-haiff" (Now they will martyr him in London town ... For the virtuous war he undertook ... Heaven he shall have). At his execution in Book XII, Wallace asks "To lat him haiff his psalter buk in sycht" (to let him have his prayer book in sight). "He gert a preyst It oppyn-befor him hauld / Quhillthai till him done all that thaiwauld" (He had a priest hold it open before him / until they were done). His actions harken back to Book I's opening line, "Our antecessowris that we suld of reide" (Our ancestors, of whom we should read).

Stylistically, the poem deploys a familiar dynamic of hero worship. The idea of Wallace as a martyr continues throughout the poem: the Virgin Mary tells Wallace in a vision in Book VII, "Thow art grantyt be the gret god abuff / Till help pepill that sufferis mekill wrang" (Thou art granted by the great God above / To help people who have suffered great wrongs). Wallace as a representative of Scotland illustrates concerns about Scotland's position on the world stage. For example, an absurd episode in Book XI set in France, where Wallace is forced to fight a lion, hints at a measure of uncertainty regarding the Old Alliance between Scotland and France.

CRITICAL DISCUSSION

Initially, *The Wallace* made a minor folk hero of Hary. In a poem attributed to Dunbar and believed to have been written eight years before *Lament* (1508), Blind Hary appears as a mythical figure. *The Dwarf's Part of the Play* (c. 1500), as William Schofield observes in *Mythical Bards and the Life of William Wallace* (1920), is "the earliest extant specimen of dramatic verse in Scots." In the play, a dwarf comes onstage and says, "I am the nakit Blynd Hary, / That lang has bene in the Fary, / Farleis to fynd." However, in the Bannatyne Manuscript (a 1568 compilation of fifteenth- and sixteenth-century poetry and other works in Scots), the same poem reads, "I am bot ane Blynd Hary" (I am but one Blind Hary). In an article for the *Chaucer Review* (1974), John Balaban concludes, "the name 'Blind Harry' was that of a popular figure, a type."

Critical explorations of *The Wallace* continue to mine the few documents that confirm Hary's existence for clues as to his identity. They also attempt to locate the poem in terms of history, nation building, and its relationship to other medieval literary works. However, the way in which *The Wallace* was published has presented numerous problems for scholars.

Opposite page:
William Wallace leading his soldiers. Wallace is the subject of The Actes and Deidis of the Illustre and Valyeant Campioun Schir William Wallace, a fifteenth-century poem by Henry the Minstrel. WILLIAM WALLACE DIRECTING HIS SOLDIERS (COLOUR LITHO), ENGLISH SCHOOL/ PRIVATE COLLECTION/ PETER NEWARK MILITARY PICTURES/THE BRIDGEMAN ART LIBRARY.

Scribe John Ramsay's 1488 manuscript survives intact, as well as fragments of the first printed edition from around 1509. But in the 1968 standard critical edition of *The Wallace,* Matthew P. McDiarmid writes that Ramsay confesses that the original manuscript "was hurriedly written" such that "at one point the intended indication of the commencement of a new Book (IX) was not properly made"; thus the work was "divided into eleven Books instead of the intended twelve retained by the editions." McDiarmid states that the oft remarked-upon mistake at the poem's end, which incorrectly states that Wallace's age at the time of his death was forty-five, is likely the fault of Ramsay.

Today *The Wallace* is often discussed alongside *The Bruce* and works by Chaucer and other English and Scottish medieval poets. Grace G. Wilson, writing in *Studies in Scottish Literature* (1990), examines the historical Wallace's support of Balliol. Reviewing centuries of *Wallace* criticism, Graeme Morton writes in the *Scottish Historical Review* (1998), "On balance, it is the literary critic rather than the historian, who is better able to place Harry." If Blind Hary treats gossip as source material, he does so to great literary effect, as with Chaucer's *Manciple's Tale* (c. 1386), in which, as Susan E. Phillips writes in *Transforming Talk: The Problem with Gossip in Late Medieval England* (2007), "in addition to making the 'textueel' appear colloquial, the Manciple uses idle talk here to make his audience into his conversational kin."

BIBLIOGRAPHY

Sources

Balaban, John. "Blind Harry and *The Wallace.*" *Chaucer Review* 8.3 (1974): 249. *JSTOR.* Web. 24 Sept. 2012.

Burns, Robert. Letter to Dr. Moore. 2 Aug. 1787. *The Works of Robert Burns.* Ed. Allan Cunningham. London: Tegg, 1840. 622–27. Web. 2 Oct. 2012.

McDiarmid, Matthew P., ed. *Hary's Wallace.* 2 vols. Scottish Text Society. Edinburgh: Blackwood, 1968. Print.

Morton, Graeme. "The Most Efficacious Patriot: The Heritage of William Wallace in Nineteenth-Century Scotland." *Scottish Historical Review* 77.204 (1998): 224–51. *JSTOR.* Web. 24 Sept. 2012.

Phillips, Susan E. *Transforming Talk: The Problem with Gossip in Late Medieval England.* University Park: Pennsylvania State UP, 2007. Print.

Schofield, William Henry. *Mythical Bards and the Life of William Wallace.* Cambridge: Harvard UP, 1920. Print.

Wilson, Grace G. "Barbour's Bruce and Hary's Wallace: Complements, Compensations and Conventions." *Studies in Scottish Literature* 25.1 (1990): 195–96. Print.

Further Reading

Fraser, James E. "'A Swan from a Raven': William Wallace, Brucean Propaganda, and *Gesta Annnalia II.*" *Scottish Historical Review* 81.211 (2002): 1–22. *JSTOR.* Web. 24 Sept. 2012.

Goldstein, R. James. "Blind Hary's Myth of Blood: The Ideological Closure of *The Wallace.*" *Studies in Scottish Literature* 25.1 (1990): 70–82. Print.

———. *The Matter of Scotland: Historical Narrative in Medieval Scotland.* Lincoln: U of Nebraska P, 1993. Print.

Homer. *The Odyssey.* Trans. Robert Fagles. New York: Penguin, 1996. Print.

McDiarmid, Matthew P., and James A. C. Stevenson, eds. *Barbour's Bruce.* 3 vols. Edinburgh: Scottish Text Society, 1985. Print.

McKim, Anne. "Scottish National Heroes and the Limits of Violence." *A Great Effusion of Blood? Interpreting Medieval Violence.* Eds. Mark Meyers and Daniel Thiery. Toronto: Toronto UP, 2004. 131–46. Print.

Skeat, W. W. "Chaucer and Blind Harry." *Modern Language Quarterly* 1 (1897): 49–50. *JSTOR.* Web. 24 Sept. 2012.

Media Adapations

Braveheart. Dir. Mel Gibson. Perf. Mel Gibson, Sophie Marceau, and Patrick McGoohan. The Ladd Company, 1995. Film.

Rebecca Rustin

ANDRÉ

A Tragedy in Five Acts

William Dunlap

OVERVIEW

First performed on March 30, 1798, *André: A Tragedy in Five Acts* by William Dunlap was the first play about the American Revolution to rise above patriotic fervor and discuss the ideological and moral quandaries raised by the war. Written in blank verse, the drama is based on the real-life execution of Major John André, a popular British officer condemned to death for his involvement with Benedict Arnold, a former American general who had defected to the British. Although he was convicted as an enemy spy, André is not portrayed as a villain but as a tragic hero whose ambitious desire for fame led to him to tempt Arnold into betraying his country. The plot revolves around the relationship between André and his fictional American friend Captain Bland, who passionately begs the character called the General (a thinly veiled George Washington) for his otherwise virtuous comrade to be spared. Bland's conflicted loyalties act as a metaphor for the fledgling country and mirror the dilemmas faced by colonists whose allegiances were equally tested as they declared independence from their mother country. Dunlap closes his play by entreating the audience to stand united, rather than being torn apart by party conflict.

Although modern critics praise *André* as Dunlap's best play, it was a dismal failure with the American public. Critics were particularly outraged by the scene in which Bland casts off his cockade (a popular symbol of American patriotism) to show his displeasure with the General's decision to hang his noble friend. As historian Sarah J. Purcell points out, "not only did the audience disapprove of the traitor appearing to be more heroic than an American officer, but the cockade … was a highly charged political symbol" in the 1790s. Although Dunlap rewrote the scene in order to restore Bland to patriotic good graces, the drama was only performed three times and was pulled from the theater's repertoire. In 1803 Dunlap rewrote the tragedy as a patriotic spectacle—an extremely popular form of entertainment—titled *The Glory of Columbia: Her Yeomanry!* Little resembling the original play, *The Glory of Columbia* boasted new characters, songs, and comic relief interwoven with nine scenes from *André*. Although the playwright himself condemned *Columbia* as the "amusement of holiday fools," it became one

of the most famous dramas in the history of the American theater, demonstrating young America's preference for patriotic spectacle over serious art.

HISTORICAL AND LITERARY CONTEXT

The real Major John André was the newly appointed head of British secret intelligence in 1780 when he entered into secret negotiations with American general Benedict Arnold, commander of the fort at West Point, New York. Arnold agreed to surrender the fort to British forces for the sum of £20,000. Returning from his final rendezvous with Arnold, André was apprehended by three American militiamen, who confiscated the papers he was carrying. Learning of André's capture, Arnold fled his post and defected to the British. André, on the other hand, was tried as a spy and sentenced to a dishonorable death by hanging. Despite an appeal to General George Washington for a more dignified death, by firing squad, André was hanged on October 2, 1780.

André was extremely popular among both Britons and Americans. He had openly sympathized with the rebellious colonies, and the compassion he showed to American prisoners of war made him a legend. Alexander Hamilton—Washington's aide-de-camp and a great admirer of André—wrote, "There was something singularly interesting in the character and fortunes of André … he united a peculiar elegance of mind and manners, and the advantage of a pleasing person." In deference to André's virtuous nature, many Americans objected to the execution and some even publicly criticized Washington. Dunlap's character Captain Bland, whose life is saved by André while he is imprisoned by the British, is a reminder of André's renowned kindness and the affection many Americans felt for him.

By 1798 the André-Arnold affair had been written about and romanticized so often that André had become part of national mythology, sometimes portrayed as martyr and sometimes as villain. Jay Fliegelman suggests that retelling André's story was America's way of dealing with the guilt and shame produced by Washington's controversial decision. He argues that "the elevating of André to the status of sacrificial lamb … was one way by which Revolutionary America relieved its guilty awareness that … it must deny gratitude to those

Key Facts

Time Period:
Late 18th Century

Genre:
Play

Events:
Benedict Arnold plot; American Revolution

Nationality:
American

WILLIAM DUNLAP: THE FATHER OF AMERICAN THEATER

Born in America in 1766, William Dunlap was one of the first professional playwrights in the United States. He contributed to the fledgling country's developing cultural identity by choosing native subject matters for his plays and using the stage to express patriotism. Despite his historical significance, Dunlap was not particularly successful during his lifetime—he was considered a respectable but struggling theater manger and a competent but not distinguished writer. Dunlap's writing suffered from sentimentality and moralistic tendencies, but Norman Philbrick argues that these faults are "overcome by the sincerity and intensity of the writer as well as the technical control exercised by a playwright who was essentially an experienced man of the theatre."

At the age of sixteen Dunlap became a professional portrait painter and was eventually sent to London to study art under Benjamin West. While in London he reveled in the dramas of the day, and upon his return to America he abandoned painting for theater, although he continued to rely on his talents as a painter for income. Dunlap entered theatrical management in his early twenties. In 1789 two of his plays were produced for the first time, the most successful being *The Father; or, American Shandy-ism.* In 1794 Dunlap's interests turned from comedy to tragedy with the staging of *The Fatal Deception, or The Progress of Guilt,* a play that pays homage to William Shakespeare. Although influenced by European drama, Dunlap sought to establish a national theater that staged American plays. In the latter part of his life Dunlap turned increasingly to history. In 1832 he wrote *A History of the American Theatre,* in which he made a strong argument for a national theater that would encourage patriotism and morality

truly deserving of it." Dunlap's treatment of André was shaped not only by previous writings on the scandal but also by European drama. Several of the plot elements resemble Thomas Otway's tragedy *Venice Preserved, or A Plot Discovered* (1682), and in Act V of *André* Bland compares himself to Otway's hero Jaffeir and André to Jaffeir's condemned friend Pierre.

A Federalist at heart, Dunlap wrote *André* during a time when America was in dire need of national unity, torn between the Democratic Republicans and the Federalists. Although some scholars suggest *André* is pro-Federalist, others argue that it speaks against the Federalist Alien and Sedition Acts passed under President John Adams that restricted free speech and immigration. However, as Sarah Purcell argues, "even if Dunlap did not intend his play to be pro-British, presenting André as an aristocratic and gentlemanly figure of honor at a time when Federalists were clamoring for war against Revolutionary France held direct political connotations." Shortly after Democratic Republican Thomas Jefferson was elected president, Dunlap revised *André.* S. E. Wilmer proposes that "with Federalism in rapid decline, Dunlap rewrote his play using Democratic Republican rather than Federalist rhetorical devices and gave it a different title that emphasized its new Democratic Republican character." The new drama overtly emphasized the virtues of the common American soldier and reduced Major André from martyr to a man responsible for his own demise. Although critics consider it Dunlap's poorest play, contemporary audiences were so enamored that it was revived regularly over the next fifty years.

THEMES AND STYLE

Central to *André* is Dunlap's declaration that men are imperfect creatures who fail in times of weakness. André, although virtuous in almost every way, tempted Arnold into betraying his country. André confesses that he "forgot my former purity of thought; / And high-ton'd honour's scruples disregarded." He recognizes that the act of bribing Arnold was "against my reason, my declared opinion; / Against my conscience, and a soldier's fame." The tragically heroic André redeems himself by admitting his guilt in the Arnold affair and acknowledging his misguided lust for fame. Bland, acting out of love for his friend, allows his emotions to blind his reason, leading to several acts of insubordination. In one passionate moment, he treasonously declares, "I will foreswear my country and her service: / I'll hie me to the Briton, and with fire, / And sword, and every instrument of death / Or devastation, join in the work of war!" Even the General is portrayed as a cruel but vulnerable father-figure. Despite these displays of weakness, Dunlap does not vilify any of the characters, suggesting that this is not a play about good triumphing over evil, but, as Joseph Ellis postulates, about "human beings under extreme stress, trying … to cope with adversity and behave virtuously."

In contrasting characters governed by reason with those ruled by emotions, Dunlap argues that rational thought leads to virtuous behavior. The most overtly emotional character is Bland, who is prone to melodramatic soliloquies and angry outbursts. Upon learning of the General's resolve to "abide by the laws of war" and execute André as a spy, Bland angrily exclaims, "The country that forgets to reverence virtue / That makes no different 'twixt the sordid wretch … And him unfortunate, whose duteous service / Is, by mere accident, so chang'd in form, / As to assume guilt's semblance, I serve not." At this point, Bland tears the cockade from his helmet to disclaim his service. Bland's emotional outbursts are contrasted with the more rational speeches of older authority figures in the play, including the General. As the plot progresses, Bland matures into a more rational character, regrets his insubordination, and even attempts to understand the General's decision to hang André.

Although Dunlap's blank verse is well crafted, the emotional zeal and maudlin lines render the tone melodramatic. Dunlap biographer Oral Sumner Coad describes the play as "artificial and sentimental," to which he adds, "The tone reaches a certain degree of intensity in places." The play is riddled with sentimental speeches, particularly from the love-sick Bland. Upon learning of André's imprisonment, Bland tenderly recalls a time when the Briton had ministered to him: "This gallant youth … like an angel, seeking good for man, / Restor'd us light, and partial liberty … He nurst and cur'd, / He lov'd and made his friend … in my heart he liv'd … Judge how my heart is tortur'd." Sentimental melodramas were common in the 1790s, and Ellis asserts that "Bland's pleas for André are precisely the kind of heartrending soliloquies that most British and American dramatists employed to win the sympathies of their audiences."

CRITICAL DISCUSSION

Contemporary critics harshly criticized Dunlap's *André* for what they understood to be antipatriotic sentiment. In his 1832 book *A History of American Theatre,* Dunlap recounts the audience's outraged reaction to Bland's tearing off his American cockade: "They thought the country and its defenders insulted, and a hiss ensued." The Democratic Republican newspaper the *Argus* deprecated Dunlap's one-sided treatment of André's story: "The brave and heroic veterans who apprehended [André], are carefully left out; men who preferred the sacred cause in which they embarked—the liberty of their country—to sordid *Lucre.*" Desiree Henderson suggests that *André* failed because Dunlap "represented the politics of the early national era through its failure, rather than its success," and in doing so, "he trod onto the dangerous and unsettled ground of national identity and memory."

Regarded by scholars as the father of the American theater, Dunlap believed that the theater was the young republic's best chance of creating a democratic community and therefore staged plays that investigated emerging civic and national characters. Over the course of his lifetime, he authored or adapted more than sixty plays, managed New York's Park Theatre, and published several biographies and American history texts. Lucy Rinehart argues that early American playwrights turned to spectacular melodramas because they had become "uncomfortable with the ways in which the political and emotional complexity of tragic history plays like *André* occasioned contradictory and unpredictable audience responses." Although he was openly critical of patriotic spectacles, Dunlap did concede to public taste and reworked his best play into a self-proclaimed "holiday drama" for "holiday fools." Some scholars suggest that he rewrote *André* into the musical spectacle *The Glory of Columbia* because his theater was failing and he desperately needed income. Dunlap wrote a number of other patriotic plays, the best-known being the musical spectacle *Yankee Chronology* (1812).

Although it was not a popular success, *André* has had a lasting impact on American drama and literature.

COLONEL ARNOLD.

Who Commanded the Provincial Troops sent against QUEBEC, through the Wilderness of Canada, and was Wounded in storming that City, under General Montgomery.

Benedict Arnold, a traitor to the American cause during the Revolutionary War, figures prominently in *André: A Tragedy in Five Acts.* COLONEL BENEDICT ARNOLD, PUB. LONDON, 1776 (MEZZOTINT), ENGLISH SCHOOL, (18TH CENTURY)/ BROWN UNIVERSITY LIBRARY, PROVIDENCE, RHODE ISLAND, USA/THE BRIDGEMAN ART LIBRARY.

André is included in most modern anthologies of American drama and is central to any discussion of theatrical depictions of the American Revolutionary War. Gary A. Richardson argues that "*André* provides Dunlap the opportunity to articulate the young nation's republican ideology to contrast its values with antecedent social codes." Allan Gates Halline contends that "the philosophical concept of man's natural evil or weakness which lies behind the Federalistic view finds decided expression in the play." Given that he was born to Loyalist parents, studied art in London, and was a great admirer of English drama, Dunlap may have had a sympathetic perspective on the humanity of America's sworn enemy. Whether or not Dunlap meant to promote the Federalist cause is debated among scholars; however, it is generally accepted that the play is an allegory with Bland representing the fledgling country. Fliegelman regards *André* as the best discussion of how "Americans finally dealt with the guilt induced by André's execution."

BIBLIOGRAPHY

Sources

Coad, Oral Sumner. *William Dunlap: A Study of His Life and Works and of His Place in Contemporary Culture.* New York: The Dunlap Society, 1917. Print.

Dunlap, William. *A History of the American Theatre.* New York: J. & J. Harper, 1832.

Ellis, Joseph J. *After the Revolution: Profiles of Early American Culture.* New York: Norton, 1979.

Fliegelman, Jay. *Prodigals and Pilgrims: The American Revolution against Patriarchal Authority, 1750–1800.* New York: Cambridge UP, 1985.

Halline, Allan Gates. "William Dunlap: 1766–1839." *American Plays.* Ed. Allan Gates Halline. New York: American, 1935.

Henderson, Desiree. "Mourning, Masculinity and the Drama of the American Revolution." *American Drama* 13.1 (2004): 31–45. *Literature Resource Center.* Web. 16 Aug 2012.

Purcell, Sarah J. *Sealed with Blood: War, Sacrifice, and Memory in Revolutionary America.* Philadelphia: U of Pennsylvania P, 2010.

Richardson, Gary A. "Nationalizing the American Stage: The Drama of Royall Tyler and William Dunlap as Post-Colonial Phenomena." *Making America / Making American Literature.* Ed. A. Robert Lee and W. M. Verhoeven. Amsterdam: Rodopi, 1996. 221–48. Print.

Rinehart, Lucy. "'Manly Exercises': Post Revolutionary Performances of Authority in the Theatrical Career of William Dunlap." *Early American Literature* 36.2 (2001): 263–93. *Literature Resource Center.* Web. 15 Aug 2012.

Wilmer, S. E. *Theatre, Society and the Nation: Staging American Identities.* New York: Cambridge UP, 2002.

Further Reading

Gates, Robert Allan. *18th- and 19th- Century American Drama.* New York: Irvington, 1984.

Johnson, Claudia. "William Dunlap." *American Writers of the Early Republic.* Ed. Emory Elliott. *Dictionary of Literary Biography.* Vol. 37. Detroit: Gale Research, 1985. *Literature Resource Center.* Web. 15 Aug 2012.

Lyons, Maura. *William Dunlap and the Construction of an American Art History.* Amherst: U of Massachusetts P, 2005.

Matthews, Brander. Introduction. *André: A Tragedy in Five Acts.* By William Dunlap. New York: The Dunlap Society, 1887. vii–xxiv. Print.

Moody, Richard. "The Glory of Columbia: Her Yeomanry!" *Dramas from the American Theatre, 1762–1909.* Ed. Richard Moody. Cleveland, OH: World, 1966. Print.

Richards, Jeffrey H. *Drama, Theatre, and Identity in the American New Republic.* Cambridge UP, 2005.

Maggie Magno

ANTIGONE

Jean Anouilh

OVERVIEW

Drawing on the work of Greek playwright Sophocles, Jean Anouilh's *Antigone,* first performed at the Théâtre de l'Atelier in Nazi-occupied Paris on February 6, 1944, is an allegory for the struggle between the French Resistance and the Vichy government during World War II. In the play, Antigone defies an edict of her uncle, Créon, the king of Thebes, by burying the body of her brother, Polynices. She stubbornly refuses to submit to Créon's authority, and he ultimately sentences her to death. Because of the play's exploration of the tension between the law and the individual, and between authority and freedom, the Vichy government and the French Resistance, though vehemently opposed, both claimed *Antigone* as work that supported their cause.

Although Anouilh completed *Antigone* in 1942, its production was delayed two years so that Nazi and Vichy censors could give the play their stamp of approval. Many renditions of Sophocles's classic Greek tragedy were performed before and during World War II, but Anouilh's version, directed by André Barsacq, stands out for its contemporary setting, use of modern slang, and timely content. Although it was initially perceived as a Nazi play championing the orderly state, as represented by Créon, many in the French Resistance came to interpret Anouilh's work as a celebration of individualism and liberation, as exemplified by the play's eponymous heroine. Thus, *Antigone,* which ran continuously from February to August 1944, serving as a call to arms for French resistors, is significant for the author's political ambiguity and the demonstration of the arbitrary nature of propaganda.

HISTORICAL AND LITERARY CONTEXT

Antigone explores the tension between authority and freedom that surrounded the Vichy government and the French Resistance—although Anouilh does not directly reference the political context in the play. The Vichy collaboration came to power after the French surrendered to Germany on June 22, 1940, and set up a collaborative government led by World War I hero Philippe Pétain. However, much of the country remained anti-Nazi and refused to acknowledge Vichy government as legitimate. An underground movement known as the French Resistance quickly sprang up to combat French collaboration. One freedom fighter,

Paul Collette, became notable for shooting at a group of collaborationists at Versailles's Légion des Volontaires Français in August 1942, seriously wounding leaders Marcel Déat and Pierre Laval. Colette's act of defiance caught the attention of many, including Anouilh.

Although Anouilh never claimed allegiance to either the collaboration or the resistance, his works were nevertheless subject to censorship by the Vichy government and Nazi occupational forces. Whereas Vichy was more concerned with issues of morality, the Nazis focused on topics of race and nationality. Anouilh admitted that *Antigone* had been inspired by Collette's defiant act but maintained that the play was strictly a theatrical drama rather than a political statement. The play eventually received approval from both German and Vichy censors and was embraced by resistors and collaborators alike. To the Germans and Vichy authoritarians, Créon was a respectable leader focused on order and upholding the law. The Resistance saw in Antigone a heroine who stood up for her beliefs in the face of death, never bending to the will of her oppressor. Thus, Anouilh's *Antigone* served as propaganda for two opposing parties, a rare feat for the World War II era.

During the Nazi occupation of France, several other playwrights reprised the performance of Greek tragedies. Plays such as Louis Barrault's rendition of Aeschylus's *Les Suppliantes* (1941), Jean Racine's *Phedre* (1941), and Anouilh's *Eurydice* (1942) retold the stories of the ancient Greek dramatists in a way that passed Nazi and Vichy censorship standards. However, few of the plays were as modern, timely, or allegorical as *Antigone.*

Anouilh's play was so well received that it continued to be performed after the liberation of France and the dissolution of the Vichy government. Following World War II, Petain, Laval, Francois Darlan, and other collaborators were deemed traitors by the French Resistance, and many were put on trial. One such collaborator was poet and critic Robert Brasillich, one of Anouilh's contemporaries. When Brasillich was sentenced to death, Anouilh circulated a petition to commute the death sentence, a risky move for a writer who had not declared his support for the resistance and whose work had received many positive reviews by pro-German sources, including collaborative writers

Key Facts

Time Period:
Mid-20th Century

Genre:
Play

Events:
World War II; Nazi occupation of France; French resistance to Vichy government

Nationality:
French

JEAN ANOUILH: THE POLITICS OF THEATER

Playwright Jean Anouilh was born in Bordeaux, France, on June 23, 1910, to François, a tailor, and Marie-Magdeleine, a violinist. The young Anouilh began writing in his early teens and then studied law at the Sorbonne. Before he embarked on a career in theater, he worked as a copywriter and screenwriter. In 1931 he married actress Monelle Valentin, who would later play the role of Antigone in the original production of the play.

During the 1930s and 1940s Anouilh became one of Europe's most popular playwrights, but his star soon faded when absurdist drama came into vogue in the late 1950s. He composed more than forty works during his lifetime, all the while maintaining that his plays—especially *Antigone*—had no political resonance. He stated that theater should be an escape from reality for the audience. Nevertheless, theatergoers and critics have readily applied political meanings to his plays, and many consider him a playwright of the Resistance. Perhaps Leonard Cabell Pronko in *The World of Jean Anouilh* (1968) best summarizes Anouilh's legacy, calling the playwright a writer "bound to the cause of man's freedom."

Alain Laubreaux and Charles Mere. However, Brasillich was ultimately executed, and Anouilh returned to his work as a playwright, attempting to avoid further political controversy.

THEMES AND STYLE

The main theme of Anouilh's *Antigone,* like that of Sophocles's original drama, is the struggle between authoritarianism, represented by Créon, and liberation, represented by Antigone. The play poses the question of whether it is more important to follow personal conviction or if maintaining order and preserving the state should be the higher priority. Créon questions Antigone's motives for disobeying him by choosing to bury her brother: "And you still insist upon being put to death—merely because I refuse to let your brother go out with that grotesque passport." Antigone replies, "I am not here to understand. That's all very well for you. I am here to say no to you, and die." Antigone's bravery and lack of fear of death parallels the French Resistance fighters' undying allegiance to their cause.

Anouilh's *Antigone* achieves its rhetorical effect by abandoning some of Sophocles's original characters, such as Tiresias and the chorus, and by restructuring the plot to begin after Antigone has buried her brother. The decisions serve to diminish Sophocles's initial focus on the mystery of who buried the body, instead highlighting the archetypical nature of Antigone and Créon's relationship. In the context of Anouilh's play, the characters seem fated to carry out their actions, as if it is human nature to both effect and

rise against tyranny. In place of the chorus is a speaker who at times functions like a Brechtian stage manager, explaining, "In the three thousand years since the first Antigone—other Antigones have arisen like a clarion call to remind men of this distinction. Their cause is always the same—a passionate belief that moral law exists, and a passionate regard for the sanctity of human dignity."

Anouilh's use of slang, contemporary language, and anachronisms gives the Greek tragedy a universal appeal and invites an interpretation of the play in the modern political context. Although the characters fulfill much the same roles as they did in the original version, the modern setting, including such locations as the bar, the bistro, and the whorehouse, lend Anouilh's version a tone of familiarity and disillusionment. The guards wear modern uniforms, hold guns, and play cards. They are representations of futility as they continue with their card game, indifferent to Antigone's fate. The speaker opines, "And there we are. All those who were meant to die have died: those who believed one thing, those who believed the contrary thing, and even those who believed nothing at all, yet were caught up in the web without knowing why."

CRITICAL DISCUSSION

Initially, many World War II-era critics viewed *Antigone* as a pro-occupation play that championed the preservation of the state and order over the rights of the individual. However, resistance audiences eventually came to see the play as a rallying cry. Kenneth Krauss, in *The Drama of Fallen France* (2004), explains, "The first reaction to Antigone in Paris in 1944 was one of indignation on the part of those sympathetic to Resistance. The word ran round that Antigone was a Nazi play." Many thought that Créon's position was more convincing, and as Krauss writes, "After a comparatively small number of performances Créon became identified in the popular view with the German Occupants." However, resisters reacted to Nazi and Vichy "ownership" of the character of Créon by staking claim to Antigone and announcing that Anouilh's true intent had been to create a play in support of the Resistance.

The disagreement over Anouilh's intended meaning has fueled the continuing significance of *Antigone* as a unique drama of the World War II era. Although subsequent productions attempted to compare Paris with the Greek city of Thebes, they failed to achieve Anouilh's ambiguity and minimalist approach. In *Defeat and Beyond: An Anthology of French Wartime Writing, 1940–1945* (1970), George Bernauer and Germaine Brée describe the similarities between ancient Greece and occupied France: "The analogies between the situations of Thebes and of France needed little stressing. The action of Sophocles' play takes place at the end of a period of plague, followed by a devastating civil war." Thus, more than half a century after its first production, Anouilh's *Antigone* remains an example of the arbitrary nature of propaganda.

Critics and historians alike read Anouilh's *Antigone* as one of the few examples of dual propaganda in modern history. In discerning Anouilh's perspective on the topic, some have referenced Anouilh's later play *L'Alouette* (1952), in which he states, "Propaganda is a soft weapon, hold it in your hands too long, and it will move about like a snake, and strike the other way." In *Jean Anouilh* (1969), Alba della Fazia finds that control over the play's meaning was completely ceded to the audience: "For many, Antigone … was a glorious heroine for having said no to Créon, the symbol of an external order unjustly imposed. Others … saw in Créon, who pleads movingly for a compromise that will allow him to continue steering the ship of state, an eloquent champion of the Vichy government's thesis of expediency."

A scene from a 1975 performance of Jean Anouilh's *Antigone* at the Theatre María Guerrero in Madrid. Ana Belén, left, played the title character. © AISA/EVERETT COLLECTION.

BIBLIOGRAPHY

Sources

Anouilh, Jean. *Antigone.* Trans. Lewis Galantière. New York: Samuel French, 1974. Print.

Bernauer, George, and Germaine Brée. "The Sides Taken." *Defeat and Beyond: An Anthology of French Wartime Writing, 1940–1945.* Ed. George Bernauer and Germaine Brée. New York: Pantheon Books, 1970. 111–12. Print.

Della Fazia, Alba. *Jean Anouilh.* New York: Twayne, 1969. Print.

Krauss, Kenneth. *The Drama of Fallen France.* Albany: State UP of New York, 2004. Print.

Pronko, Leonard Cabell. *The World of Jean Anouilh.* Berkeley: U of California P, 1968. Print.

Witt, Mary Ann Frese. "Fascist Ideology and Theater under the Occupation: The Case of Anouilh." *Journal of European Studies* 89.23 (1993): 49–69. Print.

Further Reading

Harvey, John. *Anouilh: A Study in Theatrics.* London: Yale UP, 1964. Print.

McIntyre, H. G. *The Theatre of Jean Anouilh.* Totowa: Barnes and Noble, 1981. Print.

Parker, Philip M., ed. *Jean Anouilh: Webster's Timeline History 1910–2007.* San Diego: Icon Group, 2010. Print.

Witt, Mary Ann Frese. *The Search for Modern Tragedy: Aesthetic Fascism in Italy and France.* Ithaca: Cornell UP, 2001. Print.

Media Adaptation

Antigone. Dir. Franz Peter Wirth. Perf. Andrea Jonasson, Paul Hoffmann, and Heidelinde Weis. Westdeutscher Rundfunk (WDR), 1965. Film.

Ron Horton

CATHLEEN NI HOULIHAN

W. B. Yeats, Lady Augusta Gregory

❖ *Key Facts*

Time Period:
Early 20th Century

Genre:
Play

Events:
Beginning of the Irish cultural revival; failure of Irish Home Rule movement

Nationality:
Irish

OVERVIEW

Cathleen ni Houlihan, a drama written by William Butler Yeats and Lady Augusta Gregory in 1902, depicts a rural Irish family whose wedding plans are disrupted by the arrival of a mysterious old woman who inspires the young groom to fight for his country. The Hiberno-English dialect and small-town concerns of the Gillane family are in direct contrast with the high poeticism of the Old Woman, the strange visitor whose speeches stir up nationalist feelings. Employing a centuries-old literary trope, the play personifies the nation of Ireland as an Old Woman who wanders the roads of Killala, County Mayo, in 1798, on the eve of a famous rebellion. Staged for an Irish audience in 1902, the play recalls a responsibility to liberate the colonized nation but also questions the value of the mortal sacrifice that such a rebellion entails.

Yeats and Lady Gregory wrote the play as part of the cultural revival they espoused in their *Manifesto for an Irish Literary Theatre* (1897) and in plays such as *The Countess Cathleen.* In terms of audience awareness and public reaction, *Cathleen ni Houlihan* proved to be their most galvanizing work. Stage productions emphasized the revolutionary aspects of the drama, so that the play became a rallying cry for rebellion and glamorized loss of life for independence. Though Yeats and Lady Gregory were committed to creating a dramatic tradition that united Irish people by remaining apolitical, their play resonated with the growing Irish nationalist movement. The drama warns of the high human cost of revolution, but *Cathleen ni Houlihan* is notable for its compelling nationalist message and its rousing call to rebellion.

HISTORICAL AND LITERARY CONTEXT

At the end of the nineteenth century, hopes were high among the Irish public about the prospect of Home Rule. Although the Irish Republican Brotherhood had been put down with force in 1867 and the Irish Land League, which advocated boycotts and the use of force against landlords, had been suppressed, many Irish citizens hoped that parliamentary politics would lead to a measure of autonomy. The fall of political leader Charles Stewart Parnell, however, led many Irish activists to turn from politics to cultural societies to promote a national spirit. Groups such as the Gaelic Athletic Association, the Gaelic League, and the Irish

Literary Theatre attempted to unite the Irish people by reviving the native culture and language, which had gradually disappeared under British rule.

The centenary of the failed Irish rebellion of 1798 was a call to action for Ireland's cultural leaders. Their "self-help" groups relocated the long-simmering independence movement to theater halls. As the reaction to *Cathleen ni Houlihan* suggests, Ireland's cultural heritage retained more than symbolic significance; its mythic figures could mobilize citizens to take political action. In many ways, Yeats and Lady Gregory offered an appealingly apolitical aesthetic goal while producing a work that promoted the cultural autonomy of a post-British Ireland. The intense public response to *Cathleen ni Houlihan* attests to the fact that in 1902, the production of a national Irish literature was an inescapably political pursuit.

At the turn of the century, Irish dramatists were confronted with the paradoxical task of creating a new dramatic tradition. Many authors, including Lady Gregory, Yeats, landowner Edward Martyn, and novelist George Moore, countered earlier caricatures of the "Stage Irishman" by employing Irish myth and language, as well as continental European dramaturgical techniques, to explore questions of Irish identity. In his play *Maeve,* Martyn combines mythology and Ibsenesque naturalism in his depiction of a young woman who rejects her fiancé after a dream visit from the ancient Irish queen Maeve. While *Maeve* is similar in plot to *Cathleen ni Houlihan,* Yeats and Lady Gregory's play engaged more ardent political support through a drama that, according to *The Variorum Edition of the Plays of W. B. Yeats,* contrasts "the perpetual struggle of the cause of Ireland … against private hopes and dreams."

Cathleen ni Houlihan was created long before the Irish rising in 1916, but Yeats felt a justifiable culpability for behaviors inspired by the play: "Did that play of mine send out / Certain men the English shot?" he asks in his late poem "The Man and the Echo." Yeats and Lady Gregory's work led others to create sharp satires and realist dramas. George Bernard Shaw's *John Bull's Other Island,* at first rejected by Yeats's Irish Literary Theatre, is a cutting criticism of both real and stage Irishmen. In *The Playboy of the Western World,* J. M. Synge attempts a more naturalistic portrayal of Irish peasant life and speech. Synge's play provoked riots, and the dramatist was accused of insulting Irish womanhood, which was closely linked with the purity embodied by mythical figures such as Cathleen ni Houlihan. As Ireland became a modern nation, the tropes within *Cathleen ni Houlihan* remained a potent touchstone for writers examining the Irish call to nationalism. The figure of Cathleen has been reinvented in the works of writers and filmmakers that include Sean O'Casey, James Joyce and Neil Jordan.

THEMES AND STYLE

Central to *Cathleen ni Houlihan* is a contrast between insular personal concerns and a transcendent call to national service. While Bridget Gillane reflects on her son's good fortune, the audience's awareness of the play's setting—the eve of an imminent rebellion—undercuts the significance of that personal luck. The material benefit of the dowry her son is receiving is then called into question when the Old Woman arrives and is in need of help but not of money. "If anyone would give me help he must give me himself, he must give me all," she says. When the Old Woman is revealed to represent Ireland herself, the Gillanes' earlier failure to recognize her implies a long-overlooked commitment by the Irish toward their country. Yeats and Lady Gregory portray the Gillane family sympathetically but suggest that its personal material concerns have caused it to forget its greater obligation to an independent nation.

The playwrights call attention to the characters' variations in values by attributing different speech patterns to them. Bridget and her family communicate in the formal and repetitive structures of an Irish country household, whereas the Old Woman delivers a series of transcendent poetic speeches. While the Gillanes attempt to aid the Old Woman first with food and then by splitting the much-prized 100-pound note, the Old Woman is unappeased by such material offerings. She has "her thoughts and her hopes" to console her. She leaves the Gillane household saying that her friends will help her—and when Michael follows, the audience learns through his younger brother Patrick that this desperate Old Woman has turned into a "younger girl" with the "walk of a queen." With such contrasts, *Cathleen ni Houlihan* chips away at the fleeting comforts offered by short-term material prosperity in comparison with the rewards of reclaiming a nation.

Stylistically, the play progresses from a relatable realism to a vision that recalls Catholic allegory and Irish myth. Yeats and Lady Gregory were influenced by dramatic trends as diverse as Scandinavian naturalism and Parisian symbolism. In scenes of domestic stability, the family discusses its financial betterment: "We never thought a son of our own would be wearing a suit of that sort for his wedding, or have so good a place to bring a wife to." The family's colloquial talk and concerns are interrupted, however, by the Old

CATHLEEN NI HOULIHAN: YEATS'S VISION PLAY AND THE AISLING TRADITION

In *Cathleen ni Houlihan,* W. B. Yeats draws from the aisling, or vision-poem, a bardic genre that follows a strict formula in which a poet receives a vision of a supernatural woman who recounts the misfortunes of Ireland and foretells the return of Gaelic values with the restoration of its rightful leader. Daniel Corkery writes in "The Hidden Ireland" that in the seventeenth and eighteenth centuries the aisling visitor was a personification of Ireland, "therefore a beautiful and radiant young woman." Aodhagán Ó Rathaille, the father of the aisling poem, wrote these poems as a form of Jacobite protest.

Yeats and Lady Augusta Gregory's play combines two traditional representations of Ireland: the *Spéirbhean* ("skywoman") from the aisling tradition and the *Sean Bhean Bhocht* ("poor old woman"), the latter drawing upon Celtic incarnations of the goddess of war and popularized in songs from the time of 1798 rebellion, the year of the play's events. When the Old Woman leads Michael Gillane offstage to fight in the Irish rebellion, Cathleen ni Houlihan transforms into a beautiful young queen, suggesting that the commitment of the youth to the rebellion has made Ireland young and beautiful again. The aisling remains a significant form in Irish stories, both as a means of personal reflection and political protest. Contemporary poets, including Seamus Heaney, Ciaran Carson, and Brendan Kennelly, have written about or in this tradition.

Woman's otherworldly speeches, a manifestation of Yeats's desire for a theater of estrangement combined with social vision. This contrast of language is a deliberate strategy to, as Michael McAteer puts it in *Yeats and European Drama,* "relat[e] spiritual anxiety … to the alienating effects of modern industrial capitalism." The play is a departure from the realism Yeats himself attempted earlier in *The Land of Heart's Desire,* and it is a more graceful and effective counterpoint to his *The Countess Cathleen,* in which the sinister, mystical figures are less persuasive visitors than the mysteriously compelling Old Woman.

CRITICAL DISCUSSION

At the time of the Easter Rising and subsequent civil war, Yeats was glorified for his political leadership and unparalleled poetic style, yet vilified for his elite cultural background and extremist views. In *Cathleen ni Houlihan,* Yeats created a play that cemented his connection to the nationalist movement while giving an early suggestion of his fascistic leanings. Left-wing critics such as George Orwell despised the evolution of Yeats's political values and sought to link his reactionary views with his aesthetic tastes and occult interests through his "profound hostility … to the Christian ethical code." Even as readers struggle to address the

PUCK.

GLADSTONE LAYS THE CORNER-STONE OF THE EDIFICE OF IRISH INDEPENDENCE.
It *May* be Good for Ireland—but for America—Scarcely.

problem of reconciling Yeats's politics with the power of his writing, his literary oeuvre continues to be seen as an invaluable contribution to Irish nationhood and to a world-class literary movement.

A cornerstone of the Irish Literary Revival, *Cathleen ni Houlihan* is viewed as not only a bolster to the Irish Nationalist movement but also a prescient warning of the sacrifices required by such a commitment. The poet Louis MacNeice captures the complex appeal of the play when he discusses Yeats's Irishness. Yeats, he says, possessed "the combination of an anarchist individualism with puritanical taboos and inhibitions; the half-envious contempt for England; a sentimental attitude to Irish history." The dualities MacNeice identifies in Yeats continue to be relevant to Anglo-Irish relations today. Yeats and Lady Gregory's play remains emblematic of a knotty problem in the nation's self-representation.

Cathleen ni Houlihan is a seminal work in Yeats's development as a dramatist, though critics such as Frank Hugh O'Donnell reject the values within the play. In *Yeats and European Drama,* O'Donnell says that "the form of spirituality [the play] offered [is] bogus." Even so, scholars have called *Cathleen* an artistic move forward for Yeats, who in earlier poems had also written about the Cathleen figure. This early drama heralded Yeats's later work as a mature dramatist. In *Cathleen ni Houlihan* there is, as Yeats himself says in *Certain Noble Plays of Japan,* the "distance from life which can make credible strange events." Though Yeats initially obscured Lady Gregory's role in the play's composition, much literary and biographical criticism delineates the interplay of the two authors' contributions. The themes and resolution of the play have been interpreted as a justification of the roles of the two self-appointed Anglo-Irish Protestant leaders of the Irish Literary Revival.

BIBLIOGRAPHY

Sources

Auden, W. H. "Yeats as an Example." *The Kenyon Review* 10.2 (1948): 187+. *LitFinder for Schools.* Web. 2 Aug. 2012.

Certain Noble Plays of Japan. Introduction by W. B. Yeats. Churchtown: Cuala, 1916. Print.

Clark, Rosalind. *The Great Queens: Irish Goddesses from the Morrigan to Cathleen Ni Houlihan.* Gerrards Cross: Colin Smyth, 1991. Print.

Corkery, Daniel. "The Hidden Ireland: A Study of Gaelic Munster in the Eighteenth Century (1924)." Excerpted in *Irish Writing in the Twentieth Century: A Reader.* Ed. David Pierce. Cork: Cork UP, 2000. Print.

Cusack, George. *The Politics of Identity in Irish Drama: W. B. Yeats, Augusta Gregory and J. M. Synge.* New York: Routledge, 2009. Print.

Doggett, Rob. *Deep-rooted Things: Empire and Nation in the Poetry and Drama of William Butler Yeats.* Notre Dame: U of Notre Dame P, 2006. Print.

McAteer, Michael. *Yeats and European Drama.* Cambridge: Cambridge UP, 2010. Print.

Merritt, Henry. "'Dead Many Times': *Cathleen ni Houlihan,* Yeats, Two Old Women, and a Vampire." *The Modern Language Review* 96.3 (2001): 644. *Literature Resource Center.* Web. 27 July 2012.

Orwell, George. *Collected Essays, Journalism and Letters.* New York: Harcourt, 1968. Print.

Smith, Stan. *W. B. Yeats: A Critical Introduction.* London: Macmillan, 1990. Print.

Suess, Barbara Ann. *Progress and Identity in the Plays of W. B. Yeats, 1892–1907.* New York: Routledge, 2003. Print.

The Variorum Edition of the Plays of W. B. Yeats. Ed. Russell K. Alspach, Catharine C. Alspach. London: Macmillan, 1966. Print.

Yeats, W. B. *Plays in Prose and Verse: Written for an Irish Theatre, and Generally with the Help of a Friend.* Rev. ed. London: Macmillan, 1928. Print.

———. *The Poems.* 2nd ed. Ed. Richard J. Finneran. New York: Scribner, 1997.

Further Reading

Bobotis, Andrea. "Rival Materinities: Maud Gonne, Queen Victoria, and the Reign of the Political Mother." *Victorian Studies* 49.1 (2006): 63+. *Literature Resource Center.* Web. 27 July 2012.

FitzGerald, Mary. "'Out of a Medium's Mouth': The Writing of *The Words upon the Window-pane.*" *Colby Library Quarterly* 17.2 (June 1981): 61–73. Rpt. in *Drama Criticism.* Ed. Thomas J. Schoenberg. Vol. 33. Detroit: Gale, 2009. *Literature Resource Center.* Web. 27 July 2012.

Foster, R. F. *W. B. Yeats: A Life.* Vol. 1. Oxford: Oxford UP, 1997. Print.

Lockett, Christopher. "Terror and Rebirth: *Cathleen ni Houlihan,* from Yeats to *The Crying Game.*" *Literature-Film Quarterly* 33.4 (2005): 290+. *Literature Resource Center.* Web. 27 July 2012.

Marcus, Phillip L. *Yeats and the Beginning of the Irish Renaissance.* Ithaca: Cornell UP, 1970. Print.

Pierce, David, ed. *Irish Writing in the Twentieth Century.* Cork: Cork UP, 2000. Print.

Richman, David. *Passionate Action: Yeats's Mastery of Drama.* Newark : U of Delaware P, 2000. Print.

Karen Bender

"THE CHARGE OF THE LIGHT BRIGADE"

Alfred Lord Tennyson

✥ *Key Facts*

Time Period:
Mid-19th Century

Genre:
Poetry

Events:
Crimean War;
Battle of Balaclava

Nationality:
English

OVERVIEW

"The Charge of the Light Brigade" by Alfred, Lord Tennyson, first published December 9, 1854, glorifies for posterity the doomed British cavalry charge at the October 25, 1854, Battle of Balaclava. Likely the best-known English literary work of the Crimean War, the poem is famous for its dramatization of the courageous sacrifice of those who participated in the charge, the "noble six hundred," of whom more than half were killed, wounded, or captured in the battle and its immediate aftermath. The charge itself had resulted from a miscommunication among British commanding officers, possibly aggravated by a personal enmity between military leaders Lords Cardigan and Lucan. Tennyson recast the maneuver, which was widely criticized as a "hideous blunder" on the part of the generals, as propaganda promoting the superlative valor of the common British soldier.

Tennyson drew the material for his poem from newspaper accounts of the battle; he and many others found an emblematic emotional appeal in the ill-fated charge. His work was widely appreciated for its eloquence and vividness, but its injunction to "honour the charge they made" had little lasting effect on British treatment of veterans, many of whom were left destitute and disabled at the war's end. Furthermore, the sentiment of the poem was gainsaid by many eyewitness accounts, including those of war correspondent William Russell and Allied officers present at Balaclava. Nevertheless, "The Charge of the Light Brigade" has come to be regarded as a classic of English verse, its literary quality garnering more attention as the facts of the Crimean War receded into history. Contemporary critics often regard the poem as part of a larger romantic tendency to glorify warfare by comparing it to a bygone chivalric tradition.

HISTORICAL AND LITERARY CONTEXT

The Crimean War, which Tennyson's poem would come to epitomize, began in October 1853 when the Ottoman Empire declared war on the Russian Empire over perceived encroachments on Ottoman independence. British and French forces (the Allies) joined the conflict on the Ottoman side in March 1854, hoping to use the war as a means of curbing the increasing Russian threat to the Mediterranean. The Battle of the Alma, the first major engagement of the conflict, took place on September 20, 1854, and proved a decisive victory for the Allies. British writers were concomitantly celebratory and confident; Tennyson penned several lines of a patriotic ballad commemorating the battle.

On October 25, 1854, Russian forces attempted to capture an Allied supply station at Balaclava. The resulting battle was indecisive in outcome, but the charge of the Light Brigade, an ill-fated sortie of some six hundred troops through a cannon-lined valley, captured the imagination of journalists and poets. Tennyson read about the infamous charge in the *Times,* which gave a report of the battle on November 13, 1854. As the poet laureate of the United Kingdom, Tennyson was expected to respond to such events in verse, and he found in the *Times* account the kernel of his poem: "The British soldier … is not paralyzed by feeling that he is the victim of some hideous blunder."

Tennyson's ennobling perspective on the Crimean War was far from the only—or the dominant—voice in the British press. The satirical magazine *Punch* provided a panoply of cartoons and mocking verse, ridiculing the perceived despotism and duplicity of the Russian Empire rather than making claims for the virtues of the British. *Punch* frequently fixated on the infighting among British politicians in the months leading up to the war and called attempts at peacemaking the work of traitorous "Muscovites."

When Tennyson's poem appeared in the *Examiner* on December 9, 1854, his was among a cacophony of conflicting opinions of the charge and its moral and political meaning. Where Tennyson devoted the majority of his poem to the soldiers making the charge, noting the "blunder" only in passing, *Punch* balladeers and newspaper editorials often reversed the equation, berating the generals for their mishandling of the battle. In *The British Expedition to the Crimea* (1858), Russell concurs with Tennyson that the soldiers had behaved valiantly but adds that it was a "desperate valor" that "knew no bounds, and far indeed was it removed from its so-called better part: discretion." Eventually, as the Crimean War passed from newspapers to history books, "The Charge of the Light Brigade" assumed the status of a national classic. Writing in *Victorian Poetry* in 2003, Cornelia D. J. Pearsall noted that by the 1920s, Tennyson's poem had "long [been] a memorization exercise for schoolchildren in Britain and its colonies," its "tenacity" established by continued reference in works such as Virginia Woolf's *To The Lighthouse* (1927). Emily Dickinson's poem

"To fight aloud is very brave" has been viewed by critics as a response to the jingoism of Tennyson's poem.

THEMES AND STYLE

Many writers in late 1854 found the conduct of the officers at Balaclava suspect at best and shameful at worst; Tennyson chose to tell a different story, foregrounding the gallantry of the doomed soldiers who composed the brigade itself. There is only one ominous mention ("some one had blundered") of the order that led the brigade to attempt the charge. Instead, Tennyson draws attention to the overwhelming danger faced by the cavalry, who were "storm'd at with shot and shell" from three directions. Because they braved such hazards, argues the poet, their valor is incontestable: "When can their glory fade?" The reader's sole duty is to acknowledge the heroism of the soldiers, to "Honor the charge they made, / Honor the Light Brigade."

Tennyson's narrator takes the point of view of an admiring onlooker who surveys the actions of the brigade as they charge into "the mouth of Hell." The brigade is consistently spoken of as a unified mass of six hundred—and, later in the poem, as its diminished remnant. Tennyson further infuses the conflict with a moral dimension by repeatedly invoking the biblical "Valley of Death" in place of a terrestrial battlefield, so that the charge becomes in effect a combat between valor (personified in the brigade) and evil (reified in the Russian guns). Finally, the poet focuses not on the hundreds of individual deaths but offers in their stead the summary description "horse and hero fell." By adopting this impersonal perspective, Tennyson transmutes what critics saw as the victims of a senseless mistake into willing, self-sacrificial agents fighting for a righteous cause. He also—more ambivalently, in the view of later critics—keeps the reader well clear of the gory, chaotic rout that the charge actually entailed.

Perhaps the most famous formal trait of Tennyson's poem is its galloping cadence, which emphasizes the poem's high-spirited action and provides a metrical analog for a cavalry charge. This sense of onward motion is established by a pattern known as dactylic dimeter and is immediately apparent at the poem's opening: "Half a league, half a league, / Half a league onward." In addition, as these lines illustrate, Tennyson uses repetition amply and in a variety of guises (including rhyme, anaphora, and refrain) to give the poem a sense of inertia and inevitability. In availing himself of these devices, Tennyson lays the groundwork for the poem's enduring popular appeal through a connection to the long folk tradition of the ballad. Richard A. Sylvia notes in a 1990 analysis that "The Charge of the Light Brigade" not only is a "superb ballad statement" in general but also draws specifically on a style of ballad then much in circulation in the form of broadsides.

CRITICAL DISCUSSION

Tennyson was a popular figure, and "The Charge of the Light Brigade" was widely read and appreciated.

THE LAST OF THE LIGHT BRIGADE

In writing "The Charge of the Light Brigade," Tennyson aimed to imbue the actions of Crimean War soldiers with a measure of dignity, even nobility. The war, however, was largely regarded as an embarrassment by the British, who suffered the effects of numerous tactical blunders at the Battle of Balaclava and afterward. One effect of this collective discomfiture was a lack of provision for veterans, many of whom faced old age hampered by poverty and disability.

Rudyard Kipling attempted to publicize this situation in "The Last of the Light Brigade" (1890), a poem in which a tattered band of Light Brigade veterans calls on Tennyson (by then an old man) to take their cause before the English people. The poem attracted little attention, and it is unclear whether Kipling's declaration that "the fatted souls of the English" yielded up "a cheque for enough to live on to the Last of the Light Brigade" was ever more than a fanciful wish. Widely considered to lack the impact or ingenuity of Tennyson's poem, Kipling's poem nonetheless speaks to the prestige accorded to "The Charge of the Light Brigade" decades after its composition, even as it undercuts the romanticism of the earlier work.

It appears, however, mainly to have reaffirmed contemporary opinions of the Crimean War. Nearly all accounts of the Battle of Balaclava were in agreement that the officers "had blundered" (though perhaps forgivably) and that the soldiers had demonstrated great (though perhaps blind) courage. Tennyson's work differs most clearly from other accounts in its focus on the common cavalrymen in the charge. Despite the valorization the poem gives to their actions, it ultimately failed to effect political change on their behalf. In the second half of the nineteenth century, "The Charge of the Light Brigade" would be upheld as an ironic emblem of public indifference to veterans: soldiers were commemorated in verse if they were killed in action but were left to fend for themselves if they survived. Near the end of the Victorian era, Rudyard Kipling published a "sequel" to Tennyson's poem designed to instill sympathy for the plight of disabled veterans.

In the twentieth century, critics turned their attention to Tennyson's process of composition for "The Charge of the Light Brigade," especially the ways in which he adapted contemporary prose accounts of the battle. In a 1983 piece for *PMLA,* Herbert Tucker Jr. considers that the November 13, 1854, *Times* article had provided Tennyson with not only "an emotionally congenial subject" but also "a tonic refrain to which he might build his battering stanzas." Edgar Shannon and Christopher Ricks, writing in 1985, provide a more sustained examination of the poem's genesis, concluding that the role of the *Times* had been overstated and that "no critique can adequately account for the poetic genius" of Tennyson's famous work.

More recently, "The Charge of the Light Brigade" has figured in studies that compare Tennyson's work to

The Charge of the
Light Brigade, an 1895
photogravure by Richard
Caton Woodville, depicting
the 17th Light Dragoons
(Lancers). Private Wiliam
Wightman, center, was
severely wounded and
taken prisoner. NATIONAL
ARMY MUSEUM/THE
ART ARCHIVE AT ART
RESOURCE, NY.

the wider genre of war literature. Ingrid Hanson's 2010 essay on "The Transformative Touch of Violence" notes that Tennyson's poem, often regarded as patriotic, seems much more ambiguous when read alongside other Crimean War works, such as the chivalric romances of William Morris; in his 2007 piece "Fighting Talk: Victorian Poetry," Matthew Bevis discusses this ambiguity with reference to Victorian war poems in general. Tennyson has even, for some critics, stood as the elegiac forerunner of postmodern reactions to war. In "The Two Voices" (2003), John M. Picker writes of the numerous "Tennysonian echoes" in the cultural aftermath of the September 11, 2001, terrorist attacks; especially resonant is "The Charge of the Light Brigade," which "seems a not-too-distant poetic antecedent to the kind of memorable lyric that could, but likely will not, be written" for the Afghan War of the twenty-first century.

BIBLIOGRAPHY

Sources

Bevis, Matthew. "Fighting Talk: Victorian Poetry." *The Oxford Handbook of British and Irish War Poetry*. Ed. Tim Kendall. London: Oxford UP, 2007. 7–33. Print.

Cross, Anthony. "The Crimean War and the Caricature War." *Slavonic and East European Review* 84.3 (2006): 460–80. Print.

Hanson, Ingrid. "'The Measured Music of Our Meeting Swords': William Morris's Early Romances and the Transformative Touch of Violence." *Review of English Studies* 61 (2010): 435–54. Web. 7 July 2012.

Pearsall, Cornelia D. J. "Whither, Whether, Woolf: Victorian Poetry and 'A Room of One's Own.'" *Victorian Poetry* 41.4 (2003): 596–603. Print.

Picker, John M. "The Two Voices." *Victorian Poetry* 41.4 (2003): 642–45. Print.

Russell, W. H. *The British Expedition to the Crimea.* London: Routledge, 1858. Print.

Shannon, Edgar, and Christopher Ricks. "'The Charge of the Light Brigade': The Creation of a Poem." *Studies in Bibliography* 38 (1985): 1–44. Print.

Sylvia, Richard A. "Reading Tennyson's *Ballads and Other Poems* in Context." *Journal of the Midwest Modern Language Association* 23.1 (1990): 27–44. Print.

Tucker, Herbert F., Jr. "Tennyson and the Measure of Doom." *PMLA* 98.1 (1983): 8–20. Print.

Further Reading

Boehmer, Elleke. "The Worlding of the Jingo Poem." *Yearbook of English Studies* 41.2 (2011): 41–57. Print.

Brighton, Terry. *Hell Riders: The True Story of the Charge of the Light Brigade.* New York: Macmillan, 2004. Print.

Ledbetter, Kathryn. *Tennyson and Victorian Periodicals: Commodities in Context.* Aldershot: Ashgate, 2007. Print.

Perloff, Marjorie. "Ca(n)non to the Right of Us, Can(n) on to the Left of Us: A Plea for Difference." *New Literary History* 18.3 (1987): 633–56. Print.

Tennyson, Hallam. *Alfred Lord Tennyson: A Memoir by His Son.* 2 vols. London: Macmillan, 1897. Print.

Waddington, Patrick. *"Theirs but to Do and Die": The Poetry of the Charge of the Light Brigade at Balaklava, 25 October 1854.* Nottingham: Astra, 1995. Print.

Media Adaptations

The Charge of the Light Brigade. Dir. J. Seatle Dawley. Perf. Ben F. Wilson, Richard Neill, James Gordon, and Charles Sutton. General Film Company, 1912. Film.

The Charge of the Light Brigade. Dir. Michael Curtiz. Perf. Errol Flynn, Olivia de Havilland, and Patric Knowles. Warner Bros. Pictures, 1936. Film.

The Charge of the Light Brigade. Dir. Tony Richardson. Perf. Trevor Howard, Vanessa Redgrave, and John Gielgud. United Artists, 1968. Film.

Michael Hartwell

DUSKLANDS

J. M. Coetzee

OVERVIEW

Dusklands, a novel written by South African author J. M. Coetzee in 1974, consists of two novellas that are similar in structure and theme and work together to illuminate the nature of violence and domination in imperialist advances. The first story, "The Vietnam Project," takes place in the United States during the Vietnam War and focuses on the endeavors of Eugene Dawn, a mythologist and an expert in psychological warfare at the U.S. State Department who designs a propaganda policy aimed at undermining Vietnamese culture to allow for the dominance of the U.S. military. The other story, "The Narrative of Jacobus Coetzee," is partly set in the eighteenth century and follows an armed expedition into the African interior, where it massacres an indigenous tribe. Although the two accounts are set nearly two hundred years apart, their juxtaposition links South Africa and the United States through a shared history of exerting foreign influence by dominating local cultures through psychological and physical violence.

Dusklands, published locally by a small press in South Africa, elicited immediate and mostly favorable attention. In 1977 the London publisher Secker and Warburg picked up Coetzee's second novel, *In the Heart of the Country,* which further bolstered his credentials. Since that time, Coetzee has garnered much critical acclaim and has won numerous literary prizes, including the Booker Prize in 1983 and 1999 and the Nobel Prize in Literature in 2003.

HISTORICAL AND LITERARY CONTEXT

The military involvement of the United States in Vietnam began in the 1950s and extended well into the 1970s. Despite the U.S. government's early attempts to downplay its military presence in Vietnam and then its promises of a quick victory, the reality was one of a sometimes ambiguous conflict that claimed many lives. The communistic North Vietnamese were engaged against French forces that had ruled Vietnam as a colony since 1884. The United States initially backed France and later South Vietnam under the auspices of attempting to contain the spread of communism. American involvement escalated heavily in the 1960s and reached its peak in 1968.

Meanwhile, opposition to the American presence in Vietnam continued to build. In 1970 Coetzee, then a professor at the State University of New York at Buffalo, was arrested together with forty-four other faculty members for illegally protesting U.S. involvement in Vietnam. His participation in these protests prevented him from obtaining U.S. citizenship, and he went back to South Africa, where apartheid, a form of racial segregation enforced by the government, had existed since 1948. In general, racial segregation in South Africa dated back to the colonial rule of the British and Dutch, beginning in the early 1800s. Upon returning to South Africa, Coetzee finished writing *Dusklands,* which enabled him to confront his own place in colonial history.

Dusklands is sometimes considered within a wider group of literature that analyzes the effects of colonial relationships, especially on the process of identity formation. It harks back to Daniel Defoe's *Robinson Crusoe* (1719), which is a literary reflection of the imperialist thrust of seventeenth-century Europe and has gained status as a foundational text exploring white empire building. Coetzee's book also includes references to Joseph Conrad's *Heart of Darkness* (1902) by exposing the ferocity underneath the thin veil of "civilization." There are striking similarities between Conrad's Kurtz, who wants to "exterminate the brutes," and the callous, detached language of the protagonist of "The Vietnam Project," Dawn, who "look[s] forward to Phase V and the return of total air-war." This desire is later carried out through Jacobus Coetzee's brutal massacre in "The Narrative of Jacobus Coetzee."

Coetzee's work has made a lasting impact because of the way it delves into the psychology of modernity and explores the relationships between the oppressor and the oppressed, questioning how language can be manipulated to serve the interests of those in power. He ranks among other elite South African writers who have shared his concerns, such as André Brink and Nadine Gordimer. Globally, Coetzee's work is similar in theme and style to that of Salman Rushdie, particularly the British Indian writer's 1980 book *Midnight's Children,* which exposes traditional structures of nation and history as artificial constructs and seeks to replace them with new formations suitable to the diaspora.

✥ *Key Facts*

Time Period:
Late 20th Century

Genre:
Novel

Events:
Vietnam War; apartheid; colonialism

Nationality:
South African

SAMUEL BECKETT AND MODERNISM'S INFLUENCE ON J. M. COETZEE

The term "modernism" refers to experimental literature that emerged around the turn of the twentieth century up through World War I that diverged from traditional verse forms and narrative techniques in order to find new methods of representation appropriate for modernity. Modernism encompasses a wide variety of movements in modern art and literature that are brought together by their shared concern for and anxiety over the ability for art to adequately represent the reality of the urban, industrial life in the twentieth century. Notable modernist writers include James Joyce, Virginia Woolf, T. S. Eliot, Ezra Pound, and Samuel Beckett, the last of whom had particular influence on the work of J. M. Coetzee.

Beckett's novels often focus on isolated and narcissistic heroes who are unwilling or unable to free themselves from situations in which they feel trapped and, instead of decisively acting, expend great effort contemplating their hopeless situation. In this way, they express self-reflexivity and isolation of the individual in a way that is similar to the character of Eugene Dawn in Coetzee's "The Vietnam Project." Beckett incorporates into his work meditations on the state of fiction in what literary critics call "metafiction." Coetzee studied Beckett as a PhD student at the University of Texas, and this exploration of metafiction comes across in the South African writer's work in which the reader is asked to question the process of writing and how it can be manipulated for evil ends.

THEMES AND STYLE

Dusklands examines myths and the ways in which cultures use them in the service of domination. To illuminate the psychology of the myth-making process, Coetzee sets forth situations and conflicts that arise from the intersection of self and "other," or that which is different. He aims to make connections between the dehumanizing effects of war and the psychological impact of defining racial and cultural differences as part of military tactics. In "The Vietnam Project," Dawn turns the Vietnamese into the "other" by dissecting their cultural mythology. In his mind, fundamental to the Vietnamese sense of self is "the father voice," which must be relentlessly manipulated through propaganda and further twisted through physical violence to secure successful cultural domination. Similarly, Jacobus Coetzee concerns himself with recording the differences he observes between the African natives and the Dutch settlers; he sees himself occupying the role of a father figure. However, he ultimately succumbs to fear and paranoia, believing that the "other" groups are conspiring against him. By juxtaposing the accounts of Jacobus Coetzee and Dawn, Coetzee draws attention to the ways that the U.S. foreign policy of the 1960s mirrors the brutal golden age of colonial empires.

The actions of both the United States and Coetzee's protagonists in *Dusklands* are predicated on the desire to annihilate those regarded as culturally or racially different.

Coetzee subverts the authority of historical documents and accounts, parodying them in order to further illustrate the pitfalls of imperialist attitudes. The epigraph of "The Vietnam Project" ties Dawn's report on the propaganda used in Vietnam with actual papers on the war, collected in the 1968 book *Can We Win in Vietnam? The American Dilemma*. Similarly, "The Narrative of Jacobus Coetzee" is introduced by a translator's preface, and the afterword is accompanied with purportedly scientific notes, drawing further attention to the claim that the tale is historically accurate. However, throughout the two works, the author destabilizes this authority with intertextual allusions, such as the presence of characters named Coetzee in both stories.

Stylistically, Coetzee employs sparse and economical language that reflects the detachment of the main characters. Both stories are presented as monologues, which reinforces the idea that Dawn and Jacobus Coetzee are cut off from the worlds around them and fall victim to solipsism and narcissism. The inward quality created by the monologues is especially palpable in "The Vietnam Project," in which there is no interlocutor and no outside perspective on the action. As Dawn, an expert in propaganda and mythology, becomes obsessed with the power of myth making, he slowly loses his grasp on reality. His friendly tone invites the reader to participate in his manipulation of reality. Phrases such as "by the way," "it is not in my nature," and "as you can see" give the reader access to Dawn's private thoughts and feelings as he weaves his "protective fabrications." However, his tone in his official report, as he justifies horrific violence, is cold and technical. The contrast of these two voices exposes Dawn's inner fragmentation and descent into madness; his "protective fabrications" are unable to shield him from the violent nature of his work. As Dawn's mental state disintegrates into aggressive mania, Coetzee foregrounds the damaging effect violent cultural myths can have even on the oppressors. "The Narrative of Jacobus Coetzee" uses similar language to subvert colonial texts justifying expansion.

CRITICAL DISCUSSION

Coetzee's decision to delve into the psychology of the colonizer was lauded by some commentators but criticized by others who were more politically motivated. *Dusklands* breaks from the dominant school of social realism in South Africa, instead taking a modernist, experimental approach that is rich with narrative complexity. In a review of *Dusklands,* Jonathan Crewe hails the book for bringing "the modern novel in English" to South Africa. In Stephen Watson's essay

The Landing of Jan Riebeeck, by Charles Bell, depicts the Dutch colonial administrator's 1652 arrival in South Africa. J. M. Coetzee's novel *Dusklands* critiques the Dutch colonization of South Africa. THE LANDING OF JAN RIEBEECK (1619–77) 6TH APRIL 1652, 1850 (OIL ON CANVAS), BELL, CHARLES (FL.1850)/SOUTH AFRICAN LIBRARY, CAPE TOWN, SOUTH AFRICA/THE BRIDGEMAN ART LIBRARY.

"Colonialism and the Novels of J. M. Coetzee," he welcomes Coetzee's psychological study, seeing it as a departure from the confines of "South African liberal realism" that had dominated the literary scene. However, some critics within South Africa demanded a greater degree of political engagement and found fault in Coetzee's decision to portray a general crisis of consciousness rather than the particular historical realities of apartheid in the nation. While some academics still criticize the book on this count, many more have recognized its sophistication and artistry.

As part of Coetzee's larger body of work, *Dusklands* has been influential in expressing the psychological effects of colonialism and has been widely discussed in postcolonial literary criticism. The postcolonial questions posed by Coetzee have elicited a wide range of reactions by critics. In *J. M. Coetzee and the Paradox of Postcolonial Authorship* (2009), Jane Poyner notes that through the portrayal of a series of writer protagonists, Coetzee and other "writers of conscience" risk "re-imposing the very authority they to seek to challenge." Coetzee is particularly noteworthy for examining the power of colonial language and the way this language is manipulated to silence "other" groups of people. He continues to influence South African and postcolonial critics and writers who seek to investigate the intersections of authorial authority and the politics of postcoloniality.

Coetzee's tendency to favor psychological representation over political engagement continues to be a source of debate among scholars. In his 1996 essay "*Dusklands*: A Metaphysics of Violence," Marxist critic Peter Knox-Shaw comments that in choosing to "play down the political and economic aspects of history in favour of a psychopathology of Western life … Coetzee seriously depreciates the force of context." Gordimer, writing in the *New York Times Review of Books,* expresses dismay at what she feels to be Coetzee's continued attempt to portray "an idea of survival … outside a political doctrine." Contrasting this assessment of Coetzee's fiction as apolitical, Teresa Dovey writes in *The Novels of J. M. Coetzee: Lacanian Allegories* (1988) that his work can be read as allegories of psychoanalytic processes of identity formation that take into account the materiality of language. Dovey's interpretative approach shifts Coetzee's narratives away from mimetic reflections of reality and emphasizes the textual construction of reality. Utilizing Lacanian psychoanalytic language that theorizes the construction of identity, Dovey envisions Coetzee's work as an expression of the development of the South African identity, which is inextricably linked to and determined by colonial discourse.

BIBLIOGRAPHY

Sources

Coetzee, J. M. *Dusklands.* London: Vintage, 1974. Print.

Crewe, Jonathan. Rev. of *Dusklands,* by J. M. Coetzee. *Contrast* (1974): 90–95. Web. 7 July 2012.

Dovey, Teresa. *The Novels of J. M. Coetzee: Lacanian Allegories.* Johannesburg: Ad Donker, 1988. Print.

Gordimer, Nadine. "The Idea of Gardening." Rev. of *Life & Times of Michael K,* by J. M. Coetzee. *New York Review of Books.* NYREV, 2 Feb. 1984. Web. 9 July 2012.

Head, Dominic. *J. M. Coetzee.* Cambridge: Cambridge UP, 1998. Print.

Knox-Shaw, Peter. "*Dusklands*: A Metaphysics of Violence." *Critical Perspectives on J. M. Coetzee.* Ed. Graham Huggan and Stephen Watson. London: Macmillan, 1996. Print.

Kossew, Sue. *Pen and Power: A Post-Colonial Reading of J. M. Coetzee and André Brink.* Atlanta: Rodopi, 1996. Print.

Poyner, Jane. *J. M. Coetzee and the Paradox of Postcolonial Authorship.* London: Ashgate, 2009. Print.

Watson, Stephen. "Colonialism and the Novels of J. M. Coetzee." *Research in African Literatures* 17.3 (1986): 370–92. Web. 7 July 2012.

Further Reading

Attridge, Derek. "Ethical Modernism: Servants as Others in J. M. Coetzee's Early Fiction." *Poetics Today* 25.4 (2004): 653–71. Print.

Atwell, David. *J. M. Coetzee: South Africa and the Politics of Writing.* California: U of California P, 1993. Print.

Gardiner, Allan. "J. M. Coetzee's *Dusklands*: Colonial Encounters of the Robinsonian Kind." *World Literature Written in English* 27.2 (1987): 174–84. Print.

Leist, Anton, and Peter Singer, eds. *J. M. Coetzee and Ethics: Philosophical Perspectives on Literature.* New York: Columbia UP, 2010. Print.

Lusin, Caroline. "Encountering Darkness: Intertextuality and Polyphony in J. M. Coetzee's *Dusklands* and Matthew Kneale's *English Passengers.*" *Semiotic Encounters: Text, Image and Trans-Nation.* Ed. Sarah Sackel, Walter Gobel, and Noha Hamdy. New York: Rodopi, 2009. Print.

Zamora, Lois Parkinson. "Allegories of Power in the Fiction of J. M. Coetzee." *Journal of Literary Studies* 2.1 (1986): 1–14. Print.

Elizabeth Orvis

ENDYMION, THE MAN IN THE MOON
John Lyly

OVERVIEW

Endymion, The Man in the Moon, a late sixteenth-century play by the Elizabethan playwright John Lyly, tells the story of a group of characters involved in romantic entanglements. Written as a comedy, the plot revolves around Endymion, who is in love with the moon goddess, Cynthia. Endymion's former love, Tellus, the earth goddess, casts a spell upon him that puts him into a deep a sleep, and she sends Cynthia on a search for an antidote. The plot itself is sparse; the play's effectiveness lies in its allegorical nature. With Cynthia representing Queen Elizabeth I and Tellus representing Mary, Queen of Scots, *Endymion* served as propaganda flattering Elizabeth and exposing the folly at work in the royal court, particularly as Elizabeth aged without having produced an heir to the throne.

In Elizabethan theater, Lyly was considered a top playwright; *Endymion* was commissioned by Queen Elizabeth for performance in her court. Debuting for the queen on Candlemas, Lyly's play pleased Elizabeth and secured the author a place at court. Though written to entertain, the play addresses the serious concerns about the queen's being unmarried and the future significance of the absence of a royal heir. Written in the lofty language of court, *Endymion* serves as an example of theater used as propaganda, alluding to the factionalism at court and highlighting Elizabeth's role as the "virgin queen" and as a divinely appointed ruler.

HISTORICAL AND LITERARY CONTEXT

When the play was first performed in 1587, Queen Elizabeth I had ruled Britain for nearly thirty years. The daughter of King Henry VIII and Anne Boleyn, Elizabeth took the throne in 1558, succeeding her half-sister, Mary Tudor. In 1568 Elizabeth imprisoned her Catholic cousin Mary Stuart, Queen of Scots, who was considered a threat to Elizabeth's power. The imprisonment of Mary incited a rebellion against Elizabeth, splitting the country along political and religious lines. Catholics supported Mary, while Elizabeth was championed by Protestant factions. The year before *Endymion* was first performed before Elizabeth, Mary was executed on Elizabeth's orders.

A staunch patron of the theater who sponsored her own company, the Queen's Men, Elizabeth commissioned Lyly's play, following the tradition of flattery in the Elizabethan court. Theater was commonly used to disseminate propaganda. Some scholars have suggested that the character Endymion represents Robert Dudley, Earl of Leicester, who was a close friend and suitor of Elizabeth. (Dudley supported the arts with a theater company of his own.) In such plays as *Endymion,* Elizabeth encouraged the mythmaking that depicted her as the virtuous and strong leader the country needed—particularly as a response to the growing concern over the future of England's monarchy.

During the reign of Elizabeth, the theater was accessible to all classes, and even the most common worker was able to attend regularly, making the theater an ideal vehicle for spreading propaganda to the masses. To this end, many so-called "mirror plays" emerged in which Elizabeth was contrasted with another, less favorable ruler. George Whetstone's play *Promos and Cassandra* details the dangers that befall a city when its leader is corrupt, offering an implicit comparison that encourages the audience's appreciation for their own virtuous queen. In the same way, Richard Edwards turned the myth of Damon and Pythias into a play, writing of a king who stays the execution of two men upon seeing the strength of their friendship and thus suggesting that loyalty is rewarded, especially in service to a benevolent ruler.

Endymion helped to cement a legacy that would last for centuries, for it served as a model for Lyly's contemporaries. William Shakespeare, a member of the theater company the Lord Chamberlain's Men, founded during Elizabeth's reign, used Lyly's play as inspiration for several of his plays. *A Midsummer Night's Dream,* for example, employs similar themes of star-crossed lovers, magic spells, and magic-induced slumber. The framework of Lyly's play, as well as the theme of male friendship, may have been a source for Shakespeare's *The Merchant of Venice.* Ben Jonson likewise drew on *Endymion* in his composition of *Cynthia's Revels.* Lyly's play continues to be studied in relation to both Elizabeth's court and the works of Lyly's contemporaries.

THEMES AND STYLE

At the heart of *Endymion* is the theme of love, both romantic love and the platonic love that develops between friends. Though love touches each character

† Key Facts

Time Period:
Late 16th Century

Genre:
Play

Events:
Ascension of Queen Elizabeth; execution of Queen Mary; rise of Protestantism

Nationality:
English

JOHN LYLY: ANATOMY OF A WIT

John Lyly is best known for his romance *Euphues: The Anatomy of a Wit* (1578). The novel is didactic, telling the story of Euphues—a young man blessed with wit, money, and good looks—who squanders his gifts in a life of folly. Following a series of misadventures in Naples, including the loss of a love, Euphues decides to live a life of virtue. *Euphues* was so popular in Lyly's day that it inspired its own trend of "euphuism," a style of writing marked by witty and stylized prose.

Lyly and his prose style influenced his contemporaries, including William Shakespeare, who uses similarly distinctive language in the dialogue between the courtly lovers in *Love's Labour's Lost* and in the witty exchanges between Beatrice and Benedick in *Much Ado about Nothing*. Not all the mimicry was praise, however. Shakespeare's character Falstaff mocks Lyly's overly stylized prose, and in 1609 Thomas Dekker ridiculed Lyly and euphuism, despite its being a fashionable writing style of the day.

in its own way, with the play ending in multiple marriages, the title character best embodies the theme. He follows his love, though his friend Eumenides reminds him that he is "mad" and "senseless" for desiring someone he can never possess. Even so, Endymion models true and unwavering love, a fact that he expresses to Cynthia: "I have forsaken all other fortunes to follow Cynthia, and here I stand ready to die if it please Cynthia." Endymion's words make clear the underlying message when Queen Elizabeth I is substituted for Cynthia: the appropriate response to the queen is complete devotion.

Lyly further extends his flattery of Elizabeth by contrasting Cynthia with her foil, Tellus. Tellus, a powerful goddess in her own right, is everything that Cynthia is not. Cynthia, as the moon, is presented as an unattainable beauty, a ruler who leads with intelligence and benevolence. She is described as "divine" and "delicate," and through the power of her kiss, she is the one who is able to right the wrongs by the play's end. In contrast, Tellus is vengeful, letting her jealousy overtake her senses. Whereas Cynthia is a light of the heavens, Tellus is associated with the baseness of the earth, her realm identified with "grapes" and "corn." Tellus's power puts Endymion into a deep sleep, but Cynthia's power wakes him. Tellus is destructive; Cynthia is restorative. By offering such stark comparison between the two characters, Lyly suggests to his audience that Elizabeth is preferable to Mary, Queen of Scots, or to any other, less divine ruler.

The language in the play is meant to mimic, perhaps even satirize, the overly dramatic speech heard in court life. Written in a style known as "euphuism," made famous in an earlier novel by Lyly, *Endymion* overflows with flowery language marked by inflated metaphors. Cynthia is not merely beautiful: she has a face that "neither the Summer's blaze can scorch, nor Winter's blast chap, nor the numbering of years breed altering of colors." The balanced ideas and repetitive phrases are typical of euphuism and are meant to mirror the artificiality of court life as well as elevate the language to match the theme of love and devotion, particularly that worthy of a queen.

CRITICAL DISCUSSION

If the goal of the play was to flatter Elizabeth and gain Lyly prominence in her court, then *Endymion* succeeded. Following the performance of the play at court in 1588, Elizabeth bestowed on Lyly the title Esquire of the Body. Edmund Blount, editor of Lyly's plays, wrote in 1632 that Elizabeth rewarded Lyly, suggesting that she found favor in the writer, though Blount remains vague on the subject. Perhaps because of his success at court, Lyly was particularly admired by his contemporaries, many of whom imitated his style. Lyly's writings became so popular that Shakespeare attempted to write in the style of Lyly when composing his play *Love's Labour's Lost*. Lyly's influence is also evident in the elements of magic in Shakespeare's *The Tempest*.

As a play commenting on the reign of Queen Elizabeth I, *Endymion* is often studied in an attempt to identify the men who influenced Elizabeth's personal life and political career. While critics generally agree that the characters of Cynthia and Tellus represent Elizabeth and Mary, Queen of Scots, respectively, the figure behind the character of Endymion is often debated. N. J. Halpin, writing in 1843, recognizes the Earl of Leicester in the role, while Josephine W. Bennett, nearly a century later, challenges that claim, arguing for the Earl of Oxford. Alexander Leggatt asserts that such overt speculation about political events would have made Elizabeth "livid," suggesting that the play instead pokes harmless fun at court life, "courting the Queen and courting trouble, combining flattery and warning, fantasy and political commentary."

Modern criticism of the play focuses on this delicate balance that Lyly must navigate in his text. While the flattery of Elizabeth is apparent, many critics read the play as a coded critique of the politics surrounding her court. C. M. Neufeld, for instance, argues that *Endymion* "communicates a profound anxiety about the monstrous shadow cast by the Virgin Queen." The strong element of witchcraft in Lyly's play during a time of witch hunts and trials may suggest that Elizabeth's own power, as a woman, is complicated; she is both the divinely placed ruler and the antagonistic witch.

BIBLIOGRAPHY

Sources

Bennett, Josephine W. "Oxford and *Endimion*." *Publications of the Modern Language Association* 57 (1942): 354–69. Print.

Halpin, N. J. *Oberon's Vision in the* Midsummer-Night's Dream, *Illustrated by a Comparison of Lylie's* Endymion. London: Shakespeare Soc., 1843. Print.

Leggatt, Alexander. *Introduction to English Renaissance Comedy.* Manchester: Manchester UP, 1999. Print.

Lyly, John. *Endymion.* Ed. David M. Bevington. Manchester: Manchester UP, 1997. Print.

Neufeld, C. M. "Lyly's Chimerical Vision: Witchcraft in *Endymion.*" *Forum for Modern Language Studies* 43.4 (2007): 351–69. *Humanities International Complete.* Web. 28 July 2012.

Further Reading

Bevington, David M. "John Lyly and Queen Elizabeth: Royal Flattery in *Campaspe* and *Sappho and Phao.*" *Renaissance Papers* (1966): 57–67. Print.

———. *Tudor Drama and Politics.* Cambridge: Harvard UP, 1968. Print.

Goldstein, Gary B. "Did Queen Elizabeth Use the Theater for Social and Political Propaganda?" *Oxfordian* 7 (2004): 153–69. *Shakespeare-Oxford Society.* Web. 27 July 2012.

Khomenko, Natalia. "'Between You and Her No Comparison': Witches, Healers, and Elizabeth I in John Lyly's *Endymion.*" *Early Theatre* 13.1 (2010): 37–63. *International Bibliography of Theatre and Dance with Full Text.* Web. 28 July 2012.

Pincombe, Michael. *The Plays of John Lyly: Eros and Eliza.* Manchester: Manchester UP, 1996. Print.

Rosador, Kurt Tetzeli von. "The Power of Magic: From *Endimion* to *The Tempest.*" *Shakespeare Survey* 43 (1991): 1–13. Print.

Lisa Kroger

Diana and Endymion, an eighteenth-century painting by Frans Christoph Janneck, depicts the ancient Greek myth of Endymion. John Lyly's comedy *Endymion* uses the myth as an allegory for the court of Queen Elizabeth I. DIANA AND ENDYMION, JANNECK, FRANS CHRISTOPH (1703–61)/PRIVATE COLLECTION/PHOTO © BONHAMS, LONDON, UK/THE BRIDGEMAN ART LIBRARY.

THE GOLD-CROWNED JESUS

Kim Chi-Ha

❖ *Key Facts*

Time Period:
Late 20th Century

Genre:
Play

Events:
Leadership of Park
Chung-hee, bringing
economic improvement
along with social
repression

Nationality:
Korean

OVERVIEW

The Gold-Crowned Jesus (1978), a play by Korean author Kim Chi-Ha, tells the story of a leper and social outcast who finds Jesus trapped in a stone statue. The play begins as the main character and another beggar, cold and hungry, sit on the street in a small Korean city in winter, watching society pass by. A nun, a priest, and a businessman discussing social justice and economic gain ignore their plight. The stone Jesus, who proves to be the only one concerned for the poor, begs the leper to free him by removing his gold crown and using it to help the needy. Through the leper's story, Kim, a Catholic, presents a searing admonition of those who use Christianity to justify the suffering of others. In addition, the author uses the suffering of the Jesus statue to exemplify what he views as the plight of the Korean people under the anticommunist government led by Park Chung-hee.

When *The Gold-Crowned Jesus* was published, Kim's political writings had already brought him into conflict with Park's regime, and he was in prison serving a life sentence for accusing the government of using torture to extract false confessions. Although the South Korean government tried to silence him, the rest of the world received him enthusiastically, praising his ability to give voice to human suffering. The play represents the voice of the South Korean people as one of the few texts to exemplify their suffering under Park's dictatorial government, which imposed harsh policies limiting personal freedoms, including freedoms of speech and the press. Today *The Gold-Crowned Jesus* is noteworthy as a simple and straightforward portrayal of the privations of the South Korean people and the failure of the church and the government to address those needs.

HISTORICAL AND LITERARY CONTEXT

In 1948 the Republic of Korea was divided into two countries: communist North Korea and anticommunist South Korea. A war with North Korea and a decade of shifting political leaders in South Korea followed, creating an atmosphere of upheaval. Through a 1961 military coup, Park assumed control of South Korea, promising to rebuild the war-torn country by embracing American Cold War-era positions against communism and by offering each citizen a chance to escape poverty. Although credited for strengthening

South Korea's economy, Park by the 1970s had come under criticism for turning the government into a dictatorship, controlling the press, and suppressing the speech of his opponents. Demonstrations against his government began to emerge across the country.

By 1971, the year in which Kim's play takes place, South Korea had mostly rebuilt its economy, thanks in large part to Park's efforts. However, prosperity came with a price. The government, in many ways, did not seem able to keep up with the rate of industrialization. The educational system, though growing exponentially, suffered from a lack of prepared teachers. In 1970 the collapse of a hastily constructed government housing building killed more than one hundred people, an event referenced in the beginning of Act IV of the play. South Koreans could not ignore that the government was glossing over past injustices, hoping to distract the people with new roads and better buildings. The following year was pivotal in the country's political landscape as Park won the presidential election in a close race. By the next year, he had dissolved Parliament, declaring martial law and decreasing the power of the press.

Following the Korean War and U.S. involvement in South Korean politics, literature tended to exemplify the horrors of war and the growing dissatisfaction with politics in South Korea. Novelist Hwang Sok-yong examines the effects of the separation of the two Koreas on families. Hwang's stories and plays, like Kim's, speak out against Park's dictatorship and call for freedom of speech for South Koreans. For example, Hwang's *Chang Kil-san*, serialized from 1974 to 1984, details the problems inherent in dictatorships. Yun Heung-gil echoes this distaste for the government by featuring characters who are threatened by Park's regime; some struggle with their own material well-being while others resist opponents through active rebellion. Kim's other writings, particularly the work "Five Bandits" (1970), which led to his arrest, are part of this trend of political writing that marks South Korean literature of the 1970s.

Kim's writings have secured his legacy as one of South Korea's loudest voices against Park's oppressive government. *The Gold-Crowned Jesus* added to this distinction, although the play also became known as a Christian text, proclaiming the failures of religion to meet the needs of the people. Prior to his imprisonment,

Kim was widely read in his own country. By the time *The Gold-Crowned Jesus* was published, he had become a worldwide literary figure, influencing writers and thinkers across the globe, including Japan's Kenzaburo Oe and Minjung theologians like Suh Nam-Dong.

THEMES AND STYLE

Kim's play revolves around the hypocrisy of Christians, primarily through the contrast between the characters on the street and the characters who pass by. The audience sees those in need—the leper, the beggar, and the prostitute—as they are forced to fend for themselves, while those in positions of power—the priest, the nun, and the company president—are too involved in political and theological discussion to stop and help. The priest sighs in response to the plight of the poor, saying that he does not "have any time"; he and the nun cannot decide if it is the government's or church's job to care for the poor. The company president calls the beggars "a heartless and greedy bunch," clearing his conscious of any obligation to help. Kim clarifies the "difference between Jesus and Christians" by demonstrating how the Christians have chosen to literally place their gold on a concrete statue rather than use it to care for their fellow citizens.

The wealthy in the play are presented not only as uncaring toward the street beggars but also as disturbed by the presence of the poor. The priest repeatedly states, "I'm in a hurry," while holding his nose and trying to quickly pass the leper and the beggar without incident. Similarly, the company president produces a handkerchief to cover "his nose against the odor with a great flourish," all the while looking upon the leper "with a fixed look of disdain, as if he were an undesirable insect." Through such gestures, Kim criticizes the wealthy South Koreans who turn a blind eye to the troubles that fester within the country, focusing instead on their own economic prosperity.

The play pays particular attention to language, with Kim using his skills as a poet to elucidate the state of the beggars. The beggar and the leper sing in the style of the Gaksori singers, who would perform "their ribald songs" on the street in exchange for money. In the songs, the beggar and leper repeat phrases like "dream a dream" to focus on the life they wish for themselves, a life in which they are "very well fed and clothed" and are treated to the "sizzling, sizzling, sizzling" of a barbecue grill. In reality, the repetition of the phrases only serves to highlight what they do not have, as they are forced to "mime the actions of cooking" because they do not have real food to eat. This stark depiction of hunger and need stands in direct contrast to the South Korea that Park's government attempted to portray.

CRITICAL DISCUSSION

Despite the South Korean government's attempts to silence Kim's words of dissent by imprisoning him

THE ROAD OF TORTURE: KIM CHI-HA'S POLITICAL IMPRISONMENT

Using his satirical wit, Kim Chi-Ha channels his discontent with the South Korean government in the 1970 poem "Five Bandits." The five bandits described in his poem are representative of the entities he saw as being at fault for the political and social state of South Korea: namely, government officials and businessmen. For example, the first bandit wears a suit made of money and is seen swallowing tax revenue. Another bandit controls the country while holding a golf club and a mistress in each hand. Although the caricatures represent Kim's views of the problems in his country, not everyone saw the humor in them. As a result, he was imprisoned by the South Korean government, was accused of being a spy for North Korea, and endured torture as a means of eliciting a confession.

Turning once again to writing, he penned the autobiographical poem "Torture Road" (1974), which describes the violence he was subjected to following his arrest and conviction at the hands of the Korean Central Intelligence Agency. In the poem, he relates tales of brutal treatment that he heard from fellow prisoners and stories of his own emotional turmoil, which lead him in the poem to question his own faith. Despite the bloody details, the poem ends on a hopeful note, calling for liberation for the South Korean people.

and by branding him a communist, thus alienating him from other South Koreans who feared to support him, Kim secured a reputation as a writer and activist almost immediately upon publication of his works and gained glowing reviews from critics. In the introduction to *The Gold-Crowned Jesus* (1978), Chong Sun Kim and Shelly Killen compare Kim to Albert Camus, calling Kim "a beacon of light" in the midst of a dictatorial government. The initial book reviews echo this sentiment, with Choan-Seng Song (1978) of the *Ecumenical Review* praising Kim for his ability to be "the conscience of humanity." Opinions like these, praising Kim and his ability to speak for his nation, helped to expand Kim's readership and rally support for his release from prison.

The Gold-Crowned Jesus has been regarded as one of the premier works in liberation literature. Critics have focused on Kim's activism and the effect of his writing on the political landscape of South Korea. In a 1977 article for *Bulletin of Concerned Asian Scholars*, Ko Won highlights Kim's "imageries of blood, of fire and burning, of the sword … the gun," explaining how the violent images represent South Korea's wrongs. Writing in 1984 for *Christian Century*, Deane William Ferm calls Kim "one of South Korea's foremost liberation theologians" for attempting to make Jesus real for the South Korean people. As a result of

In the play *The Gold-Crowned Jesus,* Korean poet Kim Chi-Ha depicts the liberation of a statue of Jesus. © NATIONAL GEOGRAPHIC IMAGE COLLECTION/ALAMY.

Kim's writing "the *confluence* of Christian and Korean minjung traditions." He discusses *The Gold-Crowned Jesus* as an important text in developing minjung theology—a Korean ideology that merges Christianity with idea of social justice—particularly as the sufferings of Christ can be compared with the sufferings of the characters in Kim's play. Similarly, Choan-Seng notes the relationship between Christian faith and social responsibility in *The Gold-Crowned Jesus,* calling it "a dialogue between the underprivileged people in our society and the privileged Christians who worship power and money in the Church." As such, Kim's play highlights the great divide between the way religious people ignore society's problems and the way the less fortunate experience sufferings, bringing the latter closer to Christ.

BIBLIOGRAPHY

Sources

Choan-Seng Song. "*The Gold-Crowned Jesus* and Other Writings." *Ecumenical Review* 30.4 (1978): 407–09. *Academic Search Premier.* Web. 31 Aug. 2012.

Ferm, Deane William. "Outlining Rice-Roots Theology." *Christian Century* 6.1 (1984): 78–80. Print.

Kim Chi-Ha. *The Gold-Crowned Jesus and Other Writings.* Ed. Chong Sun Kim and Shelly Killen. Maryknoll: Orbis, 1978. Print.

Ko Won. "Kim Chi-Ha: Poet of Blood and Fire." *Bulletin of Concerned Asian Scholars* 9.2 (1977): 20–25. Print.

Küster, Volker. *A Protestant Theology of Passion: Korean Minjung Theology Revisited.* Leiden: Brill, 2010. Print.

Further Reading

Ferm, Deane William. *Third World Liberation Theologies: An Introductory Survey.* Maryknoll: Orbis, 1986. Print.

Ishida, Kakuya. "S. Korean Poet: Creativity Answer to World's Problems." *Daily Yomiuri* 8 Dec. 1998: 3. Print.

Kim, Djung Kil. *The History of Korea.* Westport: Greenwood, 2005. Print.

Lee, Jin Kyung, and Choi Chungmoo. "An Autonomous Subject's Long Waiting, Coexistence: Oe Kenzaburo and Kim Chi-Ha." *Positions: East Asia Cultures Critique* 5.1 (1997): 285–313. Print.

McEnroy, Carmel E. "Friends, What Have You Done to Me? The Crucified Woman Challenges the Gold-Crowned Jesus." *Toronto Journal of Theology* 16.1 (2000): 167–86. *ATLA Religion Database with ATLA Serials.* Web. 31 Aug. 2012.

Lisa Kroger

such readings, Kim has become a writer of both Christian faith and social reform.

Although *The Gold-Crowned Jesus* is rarely discussed, modern critics read the play as an example of activist literature, focusing on Kim's roles as a voice of dissent against Park's dictatorial regime and as a leader spreading Christian thought in the liberation movement. Volker Küster in *A Protestant Theology of Passion: Korean Minjung Theology Revisited* (2010) calls

HENRY V

William Shakespeare

OVERVIEW

Believed to have been written around 1599 near the end of the reign of Queen Elizabeth I (r. 1558–1603), *Henry V* is the culminating work in William Shakespeare's Second Tetralogy of history plays, which traces the ascent of the English royal house of Lancaster. Although the entire sequence examines questions of kingship and power, the first three plays (*Richard II, Henry IV, Part 1,* and *Henry IV, Part 2*) are often considered as laying the foundation for *Henry V,* Shakespeare's portrait of the charismatic king whose unlikely triumph over the French at the Battle of Agincourt in 1415 earned him an enduring place among the most legendary figures in English history. The play focuses not only on the battle itself and the early aftermath of the victory but also on the preceding political tensions that led Henry to invade France, resuming after years of peace between the two countries the bitter conflict that became known as the Hundred Years' War.

Along with the other early history plays, *Henry V* helped to establish Shakespeare's reputation among Elizabethan audiences. In the modern era, it is widely recognized as one of Shakespeare's greatest dramatic achievements. Like many of Shakespeare's plays, *Henry V* is enigmatic and difficult to tether to a single meaning. Indeed generations of scholars have struggled to interpret the work, and debate continues over the question of Shakespeare's attitude toward his protagonist and the war he waged. While some read the play as a rousing celebration of nationalism and military prowess, others see Henry as a Machiavellian ruler whose rash decision to abandon the peace reveals his ruthlessness and moral hypocrisy. Given such ambiguity, modern stage and film directors have often interpreted *Henry V* through the lens of their own historical moment and political inclinations, using it variously to stir patriotic sentiment or deliver a strong antiwar message.

HISTORICAL AND LITERARY CONTEXT

Fought sporadically from 1337 to 1453, the Hundred Years' War was a series of conflicts between England and France over control of the vacant French throne. The Battle of Agincourt took place on October 25, 1415—Saint Crispin's Day—in northern France. Although they were outnumbered by the French, the English triumphed, and their victory began a new phase of the war. Following the battle, Henry married the French king's daughter, and their son, Henry, became heir to the throne of France.

In the years preceding the writing and performance of *Henry V,* Queen Elizabeth's power waned, as did confidence in her leadership. Although she had presided over England's glorious defeat of the Spanish Armada in 1588, conflicts with Spain and Ireland lingered until the end of her reign in 1603. During this period the English economy suffered because of poor harvests and the costs of war. As prices rose, the standard of living fell, and criticism of the queen increased. Furthermore, since Elizabeth had never married and had no children, the question of who would succeed her became an urgent public concern. Because of a lack of biographical information on Shakespeare, it is difficult or impossible to ascertain his intentions in writing *Henry V.* It seems plausible, however, that Shakespeare's valorization of Henry and portrayal of Henry as a strong ruler could have served a patriotic purpose during a difficult time in the country's history.

Although England faced economic and political uncertainty in the late sixteenth century, the arts flourished. Notable works of this era include John Lyly's *Euphues* (1578) and Edmund Spenser's *The Shepheardes Calender* (1578). Many of the most important figures in English literature, including Shakespeare and his chief literary rival—Christopher Marlowe—flourished in the 1590s, and during this period Shakespeare wrote his four-part series of plays on the House of Lancaster.

It is all but impossible to overstate Shakespeare's literary and cultural influence. *Henry V* continues to be performed and adapted for both stage and screen, and many actors view the role of Henry as one of the most challenging and complex in all of drama. Furthermore, the play's themes and its ambiguous portrayal of leadership and warfare keep it relevant, malleable, and adaptable to almost any era.

THEMES AND STYLE

The central themes of *Henry V* concern the moral complexities of both strong leadership and war. In rendering Henry as simultaneously heroic and ruthless, the play suggests that the traits that make a good leader may not necessarily make a good man. Although Henry relates to his men and is therefore able to motivate them, he also betrays many of his friends while upholding the

⁘ *Key Facts*

Time Period:
Late 16th Century

Genre:
Play

Events:
Rise of Henry V; Hundred Years' War; end of the reign of Elizabeth I

Nationality:
English

PRIMARY SOURCE

"ST. CRISPIN'S DAY SPEECH" FROM *HENRY V*

WESTMORELAND. O that we now had here

But one ten thousand of those men in England

That do no work to-day!

KING. What's he that wishes so?

My cousin Westmoreland? No, my fair cousin;

If we are mark'd to die, we are enow

To do our country loss; and if to live,

The fewer men, the greater share of honour.

God's will! I pray thee, wish not one man more.

By Jove, I am not covetous for gold,

Nor care I who doth feed upon my cost;

It yearns me not if men my garments wear;

Such outward things dwell not in my desires.

But if it be a sin to covet honour,

I am the most offending soul alive.

No, faith, my coz, wish not a man from England.

God's peace! I would not lose so great an honour

As one man more methinks would share from me

For the best hope I have. O, do not wish one more!

Rather proclaim it, Westmoreland, through my host,

That he which hath no stomach to this fight,

Let him depart; his passport shall be made,

And crowns for convoy put into his purse;

We would not die in that man's company

That fears his fellowship to die with us.

This day is call'd the feast of Crispian.

law. And while he is well aware of the horrors of war, he nonetheless rationalizes the violence that serves his political ambition. In his treatment of these issues, Shakespeare makes no definitive statement. The play neither condones moral relativism with regard to leadership and military conquest nor condemns war as an unacceptable and unnecessary atrocity.

Shakespeare uses various dramatic devices and rhetorical strategies to establish the grand setting of the play and to explore its complicated themes. Notable in *Henry V* is the role of the "Chorus," a single actor who introduces each act. In the Elizabethan era, when plays were staged without scenery, the chorus served an important function in helping the audience to visualize the setting and the events that were about to unfold. In *Henry V*, the Chorus is a source of great patriotic enthusiasm, rousing the audience, as the Shakespeare scholar Norman Rabkin describes, with his "epic romanticizations of land and sea, his descriptions of festooned fleets and nocturnal campfires and eager warriors, and his repeated invitations to imagine even more and better." Significantly, however, the scenes that follow reveal a war that is less glorious, and men less noble, than what the heady projections of the

Chorus have led the audience to expect. Some critics suggest that Shakespeare creates this discordance between Chorus and scene deliberately to render an experience of emotional conflict or ambivalence that leaves the audience uncertain: should they succumb to the allure of patriotic fervor or reject the Chorus's characterization of war as a dangerous delusion?

The playwright also explores the complicated nature of war by means of recurring metaphors, such as consumption and fire. The imagery of aggression conveys the violence of war. For example, before the Battle of Harfleur, Henry urges his men to "imitate the action of the tiger. / Stiffen the sinews, summon up the blood, / Disguise fair nature with hard-favoured rage."

The language and emotional tenor of the play fluctuate between ruminative introspection, vehement encouragement, and inspirational rallying. This range of rhetoric contributes to the ambiguity of the play's commentary on war and on Henry's style of rule. At times, Henry speaks eloquently of the difficult decisions he must make. At other times, he employs vicious imagery to inspire his troops. Still, the genius of Henry's leadership is nowhere more evident than in his famous Saint Crispin's Day speech, delivered just

He that outlives this day, and comes safe
    home,

Will stand a tip-toe when this day is nam'd,

And rouse him at the name of Crispian.

He that shall live this day, and see old age,

Will yearly on the vigil feast his
    neighbours,

And say "To-morrow is Saint Crispian."

Then will he strip his sleeve and show his
    scars,

And say "These wounds I had on
    Crispian's day."

Old men forget; yet all shall be forgot,

But he'll remember, with advantages,

What feats he did that day. Then shall our
    names,

Familiar in his mouth as household words-

Harry the King, Bedford and Exeter,

Warwick and Talbot, Salisbury and
    Gloucester-

Be in their flowing cups freshly
    rememb'red.

This story shall the good man teach his
    son;

And Crispin Crispian shall ne'er go by,

From this day to the ending of the
    world,

But we in it shall be remembered-

We few, we happy few, we band of
    brothers;

For he to-day that sheds his blood with me

Shall be my brother; be he ne'er so vile,

This day shall gentle his condition;

And gentlemen in England now-a-bed

Shall think themselves accurs'd they were
    not here,

And hold their manhoods cheap whiles
    any speaks

That fought with us upon Saint Crispin's
    day.

before the engagement at Agincourt to weary troops who know they are vastly outnumbered by the enemy and are likely to die on the field of battle. Henry gallantly dispels their pessimism and fear, dismissing the wish for additional troops with the bold contention that "the fewer men, the greater share of honour." Indeed Henry goes on to argue that honor itself is the greatest reward, promising that their survival will bring enduring glory, their heroism will become legendary, and their names will be remembered on every Saint Crispin's Day "to the ending of the world." Also key to Henry's oratory is his invocation of an intimate bond between himself and all those who would fight that day, a sacred brotherhood that would lead "gentlemen in England now abed / [to] think themselves accursed they were not here, / And hold their manhoods cheap" by comparison to the veterans of this great battle. It is this balance between brutally violent and lofty inspirational language that creates the uncertainty about Shakespeare's intended meaning.

CRITICAL DISCUSSION

The age of the play makes it difficult to determine what its early critical reception may have been. Based on what is known about Shakespeare's reputation during his lifetime, however, scholars assume that the play was, like almost all of the playwright's work, well received. Ben Jonson, a contemporary of Shakespeare and a well-known and respected writer and literary critic, held Shakespeare in high esteem. By the early eighteenth century, Shakespeare's reputation was established. The English critic Samuel Johnson, in his preface to an edition of *Shakespeare* published in 1765, stated that "Shakespeare is above all writers, at least above all modern writers." The romantics hailed Shakespeare's genius, and the Victorians revered the man who had come to be known as the Bard.

Critics have interpreted the attitude toward warfare depicted in *Henry V* in various ways. Janet M. Spencer observes that "in pursuing a foreign war, Henry exceeds the law by pressing his prerogative into issues of debatable moral legitimacy, issues that threaten to expose the origins of power." Henry's hubris leads him to invade a nonaggressive country and kill thousands of people. Furthermore, Henry never acknowledges his responsibility for the bloodshed he has initiated. Throughout the play the soaring rhetoric of the Chorus and Henry is undermined by the violent actions and coarse speech of the secondary characters who make up the king's army.

The play's openness to ideological interpretation is reflected by two of its most acclaimed film adaptations. Filmed in 1944 when the Allied victory over fascism remained uncertain, Laurence Olivier's version was intended to boost the morale of British troops, celebrating the play's nationalism and its depiction of martial glory. By contrast, the 1989 adaptation by Kenneth Branagh investigates the psychology of charismatic leadership, questions the morality of imperial conquest, and emphasizes the irredeemable human cost of war. More recently, a 2003 production directed by Nicholas Hytner for the Royal National Theater took an overtly pacifist stance, undercutting the play's high rhetoric with satire in an apparent critique of the American and British invasion of Iraq.

The discrepancies and contradictions throughout *Henry V* have become the central focus of scholars and critics. Rabkin neatly summarizes critical responses to the play by stating that critics "could hardly disagree more radically." The play's approach to complex subject matter has led not only to disagreements among critics but also to politicization by scholars, writers, and nationalists. In an article describing the relationship between Shakespeare's work and war, Werner Habicht notes that "a number of learned writers on both sides explored in high seriousness Shakespeare's own attitudes to and presentation of war and warfare, demonstrating thereby the compatibility of their findings with the military ideals of their respective nations." Interestingly, Shakespeare's play, which may or may not have been written with any intended propagandistic goals, has been routinely reimagined and reinterpreted as a work of powerful propaganda by those who view it as affirming their beliefs. It is the ambiguity of the play that allows for this repeated appropriation. Rabkin observes that "Shakespeare creates a work whose ultimate power is precisely the fact that it points in two opposite directions, virtually daring us to choose one of the two opposed interpretations it requires of us."

BIBLIOGRAPHY

Sources

Habicht, Werner. "Shakespeare Celebrations in Times of War." *Shakespeare Quarterly* 52.4 (2001): 441–55. *JSTOR.* Web. 11 July 2012.

Rabkin, Norman. "Rabbits, Ducks, and *Henry V.*" *Shakespeare Quarterly* 28.3 (1977): 279–96. *JSTOR.* Web. 11 July 2012.

Shakespeare, William. *Henry V.* Cambridge: Cambridge UP, 2005. Print.

Spencer, Janet M. "Princes, Pirates, and Pigs: Criminalizing Wars of Conquest in *Henry V.*" *Shakespeare Quarterly* 47.2 (1996): 160–77. *JSTOR.* Web. 11 July 2012.

Further Reading

Berry, Ralph. *Changing Styles in Shakespeare.* Abingdon: Routledge, 2005. Print.

Foakes, R. A. *Shakespeare and Violence.* Cambridge: Cambridge UP, 2003. Print.

Greenblatt, Stephen. *Shakespearean Negotiations: The Circulation of Social Energy in Renaissance England.* Berkeley: U of California P, 1988. Print.

Harriss, G. L. *Henry V: The Practice of Kingship.* New York: Oxford UP, 1985. Print.

Hedrick, Donald. "Advantage, Affect, History, *Henry V.*" *PMLA* 118.3 (2003): 470–87. *JSTOR.* Web. 11 July 2012.

Rabkin, Norman. *Shakespeare and the Problem of Meaning.* Chicago: U of Chicago P, 1981. Print.

Seward, Desmond. *Henry V as Warlord.* London: Sidgwick and Jackson, 1987. Print.

Wells, Stanley W., and Gary Taylor. *Modernizing Shakespeare's Spelling with Three Studies in the Text of* Henry V. Oxford: Clarendon, 1979. Print.

Media Adaptations

Henry V. Dir. Laurence Olivier. Perf. Laurence Olivier, Robert Helpmann, Felix Aylmer. United Artists, 1946. Film.

Henry V. Dir. Peter Watts. Perf. John Clements, John Garside. British Broadcasting Corporation, 1953. Television Movie.

Henry V. Dir. Kenneth Branagh. Perf. Kenneth Branagh, Simon Shepherd, and James Larkin. Samuel Goldwyn Company, 1989. Film.

Colby Cuppernull

A History of the Life and Death, Virtues and Exploits of General George Washington

Mason Locke Weems

✥ *Key Facts*

Time Period:
Early 19th Century

Genre:
Biography

Events:
Ratification of U.S. Constitution; early years of nationhood; death of George Washington

Nationality:
American

OVERVIEW

Written by Mason Locke Weems and published in 1800, *A History of the Life and Death, Virtues and Exploits of General George Washington* is a collection of anecdotes—many of dubious authenticity; some outright fabrications—about the American Revolution commander in chief and first president of the United States. Weems collected many of the stories about Washington as he traveled the Eastern Seaboard as a book salesman. His purpose in writing the work, aside from adding to his—and his publisher's—income, was to establish Washington as the ideal standard of republican virtue.

Since 1792 Weems had been traveling the back roads of America, where he had the opportunity to talk to all sorts of people in the early years of the Republic. When Washington died on December 14, 1799, Weems had already started collecting material for the biography, and the unity of the Revolutionary War—embodied by the leadership of Washington—had broken down into factions stemming partly from the debates over the ratification of the Constitution in 1787. The Federalists, led by John Adams and James Madison, favored a strong central government, while Thomas Jefferson and the Democrats wanted the least possible government interference. As a Democrat, Weems was delighted at Jefferson's election to the presidency later in 1800, but he sensed an anxiety in the people among whom he traveled—the anxiety of a lost "father" and of a "family" falling apart. One of his main goals with *A History of the Life and Death, Virtues and Exploits of General George Washington* was to ease those concerns with a binding mythology: the Founding Fathers and Washington as the "hero." Weems's collection of anecdotes had the double impact of providing colorful, quasi-legendary stories about the first president while solidifying the image of Washington desired by his readers.

HISTORICAL AND LITERARY CONTEXT

Chafing under taxes and trade restrictions by Great Britain and resentful of their lack of representation in Parliament, Britain's thirteen colonies in North America began to revolt in 1775, as small groups of colonists engaged in fighting against British soldiers. The colonies soon united and became organized, forming the Continental Army led by General George Washington, and the American Revolutionary War began. The United States declared its independence from the Crown on July 4, 1776, and five years of bloody warfare later, in August 1781, had achieved independence from Great Britain (the British House of Commons voted to make peace with their former colonies on March 5, 1782). After five years of experiment with a looser form of government coalition (Articles of Confederation), all of the state delegations to the Constitutional Convention in Philadelphia voted on September 17, 1787, to approve the final draft of the U.S. Constitution. On July 2, 1788, the document was ratified by the requisite nine states and the Constitution became the law of the land. Congress then began work on the details of forming a government.

When *History of the Life and Death, Virtues and Exploits of General George Washington* appeared in 1800, the United States was twenty-four years old and Weems was forty-one. During the War of Independence, he had been a blockade runner, taking arms and equipment to the rebellious colonies. After the war he determined to make his living helping his fellow citizens. He first became an Episcopalian clergyman and was vicar in a number of parishes, including Mount Vernon in Virginia. In the 1790s he decided that what the young country needed was not more preachers but more education, which in the early republic was synonymous with "literature." He became an itinerant bookseller, and in 1794 he became an agent for Matthew Carey, Philadelphia's preeminent publisher. Carey published inexpensive reprints of British and European literature and classical Greek and Roman texts and original works that were mainly self-help pamphlets, collections of sermons, and instruction manuals. During the last decade of the eighteenth century, Weems began to write. He developed a lively, boisterous, readable style, and everything he wrote had a didactic purpose.

One critic of Weems's Washington biography dismissed the work as "hagiography," but it was not

Weems's purpose to portray Washington as a saint. The founders of the United States unanimously regarded medieval Christianity, its saints and ceremonies, as "superstition." They were steeped in the classics, and they sought to recreate in their new country not the Rome of the popes but the Rome of Cicero and Seneca. The use of biography as a model of right and virtuous conduct dates back at least to fifth-century Greece and Xenophon's *Childhood of Cyrus* and *Memoirs of Socrates* (Xenophon, an Athenian, was notorious for preferring the austere Sparta to the rich complexities of his native city). The classical analogy most often applied to Washington was the career of the Roman aristocrat Cincinnatus (520–430 BCE), who left his farm to lead Rome through a crisis and then gave up power to return to his farm. Weems, in his enthusiasm, also likened the Founding Fathers to Old Testament prophets such as Abraham and Moses.

Even while Washington was still living, laudatory poems and essays had been pouring off the country's presses, and this became a flood upon his death. However, when Weems's biography appeared, the rest were cast aside. Throughout the nineteenth century, the Washington of the American imagination was Weems's version of Washington. Then, in the late nineteenth and early twentieth centuries, when U.S. scholars came to adopt the German methods of historical research and writing—which included a much stricter vetting of documentary evidence—*History of the Life and Death, Virtues and Exploits of General George Washington* was drastically debunked and downgraded. The last commercial edition of Weems's biography was published in 1927.

THEMES AND STYLE

The main, and virtually the only, theme of *History of the Life and Death, Virtues and Exploits of General George Washington* is the unassailable character of Washington. As Weems developed this theme through its many subsequent editions—and the book tripled in size—he concentrated increasingly on Washington's childhood and youth. The most famous episode in the book, the chopping down of the cherry tree ("Father, I cannot tell a lie …"), was not included until the fifth edition, in 1806. Never one to shy away from hyperbole—his métier, in fact—Weems went so far as to proclaim Washington as "the HERO, and the Demigod" and even "the 'Jupiter Conservator,' the friend and benefactor of men."

Weems used Washington's childhood to show what growing up in the liberty of America could do for a person's character, but he also stressed Washington's private life, maintaining:

> It is not, then, in the glare of public, but in the shade of private life, that we are to look for the man. Private life, is always real life. Behind the curtain, where the eyes of the million are not upon him, and where a man can have no

Portrait of Mason Locke Weems, c. 1810. NATIONAL PORTRAIT GALLERY, SMITHSONIAN INSTITUTION/ART RESOURCE, NY.

motive but inclination, no incitement but honest nature, there he will always be sure to act himself; consequently, if he act greatly, he must be great indeed.

Weems was also intent on portraying Washington as a simple farmer, responding to his country's need with heroic actions and wise governance and then returning, like Cincinnatus, to his plow and hearth.

The language and highly charged emotionalism of *History of the Life and Death, Virtues and Exploits of General George Washington* were part and parcel of his propagandistic intent. Weems varies widely between the evangelical fervor of a revival tent to the restrained ardor of a schoolmaster urging his pupils to take the lessons of their classical texts to heart. Still, for all of his melodrama and vagrant haranguing, he never loses control of either himself or his subject matter. Of Washington's dying, he writes, "The greatest of human beings was lying low. A life, of all others the most revered, the most beloved, was at stake. And if human skill could have saved—if the sword of genius, and the buckler of experience could have turned the stroke of death, Washington had still lived. But his hour was come." This seems, to modern ears, something of an overreaction, but many Americans at the time felt exactly that strongly about Washington—not just that he was the "father of his country" but that he was its savior as well.

CRITICAL DISCUSSION

When it first appeared, *History of the Life and Death, Virtues and Exploits of General George Washington* was an immediate popular success. Critics compared it unfavorably to Chief Justice John Marshall's scrupulously researched five-volume biography of Washington

PRIMARY SOURCE

EXCERPT FROM *A HISTORY OF THE LIFE AND DEATH, VIRTUES AND EXPLOITS OF GENERAL GEORGE WASHINGTON*

"Pa," said George very seriously, "do I ever tell lies?"

"No, George, I thank God you do not, my son; and I rejoice in the hope you never will. At least, you shall never, from me, have cause to be guilty of so shameful a thing. Many parents, indeed, even compel their children to this vile practice, by barbarously beating them for every little fault: hence, on the next offence, the little terrified creature slips out a lie! just to escape the rod. But as to yourself, George, you know I have always told you, and now tell you again, that, whenever by accident, you do anything wrong, which must often be the case, as you are but a poor little boy yet, without experience or knowledge, you must never tell a falsehood to conceal it; but come bravely up, my son, like a little man, and tell me of it: and, instead of beating you, George, I will but the more honour and love you for it, my dear."

This, you'll say, was sowing good seed!—Yes, it was: and the crop, thank God, was, as I believe it ever will be, where a man acts the true parent, that is, the Guardian Angel, by his child.

The following anecdote is a case in point. It is too valuable to be lost, and too true to be doubted; for it was communicated to me by the same excellent lady to whom I am indebted for the last.

"When George," said she, "was about six years old, he was made the wealthy

(1804–07; revised 1832), which was based on papers provided by the Washington family, but the Marshall book was written for the highly educated elite, while Weems's book was written for the American Everyman (and Everywoman). Readers thoroughly identified with the author's emotional connection to his subject, recognizing the same emotions in themselves. Many were likely intelligent enough to understand that there were factual errors and exaggerations in the book but were persuaded by the emotional truth of the work, since it coincided with their own feelings of reverence toward the man who had led them to independence and guided the first steps of the young republic.

Weems's biography enjoyed a rare success as propaganda. For years schoolchildren were taught that they could do no better than to emulate the Washington that Weems had so vividly—and single-handedly—created in his book. After a century of uncritical acceptance, the image he made of Washington has proven indelible, even when his many errors and fabrications were scrupulously exposed by scholars. If later scholarship had discovered that, contrary to Weems's glowing portrait, Washington was a venal coward or an unscrupulous opportunist, things might have been different, but no such discovery was made. The historical Washington was found to be a human being after all, but a fine and honest and honorable leader, nevertheless.

The predominant trends in the scholarship of *History of the Life and Death, Virtues and Exploits of General George Washington* are the search for documentary evidence to determine which of the anecdotes in the book can be verified as historical and the critical analysis of the character, motives, and goals of Weems. Scholars in the first trend, including Henry Adams, were quick to discover, for instance, that the cherry tree story, regardless of its undoubted worth as an exemplum, was traceable only to a completely undocumented encounter between a lady claiming to be Washington's cousin and the biographer, who pleaded for its acceptance on the grounds that she was too fine a lady to make it up. Usually, scholars in the latter trend researched a broader phenomenon—propaganda, for instance—of which Weems was merely one example, if an especially entertaining one. Neither line of inquiry has produced much in the way of controversy, mainly because no one has ever mistaken Weems's biography as a serious work of scholarship.

BIBLIOGRAPHY

Sources

Brooks, Van Wyck. *The World of Washington Irving.* New York: Dutton, 1944. Print.

Gilje, Paul A. *Encyclopedia of Revolutionary America.* Vol. 3. New York: Facts On File, 2010. 841–42. *Gale Virtual Reference Library.* Web. 11 Sept. 2012.

"Historical Writing: The Washington Myth." *American Eras. Vol. 4: Development of a Nation, 1783–1815.* Detroit: Gale, 1997. 53–54. *Gale Virtual Reference Library.* Web. 12 Sept. 2012.

Vietto, Angela. *Early American Literature, 1776–1820.* New York: Facts On File, 2010. 179–82. *Gale Virtual Reference Library.* Web. 11 Sept. 2012.

master of a hatchet! of which, like most little boys, he was immoderately fond, and was constantly going about chopping everything that came in his way. One day, in the garden, where he often amused himself hacking his mother's pea-sticks, he unluckily tried the edge of his hatchet on the body of a beautiful young English cherry-tree, which he barked so terribly, that I don't believe the tree ever got the better of it. The next morning the old gentleman, finding out what had befallen his tree, which, by the by, was a great favourite, came into the house; and with much warmth asked for the mischievous author, declaring at the same time, that he would not have taken five guineas for his tree. Nobody could tell him anything about it. Presently George and his hatchet made their appearance. "George," said his father, "do you know who killed that beautiful little cherry tree yonder in the garden?" This was a tough question; and George staggered under it for a moment; but quickly recovered himself: and looking at his father, with the sweet face of youth brightened with the inexpressible charm of all-conquering truth, he bravely cried out, "I can't tell a lie, Pa; you know I can't tell a lie. I did cut it with my hatchet."— "Run to my arms, you dearest boy," cried his father in transports, "run to my arms; glad am I, George, that you killed my tree; for you have paid me for it a thousand fold. Such an act of heroism in my son is more worth than a thousand trees, though blossomed with silver, and their fruits of purest gold."

Weems, Mason Locke. *A History of the Life and Death, Virtues and Exploits of General George Washington.* Philadelphia: Carey, 1800. *The Apotheosis of Washington.* Web. 1 Sept. 2012.

Wroth, L. C. *Parson Weems: A Biographical and Critical Study.* Baltimore: Eichelberger, 1911. Print.

Further Reading

Fast, Howard. *Citizen Tom Paine.* New York: Duell, Sloan and Pearce, 1943. Print.

Trees, Andrew S. "Washington, George." *Encyclopedia of the New American Nation.* Vol. 3. Ed. Paul Finkelman.

Detroit: Scribner, 2006. 325–29. *Gale Virtual Reference Library.* Web. 10 Sept. 2012.

Weems, Mason Locke. *The Life of Benjamin Franklin.* New York: Street & Smith, 1815. *Project Gutenberg.* Web. 9 Sept. 2012.

———. *The Life of General Francis Marion, a Celebrated Partisan Officer, in the Revolutionary War.* Philadelphia: Carey, 1809. *Project Gutenberg.* Web. 9 Sept. 2012.

Wills, Gary. *Cincinnatus: George Washington and the Enlightenment.* Garden City: Doubleday, 1984. Print.

Gerald Carpenter

KONRAD WALLENROD

A Tale from the History of Lithuania and Prussia

Adam Mickiewicz

✣ *Key Facts*

Time Period:
Early 19th Century

Genre:
Poetry

Events:
Police repression
and censorship in
Russia; increased
nationalism and
desire for sovereignty
in Russian-controlled
Poland; height of literary
Romanticism

Nationality:
Polish

OVERVIEW

Published in St. Petersburg in early 1828, Adam Mickiewicz's epic poem *Konrad Wallenrod: A Tale from the History of Lithuania and Prussia* is seen as the founding text of Polish romantic nationalism, which enflamed the literary patriotism of a generation and at least partially inspired the unsuccessful 1830–31 uprising against the Russian Empire. The poem's hero betrays the Teutonic (German) knights he commands in order to free his oppressed native land. The work translates Byronic romanticism into the context of a Polish nation deprived of a state since its late eighteenth-century partition and subsequent domination by the Russian, Prussian, and Austrian Habsburg empires. Although the Czarist censorship authorities seemingly did not recognize the allegorical character of the poem and allowed its publication and reprinting the following year, the poem's theme of national liberation and message that loyalty to one's own people, culture, and history trumps fealty to state authority resonated with its audience.

Konrad Wallenrod, which was quickly translated into several languages, was well received by Poles and others swept up in romanticist fever; by Russian poets such as Alexander Pushkin, a friend of Mickiewicz; and even by some Russian government officials. Although Mickiewicz later considered the poem flawed, stating that he wished he could buy up all remaining copies and burn them, its influence only increased as Poles struggled to liberate their nation. *Konrad Wallenrod* has maintained its status as an iconic work; in the words of George Rapall Noyes, editor of the 1944 translated *Poems,* it "is the finest fruit of the Byronic influence on the continent of Europe." However, its literary value, as part of a romantic project that sought to establish national cultures by creating new forms of language and versification, is less apparent to those outside the Polish realm.

HISTORICAL AND LITERARY CONTEXT

Konrad Wallenrod appeared at the height of the romantic literary movement, which idealized a lost past, reacting to the Enlightenment and the French Revolution and looking inward at the emotions and psyche of the individual. The poem also responds to the concerns of Poles at the dawn of the age of nationalism. In the grip of the vast and powerful Russian Empire, and after the collapse of the Napoleonic project, which had offered at least the hope of change, there was no clear path to individual or national liberation. In an era in which discussion of non-Russian national cultures was dangerous, Mickiewicz looked to the fourteenth century, when pagan Lithuanian tribes faced the militarily and politically superior Teutonic knights, to find an allegory that would make publication of his work possible. He solved the problem of tribal inferiority by constructing a story that resonated with readers of the day, involving hidden identity, divided loyalties, and the conflict between the individual and the structure of society.

In 1823 Mickiewicz was arrested in a crackdown on patriotic student groups and exiled to Russia, where he was thrust into the lap of the Russian aristocratic literary and intellectual elite. He got to know Pushkin, Russia's "national poet," who despite later anti-Polish expressions welcomed the appearance of *Konrad Wallenrod* and even tried his hand at translating it into Russian. After the suppression of the 1830–31 uprising, Mickiewicz became an extreme critic of Russia, expressed most scathingly in the poetic "Digression," appended to *Forefathers' Eve* (1823/1832). This epic work records the voyage of exile of a conspirator of the 1825 Decembrist uprising—an attempt to transform Russia to democratic constitutionalism—across a vast and cruel landscape.

Konrad Wallenrod follows a contemporary romantic literary style by creating a conflicted—or Byronic (after Lord Byron, the "patron saint" of romanticism)—hero struggling for personal and national redemption and by incorporating folkloric elements from a real or imagined national past. Mickiewicz begins this trajectory with *Grazyna* (1823), the tale of the wife of a Lithuanian leader who foils her husband's attempt at a traitorous alliance with the Teutonic knights. The poem, while lacking the complexity and literary value of *Konrad Wallenrod,* foreshadows both the theme of *Konrad Wallenrod,* which continues in his later works, and his obsession with Lithuania, which he considered his homeland despite his loyalty to a broader Polish language, culture, and nation.

Konrad Wallenrod launched romantic nationalism in Polish literature and formed the template for the national literary production of the rest of the nineteenth century. The cultural representation of a nation that does not exist politically continues to be foundational for Polish national identity and cultural memory. Its stylistic innovations were key for the development of the lyrical possibilities of the Polish language. It also inspired writers from Italy to the Balkans and beyond who were searching for ways to advance the cause of national freedom through literature. Mickiewicz's work is still memorized by Polish schoolchildren as an essential part of the national patrimony.

THEMES AND STYLE

The central themes of *Konrad Wallenrod* are the conflict between national or ethnic identity and the requirements of politics and society to suppress that identity, and the cost to the individual of acting on either side of this conflict. As a boy, the poem's tortured Lithuanian hero is kidnapped, along with Halban, a Lithuanian bard, by the Teutonic knights. Halban keeps the memory of home and culture alive, and the two escape to their native land, where Konrad marries his childhood sweetheart. Realizing that the Lithuanians' struggle against the overwhelming power of the knights is doomed, Konrad abandons his wife and country to return to the knights. As the poem opens, he is elected their grand master based on his exploits in far-flung battles. He leads the knights in battle against the Lithuanians but in service to his true homeland sabotages the campaign with delays and strategic blunders. However, Konrad's "noble treachery" leaves him a broken man, and he commits suicide; Halban survives to memorialize his deeds in song.

The work transmits its message of deception and disguise by means of a structure that is permeated with ambiguity and obscurity. In *Adam Mickiewicz in World Literature* (1956), Waclaw Lednicki notes, "*Konrad Wallenrod* was not only a poem about disguise and dissimulation, but was itself a disguise." Konrad's past and true identity are related under the alternate name of Walter Alf, in an interjection, "The Tale of the Wajdelota [Halban's title]." Other interludes—"Song" and "The Song of the Wajdelota"—establish the folkloric basis of Konrad's Lithuanian identity but are presented as mere "local color" before the assembled German knights. He carries on a dialogue with an unnamed and unseen woman locked in the castle tower, while the embedded story of Aldona, Walter's bride, indicates she must be Konrad's wife. Much of the convolution can be attributed to the need to mislead the censor. A title page motto taken from Machiavelli's *The Prince*—in the original Italian—states, "[O]ne must be both a fox and a lion," revealing but also obscuring the poem's intent. A brief preface claims the story was taken directly from history—Konrad Wallenrod was a leader of the knights, though he was said to be feckless and his tenure unremarkable; however, it asserts that the story is now completely irrelevant: "altogether a thing of the past."

MICKIEWICZ THE REVOLUTIONARY

Despite the role played by *Konrad Wallenrod* in inspiring the November 1830 Polish insurrection, Mickiewicz was notable for his absence from the struggle, news of which reached him in Rome. He felt obligated to join the uprising but dallied for months, failing to reach the battlefield before the Polish forces surrendered in September 1831. According to Noyes, the rest of Mickiewicz's life "has been regarded as a long act of expiation for his weakness in a supreme crisis." After 1834 he essentially abandoned literature for a spiritually tinged commitment to politics.

Mickiewicz's twenty-five years in exile, mostly in Paris, saw him under the spell of a cultish mystic and troubled by constant poverty, though he remained in the midst of almost continuous radical fervor. As revolution across the Continent brewed in 1848, he organized a Polish force to fight on the side of Italian independence and started a radical internationalist daily newspaper, the *People's Tribune,* which ran until the French government forced its closure. When the Crimean War broke out in 1853, he saw another chance to advance the Polish cause by organizing fighters against Russia. He went to Constantinople and began organizing a Jewish legion in support of Polish independence—remarkable in light of the region's long history of alleged Polish anti-Semitism—but contracted cholera and died on November 26, 1855, at age fifty-six.

While initially noted more for its political than its literary impact, the linguistic and poetic innovation of *Konrad Wallenrod,* in its mix of styles and rhythms, forms a landmark in Polish literature. In *European Writers: The Romantic Century* (1985), Wiktor Weintraub recognizes the unrhymed "Polish hexameter" in the middle section—"Halban's Tale"—as a "new form … one of the marvels of Polish poetry." The alternation of techniques in different sections serves to destabilize the clear nationalist import of the surface narrative. However, on a deeper level, as Anita Debska notes in *Country of the Mind: An Introduction to the Poetry of Adam Mickiewicz* (2000), "The power of language to preserve culture … is a major theme of the poem."

CRITICAL DISCUSSION

Konrad Wallenrod was immensely popular among young Poles and—despite its allegorical anti-Russian message—among Russian literati. The latter saw the work as a vindication of the 1825 Decembrist insurrection, while the older generation of neoclassicist Polish critics, guardedly praising its literary value, saw the work's hero as an immoral model for the nation's political aspirations. Concurrent events such as the treason trial of the Patriotic Society in Warsaw forced a more political interpretation onto the poem, so by the time of the November 1830 uprising, as Roman Koropeckyj writes in *Adam Mickiewicz: The Life of a*

The Battle of Grunwald, an 1878 painting by Jan Matejko depicting the Polish and Lithuanians and their battle with the knights of the Teutonic Order. Adam Mickiewicz's 1828 poem *Konrad Wallenrod* is ostensibly about these struggles but actually about nineteenth-century conflicts between Poland and Russia. ERICH LESSING/ART RESOURCE, NY.

Romantic (2008), "cadets storming the Belvedere Palace in Warsaw did so in the name of Wallenrod."

According to Weintraub, "[It] was in *Wallenrod* that Mickiewicz first laid claim to the title [Polish] national poet"—a designation he still holds. The poem's message and popularity spawned the term *Wallenrodism,* which Koropeckyj defines as "a strategy of dissimulation by the weak in their struggle against a stronger oppressor … used to characterize a specific mode of Polish behavior, praised by some, reviled by others, and exploited by patriot and scoundrel alike." Mickiewicz's activities during the last two decades of his life, when he gave up poetry for politics in service of the national cause, cemented his reputation as a spokesperson for what Noyes calls "Polish Messianism, a mystic faith that lies at the foundation of nearly all the later patriotic and romantic poetry of Poland." This vision, encapsulated in Mickiewicz's *The Books of the Polish Nation and Polish Pilgrimage* (1832), saw Poland as the "Christ of Nations," whose salvation would redeem all of the oppressed nations of the world.

While the bulk of critical attention has gone to Mickiewicz's "mature" masterpieces *Forefathers' Eve* and especially *Pan Tadeusz* (1834), *Konrad Wallenrod* cemented his reputation as the literary representative of the nation and provides clues to the internal conflict that assuming such a position caused within him. A 1960 article by Kenneth Lewalski in *American Slavic and East European Review* argues that rather than an unwieldy mix of styles and voices, the poem constitutes "a unified allegory dealing with the artist's inner conflict between political obligations on the one hand and artistic aspirations on the other." In this reading, Aldona represents "pure art," and Halban service to a political cause, with Konrad caught tragically between the two poles. Koropeckyj concurs, stating that "Mickiewicz was in a sense telling of his own willingness to sacrifice himself as an artist for the sake of his nation's political struggle."

BIBLIOGRAPHY

Sources

Debska, Anita. *Country of the Mind: An Introduction to the Poetry of Adam Mickiewicz.* Warsaw: Burchard, 2000. Print.

Koropeckyj, Roman. *Adam Mickiewicz: The Life of a Romantic.* Ithaca: Cornell UP, 2008. Print.

Lednicki, Waclaw. "Mickiewicz's Stay in Russia and His Friendship with Pushkin." *Adam Mickiewicz in World Literature.* Ed. Waclaw Lednicki. Berkeley: U of California P, 1956. 13–104. Print.

Lewalski, Kenneth F. "Mickiewicz, *Konrad Wallenrod*: An Allegory of the Conflict between Politics and Art." *American Slavic and East European Review* 19 (1960): 423–41. Web. 4 Oct. 2012.

Noyes, George Rapall. Introduction. *Poems.* Ed. George Rapall Noyes. New York: Polish Institute of Arts and Sciences in America, 1944. Print.

Weintraub, Wiktor. "Adam Mickiewicz." *European Writers: The Romantic Century.* Vol. 5. Ed. George Stade. New York: Scribner, 1985. *Scribner Writers Series.* Web. 4 Oct. 2012.

Further Reading

Ascherson, Neal. *Black Sea.* New York: Hill and Wang, 1995. Print.

Filipowicz, Halina. "Mickiewicz: 'East' and 'West.'" *Slavic and East European Journal* 45.4 (2001): 606–23. Web. 4 Oct. 2012.

Koropeckyj, Roman. *The Poetics of Revitalization: Adam Mickiewicz between* Forefathers' Eve, Part 3, *and* Pan Tadeusz. Boulder: East European Monographs, 2001. Print.

Kridl, Manfred. *Adam Mickiewicz, Poet of Poland: A Symposium.* New York: Columbia UP, 1951. Print.

Miłosz, Czesław. *The History of Polish Literature.* New York: Macmillan, 1969. Print.

Zamoyski, Adam. *Holy Madness: Romantics, Patriots and Revolutionaries 1776–1871.* London: Weidenfeld & Nicolson, 1999. Print.

Rick Esbenshade

KYNGE JOHAN

John Bale

OVERVIEW

Kynge Johan ("King John," commonly referred to as *King Johan*; ca. 1538), a play by the historian, dramatist, polemicist, and bishop John Bale, tells a highly allegorized and edited version of the story of John Lackland, king of England from 1199 to 1216, and his conflict with Pope Innocent III. It likely was performed for the first time in early 1539 at the home of the archbishop of Canterbury for an audience that likely included King Henry VIII. Bale amended the play over the years, and additions that flatter Queen Elizabeth I indicate that he may have worked on it as late as 1560. As in medieval morality plays, some characters are named after abstract concepts, such as Sedition, Nobility, and Treason. Others represent historical figures such as the titular king and Stephen Langton, the pope's preferred candidate for archbishop of Canterbury in 1207. Still others are not named, but the people they represent are made obvious—for example, Imperial Majesty clearly represents Henry VIII. In addition, Bale calls for some roles to be doubled, so that the same actor who plays Sedition also plays Stephen Langton. The play's propagandistic message, repeated throughout, is that England should declare its political, theological, and financial independence from the papacy in Rome.

The play was written during the Reformation, a period of redefinition of Christian theology that gave rise to Protestantism. This new branch of Christianity broke from Roman Catholicism, which for centuries had prevailed in western Europe. The Reformation movement, driven by theologians such as Martin Luther and John Calvin, led to upheaval and violence in many European territories. *King Johan* reflects the conflicted feelings that many English people, including the king, had about the religious changes. The play highlights the anxiety of England's split from Rome, which raised not only the threat of political instability but also the question of who was right about the fate of the Christian soul.

HISTORICAL AND LITERARY CONTEXT

After Luther launched the Reformation in Germany with his *Ninety-five Theses* (1517), Henry VIII initially maintained England's attachment to Roman Catholicism. He responded with "Declaration of the Seven Sacraments against Martin Luther" (1521), a pamphlet that drew praise from the pope. Nonetheless, Reformation ideas began to percolate in England. In the 1520s, while Bale was at the University of Cambridge, a group of students—including Thomas Cranmer, future archbishop of Canterbury—met to discuss ideas for a new Church of England. Moreover, Henry himself soon encountered difficulties in his relationship with Rome. In 1527, having only one living daughter by his wife, Catherine of Aragon (for whom he had requested papal dispensation to marry), Henry asked Pope Clement VII for an annulment. Henry wanted to remarry and produce a male heir so that England would not be vulnerable to succession disputes or loss of sovereignty by a foreign marriage. The pope, however, refused to grant Henry's request.

Henry's quarrel with the pope paved the way for England's break with Rome in the 1530s, the decade when *King Johan* was penned. In 1533 Cranmer, now archbishop of Canterbury, annulled the king's marriage, and Henry quickly remarried. The pope responded by excommunicating Henry and putting England under interdict—effectively excommunicating the whole country. Henry declared himself the head of the Church of England in 1534, and in 1536 he initiated the dissolution of Catholic monasteries in England. Yet the king did not fully embrace Protestant reforms: he continued to see the English church as Catholic, merely separated from Rome. Indeed, he made Lutheran tracts illegal in 1539. Amid this religious upheaval, Bale's play attempts to clarify the rightness of England's position.

English drama in the early sixteenth century was alive with performances at village festivals, morality plays in which Humanity battles Vice, and plays that mount traditional Catholic scenes such as the Crucifixion and the Assumption of the Virgin Mary into heaven. Playwrights of the time did not shy away from politics either. John Skelton's *Magnificence* (ca. 1520), composed as a gentle warning to the young Henry VIII, has Magnificence (the king) parrying the varied influences of characters such as Liberty and Fancy. John Heywood's *A Play of the Weather* (1533) casts the god Jupiter as a king fighting to control a court besieged by would-be usurpers. Bale, and the pro-Reformation politicians who commissioned his work, were aware of the traditionally didactic function of theater and recognized its potential as propaganda—for both the public and the reluctant king.

Key Facts

Time Period:
Mid-16th Century

Genre:
Play

Events:
Reformation; Britain's break from Catholicism

Nationality:
English

THE PROGRESS OF LEARNING

When John Bale began his studies at Cambridge, the great humanist scholar Desiderius Erasmus was just ending his residency as a professor there. Erasmus lamented the slow pace of the progress of humanism in England, which lagged behind other European nations. The "new learning," another term for Renaissance humanism, took a broader and deeper view of the works of antiquity, considering ancient Greco-Roman texts not just as analogs for Christian theology, but as works to be studied in their own right.

Bale left Cambridge before more innovative curricula were implemented, but he undertook to supplement his learning later on. Nevertheless, observes Bale scholar Thora Balslev Blatt in *The Plays of John Bale: A Study of Ideas, Technique, and Style* (1968), he cleaved to old ways of study, treating the ancient texts "in a medieval way, as mines of encyclopaedic information and collections of stories that may be used to illustrate a moral point." When a reference to classical myth appears in *King Johan,* it shines brightly against all the biblical references in the play. For instance, Dissimulation brags to Sedition about how he directs his followers: "Some read the Epistle and Gospel at High Mass / Some sing at the lectern with long ears like an ass"— referring to one of the King Midas myths, in which an angry god gives him donkey ears.

King Johan is seen as marking a transition from medieval allegorical genres to the type of historical drama that William Shakespeare would later write. It is often compared to Protestant theologian William Tyndale's *Obedience of a Christian Man* (1528), which invites readers to "consider the story of kynge John … Did not the legate of Rome assoyle [absolve] all the lordes of the realme of their due obedience which they oughte to the kynge by the ordinance of God?" The anonymously composed play *The Troublesome Reign of King John* (ca. 1591) and Shakespeare's *King John* (ca. 1611) are both thought to have drawn on Bale's work as well as historical chronicles to recount the king's less-than-chivalrous behavior toward his subjects and family.

THEMES AND STYLE

The guiding principles of *King Johan* are obedience to the king as opposed to the pope, the king's closer proximity to the divine, and the king's essential goodness as contrasted with the pope's corruption. With religious uncertainty permeating England and Henry VIII himself torn between the religion he grew up with and his irreconcilable differences with Rome, the play offers a vision of clarity. The characters of England and the Clergy are played by one actor, thus uncomfortably illuminating England's internal problems with regard to its attachment to Rome past and present. England's son Commonalty (doubled with Sedition, Stephen Langton, and Civil Order) is "poor and blind" due to "priests, canons, and monks, which do fill their belly with their sweat and labour." England urges John to allow "God's word to be taught sincerely"—such as through Protestantism—so that "the people should know to their prince their lawful duty."

A former Carmelite friar, Bale was knowledgeable enough to use the language of liturgy to lend power to his scenes. When King John refuses to accept the pope's choice, Stephen Langton, as archbishop, Private Wealth curses him with "cross, book, bell, and candle." This mystical incantation quickly morphs into a military threat: "Such enemies are up as will your realm invade." John mocks the pretense of piety—"Is this the charity of that ye call the Church?"—and points to Scripture: "The birds of the air shall speak to their great shame, / As saith Ecclesiastes, that will a prince defame." This line clearly refers to Ecclesiastes 10:20: "Curse not the king, no, not in thy thought … for a bird of the air will carry the voice." The implication is that the Roman church is so preoccupied with political power that it has lost its virtue, and Bale illustrates that loss as a departure from Scripture. The English king's familiarity with Scripture is a sign of his closeness with God.

King Johan communicates outrage over the perceived corruption of Rome via the profane language used by the characters aligned with the pope, their ungallant treatment of the widow England, and their ultimate betrayal of the king. In the play's opening scenes, Sedition snaps at England (who has just called the pope a greedy "wild boar with his church universal"): "Hold your peace, ye whore!" Sedition then proclaims his everlasting allegiance with the pope: "So long as I have a hole within my breech." Usurped Power, who represents the pope, is later revealed to have impious inclinations: "I am a man, like as another is; / Sometime I must hunt, sometime I must Alison kiss." "A better drink is not in Portugal or Spain," Dissimulation tells King John, who promptly dies from the proffered poison. In the latter portion of the play, which corresponds to the present, Imperial Majesty, representing Henry VIII, puts an end to Sedition's reign: "The Clergy accuseth thee; Nobility condemneth thee, and the Law will hang thee."

CRITICAL DISCUSSION

Commissioned under the auspices of Thomas Cromwell, Henry's chief advisor, *King Johan* was meant to convince the king and the aristocracy that England had been right to split with Rome; however, some saw it as a warning to the monarch. John Alforde, an aristocratic audience member at the 1539 performance, worried that Henry might suffer a fate similar to that of King John. Shortly afterward, escaping new anti-Lutheran laws, Bale left England for the Continent, where he continued to write anti-Catholic tracts.

The play was not forgotten, however. Records indicate that *King Johan* was performed as part of Edward VI's coronation festivities in 1547. In 1558, when Elizabeth I ascended to the throne, Bale returned to England and gained the queen's favor.

She offered him a stipend and wrote on his behalf when he attempted to recover lost property. At some point he amended *King Johan* to praise Elizabeth for "Restoring God's honour to His first force and beauty." When he made that revision and whether the new version was performed remain subjects of scholarly interest. Also of interest to scholarship are the play's significance as a transitional moment in English theater, the task Bale faced in attempting to salvage "Bad King John's" reputation, and the context of theater as propaganda in British Reformation politics, which Philip Schwyzer explores in *The Oxford Handbook of Tudor Drama* (2012).

Because *King Johan* may have been amended as late as 1560, and because the extant 1561 manuscript is partially in Bale's hand and partially in that of a scribe, the play's wording has caused disagreement among scholars. Thora Balslev Blatt's 1968 study, *The Plays of John Bale,* reveals an error in a previous editor's reading of the name of a religious order named by Clergy to show how the church is "beautiful, decked with many holy religions." The 1931 editor, J. H. P. Pafford, reads it as "Solauons," but Blatt argues that the manuscript "clearly shows that Bale has written a rather closed *c* and not an *o*"; the order was thus the same as one identified elsewhere in Bale's writings as "Ordo sclauorum." Such distinctions are helpful in parsing the play's many inside jokes and obscure references, which frequently underscore the contempt held by Bale, Tyndale, and others for the existing chronicles of England written by priests who may have been less than objective.

King John on horseback in a fourteenth-century illustration. King John is the subject of John Bale's 1538 *Kynge Johan,* one of the earliest history plays in English. HIP/ART RESOURCE, NY.

BIBLIOGRAPHY

Sources

Bale, John. *John King of England. The Dramatic Writings of John Bale, Bishop of Ossory.* Ed. John S. Farmer. Guildford: Early English Drama Society, 1966. Print.

Blatt, Thora Balslev. *The Plays of John Bale: A Study of Ideas, Technique, and Style.* Copenhagen: Gad, 1968. Print.

Fairfield, Leslie P. *John Bale: Mythmaker for the English Reformation.* West Lafayette: Purdue UP, 1976. Print.

Harris, Jesse W. *John Bale: A Study in the Minor Literature of the Reformation.* Urbana: U of Illinois P, 1940. Print.

King, John N., "Bale, John (1495–1563)." *Oxford Dictionary of National Biography.* Web. 15 Oct. 2012.

Schwyzer, Philip. "Paranoid History: John Bale's *King Johan.*" *The Oxford Handbook of Tudor Drama.* Eds. Thomas Betteridge and Greg Valker. Oxford: Oxford UP, 2012. Print.

Further Reading

Adams, Barry B. "Doubling in Bale's *King Johan.*" *Studies in Philology* 62.2 (1965): 111–120. *JSTOR.* Web. 14 Oct. 2012.

Bale, John. *John Bale's King Johan.* Ed. Barry B. Adams. San Marino: Huntington Library, 1969. Print.

———. *King Johan.* Ed. J. H. P. Pafford. Oxford: Malone Society for Oxford UP, 1931. Print.

———. "Kynge Johann." *Internet Shakespeare Editions.* U of Victoria, n.d. Web. 15 Oct. 2012.

Cavanagh, Dermot. *Language and Politics in the Sixteenth-Century History Play.* Houndmills: Palgrave Macmillan, 2003. *Google Books.* Web. 15 Oct. 2012.

Happé, Peter. *The Complete Plays of John Bale.* Cambridge: Brewer, 1985. Print.

———. *John Bale.* New York: Twayne / Simon & Schuster Macmillan, 1996. Print.

Gerhardt, Ernst. "'No Quyckar Merchaundyce Than Library Bokes': John Bale's Commodification of Manuscript Culture." *Renaissance Quarterly* 60.2 (2007): 408–433. *JSTOR.* Web. 15 Oct. 2012.

Morey, James H. "The Death of King John in Shakespeare and Bale." *Shakespeare Quarterly* 45.3 (1994): 327–31. *JSTOR.* Web. 15 Oct. 2012.

Pineas, Rainer. "The English Morality Play as a Weapon of Religious Controversy." *Studies in English Literature, 1500–1900* 2.2 (1962): 157–80. *JSTOR.* Web. 15 Oct. 2012.

Media Adaptation

The Life and Death of King John. Dir. David Giles. Perf. Leonard Rossiter, Mary Morris, and William Whymper. British Broadcasting Corporation (BBC), 1984. Television.

Rebecca Rustin

Nineteen Fourteen

Rupert Brooke

+ *Key Facts*

Time Period:
Early 20th Century

Genre:
Poetry

Events:
Outbreak of World War I

Nationality:
English

OVERVIEW

Rupert Brooke's World War I sonnets, collectively known as *Nineteen Fourteen* or *1914,* are a series of five patriotic poems written shortly after the British Empire entered the war. The poems eulogize English soldiers, including those who have not yet died, as national heroes who find repose in a glorious death. Two of the sonnets were printed in the *Times Literary Supplement* in March 1915, and all five were published in the posthumous volume *1914 and Other Poems* (1915). The sonnets resonated with an English public who expected a brief conflict with little threat to the home front. Although the war proved a grueling and protracted struggle, Brooke's work continued to draw admirers during and after the war among critics and poets.

Brooke was serving as a Royal Navy reservist at the time of the sonnets' composition. He saw action in an expedition to Antwerp, Belgium, but he did not experience the horrors of trench warfare that later poets—such as Ivor Gurney and Siegfried Sassoon—would recount. Although Brooke died in April 1915, posthumously he achieved a brief, intense fame as the leading English poet of World War I. His sonnets present an idealistic view of war that later developments, such as poison gas and unrestricted submarine warfare, rendered increasingly untenable. In the 1960s, Wilfred Owen's evocation of harsh winters and mud-slick trenches displaced Brooke's sonnets as the definitive poetic statement of the war's impact; in fact, Owen's lines on "the pity of war" were later inscribed as Brooke's epitaph. Nevertheless, the *1914* sonnets continue to occupy a prominent place in the history of war poetry.

HISTORICAL AND LITERARY CONTEXT

The United Kingdom's declaration of war on August 4, 1914, met with widespread popular approval, a sentiment reinforced by the literature, art, and popular music of the era. Britain entered the war following Germany's invasion of Belgium, of whose sovereignty Britain was a guarantor. The extreme violence against Belgian civilians that accompanied this invasion prompted an angry response in Britain. However, the British government took pains to reassure its citizens that the empire's involvement in the war would be brief and limited; in November 1914 First Lord of the Admiralty Winston Churchill articulated a policy of "business as usual" for British industry.

Brooke was one of nearly a million volunteers to respond to calls for recruits in 1914; he joined the Royal Navy Volunteer Reserve and was deployed to Antwerp. While on sick leave in England, he composed the *1914* sonnets as a reflection of his optimism and moral confidence regarding the war. On Easter Sunday 1915 the dean of St. Paul's Cathedral read Brooke's most famous sonnet, "The Soldier," to quell an anti-war protest in the church. A report on this event in the London *Times,* which included the poem, brought Brooke's war poetry to the public's attention. Brooke's idealism would not be refuted during the poet's lifetime. En route to the Battle of Gallipoli, Brooke contracted septicemia from an infected mosquito bite and died on April 23, 1915. His sonnets would, however, become inseparably linked with the disastrous battle through the efforts of Winston Churchill, who penned an obituary naming Brooke one of "England's noblest sons." Later, as the protracted fighting at Gallipoli failed to achieve a decisive result, it proved expedient for Churchill to promote Brooke's poetic vision of the war as a distraction from the mounting casualties.

During his short life, Brooke associated with many different groups of authors, but he is most commonly classed with the Georgian school of poets, the best known of whom are D. H. Lawrence and Robert Graves. Georgian poetry is characterized by a formal conservatism and frequently by an interest in specifically English natural settings. Both of these traits are evident in the *1914* sonnets, which adopt perhaps the most traditional of English forms, with frequent, wistful returns to a landscape of rippling lakes and soft breezes. Unlike Brooke, however, many Georgians lived to see their idyllic verse tempered by the grim facts of war. Graves is exemplary in this regard. Within the span of a few lines, his poem "1915" shifts from "red poppy floods" to "soul-deadening trenches" and then back to "the quiet of an English wood."

Much of the later poetry of World War I bears Brooke's imprint in that it attempts to qualify or undermine the position articulated in *1914.* Indeed, Owen's "Dulce et Decorum Est," which refutes the "old Lie" that it is sweet and fitting to die for one's country, can be seen as an almost point-for-point disputation of Brooke's sonnets. For example, Brooke reflects on the flowers and fields of England, whereas Owen foregrounds the eerie mists of a gas-laced trench;

Brooke exhibits a zealous patriotism, delivered through a first-person speaker, whereas Owen rebukes "children ardent for some desperate glory." Literary critics during the succeeding century have weighed the merit of celebratory "war poetry," evaluating both Brooke and Owen in this context and ultimately concluding that the latter poet was justified in his pessimism.

THEMES AND STYLE

Rather than portraying warfare as an unpleasant duty, the *1914* sonnets audaciously depict war as in many ways preferable to peace. In the sonnets Brooke suggests that war offers an opportunity to escape the shame and boredom of civilian life and to transmute physical poverty into spiritual largesse. The moral turbidity of peacetime life is typified in Sonnet I ("Peace") by "dirty songs and dreary, / And all the little emptiness of love." Compared to this "cold and weary" world, war appears as a positive refuge, to which the youth in the poem "turn, as swimmers into cleanness leaping." Similarly, in Sonnet II ("Safety") an honorable death is idealized as "a peace unshaken by pain forever," a respite from "the dark tides of the world."

Brooke's poems celebrate English participation in World War I by adopting the personae of idealized soldiers and by exhorting citizens at home to praise and mourn them as heroes. In each case the sonnets emphasize the abstract, moral dimensions of war, employing concrete descriptions not from the battlefield but from a remembered, tranquil English countryside. Sonnet III ("The Dead") is a veritable roll call of heroic abstractions: Holiness, Love, Pain, Honor, and Nobleness all appear, with the latter two personified as guardians of a royal heritage. According to Brooke, those who die in battle gain an ennobled moral stature; their lives are not so much sacrificed as enshrined in the memories of loved ones or as a "richer dust" in the soil itself. The sonnets combine the Christian ideal of sacrifice with the classical ideal of the warrior's noble death. This combination, which gave force to the poems, also embraces the notion of the "beautiful death," an idea that would become the basis for the myth in post–World War I English culture of the lost generation. In a pattern that later poets and critics would view with suspicion, the sonnets carefully avoid references to the physical agents of death and suffering.

In addition, Brooke authorizes his version of English nationalism by alluding to the patriotic speeches in William Shakespeare's English histories, establishing continuity between the historical England of 1399 (*Richard II*) and the nation at war in 1914. Sonnet V ("The Soldier"), for example, echoes the diction and sentiment of John of Gaunt's "This England" speech in act two of *Richard II*. Brooke champions England's natural beauty and scenes of life "under an English heaven"; similarly, in *Richard II* the ailing duke cherishes the English landscape as a "precious stone set in the silver sea" and proclaims it an "other Eden, demi-paradise." An even more striking parallel occurs

PATRIOTIC SONGS OF THE GREAT WAR

Notwithstanding Brooke's disdain for the "dirty songs and dreary" that proliferated in peacetime, British music halls played an important role in attracting recruits and maintaining civilian morale—two purposes shared by Brooke's wartime verses. The most popular music-hall songs of World War I include "It's a Long Way to Tipperary" (1912) and "Keep the Home Fires Burning" (1914), each of which in its own way assures listeners as Brooke's sonnets assure readers. "It's a Long Way to Tipperary" tells of an Irishman who, like Brooke's soldier personae, pines not for the easy comforts of civilian life but for the specific people and places that denote "home." "Keep the Home Fires Burning" expands upon many of the same aspects of patriotism found in Brooke's sonnets, exhorting those left behind to keep courage in the name of the "gallant son[s] of Britain," who are driven by honor and friendship to aid their Continental allies. Reportedly sung during long marches to the front, these songs captured the confidence of a British soldiery who had not yet been wearied by four years of fighting.

in Sonnet III ("The Dead"), which asserts an equality among soldiers that transcends socioeconomic conditions but that can be obtained only via a glorious death in war: "There's none of these," the poet asserts, "so lonely and poor of old, / But, dying, has made us rarer gifts than gold." Virtually the same idea is voiced in *Henry V,* before the famed English victory at Agincourt, when the king declares that "he to-day that sheds his blood with me / Shall be my brother." By associating his appeal to English pride with Shakespeare—the most recognizable of English poets—Brooke appeals to a sense of national unity that transcends distinctions of class and rank.

CRITICAL DISCUSSION

Brooke's sonnets came to be seen as the definitive expression of English sentiment early in the war. Fran Brearton notes that the poems "went through multiple reprintings in 1915–16 alone." The popularity of *1914* was further enhanced by a wartime government hungry for effective propaganda: Churchill, who had entered the Gallipoli conflict as First Lord of the Admiralty, was rapidly losing favor with the public. Edward Marsh, Brooke's literary executor and Churchill's political secretary, helped promote the poet as nothing short of a war hero, a project which Aaron Jaffe (2005) regards as part propaganda, part salesmanship. As noted by Elizabeth Vandiver (2010), Brooke's canonization also bore mythic overtones for early critics, because of both the classical character of his work and his burial on a remote Greek island. A number of formal imitations of the sonnets soon followed, the best known of which was May Herschel-Clarke's "The Mother," penned as an English mother's

YOUR COUNTRY'S CALL

Isn't this worth fighting for?
ENLIST NOW

as "rustic conservatives whose bland week-end verse rightly gave way to the Modernist Movement."

Since the 1970s critics have taken a more nuanced view of Brooke than did the modernists. In his 1971 study, the scholar Timothy Rogers seeks to repair the poet's critical reputation. Rogers's claims, however, have hardly been accepted without contention. Brown's review of Rogers's work, for example, offers a brief debate on Brooke's poetic merits. On a broader historical scale, for many critics Brooke represents the end of a long classical era of "war poetry." In a 2001 essay, Brearton argues that the very idea of a "war poet" signals "a reversion back … to the mythologized and heroic figure of Rupert Brooke." The *1914* sonnets are now widely considered as technically accomplished works undercut by a naive, if not disingenuous, prowar sentiment.

BIBLIOGRAPHY

Sources

Brearton, Fran. "How to Kill: The Poetry of War." *Fortnight* 398 (2001): 10–11. Print.

Brown, Terence. Rev. of *Rupert Brooke: A Reappraisal and Selection,* by Timothy Rogers. *Studies: An Irish Quarterly Review* 60.239–240 (1971): 414–15. Print.

Craik, T. W., ed. *King Henry V.* By William Shakespeare. 3rd ed. London: Arden Shakespeare, 1995. Print.

Forker, Charles R., ed. *King Richard II.* By William Shakespeare. 3rd ed. London: Arden Shakespeare, 2002. Print.

Rogers, Timothy. *Rupert Brooke: A Reappraisal and Selection.* London: Routledge, 1971. Print.

Yeats, William Butler, ed. *The Oxford Book of Modern Verse 1892–1935.* London: Oxford UP, 1936. Print.

Further Reading

Clausson, Nils. "'Perpetuating the Language': Romantic Tradition, the Genre Function, and the Origins of the Trench Lyric." *Journal of Modern Literature* 30.1 (2006): 104–28. Print.

De la Mare, Walter. "Rupert Brooke and the Intellectual Imagination." *New England Review* 20.1 (1999): 191–206. Print.

Delany, Paul. *The Neo-Pagans: Rupert Brooke and the Ideal of Youth.* New York: Free Press, 1987. Print.

Ebbatson, Roger. *An Imaginary England: Nation, Landscape, and Literature, 1840–1920.* Aldershot: Ashgate, 2005. Print.

Horne, John, and Alan Kramer. *German Atrocities, 1914: A History of Denial.* New Haven: Yale UP, 2001. Print.

Jaffe, Aaron. *Modernism and the Culture of Celebrity.* Cambridge: Cambridge UP, 2005. Print.

Lehman, John. *The Strange Destiny of Rupert Brooke.* New York: Holt, Rinehart and Winston, 1980. Print.

Norris, Margot. "Teaching World War I Poetry— Comparatively." *College Literature* 32.3 (2005): 136–53. Print.

Stallworthy, Jon. "Who Was Rupert Brooke?" *Survivors' Songs: From Maldon to the Somme.* Cambridge: Cambridge UP, 2008. Print.

expression of resignation and bravery as her son goes off to war.

As the conflict wore on, however, Brooke's popularity began to wane. Literary portrayals of the war grew darker and more complex, and those who had witnessed the abject conditions on the Western Front provided grim poetic reportage. Soldier-poets, including most famously Owen and Sassoon, wrote with the "benefit" of extensive combat experience that Brooke could not claim. In the decades after the war, Brooke had few critical allies, though the Irish poet William Butler Yeats included him in the *Oxford Book of Modern Verse* (1936); many of Brooke's counterparts had been rejected on the grounds that "passive suffering is not a theme for poetry." Nevertheless, Brooke's work was often dismissed as a specimen of the Georgian style. The critic Terence Brown explains that by midcentury, the Georgian poets had come to be viewed

Vandiver, Elizabeth. *Stand in the Trench, Achilles: Classical Receptions in British Poetry of the Great War.* London: Oxford UP, 2010. Print.

Winn, James Anderson. *The Poetry of War.* Cambridge: Cambridge UP, 2008. Print.

Media Adaptation

Brooke, Rupert. *1914.* Orchestra by Alan Gray. London: Novello and Co., 1919. Musical score.

Michael Hartwell

PARADISE LOST

John Milton

✤ *Key Facts*

Time Period:
Mid- to Late 17th
Century

Genre:
Poetry

Events:
Restoration of the
monarchy and the
Church of England under
Charles II

Nationality:
English

OVERVIEW

Written after the Restoration of Charles II, John Milton's epic poem *Paradise Lost* (1667) explores the fall of Satan and his rebel angels, as well as the fall of Adam and Eve in the Garden of Eden. In richly dense blank verse (unrhymed iambic pentameter), Milton recounts the events that led to human sin and the divine plan that ultimately allows for human salvation. According to Milton's narrator, the goal of the work is "to justify the ways of God to man"—bringing humans to a greater appreciation of God's deeds, knowledge, and compassion. At the same time, Milton develops a compelling portrait of Satan as an articulate and inspiring leader with almost egalitarian views and a seductive pride in his own capabilities. By balancing Satan's perspective with that of God and including the viewpoints of angels and human beings, Milton invites the reader to learn experientially about temptation and grace—effectively promoting what he perceived as a divine agenda.

In the aftermath of the English Protectorate, when Lord Protector Oliver Cromwell's faction had lost the power to govern, Milton published *Paradise Lost* twice: first in a ten-book version (1667) and then in an expanded twelve-book edition (1674). Although he had been allied with the unfashionable Protectorate, his contemporaries still recognized *Paradise Lost* as a rare and significant work: it was the first major epic in English since Sir Edmund Spenser's *Faerie Queene* was published beginning in 1590. Part of the appeal of *Paradise Lost* was its seemingly timeless setting and innocuous subject matter. Since the events of the epic are both cosmic and far removed from Restoration England, Milton (who had previously been incarcerated for his radical viewpoints) could promote his own religious agenda in a way that did not directly threaten the current royalist regime. By elaborating on weighty themes like good and evil, obedience, free will, and the nature of the Trinity, Milton's work subtly advocates for a personal, conscious practice of the Christian faith.

HISTORICAL AND LITERARY CONTEXT

During the Interregnum, after the beheading of King Charles I but before the accession of his son Charles II, England was led by a group of radical Protestants who had seized control of Parliament in late 1648, when their New Model Army forcibly removed members who opposed their ideas. Cromwell, the official lord protector during the Interregnum, had risen to prominence as a member of Parliament and as a soldier during the civil wars. Cromwell may not have originally intended to execute the king, but Charles's refusal to abdicate—coupled with the extensive publicity for his cause in royalist propaganda—left Parliament unable to govern authoritatively while the king lived.

Milton wrote the final version of *Paradise Lost* from about 1658 to 1663, immediately following Cromwell's death and during the gradual restoration of the Stuart monarchy. Previously he had been deeply involved in Interregnum politics. Beginning in 1649, he served as the Latin secretary for the Protectorate, producing works that justified the king's execution and condemned the exercise of tyranny. As a writer of polemical tracts and lyric verse, moreover, he advocated for the right of every person's conscience to remain "unforced," especially during periods of political upheaval. The ability of every citizen to choose a religious-political stance and to stand firm within that position remained one of the writer's major literary themes.

Like many other works from the late seventeenth century, *Paradise Lost* is grounded in biblical evidence and presents Scripture in a way that subtly advocates for a particular religious outlook. Spenser's *Faerie Queene* began this tradition in the Elizabethan era by presenting allegories of religious virtues from a militantly Protestant perspective. As the decades progressed, writers began to use biblical narratives even more explicitly as models for their own work. In 1605 the scripturally inspired work of the French writer Guillaume du Bartas was translated into English by Joshua Sylvester, and later in the century, Milton's contemporary Lucy Hutchinson published *Order and Disorder* (1679), another epic retelling of the Genesis story. Hutchinson's long poem reflects a left-leaning Protestant outlook by advocating decorous, restrained living and using plain but joyous language.

While other biblical epics experienced varying degrees of popularity, none was ultimately as influential as *Paradise Lost*. With an emphatically unrhymed style of poetry, Milton provided a stark contrast to the work of contemporaries like John Dryden, who wrote in catchy, rhymed couplets. Dryden even produced a version of *Paradise Lost* in rhyming couplets, converting it into a trendy Restoration-style piece. Ultimately, however, Milton's brand of extended sentences and enjambed, unrhymed lines would capture the imagination of the English Romantic poets, especially William Blake and William Wordsworth (the latter of whom annotated his personal copy of *Paradise Lost*). These later writers drew inspiration from Milton's blank-verse style and his subject matter, which covers themes of personal agency, guilt, indebtedness, and redemption. A mainstay of modern syllabi, *Paradise Lost* forms a crucial link between these Romantic writers and the medieval and early modern religious poets who preceded Milton.

THEMES AND STYLE

At stake in *Paradise Lost* is the question of how humans (and angels) ought to behave toward God. During a time of religiously inflected warfare in which the royalist faction worshipped in an ornate, high Anglican style and the republican faction disdained the use of elaborate images and liturgies, *Paradise Lost* showed Adam and Eve worshipping innocently in the Garden of Eden, praying in a spontaneous and heartfelt manner. Milton breaks from the republican mainstream in significant ways. First, he posits that members of the Trinity are not coequal or coeternal with the Son of God as the "first" member of "all creation." Second, he argues against the Calvinist doctrine of predestination, stating instead that humans were made "sufficient to have stood, though free to fall." By advocating for free will and an unorthodox understanding of the Trinity, Milton sketches a unique version of biblical truth and then engages in theodicy as he attempts to "justify" his God to his readers.

Part of Milton's theodicy involves creating a "fit audience"—a group of readers committed to learning experientially about God by reading Milton's epic. To educate these willing readers, Milton's first-person narrator writes twelve books filled with long, winding sentences, which must be dissected to reveal a spiritual truth. For example, in describing a charismatic, fallen angel, Milton writes, "Satan exalted sat, by merit rais'd / To that bad eminence." The first line seems to praise Satan, while the next line reveals that his merit has entirely negative consequences. As Stanley Fish argues in *Surprised by Sin*: *The Reader in* Paradise Lost (1997), the process of navigating these long, enjambed lines allows a reader to be "surprised by sin"—experiencing the Fall all over again and thereby coming to realize the necessity of God's grace. This strategy is particularly evident during Book Nine, in which Satan uses complex rhetoric to entice Eve to eat the forbidden fruit. By exposing the susceptibility of humankind on the level of language itself, Milton teaches readers about their own vulnerable nature, bringing them to a better understanding of their need for God.

Even as Milton taps biblical language and ideas, the tone and style of his epic are informed by the

JOHN MILTON: BLINDNESS AND LIGHT

In 1652 Milton lost all vision in his right eye and became almost completely blind. To make matters worse, his wife and son died within a few weeks of each other that same year, and in 1660 Milton landed in prison for his association with the republican cause. Surrounded by these oppressive circumstances, he developed a deeply spiritual attitude toward light, which he expresses in the invocation to Book Three of *Paradise Lost*. "Hail holy Light," he begins, characterizing Creation as a light-filled process. He also laments his own blindness: "[T]hou [light] / Revisit'st not these eyes."

While he expresses resentment for his inability to perceive seasonal changes or the "human face divine," he cites the example of blind poet-prophets like Homer and aspires to emulate their contributions to literature. After wrestling with these contrary impulses, he finally addresses a prayer toward celestial light: "Shine inward, and the mind through all her powers / Irradiate, there plant eyes, all mist from thence / Purge and disperse, that I may see and tell / Of things invisible to mortal sight."

classical tradition. The language of *Paradise Lost* is characterized by epic similes, for example, when Satan's fallen angel comrades are compared through an extended metaphor to swarming bees. The highly formal sentence structure and composition style hearken back to Greek and Latin models of writing, showing Milton's bid to become a great author in the tradition of Homer and Virgil. Like the *Aeneid, Paradise Lost* has twelve books, and like the *Aeneid,* the *Iliad,* and the *Odyssey,* it features frequent invocations to a muse—in this case, Urania, or Holy Light. In this classical context, Milton's work serves a propaganda-like function, proclaiming Milton's rhetorical prowess and bard-like status and promoting plain and honest human relationships with God.

CRITICAL DISCUSSION

Upon publication *Paradise Lost* was well received by Milton's allies. Republican author and member of Parliament Andrew Marvell wrote a laudatory poem about the epic—"On Milton's *Paradise Lost*" (1674)—mentioning Milton's simultaneous "gravity and ease" and his sense of religious decorum: "things divine thou treat'st of in such state / As them preserves, and thee, inviolate." Another friend, Thomas Ellwood, reacted to the work by asking Milton to address the question of "Paradise Found"—thereby inspiring Milton's later work *Paradise Regained* (1671), which covers the temptation of Jesus in the wilderness. Despite the interest of Milton's friends and allies, however, *Paradise Lost* was not a best seller. It took two years to sell the first printing of

1,300 copies, and Milton earned only ten pounds from the epic during his lifetime.

Although Milton's political viewpoints became unpopular during the period when *Paradise Lost* was published, his commitment to liberty and the freedom of individual conscience made his writings inspirational to later generations. In the eighteenth century, revolutionaries in France and America would cite him as a republican precedent. In fact, American political thinkers Benjamin Franklin and John Adams specifically alluded to *Paradise Lost* in their arguments. In England the Romantic poet William Blake wrote *Milton,* a work that—as Cato Marks points out—united aspects of Milton's prose and poetry to emphasize both political radicalism and high aesthetic standards. While praise for *Paradise Lost* and Milton's other works marked the beginning of the Romantic era and incited passion for the sublime and for blank verse, Milton became less fashionable in the nineteenth century. Sir Walter Raleigh called it "a monument to lost ideas."

In recent decades, *Paradise Lost* has become a staple of the Western literary canon, prompting scholarship that has transformed the field of English literature. When Fish published *Surprised by Sin* in 1967, describing the educable reader's reaction to Milton's text, he helped launch the field of reader-response criticism, taking literary studies in a new and promising direction. David Loewenstein points out that *Paradise Lost* is also fruitfully read in conversation with Milton's works of prose—particularly the pieces of propaganda he wrote for Cromwell's government decrying tyranny, demanding liberty, and elevating the position of the individual conscience. Just as the angel Abdiel stood alone against the power of Satan, "unshak'n, unseduc'd, unterrifi'd," the conscientious objectors that Milton highlights in his prose are heroic, if isolated, figures who fight on behalf of their beliefs.

BIBLIOGRAPHY

Sources

Campbell, Gordon. "Milton, John (1608–1674)." *Oxford Dictionary of National Biography.* Oxford: Oxford UP, 2004. Web. 17 Sept. 2012.

Fish, Stanley. *Surprised by Sin: The Reader in* Paradise Lost. 2nd ed. London: Macmillan, 1997. Print.

Loewenstein, David. "From Politics to Faith in the Great Poems?" *Visionary Milton: Essays on Prophecy and Violence.* Ed. John T. Shawcross and David V. Urban. Pittsburgh: Medieval and Renaissance Literary Studies, 2010. 269–85. Print.

Marks, Cato. "Writings of the Left Hand: William Blake Forges a New Political Aesthetic." *Huntington Library Quarterly* 74.1 (2011): 43–70. Print.

Milton, John. *Paradise Lost. Complete Poems and Major Prose.* 2nd ed. Ed. Merritt Y. Hughes. Indianapolis: Hackett, 2003. Print.

Further Reading

Dowling, Paul M. "Paradise Lost and Politics Gained: Milton Rewrites Scripture." *Cithara: Essays in the Judeo-Christian Tradition* 44.2 (2005): 16–31. Print.

Lewalski, Barbara Kiefer. "*Paradise Lost* and Milton's Politics." *Milton Studies* 38 (2000): 141–68. Print.

Lieb, Michael, and John T. Shawcross, eds. *Achievements of the Left Hand: Essays on the Prose of John Milton.* Amherst: U of Massachusetts P, 1974. Print.

Morrill, John. "Cromwell, Oliver (1599–1658)." *Oxford Dictionary of National Biography.* Oxford: Oxford UP, 2004. Web. 4 Oct. 2012.

Williams, Michael. "'More Impious than Milton's Satan?': Satan, the Romantics, and Byron." *English Studies in Africa: A Journal of the Humanities* 49.2 (2006): 109–122. Print.

Media Adaptation

Paradise Lost. Dir. Vanessa Tovell. Perf. Keith Frederick. Princeton: Films for the Humanities & Sciences, 1998. VHS.

Nancy Simpson Younger

Opposite page:
The Expulsion from Paradise, by Giuseppe Cesari. Adam and Eve being cast from the Garden of Eden is the central theme in *Paradise Lost.* V&A IMAGES, LONDON/ART RESOURCE, NY.

"PAUL REVERE'S RIDE"

Henry Wadsworth Longfellow

OVERVIEW

Henry Wadsworth Longfellow's poem "Paul Revere's Ride" (1860), set at the start of the Revolutionary War (1775–83), presents a fictionalized account of the Boston silversmith Paul Revere's midnight ride to warn Massachusetts militiamen in Lexington and Concord of British troop advancements. In thirteen stanzas featuring strong end rhymes and the easy reading style typical of Longfellow's most successful poems, "Paul Revere's Ride" conflates the daring efforts of several historical figures to create the heroic Revere. Published in the *Atlantic Monthly* during the buildup to the U.S. Civil War (1861–65), Longfellow's mythologized account of Revere's ride was intended to stir patriotic sentiments across the nation and to encourage readers to defend the Union with the same courage and zeal that the poet ascribes to his hero. The poem also contains antislavery undertones that reflect Longfellow's abolitionist principles.

On December 2, 1859, the abolitionist leader John Brown was executed for treason against the State of Virginia. Following Brown's death, Longfellow began searching for the proper imagery to express his antislavery and pro-Union positions. A visit to Boston's Old North Church in April 1860, where eighty-five years earlier Revere had arranged for lanterns to be used to indicate British troop movements, inspired Longfellow to equate the war for American independence with the coming war to end slavery and preserve the Union. The resulting poem was well received by readers sympathetic to the Union cause, gaining even wider readership after its inclusion in an 1863 collection of Longfellow's poetry, and it succeeded in elevating the little-known Revere to the status of national hero. "Paul Revere's Ride" has since become standard reading in middle-school curricula, not only because of its accessibility and demonstration of early American poetic style but also as a starting point for lessons on the Revolutionary War.

HISTORICAL AND LITERARY CONTEXT

In the spring of 1775, the conflict between Great Britain and the citizens of its Massachusetts Bay Colony reached a tipping point. With the "Boston Tea Party" in 1773, colonists had protested a tax on imported tea, dumping several shiploads of tea into Boston Harbor. The British responded by closing the port, forcing local residents to house British troops, and dissolving the local government. Revere, a member of the Massachusetts Committee of Safety and a participant in the Boston Tea Party, then secretly began to deliver updates on British activities to other colonies throughout the Northeast. Matters came to a head on April 18, 1775, as General Thomas Gage, commander of the British garrison in Boston, dispatched 1,000 troops to Concord to seize the local militia's weapons. Revere and another rider, William Dawes, set out from Boston under cover of darkness to warn residents in Lexington (where they would be joined by a third rider, Samuel Prescott) and neighboring Concord. Though Revere was detained (and subsequently released) by the British after reaching Lexington, Prescott avoided capture and reached Concord before their arrival, and the forewarned Concord militia succeeded in forcing a British retreat to Boston. The Revolutionary War had begun.

"Paul Revere's Ride" was published eighty-five years later on December 20, 1860. On that same day, South Carolina seceded from the Union in response to the election of President Abraham Lincoln, who opposed the expansion of slavery into the western territories; ten other Southern states soon followed suit. Ironically, South Carolina repeatedly referenced the American Revolution in its declaration of secession. Longfellow's poem was an attempt to frame the upcoming fight to preserve the Union as an extension of the courageous efforts of Revere and his fellow patriots during the Revolutionary War before the Confederacy could claim that narrative as its own.

When "Paul Revere's Ride" was published, its subject was little more than a rarely mentioned local legend: "Hardly a man is still alive," Longfellow writes in the first stanza, "Who remembers that famous day and year." However, the poem's portrayal in heroic terms of "the bloody work" on which "the fate of a nation" once depended ignited Northerners' patriotic zeal and helped brace them for the rampant destruction and loss of life to come. Other Northern poets made similar comparisons between the aims of the Revolution and those of the Union cause. In his "Boston Hymn" (1863), Ralph Waldo Emerson reminds readers that the colonists had rejected "tyrants great and tyrants small" in favor of a freedom that can "break your bonds and masterships" and "unchain the slave." In "The Centenarian's Tale" (1865), Walt

Whitman describes a conversation between an aging Revolutionary War veteran and a young Union soldier in which "the two, the past and present, have interchanged."

Perhaps no other poem of the period, however, links past to present, battles fought with battles to come, as does "Paul Revere's Ride." David Hackett Fischer notes in *Paul Revere's Ride* (1994) that "the insistent beat of Longfellow's meter reverberated through the North like a drum roll," stirring up the will to fight once more for the future of the nation. Unlike many other Civil War poems, "Paul Revere's Ride" continued to influence Americans in the postbellum period, making its way into elementary and middle-school curricula (despite its historical inaccuracies). Throughout the country in the late nineteenth and early twentieth centuries, monuments and works of art inspired by Longfellow's poem were dedicated to Revere. Although Longfellow was already among the most popular American poets when "Paul Revere's Ride" was published, none of his other poems has become so ingrained in the American mythos or inspired as many parodies and responses, ranging from Helen F. Moore's "The Midnight Ride of William Dawes" (1896) to Shel Silverstein's "Forgetful Paul Revere" (1996).

THEMES AND STYLE

"Paul Revere's Ride" begins with the lines "Listen my children and you will hear / Of the midnight ride of Paul Revere," signaling the speaker's intention to treat the poem as a kind of oral history passed down from one generation to the next. This breathless didacticism not only gives the speaker—and by extension the poem itself—an aura of historical and moral authority, but it also imbues the work with a swift pace and fluidity meant to evoke Revere's "steed flying fearless and fleet" and to elicit a sense of urgency in its readers. In this manner the poem is transformed into a literal and metaphorical recreation of Revere's ride, rumbling across the literary landscape, rousing readers from the slumber of indifference and alerting them to another "hour of darkness and peril and need."

Just as Longfellow amplifies Revere's heroism by attributing to him the deeds of at least three patriots, the poet explicitly links the Revolutionary War and the coming Civil War by collapsing past, present, and future in the work into an ethereal realm of living history. Because "hardly a man is still alive" to bear witness to the events described, the world of the poem is inhabited by ghosts and specters of the past: Revere awaits his signal while pondering "the dead, / In their night encampment on the hill" and is momentarily enwrapped by "the secret dread / Of the lonely belfry and the dead." He crosses the Charles River, where a British man-o-war is described as "A phantom ship"; even the buildings he passes on his ride "Gaze at him with a spectral glare." The poem is haunted not only by the ghosts of the past but also by those of patriots who will at some future time give their lives in service of the Union: in Concord sleeps an unidentified man "Who that day would be lying dead / Pierced by a British musket ball."

The historian Jill Lepore explains that "'Paul Revere's Ride' is a poem about waking the dead. The dead are Northerners, roused to war. But the dead are also the enslaved, entombed in their slavery." Longfellow acknowledges that the fight for universal freedom did not end with the Revolutionary War, nor was it likely to end at the conclusion of the coming Civil War. Revere's rallying cry, one "of defiance, and not of fear," is bound like the voices of fallen soldiers and slaves alike to "echo for evermore / … borne on the night-wind of the Past, / Through all our history, to the last." Longfellow ends the poem on a note of inclusive optimism, asserting that "the people will awaken," bolstered by the bravery of their ancestors, to defend the causes of liberty and democracy, whenever they are threatened.

CRITICAL DISCUSSION

"Paul Revere's Ride" was immediately identified as a call to arms by sympathetic Northerners who, like Longfellow, recognized the inevitability of the Civil War and the unwavering resolve required to keep the Union intact. The poem's popularity grew when it was included, under the title of "The Landlord's Tale," as the first chapter in the collection *Tales of a Wayside Inn* (1863), which sold out almost immediately and underwent two further printings over the next decade. Fischer points out that "New England antiquarians responded to Longfellow's poem with expressions of high indignation for its gross inaccuracy," citing the historian Charles Hudson's comment, made in 1868, that "we have heard of poetic license, but have always understood that this sort of latitude … should not extend to historic facts." Nevertheless, "Paul Revere's Ride" was so thoroughly integrated into the folklore surrounding the country's origins in the years after the Civil War, when the nation sought to heal the deep divisions between North and South by appealing to their common heritage, that even its historical falsities soon became a point of national pride.

Even as the turn of the century neared and as Civil War tensions began to dissipate somewhat, the poem was seen as a valuable teaching tool in American classrooms. "Just as the poem made the real events of 1775 irrelevant, so too was its original cultural work as a Civil War poem quickly forgotten," writes Angela Sorby in her *Schoolroom Poets*. "It is in this context—in the context of a secular classroom with a mandate to strengthen the Union—," she continues, "that 'Paul Revere's Ride' became an important American poem." This enduring popularity can be partially explained by the apparent simplicity of Longfellow's verse, which lends itself to memorization and recitation. This easy style, however, has also contributed to a steady decline in critical esteem among serious scholars of literature,

PRIMARY SOURCE

EXCERPT FROM "PAUL REVERE'S RIDE"

Listen my children and you shall hear

Of the midnight ride of Paul Revere,

On the eighteenth of April, in Seventy-five;

Hardly a man is now alive

Who remembers that famous day and
year.

He said to his friend, "If the British
march

By land or sea from the town to-night,

Hang a lantern aloft in the belfry arch

Of the North Church tower as a signal
light,—

One if by land, and two if by sea;

And I on the opposite shore will be,

Ready to ride and spread the alarm

Through every Middlesex village and
farm,

For the country folk to be up and to arm."

Then he said "Good-night!" and with
muffled oar

Silently rowed to the Charlestown shore,

Just as the moon rose over the bay,

Where swinging wide at her moorings lay

The Somerset, British man-of-war;

A phantom ship, with each mast and spar

Across the moon like a prison bar,

And a huge black hulk, that was magnified

By its own reflection in the tide.

Then he climbed the tower of the Old
North Church,

By the wooden stairs, with stealthy tread,

To the belfry chamber overhead,

And startled the pigeons from their perch

On the sombre rafters, that round him made

Masses and moving shapes of shade,—

By the trembling ladder, steep and tall,

To the highest window in the wall,

Where he paused to listen and look down

A moment on the roofs of the town

And the moonlight flowing over all.

Beneath, in the churchyard, lay the dead,

In their night encampment on the hill,

Wrapped in silence so deep and still

That he could hear, like a sentinel's
tread,

The watchful night-wind, as it went

Creeping along from tent to tent,

And seeming to whisper, "All is well!"

A moment only he feels the spell

Of the place and the hour, and the secret
dread

Of the lonely belfry and the dead;

For suddenly all his thoughts are bent

On a shadowy something far away,

Where the river widens to meet the bay,—

A line of black that bends and floats

On the rising tide like a bridge of boats.

Meanwhile, impatient to mount and ride,

Booted and spurred, with a heavy stride

On the opposite shore walked Paul
Revere.

Now he patted his horse's side,

Now he gazed at the landscape far and
near,

Then, impetuous, stamped the earth,

And turned and tightened his saddle girth;

But mostly he watched with eager search

The belfry tower of the Old North Church,

As it rose above the graves on the hill,

Lonely and spectral and sombre and still.

And lo! as he looks, on the belfry's height

A glimmer, and then a gleam of light!

He springs to the saddle, the bridle he
    turns,

But lingers and gazes, till full on his sight

A second lamp in the belfry burns.

A hurry of hoofs in a village street,

A shape in the moonlight, a bulk in the
    dark,

And beneath, from the pebbles, in
    passing, a spark

Struck out by a steed flying fearless and
    fleet;

That was all! And yet, through the gloom
    and the light,

The fate of a nation was riding that
    night;

And the spark struck out by that steed, in
    his flight,

Kindled the land into flame with its heat.

He has left the village and mounted the
    steep,

And beneath him, tranquil and broad and
    deep,

Is the Mystic, meeting the ocean tides;

And under the alders that skirt its edge,

Now soft on the sand, now loud on the
    ledge,

Is heard the tramp of his steed as he
    rides.

It was one by the village clock,

When he galloped into Lexington.

He saw the gilded weathercock

Swim in the moonlight as he passed,

And the meeting-house windows, black
    and bare,

Gaze at him with a spectral glare,

As if they already stood aghast

At the bloody work they would look
    upon.

It was two by the village clock,

When he came to the bridge in Concord
    town.

He heard the bleating of the flock,

And the twitter of birds among the
    trees,

And felt the breath of the morning
    breeze

Blowing over the meadow brown.

And one was safe and asleep in his bed

Who at the bridge would be first to fall,

Who that day would be lying dead,

Pierced by a British musket ball.

You know the rest. In the books you have
    read

How the British Regulars fired and fled,—

How the farmers gave them ball for ball,

From behind each fence and farmyard
    wall,

Chasing the redcoats down the lane,

Then crossing the fields to emerge
    again

Under the trees at the turn of the road,

And only pausing to fire and load.

So through the night rode Paul Revere;

And so through the night went his cry of
    alarm

To every Middlesex village and farm,—

A cry of defiance, and not of fear,

A voice in the darkness, a knock at the
    door,

And a word that shall echo for evermore!

For, borne on the night-wind of the Past,

Through all our history, to the last,

In the hour of darkness and peril and
    need,

The people will waken and listen to hear

The hurrying hoof-beats of that steed,

And the midnight message of Paul Revere.

Portrait of Paul Revere. Although it contains many historical inaccuracies, "Paul Revere's Ride" created a national legend. © GL ARCHIVE/ ALAMY.

not only for "Paul Revere's Ride" but for all of Longfellow's once-celebrated works. Nevertheless, despite its loose treatment of fact and out-of-fashion literary style, the poem retains its status as a touchstone of American history. Ray Raphael notes that "Longfellow himself made history in two ways: he conjured events that never happened, and he established a new patriotic ritual. For nearly a century to follow, nearly every school child in the United States would hear or recite 'Paul Revere's Ride.'"

Longfellow's fall from favor among modern critics has resulted in a general lack of recent literary studies of the work, though there was a brief period of renewed appreciation surrounding the 150th anniversary of the poem in 2010. Lepore points out that "decades of schoolroom recitation have not only occluded the poem's meaning but have also made it exceptionally serviceable as a piece of political propaganda, not least because political propaganda and juvenilia have rather a lot in common." Indeed, the myth of Revere's ride is frequently invoked for political purposes of all sorts, and a failure to recall, however vaguely, the poem's central narrative is seen as borderline un-American. During the 2008 presidential election, for example, the vice presidential candidate Sarah Palin was roundly panned for claiming that Revere "warned the British that they weren't gonna be takin' away our

arms." The resulting uproar proved how central to the American identity Longfellow's account of Revere's ride has become and hinted at the power of poetic narratives to shape our understanding of history and its bearing upon our lives.

BIBLIOGRAPHY

Sources

Emerson, Ralph Waldo. *Ralph Waldo Emerson: Collected Poems and Translations.* Ed. Harold Bloom and Paul Kane. New York: Literary Classics of the U.S., 1994. Print.

Fischer, David Hackett. *Paul Revere's Ride.* New York: Oxford UP, 1994. Print.

Lepore, Jill. "How Longfellow Woke the Dead." *American Scholar* 81 (2011): 2–15. Print.

Longfellow, Henry Wadsworth. *Henry Wadsworth Longfellow: Poems and Other Writings.* New York: Literary Classics of the U.S., 2000. Print.

Raphael, Ray. *Founding Myths: Stories That Hide Our Patriotic Past.* New York: New, 2004. Print.

Sorby, Angela. *Schoolroom Poets: Childhood and the Place of American Poetry, 1865–1917.* Durham: U of New Hampshire P, 2005. Print.

Whitman, Walt. *Complete Poetry and Selected Prose.* New York: Literary Classics of the U.S., 1982. Print.

Further Reading

Martello, Robert. *Midnight Ride, Industrial Dawn: Paul Revere and the Growth of American Enterprise.* Baltimore: Johns Hopkins UP, 2010. Print.

Middlekauff, Robert. *The Glorious Cause: The American Revolution, 1763–1789.* New York: Oxford UP, 2005. Print.

Miller, Joel. *The Revolutionary Paul Revere.* Nashville: Thomas Nelson, 2010. Print.

"Overview: 'Paul Revere's Ride.'" *Poetry for Students.* Vol. 2. Ed. Marie Rose Napierkowski. Detroit: Gale, 1998. *Literature Resource Center.* Web. 17 Aug. 2012.

Ruland, Richard. "Longfellow and the Modern Reader." *English Journal* 55.6 (1966): 661–68. Print.

Triber, Jayne E. *A True Republican: The Life of Paul Revere.* Amherst: U of Massachusetts P, 1998. Print.

Media Adaptations

The Midnight Ride of Paul Revere. Dir. Charles Brabin. Perf. Augustus Phillips, Carlton S. King, and Harry Linson. Edison Company, 1914. Film.

The Midnight Ride of Paul Revere. Dir. Charles J. Brabin. Cast Augustus Phillips, Carlton King, Richard Tucker et al. United States: K.E.S.E., 1917. Film.

Jacob Schmitt

THE PEACH BLOSSOM FAN

Kong Shangren

OVERVIEW

Composed by Kong Shangren in the early decades of the Qing dynasty, *Taohua shan* (1699; *The Peach Blossom Fan*) is a drama that portrays the unraveling of a romantic relationship during the political upheaval in China at the end of the seventeenth century. Set between 1643 and 1646, as the decadent and corrupt Ming dynasty gave way after nearly three hundred years to the invading Manchus and the new Qing order, the play revolves around the ill-fated romance of two star-crossed lovers, the poet Hou Chaozong and the courtesan Li Xiangjun. With forty scenes and more than thirty characters, many of whom are grounded in historical precedent, *The Peach Blossom Fan* is a sprawling and complex drama that makes a moralistic call for a return to Confucian ideals after an extensive period of declining political and personal integrity in China.

After it was completed in 1699, *The Peach Blossom Fan* was rapidly disseminated and widely performed and mimicked. However, it also drew the ire of the new Manchu imperial leadership for its lament for the golden age of the Ming dynasty and for traditional Confucian values. As a result, Kong was dismissed from his position as a scholar within the Imperial Academy soon after *The Peach Blossom Fan*'s initial performance for the Qing emperor. The drama reflects a growing consensus that the Ming dynasty's decline and eventual downfall after centuries of prosperity and vitality was largely the product of the abuse of power among the dynasty's elite. Today *The Peach Blossom Fan* is widely admired not only for its historical insight but also for its poeticism and artfulness. Considered a canonical work of Chinese drama, Kong's play is an invaluable document of the Ming empire's political, cultural, and moral decline.

HISTORICAL AND LITERARY CONTEXT

When it fell in 1644, the Ming dynasty had ruled for 276 years. During that period, Chinese political and social life was characterized by its stability and orderliness at the expense of significant growth and advancement. By the early seventeenth century, however, the dynasty was in rapid decline due to widespread governmental corruption, factional conflict among the powerful, and a series of unstable rulers. Several famines catalyzed a movement for rebellion, which in 1644 toppled the dynasty. However, the rebels were soon defeated by the Chinese general Wu San-kuei, who invited the Manchurian empire to take control of China. The Manchus quickly took over northern China and established the Qing dynasty. Meanwhile, members of the Ming court fled in shambles to Nanking and attempted to reestablish their rule. Within a few months, however, the Manchus had conquered the south and finished off the Ming dynasty forever. It was this last, desperate attempt to save the Ming dynasty that provided Kong with the material for *The Peach Blossom Fan*.

By the time Kong wrote *The Peach Blossom Fan* in 1699, the Qing dynasty was firmly entrenched in China, but the cause of the Ming collapse was still a source of much speculation and regret among many Chinese, who were now living with foreigners occupying the imperial throne. By the 1690s, although there were a few elderly people who could recall life in Ming China, the old order had been largely relegated to the historical past. Kong was born in 1648, three years after the Ming collapse, and was a descendant of the Chinese philosopher Confucius. Kong spent many years as a scholar of his influential ancestor. An authority on ancient rites and music, he was made a doctor of the Imperial Academy by the Qing emperor Kangxi. In writing the play, Kong interviewed Ming loyalists and extensively researched the historical events of the fall of the Ming dynasty and Ming loyalist resistance. Thus, the drama, when it was completed after three revisions, offers a warning against the kind of institutional and personal immorality and corruption that led to the Ming collapse.

In form and content, *The Peach Blossom Fan* is representative of the dramatic works produced at the end of the seventeenth century in southern China. Unlike the drama of northern China, which was characterized by a four-act structure and a narrative focus on a single character, the drama of southern China during this era was loose and long and featured large, ensemble casts. With its forty scenes and thirty-one principle characters, *The Peach Blossom Fan* is typical of this regional dramatic form. Its focus on the Ming-Qing transition and the lasting legacy of the Ming Empire was common to early Qing literature from throughout China—including firsthand accounts, memoirs, reenactments, and veiled allegories. *The Peach Blossom*

✣ *Key Facts*

Time Period:
Late 17th Century

Genre:
Play

Events:
Downfall of the Ming dynasty

Nationality:
Chinese

KUNQU AND CHINESE OPERA

The Peach Blossom Fan has been regarded as a paragon of kunqu-style opera. *Kunqu* refers to one of nearly four hundred styles of region-ally developed operatic forms in China; however, it stands out as the mother of traditional Chinese opera and one of the oldest and most influential forms. Emerging from the Kunshan region in the Jiangsu province, the style dates from the late Yuan dynasty (c. fourteenth century), when it was pioneered by musician Gu Jian. Combining music of the area with local dialect, Gu performed and improved *Nanxi* oper-atic style to create kunqu. The style's rhythms have been called "mild, smooth, and melodious," typically accompanied by a reed instrument; bamboo flute; and *pipa,* or Chinese lute.

In the early Ming dynasty, musicians formalized and distilled the style, which also broadened its appeal. The success of Liang Shengyu's *Wanshaji,* an early kunqu opera, established the style's *Kunquiang* rhythm scheme as one of the four primary operatic musical tunes, char-acterized by slow and elaborate melodies. During the Ming dynasty, kunqu became a popular operatic form throughout all of China. However, as tastes changed in the early Qing dynasty, kunqu gave way to other styles, and by the early twentieth century the form had almost disappeared. In 2001 the United Nations Educational, Scientific and Cultural Organization (UNESCO) recognized kunqu's vast influ-ence on cultural works and ensured the preservation of kunqu pieces in the future.

Fan stands out because it directly deals with the Ming collapse. Formally, the play belongs to the *kunqu* style of Chinese opera, which dominated in the sixteenth and seventeenth centuries. The play is often compared to Hong Sheng's *The Palace of Eternal Life* (1688), also a historical kunqu that interweaves love and politics.

In the centuries following its illustrious debut, *The Peach Blossom Fan* cemented its place in the canon of Chinese drama and was revived and revised at vari-ous times for its propagandistic potential. A major success for Kong, the play was passed around among Qing courtiers and performed throughout the realm. It soon became a classic piece of Chinese theater and today is regarded as a masterpiece of kunqu-style drama. After falling into obscurity, the play was reis-sued by late-Qing scholar Liang Qichao in the early twentieth century. Liang reframed the play as a work of ethnic nationalism, capitalizing on Kong's warn-ing that the enemy within can bring about a nation's demise. The play has been subject to numerous adap-tations, including rewritings that set the lovers in World War II-era China. In 1937, for example, the playwright Ouyang Yuqian rewrote the drama's end-ing so that Hou surrenders to, rather than resists, the Manchus. Ouyang's revision was meant as an indict-ment of the contemporary Chinese traitor and Japa-nese collaborationist Wang Jingwei.

THEMES AND STYLE

The central theme of *The Peach Blossom Fan* is that moral decay leads to personal turmoil and political collapse. Aiming to deflate the glorified Ming dynasty but praise its loyal subjects, Kong portrays the fall as an inevitable outcome of the fecklessness of the ruling elite and the loss of traditional Confucian ideals. The fate of the play's protagonists, Hou and Li, whose love is tragically undone by the circumstances of the Ming collapse, is indicative of the human cost of institu-tional corruption. The eponymous peach blossom fan also proves a powerful symbol of this theme. Initially a love token from Hou, it is splattered with Li's blood when she attempts suicide after being separated from Hou and being forced to marry another man. Amid the devastation of dynastic collapse, the lovers' fervor is depicted as typical of the imprudence that caused the Ming downfall. At the play's end, the lovers each repair to monastic life and temperance prevails.

The play achieves its rhetorical effect through appeals to an underlying national morality that must be preserved for the prosperity and stability of Chinese society and culture. One way in which Kong makes this appeal is by selecting as his protagonist Hou, who had been a prominent member of the Revival Club, a group devoted to returning China to a foundation of Confucian ideals. As a result of their critique of ram-pant corruption, members of the Revival Club were nearly wiped out by the Ming emperor Wei Chung-hsien. In selecting this historical figure as his play's tragic hero, Kong emphasizes the notion that the Ming collapse was an outcome not of Manchu aggression or of blind fate but of a deterioration of values that remained integral to Chinese identity and prosperity.

The Peach Blossom Fan adheres to the style of southern Chinese dramatic works. Classified as a kunqu-style opera, it is marked by a lyrical poetic structure, choreography, singing parts, traditional cos-tumes, and an extensive length. The work is identified as a masterpiece for its skillful use of kunqu conven-tions, which critic Chun-jo Liu in the *Journal of Asian Studies* (1977) describes as "glorious" and "graceful." As a dramatic work, *The Peach Blossom Fan* is intended for live performance, and the original Chinese work includes several musical interludes. Nevertheless, the tone of the play is sober. In some of the first lines of the prologue, the master of ceremonies sings a lament: "I extirpate old sorrow from my breast, / And where there's wine and song I'm apt to linger. / When filial duty and loyalty reign, the universe will thrive / And the fruit of longevity grow superfluous." As the play proceeds and recounts the unraveling of not only a great love but also a great dynasty, *The Peach Blossom Fan* assumes a melancholic and elegiac mood.

CRITICAL DISCUSSION

When *The Peach Blossom Fan* first appeared in 1699, it was well received by audiences from all echelons of society. Extremely popular, the play had a significant impact on spectators, allowing them to come to terms with the lasting effects of the Ming downfall. Audiences expressed a deep emotional resonance. Lynn Struve in *Chinese Literature: Essays, Articles Reviews* (1980) quotes censor-in-chief Li Nan as stating, "Viewing *The Peach Blossom Fan* is like gazing at rare treasures. The heart should be stilled as signs of pleasure and approval come forth." Struve writes that even Emperor Kangxi was moved, as he "stamped his feet, frowned and declared that although Emperor Zhu Yousong did not want to perish, he could not escape his fate." After initial performances in 1699, the production toured the country, playing to packed theaters. However, both playwright and play soon fell out of favor; Shangren was exiled from the Imperial Court for unknown reasons and operatic fashion changed.

Despite falling into obscurity during the nineteenth century, *The Peach Blossom Fan* cemented its place in the canon of Chinese literary history after its rediscovery in the early twentieth century and has since been lauded as the "swan song" of southern dramatic styles and as an encapsulation the Ming-Qing dynastic transition era. One of only a few dozen kunqu operas still performed regularly, *The Peach Blossom Fan* continues to dazzle audiences in the twenty-first century as contemporary performances highlight the piece's lyrical fluidity and its artistic treatment of sensitive issues. Scholars also enthusiastically greeted the first English-language translation, completed in 1976 by Ch'en Shih-hsiang, Harold Acton, and Cyril Birch.

Much scholarship has focused on the role of history in *The Peach Blossom Fan*, as well as on the play's role in history. As a fictional historical account, the play is often looked to as a representation of the late Ming era and has been included in scholarly discussions of that genre's parameters and success. Scholar Tina Lu in *Persons, Roles, and Minds: Identity in Peony Pavilion and Peach Blossom Fan* (2001) dismisses questions of historical accuracy, instead considering the representation of identity and cultural roles. Wai-yee Li asserts in the *Journal of the American Oriental Society* (1995) that the play destabilizes a definitive sense of history "by drawing attention to how the present produces and organizes the past"; in doing so "the play defines the conditions of historical understanding, articulating time as the ambivalence that affects historical knowledge." Li asserts that the temporal distance between the events portrayed and the production of the play is central to the play's success and its continued relevance.

BIBLIOGRAPHY

Sources

Li, Wai-yee. "The Representation of History in the Peach Blossom Fan." *Journal of the American Oriental Society* 115.3 (1995): 421–33. Print.

Liu, Chun-Jo. Rev. of *The Peach Blossom Fan*, by K'ung Shang-jen. *Journal of Asian Studies* 37.1 (1977): 97–99. Print.

Lu, Tina. "Introduction to *Taohua shan*." *Persons, Roles, and Minds: Identity in Peony Pavilion and Peach Blossom Fan*. Stanford: Stanford UP, 2001. 145–59. Print.

Shang-jen, K'ung. *The Peach Blossom Fan*. Trans. Chen Shih-hsiang, Harold Acton, and Cyril Birch. Berkeley: U California P, 1976. Print.

Struve, Lynn A. "History and The Peach Blossom Fan." *Chinese Literature: Essays, Articles, Reviews* 2.1 (1980): 55–72. Print.

Further Reading

Li, Wai-yee. "Early Qing to 1723." *The Cambridge History of Chinese Literature*. Vol. 2. Ed. Kang-I Sun Chang and Stephen Owen. Cambridge: Cambridge UP, 2010: 239–44. Print.

Owen, Stephen. "'I Don't Want to Act as Emperor Any More': Finding the Genuine in *Peach Blossom Fan*." *Trauma and Transcendence in Early Qing Literature*. Ed. W. L. Idema, Wai-yee Li, and Ellen Widmer. Cambridge: Harvard UP, 2006. 488–512. Print.

Strassberg, Richard E. *The World of K'ung Shang-jen*. New York: Columbia UP, 1983. Print.

A silk painting depicting two mandarins of the Ming dynasty court. Kong Shangren wanted to make clear the historical lessons of the collapse of the Ming dynasty through *The Peach Blossom Fan*. GIANNI DAGLI ORTI/ THE ART ARCHIVE AT ART RESOURCE, NY.

Tu, Lien-che. "K'ung Shang-jen." *Eminent Chinese of the Ch'ing Period.* Vol. 1. Ed. Arthur W. Hummel. Washington, DC: U.S. Government Printing Office, 1943. 434–35. Print.

Volpp, Sophie. "The Theatricality of the 'Vernacular' in Kong Shangren's *Taohua Shan* (*The Peach Blossom Fan*)." *Worly Stage: Theatricality in Seventeenth-Century China.* Cambridge: Harvard UP, 2011. Print.

Wang, C. H. "The Double Plot of *T'ao-hua shan.*" *Journal of the American Oriental Society* 110.1 (1990): 9–18. Print.

Zeitlin, Judith T. "'Notes of Flesh' and the Courtesan's Song in Seventeenth-Century China." *The Courtesan's Arts: Cross-Cultural Perspectives.* Ed. Martha Feldman and Bonnie Gordon. Oxford UP, 2006. 92–95. Print.

Media Adaptation

Peach Blossom Fan. Dir. Jing Sun. Perf. Wangdanfeng and Feng Zhe. Xi'an Film Studio, 1963. Film.

Elizabeth Boeheim

PRISON WRITINGS
My Life Is My Sun Dance

Leonard Peltier

OVERVIEW

Published in 1999, *Prison Writings: My Life Is My Sun Dance,* a memoir by Leonard Peltier, reflects on the author's role in the notorious 1975 slaying of two government agents during a shoot-out between the FBI and the American Indian Movement (AIM) on the Pine Ridge Reservation in South Dakota. An Anishinabe-Dakota activist, Peltier claimed he was innocent; however, he was sentenced to two consecutive life sentences in prison. Presenting himself as a warrior who was framed by the FBI and was sacrificed while fighting for his people, he situates his personal story in the vast history of American Indian struggles with the U.S. government over lands and cultural practices. In a tone that is both political and spiritual, the memoir openly makes a case for Peltier's innocence and concludes with a plea by Peltier's editor and collaborator on behalf of the Leonard Peltier Defense Committee.

At the time *Prison Writings* appeared, the story of Peltier as a likely victim of wrongful imprisonment was already well known due to two works: *In the Spirit of Crazy Horse* (1983), Peter Matthiessen's nonfiction book examining the FBI's war on AIM, and *Incident at Oglala* (1992), Michael Apted's documentary film about the Pine Ridge shoot-out. As such, *Prison Writings* was a highly anticipated work. Reviewers, giving it a sympathetic and enthusiastic reception, compared it favorably to the prison memoirs of Mahatma Ghandi, Martin Luther King Jr., and Nelson Mandela. As a polemic published when Peltier was awaiting the verdict on a plea for presidential clemency, the book allocates to Peltier a heroic role, one intended to be emblematic of the plight of subjugated and marginalized peoples everywhere.

HISTORICAL AND LITERARY CONTEXT

Prison Writings speaks to a long history of American Indian struggles for rights and justice in the face of colonial encroachment. This history was on the minds of AIM activists in the years leading up to the Pine Ridge shoot-out as AIM began as a grassroots organization addressing poverty, inadequate housing, and police harassment in the urban native community. It blamed these ills on the federal government for failing to honor treaties granting and safeguarding Indian

rights to certain lands and resources. In 1972 AIM took its grievances to Washington, D.C., where its members occupied the Bureau of Indian Affairs (BIA) headquarters, an action that earned the leaders, including Peltier, the FBI's label of "key extremists." Three years later, the AIM and a thirty-two-year-old Peltier were at Pine Ridge to protect traditional Lakota, who wanted independence from the federal government and from a BIA-backed tribal government known for its corruption and brutality. As such, the shoot-out was conflict laden with political, economic, and cultural stakes.

When *Prison Writings* was published, Peltier had been in prison twenty-three years. Although several appeals for a retrial and parole had been filed on his behalf, all had been denied—even after it became public knowledge that the FBI had used falsified testimonies and fabricated evidence to prosecute him for the killing of agents Jack Coler and Ronald Williams. Awaiting the verdict on a plea for executive clemency made in 1993, Peltier intended for his memoir to set the record straight: he was not a criminal but a spiritual leader serving an endangered people.

Matthiessen's book and Apted's film made Peltier's story famous. Both contextualized the shoot-out in the larger history of competing interests over Indian lands, and each made a case against the FBI for deliberately neutralizing Peltier as a political leader. *Prison Writings* evokes a more intimate sense of the emotional and cultural stakes of his incarceration. As a justification of Peltier's activism and an indictment of his punishment, the memoir shares much with Martin Luther King Jr.'s "Letter from Birmingham Jail" (1963). Meanwhile, as a disclosure of how prison life feeds the radical imagination, *Prison Writings* belongs in a tradition that includes *The Autobiography of Malcolm X* (1965), Eldridge Cleaver's *Soul on Ice* (1965), and Mumia Abu-Jamal's *Live from Death Row* (1995).

Prison Writings contributes to the conception of Peltier as a folk hero and undoubtedly helped to renew interest in his cause. Following its publication, supporters declared November 1999 Leonard Peltier Freedom Month, staging events outside the White House in the hope of having his case reopened. In response the FBI Agents Association lobbied with an open letter and national ad campaign arguing against clemency.

❖ *Key Facts*

Time Period:
Late 20th Century

Genre:
Memoir

Events:
Founding of American Indian Movement (AIM); Pine Ridge shootout

Nationality:
Anishinabe-Dakota (Native American)

LEONARD PELTIER IN MUSIC

Numerous singers and songwriters have sympathetically invoked and alluded to Leonard Peltier and his story in their work. In 1998 Robbie Robertson, former guitarist and songwriter of the Band, released *Contact from the Underworld of Redboy,* an album inspired by Native American music. It includes the track "Sacrifice," featuring the voice of Peltier speaking over the telephone. Toad the Wet Sprocket asks on their 1997 album *Coil,* "What have you done with Peltier?" in "Crazy Life," a song suggesting that a change in Peltier's fortunes is on its way.

In a much more confrontational vein, the video for Rage Against the Machine's 1994 single "Freedom" shows the band playing against a backdrop that reads "freedom for Peltier." The performance is cut with documentary footage from the Peltier case, captions extracted from Matthiessen's *In the Spirit of Crazy Horse,* and reenacted scenes of the Pine Ridge shoot-out from Apted's *Incident at Oglala.* From Buffy Sainte-Marie and Little Steven to U2, Dead Prez, and French singer Renaud, artists and musicians continue to tap the range of emotions Peltier's story provokes, from heartfelt sorrow to bitter outrage.

Although Peltier remains in prison without commutation, his story continues to draw support from peace workers around the world and from human rights organizations, such as Amnesty International, for which Peltier has become a symbol of U.S.-Indian relations at their most fraught.

THEMES AND STYLE

The subtitle of the memoir, *My Life Is My Sun Dance,* signals Peltier's main theme: his predicament is cause for spiritual concern. As he describes it, the Sun Dance ceremony involves prayer, fasting, and ritual piercing of the flesh as an offering to the Great Spirit. "A man who has Sun Danced," he writes, "has a special compact with Pain. And he'll be hard to break." So the Sun Dance suggests *survivance,* a key word in Native American studies, for Peltier the prisoner. But more than this, it provides a sacred connection to all humanity. Peltier explains, "For the rest of your life, once you have made that sacrifice of your flesh to the Great Mystery, you will never forget that greater reality of which we are each an intimate and essential part and which holds each of us in an embrace as loving as a mother's arms." With individual survivance comes social responsibility. Thus, Peltier also describes his life as "a prayer for my people" and his autobiography as "the story of my people." This overarching theme, in which "the political and the spiritual are one," asks the reader to take Peltier's side as the struggle of not just one man but of a whole people.

Drawing on a worldview that both acknowledges and disavows the authority of the United States, Peltier's traditional Indian perspective makes for compelling

rhetorical choices. He describes himself as "a native of Great Turtle Island," another name for the North American continent that dispenses entirely with the idea of an America nation except as an occupying presence. Although he claims, "I write this book to bring about a greater understanding of what being an Indian means," he also puts pressure on what being an American means. This is evident when he states, "Read your own Declaration of Independence, America," and again when he asks, "America, when will you live up to your own principles?" His grievance, as a prisoner and an American Indian, is that the United States does not "live up to its own laws, its own Constitution," an assertion he underlines by accusing the country of concocting "an illegal government conspiracy to frame and imprison—if not outright murder—a whole generation of Native American activists."

Peltier is often incendiary in his indictment of white America as racist and corrupt. Yet he is conscious that he, too, stands indicted, accused of the slaying of two federal agents. As such, he often displays emotional appeals of a different sort. He confesses, "I have no apologies, only sorrow. I can't apologize for what I haven't done. But I can grieve, and I do. Every day, every hour, I grieve for those who died at the Oglala firefight in 1975 and for their families—for the families of FBI agents Jack Coler and Ronald Williams." Even if Peltier never wholly relinquishes his bitterness for America's crimes, this compassion leads him to imagine a "great healing" ahead, when "we will begin to look upon one another with respect and tolerance instead of prejudice, distrust, and hatred."

CRITICAL DISCUSSION

While Peltier's story received some critical attention, serious criticism about *Prison Writings* is in its infancy. Some publications treat it in the context of the sociology of prison life, reading it as a litmus test for classic analyses of carceral writings or of discourse analysis, tracing the way Peltier's memoir both relies on and deviates from Western literary conventions. Of the few articles that discuss the text in its own right, Deena Rhyms's "Discursive Delinquency in Leonard Peltier's *Prison Writings,*" published in a 2002 issue of the journal *Genre: Forms of Discourse and Culture,* stands out for its explanations of the way Peltier puts language and form to work for political and spiritual purposes. Rhyms's insights into the ways "Peltier writes against the master-discourses of law and Christianity" are especially useful for thinking about the prison memoir as politically rich in both content and form.

Peltier's book makes a major contribution to the understanding of prison life and prison writing. As a cultural document that records, for example, how Indian prisoners in Leavenworth penitentiary manage to carry on their religious sweat lodge ceremonies, it yields rich insights into what it means to be an American Indian in a U.S. prison. Polemically, making a case both for Peltier and against the U.S. government, it puts serious pressure on some of America's most fundamental institutions and practices, especially in terms of legal, judicial, and penal systems. Consciously crafting an aesthetic vision that disavows the orthodox American way of life, it is a genuinely radical work, and critics have only just begun to explore it for its sociological insights and rhetorical choices.

As of the early twenty-first century, scholarly interest in Peltier's memoir is slowly gathering momentum. Janna Knittel, in *American Indian Rhetorics of Survivance: Word Medicine, Word Magic* (2006), considers Peltier's rhetoric in relation to oral tradition. Similarly useful studies seek to contextualize Peltier in terms of the way the public perceives the prison system and how Peltier's text relates to other prison memoirs, such as Abu-Jamal's *Live from Death Row*. Also of note are D. Quentin Miller's examination of the racial implications of *Prison Writings* as a nonwhite prison narrative potentially read by white readers in an essay in *Prose and Cons: Essays on Prison Literature in the United States* (2005) and Caroline Woidat's study of conspiracy culture surrounding Peltier's case in a 2006 essay in *Journal of American Culture*. As these select works show, interest in *Prison Writings* ranges widely in terms of exploring the work's political, social, and aesthetic significance.

BIBLIOGRAPHY

Sources

Bennett, Juda. "Writing into the Prison-Industrial Complex." *Prose and Cons: Essays on Prison Literature in the United States.* Ed. Quentin D. Miller. Jefferson: McFarland, 2005. 203–216. Print.

Knittel, Janna. "Sun Dance behind Bars: The Rhetoric of Leonard Peltier's *Prison Writings*." *American Indian Rhetorics of Survivance: Word Medicine, Word Magic.* Ed. Ernest Stromberg. Pittsburgh: U of Pittsburgh P, 2006. 110–28. Print.

Miller, D. Quentin. "'On the Outside Looking In': White Readers of Nonwhite Prison Narratives." *Prose and Cons: Essays on Prison Literature in the United States.* Ed. Quentin D. Miller. Jefferson: McFarland, 2005. 15–32. Print.

Rhyms, Deena. "Discursive Delinquency in Leonard Peltier's *Prison Writings*." *Genre: Forms of Discourse and Culture* 35.3–4 (2002): 563–74. Print.

Riley, John. "The Pains of Imprisonment: Exploring a Classic Text with Contemporary Authors." *Journal of Criminal Justice Education* 13.2 (2002): 443–61. Print.

Woidat, Caroline M. "The Truth Is on the Reservation: American Indians and Conspiracy Culture." *Journal of American Culture* 29.4 (2006): 454–67. Print.

Further Reading

Arden, Harvey. *Have You Thought of Leonard Peltier Lately?* Houston: HYT, 2004. Print.

Ball, Dewi Ioan, and Joy Porter. *Competing Voices from Native America.* Santa Barbara: Greenwood, 2009. Print.

Matthiessen, Peter. *In the Spirit of Crazy Horse.* New York: Penguin, 1983. Print.

Rhyms, Deena. *From the Iron House: Imprisonment in First Nations Writing.* Waterloo: Wilfrid Laurier UP, 2008. Print.

Media Adaptation

Incident at Oglala: The Leonard Peltier Story. Dir. Michael Apted. Miramax Films, 1992. DVD.

David C. Aitchison

At the 1992 Fort Snelling State Park Pow Wow in Mendota Heights, Minnesota, a car bears a bumper sticker supporting Leonard Peltier's release from prison. © STEVE SKJOLD/ALAMY.

SAINT JOAN

George Bernard Shaw

✢ *Key Facts*

Time Period:
Early 20th Century

Genre:
Play

Events:
World War I; Hundred
Years' War

Nationality:
English

OVERVIEW

George Bernard Shaw's *Saint Joan* (1923) is both a recounting of the trial and execution of Joan of Arc and an indictment of the human tendency to condemn cruelties of the past while remaining blind to similar suffering in the contemporary world. Presented in six scenes, the play is introduced by a lengthy preface elucidating some of the work's central themes and concludes with an epilogue set twenty-five years after Joan's execution. Both Joan and her inquisitors are shown as reasonable and "right" in their respective viewpoints, and Shaw's portrayal of Joan's anguish over the loss of "the wind in the trees, the larks in the sunshine, the young lambs crying through the healthy frost" expresses not merely her own agony or that of the troops who carried her image into battle but also the anguish of soldiers and political prisoners everywhere.

During World War I, Joan of Arc became a potent symbol for the French, as Germany bombed the land where she had fought. It is perhaps unsurprising that Shaw, who was known for his politically inflected theater, should have chosen to explore her story at a time when her image was being used to promote French nationalism and the righteousness of the Allied cause. While *Saint Joan* was well received as drama, Shaw was criticized on grounds of historical and religious inaccuracy. Notwithstanding such objections, his broader engagement with questions about the deficiency of human judgment and its implications for succeeding generations have cemented his reputation as an important dramatist.

HISTORICAL AND LITERARY CONTEXT

Many books have been written about Joan of Arc, a fascinating figure both for the drama of her story and for the significant documentation surrounding her trial and execution. The Maid of Orléans, as she is sometimes known, was a peasant girl from eastern France who, during the Hundred Years' War, led the armies of Charles VII in a series of victories against the English. Claiming that she heard voices and was the agent of God's will, Joan was eventually captured by the Burgundian allies of the English and then delivered to the English seat in occupied Rouen, where she was tried for heresy and burned at the stake on May 30, 1431. Twenty-five years after her death, she was

found innocent of the charges of heresy and declared a martyr by Pope Callixtus III. She was canonized in 1920, several years before Shaw published his play, and remains the patron saint of France.

Years before writing *Saint Joan,* Shaw had expressed an interest in Joan of Arc and, according to his own admission, had read all of the important biographical studies of her life and numerous stage adaptations (many of them melodramatic) of her story. World War I had sentimentalized Joan's heroism, with Allied soldiers carrying her image into battle, and calls for her immediate canonization were renewed. In his essay in *George Bernard Shaw* (1978), Eldon C. Hill notes that the playwright declared that he might not have been inspired finally to undertake the work had there not been "a world situation in which we see whole peoples perishing and dragging us toward the abyss which has swallowed them, all for want of any grasp of the political forces that move civilization."

Treatments of Joan of Arc abound in all genres and vary from the sympathetic to the skeptical; indeed, Shaw discusses a number of them in his preface. Voltaire's "La Pucelle" (1730), a satirical poem mocking the veneration of a peasant girl and a post-Enlightenment belief in miracles, stands in sharp contrast to the response by Friedrich Schiller in his tragic play *Die Jungfrau von Orleans* (1801). Schiller portrays Joan as a romantic heroine who falls in love with an enemy soldier but chooses to spare his life and suffers guilt over her traitorous behavior until she dies, unlike the historical Joan, in the heat of a battle. Anatole France's biography *Vie de Jeanne d'Arc* (1908)—a book that elicited severe criticism from Shaw—casts Joan's visions as hallucinations and questions both her mission and her reputation as a skilled commander and battle strategist. More directly related to *Saint Joan* is *Jeanne d'Arc* (1906) by Percy McKay, who, like Shaw, drew from T. Douglas Murray's English translation of Joan's trial transcripts and rehabilitation proceedings of 1456.

Saint Joan shored up Shaw's post-World War I reputation (his pacifism had alienated many friends and supporters) and, with the exception perhaps of *Pygmalion* (the basis for *My Fair Lady*), remains his best-known and most acclaimed work. Most critics agree that *Saint Joan* is largely responsible for Shaw's receiving the 1925 Nobel Prize in Literature. Adaptations of the play are numerous and have starred such celebrated actresses as Sybil Thorndike (for whom Shaw wrote the role of Joan), Joan Plowright, Lynn Redgrave, and Judi Dench. A revival of the play won a Tony in 1993. *Saint Joan* was also adapted for the screen by Graham Greene, although in a revised and condensed version with an eye to preventing a boycott by the Catholic Church.

THEMES AND STYLE

Central to Shaw's conception of *Saint Joan* is the notion, stated in the preface, that "the trial and execution in Rouen might have been an event of today; and we may charge our consciences accordingly." Shaw conceives of Joan's crimes not as heresy but as extraordinary feats. He presents Joan as a "genius" who, in her excellence, her powers of imagination, her military prowess, and her ability to argue and persuade, inspired fear and anger. Contrary to popular conceptions of the particular villainy of bishop Pierre Cauchon and the ecclesiastic court, Shaw presents them as ordinary and even reasonable within their fifteenth-century framework. Cauchon, for example, raises his eyebrows at English chaplain John de Stogumber's uncritical nationalistic assertion that "no Englishman is ever fairly beaten" and insists that a French court must decide the validity of the charges against Joan, whom the Earl of Warwick has already convicted as "a sorceress" and Stogumber has called an "arrant witch."

As text rather than as performance, *Saint Joan* is wrapped neatly in Shaw's explication, most directly in his preface, with its rather lengthy elaboration of his views on religion, on Joan in history and literature, and on the relation of the play's events to contemporary society. The epilogue, a dream sequence that details Joan's rehabilitation and eventual status as a saint, provides further indications of Shaw's intentions. Having appeared, Joan asks the assembled cast of characters whether, in light of her exculpation, she might return to Earth and be treated differently. The characters answer in the negative, Cauchon perhaps most eloquently: "The heretic is always better dead. And mortal eyes cannot distinguish the saint from the heretic."

Cauchon's words exemplify the overall measured tone of *Saint Joan* and serve to illustrate Shaw's assertion in the preface that "there are no villains in this play." While Cauchon is indeed responsible for Joan's trial and thus, ultimately, for her execution, he is not presented by Shaw as evil and is indeed kindly disposed toward Joan. Moreover, Joan, who claims to have had divine visitations, is rational in her arguments and often witty in her responses to her inquisitors. She is not at all crazy. While the play's tone is typically Shavian, with characters discoursing at length about ideas, the last line hints at Shaw's genuine despair about the human condition and the implication for present and future generations. Joan, lit by white radiance, cries out, "Oh God that made this beautiful

GEORGE BERNARD SHAW'S LIFE FORCE

George Bernard Shaw was inspired by the philosopher Henri Bergson's *Creative Evolution* (1907), which expounds the notion that a vital force or impulse underlies and defines the evolution of human life. Shaw's version of the theory was also influenced by Samuel Butler's *Life and Habit* (1878), which promotes the Lamarkian view that beneficial habits can be acquired and passed from parent to offspring. In his preface to *Saint Joan*, Shaw writes that "there are forces at work which use individuals for purposes far transcending the purpose of keeping these individuals alive and prosperous." For Shaw, the Life Force is most strongly expressed by individuals, such as Joan, who are exceptional in their expression of will "in the pursuit of knowledge and social readjustments."

Shaw's theory of the Life Force is illustrated most fully in *Back to Methuselah* (1921), a sequence of five plays sometimes (mistakenly) classed as science fiction. The plays, which begin in 4004 BCE with Adam and Eve, develop the theory that modern civilization cannot advance to a state of satisfactory governance because human beings do not live long enough to learn how to govern and then apply that knowledge. In *Methuselah* humanity acquires the ability to pass on learned traits, and humans eventually prolong life enough to establish the peaceful utopia of the fifth play, *As Far as Thought Can Reach* (set 31,920 CE), wherein humans evolve to disembodied energy and presumably live in peace.

earth, when will it be ready to receive Thy saints? How long, O Lord, How long?"

CRITICAL DISCUSSION

Saint Joan opened to mixed reviews, with its early American notices giving no indication that the play would eventually be considered a masterpiece of modern drama. T. S. Eliot, who reviewed the play's London opening, famously suggested that Shaw was guilty of "deluding the numberless crowd of sentimentally religious people who are incapable of following an argument to a conclusion," adding that "the potent ju-ju of the Life Force is a gross superstition." Eliot also dubbed *Saint Joan* the "most superstitious" portrayal of Joan of Arc, a variant of the objection raised by other critics that Shaw's heroine flies in the face of historical fact.

Saint Joan's legacy does not lie in being a historically accurate account of the life of Joan of Arc but rather rests in its accounting of the susceptibility of human beings to venerating false or harmful systems—a susceptibility that did not end with the Middle Ages. While Shaw was critical of religious persecution and feudalism, he also objected to the modern "enlightened practices" of vivisection and psychotherapy and writes disapprovingly in his preface that "modern science is

Joan of Arc at the Coronation of Charles VII in Reims Cathedral, painting by Jean Auguste Dominique Ingres, 1854. © ALFREDO DAGLI ORTI/ THE ART ARCHIVE/CORBIS.

upon (close as it came on the heels of the Allied victory), spoke to the uneasy consciousness of French political and economic instability. Other critics of the play have examined Shaw's religious beliefs or his representation of Joan as an agent of the Life Force, a concept discussed throughout his long writing career.

making short work of hallucinations without regard to the vital importance of the things they symbolize." What these things might be and what makes Saint Joan a compelling play continue to interest contemporary scholars.

Saint Joan is often analyzed in tandem with other portrayals of Joan of Arc, although many critical studies focus on *Saint Joan* exclusively. Craig Hamilton, in his 2000 essay in *Modern Drama,* calls Joan of Arc "the Grand Canyon of France," a potent symbol loaded with numerous cultural meanings. Hamilton analyzes the factors that made the 1925 Paris premiere so successful, concluding that the popularity of the play in France was largely attributable to the identification with Joan's nationalism, which, while perhaps frowned

BIBLIOGRAPHY

Sources

Eliot, T. S. "A Commentary: *St. Joan.*" *Criterion* 3 (1924): 1–5. Print.

Hamilton, Craig. "Constructing a Cultural Icon: *Nomos* and Shaw's *Saint Joan* in Paris." *Modern Drama* 43.3 (2000): 359–75. *Literature Resource Center.* Web. 10 Aug. 2012.

Hill, Eldon C. "The Climax of a Career." *George Bernard Shaw.* Twayne, 1978. 131–33. Rpt. in *Drama for Students.* Ed. Elizabeth Thomason. Vol. 11. Detroit: Gale, 2001. *Literature Resource Center.* Web. 9 Aug. 2012.

Shaw, George Bernard. *Saint Joan: A Chronicle Play in Six Scenes and an Epilogue.* New York: Penguin, 2009. Print.

Further Reading

Bentley, Eric. *Bernard Shaw.* New York: Applause, 2002. Print.

Bloom, Harold, ed. *George Bernard Shaw's* Saint Joan: *Modern Critical Interpretations.* New York: Chelsea, 1987. Print.

Crompton, Louis. "A Hagiography of Creative Evolution." *George Bernard Shaw's* Saint Joan. Ed. Harold Bloom. New York: Chelsea, 1987. 31–52. Print.

Holroyd, Michael. *Bernard Shaw: The One-Volume Definitive Edition.* New York: Norton, 2005. Print.

Peters, Julie Stone. "Joan of Arc Internationale: Shaw, Brecht, and the Law of Nations." *Comparative Drama* 38.4 (2004): 355+. *Literature Resource Center.* Web. 9 Aug. 2012.

Pharand, Michel W. *Bernard Shaw and the French.* Gainesville: UP of Florida, 2000. Print.

Tyson, Brian F. *The Story of Shaw's* Saint Joan. Kingston: McGill-Queen's UP, 1982. Print.

Media Adaptations

Saint Joan. Dir. Widgey R. Newman. Perf. Sybil Thorndike. Lee De Forest Films, 1927. Film.

Saint Joan. Dir. and prod. Otto Preminger. Cast Richard Widmark, Richard Todd, Anton Walbrook, et al. Screenplay by Graham Greene. Music by Mischa Spoliansky. Warner Home Video, 1994, © 1957. VHS.

Daisy Gard

THE TRIAL OF DEDAN KIMATHI

Ngugi wa Thiong'o

OVERVIEW

The Trial of Dedan Kimathi (1976), a play written by Ngugi wa Thiong'o in collaboration with Micere Githae Mugo, celebrates the heroic role played by Field Marshall Dedan Kimathi in the Mau Mau resistance against British colonial rule in Kenya in the 1950s. The play takes its content from the actual trial and court-ordered execution of Kimathi at the Kamiti Maximum Security Prison on February 18, 1957. However, the authors forsake a realistic treatment of these events in favor of an imaginative reconstruction that intercuts the story of Kimathi's last days in jail with flashback and dream sequences and intervals of song, dance, and mime drawn from the oral tradition of the Gikuyu tribe. In combination, the various episodes identify Kimathi with the great heroes of ancient African legend and describe several centuries of the oppression of Kenya's masses, leading up to their courageous fight for national independence. Ngugi and Mugo sought to activate memories of Kimathi and the anticolonial period to motivate the people of Kenya to rebel against a neocolonial government they felt had betrayed the revolution.

As an attempt to rewrite the popular struggle back into an official British and neocolonial historical record notorious for marginalizing the role of the masses in the transition from colonialism to independence—finally achieved in 1963—*The Trial of Dedan Kimathi* is one of several political works written by Ngugi expressing his Marxist convictions. (Given Ngugi's much greater literary stature, the play is generally discussed in terms of the development of his career rather than that of Mugo's, one of his colleagues at the University of Nairobi.) The debut of *The Trial of Dedan Kimathi* at Nairobi's National Theatre was restricted to only four nights by the post-independence government of Jomo Kenyatta. Crowds enthusiastically embraced the play, but establishment critics subjected it to a barrage of attacks. *The Trial of Dedan Kimathi* has since been judged central to Ngugi's lifelong project to restore agency to Kenya's disenfranchised poor.

HISTORICAL AND LITERARY CONTEXT

The Gikuyu, the largest ethnic group in Kenya, suffered most from the British expropriation of tribal lands in the fertile central region of Kenya, and it was they who comprised the majority population of the Mau Mau, a nationalist resistance movement formed in the forests of Kenya with the aim of combating the institutionalized racism of the British through their violent removal from rule. Kimathi was highly influential in organizing the guerilla forest fighters in a bitter civil war of several years that pitted the Gikuyu Land Freedom Army against the occupying British and Gikuyu loyalists. Kimathi was captured by government authorities in 1956, charged with murder and terrorism, and sentenced to hang. The strength of the Mau Mau dwindled with Kimathi's execution, but among the common people of Kenya, his efforts are considered fundamental to the eventual withdrawal of the British in 1963.

The Trial of Dedan Kimathi addresses the colonial legacy of capitalism that the authors, in accordance with their Marxist beliefs, perceived to be compromising the African identity of the 1970s. As further evidence of Ngugi's Marxist orientation, he was convinced of the revolutionary character of the anticolonial struggle, in sharp contrast to the neocolonial state's official account of its genesis, which downplayed the significance of the Mau Mau as part of a strategic effort to portray the process of liberation as one of negotiation and conciliation. Thus, whereas Kimathi is viewed by the majority of the peasants of Kenya as the hero of the revolution, he emerges from colonialist and neocolonialist writings about the Mau Mau as a dangerous and unbalanced subversive. *The Trial of Dedan Kimathi* was written to counteract this perspective, especially as it had taken shape in a recent play by Kenya National Theatre dramatist Kenneth Watene titled *Dedan Kimathi* (1974), which had caused a storm of controversy among Kenyan intellectuals for its portrait of Kimathi as a brutal, self-obsessed paranoiac.

The Trial of Dedan Kimathi was the immediate forerunner to *Ngaahika Ndenda* (1977, cowritten with Ngugi wa Mirii; *I Will Marry When I Want*), the first play Ngugi would write for the people's theater he established in 1977 in his native village of Kamiriithu. This grassroots production, in combination with the publication of *The Trial of Dedan Kimathi* and Ngugi's novel *Petals of Blood* (1977), another scathing critique of capitalism, proved too threatening for the government of Kenyatta (1964–78). The state withdrew the play's license and imprisoned Ngugi without charge for over a year. In 1982, four years following Ngugi's

✦ Key Facts

Time Period:
Late 20th Century

Genre:
Play

Events:
Growth of anticolonialism; Kenyan independence movement; spread of Marxist thought

Nationality:
Kenyan

SACRIFICE FOR THE CAUSE

Ngugi wa Thiong'o was arrested and detained by the Kenyan state in December 1977. Although no charges were ever formally filed against him, it is generally understood that his repeated public criticisms of the neocolonial government of Jomo Kenyatta, as well as his establishment of a community theater at Kamiriithu, represented serious threats to the interests of Kenya's national bourgeoisie. Despite public outcry and an attempt by Amnesty International to secure his release, Ngugi remained incarcerated at the Kamiti Maximum Security Prison until mid-December 1978. While there, Ngugi wrote *Caitaani mutharaba-ini* (1980; *Devil on the Cross*), the first modern novel in the Gikuyu language, on sheets of toilet paper from his cell. He also wrote an important prison memoir, *Detained* (1981).

Biographers have reported that Ngugi suffered great anguish when *Devil on the Cross* was temporarily confiscated by prison guards for three weeks in the fall of 1978. After Ngugi's release, *Devil on the Cross,* a damning critique of postcolonial politics in Kenya, sold out in two Gikuyu editions and one in Swahili within two years.

release, the theater was torn down and Ngugi went into exile, having already been stripped of his appointment at the University of Nairobi.

Ngugi's detention only increased his influence, making him a world-famous spokesperson on neocolonial oppression. In prison, he made the decision to write future novels and plays only in Gikuyu or Swahili rather than English because he believed it impossible for literature written in the language of the colonizer to be a source of revolutionary inspiration to the people of Africa. His decision is especially meaningful when read in the context of the preface to *The Trial of Dedan Kimathi,* in which the authors write: "We believe that Kenyan literature—indeed all African Literature, and its writers, is on trial. We cannot stand on the fence. We are either on the side of the people or on the side of imperialism."

THEMES AND STYLE

The Trial of Dedan Kimathi establishes a series of contrasts between radical nationalism on the one hand and colonialism and its pervasive legacy in post-independence Kenya on the other hand. The play draws on the recent memory of Kimathi and the Mau Mau to explore a long history of imperial oppression dating back to the times of slavery and to make an immediate call to the peasants to mobilize against their continuing exploitation by capitalist interests. The actual courtroom trial of Kimathi frames the narrative of four additional trials, which include torture and bribery, that Kimathi resists before his sentencing. These embedded trials all serve to contrast the courage and loyalty of Kimathi with the duplicity and avarice of the colonials and loyalists.

A subplot tells the story of Boy and Girl, symbolic of Kenya's next generation, whose thinking is molded by a character named Woman, a representative of the reproductive capacity of the Mau Mau ideology. Woman convinces the children to save Kimathi by smuggling a gun into his courtroom, symbolic of the necessity for armed resistance against the imperialist enemy.

The four temptations of Kimathi contain a great deal of didactic material, much of it delivered in Marxist rhetoric directed at the Kenyan audience. Kimathi's speech is defiant and assured, resounding in its affirmation of the validity of the peasants' struggle. The authors regularly employ such words and phrases as "oppressed," "oppressors," "labour power," and "justice for the people" to impress upon the audience the urgency of carrying on the goals of the Mau Mau in post-independence Kenya. The travesty of justice that is Kimathi's trial forms a contrast to Kimathi's democratic trial of Mau Mau traitors in the forest. Kimathi forgives those who have betrayed him in a scene that, as Patrick Williams argues in his 1999 article in *Ngugi wa Thiong'o,* "humanises Kimathi in opposition to received versions of him as a ruthlessly efficient—or simply ruthless—Mau Mau leader."

At the same time, the authors make strong emotional appeals that invite the audience to internalize the transcendent spirit of Kimathi and the ancestral folk heroes. The Boy and Girl underscore the mythic qualities of Kimathi by detailing his superhuman accomplishments. The Boy claims that Kimathi can turn himself into an airplane to elude his enemies, and the Girl reports that Kimathi can walk one hundred miles on his belly. At the climax, when Kimathi is led off to his death, the Boy and Girl stand up, crying in unison "not dead," signifying that Kimathi's courage and commitment live on. The indigenous language, suppressed by the British conquerors, becomes a tool of liberation as well. In the final scene, a large crowd of workers and peasants join onstage to sing one of the many Gikuyu freedom anthems included in the play. By Ngugi's own account of the opening night performance, as quoted in *Contemporary Black Biography,* the direct appeal to the people's consciousness was highly successful: "As the actors performed their last song and danced through the middle aisle of the auditorium, they were joined by the audience. They all went outside the theatre building, still dancing. What had been confined to the stage had spilled out into the open air, and there was no longer any distinction between actors and audience."

CRITICAL DISCUSSION

The reception of *The Trial of Dedan Kimathi* was politically charged from the outset. The play premiered at the Nairobi National Theatre to sold-out performances, but it was restricted to only four nights to give room to two imported productions brought in for the UNESCO conference being held in Nairobi. In an article in the *Daily Nation* in October 1976, Ngugi publicly criticized Kenyatta's government for failing to accord the play better treatment, especially given that it had already been selected as one of Kenya's official entries for the 1977 Festac Festival of Arts and Culture in Lagos, Nigeria. As Ngugi recalled several years later, "The conflict over the performance space was also a struggle over which cultural symbols and activities would represent the new Kenya."

Ngugi has achieved enormous international stature as a writer and activist since his exile; all of his writings, including *The Trial of Dedan Kimathi,* are judged foundational to the articulation of an authentic post-independence African identity. Ngugi was considered a major threat to the neocolonial government of Daniel Arap Moi (1978–2002), who attempted to halt the growing popularity of Ngugi's politics among the people of Kenya, as well as the spread of community theater. Evan Maina Mwangi, a student at the University of Nairobi in the late 1990s and early 2000s, revealed that there was an organized campaign there against Ngugi: "It was an open secret that some of the professors at the time were hired and promoted with specific terms of reference to reduce the popularity of Ngugi's creed in the country and to teach students to be loyal to the government." Mwangi went on to report that theater personalities associated with Ngugi, including Mugo, had all been exiled.

Ngugi's fame has brought increased critical attention to *The Trial of Dedan Kimathi.* It is mainly still read as a work of left-wing nationalism meant to inspire people to carry on Kimathi's legacy and to revise distortions in the official historical record. The commentary of Oyeniyi Okunoye in *History in Africa* is representative: "The play becomes the more significant because it links the three major phases of the African historical experience: the precolonial, the colonial, and the post-independence eras. Its appropriation of Marxist historiography facilitates the universalization of the experience it mirrors, making the world of the play that of the oppressor and the oppressed." Still, some critics have urged that the play's didactic message is made much more powerful by virtue of a sophisticated aesthetic strategy incorporating allegory, symbolism, metaphor, and legend derived from the Gikuyu oral tradition.

BIBLIOGRAPHY

Sources

Mwangi, Evan Maina. "Gender and the Erotics of Nationalism in Ngũgũ wa Thiong'o's Drama." *Drama Review* Summer 2009: 90–112. *Project Muse.* Web. 30 July 2012.

"Ngugi wa Thiong'o." *Contemporary Black Biography.* 2007. *Encyclopedia.com.* Web. 3 Aug. 2012.

Ngugi wa Thiongo'o, with Micere Githae Mugo. *The Trial of Dedan Kimathi.* London: Heinemann, 1981. Print.

Okunoye, Oyeniyi. "Dramatizing Postcoloniality: Nationalism and the Rewriting of History in Ngugi and Mugo's *The Trial of Dedan Kimathi.*" *History in Africa* 28 (2001): 225–37. *JSTOR.* Web. 30 July 2012.

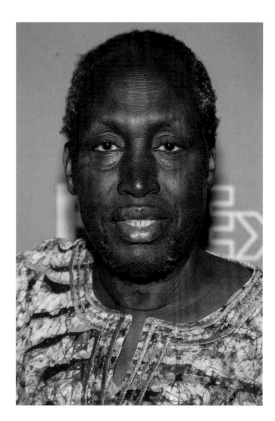

Ngugi wa Thiong'o, author of *The Trial of Dedan Kimathi,* in 2007. © ZUMA WIRE SERVICE/ALAMY.

Williams, Patrick. "The Struggle Betrayed." *Ngugi wa Thiong'o.* Manchester: Manchester UP, 1999. 78–120. Print.

Further Reading

Brown, Nicholas. "Revolution and Recidivism: The Problem of Kenyan History in the Plays of Ngugi wa Thiong'o." *Research in African Literatures* 30:4 (1999): 56–73. *Project Muse.* Web. 30 July 2012.

Dasylva, Ademola O. "Playing with History, Playing with Words: Ngugi and Mugo's *The Trial of Dedan Kimathi.*" *Matatu* 2011: 531–44. *Literature Online.* Web. 31 July 2012.

Gikandi, Simon. "On Culture and the State: The Writings of Ngũgĩ wa Thiong'o." *Third World Quarterly* Jan. 1989: 148–56. *JSTOR.* Web. 30 July 2012.

Kahiga, Samuel. *Dedan Kimathi: The Real Story.* Nairobi: Longman Kenya, 1990. Print.

Lovesey, Oliver. "Ngugi wa Thiong'o's Postnation: The Cultural Geographies of Colonial, Neocolonial, and Postnational Space." *Modern Fiction Studies* 48.1 (2002): 139–68. Rpt. in *Contemporary Literary Criticism.* Ed. Jeffrey W. Hunter. Vol. 275. Detroit: Gale, Cengage, 2009. 166–80. *Literature Criticism Online.* Web. 31 July 2012.

Ngugi wa Thiong'o. *Devil on the Cross.* London: Heinemann, 1987. Print.

Sinha, Nandita. *Ngugi and Mugo's "The Trial of Dedan Kimathi": A Reader's Companion.* New Delhi: Asia Book Club, 2004. Print.

Watene, Kenneth. *Dedan Kimathi: A Play.* Nairobi: Transafrica, 1974. Print.

Janet Mullane

THE VIOLENCE OF LOVE

Archbishop Oscar Romero

OVERVIEW

Published in 1988, James Brockman's compilation of Archbishop Oscar Romero's homilies, *The Violence of Love,* serves to critique El Salvador's violent civil war from the 1970s into the early 1990s. Assassinated in 1980, Romero passionately celebrates the examples of Jesus Christ, Catholic saints, Christian apostles, and others who fought violence and persecution through selflessness and love. His sermons denounce the acts of "murder," "torture," "atrocity," and "injustice" directed by governmental and paramilitary forces. While never endorsing guerrilla movements, Romero stresses the importance of finding liberation and justice through the Christian example of sacrifice and suffering rather than political or military campaigns. Through the words of an assassinated priest who preached Christian nonviolence and service, "the violence of love," Brockman provides readers with a martyr whose very example inspires others to condemn the repression and brutality that dominated the Salvadoran civil war.

In the midst of various Central and South American so-called "dirty" wars, various religious figures demanded more attention to the needs of impoverished peoples and reproached oligarchic governments and military dictatorships. Because of the disparate inequality in El Salvador, many religious officials witnessed to the needs of their parishioners and questioned both counterinsurgency tactics and guerrilla warfare. Romero's language embodies these sentiments. Following the archbishop's assassination in the middle of the Salvadoran civil war, various writers, activists, and organizations published Romero's words in order to bring attention to the economic ills and human rights violations in the Central American nation. While the oligarchic government and guerrilla insurgency fought, Romero provided an example for an alternative path that questioned the status quo and uplifted the Salvadoran people without accepting either side in the civil war. Romero's martyrdom inspired numerous religious and social activists to examine El Salvador due in great part to works such as that of Brockman.

HISTORICAL AND LITERARY CONTEXT

In El Salvador, an oligarchy dominated the government, and an entrenched military eliminated projects or spokespersons that offered reform. Additionally, the military received significant military and financial aid from the U.S. government. Numerous organizations of students, peasants, and workers opposed the repression. Inspired by the Cuban Revolution and later Nicaragua's Sandinistas, leftist insurgents organized guerrilla movements to destabilize this government. One group of opponents to military repression was religious, prominently Catholic, activists. Some Catholic activists, often influenced by "liberation theology" and the 1968 Medellín conference, stressed the need to serve not only the spiritual needs but the physical needs of the people. These pastors utilized Christian scripture and Catholic theology to discuss social ills and economic inequality, especially useful in a predominantly Catholic nation. Although some activists joined insurgencies, the majority focused upon their parishioners. The military junta and paramilitary organizations, or "death squads," did not make such distinctions and targeted many such activists.

Appointed archbishop of San Salvador in February 1977, Romero witnessed the next month the escalation of military and paramilitary repression when these forces gunned down his friend, the priest Rutilio Grande. Two months later, extreme right-wing organizations killed another priest, Alfonso Navarro. Romero's homilies for these priests set forward his vision of Christian love and sacrifice that criticized the brutal actions of the extreme right. Brockman uses these words to introduce readers to Romero. Romero described those "whose hands are bloodied with Father Grande's murder" and "who shot Father Navarro" as those "who have killed, who have tortured, who have done so much evil." Never endorsing violence, Romero told them to repent and seek "forgiveness." At the funeral for Grande, Romero spoke of "a church that walks serene, because it bears the force of love." It is from this argument for Christian nonviolence and service to the poor that Brockman pulls the title for his text. "We have never preached violence, except the violence of love, which left Christ nailed to a cross," Romero said November 27, 1977. "It is the violence of love, of brotherhood."

This language of Christian nonviolence and service followed the 1968 Latin American Episcopal Conference at Medellín, Colombia, where 130 Catholic bishops claimed a Christian duty to address parishioners' social problems. At Medellín, many Catholic bishops and activists used the reforms from the 1962–65 Vatican II council to lambast poverty, inequality, and structural violence and oppression, as well as armed violence and repression. Throughout the 1970s Catholic bishops in Central and South American countries including Brazil, Ecuador, and Guatemala spoke against oligarchic governments and military regimes and highlighted the vast economic and social inequities defining Latin America. On November 27, 1978, Romero noted his debt to these discussions. Included in Brockman's compilation, the homily outlined Romero's philosophy, stating, "I say … what Medellín says: Christians are peacemakers, not because they cannot fight, but because they prefer the force of peace."

Similarly, Brockman's decision to inscribe Romero's homilies was not a lone event, for priests, activists, and authors utilized Romero's legacy to condemn Latin America's authoritarian governments. Death squads threatened numerous Christian activists, so critics co-opted Romero and other victims of extreme right-wing repression to defend Christian nonviolence and service to the oppressed. When the military brutally murdered four U.S. churchwomen in 1980, international and religious criticism helped end temporary U.S. aid to the Salvadoran regime. Not only did Brockman produce *The Violence of Love*; he also published *The Church Is All of You: Thoughts of Archbishop Oscar A. Romero* and *Romero, a Life*.

THEMES AND STYLE

The Violence of Love uses Romero's example of Christian sacrifice and service to attack the violence of the Salvadoran civil war. Brockman utilizes Romero's homilies to continuously stress this message, beginning with the priest's opposition to both "revolutionary violence" and "institutionalized violence" based upon the Catholic faith. Romero claims, "True hope is not found in a revolution of violence and bloodshed." Rather, it lies in "self-sacrifice" and "giving up many comforts" as in Christ's example. This message urges El Salvador's oligarchy and military to abandon "violence, kidnapping, and terrorism" for "love, reconciliation, and pardon." Romero's homily of December 31, 1977, embodies this message. "The church … believes that in each person is the Creator's image," Romero declares, "and that everyone who tramples it offends God. As holy defender of God's rights and of his images, the church must cry out." His final homilies explicitly condemn an oligarchy that kills peasants and teachers.

With Romero's homilies, Brockman presents a Christian rebuttal to any justification of the civil war's atrocities. Since paramilitaries persecuted those who worked with the poor, Brockman uses Romero's words to celebrate these victims and undermine the junta's ideological claims. "What we are saying is that Christ declared, 'The Lord has sent me to preach good news to the poor.'" By positioning this criticism against violence and structural inequality in Catholic doctrine, Romero's message, "Do not hate," and Brockman's

MONSEÑOR ROMERO ON THE INTERNET AND ON FILM

Oscar Romero's symbol as a martyr and advocate for social justice endures. Numerous websites detail his history and legacy. The most useful and comprehensive website is hosted by the Kellogg Institute for International Studies at the University of Notre Dame for Latin American/North American Church Concerns (LANACC). The website includes a timeline for the Salvadoran civil war, a brief timeline-biography of Romero, and lists of relevant books, movies, and websites. In 2010 LANACC and the Kellogg Institute produced *Monseñor: The Last Journey of Oscar Romero*. The film's director, Reverend Robert Pelton, had met and was inspired by Romero in 1979. The film follows the last three years of Romero's life, resulting in an overlap with material from *The Violence of Love*.

Romero (1989) remains the more popular movie on Romero's work in El Salvador. The actor Raul Julia portrays Romero and depicts the man's evolution from a timid priest into a symbol for Christian action among the impoverished and victimized. Pivotal to the movie are not only the priest's words but his actions. Scenes of his refusal to submit to military authorities and his service among the nation's poor illustrate the power of his work and the legacy of his martyrdom.

compilation gain authority in an overwhelmingly Catholic nation. By grounding the critique of the Salvadoran regime in Catholic theology, Romero and Brockman provide an alternative path for the nation. "The history of salvation will be Salvador's history," Romero warns, "when we Salvadorans seek in our history the presence of God the savior." The victims of repression and inequality thus become the poor whom Christ and therefore all Christians must serve.

At the core of *The Violence of Love* is Romero's passionate appeal to Christian sacrifice and selflessness. He repeatedly denounces the assassinations of peasants, workers, and especially religious activists, and he presents them as examples and heroes. Throughout his homilies are the names of slain priests and laity who worked to uplift the poor. "The church must suffer for speaking the truth, for pointing out sin, for uprooting sin," Romero alleges. His homilies are more than text; they are directly addressing the oppressors and the oppressed with a direct plea for peace. "I cry out in the name of suffering, of those who suffer injustice," Romero declares, "but only to say to the criminals: Be converted! Do not be wicked!" He concludes that he and other activists "only preach the subversive witness of the Beatitudes, which have turned everything upside down to proclaim blessed the poor, blessed the thirsting for justice, blessed the suffering." This emotional plea reinforces the contrast between the violence of the oligarchic military junta and *The Violence of Love*.

Oscar Romero, Archbishop of San Salvador, celebrating mass in 1979. Romero was assassinated on March 24, 1980, during mass at a small hospital chapel. © ALAIN KELER/ SYGMA/CORBIS.

CRITICAL DISCUSSION

This Christian critique of the Salvadoran government's repression led to Romero's martyrdom. The night before, he had begged the military regime and paramilitary forces to stop. "We know that every effort to better society," Romero spoke March 24, 1980, in the last homily Brockman could include in *The Violence of Love,* "is an effort that God blesses, that God wants, that God demands of us." An anonymous gunman then shot Romero as he gave mass at the altar. At the funeral on March 30, a gathering of at least 50,000 peasants and religious officials attended the San Salvador Cathedral to testify to Romero's inspiration. To suppress the gathering and Romero's legacy, snipers in the government's National Palace fired upon the crowd and set off bombs. This bloodshed and Romero's assassination further contributed to the violence. Paramilitary forces killed more people, insurgents finished the formation of the Farabundo Martí National Liberation Front, and the nation plunged deeper into war.

Romero's legacy spread as the extreme right increased its repression of Christian activists and innocent people. The oligarchic military junta labeled murdered Salvadoran priests, U.S. nuns, and thousands of peasants as "communists" and "subversives." Consequently, authors and activists utilized Romero's writings in order to condemn this repression and violence. Many criticized U.S. military and financial support for the regime. Romero's homilies and speeches spread throughout El Salvador, the earliest, *Cese la represión* (Stop the Repression) and *Monseñor*

Romero, published within months of his assassination. Inspired by Romero, Brockman compiled *The Church Is All of You: Thoughts of Archbishop Oscar A. Romero* before producing *The Violence of Love.* The murders of other Catholic activists in El Salvador gave rise to similar compilations. After military forces killed six Jesuit priests and two women at the University of Central America in 1989, activists published *Companions of Jesus: The Jesuit Martyrs of El Salvador* to condemn the atrocities.

Romero's assassination inspired discussions and programs on Latin America's socioeconomic development. Theologian Jon Sobrino and scholar Phillip Berryman claim that Romero's martyrdom inspired Sobrino and other religious officials' service among the poor. Books, articles, testimonies, and even daily devotionals detail Romero's life. Scholarly, religious, and activist groups continue to discuss his example, commemorating the assassination's twenty-fifth anniversary in 2005. Repeated in books, magazines, movies, and websites, his prophetic words epitomize his legacy: "As a Christian I do not believe in death without resurrection. If they kill me I will rise again in the Salvadoran people."

BIBLIOGRAPHY

Sources

Berryman, Phillip. *Liberation Theology: Essential Facts about the Revolutionary Movement in Latin America and Beyond.* Philadelphia: Temple UP, 1987. Print.

Brockman, James R. *Romero, a Life.* Maryknoll: Orbis, 2005. Print.

Romero, Oscar. *The Violence of Love: The Pastoral Wisdom of Archbishop Oscar Romero.* Ed. James R. Brockman. San Francisco: Harper & Row, 1988. Print.

———. *Voice of the Voiceless: The Four Pastoral Letters and Other Statements.* Trans. Michael J. Walsh. Maryknoll: Orbis, 1985. Print.

Sobrino, Jon. *Companions of Jesus: The Jesuit Martyrs of El Salvador.* Maryknoll: Orbis, 1990. Print.

Whitfield, Teresa. *Paying the Price: Ignacio Ellacuria and the Murdered Jesuits of El Salvador.* Philadelphia: Temple UP, 1994. Print.

Further Reading

Berryman, Phillip. *Stubborn Hope: Religion, Politics and Revolution in Central America.* Maryknoll: Orbis, 1995. Print.

Danner, Mark. *The Massacre at El Mozote: A Parable of the Cold War.* New York: Vintage, 1993. Print.

Lernoux, Penny. *Cry of the People: The Struggle for Human Rights in Latin America—The Catholic Church in Conflict with U.S. Policy.* New York: Penguin, 1991. Print.

Levine, Daniel, ed. *Religion and Political Conflict in Latin America.* Chapel Hill: U of North Carolina P, 1986. Print.

Rosenberg, Tina. *Children of Cain: Violence and the Violent in Latin America.* New York: Penguin, 1992. Print.

Sigmund, Paul E. *Liberation Theology at the Crossroads: Democracy or Revolution?* New York: Oxford UP, 1990. Print.

Smith, Christian. *The Emergence of Liberation Theology: Radical Religion and Social Movement Theory.* Chicago: U of Chicago P, 1991. Print.

Steigenga, Timothy J., and Edward L. Cleary, eds. *Conversion of a Continent: Religious Change in Latin America.* New Brunswick: Rutgers UP, 2007. Print.

Stoll, David. *Is Latin America Turning Protestant?: The Politics of Evangelical Growth.* Berkeley: U of California P, 1990. Print.

Aaron Moulton

THE WHITE-HAIRED GIRL

Ho Ching-chih, Ting Yi

✥ *Key Facts*

Time Period:
Mid-20th Century

Genre:
Opera

Events:
Rise of Mao Zedong;
communist revolution
in China

Nationality:
Chinese

OVERVIEW

The White-Haired Girl, a modern Chinese Communist opera written by Ho Ching-chih and Ting Yi and first performed in April 1945, dramatizes the oppression of a poor farmer, Yang, and his daughter, Xi'er, by a greedy landlord. The original play depicts the debtor father's forced sale of his daughter and his consequent suicide, followed by the daughter's rape and impregnation by the landlord. Xi'er escapes into a cave, where her hair turns white from lack of light and nutrition. Scavenging food from a nearby temple, she is mistaken for a white-haired goddess for several years until Communist cadres arrive and expose this illusion. The Communists then restore Xi'er to society and bring the landlord to justice. Drawn from an oral folktale circulating in the early 1940s and dramatized through an adaptation of the popular *yangko* ("rice-sprout song") peasant dance, this modern opera stands out in Communist Chinese history as one of the most successful utilizations of long-beloved folk art to spread revolutionary ideas to the people.

The play was written and produced by students of Lu Hsun College in Ya'nan, in direct response to the call sounded by Communist leader Mao Zedong for the reformation of Chinese literature and art into forms and themes that would serve the interests of the common people. Wildly popular from its first opening, *The White-Haired Girl* was performed thirty times in Ya'nan alone. Following its Ya'nan premier, the play was revised and performed by the classically trained Peking (Beijing) Opera. During the Cultural Revolution (1966–76), it was transformed into a ballet. *The White-Haired Girl* eventually became a film and a television stage drama, making it accessible to Western audiences as well. The Communist Party ultimately honored *The White-Haired Girl* as one of the eight most exemplary revolutionary works of art.

HISTORICAL AND LITERARY CONTEXT

Mao began advocating the use of Chinese folk literature and art in the 1930s. His most famous speech on the topic was given at the Ya'nan Forum on Literature and Art in 1942, three years before *The White-Haired Girl* was penned. Mao believed that writers should live among the common people, drawing artistic material from folk culture rather than from the classical Chinese or modern foreign art forms that had constituted China's primary theater offerings prior to Mao's intervention.

Conforming to Mao's prescription, the authors of *The White-Haired Girl* seized on the *yangko* dance, which was wildly popular among the peasant farmers, to ensure the opera's broad appeal. This exhilarating dance, originally a somewhat comic, even sexual, fertility rite celebrating the arrival of spring, was transformed into modern opera through several changes in theme and elaborations in form. As early as 1937, Communist groups had been using the "rice-sprout" dance for propagandist purposes—developing it into dramatic narratives that depicted the revolutionary struggles of the poor against the rich and against the Japanese who invaded China during that period. Scholar J. Norman Wilkinson notes that, as propagandists, the authors' primary goals with *The White-Haired Girl* were to create support for the changes in policy being put forward by Mao and to provide a model for proletarian unity and courage.

Although *The White-Haired Girl* was not the only *yangko* opera—the first was *Brother and Sister Pioneers* (1943), also created at Lu Hsun College—it was clearly the most successful, followed closely in popularity only by a later revolutionary ballet called *The Red Detachment of Women* (1964). Consistent with Chinese theater's practice of continually perfecting its major hits, *The White-Haired Girl* was adapted tirelessly for decades, for both political and aesthetic reasons. One of the first major adaptations came in 1949, when the Communist Party declared itself the official government of China. Classical operas were banned or altered drastically, and, as Wilkinson remarks, the formally trained Peking Opera performers were required to adapt their traditional acting style to achieve a more "natural" and "realistic" effect in their performances of *The White-Haired Girl.*

The next major innovation followed the start of the Cultural Revolution in 1966, when the opera was made into a ballet and the plot was modified to make it more consistently "revolutionary." It was at this point that the Communist Party named *The White-Haired Girl* as one of the *yangbanxi* ("model dramas"), which comprised eight exemplary works of modern revolutionary art. Wilkinson explains that the party's aim was to persuade the Chinese proletariat to emulate the virtues of Yang, Xi'er, and her fiancé, Dachun, whom the Communists considered idealized models of revolutionary heroism. Although China is not the only country to have provided official models of behavior to influence social practices, scholar Paul Clark emphasizes that China does have an especially long and successful history of establishing moral authority through such means. That history doubtless helped to ensure the triumph of *The White-Haired Girl* as an influential piece of propaganda that is also considered a classic in China today.

THEMES AND STYLE

The sharp contrast between traditional and modern societies and the meaning of proletariat liberation constitute the central thematic axes of the opera. In line with Mao's artistic precepts, the play resists cultural imperialism by drawing deliberately from Chinese folk traditions rather than from the modern Western dramas that had begun to influence Chinese theater before the revolution. At the same time, *The White-Haired Girl* undercuts the superstitious beliefs found in those older Chinese folk tales. For example, paper gods, hung by the door of the family house, are supposed to "keep out all devils, great and small," but they give Xi'er and her father no protection against a systemic evil. Furthermore, the white goddess of the play's title is exposed by Communist cadres to be merely another human girl victimized by wealthy men. The play constantly foregrounds the corruption, heartlessness, and greed of the ruling class, characterized by the landlord Huang and his mother, who exploit their peasants and torture their house servants. Admitting that he does not care about the poor, Huang offers the conventional assumptions held in a hierarchical society as justification: that "the only way to get rich is at the expense of the poor" and that "the poor, of course, must go cold and hungry, because that's their destiny, fixed by fate." Perhaps the most disturbing fact of this "fate" is that the traditional system, at least as portrayed in the play, allows no avenue of appeal for the wronged peasants, for there can be no justice when the magistrate and the head of the district are "hand in glove with the rich."

In the eyes of the Communist Party, the central priority of *The White-Haired Girl* is to show Chinese audiences that, with courage and unity, it is possible to break out of that helpless position. Perhaps the most effective tactic employed by the writers is the grafting of new meanings onto already familiar and beloved literary forms and themes. The original play's sixteen scenes and five acts are composed of sung sections alternated with spoken dialogue, a structure already common to Chinese theater. Several themes, such as the haunting of an evil man by a hungry ghost and a child's seeking vengeance on behalf of a parent, are familiar as well. Those well-known cultural elements enabled Chinese spectators to embrace the play

REVENGE: AN OLD PLOT IN NEW CHINA

Although *The White-Haired Girl* is characteristic of the innovation and modernization taking place in Chinese culture since the 1940s, it owes much of its success to its sourcing of an already popular plot in Chinese folktales: the punishment of the corrupt and wealthy and the avenging of the poor by an intervening force. Before the revolution, this force generally took the shape of a good king, a just official, a supernatural power, or a Robin Hood-type figure. In *The White-Haired Girl,* the Eighth Route Army arrives on the people's behalf—but this Communist force empowers the people to rise up and avenge themselves.

The vengeful goddess figure also appears frequently in Chinese legend. In *Five Chinese Communist Plays,* Martin Ebon points out how, as *The White-Haired Girl* was adapted over the years in response to political pressures, the characters grow progressively more idealized and heroic. Xi'er becomes increasingly like a mythic goddess of folklore—a "red goddess with white hair." Yet even in the earliest version of the play, she has a fearless quality by the end; despite all she has been through, she has never given up, crying out defiantly, "I'm a fire you'll never put out! I'm a tree you'll never uproot!"

at once, easing the process of questioning old belief systems that would impede the kind of revolution depicted in the play.

While the play begins with simple words and gestures of affection between family members, the language and delivery of the lines grow increasingly anthemic as the play progresses. With the arrival of the Eighth Route Army on the day of reckoning, the characters' speeches coalesce into a collective voice that lists the landlord's many crimes against the poor: "[S]o much rent you squeezed, so much money too, there's no counting the tragedies caused by you!" This joint voice also celebrates the new future opening up before them: "A new life starts today! Age-old feudal bonds today are cut away! We will be our own masters from now on!"

CRITICAL DISCUSSION

Immediately hailed as a success by Chinese audiences, *The White-Haired Girl* eventually was also praised by critics for its innovative combination of old and new cultural elements. Communist Party representatives, considering *The White-Haired Girl* primarily in terms of its propagandistic effectiveness, initially approved of the play. However, several elements seen as the cultural residue of old China—such as the helpless suicide of Xi'er's father and the rape of Xi'er—disturbed some critics, including Comrade Jiang Qing, wife of Mao and a leading figure in the Communist reformation of art and literature. When the play was later revised,

A performance of *The Red Detachment of Women* produced in Beijing, China, in 2006. Like *The White-Haired Girl,* it is a dramatic dance production with political overtones. © TAO IMAGES LIMITED/ALAMY.

many of those "counterrevolutionary" elements were altered to make the characters even more exemplary models of revolutionary heroism. Meanwhile, in the West, few academic critics had access to *The White-Haired Girl* during its first thirty years, as is evident in the introduction-style scholarship that did emerge in the early 1970s. Wilkinson's "'The White-Haired Girl': From 'Yangko' to Revolutionary Modern Ballet" (1974) and other criticism of the 1970s focused on tracing the relationship between the modern opera/ballet form and the older cultural themes and forms. Francis L. K. Hsu, writing in 1977, defended *The White-Haired Girl* against American art critics' derision of Chinese theater in general; he argued that their low opinion was largely a result of their misunderstanding of Chinese culture.

For most critics, the greatest significance of *The White-Haired Girl* lies in its illustration of what critic Xiaomei Chen calls the "intimate and ironic relationship between theater and politics." Chen's significant *Acting the Right Part: Political Theater and Popular Drama in Contemporary China* (2002) examines the history of the public reception of *The White-Haired Girl* to emphasize the theatricality of public life in China. Chen cites Chinese critic Meng Yue, who demonstrates how the play exemplifies the process by which a new political regime and culture shores up authority by weaving itself into the values and forms of the existing culture.

The history of *The White-Haired Girl's* public reception and its many permutations over the years

also have prompted many scholars to declare the opera one of the richest sites for understanding the processes of modernization in China. Recent scholarship pushes back against the popular notion that communism was the sole arbiter of 20th-century Chinese aesthetics. Clark, examining the Cultural Revolution through the lens of the arts, focuses heavily on formal innovations made by artists during the period. Clark admires the way *The White-Haired Girl* combines Western dance forms such as ballet with Chinese folk forms to produce a modern, distinctively Chinese performance style, and he concludes that Chinese model operas played a major role in establishing a new revolutionary culture.

BIBLIOGRAPHY

Sources

Chen, Xiaomei. *Acting the Right Part: Political Theater and Popular Drama in Contemporary China.* Honolulu: U of Hawaii P, 2002. Print.

Clark, Paul. *The Chinese Cultural Revolution: A History.* Cambridge, UK: Cambridge UP, 2008. Print.

Ebon, Martin, ed. *Five Chinese Communist Plays.* New York: John Day, 1975. Print.

Hsu, Francis L. K. "Intercultural Understanding: Genuine and Spurious Author(s)." *Anthropology & Education Quarterly* Nov. 1977: 202–09. *JSTOR.* Web. 15 Aug. 2012.

Wilkinson, J. Norman. "'The White-Haired Girl': From 'Yangko' to Revolutionary Modern Ballet." *Educational Theatre Journal* May 1974: 164–74. *JSTOR.* Web. 15 Aug. 2012.

Further Reading

Chen, Xiaomei. *The Columbia Anthology of Modern Chinese Drama.* New York: Columbia UP, 2010. Print.

Du, Mingxin. *The Red Detachment of Women. Five Chinese Communist Plays.* Ed. Martin Ebon. New York: John Day, 1975. Print.

Durdin, Tillman. "Popular Ballet Is Reminiscent of 'Uncle Tom's Cabin.'" *The New York Times Report from Red China.* Ed. Frank Ching. New York: Quadrangle, 1971. 325. Print.

Grasso, June, Jay Corrin, and Michael Kort. *Modernization and Revolution in China.* Armonk, NY: Sharpe, 1991. Print.

Marchetti, Gina. "Two Stage Sisters: The Blossoming of a Revolutionary Aesthetic." *Jump Cut* 34 (1989): 95–106. Print.

Roberts, Rosemary A. "Maoist Women Warriors: Historical Continuities and Cultural Transgressions." *Chinese Revolution and Chinese Literature.* Ed. Tao Dongfeng, Yang Xiaobin, Roberts, and Yang Ling. Newcastle upon Tyne, UK: Cambridge Scholars, 2009. 139–62. Print.

Sun-Childers, Jaia, and Douglas Childers. *The White-Haired Girl: Bittersweet Adventures of a Little Red Soldier.* New York: Picador USA/St. Martin's, 1996. Print.

Zhao, Hongfan. *Modern Chinese Drama.* Trans. Matthew Truman. San Francisco: Long River, 2011. Print.

Media Adaptations

The White-Haired Girl. Conductor Fan Shengwu. Orchestra by Shanghai Ballet. [S.l.]; KK Productions, © 1992. CD.

The White-Haired Girl. Dir. Choui Khoua and Bin Wang. Perf. Qiang Chen, Baiwan Li, and Hua Tian. Changchun Film Studio. 1950. Film.

Sarah Gardam

PREDICTIONS AND PRESCRIPTIONS

ALAS, BABYLON

Pat Frank

OVERVIEW

Alas, Babylon, a novel by Pat Frank published in 1959, is a postapocalyptic novel, describing the aftershocks of a nuclear event in a small town in Florida. After the Soviet Union drops a nuclear bomb on the United States, the protagonist Randy Bragg awakes to find the majority of the cities in the country gone, including nearby Orlando. The plot follows different members of society, detailing how each person deals with a civilization in ruins. Effectively capturing the anxieties of the Cold War era, *Alas, Babylon* offers a grim look at the effects of war in a nuclear age.

Following a trend of films and novels featuring nuclear incidents in the 1950s, *Alas, Babylon* marks one of the first of many speculative fiction novels that became popular in the 1960s. Upon its publication, the novel was met with mixed reviews, though it was praised for its ability to show the human effects of nuclear war. Rather than focusing on a depiction of nuclear warfare, Frank's novel explores the toll a nuclear war takes on society, particularly the strains placed on civilian relationships. It echoes the fears of Americans as they faced a cold war that threatened every day to turn to nuclear devastation. Nuclear weaponry no longer seemed something of science fiction; instead, the United States lived in the dark reality that a mushroom cloud could appear at any time. Considered to be one of the first postnuclear holocaust novels written from the perspective of a group of survivors, *Alas, Babylon* is noteworthy in its influence on novels that would follow in the genre.

HISTORICAL AND LITERARY CONTEXT

At the end of World War II, postwar Europe became a divided continent, with the Soviets controlling the east and the Allies the west. By 1947 there was growing concern among British and American leaders that the Soviet Union might attack Western Europe. Tensions increased during the early 1950s, when the United States and the Soviet Union both developed a new type of nuclear weapon—the hydrogen bomb—which was capable of producing a much greater explosion than the nuclear weapons that had preceded it. In 1951 the insurance company Mutual of Omaha created an advertisement detailing how to survive a nuclear attack, instructing people in the event of a nuclear blast to drop to the ground immediately and protect themselves from the ensuing searing flash. Schoolchildren were taught to seek cover under their desks if a nuclear bomb was dropped.

At the time *Alas, Babylon* saw publication, nuclear technology had become part of American culture, generating not only fear of nuclear annihilation but also anticipation of the potential benefits of nuclear technology. The term *atomic* often carried a positive connotation, suggesting the exciting possibilities of a new era. Infiltrating popular culture, the word became common in comic books and science fiction movies, including *Them!* (1954), which features monster ants that are a result of nuclear radiation. *Alas, Babylon* marks a departure from the campy science fiction common in the 1950s as it takes a real and unflinching look at a possible future.

American novelists in the decade capitalized on the public's fears of a potential Soviet invasion. Pulp novels such as Joseph L. Whatley's *Purgatory of the Conquered* (1956) depicted a future in which the United States becomes a communist country. These novels, however, did not share Frank's vision of a nuclear holocaust; rather, they tended to focus on what the United States would be like under the control of the Soviet Union, drawing upon fears of communism more than any anxieties based on nuclear warfare. Nevil Shute's 1957 novel *On the Beach* comes closest to the themes explored in *Alas, Babylon.* Shute, like Frank, centers his novel on a group of survivors as they attempt to navigate a world forever changed by a war involving multiple bombings that effectively bring about worldwide holocaust.

Following the precedent set by Shute's novel and its popular 1959 film adaptation, *Alas, Babylon* anticipated the fears of nuclear devastation that would paralyze the United States during the Cuban missile crisis of 1962. Even with Frank's acute ability to paint a cultural moment, his novel was met with mixed reviews upon its initial publication. Nevertheless, the novel has maintained a legacy as one of the more popular texts of holocaust fiction that came out of the early nuclear era. *Fail-Safe,* a 1962 novel coauthored by Eugene Burdick and Harvey Wheeler, explores the same themes of nuclear holocaust and cold war anxiety, and writer David Brin has cited *Alas, Babylon* as an important text as he was composing his own postapocalyptic novel, *The Postman* (1985).

⁜ *Key Facts*

Time Period:
Mid-20th Century

Genre:
Novel

Events:
Cold War; nuclear proliferation

Nationality:
American

PAT FRANK: AUTHOR OF THE APOCALYPSE

Alas, Babylon was only one of Pat Frank's ventures into the possible future of the Cold War. He wrote several novels that explore similar themes of atomic apocalypse. Two years prior to *Alas, Babylon*, Frank published *Forbidden Area*, a thriller-style novel that tells the story of a young couple who face the imminent destruction of the United States at the hands of the Soviets. The satiric novel *Mr. Adam*, published in 1946, details the effects of a nuclear power plant explosion that leaves all of the men on earth sterile. When a baby girl is born, it is discovered that the title character is the only man capable of reproduction; Mr. Adam thus becomes mankind's last hope for survival.

In 1962, the year of the Cuban missile crisis, Frank penned a nonfiction book, *How to Survive the H-Bomb, and Why*. The book, as suggested by the title, details not only the probability of a nuclear attack on the United States but also describes what would happen if such an event were ever to occur. Frank's handbook tells of what difficulties would befall the survivors, such as loss of electricity and transportation, and instructs readers how to survive.

THEMES AND STYLE

At the heart of *Alas, Babylon* is the theme of survival and resilience, both on a global scale in the face of worldwide disaster and on the personal level, as a group of survivors attempts to maintain relationships as well as their own humanity. Readers are given a bleak view of war in which weapons of mass destruction threaten to annihilate everyone; as one character notes, "Nobody's winning. Cities are dying and ships are sinking and aircraft is going in, but nobody's winning." In the midst of the chaos, life continues, surviving against the odds. The survivors bury their dead, plant gardens for food, and even engage in mock ceremonies to preserve some normalcy. One young couple gets married, the best man "clad in a tentsized, striped bathrobe." Frank portrays the nuclear holocaust with careful attention to human emotion, emphasizing the characters' strength against the human toll such an event would take.

Frank reminds his readers of the effects of a widespread nuclear disaster and the enormous consequences of waging nuclear war. While focusing much of the action on protagonist Randy Bragg, Frank periodically deviates from the main narrative to describe how other survivors are faring. Usually, the report is grim, as in the case of Lavinia McGovern, a diabetic, who dies once the insulin upon which she is dependent can no longer be refrigerated to preserve it. Frank also writes of the less significant effects of nuclear war, as when Randy reminisces about the "painful luxuries" of his life before the mushroom cloud, such as hot showers, sweets, and his record player.

Frank's style is simple and straightforward, suggestive of military-speak or the mundane daily task list that would befall the nuclear bomb survivor. Slang or regional dialect is notably absent from the text; even emotional scenes are described in simple, declarative sentences: "They buried Porky Logan Friday morning. It was a ticklish and exhausting procedure." Rather than describing any emotions of mourning, Frank details the obstacles Randy must overcome when burying Porky, given that the funeral parlor is locked and the local undertaker must be led by gunpoint to get the man properly buried. The detached, simple style of the prose serves to highlight the plight of the survivors, who do not have the luxury of time to process more complex emotions such as grief. Their only goal is to survive the radioactive fallout.

CRITICAL DISCUSSION

Some critics, particularly science fiction enthusiasts, were not impressed with Frank's simplistic style. Floyd C. Gale, in a review for *Galaxy* in 1959, complains that "Frank stopped too soon with too little," giving *Alas, Babylon* three out of five stars. Despite receiving mixed reviews, the novel was a best seller, with more than thirty printings in six years. Although Frank's novel could easily have been dismissed, it continues to be read more than fifty years later, perhaps due to the adaptations of the novel that followed its initial publication. In 1960, CBS produced a TV adaptation for the network's *Playhouse 90* program. Three years later, Frank's novel was adapted as a play by Anne Coulter Martens.

Cementing its legacy as a classic work of postnuclear fiction, Frank's novel is regarded both as a warning of nuclear war and a reminder of the hope that the country maintained regarding the possibilities of nuclear power in the mid-twentieth century. Jeffrey L. Porter claimed that the novel "would have readers believe that something very good can come out of disaster," playing on the tension that Americans felt between the promise of nuclear energy and the ever-present threat of global disaster. It is Frank's ability to so clearly capture the fears, hopes, and beliefs of his time that makes *Alas, Babylon* a text that is still read by contemporary readers.

Today, Frank's novel is discussed as a part of nuclear-era apocalyptic fiction, alongside texts such as *On the Beach* and Phillip Wylie's *Tomorrow!* (1954). Modern critics look at *Alas, Babylon* as a window into the culture of the 1950s-era United States, particularly the idea of the importance of the nuclear family unit during the Cold War period. For example, Richard Schwartz notes that the family unit in Frank's novel is maintained, perhaps even strengthened, throughout the chaos caused by the nuclear bomb; survival requires "the protagonist ... to become a better, more responsible person and to form and head a family of his own." Jacqueline Foertsch observes that Frank's group of survivors become a microcosm

Mushroom cloud during atomic weapons test in the 1950s. Pat Frank's novel *Alas, Babylon* imagines the effects of nuclear war on a small American town. © ROGER RESSMEYER/ CORBIS.

of American society, as the African American characters, who are treated fairly by Randy, find themselves facing "misgivings and outright hostilities" from the group's other members as they integrate into Randy's "family," thus perhaps echoing the decade's evolving attitudes toward race.

BIBLIOGRAPHY

Sources

Frank, Pat. *Alas, Babylon.* New York: Harper Perennial, 1959. Print.

Foertsch, Jacqueline. "'Extraordinarily Convenient Neighbors': African-American Characters in White-Authored Post-Atomic Novels." *Journal of Modern Literature* 30.4 (2007): 122–38. *MLA International Bibliography.* Web. 15 Aug. 2012.

Gale, Floyd. C. "Galaxy's 5 Star Shelf." Rev. of *Alas, Babylon,* by Pat Frank. *Galaxy Magazine* Dec. 1959: 150.

Porter, Jeffrey L. "Narrating the End: Fables of Survival in the Nuclear Age." *Journal of American Culture* 16.4 (1993): 41–47. *MLA International Bibliography.* Web. 15 Aug. 2012.

Schwartz, Richard A. "Family, Gender, and Society in 1950's American Fiction of Nuclear Apocalypse: *Shadow on the Hearth, Tomorrow!, The Last Day,* and *Alas, Babylon.*" *Journal of American Culture* 29.4 (2006): 406–24. *MLA International Bibliography.* Web. 15 Aug. 2012.

Further Reading

Boyer, Paul S. *By the Bomb's Early Light: American Thought and Culture at the Dawn of the Atomic Age.* New York: Pantheon, 1985. Print.

Brin, David. *The Postman.* Toronto: Bantam, 1985. Print.

———. *Through Stranger Eyes: Reviews, Introductions, Tributes, and Iconoclastic Essays.* Ann Arbor, MI: Nimble, 2008. Print.

Curtis, Claire P. *Postapocalyptic Fiction and the Social Contract: "We'll Not Go Home Again."* Lanham, MD: Lexington, 2010. Print.

Franklin, Bruce H. *War Stars: The Superweapon and the American Imagination.* New York: Oxford UP, 1988. Print.

Sullivan, C. W., III. "*Alas, Babylon* and *On the Beach*: Antiphons of the Apocalypse." *Phoenix from the Ashes: The Literature of the Remade World.* NY: Greenwood, 1987: 37–44. *MLA International Bibliography.* Web. 14 Aug. 2012.

Weart, Spencer R. *Nuclear Fear: A History of Images.* Cambridge: Harvard UP, 1988. Print.

Zimbaro, Valerie P. *Encyclopedia of Apocalyptic Literature.* Santa Barbara: ABC-CLIO, 1996. Print.

Media Adaptation

"Alas, Babylon." Playhouse 90. Dir. Robert Stevens. Perf. Dana Andrews, Robert Crawford Jr., and Judith Evelyn. Columbia Broadcasting System, KCBS-TV. Los Angeles. 3 Apr. 1960. Television.

Lisa Kroger

ATLAS SHRUGGED

Ayn Rand

✦ **Key Facts**

Time Period:
Mid-20th Century

Genre:
Novel

Events:
Heightening of Cold
War tension; Bolshevik
Revolution; growing
jingoism

Nationality:
American

OVERVIEW

Russian-born American writer Ayn Rand's *Atlas Shrugged* (1957) is a philosophical novel set in a dystopian United States, where society's most intelligent and productive citizens go on strike to protest increasing governmental regulation and taxation and the collectivist leadership's support of the parasitic, unambitious masses through major social programs. The novel's title is a reference to the mythological figure of Atlas, who is tasked with holding the heavens upon his shoulders. Rand's capitalist protagonists, no longer willing to support the rest of civilization, shrug off the unwanted responsibility. The author argues that any government is doomed to collapse when it stifles individual creativity and free enterprise; she denounces any restriction imposed on individuals to serve the collective. Initially titled *The Strike*, the novel is overtly theoretical and procapitalist, promoting antisocialist views and laissez-faire policies as an antidote to expansive government intervention.

Despite the conservative Cold War context of the novel's publication, early critics disliked *Atlas Shrugged*. Reviewers dismissed the novel as an immoral endorsement of self-interest and greed; however, readers embraced the depiction of the indefensible stifling of Americans' entrepreneurial and creative spirit. Rand wrote no further works of fiction, turning to nonfiction in order to develop the themes and concepts put forth in *Atlas Shrugged*. Collectively, these writings articulate her philosophy of objectivism, which promotes reason, the dispassionate assessment of reality, self-interest, strong rights of private property, and laissez-faire government. The novel remains immensely popular, particularly among right-wing conservatives, for its glorification of human achievement and advocacy of rationality, individualism, and capitalism.

HISTORICAL AND LITERARY CONTEXT

Rand wrote *Atlas Shrugged* in the wake of World War II, after the totalitarian governments in Germany and Italy were overthrown and socialist and communist systems took root in parts of Europe, China, Korea, and Cuba. In 1947, fearing the spread of new totalitarian regimes, U.S. President Harry S. Truman announced his doctrine of communist containment, which helped initiate the Cold War. Support for socialist and communist ideals plummeted among Americans, and communist sympathizers became enemies of the state for their alleged opposition to the ideals of freedom and democracy.

Atlas Shrugged was published at the height of the Cold War, amid a flurry of U.S. government-sponsored propaganda intended to build patriotic sentiment and to incite anxiety about the global spread of communism. In the 1930s and 1940s, President Franklin Delano Roosevelt's New Deal and World War II had greatly expanded the reach of the federal government, and some feared that unchecked growth could lead to a near-socialist state that would fund colossal social programs through heavy taxation of citizens. During the second Red Scare of 1947 to 1957, U.S. Senator Joseph McCarthy heightened the widespread paranoia, blacklisting alleged Soviet sympathizers and conducting trials against them. Many mainstream readers embraced procapitalist works by writers such as Rand who condemned socialism, communism, and fascism as deeply and inherently unjust. As a child in Russia, Rand had personally witnessed the 1917 October Revolution and was adamant in her denunciation of the Bolsheviks and their institution of a socialist regime.

Part of a long tradition of dystopian literature, *Atlas Shrugged* is one of many twentieth-century novels that feature an authoritarian government. Other notable examples in this genre are Aldous Huxley's *Brave New World* (1932) and George Orwell's *Nineteen Eighty-Four* (1949). Both describe nations under the thumb of a totalitarian regime that suppresses individuality and rules through fascism and coercion. Rand's three major fictional works before *Atlas Shrugged* also treat themes of tyranny triumphing over individual freedom. *We the Living* (1936) addresses this subject in the context of Soviet Russia; in the future society depicted in *Anthem* (1938), the collective has subsumed the individual, substituting the word "we" for "I"; and *The Fountainhead* (1943) portrays a young man's resistance to compulsory servility and the unquestioning conformists who thwart him.

Rand's legacy has been political rather than literary. She has particularly inspired Republicans—though she is pro-choice and an atheist—and libertarians through her ability to promote a platform of laissez-faire capitalism to a wide audience. One of the earliest defenders of *Atlas Shrugged* was the economist

Alan Greenspan, who later chaired the Federal Reserve (1987–2006). He enthusiastically adopted objectivism and wrote multiple articles on it throughout the 1950s and 1960s. He also contributed several essays to Rand's 1966 collection *Capitalism: The Unknown Ideal*. Rand elaborated on her philosophies in three newsletters she produced—*The Objectivist Newsletter* (1962–66), *The Objectivist* (1966–71), and *The Ayn Rand Letter* (1971–76)—and in several books of nonfiction, including *The Virtue of Selfishness* (1964) and *Introduction to Objectivist Epistemology* (1967). After the 2008 global financial crisis, commentators on both sides of the political divide revived *Atlas Shrugged*, some finding in it possible roots of the crash and others advocating its proposals as a way out of the quagmire.

THEMES AND STYLE

The primary theme of *Atlas Shrugged* is the idea that human achievement is based on the necessary primacy of the individual over the collective. The novel's protagonists are brilliant capitalist mavericks and models of success: Dagney Taggart is the operating vice president of a railroad company that is struggling under the state's collectivist policies; Francisco D'Anconia is a copper magnate; Henry "Hank" Reardon presides over American steel production; and the inventor John Galt leads the strike that brings down the government, describing himself as "the man who's taken away your victims and thus destroyed your world." All are heroes who defend the individual's right "to think, to work and to keep the results." Social growth and prosperity depend on this "rational selfishness," which is embodied in the oath Galt's strikers must take: "I swear by my life and my love of it that I will never live for the sake of another man, nor ask another man to live for mine." Rand's antagonists are incompetent and weak, refusing to think for themselves; they represent the government-supported masses, most of whom are "mooches" and "looters" living off the collective resources and within its mindset.

All aspects of the novel—plot, characters, narrative strategies, and tone—reflect rationality as a primary value, each contributing its share to the illustration of objectivism. The third-person point of view lends a seeming objectivity to the author's argument; however, the narrator frequently offers commentary on and insight into the characters' inner lives, thoughts, and emotions, applying Rand's philosophy to the story as it unfolds and portraying its content as political reality. Consequently, the characters serve as avatars of either individualism or collectivism operating under the author's worldview. Similarly, Rand uses conflict primarily to draw broad philosophical conclusions rather than to build tension.

The novel's tone is detached and rational. Rand makes little attempt to disguise her views: her narrator's frequent asides are often overtly contemptuous or cynical. Dialogue is often stilted. Many of the characters

ATLAS SHRUGGED AND THE 2012 PRESIDENTIAL RACE

In 2012 Republican presidential candidate Mitt Romney's choice of Wisconsin congressman Paul Ryan as his running mate focused nuanced attention on Ayn Rand and *Atlas Shrugged*. Earlier in his career Ryan was an outspoken proponent of Rand's philosophy, had been a guest speaker at the Rand-inspired Atlas Society, and had, in interviews, confessed to giving out copies of *Atlas Shrugged* as staff Christmas gifts. As a candidate for the vice presidency, however, Ryan distanced himself from the author he once credited with being a major inspiration for his political career.

Although *Atlas Shrugged* has often been criticized as a heartless endorsement of greed, particularly by American liberals, Ryan's reticence to embrace Rand in 2012 stemmed not from her polarizing economic views but from her atheism. Ryan, a conservative Catholic courting an increasingly socially conservative sector of the Republican Party, openly embraced his religion as a grounding for his political positions. Rand, whose novel he once saw as powerful propaganda for small, limited government and unfettered free market capitalism, thus became a dangerous ally. Although Rand's abhorrence of religion had long been overlooked by her fans on the far right, Ryan's change of position suggests a reevaluation of the value of her work as propaganda among American conservatives.

speak in didactic monologues void of subtext or ambiguity; the most notorious of these are D'Anconia's lengthy discourse on money as the root of all good and Galt's three-hour speech over a hijacked radio channel explaining Rand's objectivist philosophy. An unapologetic novel of ideas, *Atlas Shrugged* maintains an ironic distance from sentimentality. As Galt coolly tells Taggart near the end of the novel, "No one's happiness but my own is in my power to achieve or to destroy."

CRITICAL DISCUSSION

Atlas Shrugged was an immediate popular success, almost instantly appearing on the *New York Times* best-seller list and remaining there for more than five months. Polls showed that some readers counted it among the books that had most changed their lives. Many reviewers panned the novel, however, censuring both the quality of its writing and the ideas it promoted. Most critics felt it was heavy-handed, calling it black and white; by turns melodramatic and moralistic; excessively dogmatic; and offensively selfish. Those who were overt about their place on the political spectrum expressed greater outrage or enthusiastic approval.

In the intervening decades *Atlas Shrugged* has become one of the most renowned and influential twentieth-century novels. Yaron Brook, president and executive director of the Ayn Rand Institute, notes

Ancient Roman statue of the titan Atlas supporting the heavens on his shoulders. Ayn Rand's *Atlas Shrugged* likens industrialists and inventors to the heroic, overburdened titan of Greek mythology. © MIMMO JODICE/CORBIS.

commented on the book's continued social impact and prominent role in shaping American political ideology. In the introduction to *Ayn Rand's* Atlas Shrugged: *A Philosophical and Literary Companion* (2007), business professor Edward Younkins writes that the novel is still "a blueprint for the future and a potential for social change." His collection of essays (which he concedes were all contributed by "enthusiastic admirers" of *Atlas Shrugged*) broadened the scope of Rand scholarship, treating the philosophical, historical, aesthetic, literary, and sociological aspects of the book and its legacy. Almost a political litmus test, Rand's final novel is both celebrated and reviled for its ideas and their powerful impact on American views of the purpose of government.

BIBLIOGRAPHY

Sources

Brook, Yaron. "Is Rand Relevant?" *Wall Street Journal.* Dow Jones & Company, 14 Mar. 2009. Web. 20 June 2012.

Fletcher, Max E. "Harriet Martineau and Ayn Rand: Economics in the Guise of Fiction." *American Journal of Economics and Sociology* 33.4 (1974): 367–79. Web. 4 July 2012.

Rand, Ayn. *Atlas Shrugged.* New York: Plume, 1999. Print.

Younkins, Edward W. Introduction. *Ayn Rand's* Atlas Shrugged: *A Philosophical and Literary Companion.* Ed. Younkins. Hampshire: Ashgate, 2007. Print.

Further Reading

Berliner, Michael, ed. *Letters of Ayn Rand.* Trans. Dina Garmong. New York: Dutton, 1995. Print.

Binswanger, Harry, ed. *The Ayn Rand Lexicon: Objectivism from A to Z.* New York: New American Library, 1986. Print.

Burns, Jennifer. *Goddess of the Market: Ayn Rand and the American Right.* New York: Oxford UP, 2009. Print.

Gladstein, Mimi. *The New Ayn Rand Companion.* Westport: Greenwood, 1999. Print.

Harriman, David, ed. *The Journals of Ayn Rand.* New York: Plume, 1997. Print.

Peikoff, Leonard. *Objectivism: The Philosophy of Ayn Rand.* New York: Meridian, 1993. Print.

———, ed. *The Voice of Reason: Essays in Objectivist Thought.* New York: Meridian, 1990. Print.

Rand, Ayn. *Capitalism: The Unknown Ideal.* New York: New American Library, 1967. Print.

———. *The Virtue of Selfishness: A New Concept of Egoism.* New York: New American Library, 1964. Print.

Media Adaptations

Atlas Shrugged: Part I. Dir. Paul Johansson. Perf. Taylor Schilling, Grant Bowler, and Paul Johansson. Strike Productions, 2011. Film.

Atlas Shrugged II: The Strike. Dir. John Putch. Perf. Samantha Mathis, Jason Beghe, and Esai Morales. 2012. Film.

in a 2009 article in the *Wall Street Journal,* "Pundits including Rush Limbaugh and Rick Santelli urge listeners to read [Rand's] books, and her magnum opus, *Atlas Shrugged,* is selling at a faster rate today than at any time during its fifty-one-year history." Its popularity has been partly sustained by private organizations that fund education and outreach based on Rand's ideas, including the Ayn Rand Institute (founded in 1985), which teaches courses through its Objectivist Academic Center and distributes free copies of Rand's books to high school and university students and teachers; it also sponsors nationwide essay contests, campus clubs, scholarships, conferences, lectures, and media appearances that promote Rand's books and philosophies. Business professor and former banker John Allison has offered up to two million dollars in grants to some colleges contingent on their instituting courses on capitalism that use *Atlas Shrugged,* contributing to the national debate about charitable donations with stipulations. Public sales of the book spiked after the 2008 stock market crash and again during the 2012 presidential race, when Republican vice presidential candidate Paul Ryan declared that his system of values was based on *Atlas Shrugged.*

The dominant trend in scholarship of the novel focuses on its political and economic aspects. In a 1974 article for the *American Journal of Economics and Sociology,* Max E. Fletcher refers to Rand as a "purpose writer" whose mission is to "convert [her] reading public to a firm belief in the principles of a self-regulating market system." Many critics have

Colby Cuppernull

CAPITALISM AND FREEDOM

Milton Friedman

OVERVIEW

Milton Friedman's *Capitalism and Freedom,* a book of economic theory published in 1962, argues that economic freedom, as manifested in free-market capitalism, is a necessary condition for political liberty. Throughout the book, Friedman asserts that the role of government should be limited to enforcing laws, supporting the public good, and regulating the money supply. Friedman analyzes various aspects of U.S. society, including international trade, fiscal policy, education, racial and religious discrimination, and social welfare programs, almost always concluding that a substantially reduced degree of governmental intervention results in both a better economy and a freer society. The book stands as one of the seminal twentieth-century arguments for laissez-faire capitalism.

Friedman's economic ideas held little sway in the intellectual climate of 1962, when government intervention in the wake of the New Deal was more readily accepted. The prevailing economic theory among U.S. economists and policymakers was Keynesianism, which supported the principles of a free market but advocated a more active governmental role in maintaining a stable economy. In the decades since its publication, however, *Capitalism and Freedom* has grown substantially in stature, influencing late-twentieth-century economic policy and becoming an intellectual touchstone for countless economic writings. Friedman, who served as an economic advisor to U.S. President Ronald Reagan, is now considered to be among the most important economists of the twentieth century, and his impact on economic policy and theory still endures.

HISTORICAL AND LITERARY CONTEXT

The Great Depression, which was triggered by the U.S. stock-market collapse of October 1929 and deepened by subsequent steep worldwide economic decline over the next few years, led to a substantial reevaluation and reconfiguration of existing economic policy. The market theories of the English economist John Maynard Keynes, whose influential 1936 text *The General Theory of Employment, Interest and Money* challenged the then-dominant belief in a self-stabilizing competitive market, inaugurated what came to be termed a "Keynesian Revolution," in which the government played an increased economic role by such means as controlling monetary policy and regulating how business could be conducted. Keynesianism remained the foremost economic paradigm for several decades before falling out of favor during the economic downturn in the 1970s, and it led to profound and lasting changes in governmental structure and economic policy.

At the time *Capitalism and Freedom* was published, Keynesian economics were being used to justify large and growing federal expenditures on U.S. economic infrastructure and social welfare in the aftermath of the Great Depression. The apparent success of Keynesian policy, given the relative prosperity of the post-World War II period, had led to a largely bipartisan expansion of governmental controls over many aspects of U.S. society. Friedman's book counters this orthodoxy, arguing that in almost every instance, governmental intervention hinders the economy rather than helps and, moreover, fundamentally stands in opposition to the ideals toward which a free society should strive.

Economists in the early 1960s mostly favored active government involvement in the economy, since they feared that without such action another depression would occur. Friedman's work, largely out of step with the intellectual mainstream, was a product of the "Chicago school" of economics, which initially referred to a group of economists—including Friedman, George Stigler, and Ronald Coase—who taught in the economics department at the University of Chicago and strongly supported free markets in opposition to Keynesianism. An important textual influence on *Capitalism and Freedom* is the 1944 polemic *The Road to Serfdom* by Austrian economist F. A. Hayek. His arguments, linking tyranny and the loss of individual freedom with collectivism and central planning, prefigure Friedman's similar conviction that political freedom is dependent on economic freedom.

Economists within the then-fledgling conservative movement took *Capitalism and Freedom* seriously, but its publication did not draw widespread notice. The arguments in the book gained traction, eventually exerting a great influence on economic analysis and theory. After the downfall of Keynesianism in the 1970s, *Capitalism and Freedom* came to be seen as one of the preeminent economic statements of the twentieth century, and it has sold more than one-half million copies. In 1976 Friedman was awarded the

Key Facts

Time Period:
Mid-20th Century

Genre:
Economic Philosophy

Events:
Rise of federal expenditures on national defense, infrastructure, and social welfare under Presidents Eisenhower and Kennedy

Nationality:
American

MONETARISM

Milton Friedman was the most prominent exponent of the economic philosophy known as monetarism, which exerted considerable influence on public policy in the 1980s and remains (in modified form) an important part of contemporary economics. Although monetarism forms the basis of some of the assertions made in *Capitalism and Freedom,* it is elaborated in much greater detail in Friedman's 1953 essay collection *Essays in Positive Economics* and his 1963 book *A Monetary History of the United States, 1867–1960,* the latter cowritten with Anna Jacobson Schwartz, another monetarist of note.

Monetarist economics is heavily indebted to the premises of Keynesianism but departs from it in crucial ways. For example, it argues against the Keynesian belief in expansionary fiscal policy as a response to economic recession. In contrast to Keynesianism's emphasis on government expenditures as a means of stabilizing the economy and controlling inflation, monetarists emphasize the importance of monetary policy, particularly stressing the need to control the growth of the money supply, which, in the monetarist view, is linked inexorably to inflation. Inflation, to Friedman and his fellow monetarists, is solely a product of variation in the money supply. As a consequence, expanding the money supply is inevitably counterproductive and leads only to further inflation and, in turn, greater stagnation and recession.

Nobel Prize in Economics. Given his enduring prominence in the field, contemporary economists—even those such as Keynes-influenced Paul Krugman, also a Nobel Prize winner—are invariably obliged to engage with Friedman's conclusions.

THEMES AND STYLE

Central to *Capitalism and Freedom*'s assertions is the idea that political liberty cannot exist in a society that denies its citizens the ability to participate freely in a private economy. In light of the extreme complexity and interdependence of human societies, "there are," Friedman states, "only two ways of co-ordinating the economic activities of millions. One is central direction involving the use of coercion—the technique of the army and of the modern totalitarian state. The other is voluntary co-operation of individuals—the technique of the marketplace." This latter technique takes the form of free exchange within an economy centered on private enterprise, which, as long as it remains truly free, "prevents one person from interfering with another in respect of most of his activities." This system of voluntary exchange, which "gives people what they want instead of what a particular group thinks they ought to want," is undermined by the coercive element introduced by government intervention and results in a fundamental loss of freedom. Friedman contends that "underlying most arguments against the free Market is a lack of belief in freedom itself."

Friedman's arguments are couched in a rhetorical appeal to the principles of classical liberalism. He defines his viewpoint as being liberal, though he takes care to point out that he uses the word "liberal" in its nineteenth-century sense, denoting a belief in personal liberty and economic freedom. Friedman views the more recent notion of liberalism—"a readiness to rely primarily on the state rather than on private voluntary arrangements"—as a corruption of the term, and he makes a point of reclaiming it in his own arguments. To that end, his economic analysis is frequently accompanied by discussions of whether a given market arrangement is compatible with liberal principles. When speaking of a paternalistic rationale for public housing, for example, he asserts that "the liberal will be inclined to reject this argument for responsible adults." Similar invocations of liberalism, which serves as Friedman's avowed philosophical foundation, appear throughout the text.

Friedman employs a lucid and straightforward style that avoids potentially confusing verbiage and prioritizes ease of comprehension. The text, which is relatively short on economic jargon and often provides detailed explanations of specific terms, seems directed not only at the field of practicing economists but also at a more general audience. It largely maintains an even (but rhetorically conscious) tone and avoids excessively emotional language, though its arguments are made forcefully. Its expository approach tends toward the posing of questions that are then immediately answered, as when Friedman, speaking of a hypothetical rise in government expenditures, asks "how much of the rise in expenditures will be offset?" and then proceeds to answer his own inquiry throughout the next few paragraphs. Friedman's professorial delivery befits the book's origins as a series of academic lectures.

CRITICAL DISCUSSION

Upon its initial release, *Capitalism and Freedom* attracted almost no attention from society at large, and not a single major mainstream media outlet in the United States published a review of the book. Its reception in economic journals was mixed and largely skeptical, but some of these reviewers, though not wholly persuaded by Friedman's conclusions, were respectful of his socioeconomic analysis to varying degrees. For example, Abba P. Lerner, writing in the *American Economic Review,* asserts that while Friedman's "pessimistic antigovernmentism leads him to some strange extremes," *Capitalism and Freedom* is nonetheless "an important book that will provoke much thinking and rethinking."

The views expressed in *Capitalism and Freedom* exercised a substantial influence, both directly and indirectly, on the economic policies of later decades. A brief memorial profile of Friedman published in the *Economist* shortly after his death in 2006 asserts that "Friedman laid the foundation of modern theories of consumption." His ideas formed part of the ideological background for the market deregulation that occurred under Reagan and UK Prime Minister Margaret Thatcher in the 1980s, and some of Friedman's suggested reforms, such as a flat income tax rate and a school voucher program, have been implemented by various governments. Likewise, the establishment of the North American Free Trade Agreement in 1994 and the World Trade Organization in 1995 was partly fueled by the free-market arguments of Friedman's work, making it an important precursor to modern globalization. Much recent scholarship is devoted to assessing the ramifications of his legacy.

Scholars today tend to discuss *Capitalism and Freedom* in conjunction with his other writings and with his economic views in general. William Frazer's 1994 study *The Legacy of Keynes and Friedman,* which examines the two economists in detail and discusses their influence in the works of later economists, is one of a large number of works analyzing Friedman's economic and ideological impact. His influence is discussed in far more negative terms in recent texts such as Naomi Klein's *The Shock Doctrine* (2007), which asserts that, contrary to Friedman's statements linking unfettered capitalism with political freedom, "this fundamentalist form of capitalism has consistently been midwifed by the most brutal forms of coercion."

Economist Milton Friedman in 1983. © ROGER RESSMEYER/CORBIS.

BIBLIOGRAPHY

Sources

Frazer, William. *The Legacy of Keynes and Friedman: Economic Analysis, Money, and Ideology.* Westport: Praeger, 1994. Print.

Friedman, Milton. *Capitalism and Freedom.* Chicago: U of Chicago P, 1962. Print.

"A Heavyweight Champ, at Five Foot Two—Milton Friedman." *The Economist* 25 Nov. 2006: 80. *General OneFile.* Web. 28 Aug. 2012.

Klein, Naomi. *The Shock Doctrine: The Rise of Disaster Capitalism.* New York: Metropolitan/Henry Holt, 2007. Print.

Lerner, Abba P. Rev. of *Capitalism and Freedom,* by Milton Friedman. *The American Economic Review* 53.3 (1963): 458–60. Print.

Further Reading

Congdon, Tim G. *Money in a Free Society: Keynes, Friedman, and the New Crisis in Capitalism.* New York: Encounter Books, 2011. Print.

Friedman, Milton. *Essays in Positive Economics.* Chicago: U of Chicago P, 1953. Print.

Friedman, Milton, and Rose Friedman. *Free To Choose: A Personal Statement.* New York: Harcourt, 1980. Print.

Friedman, Milton, and Anna Jacobson Schwartz. *A Monetary History of the United States, 1867–1960.* Princeton: Princeton UP, 1963. Print.

Hayek, F. A. *The Road to Serfdom.* Chicago: U of Chicago P, 1944. Print.

Hirsch, Abraham, and Neil de Marchi. *Milton Friedman: Economics in Theory and Practice.* Ann Arbor: U of Michigan P, 1990. Print.

Keynes, John Maynard. *The General Theory of Employment, Interest and Money.* London: Macmillan, 1936. Print.

Leeson, Robert. "The Legacy of Milton Friedman." *International Journal of Applied Economics and Econometrics* 16.4 (2008): 188–201. Print.

Palley, Thomas I. "Milton Friedman and the Monetarist Counter-Revolution: A Re-Appraisal." *Eastern Economic Journal* 19.1 (1993): 71–81. Print.

James Overholtzer

"CASSANDRA"

Florence Nightingale

✣ *Key Facts*

Time Period:
Mid-19th Century

Genre:
Essay

Events:
Crimean War; advent
of women's suffrage
movement in England

Nationality:
English

OVERVIEW

Written by Florence Nightingale in 1852, "Cassandra" outlines the English nurse and social reformer's frustration with the ways in which family life and gender expectations entrapped women into useless, frustrating lives. Part of an 800-page philosophical and spiritual work titled *Suggestions for Thought to Seekers after Religious Truth,* the essay, and *Suggestions* in general, seems to have been written primarily for Nightingale's own emotional relief rather than addressed to a particular audience. In essence, "Cassandra" speaks to the frustrations Nightingale faced as a well-to-do woman: with no need for a profession, she passed her day in an endless round of fancy sewing and social visits but had no time of her own. This life, she states, can lead women to nervous exhaustion and despair; Nightingale herself was suicidal when she first composed the work.

"Cassandra" and *Suggestions* were never publicly published during Nightingale's lifetime. After completing the initial draft, she began working as a nurse in the Crimean War (1853–56) and rapidly became one of England's most famous individuals for her admirable performance there. When she returned to England, she significantly rewrote "Cassandra" (changing its format from novel to essay) and privately published *Suggestions* in 1860. Nightingale then sent copies to six intellectuals for comments. Although John Stuart Mill, a prominent philosopher, admired it greatly, Nightingale heeded the more cautious approaches of her other readers, including University of Oxford classical scholar Benjamin Jowett, who suggested substantial revisions and a less radical tone. Perhaps because of her new success—her *Notes on Nursing* sold 15,000 copies in its first month—and her new projects, including founding a nursing school, Nightingale chose not to attempt a wider distribution for *Suggestions.* "Cassandra" was first published in 1928 as an appendix to a history of women's suffrage and has been hailed as a classic feminist work ever since.

HISTORICAL AND LITERARY CONTEXT

"Cassandra" dramatizes the problems that Nightingale saw as endemic to middle- and upper-class women in the nineteenth century: psychological and intellectual entrapment. Nightingale, the daughter of wealthy parents whose mother, in particular, was highly conventional, suffered from exactly these problems. While far better educated than many women of her time, she was expected to spend her time on needlework and social calls. Her experience thus exemplified the way in which women were trapped by the nineteenth-century "cult of domesticity": a belief that the home was a woman's "proper sphere" and her duty was to create a refuge of purity and piety to which men could retreat. This worldview naturally prevented employment outside the home: women were expected to be available to their husbands, children, and family at all times.

Nightingale did find a way, shortly after writing "Cassandra," to escape from the cult of domesticity by training as a nurse. After gaining skills in Germany, she went to Scutari, in modern Turkey, where the British army was engaged in the Crimean War against Russia. There, in six months, she reduced Britain's mortality rate from 42 to 2.2 percent, making her a national hero. Nightingale revised "Cassandra" in 1859 after her return from the Crimea, when not only her own situation was radically different but also popular opinion was beginning to change. Although women would not be allowed to initiate divorce (except under extreme circumstances) until 1890 or receive the right to vote until 1918, the first bill for women's suffrage was introduced in 1867, and in 1870 women were given the right to control property they acquired after they married (prior to that, all money earned by a woman automatically belonged to her husband, even if the couple was separated). While numerous men and women were working for these causes by the end of the 1850s, Nightingale declined to get involved in the legal actions (or even, for many years, publicly support them), arguing that employment for women was a far more pressing question than their legal status.

"Cassandra" can be placed within a British tradition of nineteenth-century essays about women's rights, beginning with author and early feminist Mary Wollstonecraft's *A Vindication of the Rights of Women* (1792). During the mid-nineteenth century, essays about women's legal and occupational rights were a popular subgenre, including works by activists Barbara Bodichon (*Women and Work,* 1857) and Bessie Rayner Parkes (*Essays on Women's Work,* 1865). Although the novel was considered an increasingly "feminine" genre, leaving essays as the "masculine" arena, there were a number of prominent midcentury female essayists, including Harriet Martineau and Mary Russell Mitford.

As soon as "Cassandra" was published, it was hailed as a classic women's rights text. Critics see it as important not only in terms of what it says about women's rights but also how it says it: Nightingale's forceful, vivid language creates a "masculine" voice that supports women's right to be taken seriously as intellectuals. According to Elaine Showalter in her 1981 article "Florence Nightingale's Feminist Complaint," the topics that Nightingale raises remain relevant. Showalter argues that Nightingale "has much to say to our time, especially about the development of women who burn themselves out in the struggle against mothers and sisters and who demand freedom from women's culture as much as from women's sphere."

THEMES AND STYLE

The central theme of "Cassandra" is the manner in which domestic life stifles women and keeps them from reaching their full potential. "Women," Nightingale writes, "are never supposed to have any occupation of sufficient importance not to be interrupted, except 'suckling their fools.'… They have accustomed themselves to consider intellectual occupation as a merely selfish amusement." Women thus suffer from "Death of Thought from Starvation, or Death of Moral Activity from Starvation." Nightingale strikingly blames women as much as men for their position, noting that "women themselves have accepted this, have written books to support it, and have trained themselves so as to consider what-ever they do as not of such value to the world or to others, but that they can throw it up at the first claim of social life." To solve this impasse, women must step away from their easy, if stifling, lives, and some must sacrifice themselves: "Better have pain than paralysis! A hundred struggle and drown in the breakers. One discovers the new world. But rather, ten times rather, die in the surf, heralding the way to that new world, than stand idly on the shore!"

One of the most striking rhetorical effects in "Cassandra" is the use of choppy, fragmented vignettes written in the third person. Whereas the initial draft was composed as an autobiographical novel, the published version has neither a clear narrator nor even a main character (the Cassandra of the title comes from the earlier version, when the heroine, Nofriana, renames herself after the Greek prophetess Cassandra, doomed to know the future but not be believed). The essay moves between describing the condition of women in general and directly apostrophizing its reader, as well as the larger voice of society, often in the same sentence, as in this point about marrying wisely: "It is very well to say 'be prudent, be careful, try to know each other.' But how are you to know each other? Unless a woman had lost all pride, how is it possible for her, under the eyes of all her family, to indulge in long exclusive conversations with a man?"

Women Sewing (1863) by Odoardo Borrani. In her 1852 essay "Cassandra," Florence Nightingale laments the fact that women are expected never to engage in important work. SCALA/WHITE IMAGES/ART RESOURCE, NY.

The text of "Cassandra" is also remarkable for its display of overt anger. "Behind his destiny," writes Nightingale about the problems of marriage, "woman must annihilate herself, must only be his complement … if she has any destiny, any vocation of her own, she must renounce it in nine cases out of ten.… A man gains everything by marriage: he gains a 'helpmate,' but a woman does not." Nightingale explicitly argues that expressing this anger, or complaining, is necessary: "The great reformers of the world turn into great misanthropists, if circumstances or organizations do not permit them to act. Christ, if He had been a woman, might have been nothing but a great complainer." In addition to direct complaints, Nightingale employs vivid images to illustrate her claims, as in the description of women dying in the surf.

CRITICAL DISCUSSION

Although "Cassandra" was not published in Nightingale's lifetime, it was circulated among several prominent intellectuals to whom Nightingale had ties. Scholar Jowett found it original and striking, but, as a conservative, he did recommend that she "soften" the "antagonisms" of the text. Philosopher Mill wrote that he had "seldom felt less inclined to criticism than in reading this book," adding that "the mere fact that

PRIMARY SOURCE

EXCERPT FROM "CASSANDRA"

Why have women passion, intellect, moral activity – these three – and a place in society where no one of the three can be exercised? Men say that God punishes for complaining. No, but men are angry with misery. They are irritated with women for not being happy. They take it as a personal offence. To God alone may women complain, without insulting Him! And women, who are afraid, while in words they acknowledge that God's work is good, to say, Thy will be *not* done (declaring another order of society from that which He has made), go about maudling to each other and teaching to their daughters that 'women have no passions'. In the conventional society, which men have made for women, and women have accepted, they *must* have none, they *must* act the farce of hypocrisy, the lie that they are without passion – and therefore what else can they say to their daughters, without giving the lie to themselves? …

It seems as if the female spirit of the world were mourning everlastingly over blessings, *not* lost, but which she has never had, and which, in her discouragement, she feels that she never will have, they are so far off.

The more complete a woman's organization, the more she will feel it, till at last there shall arise a woman, who will resume, in her own soul, all the sufferings of her race, and that woman will be the Saviour of her race.

Jesus Christ raised women above the condition of mere slaves, mere ministers to the passions of the man, raised them by his sympathy, to be ministers of God. He gave them moral activity. But the Age, the World, Humanity, must give them the means to exercise this moral activity, must give them intellectual cultivation, spheres of action.

There is perhaps no century where the woman shows so meanly as in this. Because her education seems entirely to have parted company with her vocation; there is no longer unity between the woman as inwardly developed, and as outwardly manifested.

In the last century it was not so. In the succeeding one let us hope that it will no longer be so.

But now she is like the Archangel Michael as he stands upon Saint Angelo at Rome. She has an immense provision of wings, which seem as if they would bear her over earth and heaven; but when she tries to use them, she is petrified into stone, her feet are grown into the earth, chained to the bronze pedestal.

The dying woman to her mourners:—'Oh! if you knew how gladly I leave this life, how much more courage I feel to take the chance of another, than of anything I see before me in this, you would put on your wedding-clothes instead of mourning for me!'

'But', they say, 'so much talent! so many gifts! such good which you might have done!'

'The world will be put back some little time by my death', she says; 'you see I estimate my powers at least as highly as you can; but it is by the death which has taken place some years ago in me, not by the death which is about to take place now'. And so is the world put back by the death of every one who has to sacrifice the development of his or her peculiar gifts (which were meant, not for selfish gratification, but for the improvement of that world) to conventionality.

'My people were like children playing on the shore of the eighteenth century. I was their hobby-horse, their plaything; and they drove me to and fro, dear souls! never weary of the play themselves, till I, who had grown to woman's estate and to the ideas of the nineteenth century, lay down exhausted, my mind dosed to hope, my heart to strength.'

'Free – free – oh! divine freedom, art thou come at last? Welcome, beautiful death!'

Let neither name nor date be placed on her grave, still less the expression of regret or of admiration; but simply the words, 'I believe in God'.

these are the opinions of such a woman as all the world knows you to be, is a fact which it would be of as much use to the world to know, as almost anything which could at this time be told to it." Mill's own famous work on women's rights, *The Subjection of Women,* was published in 1869, and recent scholars have suggested that Nightingale's work may have significantly shaped Mill's own thinking.

"The suppression of … 'Cassandra,'" writes Showalter, "is one of the most unfortunate sagas of Victorian censorship of female anger, protest, and passion. The continued neglect of the work today

deprives us … of a major text of English feminism, a link between Wollstonecraft and Woolf." Since its publication in 1928, "Cassandra" has been hailed as crucial to feminist thought: when Woolf first read the essay, she termed it more like screaming than writing. Feminist scholarship has frequently returned to it as a key text in both its frank depiction of the problems of domesticity and its bold rendering of the anger and despair such conditions cause.

Although the most common critical approach to "Cassandra" has been its importance as a feminist text, other avenues of exploration have considered not only the political messages Nightingale delivers but also the format in which she delivers them. Many critics have wrestled with Nightingale's choice to shift the narration in "Cassandra" from a more conventional autobiographical novel to its essay form. Some have seen this format choice as one that allowed Nightingale to leave behind feminized interiority and subjectivity, a view that George Landow in his essay in *Victorian Sages and Cultural Discourse* (1990) extends to argue that Nightingale's "sage-writing" de-sexes the traditionally masculine male essay form. Other critics, however, read the shift to an essay form as one that betrays her fear of both fantasy and "feminine" weakness. In addition, some scholars have engaged with the religious iconography of "Cassandra"—the whole of *Suggestions* deals with Nightingale's vision of religion, and "Cassandra" posits the possibility of a new female Jesus. Ruth Jenkins, in her 1994 article "Rewriting Female Subjection," writes that "rather than accepting a patriarchal interpretation of divine design that conflicts with her own desires, Nightingale reappropriates and rewrites the Judea-Christian narrative of prophetic lineage and incarnation as female."

FLORENCE NIGHTINGALE AT HOME

While Florence Nightingale's attack on female domesticity certainly reflects the experiences of many women of her time and class, the details of her autobiography shed light upon why she might have reacted so violently. Born the second daughter of a well-to-do family, Florence (named after the city in Italy where she was born) identified closely with her father, who taught her classics and mathematics, while her sister Parthenope (known to the family as Parthe, or Pop) bonded closely with her mother, a very correct, socially focused upper-class Englishwoman.

Although younger, Florence was both more intellectually gifted and physically beautiful than Parthenope. Rather than openly expressing her resentment of Florence, Parthenope turned to illness and hysteria as a way to control Florence's movements. When Florence first tried to leave to become a nurse, for instance, Parthenope had multiple full-fledged hysterical fits, complaining of the "agony" of mysterious pains and declaring that Florence's behavior was, literally, killing her. It was not until her mother's illness and death, and Parthenope's own late marriage (to a man who had first courted Florence), that Florence was able to move into a less contentious relationship with the female members of her family.

BIBLIOGRAPHY

Sources

Jenkins, Ruth Y. "Rewriting Female Subjection: Florence Nightingale's Revisionist Myth of 'Cassandra.'" *Weber Studies* 11.1 (1994): 16–26. Print.

Landow, George P. "Aggressive (Re)Interpretations of the Female Sage: Florence Nightingale's *Cassandra*." *Victorian Sages and Cultural Discourse: Renegotiating Gender and Power.* Ed. Thais E. Morgan. London: Rutgers UP, 1990. 32–45. Print.

Minkea, Francis E., and Dwight W. Lindley, eds. *The Later Letters of John Stuart Mill.* Toronto: U of Toronto P, 1972. Print.

Poovey, Mary, ed. *Florence Nightingale*: Cassandra *and Other Selections from Suggestions for Thought.* New York: New York UP, 1993. Print.

Showalter, Elaine. "Florence Nightingale's Feminist Complaint: Women, Religion, and Suggestions for Thought." *Signs* 6.31 (1981): 395–412. Print.

Further Reading

Barritt, Evelyn R. Rev. of *Cassandra: An Essay,* by Florence Nightingale. *American Journal of Nursing* 81.5 (1981): 1059–61. *JSTOR.* Web. 10 Sept. 2012.

Bogdanou, Christina. *Revisioning Cassandra: Defying Daughters and Master Narratives in Florence Nightingale's "Cassandra" and Margarita Karapanou's "Kassandra and the Wolf."* Diss. University of California, Los Angeles, 2004. *ProQuest Dissertations & Theses.* Web. 10 Sept. 2012.

Bostridge, Mark. "Women of the World Unite." *Guardian.* Guardian News and Media, 28 Jan. 2005. Web. 25 Sept. 2012.

Dossey, Barbara M. "Florence Nightingale: A 19th-Century Mystic." *Journal of Holistic Nursing* 16.2 (1998): 111–64. *Sage.* Web. 10 Sept. 2012.

Kahane, Claire. "The Aesthetic Politics of Rage." *States of Rage: Emotional Eruption, Violence, and Social Change.* Ed. Renee R. Curry and Terry L. Allison. New York: New York UP, 1996.

Pugh, Evelyn L. "Florence Nightingale and J. S. Mill Debate Women's Rights." *Journal of British Studies* 21.2 (1982): 118–38. *JSTOR.* Web. 8 Sept. 2012.

Selanders, Louise C. "Florence Nightingale: The Evolution and Social Impact of Feminist Values in Nursing." *Journal of Holistic Nursing* 16.2 (1998): 227–43. *Sage.* Web. 10 Sept. 2012.

Smith, Frances T. "Florence Nightingale: Early Feminist." *American Journal of Nursing.* 81.6 (1981): 1020–24. *JSTOR.* Web. 8 Sept. 2012.

Snyder, Katherine V. "From Novel to Essay: Gender and Revision in Florence Nightingale's 'Cassandra.'" *The Politics of the Essay: Feminist Perspectives.* Ed. Ruth-Ellen Boetcher Joeres and Elizabeth Mittman. Bloomington: Indiana UP, 1993. Print.

Abigail Mann

EIGHTEEN HUNDRED AND ELEVEN

Anna Laetitia Barbauld

❖ *Key Facts*

Time Period:
Early 19th Century

Genre:
Poetry

Events:
Napoleonic Wars

Nationality:
English

OVERVIEW

Eighteen Hundred and Eleven, a long poem in 334 lines by Anna Laetitia Barbauld written in 1812, criticizes Great Britain's participation in the Napoleonic Wars (1803–1815). The poem asserts that Britain suffered financial and cultural setbacks as a result of the conflict. Barbauld crafts the poem so that it offers a historical viewpoint of Britain's scientific and cultural innovation and then contrasts that with predictions that the nation will no longer be a world power. The text effectively argues that Britain's dominance will be superseded by that of its former colonies and the emerging republics of South America, a sentiment that much of the nation did not share. *Eighteen Hundred and Eleven* calls into question Britain's motivation for and the consequences of entering the war. As a result, the poem was deemed unpatriotic by many of her fellow citizens, including writers and artists. Barbauld's poem serves as a contrast to the patently nationalistic writing generated by her colleagues.

Barbauld was a well-known poet, political essayist, literary critic, and editor during the late eighteenth and early nineteenth centuries. However, the reaction to *Eighteen Hundred and Eleven* was so negative that it largely ended her literary career. Though she continued to write, she published comparatively little poetry in the ensuing years. The text reflects Barbauld's own views on the war, which she considered an inexcusable waste of life and talent. It also rejects the prevailing British sentiment, which held that the war should be won at any cost in order to stop Napoleon Bonaparte from conquering Europe. The poem is notable for its very public critique of the government and popular opinion, and it is also one of the most important feminist critiques of the war.

HISTORICAL AND LITERARY CONTEXT

Britain's complicated involvement in the Napoleonic Wars, including its controversial blockade of French ports, was a major reason that Barbauld wrote *Eighteen Hundred and Eleven.* Napoleon's desire to expand the French empire had left Britain scrambling to defend its colonies and commercial interests in the West Indies. England became more entangled when, in 1808, it sent troops to the Iberian Peninsula for Spain in what would be known as the Peninsular War (1808–1813). Britain and Spain's forces eventually drove Napoleon out of the peninsula, but it was not until 1815 that he was completely defeated at Waterloo and exiled to St. Helena. By then, the British government had spent some £1,650,000,000 or more to finance its part in the war. More than 300,000 of its troops had been killed or were missing in action. *Eighteen Hundred and Eleven* highlights these costs at a time when Britain was already suffering from financial hardship.

In 1811, the year of the poem's title, Britain's King George III was declared mentally unfit to rule, the Luddite uprisings began, and extremely high unemployment and widespread food shortages continued unabated. Barbauld does not mention these issues specifically, but the tension and discontent of the time are part of the emotional tenor of the poem. Then, in 1812, the year the poem was published, Prime Minister Spencer Perceval was assassinated in the House of Commons, the Peninsular War entered a critical stage, and Napoleon invaded Russia. That same year, England entered into the War of 1812 (1812–1815) with the United States, which had imposed trade restrictions on England in response to that country's blockade of European ports as part of its involvement in the Napoleonic Wars. Barbauld, whose poem appeared several months before the War of 1812 began, had warned that current and former British colonies would begin to stand up to the monarchy, a prediction that further angered the British public.

Not surprisingly, many Romantic-era authors commented on the Napoleonic Wars in their writing. Samuel Taylor Coleridge's 1798 poem *Fears in Solitude* describes the horrors of the war, while Robert Southey's *Ode Written During the Negotiations with Bonaparte, in January 1814* contends that England should abandon peace negotiations with France and destroy Napoleon. Although Barbauld was not the only poet to condemn the war, her criticism was unique and decidedly gendered. In her essay 'The Wealth of Nations' or 'The Happiness of Nations'?, Karen Hadley states "that [Barbauld's] text challenges some of the gendered stereotypes that her more recent critics have observed, where she addresses the gendered logic of enlightenment hegemony." The poem points out the terrible human costs of the war, as well as the social and political problems of England's male-dominated capitalist society.

The predominantly negative initial reaction to *Eighteen Hundred and Eleven* was such that Barbauld's peers, even her friends, expressed their displeasure. However, one friend, Maria Edgeworth, supported Barbauld privately and wrote to her that "it is not their criticism on your poem which incenses me, it is the odious tone in which they dare to speak of the most respectable and elegant female writer that England can boast. The public, the *public* will do you justice!" Indeed, Maggie Favretti states in *The Politics of Vision* that the impact of the poem was felt in feminist circles: "Barbauld's voice is distinctly feminine as far as the feminine role of moralist was developing into the nineteenth century."

THEMES AND STYLE

Eighteen Hundred and Eleven focuses mainly on the consequences of war and the author's dire prediction about England's future. Although the English public was mostly in favor of the war, contemporary political and social disruptions had created a tense environment, something Barbauld also alludes to in her text:

> To the stern call still Britain bends her ear,
> Feeds the fierce strife, the alternate hope and
>   fear;
> Bravely, though vainly, dares to strive with Fate,
> And seeks by turns to prop each sinking state.
> Colossal power with overwhelming force
> Bears down each fort of Freedom in its course.

These lines offer the reader a sense of the political upheaval England was experiencing. The author also genders the conflict with this passage, as well as throughout the rest of the poem, speaking of the "Colossal power" as male and "Freedom" as female. Barbauld's insertion of gender politics gives further dimension to the theme of conflict and political tension.

The contrast is made even more striking as the narrator alternates between discussion of impending cultural demise and praise for England's traditions: "Thine are the laws surrounding states revere, / Thine the full harvest of the mental year, / Thine the bright stars in Glory's sky that shine, / And arts that make it life to live are thine." These lines, which demonstrate the sincere patriotism of the writer, alternate with lines that question England's role in the war. As Hadley argues, the criticism extends beyond war: "Barbauld constructed the narrative as such to provide a logic which criticizes not only England's actions but also Western bourgeois culture in general." Barbauld is also concerned with how masculine ambition has polluted the idealistic aims of the Enlightenment culture that England considered important to its reputation as the world's greatest power.

Stylistically, the poem combines lofty, heightened language with repeated references to mythology and significant events in England's history. Barbauld estab-

ANNA BARBAULD: A WRITER'S LIFE

Anna Laetitia Aikin was born June 20, 1743, in Leicestershire, England, to John Aikin, a Nonconformist minister, and his wife, Jane. During her childhood, she was educated mainly by her father, who allowed her to study French, Italian, Greek, and Latin. The family moved to Warrington, England, when she was fifteen so that her father could teach at the Warrington Academy. Anna was surrounded there by intellectuals such as Joseph Priestley and Gilbert Wakefield, and she spent the next fifteen years learning from these men. In 1773, with the encouragement of her brother, John Aikin, Anna published her first volume of poetry, titled *Poems*. The book was so popular that it went through four editions that first year.

A year later, she married Rochemont Barbauld and continued to write poems and essays, as well as books for children. Her popularity and reputation as an author grew, and her home became a center for dissenting intellectuals. She also became more politically and socially conscious, tackling issues such as the French Revolution and the injustices of slavery in her writing. In 1793, using the pseudonym "A Volunteer," she published a political pamphlet on national reform, *Sins of Government, Sins of the Nation,* based on individual morality. Following the hostile public response to her best-known political poem, *Eighteen Hundred and Eleven,* Barbauld largely, though not completely, retired from public activism. She died in Stoke-Newington, England, on March 9, 1825.

lishes the poem as thoroughly British with lines such as these: "With fond adoring steps to press the sod / By statesmen, sages, poets, heroes trod; / On Isis' banks to draw inspiring air, / From Runnymede to send the patriot's prayer." The historical allusions also provide a basis for her prediction that England will eventually be eclipsed by the republics of the Americas. Maggie Favretti asserts that Barbauld's "skillfully phrased heroic couplets" portray Britain's history so as to "describe the dismal state of affairs in 1811, to identify what went wrong, and finally to explore what will happen after Britain loses its status as the seat of civilization." These lines' exploration—commanding and authoritative yet elegiac—match the poem's emotional tenor, mourning what the poet believes to be the inevitable downfall of the British empire.

CRITICAL DISCUSSION

For the most part, reaction to *Eighteen Hundred and Eleven* was scathing. Immediately after the poem was published, John Wilson Croker wrote in the *Quarterly Review,* "Our old acquaintance Mrs. Barbauld turned satirist! The last thing we should have expected, and, now that we have seen her satire, the last thing that we could have desired." Croker derides Barbauld and her poem further, stating that writing about politics actually degrades her poetry. Even her

close friend Henry Crabb Robinson was critical, writing in his *Diaries:*

> I certainly wish she had not written it, though it is written in a pleasing style. For the tone and spirit of it are certainly very bad. She does not content herself with expressing her fears lest England should perish in the present struggle; she speaks with the confidence of a prophet of the fall of the country as if she had seen in a vision the very process of its ruin.

Some reviews, however, were relatively positive. For example, the *Monthly Repository* said that Barbauld had crafted a "deeply interesting poem" full of "solemn truths."

As part of Barbauld's larger body of work, *Eighteen Hundred and Eleven* stands out as the most openly political. William Keach writes in "A Regency Prophecy and the End of Anna Barbauld's Career": "She not only wrote no more of what he [Croker] calls 'satire' and 'party pamphlets in verse,' she wrote no more for publication at all." In fact, Barbauld did continue to publish both poetry and prose, but the public reception of *Eighteen Hundred and Eleven* seriously affected her public standing. More recent scholars have pointed to Barbauld's poem as a good example of a dissenting voice during that period in Britain's history. Some earlier critics nevertheless felt the poem was patriotic at the core. In 1876, Jerom Murch stated in *Mrs. Barbauld and Her Contemporaries* that "some

of the most impassioned parts of her poem are those which breathe the most ardent love of her native land."

Barbauld's work, including *Eighteen Hundred and Eleven,* has experienced a resurgence in popularity, especially among feminist scholars. The poem is discussed not only as a warning of Britain's decline but also as a critique of traditional gender roles. Favretti states that in the poem, Barbauld "commandingly stakes out her political position concerning gender and the etiology of destruction." Scholars also point out that the criticism surrounding *Eighteen Hundred and Eleven* was itself quite gendered. Favretti writes, "For the male readers … the prophecy of the end of the British empire as a result of the gentleman's failure to fully comprehend and stabilize the competing interests in the world struck too close to home."

BIBLIOGRAPHY

Sources

Croker, John Wilson. "*Eighteen Hundred and Eleven:* A Poem By Anna Letitia Barbauld." *The Quarterly Review* 7 (June 1812): 309. Print.

"*Eighteen Hundred and Eleven.* A Poem By Anna Laetitia Barbauld." *The Eclectic Review* 8 (May 1812): 475. Print.

Favretti, Maggie. "The Politics of Vision: Anna Barbauld's *Eighteen Hundred and Eleven.*" *Women's Poetry in the Enlightenment: The Making of a Canon, 1730–1820.* Ed. Isobel Armstrong and Virginia Blain. Houndmills: Macmillan P, 1999. 99–110. Rpt. in *Nineteenth-Century*

Literature Criticism. Vol. 185. Ed. Russel Whitaker and Kathy D. Darrow. Detroit: Gale, 2008. *Literature Resource Center.* Web. 8 July 2012.

Hadley, Karen. "'The Wealth of Nations', or 'The Happiness of Nations'? Barbauld's Malthusian Critique in *Eighteen Hundred and Eleven.*" *CLA Journal* 45.1 (Sept. 2001): 87–96. Rpt. in *Nineteenth-Century Literature Criticism.* Vol. 185. Ed. Russel Whitaker and Kathy D. Darrow. Detroit: Gale, 2008. *Literature Resource Center.* Web. 8 July 2012.

Keach, William. "A Regency Prophecy and the End of Anna Barbauld's Career." *Studies in Romanticism* 33.4 (1994): 569–77. Rpt. in *Nineteenth-Century Literature Criticism.* Vol. 185. Ed. Russel Whitaker and Kathy D. Darrow. Detroit: Gale, 2008. *Literature Resource Center.* Web. 8 July 2012.

Le Breton, Anna Letitia. *Memoir of Mrs. Barbauld, Including Letters and Notices of Her Family and Friends.* London: George Bell, 1874. 155–56. Print.

Murch, Jerom. *Mrs. Barbauld and Her Contemporaries: Sketches of Some Eminent Literary and Scientific Englishwomen.* London: Longmans, Green & Co., 1877. Rpt. in *Nineteenth-Century Literature Criticism.* Vol. 185. Ed. Russel Whitaker and Kathy D. Darrow. Detroit: Gale, 2008. *Literature Resource Center.* Web. 8 July 2012.

Robinson, Henry Crabb. *Henry Crabb Robinson on Books and Their Writers.* 3 vols. Ed. Edith J. Morley. London: J. M. Dent and Sons, 1938. Web. 8 July 2012.

Further Reading

Bainbridge, Simon. *British Poetry and the Revolutionary and Napoleonic Wars: Visions of Conflict.* New York: Oxford University Press, 2003. Print.

Behrendt, Stephen C. *British Women Poets and the Romantic Writing Community.* Baltimore: Johns Hopkins UP, 2009. Print.

Crisafulli, Lilla Marie, and Cecilia Pietropoli, eds. *Romantic Women Poets: Genre and Gender.* Amsterdam: Rodopi, 2007. Print.

Crocco, Francesco. "The Colonial Subtext of Anna Letitia Barbauld's *Eighteen Hundred and Eleven.*" *Wordsworth Circle* 41.2 (2010): 91+. *Literature Resource Center.* Web. 9 July 2012.

McCarthy, William. *Anna Letitia Barbauld: Voice of the Enlightenment.* Baltimore: Johns Hopkins University Press, 2008. Print.

McDonagh, Josephine. "Barbauld's Domestic Economy." *Romanticism and Gender.* Ed. Anne Janowitz. Cambridge: D. S. Brewer, 1998. 62–77. Rpt. in *Nineteenth-Century Literature Criticism.* Vol. 185. Ed. Russel Whitaker and Kathy D. Darrow. Detroit: Gale, 2008. *Literature Resource Center.* Web. 9 July 2012.

Watkins, Daniel P. *Anna Letitia Barbauld and Eighteenth-Century Visionary Poetics.* Baltimore: The Johns Hopkins UP, 2012. Print.

Hannah Soukup

THE FIRE NEXT TIME

James Baldwin

✦ *Key Facts*

Time Period:
Mid-20th Century

Genre:
Essays

Events:
Civil rights movement;
desegregation; murder
of civil rights leader
Medgar Evers; bombing
of the 16th Street Baptist
Church in Birmingham,
Alabama

Nationality:
American

OVERVIEW

Written by James Baldwin and published in 1963 at the height of the civil rights movement, *The Fire Next Time* is a book that contains two essays on the subjects of black identity and race relations in the United States. The first essay, "My Dungeon Shook: Letter to My Nephew on the One Hundredth Anniversary of the Emancipation," is a deeply personal description of the effects of racism, containing both a warning for young blacks and a call for pride and steadfastness. The second, and much longer, essay, "Down at the Cross: Letter from a Region in My Mind," examines both Christianity and Islam in terms of the African American experience and discusses the deep divide between white and black America.

The Fire Next Time emerged from a period of political and intellectual ferment in the United States, as segregation and other forms of racial discrimination were openly challenged, both in the courts and by grassroots activists in the streets. The topic of race, once only discussed in fearful whispers, became part of the national debate as reformists and militants argued over the most effective strategies for change. With the publication of *The Fire Next Time,* Baldwin, an African American who was already a respected novelist and essayist, gained stature as one of the most important contemporary American writers. "Down at the Cross" was first published in the *New Yorker,* and liberal white readers were both shaken and riveted by Baldwin's passionate and lucid description of the experience of being black in a racist society. *The Fire Next Time* soon became required reading for students of the civil rights movement and a classic of African American literature.

HISTORICAL AND LITERARY CONTEXT

While the 1863 Emancipation Proclamation legally ended slavery in the United States, numerous laws limiting the rights of African Americans remained in effect. While many of these laws existed in the South, unwritten policies and deeply racist attitudes existed throughout the nation. From the time of the Civil War, activists struggled against the repression and discrimination that resulted from these racist attitudes and policies, forming organizations such as the National Association for the Advancement of Colored People (NAACP) in 1909. During World War II many African Americans not only served their country but also had the opportunity to leave it and experience life in the less racially polarized cultures of Europe. They returned less willing to endure the limitations on their lives and the contempt and hostility with which they were often treated by white Americans. As a result, civil rights activism increased. A determined campaign of demonstrations, boycotts, and court cases challenged racial discrimination and led to massive legal changes.

By the early 1960s the growing civil rights movement continued to make gains while still facing bitter opposition from racist whites. The first black student enrolled in the University of Mississippi in 1962, setting off violence that was quelled by the deployment of five thousand federal troops. In 1963 movement leader Medgar Evers was murdered in front of his home in Mississippi, and four young girls in Alabama died when their church, a center for civil rights meetings, was bombed. It was in this atmosphere that Baldwin wrote the heartfelt analysis he published as *The Fire Next Time.* The essays it contains offer a clear message to white readers: the racist society must change or it will implode.

As post-slavery blacks began to form vibrant urban communities during the early 1900s, African American literature flourished, with such writers as James Toomer (*Cane,* 1923), James Weldon (*God's Trombones,* 1923), and Zora Neale Hurston (*Their Eyes Were Watching God,* 1937) beginning to unravel the complex experience of black Americans. Richard Wright's 1940 novel *Native Son* is an unflinching exposé of the devastating effects of racism on the human spirit that deeply affected Baldwin, who responded with his first overtly political work, a book of essays he titled *Notes of a Native Son,* published in 1955. Like Wright, Baldwin developed much of his early writing while living in France, feeling that in the United States he would be categorized and patronized because he was black.

With the publication of *The Fire Next Time,* Baldwin took his place among the most persuasive writers of the civil rights movement. While conservative whites and some radical blacks criticized the book, many progressives of all races welcomed it, and in the twenty-first century it remains Baldwin's best-known work. His warnings about the cycle of vengeance and the violence that would result from the racism deeply imbedded in U.S. culture seemed to be borne out by future events, such as the assassination of Martin Luther King Jr. in 1968 and the growth of militant black and white movements. Fern Marja Eckman wrote the first biography of Baldwin, *The Furious Passage of James Baldwin,* published in 1966.

THEMES AND STYLE

The central focus in *The Fire Next Time* is the utter degradation of African Americans under racism and its effect on black identity. The book also confronts the ignorance of white people in general about this struggle. It states, "The brutality with which Negroes are treated in this country simply cannot be overstated, however unwilling white men may be to hear it." Baldwin makes the point repeatedly that racism robs people of color of their humanity and that this damage begins in childhood. He writes, "Negroes in this country … are taught really to despise themselves from the moment their eyes open on the world." In addition, in "Down at the Cross," Baldwin examines the seductive power of religion. Christianity, even though it provided him with an escape from debilitating anger, is ultimately viewed as a white man's religion. He writes, "But God … is white. And if His love was so great, and if He loved all His children, why were we, the blacks, cast down so far?" Islam, as practiced by radical black Muslims, offers a satisfying prediction of black dominance but is ultimately too vengeful. Ultimately, Baldwin comes back to humanity, writing, "Color is not a human or a personal reality; it is a political reality."

As a young man, Baldwin was a Christian minister, and he employs the compelling cadences of a sermon throughout his book. Biblical allusions appear frequently, beginning with the title, which is a reference to God's promise to Noah after the flood. Baldwin repeats this prediction in several ways. He writes, "America and all the Western nations will be forced to reexamine themselves and … discard … the assumptions that have been used to justify their lives and their anguish and their crimes so long," and "A bill is coming in that I fear America is not prepared to pay." In "My Dungeon Shook" Baldwin uses the device of a letter to a beloved child to give his message force and immediacy: "You can only be destroyed by believing that you really are what the white world calls a *nigger*. I tell you this because I love you, and please don't you ever forget it."

Baldwin, who died in 1987, was a novelist and playwright as well as an essayist, and his nonfiction writing in *The Fire Next Time* is lyrical and absorbing, with long, fluid sentences and poetic metaphors:

> Perhaps the whole root of our trouble, the human trouble, is that we will sacrifice all the beauty of our lives, will imprison ourselves in totems, taboos, crosses, blood sacrifices, steeples, mosques, races, armies, flags, nations, in order to deny the fact of death, the only fact we have. It seems to me that one ought to rejoice in

THE OTHER AMERICAN IN PARIS

James Baldwin spent much of his writing career outside the United States. From 1948 to 1957 he lived in Paris, and like hundreds of other African Americans, he was drawn to France because it offered a rich cultural atmosphere and a chance to escape the oppressive racism that seemed intrinsic to U.S. society. In the years between World War II and the growth of the civil rights movement in the 1960s, a number of other black American writers, musicians, and artists lived in Europe and Africa, feeling that they would never be allowed to express their full humanity in their homeland.

This migration originated after World War I, when black soldiers who participated in the liberation of France were welcomed as heroes. While France was certainly not devoid of racism, French society was much more integrated than U.S. society, and artists, such as singer and dancer Josephine Baker and writer Langston Hughes, found both acceptance and freedom to develop their craft while living in Paris during the 1920s. A similar wave of black expatriation followed World War II, including Baldwin and other influential writers, such as Chester Hines and Richard Wright, who lived in Paris from 1947 until his death in 1960.

> the fact of death—ought to decide, indeed, to earn one's death by confronting with passion the conundrum of life.

Both essays are written in a deeply personal, almost intimate, idiom, even when making a political point: "If we—and now I mean the relatively conscious whites and the relatively conscious blacks, who must, like lovers, insist on, or create, the consciousness of others—do not falter in our duty now, we may be able … to end the racial nightmare … and change the history of the world."

CRITICAL DISCUSSION

The mainstream press received *The Fire Next Time* with enthusiasm. Sheldon Binn, writing in the *New York Times,* calls it "masterful," saying of Baldwin's writing, "His heart guides his pen. His experience tells the tale in staccato clarity." A *Time* magazine article states, "There is not another writer—white or black—who expresses with such poignancy and abrasiveness the dark realities of the racial ferment in North and South." The book's strong language and cautionary vision were, however, controversial; F. W. Dupee complains in the *New York Review of Books* that Baldwin "replaces criticism with prophecy," weakening "his grasp of his … great theme." Some radical black activists rejected Baldwin's conciliatory tone. In his 1968 book, *Soul on Ice,* Eldridge Cleaver directs barbs at Baldwin's homosexuality and describes his work as "the most shameful, fanatical, fawning, sycophantic love of the whites … of any black American writer of note in our time."

In The Fire Next Time, *author James Baldwin, pictured here in New Orleans in 1963, discusses issues including race and religion.* © STEVE SCHAPIRO/CORBIS.

The Fire Next Time remains the best known of Baldwin's works and one of the most enduring expressions of the sensibility that drove the radical civil rights movement of the 1960s. The text is often assigned reading in high school and college courses in the United States, and Baldwin's authoritative voice offers a clear and disturbing picture of 1960s white America through black eyes. Critic Darryl Pinckney affirms the work's influence on one of the most turbulent periods in U.S. history. In the *New York Review of Books* he writes, "The climate of the times—perilous sit-ins and voter registration drives, murders and marches, songs of toil and deliverance—had everything to do with the sensation created by *The Fire Next Time.*"

Baldwin's reputation declined somewhat after *The Fire Next Time* appeared. *Time* magazine, which had featured him on its May 17, 1963, cover, refused to print an article about him in 1973, calling him "passé." During the early 1980s Baldwin came out

publicly as homosexual, causing civil rights movement leaders to distance themselves from him and some critics to evaluate his work in the light of their own homophobia. Stanley Crouch, in a 1988 article in the *Village Voice,* disparages Baldwin's writing in *The Fire Next Time* as "coated with the effete sheen of the homosexual straining to present himself as part of an elite." Since Baldwin's death in 1987, other scholars have reexamined his writing as an expression of his complex identity. A number of twenty-first-century works, such as Douglas Field's *A Historical Guide to James Baldwin* (2009), confirm the author's importance in literature, politics, and history.

BIBLIOGRAPHY

Sources

Binn, Sheldon. Rev. of *The Fire Next Time,* by James Baldwin. *New York Times.* The New York Times Company, 31 Jan. 1963. Web. 6 Sept. 2012.

Campbell, James. "Son of the Preacher Man: The Baptism of James Baldwin." *London Magazine* 19.9–10 (1979): 103–10. *Literature Resource Center.* Web. 6 Sept. 2012.

Cleaver, Eldridge. *Soul on Ice.* New York: McGraw-Hill, 1968. Print.

Crouch, Stanley. "The Rage of Race." *Village Voice* 33.2 (1988): 35. *Literature Resource Center.* Web. 6 Sept. 2012.

Dickstein, Morris, ed. *Critical Insights: James Baldwin.* Ipswitch: Salem Press, 2011. Print.

Dupee, F. W. "James Baldwin and the 'Man.'" Rev. of *The Fire Next Time,* by James Baldwin. *New York Review of Books.* NYREV, Feb. 1963. Web. 8 Sept. 2012.

"The Nation: Races: Freedom—Now." *Time* 17 May 1963: 23–7. Print.

Pinckney, Darryl. "The Magic of James Baldwin." Rev. of *James Baldwin: Collected Essays,* by James Baldwin. *New York Review of Books* 19 Nov. 1998: 64–74. Print.

Further Reading

Balfour, Lawrie. *The Evidence of Things Not Said: James Baldwin and the Promise of American Democracy.* New York: Cornell UP, 2001. Print.

Field, Douglas. *A Historical Guide to James Baldwin.* New York: Oxford UP, 2009. Print.

King, Lovalerie, and Lynn Orilla Scott. *James Baldwin and Toni Morrison: Comparative Critical and Theoretical Essays.* New York: Palgrave-Macmillan, 2006. Print.

Nabers, Deak. "Past Using: James Baldwin and Civil Rights Law in the 1960s." *Yale Journal of Criticism* 18.2 (2005): 221–42. *Literature Resource Center.* Web. 6 Sept. 2012.

O'Neale, Sondra A. "Fathers, Gods, and Religion: Perceptions of Christianity and Ethnic Faith in James Baldwin." *Critical Essays on James Baldwin.* Ed. Fred L. Standley and Nancy V. Burt. Boston: G. K. Hall, 1988. 125–43. *Literature Resource Center.* Web. 6 Sept. 2012.

Teachout, Terry. "Nobody Knows His Name." *National Review* 50.1 (1998): 50. *Literature Resource Center.* Web. 6 Sept. 2012.

Tina Gianoulis

THE GROUP

Mercy Otis Warren

OVERVIEW

First appearing in the *Boston Gazette* on January 23, 1775, *The Group* by Mercy Otis Warren is a satirical play deriding the Loyalist position during the American Revolution. Using thinly veiled, absurdly named characters to portray prominent Loyalist or Tory public figures, Warren's play imagines the apocalyptic consequences of the dissolution of the Massachusetts Charter in favor of a Tory governing council that is driven only by greed and love of power. Written in iambic pentameter with irregular rhyming couplets, the two-act play features almost no action, mostly relying on soliloquy from an abundance of characters. The soliloquies serve to reinforce the play's main thesis: prominent Tory politicians are treacherous and greedy, choosing a love of power over their own nation, while the unseen patriots are noble, brave, and ultimately on the correct side of history.

Written in the wake of the so-called Intolerable Acts—and particularly responding to the Massachusetts Government Act that weakened colonist power in the Massachusetts colony—*The Group* was first mailed by Warren's husband to John Adams, who praised the play as "Genius" and sent it on to the press. After appearing in the *Boston Gazette,* portions of the play were printed in the *Massachusetts Spy* and circulated in pamphlet form in Philadelphia and New York. Published anonymously, *The Group* would appear only a few months before the Battle of Lexington and Concord, which marked the beginning of the Revolutionary War. Although she has been largely forgotten, Mercy Otis Warren was a significant political voice of her time and is all the more noteworthy for being a female voice in a revolution created and controlled by men.

HISTORICAL AND LITERARY CONTEXT

In the wake of the Boston Tea Party, the so-called "Intolerable Acts" or Coercive Acts passed down from the British Parliament in 1773 were intended to quash revolutionary spirit in the colonies. Instead, these acts deepened tensions, especially in Massachusetts, the colony most affected by the restrictive measures. Particularly egregious to the citizens of Massachusetts was the Massachusetts Government Act, which went into effect in May 1774. This act abrogated the Massachusetts Charter and took away the colonists' right to elect council members and many other civil officers.

Warren satirizes these "mandamus councilors" and their internal debates in *The Group.*

Tensions formed not only between Britain and its colony but also among the colonists themselves, many of whom struggled with different ideas of patriotism under the rule of a colonial power. Those who wanted to remain loyal to Britain were called Loyalists or Tories; the Whigs or Patriots, which included Warren and her husband, were in favor of self-government for the colonies. In September 1774 the First Continental Congress met with delegates from twelve colonies and declared a boycott on British goods. Even among the delegates, tensions between Loyalists and Whigs were high.

The political situation of the time provided a muse for many colonist authors, who had largely lacked an artistic heritage of their own. In 1775 American drama was still in its infancy. The first play written by an American had been performed only ten years earlier. Warren had a contemporary in Jonathan Sewall, who wrote plays defending the British cause including *A Cure for the Spleen* (1775). Like Warren's plays, Sewall's were not written to be performed but rather served as political satire for circulation and discussion. However, political discourse continued beyond the world of drama: lawyer Daniel Leonard (represented as Beau Trumps in *The Group*) wrote pro-Tory essays under the pseudonym "Massachusettensis," and John Adams responded with his propatriot "Novanglus" essays. One of the most famous works of the Revolution, Thomas Paine's *Common Sense,* would be published a year later in 1776.

Written a few months before war began, *The Group* entered a highly charged political world. Warren, who had written two other political plays as well as poetry, would go on to write full five-act plays and a three-volume *History of the Rise, Progress, and Termination of the American Revolution,* and would eventually take credit for *The Group.* Although Warren remains largely a footnote in history and her plays may seem lacking in drama to modern audiences, she is a figure of scholarly focus as a female political writer at a time when politics and writing were largely confined to men.

THEMES AND STYLE

In lieu of a plot or dramatic action, *The Group* achieves political satire by imagining conversations between British-appointed councilors who are caricatured as

❖ Key Facts

Time Period:
Late 18th Century

Genre:
Play

Events:
Increased tensions between Britain and its American colonies; Boston Tea Party; passage of the so-called "Intolerable Acts," or Coercive Acts; First Continental Congress declares boycott on British goods

Nationality:
American

WHO WAS MERCY OTIS WARREN?

Mercy Otis Warren was surrounded by extraordinary people and unusual circumstances all her life. She was born in 1728 in Barnstable, Massachusetts, the third of thirteen children. Her great-grandfather had been a passenger on the *Mayflower*, and her father, James Otis Sr., had served as attorney general of the Province of Massachusetts Bay. Her brother, James Otis Jr., is said to have coined the phrase "taxation without representation is tyranny" and would later be elected to the Massachusetts provincial assembly like his father. As children, Mercy's brothers were educated by the Reverend Jonathan Russell. The young Mercy joined them in their education, taking the same courses that would prepare her brothers to attend Harvard.

At the age of twenty-six, she married James Warren, a merchant and farmer who would go on to become the president of the Massachusetts Provincial Congress. The marriage was apparently a happy one, and James encouraged Mercy's writing. A friend of many prominent colonial women, including Abigail Adams and Martha Washington, Mercy was the mother of five sons and seems to have seamlessly existed in both the domestic and political spheres. Her background and talents made her a woman particularly suited for this extraordinary period.

greedy buffoons. Although some of the characters express doubts about their decision to be loyal to the British government, they ultimately submit because of their "itch" for "titled place, some honorary post, some small distinction" and their love of money. Through the course of their conversations, it becomes clear that bloodshed is occurring behind the scenes. Although the councilors do not seem to care how much blood is spilled so long as they maintain their positions, they describe the patriots as righteous men who "fight for freedom" and who will ultimately be crowned with "glory and victory and lasting fame."

Warren uses a combination of sentimentality and absurdity to appeal to an already sympathetic and highly knowledgeable insider audience. The characters are absurdly named (e.g., Crusty Crowbar and Hum Humbug) and are meant to represent real Tory political figures who might not be familiar to every colonist. By allowing her characters to "defend" themselves, Warren ensures that they appear repulsive, corrupt, and absurd. Another facet of their corruption, aside from their love of money and power, is their callous treatment of women. For example, Simple Sapling, when asked if his wife would mind housing troops, implies that his wife will sleep with the soldiers to "help her husband's fame" and that she should "solicit charity abroad" if she opposes this plan. Hateall expresses contempt for his wife, "nut-brown Kate," and declares the "willow Twig" a weapon against "each rebellious dame who dare oppose her husband's will." The play closes with

a speech from an unnamed woman, who is presumably a wife of one of the Tories and has been watching all of the action. She mourns the bloodshed occurring around her and calls the patriots "heroes" and "Virtue's sons." The condemnation of cruelty to women allows for a protofeminist reading of the text and heightens the play's sense of repulsion by the cruel characters.

Warren's sentimental and emotion-driven style is further illustrated through the use of lofty language. The speeches are frequently written in rhyming iambic pentameter, and there are many allusions to ancient Rome and to modern politics, suggesting the intended audience was well read. The characters frequently speak of abstract notions, such as "the scale which virtue holds to reason," as if abstractions were fixed quantities. The satire of the play is broad, and the characters are either good or unreasonably evil, hating "the leaders of these restless factions for their generous attempts to be free." Adding to the absurdity is the play's apocalyptic early stage direction that the main characters are to be "attended by a swarm of court sycophants, hungry harpies, and unprincipled danglers … led by Massachusettensis in the form of a basilisk." The play is both serious and comic, and this extreme juxtaposition helps Warren contrast the moral imperative of the patriots with the absurdity of the Loyalists.

CRITICAL DISCUSSION

The Group was very popular with its American audience and was reprinted in several different forms. Because Warren was a woman of prominence in early American society, her writing was praised by family friends George Washington, Alexander Hamilton, and Thomas Jefferson, among others. Outside of Warren's family, the earliest reader was John Adams, who was an ardent fan. In *The Muse of the Revolution: The Secret Pen of Mercy Otis Warren and the Founding of a Nation* (2009), Nancy Rubin Stuart quotes Adams as declaring, "of all the genius's which have yet arisen in America, there have been none, superior, to one, which now shines, in this happy, this exquisite faculty." Judith Sargent Murray, an American writer and early feminist, also praises Warren's plays as elegant.

Although *The Group* is Warren's best-known play, she has fallen out of historical favor and is mainly studied in conjunction with other female writers. By the time of her death at age eighty-six, she seemed to have been forgotten, having only an eight-word elegy. Part of *The Group*'s failure to endure is its specificity to its time period. In addition to alluding to specific political figures of Boston in the 1770s, the play has little to offer beyond its political purpose because it lacks a plot or real characters. As Jared Brown in *The Theatre in America During the Revolution* (1995) writes, "since the characters are presented as the embodiments of fanatical avarice, willing to sell out their country for personal gain, the play is reduced to the level of a diatribe." The fanatical and sentimental language of the play therefore contributes to the problem of its timeliness as the urgency of the Revolution was not as relevant to later audiences.

The Group is typically discussed as a rare example of a female-authored text written at a critical time in American history. Many modern critics have called Warren an early feminist writer. Katharina Erhard in *Amerikastudien* (2005) notes in an observation about one of Warren's other plays, which also applies to *The Group,* "women's bodies police a republic's borders." Benjamin Franklin V in *The Plays and Poems of Mercy Otis Warren* (1980) examines the way in which *The Group* relates the evil of "wives [who] cannot direct their own lives" with colonists who cannot direct their own affairs. Warren's anonymity and loss of female identity also has been a topic of discussion. In a 2000 article for *Theatre Journal,* Gay Gibson Cina writes about the ways in which anonymity "enabled her to broaden her choice of weapons to include satire" but included other disadvantages. Thus, Warren's participation in political writing as a woman makes her a revolutionary figure.

A statue of *The Group* author Mercy Otis Warren in Barnstable, Massachusetts. © NORTH WIND PICTURE ARCHIVES/ ALAMY.

BIBLIOGRAPHY

Sources

Brown, Jared. *The Theatre in America during the Revolution.* New York: Cambridge UP, 1995. Web. 18 Sept. 2012.

Cina, Gay Gibson. "Black and Unmarked: Phillis Wheatley, Mercy Otis Warren, and the Limits of Strategic Anonymity." *Theatre Journal* Dec. 2000: 465–95. *JSTOR.* Web. 18 Sept. 2012.

Erhard, Katharina. "Rape, Republicanism, and Representation: Founding the Nation in Early American Women's Drama and Selected Visual Representations." *Amerikastudien / American Studies* 50.3 (2005): 507–34. *JSTOR.* Web. 18 Sept. 2012.

Franklin, Benjamin, V. *The Plays and Poems of Mercy Otis Warren.* New York: Scholars' Facsimiles & Reprints, 1980. Print.

Richards, Jeffrey H. *Mercy Otis Warren.* New York: Twayne, 1995. Print.

Stuart, Nancy Rubin. *The Muse of the Revolution: The Secret Pen of Mercy Otis Warren and the Founding of a Nation.* Boston: Beacon, 2009. Web. 2 Oct. 2012.

Further Reading

Cohen, Lester H. "Explaining the Revolution: Ideology and Ethics in Mercy Otis Warren's Historical Theory." *William and Mary Quarterly* Apr. 1980: 200–218. *JSTOR.* Web. 18 Sept. 2012.

Davies, Kate. *Catherine Macauley and Mercy Otis Warren: The Revolutionary Atlantic and the Politics of Gender.* New York: Oxford UP, 2006. Print.

Oreovicz, Cheryl Z. "Mercy Otis Warren (1728–1814)." *Legacy* 13.1 (1996): 54–64. *JSTOR.* Web. 18 Sept. 2012.

Richards, Jeffrey H. *Early American Drama.* New York: Penguin, 1997. Print.

Sarkela, Sandra J. "Freedom's Call: The Persuasive Power of Mercy Otis Warren's Dramatic Sketches, 1772–1775." *Early American Literature* 44.3 (2009): 541–68. *General OneFile.* Web. 17 Sept. 2012.

Showalter, Elaine. *A Jury of Her Peers: American Women Writers from Anne Bradstreet to Annie Proulx.* New York: Knopf, 2009. Print.

Teunnisen, John J. "Blockheadism and the Propaganda Plays of the American Revolution." *Early American Literature* 7.2 (1972): 148–62. *JSTOR.* Web. 18 Sep. 2012.

Emily Jones

THE IMPENDING CRISIS OF THE SOUTH

How to Meet It

Hinton Rowan Helper

❖ *Key Facts*

Time Period:
Mid-19th Century

Genre:
Nonfiction

Events:
Slavery debate; lead-up
to American Civil War

Nationality:
American

OVERVIEW

The Impending Crisis of the South: How to Meet It was published in 1857 by North Carolinian Hinton Rowan Helper with the aim of revealing what he believed to be the harm the slave system caused not only to slaves but also to Southern society as a whole and to the Southern economy in particular. Combining extensive factual research with a sometimes bitterly polemical tone, Helper's volume set out to make, through a comparison between free and slaveholding states, the case for immediate emancipation. Unlike the work of Northern abolitionists, who focused on the immorality of slavery and the suffering of slaves, Helper's focus was on the subordination of the non-slaveholding majority in the South to their powerful slaveholding neighbors, an argument he hoped would resonate with others who shared his racial and class status. He also believed that slavery was an economic failure and that the institution actually impeded the growth of the South.

The Impending Crisis appeared in the last years before the American Civil War (1861–65), at a time when sectional tensions were already high, and played a role in exacerbating those tensions. Reactions were split along regional lines, with Northerners and Republicans generally praising the book and Southerners and Democrats generally rejecting it. In the months following militant abolitionist John Brown's raid on the federal arsenal at Harper's Ferry, which likewise deepened sectional divides, Democrats were particularly inclined to view the book's message as dangerously divisive. Republicans' plans to make use of a shortened version of the book in the 1860 presidential campaign created conflict in both the U.S. Congress and the country itself. Abolitionists praised the book at the time of publication, but later readers have put more emphasis on the racist underpinnings of Helper's colonizationist stance, which envisioned not only the freeing of enslaved African Americans but also their permanent removal from the United States.

HISTORICAL AND LITERARY CONTEXT

The Impending Crisis draws on and extends a Southern antislavery tradition dating back to the founding fathers, including Thomas Jefferson and James Madison, whom Helper quotes in his book. Until about 1830, many slaveholders regarded slavery as an evil to be eradicated if possible, and they advocated approaches that usually involved colonization: deportation of emancipated slaves to Africa. By the time Helper wrote his thesis, the view of slaveholders had shifted and they increasingly embraced an overtly pro-slavery patriarchal ideology.

Sectional tensions increased after the controversial 1857 Dred Scott decision, in which the U.S. Supreme Court ruled that slavery was legal in all U.S. territories, effectively nullifying the Missouri Compromise of 1820—which had temporarily resolved the extension of slavery issue—as unconstitutional. Helper's own sectional experience helped to shape his views; he was born and raised in North Carolina's Central Piedmont, a region where slavery was not crucial to the economy as it was in the eastern part of the state. Early scholarship suggested that Helper grew up in poverty, providing an explanation for his resentment of the planter class. However, more recent archival research by scholar David Brown suggests that Helper came from a family of landowners and skilled craftspeople.

The immediate motivation for Helper's writing *The Impending Crisis* seems to have been the censorship of passages he wrote in his first book, *Land of Gold* (1855). The passages, critical of urban slavery, were censored by book's editor, Charles Mortimer, a slaveholder. Helper felt that the rights of white citizens to free speech were being limited by powerful slave owners. His sense of injustice was heightened when he was caught up in an anti-Republican mob in Baltimore, Maryland, in 1856 and when another North Carolina native, prominent chemistry professor Benjamin Sherwood Hedrick, lost his faculty job at the University of North Carolina for publicly supporting a Republican candidate. The excised passages from *Land of Gold* formed the nucleus of *The Impending Crisis*. Helper fleshed out his argument by drawing on newspapers, speeches, economic statistics, and conversations with fellow Republicans to provide an intellectual framework for his protest of the slaveholders' power over not only slaves but also free white fellow-citizens.

The Impending Crisis played a central role in debates over slavery in the years immediately preceding the American Civil War, but its longer-term influence was limited because of Helper's colonizationist stance and by the increasingly virulent racism expressed in his later works such as *Nojoque: A Question for a Continent* (1867), *The Negroes in Negroland; The Negroes in America, and Negroes Generally* (1868), and *Noonday Exigencies in America* (1871). Helper had never envisioned the approach to emancipation embodied by the Fourteenth Amendment, which not only abolished slavery but also recognized former slaves as citizens. Helper and his work had little to contribute to the long struggle for full civil rights for African Americans; instead, *The Impending Crisis* and Helper's subsequent works on race serve as a reminder that support of abolition and belief in racial equality did not necessarily go hand in hand.

THEMES AND STYLE

Throughout *The Impending Crisis*, Helper's primary focus is on white Southerners and their relationships with each other. He is especially interested in the relations between slaveholders, whom he repeatedly calls "oligarchs," and "non-slaveholders" like himself. Helper announces in the preface to *The Impending Crisis* that his purpose is not "to cast any unmerited opprobrium upon slaveholders or to display any special friendliness or sympathy for the blacks" but to examine slavery "with reference to its economic aspects as regards the whites." At times he does take on the "humanitarian and religious aspects" of slavery (as, for instance, in Chapters III–VII, where he presents declarations from a variety of sources against slavery), but that is not his primary goal. An explanation of "How Slavery Can Be Abolished"—the focus of Chapter II— appears to be a secondary goal; Helper's main focus is on the why rather than the how of abolition.

Much of Helper's argument is made through comparisons between the South and the North. Chapter I explicitly offers a "comparison between the Free and the Slave States," and Chapter VIII, "Free Figures and Slave," offers statistical comparisons of everything from "tonnage, exports, and imports" and "miles of canals and railroads in operation" to lists of federal officeholders from slave and free states. Chapter IX continues a comparison of commodities, and the final chapter, XI, deplores the state of Southern literature and the relative dearth of "periodical and general literature" and of publishers in the South. Presenting himself as a "true hearted southerner, whose ancestors have resided in North Carolina between one and two hundred years," Helper describes himself as "abashed and chagrined at the disclosures of the comparison thus instituted."

The Impending Crisis incorporates both carefully researched analytical arguments and strongly polemical statements. The analytical arguments stem at least in part from Helper's desire to distinguish his book from a genre he mentions in the preface: "the most popular anti-slavery literature of the day"—"novels"

SOUTHERN PROSLAVERY ARGUMENT IN 1857: GEORGE FITZHUGH

In the same year that Hinton Rowan Helper's *The Impending Crisis* appeared, George Fitzhugh, a leading advocate of the patriarchal or paternalist view of slavery, published his second book, *Cannibals All! Or Slaves without Masters*. As in his earlier *Sociology for the South; or the Failure of Free Society* (1854), Fitzhugh argued that Northern workers in the capitalist system were even less protected than slaves, because their interests and those of their employers were opposed to each other. These opposing interests, Fitzhugh argued, made the much-vaunted class mobility of the North a myth.

Fitzhugh saw relationships between masters and slaves as governed not only by the economic self-interest of the masters but also by mutual affection between the two races, parallel to that between a parent or guardian and a dependent child. The cornerstone of this patriarchal proslavery argument was the belief that people of African descent were, by nature, suited only to occupy the child's position in the metaphorical plantation family; any recognition of racial equality would, of course, have undermined the argument entirely. Although Fitzhugh and Helper differed in their conclusions, they agreed on this point: neither could envision a system in which African Americans were free, equal citizens.

written by "Yankee wives." Although Helper assures his reader that he has "nothing to say" against this literature, he argues that while "it is well enough for women to give the fictions of slavery; men should give the facts." These facts appear throughout the work, in quotations from letters replying to Helper's requests for information, in tables of figures, and in prose. Even these examples, however, can easily swerve into impassioned argument; in one passage in Chapter 1, "Comparison between the Free and the Slave States," Helper turns a list of products manufactured primarily in the North into proof that "in one way or another we [Southerners] are subservient to the North everyday of our lives," from an "infancy in which we are swaddled in Northern muslin" to a final trip "to the grave in a Northern carriage, entombed with a Northern spade, and memorized [sic] with a Northern slab!"

CRITICAL DISCUSSION

Initial reactions to *The Impending Crisis* were, predictably, positive in the North, especially among abolitionists, and negative in the South. Helper's work received favorable reviews in antislavery papers, including the *National Era, National Anti-Slavery Standard,* and *Liberator.* Southern newspapers, including the *Carolina Watchman, Raleigh Standard,* and *Fayetteville Observer,* panned the book, sometimes without reading it, and labeled Helper a traitor to the region of his birth.

A row of slave cabins on a Southern plantation in the 1800s. © NORTH WIND PICTURE ARCHIVES/ ALAMY.

time," including many Northern abolitionists. In his 2004 *Journal of Southern History* article, David Brown takes a more positive view of *The Impending Crisis,* conceding the racism of Helper's later books but arguing that, in 1857, "Helper outlined a surprisingly inclusive conception of humanity" and that "his religious ethos posited equality before God." Victoria Bynum, in *The Long Shadows of the Civil War* (2010), follows Brown in concluding that "Helper objected to slavery on the same grounds as did most Northerners: because it was morally wrong to enslave human beings, and because it privileged one class over another, creating an economically backward society in the process."

BIBLIOGRAPHY

Sources

Brown, David. "Attacking Slavery from Within: The Making of *The Impending Crisis of the South." Journal of Southern History* 70.3 (Aug. 2004): 541–76. *Proquest.* Web. 17 July 2012.

Bynum, Victoria E. *The Long Shadow of the Civil War: Southern Dissent and Its Legacies.* Chapel Hill: U of North Carolina P, 2010. Print.

Helper, Hinton Rowan. *The Impending Crisis of the South: How to Meet It.* 1857. Ed. George M. Fredrickson. Cambridge: Harvard UP, 1968. Print.

Further Reading

Brown, David. *Southern Outcast: Hinton Rowan Helper and "The Impending Crisis of the South."* Baton Rouge: Louisiana State UP, 2006. Print.

Escott, Paul D. *What Shall We Do with the Negro?: Lincoln, White Racism, and Civil War America.* Charlottesville: U of Virginia P, 2009. Print.

Fitzhugh, George. *Cannibals All! Or Slaves without Masters.* 1857. Ed. C. Vann Woodward. Cambridge: Harvard UP, 1966. Print.

———. *Sociology for the South; or the Failure of Free Society.* Richmond: Morris, 1854. *Google Book Search.* Web. 20 July 2012.

Foner, Eric. *Free Soil, Free Labor, Free Men: The Ideology of the Republican Party before the Civil War.* New York: Oxford UP, 1970. Repr. with new introduction, New York: Oxford UP, 1995. Print.

Helper, Hinton Rowan. *Nojoque: A Question for a Continent.* New York: Carleton, 1867. *Google Book Search.* Web. 20 July 2012.

———. *The Negroes in Negroland; The Negroes in America, and Negroes Generally.* New York: Carleton, 1868. *Google Book Search.* Web. 20 July 2012.

———. *Noonday Exigencies in America.* New York: Bible Brothers, 1871. *Google Book Search.* Web. 20 July 2012.

Stampp, Kenneth M. *America in 1857: A Nation on the Brink.* New York: Oxford UP, 1990. Print.

Williams, David. *Bitterly Divided: The South's Inner Civil War.* New York: Norton, 2008. Print.

Underlying these reviews, however, was the fact that Helper used his work to attack the slave system and the Southern view that slaves were treated better than Northern workers. Helper's views placated the North while they alienated the South.

One of Helper's strongest supporters was Republican Party organizer Horace Greeley, an antislavery advocate and publisher of the *New York Daily Tribune.* Greeley helped publish a compendium, or condensed version, of Helper's work that further inflamed political tensions on the eve of the Civil War. With Greeley's help, Helper had, in March 1859, gathered endorsements from sixty-eight Republican members of Congress. In December 1859, in the midst of tensions following John Brown's attempt to seize the federal arsenal at Harper's Ferry, the Democratic *New York Herald* publicized the names of the endorsers. This led to discord among members of the House in electing its speaker because Democratic Representatives treated support of Helper's book as tantamount to support of class war in the South. Although the link is not direct, some scholars believe that the Congressional divisions that hardened during this struggle helped hasten the Civil War.

In the twentieth century, scholarship on *The Impending Crisis* focused not only on the political impact of Helper's work but also on the racism underlying it. George Frederickson, a prominent scholar of American ideas about race, argued in his introduction to a 1968 reprint of *The Impending Crisis* that Helper's work was "worthy of study" because "his racism and cultural intolerance were extreme manifestations of beliefs which were shared by most Americans of his

Catherine E. Saunders

THE JAPAN THAT CAN SAY NO

Shintaro Ishihara, Akio Morita

OVERVIEW

In 1989 a collection of essays written by Shintaro Ishihara and Akio Morita and published under the title *No to Ieru Nihon* (*The Japan That Can Say No*) caused a significant global commotion with its criticisms of U.S. economic and military policies and its call for Japan to take a more independent stance on numerous international issues. In its original Japanese version, the book is divided into eleven chapters, five by Ishihara and six by Morita. There are numerous provocative statements, most of which come from Ishihara. For instance, in one essay he describes the United States as a racist nation and supports this contention by suggesting that it dropped atomic bombs on Hiroshima and Nagasaki but did not attack the Germans in the same manner because they are white and not Asian. Ishihara also urges Japan to wrest greater control of its national defense from the U.S. military. He refers to Japan Prime Minister Yasuhiro Nakasone as U.S. President Ronald Reagan's lapdog and strongly suggests selling semiconductors to the Soviets as a way of shifting the international balance of power. The book is specifically designed to stir nationalistic emotions.

The Japan That Can Say No was, in part, a response to years of unproductive trade negotiations between Japan and the United States. The U.S. government was consistently pressuring Japan to open markets to more foreign goods, while Japan resisted these pressures in order to protect its own businesses. When an English translation of the book was published by the Pentagon soon after the original Japanese version was released, U.S. political and business leaders were outraged. Morita was so embarrassed by the book's harsh reception that he refused to allow his sections to be officially translated into English or be included in any future printings.

HISTORICAL AND LITERARY CONTEXT

During the 1970s and 1980s, a strong codependency developed between the United States and Japan on economic and security matters. Japanese leaders felt less threatened by China and North Korea with the might of U.S. forces at their nation's doorstep, while the United States relied on Japan as an ally against the Soviet Union. Nevertheless, Japan clearly had a subservient role in this relationship, which angered many Japanese, including Ishihara. He has recalled in interviews and essays an incident as a boy in Japan in 1946 when he was struck by a U.S. soldier for not moving out of the way as the soldier and his companions passed him. The incident influenced many of his actions over the next forty years as he became one of the nation's most popular novelists and an admired politician.

Originally, *The Japan That Can Say No* was printed in Japanese and available only in Japan. The book was an immediate commercial success, and the Pentagon noticed. Within several months a pirated English version was published by the Defense Advanced Research Projects Agency. U.S. politicians and business leaders were incensed by, among other things, the book's suggestion that Japan's sophisticated technology sector should be used as leverage against U.S. trade demands. After all, the country's ballistic missiles were dependent on Japanese semiconductor chips, and denying that technology to the United States and offering it instead to the Soviets had the potential to cause a massive shift in the international power balance. The criticism was so intense that Morita, then the chairman of Sony and an unofficial ambassador to the United States, disavowed the book while Ishihara complained that the unofficial translation was filled with mistakes, omissions, and intentional distortions.

The book's themes were drawn largely from Ishihara's previous experiences, published works, and political philosophy. He initially made a name for himself as a novelist. At age twenty his first novel, *Season of the Sun* (1955), about teen rebelliousness in post-World War II Japan, won the Akutagawa Prize, Japan's most coveted literary award. His 1982 novel *Lost Country*, which speculates on Japanese life under Soviet domination, can also be seen as an influence on *The Japan That Can Say No.* As for Morita, many of the nationalistic concepts in *The Japan That Can Say No* can be seen in his autobiography *Made in Japan* (1986). For example, Morita writes in his autobiography, "When the United States Government criticizes Japanese policy or makes specific requests, the Japanese Government should respond with rational explanations of its positions and counterarguments instead of saying nothing, appearing to acquiesce, or simply saying 'no.'"

The Japan That Can Say No sparked a spirited debate about Japan's place in the international community,

Key Facts

Time Period:
Late 20th Century

Genre:
Essays

Events:
Increased economic and geopolitical interdependency between Japan and the United States under Japanese Prime Minister Yasuhiro Nakasone and U.S. President Ronald Reagan

Nationality:
Japanese

COURTING THE PUBLIC IN *THE JAPAN THAT CAN SAY NO*

Much of the commercial success of *The Japan That Can Say No* can be attributed to its populist rhetoric. Shintaro Ishihara, an important figure in Japan's Liberal Democratic Party, contributed many pieces to the volume that originated in his political speeches. In a 1996 article on the book, scholar Morris F. Low notes that it began as little more than "a string of anecdotes and rhetoric" that was transformed into book form by editors. Such rhetoric was intended primarily to rouse public sentiment in support of the party. The message of Japanese cultural and economic superiority and the assertion of America's flaws comforted and empowered Japanese citizens regarding their place in a changing world.

The composition and publication decisions involved in Ishihara and Morita's book also contributed to its popularity. Its rhetoric demonstrates that the authors' intended audience was average citizens rather than intellectual elites. The first Japanese edition of the text was published as a mass-market paperback by Kobunsha, a press best known for its magazines and popular novels. The volume was priced within the reach of the general public, and it quickly sold more than a million copies. The American furor over the book only enhanced sales and interest within Japan.

directly influencing works such as *China Can Say No,* a collection of essays published in 1996. Other similarly themed texts include *Global Security: North American, European, and Japanese Interdependence in the 1990s* (1991) by Eric Grove and *Bridging Japanese/North American Differences* (1994) by William Gudykunst and Tsukasa Nishida. Though *The Japan That Can Say No* has since receded into history, its statement concerning the value and interconnectivity of nations in the international community is still relevant today, especially as the economy becomes more globalized.

THEMES AND STYLE

The basic theme of *The Japan That Can Say No* is that Japan has been looked down upon and taken advantage of by other nations, specifically the United States, and must now do what is in its own best interests. In one of Ishihara's essays, he states, "In these days Japan seems to be flattered by all nations … but we Japanese have, besides money, a tradition and culture of which we can boast to the rest of the world … and high technology that neither the United States nor the Soviet Union can ignore." The authors wish to remind the Japanese people of their history and values in order to foster a sense of nationalism. To emphasize this point, Ishihara writes:

> The Japanese world view appears to be very peculiar, in the sense that in our mind Japan and the rest of the world do not form a single

circle. This may be due to linguistic differences as well as geographical factors nurtured by our climate. The rest of the world forms a separate world that exists outside and parallel to Japan, not making one world.

The Japan That Can Say No achieves its rhetorical effect through aggressive and emotional appeals. Rather than calmly present bland facts and figures, the work aims to rouse Japan from its passivity. Much of the writing is inflammatory, especially in Ishihara's pieces, as when he accuses the United States of being racist and bigoted. Certain passages even verge on threats: "If, for example, Japan sold chips to the Soviet Union and stopped selling them to the U.S., this would upset the entire military balance."

The book's title sets a passionate tone, implying that Japan has been a "yes man" to the United States and it is time to say "no." From there, the authors continually indict U.S. policies and attitudes. The message could not be clearer: Japan, despite so many strengths and resources, has allowed itself to be demoted to a second-class nation, a child among the adult superpowers. To gain international respect, writes Ishihara, Japan has no choice but to stand up to the United States: "Only through becoming aware of the 'no' they utter themselves can the Japanese join the world community as adult members…. No other nation will pay serious attention to the Japanese who cannot say 'no' to the United States."

CRITICAL DISCUSSION

The initial reaction to *The Japan That Can Say No* was not as positive as the authors had expected. Though many readers in Japan agreed with the contents of the book, professional critics warned of a strong backlash from the United States. A review by Shumpei Kumon in the *Journal of Japanese Studies* states that "the book has turned out to be an immature and dangerous way to give vent to the burgeoning nationalism of a new economic superpower. I cannot but see in Ishihara's new book the old hero of [*Season of the Sun*], who has grown up just enough that he now feels he can do what he wants vis-à-vis the United States." In the United States, management icon Peter Drucker weighed in with a piece in the *New York Times Book Review*: "In the end, his tongue and his pen simply made too many enemies. And so this book can be considered a loser's attempt to get back into the running." Ivan Hall's review concluded, "Both the substantive points and emotional temperature of the original come across not so much inaccurately as inelegantly."

The negative publicity actually served to catalyze discussion and analysis over the next decade on Japanese-U.S. economic relations. Many important publications appeared on the subject, such as *Parallel Politics: Economic Policymaking in the United States and Japan* (1991) by Samuel Kernell and *The End of the*

U.S. President Jimmy Carter and Japanese Prime Minister Masayoshi Ohira toasting at a state visit before an economic conference in 1979. In *The Japan That Can Say No*, Shintaro Ishihara and Akio Morita discuss Japan's economic and political strength, especially in relation to the United States. © CORBIS.

Nation State: The Rise of Regional Economies (1996) by Kenichi Ohmae. Ironically, then, *The Japan That Can Say No* accomplished its goal: to raise awareness of the relationship between the two nations and produce a more intense and honest dialogue.

Today, *The Japan That Can Say No* has been relegated to the status of historical footnote. For one, the worldwide financial crisis of the late 2000s created new economic and geopolitical rules and relationships. The United States and Japan are now closer allies than ever, partially because of the economic ascendance of China. Not only is China an economic threat to both nations, but it also has a long, difficult history with Japan. Politically, the world has also changed considerably since *The Japan That Can Say No* was published, as the Cold War has been replaced by the War on Terror. Indeed, on both political and economic levels, many of the accusations leveled in the book have been rendered obsolete.

BIBLIOGRAPHY

Sources

Drucker, Peter. "Our Irritable Friend" *New York Times Book Review* 13 Jan. 1991. Print.

Hall, Ivan P. "The Japan That Can Say 'No': The New U.S.-Japan Relations Card." *Journal of Asian Studies* 49.3 (1990): 660–62. *JSTOR.* Web. 26 Sept. 2012.

Heine, Steven. "From Art of War to Attila the Hun: A Critical Survey of Recent Works on Philosophy/ Spirituality and Business Leadership." *Philosophy East and West* 58.1 (2008): 126–43. *JSTOR.* Web. 26 Sept. 2012.

Ishihara, Shintaro. *The Japan That Can Say No.* Trans. Frank Baldwin. New York: Simon & Schuster, 1991. Print.

Kumon, Shumpei. Rev. of *The Japan That Can Say No,* by Shintaro Ishihara and Akio Morita. *Journal of Japanese Studies* 16.2 (1990): 427–36. *JSTOR.* Web. 26 Sept. 2012.

Miyoshi, Masao. Rev. of *The Japan That Can Say No,* by Shintaro Ishihara and Akio Morita. *Transition* 52 (1991): 158–64. *JSTOR.* Web. 26 Sept. 2012.

Morita, Akio, Edwin M. Reingold, and Mitsuko Shimomura. *Made in Japan: Akio Morita and Sony.* New York: E. P. Dutton, 1986. Print.

Further Reading

Grove, Eric. *Global Security: North American, European, and Japanese Interdependence in the 1990s.* London: Brassey's, 1992. Print.

Gudykunst, William, and Tsukasa Nishida. *Bridging Japanese/North American Differences.* Thousand Oaks: Sage, 1994. Print.

Kernell, Samuel. *Parallel Politics: Economic Policymaking in the United States and Japan.* Washington, DC: Brookings Institute, 1991. Print.

Ming, Ben She Yi. *China Can Say No.* China: Industrial & Commercial Joint Press, 1996. Print.

Ohmae, Kenichi. *The End of the Nation State: The Rise of Regional Economies.* New York: Free Press, 1996. Print.

Ozawa, Ichiro. *Blueprint for a New Japan: The Rethinking of a Nation.* New York: Kodansha America, 1994. Print.

Vogel, Ezra. *Japan as Number One: Lessons for America.* Cambridge: Harvard UP, 1999. Print.

Jim Mladenovic

"NUESTRA AMÉRICA"

José Martí

✣ *Key Facts*

Time Period:
Late 19th Century

Genre:
Essay

Events:
Latin American
independence
movement; Cuban
independence
movement; Ten Years'
War

Nationality:
Cuban

OVERVIEW

"Nuestra América" ("Our America") is an essay written by Cuban intellectual and revolutionary José Martí that was first published in *La Revista Ilustrada de Nueva York* (The New York Illustrated Magazine), on January 1, 1891. In the work, Martí proposes an authentically Latin American identity that is completely independent from European influence. In lofty, poetic prose, "Nuestra América" warns the Latin American intelligentsia of the threat that the United States and European powers pose to the sovereignty of Latin American nations. Martí calls for a Pan-Latin American unity in order to confront this external threat, and he critiques the Creole elite within the region for buying into the ploys of Anglo America and living their lives in imitation of everything European. The essay challenges the binary perception of civilization versus barbarism, privileging the "civilized" North over the "barbaric" South, and instead introduces a model that celebrates the unique identity and traits of Latin America, advocating for a political system that responds to the specific needs and reality of Latin America.

When "Nuestra América" was first published, Martí was residing in New York, seeking financial and political support for the cause of Cuban independence. His time in the United States helped show him the workings of U.S. imperialism to which he responds in the essay. Following its publication, "Nuestra América" received a positive reaction from progressive Latin Americans throughout South and Central America, while it was either condemned or ignored by the more conservative Latin American elite whose interests lay in fostering foreign investment and economic assistance from the United States and Europe. Martí's best-known political essay, "Nuestra América" is often regarded as the foundational text for Latin American nation building. The essay expresses the growing dissatisfaction of the Latin American masses with the oppressive imperial/colonial presence of Spain and the United States, among other countries, and the desire of the people to establish completely autonomous states. Martí's "seemingly impenetrable" prose, according to author Laura Lomas in her book, *Translating Empire,* is clearly written for a highly educated, intellectual audience and serves as a call to Latin American political and intellectual leaders to address the needs and demands of their people.

HISTORICAL AND LITERARY CONTEXT

By the time "Nuestra América" was first published in 1891, the struggle for independence had been taking place in Cuba for more than two decades. Unhappy with the racist, repressive governance of Spain, Cubans rose up twice against the crown—in the Ten Years' War (1868–1878) and in the Little War (1879–1880)—but both revolutionary attempts ultimately failed. The cruel acts of violence committed by the Spanish during the Ten Years' War further incensed Cuban colonists. These acts include the execution in 1871 of eight medical students for supposedly scratching the tombstone of a Spanish journalist, as well as the capture and execution of fifty-three people from the steamship *Virginius* in 1873. In response to the Cuban people's growing unrest, Martí sought support in the United States, Latin America, and Europe beginning in the early 1880s for a third (and final) war for Cuban independence.

In the late nineteenth century, Spain was quickly losing popularity among Cubans. Many former supporters had finally been convinced of the unjust nature of Spanish rule after the numerous atrocities committed by Spanish authorities during the Ten Years' War. At the same time, virulently racist Spanish propaganda attempted to divide the Cuban revolutionaries by spreading rumors that military leader Antonio Maceo, who was mulatto, was trying to start a racial war against white Cubans, which exacerbated the racist prejudices of his fellow Cuban officers. The propaganda had little effect on the movement or on Maceo's reputation, however, and indeed it was he and fellow revolutionary leader Máximo Gómez who garnered support throughout Cuba while Martí was fundraising abroad. They were able to recruit large numbers of men for the growing revolutionary army, often through the clandestine printing and distribution of leaflets calling for participation in the movement for independence.

The central debate in the Latin American intellectual sphere during this period was that of civilization versus barbarism, a European-influenced model for viewing the region as divided between the "civilized," cultured city dwellers and the uneducated, "barbaric" rural inhabitants of Latin America. "Nuestra América" responds in part to this polemic, which is most commonly associated with Domingo Faustino Sarmiento's

1845 work *Facundo: Civilización y barbarie* (*Facundo: Civilization and Barbarism*). Political essays by other Latin American progressive intellectuals began to appear in several independent periodicals in Central and South America, including *El Partido Liberal* (Mexico City), *La Nación* (Buenos Aires), and *La Opinión Nacional* (Caracas). Martí's essay contributes to the political dialogue opened up by these publications, drawing on the notions of Pan-Latin American identity that had already been introduced by Mexican reformers, including Guillermo Prieto and Ignacio Manuel Altamirano. "Nuestra América" further develops Martí's political ideology, which is present in earlier form in his 1883 "Respeto a Nuestra América" (Regarding Our America) and a 1889 work that is also titled "Nuestra América."

"Nuestra América" emerged during a critical period for the transitioning Latin American region that was still struggling with nation formation and the establishment of political and social systems independent from former colonial powers. Most Spanish colonies in the region obtained their independence from Spain by 1820; Cuba and Puerto Rico, in contrast, remained under the Spanish crown until the Spanish-American War of 1898. Martí wrote "Nuestra América" following a series of inter-American conferences, where he was "instrumental in convincing the Latin American representatives to reject U.S. proposals antithetical to their interests," according to author Susana Rotker, writing in the book *José Martí's "Our America."* The essay was quite successful in gaining the support of a wider mass of Latin Americans and in forging solidarity among its various countries.

THEMES AND STYLE

Central to the message of "Nuestra América" is a warning to the Latin American people about the threat posed by U.S. and European imperialist interests to the sovereignty of Latin American countries. Stressing the importance of solidarity among these nations to confront this threat, Martí writes: "Nations that do not know one another should quickly become acquainted, as men who are to fight a common enemy." Martí attempts to persuade his audience to adequately prepare for the looming threat of Anglo American economic and political dominance, warning that "the tiger lurks behind every tree, lying in wait at every turn," meaning that the threat of imperialism was still looming large for Latin America.

Martí wrote "Nuestra América" in a verbose, poetic style meant to speak to highly educated, intellectual Latin Americans. By calling on the cultured sons of Latin America to right the wrongs of past generations, Martí reveals his own elitism in his belief that the educated few must guide the ignorant masses. He writes, "The uncultured masses are lazy and timid in the realm of intelligence, and they want to be governed well. But if the government hurts them, they

THE CUBAN WAR OF INDEPENDENCE

The Cuban War of Independence (1895–1898) was the last of three wars that Cuba fought for its liberation from Spain, concluding the fight that had begun in the Ten Years' War (1868–1878) and in the Little War (1879–1880). Many early leaders in the struggle for independence, including revolutionary Carlos Manuel de Céspedes, also advocated for the abolition of slavery, which was finally achieved in 1884. The Ten Years' War, sometimes referred to as the Big War, is noted for the leadership of Céspedes in his attack on Yara on October 11, 1868. The death and imprisonment of several key leaders and the dissolution of the constitutional assembly by the end the Ten Years' War left a great deal of dissatisfaction among the supporters of the revolutionary army. This resulted in a new rebellion in August 1879, initiated by several generals, including José Maceo, Calíxto García, and Guillermo Moncada, but this action lasted little more than a year because of the wish of the populace for a return to peace.

The Cuban War of Independence (*Guerra de Independencia*) began on February 24, 1895, under Martí's leadership and started simultaneously in four different areas of the island. The final three months of the war escalated into the Spanish-American War (1898) as the United States declared war on Spain. In response to U.S. military advances, Spain quickly signed a peace agreement in July 1898 that led to a formal treaty in December that ended Spanish rule of Cuba. The United States governed Cuba for two years until the election of Cuba's first national government on May 20, 1902, a date that would later be celebrated annually as *Día de la República* (Republic Day) throughout Cuba.

shake it off and govern themselves." This appeal to the superiority of the cultured elite gains the interest and potential support of individuals who may not have responded to a more informal type of rhetoric. Martí's use of the first-person, collective "we" throughout the essay belies both an elitist and collectivist tone, at times addressing the educated, cult Latin Americanist and at other times emphasizing the unity and commonalities among the peoples of Latin America. The title itself, "Nuestra América," claims a collective ownership of the Americas, striving to facilitate solidarity within the region.

The abstract, figurative language Martí employs in "Nuestra América" at times renders its comprehension difficult, since it commonly introduces vague symbols rather than concrete examples or facts. He writes, "Poetry shears off its Zorrilla-like locks and hangs its red vest on the glorious tree. Selective and sparkling prose is filled with ideas." By referencing the Spanish romantic poet José Zorrilla y Moral as a symbol of an irrelevant cultural past, Martí criticizes the Latin American elite who still cling in desperation to outdated tradition. This approach is necessary

Statue of Cuban national hero José Martí in Cienfuegos, Cuba. © IMAGES & STORIES/ ALAMY.

conservative Latin American elite was quick to condemn it, if they acknowledged it at all. Although Martí was writing from New York, most U.S. citizens were unaware of the politically transformative prose being written on their own soil. Lomas writes, "Some of the earliest modernist writing was insisting upon another America within earshot of North America's leading authors, and yet remained largely unknown to them." By 1891, however, Martí's Spanish-speaking contemporaries, specifically the intellectuals who engaged with his work, including Ruben Dario (Nicaragua), Miguel de Unamuno (Spain), and Amado Nervo (Mexico), were very familiar with Martí and his work.

Contemporary scholarship regards "Nuestra América" as the most significant of Martí's political writings and views the essay as fundamental to Latin American nation building in the late nineteenth and early twentieth centuries. Scholars studying the Cuban independence period often analyze "Nuestra América" in comparison with other political writings by Martí, such as "¡A Cuba!" (1894) and *Manifiesto de Montecristi* (1895), noting the transformation from a more lofty philosophical work ("Nuestra América") to more concrete political documents expounding on the specific cause of Cuban independence. Latin American revolutionaries of the twentieth century, including Che Guevarra, Fidel Castro, and Hugo Chávez, lauded Martí's political vision and incorporated it into their respective political systems. The Cuban exile community in Miami, Florida, has also embraced Martí as a hero and a symbol of their idealized vision of Cuba, manipulating Martí's decidedly antielitist, anti-imperial ideology to fit into their politically conservative stance on the reality of their homeland.

"Nuestra América" is a foundational text of Latin American literature that is incorporated into the majority of university courses in the United States on the postindependence period and is regarded as fundamental in the construction of national Latin American and Pan-Latin American identities in the region. Much scholarship focuses on Martí's inversion of the "us" (Europe) versus "them" (Latin America) binary, and on the attention he draws to the United States as a potential threat. Lomas, in his book *Translating Empire,* explores Martí's criticism of the United States, asserting that his text enables us to "read 'America' from the Latino migrant's distinct linguistic, cultural, historical, and political position. Reading with a literary imagination, we can see how a shift of 'America' to the prior, now nondominant Latin American Spanish hemisphere, makes 'other' the term that once described the unmarked 'us.'" Another issue addressed by many scholars is the cautious criticism that Martí directs at Latin American political leaders. In his book, *José Martí's "Our America,"* editor Jeffrey Belnap writes, "At the same time, then, that 'Our America' addresses itself to the Latin American intelligentsia in order to awaken it to the external danger

for Martí to exemplify his true message by adopting a clearly distinct, fundamentally Latin American literary approach. The poetry and prose emerging from this region, Martí claims, must be uniquely Latin American in nature, and writers must excise the remnants of European literary style from their work.

CRITICAL DISCUSSION

When "Nuestra América" was published, it received a mixed response from the Pan-Latin American audience to whom it was addressed. Latin American exiles residing in the United States and well-read intellectuals living in Latin America reacted to the highly emotional address. Progressive Latin Americans throughout the region found the work inspiring and embraced its central message, but the more

posed by the United States, the essay carefully confronts this same class with an articulation of its own internal enemy: the intellectual orientation that turns the ruling class toward Europe and away from its own peoples."

BIBLIOGRAPHY

Sources

Belnap, Jeffrey, and Raúl Fernández, eds. *José Martí's "Our America": From National to Hemispheric Cultural Studies.* Durham: Duke UP, 1998. Print.

Gray, Richard B. "José Martí and Social Revolution in Cuba." *Journal of Inter-American Studies* 5.2 (1963): 249–56. Print.

Lomas, Laura. *Translating Empire: José Martí, Migrant Latino Subjects, and American Modernities.* Durham: Duke UP, 2008. Print.

Martí, José. "Our America." *Elaine O'Brien Latin American and Latino/a Art,* California State University, Sacramento. RTF file. Web. 29 Jan. 2013.

Rotker, Susana. "The (Political) Exile Gaze in Martí's Writing on the United States." *José Martí's "Our America": From National to Hemispheric Cultural Studies.* Eds. Jeffrey Belnap and Raúl Fernández. Durham: Duke UP, 1998, 56–90. Print.

Further Reading

Gillman, Susan Kay. "The Epistemology of Slave Conspiracy." *Modern Fiction Studies* 49.1 (2003): 101–23. Print.

Hatfield, Charles. "The Limits of Nuestra América." *Revista Hispánica Moderna* 63.2 (2010): 193–202. Print.

Ramos, Julio. *Divergent Modernities: Culture and Politics in Nineteenth-Century Latin America.* Trans. John D. Blanco. Durham: Duke UP, 2001. Print.

Retamar, Roberto Fernandez. "About My Writing on Martí's Work." *World Literature Today* 76.3–4 (2002): 17–23. Print.

Rodriguez-Luis, Julio, ed. *Re-Reading José Martí (1853–1895): One Hundred Years Later.* Albany: State U of New York P, 1999. Print.

Rotker, Susana. *The American Chronicles of José Martí: Journalism and Modernity in Spanish America.* Trans. J. French and K. Semler. Hanover: UP of New England, 2000. Print.

Ward, Thomas. "From Sarmiento to Martí and Hostos: Extricating the Nation from Coloniality." *European Review of Latin American and Caribbean Studies* 83 (2007): 83–104. Print.

Katrina White

"PATH OF THUNDER"

Christopher Okigbo

❖ *Key Facts*

Time Period:
Mid-20th Century

Genre:
Poetry

Events:
Nigerian independence
from British colonial
rule; establishment of
the Republic of Biafra;
Nigerian Civil War

Nationality:
Nigerian

OVERVIEW

"Path of Thunder," a collection of six poems written from December 1965 to May 1966 by Christopher Okigbo and published posthumously in 1968, prophesies the state of post-civil war Nigerian politics. He urges his audience to avoid falling into the same cycle of corruption he sees as synonymous with rulers made complacent by colonial influence. Deeming himself a "prodigal" turned "town crier," he acknowledges the need to preserve and return to African traditions to form a new unbiased government in which all the peoples of his native Nigeria had a voice. "Path of Thunder" marks a strong shift in Okigbo's poetic intentions from traditional symbolism to political prophecy. His untimely death fighting for Igbo rights in the Nigerian-Biafran Civil War made him a martyr for the revolution and helped these final poems become the most memorable piece of war propaganda from that era.

"Path of Thunder" was written two years prior to the July 6, 1967, outbreak of the Nigerian-Biafran War. Okigbo fought for revolutionary forces supporting the secession of the predominately Igbo southeastern region of Nigeria to become the Republic of Biafra. Okigbo returned to the customs of his Igbo ancestors, imbuing the poem with a song-like rhythm, decreeing his powerful prophecy of the events surrounding Biafran secession. Although Biafran forces lost the war, the oppression and struggle of the Igbo people live on through the literature of Okigbo, Chinua Achebe, and other Nigerian authors. Okigbo's "Path of Thunder" remains a timely warning to future activists to beware the outcome of their respective fights, lest they become that which they seek to depose.

HISTORICAL AND LITERARY CONTEXT

Although "Path of Thunder" was written in the years preceding the secession of the Republic of Biafra on May 30, 1967, it predicted the events leading up to this event by examining the neocolonial Nigerian government. Upon gaining its independence from direct colonial rule in 1960, Nigeria was divided into three sections: North (Hausa,) West (Yoruba,) and East (Igbo). The Igbo, who had long withstood colonial rule, deemed this division unfair as the land, with its rich oil reserves, was given to the new leaders of the succeeding regime. Okigbo's poem examines this unequal division of resources and power to warn future

Biafran secessionists against falling into the same cycle of corruption and abuse of power. According to Chukwuma Azuonye in an essay in *The Gong and the Flute: African Literary Development and Celebration* (1994), Okigbo through his poetry "reveals his dissatisfaction with the myopic and indecisive conduct of the regime of [Igbo] General Ironsi ... despite the popular reception of his regime throughout the country, his policy of appeasement toward the North as if to mollify its elite over the loss of its leaders was a position of weakness which undermined the force of his decrees."

"Path of Thunder" was written during the period of political unrest preceding the January 15, 1966, coup and the July 29, 1966, countercoup. The first poem in the collection was written in December 1965, just two months after a major incident of electoral fraud in Western Nigeria, which led to the January coup. Okigbo passed the poems to his editor shortly before moving to Eastern Nigeria to join the Biafran secessionists. "Path of Thunder" was first published in the same 1968 issue of *Black Orpheus* that contained Christopher Okigbo's obituary. In an essay in *Critical Perspectives on Christopher Okigbo* (1984), N. J. Udoeyop describes the loss of one of Africa's great revolutionary voices: "The poet saw in the secessionist cause the possibility of fusing the struggle for the ideal poetry and the ideal nation into one effort. The two struggles met one and the same end; and the man did not survive the harsh reality of war." Okigbo's "Path of Thunder" is a near perfect piece of Biafran secessionist propaganda; the poet not only lived his words but also died fighting for the truths represented therein.

Christopher Okigbo's poetry follows the tradition of anticolonial and secessionist propaganda prevalent during this period of political unrest in Nigeria and the African continent. Two of his contemporaries, Chinua Achebe and Ken Tsaro-Wiwa, also wrote about Igbo culture, addressing themes similar to those expressed in "Path of Thunder." Achebe's *Things Fall Apart* (1958) follows a fierce Igbo warrior, Okonkwo, whose way of life is swallowed up by corrupt colonial and neocolonial governments. The protagonist dies at the end of the novel after attacking a government messenger with a machete. Tsaro-Wiwa's poems, written before Okigbo's passing, eerily foreshadow the poet's death. "Night Encounter" and "Silence," which appear in the same edition of *Black Orpheus* as "Path of Thunder," sympathize with secessionist soldiers who face death for challenging the corrupt Nigerian government.

The prophetic nature of "Path of Thunder" and Okigbo's death in battle earned him respect as a revolutionary poet and martyr. Although his life was short and his body of work small, Okigbo predicted the bloody coups of 1966, the Nigerian-Biafran Civil War in which he fought, and the plight of future neo-colonial Nigerian governments. He is also the subject of Ali Mazrui's novel, *The Trial of Christopher Okigbo* (1971), which examines the responsibility of the artist in society by putting Okigbo on trial for putting societal needs above his art and endorsing patriotism over creativity. In Achebe's *Anthills of the Savannah* (1987), the hero, Chris Oriko, is a martyr based on Okigbo's life experiences and death. The poet is also remembered in *Don't Let Him Die: An Anthology of Memorial Poems for Christopher Okigbo* (1978) and a collection of contemporary African poetry in the spirit of Okigbo titled *Crossroads* (2007), released on the fortieth anniversary of his death.

THEMES AND STYLE

The main theme of "Path of Thunder" is a prophetic meditation on the future of Nigerian government and postcolonial African politics in general. The final poem, "Elegy for Alto," contains Okigbo's prophecy for the direction of Nigerian politics and for his own future. He states, "Earth, unbind me; let me be the prodigal … An old star departs, leaves us here on the shore / Gazing heavenward for a new star approaching; / The new star appears, foreshadows its going / Before a going and coming that goes on forever." He calls for political leaders to embrace the different cultural traditions in all regions of Nigeria, allowing for equality in government and distribution of resources. Although he hopes for an idyllic future, Okigbo predicts the inevitability of political unrest, corruption, and neo-colonial influence, as is evident in the following lines: "The Eagles have come again, / The eagles rain down on us— / Politicians are back in giant hidden steps of howitzers or detonators— / The Eagles descend on us, / Bayonets and cannons— / The Robbers descend on us to strip us of our laughter, of our thunder."

"Path of Thunder" is broken into six poems or movements: "Thunder Can Break," "Elegy of the Wind," "Come Thunder," "Hurrah for Thunder," "Elegy for Slit-Drum," and "Elegy for Alto." "Thunder Can Break" describes Nigeria's revolt against British colonial rule, while "Elegy of the Wind" urges a more vocal, direct approach to a government rooted in cultural traditions of the past. "Come Thunder" predicts future unrest or civil war, stating, "The death sentence lies in ambush along the corridors of power." "Hurrah for Thunder" warns the new government to avoid the corruption of colonial influence, and "Elegy for the Slit-drum" further addresses corruption in the new

CHRISTOPHER OKIGBO: NIGERIAN POET

Christopher Ifekandu Okigbo was born in Nigeria on August 16, 1932. Although he was brought up in a Christian household, he adopted the traditional religion of the Igbo people. He attended several universities in Nigeria and later worked as an assistant librarian and teacher at the University of Nigeria. Okigbo worked as a teacher, librarian, jazz saxophonist, soldier, and publisher, but he is most famous for his poetry. In his short life, he published three collections of poems: *Heavensgate* (1962), *Limits* (1964), and *Silences* (1965). His most famous volume, *Labyrinths with Path of Thunder* (1971), was published posthumously.

Okigbo's poems garnered much critical acclaim, and though his early work was classical in nature, his later work became much more politically motivated. He rejected negritude, refusing the Langston Hughes Award for African Poetry at the 1966 Festival of Negro Arts on the grounds that art should not be confined to race. In 1966 he returned to Eastern Nigeria to support the secession of Biafra from the oppressive North. Rather than serving his country as a speaker or public official, he chose to fight on the front lines, dying in the battle of Nsukka, the university town where he had been educated as a poet.

government and calls for peace and equality among all regions of Nigeria. The final poem, "Elegy for Alto," contains Okigbo's political prophecy. Taken as one poem in six movements, "Path of Thunder" describes the climate before, during, and after the first 1966 coup that led to the brutal civil war in which the poet met his demise.

In "Path of Thunder," Okigbo uses traditional Igbo myths, folk chants, and musical instruments to convey his message. The poem's musical nature—incorporating the sounds of town-crier chants, native drums, and thunder bursts—sets an emphatic tone that is pertinent, loud, and unavoidable. By using native drums and chants and invoking his role as a prodigal town crier, Okigbo acknowledges the necessity of embracing his own cultural identity as well as Africa's past in an attempt to avoid corruption and an endless cycle of abuse at the hands of new government officials. In "Hurrah for Thunder," he calls for direct action: "If I don't learn to shut my mouth I'll soon go to hell, / I, Okigbo, town-crier, together with my iron bell." Thus, he stresses the need to stand up for his beliefs although the likely outcome is his own demise. Azuonye describes "Path of Thunder" as "not a fulfillment but a promise of the revolutionary direction of the unrealized future of Okigbo's poetry." The fact that the poet died before the publication of this final work does not lessen Okigbo's transformation into a performance-oriented poet drawing on the inspiration of the African oral tradition to educate and inform his readers to the state of things to come.

Biafran refugees in the Nigeria/Biafra conflict, 1968. Poet Christopher Okigbo, who created the poem series "Path of Thunder," died in the conflict. AP PHOTO/KURT STRUMPF.

CRITICAL DISCUSSION

While "Path of Thunder" was embraced by Biafran secessionists and refuted by the "iron" government he criticizes as corrupt, critical reaction to the poem goes well beyond political ideologies. Okigbo's work was received with mixed reviews: government officials saw it as an act of dissension, while literary critics and other poets saw it as a remarkably complex poem with many meanings. It was also seen as a prophecy of war, a war in which Okigbo eventually paid the ultimate price for his beliefs. In a 1970 review in *Books Abroad* of the issue of *Black Orpheus* in which the poem—and Okigbo's obituary appears—Bernth Lindfors referrs to "Path of Thunder" as "the most exciting reading" in the issue, "a prophetic record of the torment and trauma of a nation in tragic grip of self-recognition."

Literary critics have seen "Path of Thunder" as a transitional set of poems for Okigbo toward a future that was never realized due to his untimely death. In *Christopher Okigbo: Creative Rhetoric,* Sunday Anozie (1972) states: "Nothing can be more tragic to the world of African poetry … than the death of Christopher Okigbo, especially at a time when he was beginning to show maturity and coherence in his vision of art, life and society, and greater sophistication in poetic form and phraseology." Okigbo's legacy as a sociopolitical poet and prophet sparked a wave of support from his Igbo compatriots and the world at large. His commitment not only to speak out against oppression but also to actively fight for the causes he held most dear led Okigbo to pay the ultimate price. However, his death was not in vain. "Path of Thunder"

inspired revolutionary poets, both in his native Nigeria and worldwide. The Christopher Okigbo Foundation, established in 2005, preserves his legacy, publishing lost manuscripts and holding symposiums on the influence of Okigbo's work on the modern world. The foundation's website describes its mission "to give Christopher Okigbo the place he deserves internationally and to further the poet's humanist vision and ideal through promotion of contemporary creation in Nigeria and cultural exchange worldwide. … When civilizations are long gone, only the Arts remain as testimony of our evolution."

"Path of Thunder" stands as the final prophetic words of an artist committed to fighting and inevitably dying for his beliefs. Filmmaker Branwen Kiemute Okpako's *The Pilot and the Passenger* is a biographical film about Okigbo that blends interviews with contemporaries and readings of his poetry with images of Nigeria and traditional music and discussion of cultural myths. This film and dozens of other novels, poems, and essays on the lingering influence of Christopher Okigbo's works on contemporary African writings and world literature were discussed at the Christopher Okigbo International Conference held at the University of Massachusetts in September 2007. In *Critical Essays on Christopher Okigbo* (2000), Robert Fraser describes the poet's greatest piece of propaganda: "'Path of Thunder' is strident, explicit, outright art: its reiterated images and ritualistic repetitions speak of a state of rapt possession in which a priest, one gifted with divine knowledge, utters his declamations and judgments. It is poetry of foresight and warning: in the full Old Testament sense, poetry of prophecy."

BIBLIOGRAPHY

Sources

Anozie, Sunday. *Christopher Okigbo: Creative Rhetoric.* London: Evan Brothers, 1972. Print.

Azuonye, Chukwuma. "'I, Okigbo, Town-Crier': The Transition from Mythopoeic Symbolism to a Revolutionary Aesthetic in Path of Thunder." *The Gong and the Flute: African Literary Development and Celebration.* Ed. Kalu Ogbaa. Westport: Greenwood, 1994. 19–36. Print.

Christopher Okigbo Foundation. "C. Okigbo: 1932–1967." *Christopher Okigbo Foundation.* Christopher Okigbo Foundation, n.d. Web. 4 Sept. 2012.

Fraser, Robert. "Christopher Okigbo." *Critical Essays on Christopher Okigbo.* Ed. Uzoma Esonwanne. New York: G. K. Hall, 2000. 230–59. Print.

Lindfors, Bernth. Rev. of *Black Orpheus,* ed. Theo Vincent. *Books Abroad* 44.3 (1970): 404–7. Print.

Okigbo, Christopher. *Labyrinths and Paths of Thunder.* New York: African Publishing Corp., 1971. Print.

Udoeyop, N. J. "Extract from 'Okigbo: A Branch of Giant Fennel.'" *Critical Perspectives on Christopher Okigbo.* Ed. Donatus Ibe Nwoga. Washington, D.C.: Three Continents, 1984. Print.

Further Reading

Achebe, Chinua, and Dubem Okafor, eds. *Don't Let Him Die: An Anthology of Memorial Poems for Christopher Okigbo.* Enugu: Fourth Dimension, 1978. Print.

Izevbaye, D. S. "Death and the Artist: An Appreciation of Okigbo's Poetry." *Research in African Literatures* 13.1 (1982): 44–52. Print.

Knipp, Thomas R. "Okigbo and 'Labyrinths': The Death of a Poet and the Life of a Poem." *Research in African Literatures* 26.4 (1995): 197–205. Print.

Mazrui, Ali Al'Amin. *The Trial of Christopher Okigbo.* London: Heinemann, 1971. Print.

Nwoga, Donatus Ibe, ed. *Critical Perspectives on Christopher Okigbo.* Washington, D.C.: Three Continents, 1984. Print.

Oguejiofor, Patrick Tagbo, and Uduma Kalu, eds. *Crossroads: An Anthology of Poems in Honor of Christopher Okigbo (1933–67) on the 40th Anniversary of his Death and on his 75th Birthday Anniversary.* Lagos: Apex Books, 2008. Print.

Ron Horton

THE QUIET AMERICAN

Henry Graham Greene

❖ *Key Facts*

Time Period:
Mid-20th Century

Genre:
Novel

Events:
Cold War; French
occupation of Vietnam

Nationality:
English

OVERVIEW

The Quiet American, a novel by Henry Graham Greene published in 1955, follows the uneasy relationship between a British war correspondent, Thomas Fowler, and an American economic attaché, Alden Pyle, during the French occupation of Vietnam. The two men hold opposing views on the West's involvement in Indochina. Narrated in the first person by Fowler, the story hinges on the contrast between Fowler's jaded realism and Pyle's untested optimism. Their arguments can be viewed on more universal levels as well, regarding the wisdom of involving oneself in the affairs of others. The book implicitly argues that Pyle's view of his country's foreign policy as a force for good is misguided and will ultimately have catastrophic effects for both countries.

During the early 1950s it was becoming increasingly clear that France was losing its struggle to control its colonies in Southeast Asia, which it had maintained since the 1880s. The emergence of the Communist-ruled People's Republic of China in 1949 had a massive impact on the region and spurred the cause of Viet Minh forces in Vietnam. In 1954 Indochina won its independence and France relinquished its claims on the peninsula. At this time, the United States, alarmed by the potential spread of communism, began to assert itself more vigorously in the region. Fowler and Pyle serve as allegorical foils: Fowler represents weary acceptance of the world as imperfect and immutable, while Pyle adheres to an idealistic worldview, insisting that change and betterment are possible. *The Quiet American,* and its thesis that actions taken with the best of intentions often have disastrous results, has served as a warning against the perils of international intervention that resonates up to the present day.

HISTORICAL AND LITERARY CONTEXT

The Quiet American is set during the moment when the French colonial army and its allies found themselves mired in a losing battle against the communist Viet Minh forces. By the mid-1950s the Viet Minh were becoming bolder in their guerrilla campaign against the French occupying forces. In a preface to the novel, Greene points out that *The Quiet American* does not maintain a strict adherence to historical events. However, Greene had visited Vietnam in the early 1950s and reported extensively on the experience for the *London Times.* Additionally, during this time he was secretly working as an operative for British intelligence and had knowledge of covert activities in the region. Years later, in his memoirs, Greene admitted that there was more direct reporting in *The Quiet American* than in any of his other novels. The book does seem to parallel the author's journalistic impression that Catholic populations in Vietnam were being crushed between nationalistic and U.S.-backed forces.

The Quiet American was published at a time when European colonialism was on the wane. Years of costly occupation following World War II had stretched the defenses of many countries, including Great Britain and France, to the breaking point, drained their treasuries, and cost many lives. The British Fowler represents this jaded worldview. As the age of European interventionism faded, the United States launched a cold war against the Soviet Union to contain the spread of communism. Pyle, the well-intentioned American for whom the book is titled, arrives in Saigon with the belief that he knows how to succeed where the old colonial forces have failed. As a reporter who had traveled the world extensively, Greene was uniquely positioned to chronicle the actions of these two men on the global stage.

At the time of its publication, many critics viewed *The Quiet American* as a departure from Greene's earlier work. His novels immediately preceding it, *The Power and the Glory, The Heart of the Matter,* and *The End of the Affair,* deal largely with religious themes, while *The Quiet American* strikes a more political tone. Greene himself was coy about whether or not it was a political novel, but even on a cursory read it is difficult to ignore the book's commentary on the perils of colonialism. These views were not particularly new, however. Joseph Conrad's *The Heart of Darkness,* published in 1899, detailed the horrors of the occupation of the Belgian Congo, and E. M. Forster's *A Passage to India,* published in 1924, dealt with complications surrounding Britain's colonial interests in India. Both of these works had at least a passing influence on *The Quiet American.*

The Quiet American had an enormous cultural and literary impact upon publication. Like Greene's other work, the book was widely read by both academic scholars and the public in general. While most Cold War novels, particularly popular novels, tended to adopt a pro-Western position, *The Quiet American* maintains a less enthusiastic view of Western actions. Its message of anti-interventionism would go on to inform and critique U.S. involvement in Latin America and the Middle East throughout the twentieth century and into the twenty-first century. *The Quiet American* was adapted for film twice, once in 1958 and again in 2002.

THEMES AND STYLE

The central thesis of *The Quiet American* is that actions taken with the best of intentions often have negative consequences. Fowler, who befriends Pyle, describes him as earnest but naïve, noting that "he was as incapable of imagining pain or danger to himself as he was incapable of conceiving the pain he might cause others," and yet "he was determined … to do good, not to any individual person but to a country, a continent, a world." Fowler, however, understands the danger of innocence, calling it "a dumb leper who has lost his bell, wandering the world, meaning no harm." When he learns that Pyle orchestrated a bombing that killed more than fifty innocent women and children, Fowler is forced to take action to thwart Pyle. "Sooner or later," Fowler claims near the end of the novel, "one has to take sides. If one is to remain human." Thus, the novel stands as a warning against reckless adventurism, however well intentioned.

The Quiet American is often praised for its nonlinear narrative arc. The fact that Pyle dies is revealed within the first few pages of the book. The rest of the story unfolds in an intricate series of flashbacks juxtaposed with the present. Greene slowly reveals not only who killed Pyle but also how and why. The novel's first-person perspective from Fowler's point of view provides the reader unfiltered access to his thoughts on the dim state of the French occupation of Vietnam. When Fowler and Pyle argue about what should be done, the arguments tend to be one sided, as the reader has no way of knowing Pyle's interior thoughts. For example, because Fowler is narrating the story, he can say Pyle "had pronounced and aggravating views on what the United States was doing for the world," and the reader has no way of determining what those views are or whether they have merit. In this way, Greene is able to manipulate the argument to emphasize the strength of Fowler's views.

Fowler presents himself as a world-weary correspondent who has come to view the French occupation and the accompanying insurgency in a blasé manner. At times, his narration adopts a sneering tone that betrays his disdain for Pyle, such as when he mocks Pyle's interest in academics, saying Pyle "had taken a degree in—well, one of those subjects Americans can take degrees in: perhaps public relations or theatrecraft, perhaps even far Eastern studies." The love triangle that forms when Pyle declares his interest in Fowler's Vietnamese mistress, Phuong, can be seen as an allegory for the struggle for neocolonial hold over Southeast Asia.

A MASTER CRAFTSMAN

What sets Graham Greene apart from many of his contemporaries, and likely contributed to his immense popularity as a writer, was his ability to meld serious topics such as religion and politics with stories that included intrigue and suspense. Greene was careful, however, to draw distinctions between his books based on their relative seriousness. He referred to works that relied more heavily on melodrama or on less complexly drawn characters as "entertainments." These books also tended to have happy endings. While *The Quiet American* includes many elements that make for a dramatic story, the depth of the characters and the seriousness of its subject matter place it firmly in the category Greene referred to as his "novels."

Today, Greene is often viewed as one of the masters of the spy novel. Undoubtedly, his writing benefitted from the fact that, during his world travels, he served as an operative for MI6, Britain's secret service. He was stationed in Sierra Leone during World War II and was initially recruited into the service by his sister, Elisabeth, due to his access to exotic parts of the world. Green acknowledged how much this experience influenced his writing when he dedicated his book *The Human Factor* to his sister, "who cannot deny some responsibility."

CRITICAL DISCUSSION

Greene was a successful novelist by the time he wrote *The Quiet American,* yet this work received mixed reviews upon publication. While many critics praised it as a piece of fiction, some reviewers in the United States objected to what they perceived as its caricature of U.S. ideals and virtues. A *Time* magazine editorial said that "Greene would have written a far better book if his anti-Americanism had not led him to the absurd extremity of suggesting that ice cream sodas are the opium of the people." Others were incensed by the book's implication that it would be wiser to succumb to the spread of communism. The *Saturday Evening Post* argued that the novel "implies that the communists love the Asian peasants and that American shouldn't help anti-communists … even if the Reds conquer all Asia."

As U.S. involvement in Vietnam grew during the 1960s and 1970s, scholars developed a deeper appreciation of Greene's depiction. Many of the tropes in *The Quiet American,* such as government censorship of the press, hazy battlefield reporting, and an amorphous definition of friend and ally, became commonplace to the U.S. experience in Vietnam. According to Karen Steigman in her 2012 essay in *College Literature,* "*The Quiet American* has been read as a particularly prescient and trenchant anti-American allegory of US security policy in East Asia." Greene's novel has also been studied for its accurate depiction of the United States' overseas involvement beyond the Asian sphere. Critic Maria Couto writes that "the subject

Brendan Fraser (center) plays Alden Pyle in a scene from the 2002 film adaptation of Graham Greene's 1955 novel *The Quiet American*. © MIRAMAX/COURTESY EVERETT COLLECTION.

of Greene's satire has always been America's foreign policy which pretends to protect the 'free world' [but which] in fact often means only one objective: American interests."

U.S. foreign policy in the twenty-first century has brought about a new reason for scholars to turn to *The Quiet American*. In his essay in *Critical Zone 2: A Forum of Chinese and Western Knowledge* (2006), William Spanos praises the novel for its "uncanny relevance to the contemporary American occasion: 9/11 and America's global war on terrorism." Steigman notes that Greene's book "has headlined both sides of the debate about the US wars in Iraq and Afghanistan." Other critics have pointed out how U.S. military excursions in both countries started off triumphantly but soon stagnated and began to rapidly deteriorate, resulting in immense loss of life and property. In light of such outcomes, it is difficult not to see the wisdom in Fowler's comment, "I never knew a man who had better motives for all the trouble he caused."

BIBLIOGRAPHY

Sources

Couto, Maria. *Graham Greene: On the Frontier: Politics and Religion in the Novels.* New York: St. Martin's, 1988. Print.

Davis, Robert Gorham. Rev. of *The Quiet American,* by Graham Greene. *New York Times.* The New York Times Company, 11 Mar. 1956. Web. 20 Sept. 2012.

"Greene Hell of Indo-China." Rev. of *The Quiet American,* by Graham Greene. *Time* 12 Mar. 2012. Print.

Hawtree, Christopher. "A Muse on the Tides of History: Elizabeth Dennys." *Guardian.* Guardian News and Media, 9 Feb. 1999. Web. 2 Oct. 2012.

Kunkel, Francis L. *The Labyrinthine Ways of Graham Greene.* Mamaroneck: Paul P. Appel, 1960. Print.

Spanos, William. "Who Killed Alden Pyle? The Oversight of Oversight in Graham Greene's *The Quiet American.*" *Critical Zone 2: A Forum of Chinese and Western Knowledge.* Ed. Q. S. Tong, Wang Shouren, and Douglas Kerr. Hong Kong: Hong Kong UP, 2006. Print.

"To Get Rave Reviews Write an Anti-U.S.A. Novel!" Rev. of *The Quiet American,* by Graham Greene. *Saturday Evening Post* 6 Oct. 1956. Print.

Steigman, Karen. "The Literal American: Rereading Graham Greene in an Age of Security." *College Literature* 1–26. MLA *International Bibliography.* Web. 28 Jan. 2013.

Further Reading

Diemert, Brian. "Graham Greene." *Mystery and Suspense Writers: The Literature of Crime, Detection, and Espionage.* Ed. Robin W. Winks and Maureen Corrigan. New York: Scribner, 1998. *Literature Resources from Gale.* Web. 2 Oct. 2012.

Greene, Richard, ed. *Graham Greene: A Life in Letters.* New York: W. W. Norton, 2007. Print.

Hitchens, Christopher. "I'll Be Damned: Graham Greene's Most Fervent Loyalty Was to Betrayal." *Atlantic* Mar. 2005: 105+. *Literature Resources from Gale.* Web. 2 Oct. 2012.

Lane, Anthony. "Love and War." *New Yorker* 2 Dec. 2002: 117. *Literature Resources from Gale.* Web. 2 Oct. 2012.

Palm, Edward F. "*The Quiet American* Revisited: Orientalism Reconsidered." *War, Literature & The Arts* 23.1 (2011). *Literature Resources from Gale.* Web. 2 Oct. 2012.

Sherry, Norman. *The Life of Graham Greene: Volume III: 1955–1991*. New York: Penguin, 2004. Print.

Thompson, Hunter S. "Hunter S. Thompson, The Art of Journalism No. 1." *Paris Review*. The Paris Review, Fall 2000. Web. 2 Oct. 2012.

White, Charles Dodd. "Graham Greene's *The Quiet American*." *Explicator* 67.1 (2008): 33+. *Literature Resources from Gale*. Web. 2 Oct. 2012.

Media Adaptations

The Quiet American. Dir. Joseph L. Mankiewicz. Perf. Audie Murphy, Michael Redgrave, and Claude Dauphin. United Artists, 1958. Film.

The Quiet American. Dir. Phillip Noyce. Perf. Michael Caine, Brendan Fraser, and Do Thi Hai Yen. Miramax Films, 2002. Film.

Giano Cromley

THE STATE AND REVOLUTION

Vladimir Ilyich Lenin

❖ *Key Facts*

Time Period:
Early 20th Century

Genre:
Treatise

Events:
World War I; Russian
Revolution of 1917;
Bolshevik assumption
of power under Vladimir
Ilyich Lenin

Nationality:
Russian

OVERVIEW

The State and Revolution, published in 1918 by Russian communist leader Vladimir Ilyich Lenin, is an analysis of the writings of Karl Marx and Friedrich Engels on the proposed violent overthrow of capitalism and the cooperative socialist system that would take its place. Optimistic and utopian in tone, *The State and Revolution* offers Lenin's vision of the future, not only for the Russian people but also for the working classes around the world, whom he predicted would dismantle oppressive regimes based on the accumulation of wealth and power and develop a collective ethic that would eventually make the idea of a governing state unnecessary. As a part of his radical discourse, Lenin offers severe criticism of more moderate socialist theorists, whom he views as "opportunists" weakening the movement.

Lenin began work on an essay titled "Marxism on the State" while living in exile in Western Europe between 1905 and 1917. During this turbulent period, popular unrest in Russia led to two revolutions, the abdication of the tsar, and the formation of a provisional government. Lenin returned to Russia in 1917 to take a leadership role in the rapidly evolving political change. He distilled his radical interpretation of socialist theory into *The State and Revolution,* which, published just after the revolution, became a major influence on socialist and anarchist thought into the next century.

HISTORICAL AND LITERARY CONTEXT

The reverence for scientific thinking and humanitarian ideals that characterized the eighteenth-century Age of Enlightenment sparked democratic political movements throughout Western Europe and led to revolutions in America and France, the Greek War of Independence, and various unsuccessful revolutions in South America. By the early 1800s these modern ideas of equality and self-rule had begun to spread to Russia, which was still under the control of a repressive feudalistic monarchy. At the end of 1825, leaders of the Decembrist Revolt demanded the creation of a Russian constitution to ensure basic rights for the common people. The tsarist army repressed the Decembrists, but unrest continued. During this period, tsarist officials sought to neutralize any reformist or revolutionary organizations by execution or via exile to Siberia

and Western Europe. In January 1905 the massacre by government forces of hundreds of peaceful demonstrators in St. Petersburg led to a massive uprising, forcing Tsar Nicholas II to establish a democratic constitution and an elected parliament. However, the newly established Duma had little power, and real change was slow to come. Tsarist officials engaged in a concerted campaign to retract or gut all the concessions that had been made in a combination of manipulation, repression, and neutralization.

In 1914 precarious European alliances collapsed, plunging Russia, along with the rest of Europe, into World War I. With little faith in the tsar's leadership, millions killed in the fighting, and starvation at home, the Russian people once again rebelled. Almost one hundred thousand women took to the streets on International Women's Day, February 23, 1917, demanding food and peace. More militant demonstrations followed, and thousands of soldiers, sent to suppress the protest, mutinied and joined the workers in the streets. By March the tsar and his heirs abdicated power, and members of the Russian parliament formed a provisional government. But many Russian radicals were dissatisfied with the new moderate and increasingly ineffectual administration, and in October 1917, under the leadership of Lenin, the Bolshevik faction took over St. Petersburg, the seat of the provisional government.

The Industrial Revolution, which swept Europe during the eighteenth and nineteenth centuries, transformed the lives of working people, creating a vast new class of impoverished and often exploited laborers and inspiring a new wave of social theorists determined to create a more just and equitable society. Two of the most influential writers of this movement were German philosophers Karl Marx and Friedrich Engels, who collaborated in 1848 to produce the *Communist Manifesto,* which advocated a more communal society governed by the proletariat, or working class. Dutch astronomer Anton Pannekoek was another pioneer of socialist thought. Some of his articles, including "Labor Movement and Socialism" (1908) and "Marxist Theory and Revolutionary Tactics" (1912), influenced early activists. In Russia such writers as Georgi Plekhanov (*The Bourgeois Revolution,* 1891) and Nikolai Bukharin ("The Imperialist Pirate State," 1916) applied Marx's and Engels's principles to their own history and culture.

Still studied decades after the collapse of the government he helped to build, Lenin's analysis in *The State and Revolution* remains a vehicle for important insights into the development of the Soviet communist state. The work not only influenced Soviet leaders from Joseph Stalin in the 1920s to 1950s to Mikhail Gorbachev in the 1980s, but it has been an inspiration to leaders of other communist regimes, such as China's Mao Zedong. It has also become a classic polemic of utopian political vision for the radical left and of authoritarianism for the conservative right.

THEMES AND STYLE

In the preface to his book, Lenin sets himself the task "of explaining to the masses what they will have to do before long to free themselves from capitalist tyranny." The visionary passion of *The State and Revolution* is founded on Lenin's admiration for the intrinsic capability of working people to do what they "have to do." He repeats this theme throughout: "Instead of the special institutions of a privileged minority ... the majority itself can directly fulfill all these functions.... The *mass* of the population will rise to taking an *independent* part, not only in ... elections, *but also in the everyday administration of the state.*" In his demand for complete overthrow of the contemporary repressive regime, he calls on the authority of Marx: "Marx's idea is that the working class must *break up, smash* the 'ready-made state machinery,' and not confine itself merely to laying hold of it." However, Lenin's view of the future is neither harsh nor angry but idealistic: "The state will be able to wither away completely when society adopts the rule: "From each according to his ability, to each according to his needs"; that is, "when people have become so accustomed to observing the fundamental rules of social intercourse ... that they will voluntarily work according to their ability."

Lenin makes an emotional appeal to his readers by calling up the drama of the recent revolution. "Prior to January 22, 1905, the revolutionary party of Russia consisted of a small group of people, and the reformists ... derisively called us a 'sect.' ... Within a few months, however ... hundreds ... 'suddenly' grew into thousands; the thousands became the leaders of between two and three million proletarians.... In this way dormant Russia was transformed into a Russia of revolutionary proletariat and a revolutionary people." He criticizes more moderate Marxists such as Karl Kautsky by contrasting his own "correct" interpretation of the master: "In these circumstances, in view of the unprecedentedly widespread distortion of Marxism, our prime task is to *re-establish* what Marx really taught on the subject of the state," in order that the "distortion by the 'Kautskyism' now prevailing may be documented and clearly demonstrated."

While he uses academic and historical references that tend to make his text somewhat obscure to those unfamiliar with the basics of socialist rhetoric, Lenin's writing style is forthright and accessible, as when he

SUPPRESSING THE OPPOSITION: THE FAILURE OF AN IDEAL

In 1991 the Union of Soviet Socialist Republics (USSR), the communist nation that emerged from the ideals and actions of revolutionaries such as Vladimir Ilyich Lenin, dissolved, becoming fifteen separate nations. The dissolution of the USSR had its roots as far back as the aftermath of the 1917 revolution, when the new communist government began using repressive measures to enforce compliance with economic and political change. Marxist revolutionary Rosa Luxemburg articulated concerns about these tactics: "Socialism in life demands a complete spiritual transformation in the masses degraded by centuries of bourgeois class rule.... No one knows this better, describes it more penetratingly, describes it more stubbornly than Lenin. But he is completely mistaken in the means he employs," she writes. "Decree, dictatorial force of the factory overseer, draconic penalties, rule by terror—all these things are but palliatives. The only way to a rebirth is the school of public life itself, the most unlimited, the broadest democracy and public opinion. It is rule by terror which demoralizes."

Lenin's *State and Revolution* was written to instruct and encourage its readers, who were presumably en route to the new society the Bolsheviks envisioned. From any number of perspectives, it is clear the USSR made only the most halting steps with virtually no progress toward the new society that Lenin believed could and would come to exist. During the 1980s the Soviet Union faced an economy drained by decades of its arms race with the United States, an unstable political landscape with more than a hundred uneasily united ethnic groups, and international scrutiny over a devastating accident at its Chernobyl Nuclear Plant. President Mikhail Gorbachev sought to ease his country's problems by the introduction of two programs: *glasnost,* or openness, and *perestroika,* or rebuilding. The freedoms of speech and press that resulted from glasnost led to an outpouring of debate and dissent that eventually led to demands for autonomy from the republics and the end of the union.

describes "the conversion of the representative institutions from talking shops into 'working' bodies." His writing even approaches the humorous, such as in the "Postscript to the First Edition," in which he explains his failure to complete an intended final chapter on the 1905 and 1917 revolutions: "It is more pleasant and useful to go through the 'experience of revolution' than to write about it."

CRITICAL DISCUSSION

Upon its publication, Lenin's treatise on Marxism and the revolution became an immediate part of the vigorous political debate of the time. His fellow revolutionary Leon Trotsky called it a work of "immeasurable importance" because "it constituted the scientific introduction to the greatest revolution in history." Socialist historian Ian Birchall notes his article in *International Socialism*, "At the time of its first publication, this vital

A 1917 painting of Vladimir Ilyich Lenin, author of *The State and Revolution*. AP PHOTO.

book received a far warmer welcome among anarchists than among the orthodox Marxists of the day." In *Lenin's Moscow* (1987), French communist Alfred Rosmer described the horror with which some greeted Lenin's work. "'It isn't Marxist,' they shrieked.... On the other hand, for revolutionaries situated outside the mainstream of orthodox Marxism … [*The State and Revolution*] was a pleasant revelation…. They read and re-read this interpretation of Marx, which was quite unfamiliar to them." In the United States, a reviewer for the New Orleans *Times-Picayune* expressed a more conservative view in 1927, describing the book as "an alarming treatise in many ways."

Trotsky called *The State and Revolution* Lenin's "secret last will and testament" and suggested its greatest legacy was as a declaration of communist ideals, values, and dreams. In his introduction to the 1992 edition, Robert Service called the work "a choral ode to action, intolerance, combat and collectivism, the anthem of Bolshevism in its revolutionary era." Though the work is clearly a product of a particular ideology at a unique time in history, it remains vibrant in expression of a belief in the power of ordinary people to take control of their lives and build an understanding of their collective interests to create a just and fair society.

Many scholars have viewed *State and Revolution* as a utopian departure from Lenin's usual pragmatic political analysis. In a 1952 essay in the *American Slavic and East European Review,* historian Robert V. Daniels described it as an "argument for utopian anarchism"

and "a work conforming neither to Lenin's previous thought nor to his subsequent practice." Adam Ulam concurs in his book *The Bolsheviks* (1998): "No work could be more *un*-representative of its author's political philosophy and his general frame of mind." However, Rodney Barfield, writing for *Slavic Review,* views *The State and Revolution* not as a manifesto but as a "theoretical work looking into the future," representing Lenin's "fundamental philosophy of man, his inner conviction of human nature, his ideals for a more humane world." Neil Harding, who has written several analyses of Lenin's work, describes *The State and Revolution* as a "vision of genuine direct democracy and genuine freedom."

BIBLIOGRAPHY

Sources

Barfield, Rodney. "Lenin's Utopianism: *State and Revolution." Slavic Review* 30.1 (1971): 45–56. Rpt. in *Twentieth-Century Literary Criticism.* Ed. Scot Peacock. Vol. 67. Detroit: Gale Research, 1997. *Literature Resource Center.* Web. 13 Aug. 2012.

Birchall, Ian. "Another Side of Anarchism." *International Socialism: A Quarterly Journal of Socialist Theory.* International Socialism, Summer 2010. Web. 14 Aug. 2012.

Daniels, Robert V. "*The State and Revolution*: A Case Study in the Genesis and Transformation of Communist Ideology." *American Slavic and East European Review* 11–12 (1952). *Google Books.* Web. 13 Sept. 2012.

Evans, Alfred B. "Rereading Lenin's *State and Revolution.*" *Slavic Review* 46.1 (1987): 1–19. Rpt. in *Twentieth-Century Literary Criticism.* Ed. Scot Peacock. Vol. 67. Detroit: Gale Research, 1997. *Literature Resource Center.* Web. 13 Aug. 2012.

Harding, Neil. *Lenin's Political Thought.* New York: St. Martin, 1977. Print.

Luxcmburg, Rosa. *The Russian Revolution, and Marxism or Leninism.* Ann Arbor: U of Michigan P, 1961.

Rev. of *The State and Revolution. Times-Picayune* (New Orleans) 15 May 1927: 112. *America's Genealogy Bank.* NewsBank. Web. 14 Aug. 2012.

Rosmer, Alfred. *Lenin's Moscow.* London: Bookmarks, 1987. Print.

Service, Robert. Introduction. *The State and Revolution.* By Vladimir Lenin. New York: Penguin, 1992. xi–xlviii. Print.

Trotsky, Leon. *History of the Russian Revolution. 1932.* Chicago: Haymarket, 2007. Print.

Ulam, Adam Bruno. *The Bolsheviks: The Intellectual and Political History of the Triumph of Communism in Russia.* Cambridge: Harvard UP, 1998. Print.

Further Reading

Bottomore, Tom, ed. *A Dictionary of Marxist Thought.* Oxford: Blackwell, 1988. Print.

Felshtinsky, Yuri. *Lenin and His Comrades: The Bolsheviks Take Over Russia 1917–1924.* New York: Enigma, 2010. Print

Gooding, John. *Socialism in Russia: Lenin and His Legacy, 1890–1991.* New York: Palgrave Macmillan, 2002. Print

Lee, Stephen J. *Lenin and Revolutionary Russia.* New York: Routledge, 2003. Print.

Pannekoek, Anton, and Lance Byron Richey. *Lenin as Philosopher: A Critical Examination of the Philosophical Basis of Leninism.* Milwaukee: Marquette UP, 2003. Print.

Pipes, Richard. *A Concise History of the Russian Revolution.* New York: Vintage, 1995. Print.

Budgen, Sebastian, Eustache Kouvélakis, and Slavoj Zizek, eds. *Lenin Reloaded: Towards a Politics of Truth.* Durham: Duke UP, 2007. Print.

Tina Gianoulis

SUPPRESSION AND SCAPEGOATING

ANIL'S GHOST

Michael Ondaatje

OVERVIEW

Set in Sri Lanka during the civil unrest of the late twentieth century, Michael Ondaatje's novel *Anil's Ghost* (2000) is a somber meditation on the human costs of war and political violence. It tells the story of Anil Tissera, a Sri Lanka-born forensic anthropologist sent by an international human rights organization to investigate the growing number of murders on the island. Sarath Diyasena is an archaeologist assigned by the government to work with Anil. Divided into eight sections, the novel follows Anil and Sarath as they investigate the bones of a recent murder victim that were found among older bones in an ancient burial site. Meanwhile, Sarath's brother, Gamini, works in the emergency ward of the Colombo hospital and is struggling to help the living victims of the violence. Through the novel, Ondaatje, a native of Sri Lanka, offers an indictment of state-sponsored terrorism and its lasting consequences for individuals and national histories.

When *Anil's Ghost* was published, significant peace efforts were under way in Sri Lanka. Two decades of civil unrest had left many people dead, and many more were displaced, living in poverty in refugee camps. Despite the number of casualties, however, the conflicts had not received significant international attention. The success of *The English Patient* (1992) had brought Ondaatje a wide audience, and *Anil's Ghost* was well received by critics, winning the Canadian Governor General's Award for fiction in 2000. The novel was also favorably reviewed in the United States, and Ondaatje was praised in the *New York Times* for "making the blood of his own country real."

HISTORICAL AND LITERARY CONTEXT

Tension had long simmered between Sri Lanka's two largest ethnic groups, the majority, consisting largely of Buddhist Sinhalese, and the minority, consisting mainly of Hindu Tamils. Beginning in 1983, Sri Lanka was gripped by violent civil unrest as various groups fought against the government. Insurgents from the south and, more significantly, from a separatist group in the north called The Liberation Tigers of Tamil Eelam (LTTE), caused thousands of casualties. Further, rumors persisted of covert governmental involvement in the slaughter. Politically motivated kidnappings were common, and the victims of such

crimes permanently vanished, leaving families in turmoil and disbelief. By the late 1990s, many people were dead or displaced, and there was no obvious end to the violence in sight.

Anil's Ghost provides a view of the violence in Sri Lanka through Western eyes at a time when Western countries had officially named the LTTE a terrorist organization and had become at least marginally involved in brokering peace. In 2000 the Sri Lankan government, together with the LTTE, invited Norway to take the role of facilitator in the forthcoming peace process. Nevertheless, in the West the violence was largely considered peripheral to the conflicts taking place in the Middle East, which had captured world attention.

As a novelist and poet, Ondaatje had been interested in grappling with the weighty subject of war, most notably in 1992's Booker Prize winner *The English Patient,* which focuses on a badly burned pilot, his nurse, and several others holed up in a half-destroyed Italian villa at the end of World War II. The novel spawned an Academy Award-winning film, generating additional interest in Ondaatje's work.

Ondaatje is arguably the best-known writer of Sri Lankan birth, and *Anil's Ghost* is often read for that reason. Ondaatje, who has spent most of his career as a Canadian citizen, writes in English. His subject matter is most often outside the country of his birth, but his fictionalized memoir *Running in the Family* is also set in Sri Lanka. Ondaatje goes to great lengths to avoid *Anil's Ghost,* or his body of work in general, being seen as "representative" of Sri Lanka. He does admit, however, that the civil war's destruction of his home country has been for him "the same kind of obsession Anil has with the skeleton—not letting go of it." Ondaatje used his Booker prize money to establish an annual literary prize, the Gratiaen, for the best work by a resident Sri Lankan writing in English.

THEMES AND STYLE

Anil's Ghost is about the experience of living in the shadow of violence; it is not a single story of war, or of one war, but a multiplicity. Early in the novel Sarath talks to Anil about life in Sri Lanka, saying, "Everyone's scared, Anil. It's a national disease." Indeed, each of the main characters in *Anil's Ghost* experiences significant fear. Anil, in particular, spends much of the novel

✤ *Key Facts*

Time Period:
Early 21st Century

Genre:
Novel

Events:
Sri Lanakan civil unrest

Nationality:
Canadian

MICHAEL ONDAATJE: A "REAL SALAD"

Michael Ondaatje was born in Colombo, Sri Lanka, in 1943. His father, Mervyn, a tea and rubber plantation supervisor, was an alcoholic known for his drunken antics, some of which are recounted in Ondaatje's fictionalized autobiography, *Running in the Family.* Mervyn's alcoholism ultimately contributed to his divorce from Michael's mother, who then moved to England. Michael traveled to England alone to join his mother, and his boat journey inspired some of the details in his acclaimed novel *The Cat's Table,* published in 2011.

In 1962 Ondaatje immigrated to Canada, where he pursued his education at the University of Toronto and then Queen's University. A resident of Toronto since 1970, Ondaatje has taught English literature at York University and Glendon College. In addition to teaching, Ondaatje has published poetry, criticism, and six critically acclaimed novels. In an interview with Maya Jaggi that followed the publication of *Anil's Ghost,* Ondaatje calls his background "a real salad" and acknowledges that his mixed Tamil, Sinhalese, and Dutch heritage may have inclined him to take a multiperspective approach in writing about the Sri Lankan conflict and to avoid expressing an opinion about any single view of the violence.

unsure about Sarath's alliances, wondering whether he might be in collusion with the government to bury evidence of murders, such as that of "Sailor," the victim whose bones have been found in the midst of a government controlled burial site. Ultimately, however, Anil is able to submit her report on Sailor and leave the country, much like "one of those journalists who file reports about flies and scabs while staying at the Galle Face Hotel." In an important way, Western experiences of third-world violence are very different from the experiences of those who are born to it and who must build personal and professional lives in its midst. Although Anil was born in Sri Lanka, she is not "of" the country in the way that Sarath and Gamini are. Her connections to her few remaining family members are tenuous, and they know her from her past glories as a swimmer—not in her present life as an archaeologist doing important work.

In an interview about the novel, Ondaatje expresses his desire to avoid creating a "statement" or asserting "the 'true and only' story" of the war. Perhaps to that end, *Anil's Ghost* is divided into eight sections, each loosely focused on a particular character, each prefaced by an italicized vignette framing what is to follow. The first section, "Sarath," is introduced by a story of a dig in Guatemala where Anil encounters a woman sitting over the bodies of her husband and son. Anil cannot forget the woman's grief, but she also cannot entirely describe it, recognizing that "each afternoon of the week she [the woman] was part of

this" in a way that Anil has not been. There are parallels between Guatemala and Sri Lanka, just as there are parallels between Anil's relationships to each scene. Meanwhile, Palipana, a Sinhala epigraphist and Sarath's former teacher, reflects not on the parallels but on the differences between Eastern and Western experiences, observing that "The West saw Asian history as a faint horizon where Europe joined the East"; but for Palipana, who sees his country "in fathoms and colors," Europe is merely "a landmass on the end of the peninsula of Asia." As critics have noted, Ondaatje deliberately extends the novel beyond Anil's departure from Sri Lanka, thus making clear that the story does not end when Western eyes leave.

The multiplicity of stories in *Anil's Ghost* are elaborated in lyrical language, which often contradicts the horror attached to, for example, the bones of murder victims. Describing a lecture from early in her forensic studies, Anil remembers writing only one statement in her notebook, "The bone of choice would be the femur." She lovingly recalls the way the lecturer said it "offhand," but as if "this piece of information were the first rule needed before they could progress to greater principles." For Anil, the beauty of forensics is that it starts with a leg bone and progresses to a whole system of knowledge. Similarly, Ondaatje starts with the emotion attached to one event, one thing, or one person and expands outward to describe something as large and multi-storied as a war.

CRITICAL DISCUSSION

Anil's Ghost was published to largely favorable reviews, with some critics describing it as Ondaatje's best work to that point. Writing in the *New York Times,* Richard Eder praises Ondaatje's subtlety, opining that "Ondaatje's moral urgency comes less as statement than as asides; not as a directed beam but as a series of cross-reflections and refractions." Less favorably, Tom LeClair of the *Nation* criticizes the novel as "apolitical," complaining that "for Ondaatje, 'real' words are those the poet can sneak into the minds and mouths of highly educated and exquisitely sensitive characters," avoiding engagement with the war's real victims and their families.

Anil's Ghost strengthened Ondaatje's reputation as a postmodern experimenter par excellence, particularly with regard to his treatment of identity and history in an increasingly globalized world. Indeed, in his introduction to *Comparative Cultural Studies and Michael Ondaatje's Writing,* Steven Tötösy de Zepetnek suggests that it is this sensibility that has attracted so many scholars to Ondaatje's work.

Much of the scholarly work on *Anil's Ghost* focuses on issues of identity as filtered through the lens of postcolonialist theory and particularly responds to criticism that the novel is "apolitical." Margaret Scanlan, for instance, suggests that "Ondaatje's unwillingness to take sides or offer solutions may owe as much to local conditions as to postmodernist theory."

Further, Scanlan asserts that the Sri Lankan political situation itself seems to echo postmodern notions of "the collapse of grand narratives, the fragility and impermanence of identity, the failure of history to provide us with a coherent account of our origins, and the moral ambiguities of action and character in a world where cause and effect are endlessly complex." Wendy Knepper examines *Anil's Ghost* as an example of the postcolonial crime or detective novel. Knepper builds on Scanlan's claim that in *Anil's Ghost*, direct political rhetoric by Ondaatje is replaced by his recreation of the "experience of terror" through poetic language and "fragmentary narrative techniques." Seeking to refine Scanlan's position, Knepper proposes that "more than introducing terror and doubt, … the novel calls into question the meaning and role of 'poetic justice' in society, prompting the reader to examine critically the assumptions about truth that inform Western concepts of social justice." Furthermore, she states that a "closer interrogation" of Ondaatje's strategy "reveals that such poetics are never simple or apolitical."

BIBLIOGRAPHY

Sources

Tötösy de Zepetnek, Steven, ed. *Comparative Cultural Studies and Michael Ondaatje's Writing.* West Lafayette: Purdue UP, 2005. Print.

Eder, Richard. "A House Divided." *New York Times.* New York Times, 14 May 2000. Web. 12 July 2012.

Jaggi, Maya. "Michael Ondaatje in Conversation with Maya Jaggi." *Wasafiri* 16.32 (2000): 5–11. Web. 11 July 2012.

Knepper, Wendy. "Confession, Autopsy and the Postcolonial Postmortems of Michael Ondaatje's *Anil's Ghost.*" *Postcolonial Postmortems: Crime Fiction from a Transcultural Perspective.* Ed. Christine Matzke and Susanne Mühleisen. New York: Rodopi, 2006. 35–57. Rpt. in *Contemporary Literary Criticism.* Vol. 322. Ed. Jeffrey W. Hunter. Detroit: Gale, 2012. *Literature Resource Center.* Web. 11 July 2012.

LeClair, Tom. "The Sri Lankan Patients." *Nation.* Nation, 19 June 2000. Web. 11 July 2012.

Ondaatje, Michael. *Anil's Ghost.* New York: Knopf, 2000. Print.

Scanlan, Margaret. "*Anil's Ghost* and Terrorism's Time." *Studies in the Novel* 36.3 (2004): 302–317. Rpt. in *Contemporary Literary Criticism.* Vol. 322. Ed. Jeffrey W. Hunter. Detroit: Gale, 2012. *Literature Resource Center.* Web. 11 July 2012.

Further Reading

Burrows, Victoria. "The Heterotopic Spaces of Postcolonial Trauma in Michael Ondaatje's *Anil's Ghost.*" *Studies in the Novel* 40.1–2 (2008): 161+. *Literature Resource Center.* Web. 11 July 2012.

Burton, Antoinette. "Archive of Bones: *Anil's Ghost* and the Ends of History." *Journal of Commonwealth Literature* 38.39 (2003): 39–56. Rpt. in *Contemporary Literary Criticism.* Vol. 322. Ed. Jeffrey W. Hunter. Detroit: Gale, 2012. *Literature Resource Center.* Web. 11 July 2012.

Kanaganayakam, Chelva. "In Defense of *Anil's Ghost.*" *Ariel* 37.1 (2006): 5–26. Rpt. in *Contemporary Literary Criticism.* Vol. 322. Ed. Jeffrey W. Hunter. Detroit: Gale, 2012. *Literature Resource Center.* Web. 11 July 2012.

Kertzer, Jon. "Justice and the Pathos of Understanding in Michael Ondaatje's *Anil's Ghost.*" *English Studies in Canada* 29.3–4 (2003): 116+. *Literature Resource Center.* Web. 11 July 2012.

Ratti, Manav. "Michael Ondaatje's *Anil's Ghost* and the Aestheticization of Human Rights." *ARIEL* 35.1–2 (2004): 121+. *General OneFile.* Web. 11 July 2012.

Shounan, Hsu. "Engaged Buddhism and Literature: The Art for Peace in Michael Ondaatje's *Anil's Ghost.*" *Tamkang Review* 37.3 (2007): 5–33. Rpt. in *Contemporary Literary Criticism.* Vol. 322. Ed. Jeffrey W. Hunter. Detroit: Gale, 2012. *Literature Resource Center.* Web. 11 July 2012.

Daisy Gard

Sri Lankan woman making religious offerings on behalf of a missing relative. A Sri Lankan forensic pathologist uncovers secrets about her homeland in Michael Ondaatje's 2000 novel *Anil's Ghost.* AP PHOTO/ GEMUNU AMARASINGHE.

THE ARRAIGNMENT OF LEWDE, IDLE, FROWARD AND UNCONSTANT WOMEN OR THE VANITY OF THEM

Joseph Swetnam

✣ *Key Facts*

Time Period:
Early 17th Century

Genre:
Pamphlet

Events:
Increase in female
monarchs; improvements
in printing

Nationality:
English

OVERVIEW

Initially published as a pamphlet under the pseudonym Thomas Tel-Troth, *The Arraignment of Lewde, Idle, Froward and Unconstant Women or the Vanity of Them* (1615) by Joseph Swetnam is a misogynist invective against the conduct and nature of women. Filled with examples from a variety of classical and biblical texts, Swetnam's scurrilous tract condemns women as depraved, feeble, and responsible for the presence of evil in the world. In the dedicatory epistle, Swetnam claims to attack only degenerate women while lauding "wise, virtuous, and honest Women," but the pamphlet is essentially a rambling diatribe against women, regardless of class. Presented as a warning to young men about the dangers of women, *The Arraignment* is Swetnam's antifeminist contribution to the *querelle des femmes,* or "argument about women," a longstanding debate that experienced renewed vigor during the Renaissance.

Despite being censured by both contemporary and modern critics as unorganized, unsophisticated in language, and rhetorically weak, *The Arraignment* was so popular that it was reprinted regularly throughout the seventeenth century and several times in the eighteenth century. Swetnam's treatise incited a major pamphlet war that elicited a round of printed rebuttals, including a comedic play titled *Swetnam the Womanhater Arraigned by Women* (1620). Three of the counterattacks were specifically directed at Swetnam, and the authors claimed to be women. Although these confutations were largely ignored at the time, modern scholars regard them as evidence of a change in the *querelle des femmes* and as some of the first examples of a feminist debate in England.

HISTORICAL AND LITERARY CONTEXT

The question regarding a woman's worth has long been a subject of interest in Western literature. In the late eighth century BCE, the Greek poet Hesiod penned a tale of the mythical first woman, Pandora, who unleashes chaos into the world and is characterized by "lies, and wheedling words of falsehood, and a treacherous nature." Later Greek treatments range from Aristophanes's bawdy banter to Aristotle's reasoned argument for the inferiority of women. Classic Roman literature is less misogynistic, although Juvenal's poem *Sixth Satire* (first century CE) berates women's lustfulness, greed, jealousy, superficiality, cruelty, and shrewish behavior. Early Christian writing supports an antifeminine reading of the creation story, disparages sex and marriage, and presents women as sources of temptation.

Medieval writers formalized the literary debate about the nature of women by mounting unrestrained attacks and counterattacks on them. Authors on both sides of the question relied heavily on stock anecdotes and common arguments. Fourteenth-century English poet Geoffrey Chaucer dedicates much of *The Canterbury Tales* to the subject of women and marriage, amiably advancing both the misogynistic arguments and the defenses of earlier literature. In the sixteenth century, with an atypical number of female monarchs ruling, discussions of women's capabilities and their aptitude to rule were of great interest to English citizens. Additionally, printing improvements during this time led to an increased number of pamphlets about women that featured highly charged rhetoric and attracted a wide readership. Extensive dissemination of these attacks on women spurred numerous defenses, leading to the "pamphlet wars." Swetnam created a lucrative business opportunity by inciting his own pamphlet war with *The Arraignment.*

The Arraignment draws heavily on earlier works, as was the rhetorical convention of the time. In *Ester hath hang'd Haman* (1617)—one of the rebuttals to *The Arraignment*—Ester Sowernam accuses Swetnam of lifting much of his material from John Lyly's extremely popular *Euphues* (1578): "Alas, silly man, he objecteth nothing but what he hath stolen out of English writers, as *Euphues.*" In *The Romance of the New World: Gender and the Literary Formations of English Colonialism,* Joan Pong Linton describes *Euphues* as "a 'surfeiter of love' who finds all women to be foul monsters underneath their perriwigs, paint, and fashionable attire." Swetnam also borrows from biblical and classical examples to support his thesis. For example, he cites David, Solomon, and Samson as victims of seduction. Scholars suggest that the retelling of common misogynist anecdotes and arguments combined with bawdy humor and a playful tone account for the immense popularity of *The Arraignment.*

Although Swetnam claims in *The Arraignment* that his tract is "hurtful to none," the writers who launched counterattacks evidently disagreed. The first defense to appear, Daniel Tuvil's *Asylum Veneris; or, A Sanctuary for Ladies* (1616), argues for the education of and some public roles for women. Swetnam's diatribe also elicited three direct responses written by women: Rachel Speght, Ester Sowernam, and Constantia Munda, the latter two most likely being pseudonyms. These learned and coherent rebuttals carefully deconstruct Swetnam's argument, generously mocking his style, flawed logic, and muddling of classical and biblical texts. While many critics criticize Swetnam's tract as a mere conglomeration of contemporary misogynist thought, scholars regard the three females who rebutted his work as trailblazers in early English feminism whose responses are not mere defenses but investigations into gender ideology.

THEMES AND STYLE

The central theme of *The Arraignment* is the inherently corrupt nature of women. Swetnam cites Eve as the primary example of woman's evil nature, proclaiming that she "was no sooner made but straightway … procured man's fall." He also claims that because Eve was made from Adam's crooked rib, women are incapable of leading a good life. Swetnam locates the source of woman's evil in her flesh:

> Between their breasts is the vale of destruction; and in their beds there is hell, sorrow, and repentance … Then who can but say that women sprung from the Devil? Whose heads, hands, and hearts, minds and souls are evil, for women are called the hook of all evil because men are taken by them as fish is taken from a hook.

Thus, Swetnam contends that women—the by-products of the devil—exploit their bodies to trap and manipulate men.

The tract achieves its rhetorical effect by reiterating commonplace anecdotes and examples from the debates about women, especially those from the preceding century in England. For example, Swetnam retells a rustic vignette to prove all women are alike underneath, regardless of rank:

> Jone is as good as my lady; according to the Country-mans Proverbe, who gave a great summe of money to lye with a Lady, and going homewards, he made a grievous mone for his money, and one being on the other side of the hedge, heard him say, that his Jone at home was as good as the lady.

LA QUERELLE DES FEMMES IN RENAISSANCE ENGLAND

The long-debated "argument of women" was taken up with new vigor in England during the Renaissance. While the discussion of a woman's worth was of great importance to the general public, few well-known English authors engaged in the debate. Rather, clerics, polemicists, and anonymous authors kept it going through treatises in the form of pamphlets. In *Half Humankind: Contexts and Texts of the Controversy about Women in England, 1540–1640,* Katherine Usher Henderson and Barbara F. McManus claim that these tracts "were written for a middle-class audience living in an increasingly urban, commercial, and individualist world"—a shift from previous aristocratic and courtly treatises.

Renaissance writers who wished to attack women turned to classical antiquity and the Bible for examples to prove female inferiority. English writers who wished to defend women may have been inspired by the translated works of Continental authors who wrote about women, including Christine de Pisan, Cornelius Agrippa, Dutch humanist Erasmus, and Spanish humanist Juan Luis Vives. A student of humanism, Sir Thomas Elyot published a treatise in praise of women, *The Defense of Good Women* (1540), in which he argues that they should be educated. Around the same time, *The Schoolhouse of Women* (an attack on women) and *Mulierum Paean* (a defense) began a pamphlet war that dominated the middle of the sixteenth century. By the end of the sixteenth century in England, it had become routine for men to write pamphlets criticizing women in order to exhibit their rhetorical prowess and to tell bawdy stories. These attacks eventually evoked formal responses from female writers, marking the dawn of feminism in England.

In her article in *The Renaissance Englishwoman in Print: Counterbalancing the Canon,* Ann Rosalind Jones argues that Swetnam's "main ploy is to mix classical and biblical criticism of women and then to modernize it in the direction of pragmatic cynicism." For example, Swetnam echoes the biblical notion that woman is a helpmeet to man, but then reverses this argument in a comical twist: "Moses describeth a woman thus: 'At the first beginning' saith he, 'a woman was made to be a helper unto man.' And so they are indeed, for she helpeth to spend and consume that which man painfully getteth." Jones suggests that in gathering traditional anecdotes, reversing common examples, and retelling contemporary jokes, Swetnam "was assembling a jestbook, which as a genre could break rules of realism and propriety."

Stylistically, *The Arraignment* is distinguished by its contradictory tones. On the one hand, Swetnam promises amusement to "the ordinary sort of giddy-headed young men" in the form of a "Beare-bayting of Women." However, when addressing women, he adopts a contemptuous tone: "Whatever you think

privately, I wish you to conceale it with silence, lest in starting up to find fault, you prove yourselves guilty of those monstrous accusations which are here following against some women." Contradictions are prevalent throughout *The Arraignment,* suggesting the playfulness of a court jester. For example, even though Swetnam counsels men on how to choose a good wife, he also claims there are no good wives: "Commonly Beauty and Pride goeth together, and a beautiful woman is for the most part costly, and no good Huswife; and if she be a good Huswife, then no servant will abide her fierce cruelty, and if she be honest and chaste, then commonly she is jealous." Despite the "monstrous accusations" he makes about females, Swetnam maintains that his pamphlet is merely a pleasurable pastime and should not be taken seriously.

CRITICAL DISCUSSION

When *The Arraignment* was first published in 1615, it was tremendously popular, as evidenced by its republication that same year. However, it also elicited the three aforementioned responses, all of which were written by women who took "the toyes of an idle head" very seriously. In the carefully constructed *A Mouzell for Melastomus* (1617), Speght accuses Swetnam of blasphemy, arguing that his characterization of women as a curse on mankind shows ingratitude toward God and demonstrates a poor understanding of scripture. In *Ester hath hang'd Haman,* Sowernam reverses Swetnam's arguments back onto him: "That which giveth quality to a thing, doth more abound in that quality, as fire which heateth, is it selfe more hot: … So, if woman received her crookednesse from the rib, how doth man excel in crookednesse, who hath more of those crooked ribs?" The third rebuttal, *The Worming of a Madde Dog* (1617) by Munda, calls Swetnam "Cerberus the Jaylor of Hell."

Despite such criticism, *The Arraignment* continued to be immensely popularity for the next century and was even twice translated into Dutch. Its playful nature and collection of contemporary anecdotes and jokes greatly appealed to the English middle class. While modern scholars have often analyzed Swetnam's misogynistic contribution to the *querelle des femmes,* they have just as frequently been interested in the responses to his tract. Katherine Usher Henderson and Barbara F. McManus contend in *Half Humankind: Contexts and Texts of the Controversy about Women in England, 1540–1640* that the Swetnam controversy was significant because "for the first time in England women began to write in their own defenses and for the first time anywhere significant numbers of women began to publish defenses."

In recent years, scholars have found Swetnam's pamphlet and the corresponding responses to be of considerable value because they shed light on the *querelle des femmes,* elucidate the development of early feminism, and provide a window into the economics of writing and publishing in the early modern era. While many commentators criticize Swetnam's dependence on anecdotes as highly unoriginal, Diane Purkiss argues in *Women, Texts and Histories 1575–1760* that his "deployment of a rhetoric of citation goes beyond the mere reiteration of the familiar, creating at certain points an intertextual *bricolage* of considerable subversive power." In Jones's view, Swetnam's tract did not have to be "learned or coherent" because his goal was "to turn the *Querelle des femmes* into a predictable and profitable farce, capable of amusing as many readers as possible." Although Swetnam's intentions may have been mercenary, his tract seems to have fueled early feminism in England. Henderson and McManus argue that the pro-feminine rebuttals to Swetnam "helped build the foundation for a more activist feminism by fostering in women the conviction of their own intellectual and moral worth."

BIBLIOGRAPHY

Sources

Banks, J. *The Works of Hesiod, Callimachus and Theognis.* London: George Bell and Sons, 1876. Print.

"Defense of Women Pamphlets in Early Modern England." *Literature Criticism from 1400 to 1800.* Ed. Lawrence J. Trudeau. Vol. 191. Detroit: Gale, Cengage Learning, 2011. 102–222. Gale, *Cengage Learning Trial Site. Literature Criticism Online.* Web. 26 July 2012.

Henderson, Katherine Usher, and Barbara F. McManus. *Half Humankind: Contexts and Texts of the Controversy about Women in England, 1540–1640.* Urbana: U of Illinois P, 1985. Print.

Jones, Ann Rosalind. "Counterattacks on 'the Bayter of Women': Three Pamphleteers of the Early Seventeenth Century." *The Renaissance Englishwoman in Print: Counterbalancing the Canon.* Ed. Anne M. Haselkorn and Betty S. Travitsky. Amherst: Massachusetts UP, 1990. 45–62. *Literature Criticism from 1400 to 1800.* Vol. 191. Detroit: Gale, 2011. *Literature Resource Center.* Web. 22 July 2012.

Linton, Joan Pong. *The Romance of the New World: Gender and the Literary Formations of English Colonialism.* Cambridge: Cambridge UP, 2006. Print.

Munda, Constantia. *The Worming of a mad Dog.* Rpt. in Henderson and McManus 244–263.

Purkiss, Diane. "Material Girls: The Seventeenth-Century Woman Debate." *Women, Texts and Histories 1575–1760.* Ed. Clare Brant and Diane Purkiss. London; New York: Routledge, 1992. 69–101. Print.

Sowernam, Ester. *Ester hath hanged Haman.* Rpt. in Henderson and McManus 217–243.

Swetnam, Joseph. *The Arraignment of Lewd, idle, froward, and unconstant women.* Rpt. in Henderson and McManus 189–216.

Further Reading

Alfar, Cristina León. *Fantasies of Female Evil: The Dynamics of Gender and Power in Shakespearean Tragedy.* Newark: U of Delaware P, 2003. Print.

Opposite page:
Jezebel, a painting by John Byam Liston Shaw (1896). In *The Arraignment of Lewde, Idle, Froward and Unconstant Women or the Vanity of Them,* Joseph Swetnam uses the biblical character of Jezebel as an example of a less-than-virtuous woman. *JEZEBEL,* 1896, SHAW, JOHN BYAM LISTON (1872–1919)/ © RUSSELL-COTES ART GALLERY AND MUSEUM, BOURNEMOUTH, UK/THE BRIDGEMAN ART LIBRARY.

Brown, Meg Lota. "Rachel Speght (1597-after 1630)." *Seventeenth-Century British Nondramatic Poets, Second Series.* Ed. M. Thomas Hester. *Dictionary of Literary Biography Complete Online.* Web. 28 July 2012.

Crandall, Coryl. "The Cultural Implications of the Swetnam Anti-Feminist Controversy." *Journal of Popular Culture* 2 (1968): 136–148. Print.

Jones, Ann Rosalind. "From Polemical Prose to the Red Bull: The Swetnam Controversy in Women Voices Pamphlets and the Public Theater." *The Project of Prose in Early Modern Europe and the New World.* Ed. Elizabeth Fowler and Roland Greene. Cambridge, 1997. 122–137. Print.

Kelly-Gadol, Joan. "Early Feminist Theory and the *Querelle des femmes,* 1400–1789." *Signs* 8 (Autumn 1982): 2–28. Print.

Kemp, Theresa D. *Women in the Age of Shakespeare.* Santa Barbara: ABC-CLIO, 2010. Print.

Nevitt, Marcus. *Women and the Pamphlet Culture of Revolutionary England, 1640–1660.* Hampshire: Ashgate Publishing, 2006. Print.

"Rachel Speght (1597?–1630?)." *Literature Criticism from 1400 to 1800.* Ed. Thomas J. Schoenberg and Lawrence J. Trudeau. Vol. 97. Detroit: Gale, 2004. 242–288. *Literature Criticism Online.* Web. 28 July 2012.

Shepherd, Simon. *The Woman's Sharp Revenge: Five Women's Pamphlets from the Renaissance.* New York: St. Martin's Press, 1985. Print.

Maggie Magno

THE COMMITTEE
Sonallah Ibrahim

OVERVIEW

The Committee, by Sonallah Ibrahim, was published in 1981, at the end of Anwar Sadat's presidency. The novel tells the story of a well-educated Egyptian man's encounter with a shadowy authority known simply as "the committee." It is unclear whether the narrator was summoned to the initial meeting or if he requested it, and the reader never learns its purpose. After performing a number of tasks demanded by the committee, the narrator murders one of its members and is sentenced to death by autocannibalism. The insidious power of the committee, exercised through its restriction of information, which in turn grants it control over history and narrative, is described in even-toned, minimalist prose. Even though the narrator makes a conscious effort to consistently present the "correct" narrative to the committee, his benign, uncritical inclusion of every piece of information he can find on a certain public figure inadvertently creates a subversive counter-narrative.

Enthusiastically received by scholars of Arabic literature, *The Committee* has generated a large body of scholarship. Although it is not a work of realism, *The Committee* draws from contemporary political and economic realities and—along with other creative works by Ibrahim, such as *The Smell of It* (1966) and *Zaat* (1992)—serves as a historical document. It is an excellent example of the trend toward experimentation characteristic of the group of Arab writers known as the "generation of the sixties." *The Committee* is notable for its complex criticism of censorship, which is described as the function of both global forces and more local forms of power.

HISTORICAL AND LITERARY CONTEXT

After the 1952 Revolution, Egypt witnessed several decades of rapid economic and political change. During his presidency, from 1956 until his death in 1970, Gamal Abdel Nasser ushered in a period of hopeful pan-Arab nationalism. Within Egypt, economic policies based on state socialism and protectionism improved the living conditions of the lower classes, and Nasser became a hero after standing up to Western imperialism by nationalizing the Suez Canal in 1956. However, the 1967 Arab defeat in the Six-Day War against Israel dealt a devastating blow to the economy, and when Anwar Sadat became president in 1970, he was intent on following a program of "de-Nasserization." This included Westernization and an economic *infitah,* or open-door, policy that encouraged foreign investment and led to privatization, rampant consumerism, inflation, and the growth of income inequality. Sadat's desperation for economic stability contributed to his decision to pursue a separate peace with Israel, which failed to meaningfully address the status of the West Bank and the Gaza Strip. This ostracized Egypt from the rest of the Arab world and led to closer ties with the United States.

When *The Committee* first appeared as a short story in 1979, it foreshadowed the censorship of the Sadat era, even as it reflected on the political oppression of Nasser's rule. Under Nasser, the *mukhabarat,* a far-reaching intelligence network, had come into existence to monitor "enemies" of the government, including Islamist and communist groups. In 1959, 250 suspected communists were arrested, including Ibrahim, who was sentenced to seven years in prison. In 1981, the same year *The Committee* was published as a full-length novel, Sadat arrested 1,500 Egyptians who were perceived as a threat to him or his policies, including members of Islamist organizations, feminists, journalists, and intellectuals. He was backed by the 1980 "Law of Shame," which effectively reinstituted the restraints on freedom of expression that he himself had loosened when he took power. One month later, in October 1981, Sadat was assassinated by militant Islamists.

In the years following the Six-Day War, the optimism of the 1952 Revolution was replaced by an atmosphere of "rejection and disillusion" that found expression in the work of a group of writers known as the "generation of the sixties." Many Egyptian novelists, such as Yusuf al-Qaid and Jamal al-Ghitani, began to approach reality with a cynicism and experimentalism that challenged dominant narratives and that were in sharp opposition to the idealism and straightforward realism typified by authors such as Yahya Haqqi and Naguib Mahfouz. New narrative forms were deemed necessary in part to escape state censorship. Sonallah Ibrahim's *The Smell of It* (1966), with its antihero narrator, is regarded as the first significant Arabic work in this new direction.

Although *The Committee* was published at the end of Sadat's presidency, its themes and message

+ *Key Facts*

Time Period:
Late 20th Century

Genre:
Novel

Events:
Presidencies of Anwar Sadat and Gamal Abdel Nasser

Nationality:
Egyptian

PRIMARY SOURCE

EXCERPT FROM *THE COMMITTEE*

One of the officers, who had come into the room during the conversation and so heard part of it, said, "Didn't you think about the significance of what you were doing and its effects?"

Defending myself, I said, "My research was strictly objective. I covered nothing but proven facts and logical explanations. I have almost finished collecting and organizing the required information. I need only distill the important points and weave them into a well-ordered analysis."

"This is precisely why we want to give you some advice," Stubby said angrily.

The rest of the Committee members had begun to congregate near me. The two women sat on the edge of the bed, and one of the officers sat beside them. Next to them, another officer sat on the armchair. The third officer and some other members joined the Blond at the table. Others leaned on the arms of the chair, the wardrobe, and the door. Stubby held out some index cards. Among them I noticed the ones with the notes from the American magazines. They passed them around in silence, then began to look at me. They formed a semicircle surrounding me. I faced them again imploringly, "I chose the Doctor after much thought and scrutiny. The selection of the most luminous personality in the Arab world is an exceedingly difficult matter because of the number of countries, the spread of education, the proliferation of communications, and consequently..."

Stubby interrupted me angrily, "And consequently the existence of many luminous personalities. You admit to it."

SOURCE: *The Committee*, translated by Mary St. Germain and Charlenen Constable, pp. 69–70. Syracuse University Press, 2001. Copyright © 2001 by Syracuse University Press. All rights reserved. Reproduced by permission.

continued to resonate throughout the Arab world after his death. In 2003 Ibrahim publicly refused the Arab Novel Award given by the Egyptian Ministry of Culture, stating: "it is awarded by a government that … lacks the credibility of bestowing it." Farouk Hosni, the Minister of Culture, quickly responded that such a refusal should be viewed as a source of pride for the Egyptian government because it "represented solid proof of democratic practices and freedom of speech."

THEMES AND STYLE

The Committee is centrally concerned with the control of knowledge and the intellectual urge to create a counter-narrative that challenges dominant representations of history. When the narrator first goes to see the committee, the reader learns that its members work in a language other than Arabic. In addition to differentiating the narrator's language of opposition from the language of oppression, this characterization identifies the committee as a global, rather than a merely national or regional, power. Censorship and oppression function differently here than they do in the actual nation state, and the narrator is defenseless before the committee's pervasive authority. Although the committee knows everything about the narrator, he fails to locate any information about its members. The idea of an imbalance in power stemming from unequal access to knowledge is echoed when the narrator is later asked by the committee to prepare "a study on the greatest contemporary Arab luminary." When all information on the narrator's chosen subject, "the Doctor," is subsequently removed from the archives, it is only through careful work on the unpoliced margins that he is able to construct a narrative. However, this uncritical study represents a subversive counter-narrative that links contemporary problems to governmental policies and specific historical events. The narrator is urged to abandon the project, leading him to finally challenge the committee: "Your group will gradually lose what authority it has, while the power of those like me to confront and resist it will grow."

Ibrahim's text embodies this challenge. During his first interview with the committee, the narrator is invited to talk at length on two issues: a century-defining "momentous event" and the Great Pyramid. Both of these analyses, related in the voice of an intellectual, as well as the narrator's subsequent research on "the Doctor," allow for an exploration of dominant narratives, as well as the creation of new histories. When the committee members come to the narrator's apartment, they discover a collage that he has created by assembling photographs of prominent public figures to create a picture. The narrator explains to the committee: "As you know, there is a whole school of art whose work is founded on a similar basis. At first this appears extremely simple, but to get worthwhile results you have to successfully link originality and novelty on the one hand with profundity on the other." The narrator's reflection on his art parallels the author's own attempt to satirize reality through its rearrangement while also making a meaningful statement.

Stylistically, *The Committee* shocks its readers by relating appalling events in emotionless, straightforward language that relocates the exceptional horrors of the text within the ordinary and everyday. This is perhaps clearest in the final lines of the novel, when the narrator carries out the committee's prescribed punishment: "I stayed in my place, tranquil, elated, until dawn. Then I lifted my wounded arm to my mouth and began to consume myself." There is no sense of horror at this act of autocannibalism. The only real emotion displayed by the narrator surfaces in his interactions with individuals other than the members of the committee, such as an altercation he has with a fellow bus passenger. The narrator's dramatic response to these injustices cause them to fade into the

background, while his lack of outrage in the face of the committee highlights the pernicious suppression of the intellectual.

CRITICAL DISCUSSION

The Committee received enthusiastic reviews from scholars of Arabic literature following the publication of an English translation in 2001. Comparisons with Kafka abound. In his afterword to the English translation, Roger Allen asserts that "Sonallah Ibrahim can be regarded as a true peer of Franz Kafka in his ability to make use of a disarmingly undramatic level of discourse to convey a reality that is genuinely disturbing in its routine callousness." In her essay "Sonallah Ibrahim and the (Hi)story of the Book," Samia Mehrez draws attention to Ibrahim's "consistent and audacious representation of the politics of writing and publishing in the Arab world" and, referring to *The Committee,* argues that "this Kafkaesque novel represents the nightmarish dimensions of Ibrahim's collision with the political authorities, and the literary establishment, as he experienced it."

The Committee has been regarded as a warning not just about censorship and the suppression of intellectual freedom, but also as a condemnation of certain kinds of economic policy. Although the events of the novel unfold in a parallel reality, the trajectory is informed by contemporary Egypt, specifically the local effects of globalization and Sadat's open-door economic policies, both signaled by repeated references to Coca-Cola. In her article "'This Reality Is Deplorable': The Egypt of Sonallah Ibrahim," Andrea

Haist calls the text a "sarcastic settling of scores with the Sadat era." Christopher Stone similarly points to the text as "proof of the continued dominance of capitalism and the concomitant production of narrative, both modernist and realist, that reflect the angst that is capitalism's inevitable by-product."

Recent scholarship has focused a great deal on the relationship of the text to current discussions on globalization. In her book, *Gender, Nation, and the Arabic Novel: Egypt, 1892–2008* (2012), Hoda Elsadda states that "Ibrahim's project is to expose the glocal hegemony of the new world order, especially its impact on the lives of individuals." Muhsin J. al-Musawi argues in his article, "Engaging Globalization in Modern Arabic Literature: Appropriation and Resistance," that "*The Committee,* especially in its emphasis on 'Coca-Colonization' and 'world-wide cultural standardization,' has significance for cultural studies, too."

BIBLIOGRAPHY

Sources

Allen, Roger. Afterword. *The Committee.* By Sonallah Ibrahim. Trans. Mary St. Germain and Charlene Constable. Cairo: American U in Cairo P, 2000. 159–66. Print.

Elsadda, Hoda. "Defeated Masculinities in Sonallah Ibrahim." *Gender, Nation, and the Arabic Novel: Egypt, 1892–2008.* Syracuse: Syracuse UP, 2012. 119–41. Print.

Haist, Andrea. "'This Reality Is Deplorable': The Egypt of Sonallah Ibrahim: Between Media Representation and Experienced Everyday Reality." *Arabic Literature:*

Postmodern Perspectives. Ed. Angelika Neuwirth, Andreas Pflitsch, and Barbara Winckler. London: Saqi, 2010. 158–70. Print.

Mehrez, Samia. "Sonallah Ibrahim and the (Hi)story of the Book." *Egyptian Writers between History and Fiction: Essays on Naguib Mahfouz, Sonallah Ibrahim, and Gamal al-Ghitani.* Cairo: American U in Cairo P, 1994. 39–57. Print.

al-Musawi, Muhsin J. "Engaging Globalization in Modern Arabic Literature: Appropriation and Resistance." *Modern Language Quarterly* 68.2 (2007): 305–29. Print.

Stone, Christopher. "Georg Lukács and the Improbable Realism of Sonallah Ibrāhīm's *The Committee.*" *Journal of Arabic Literature* 41 (2010): 136–47. Print.

Further Reading

Ibrahim, Sonallah. *The Smell of It.* Trans. Denys Johnson-Davies. London: Heinemann, 1971. Print.

———. *Zaat.* Trans. Anthony Calderbank. New York: American U in Cairo P, 2001. Print.

Marsot, Afaf Lutfi Al-Sayyid. *A Short History of Modern Egypt.* New York: Cambridge UP, 1985. Print.

Mehrez, Samia. *Egypt's Culture Wars: Politics and Practice.* New York: American U in Cairo P, 2010. Print.

Stagh, Marina. *The Limits of Freedom of Speech: Prose Literature and Prose Writers in Egypt under Nasser and Sadat.* Stockholm: Almquist and Wiksell, 1993. Print.

Allison Blecker

THE CRUCIBLE

Arthur Miller

OVERVIEW

Arthur Miller's 1953 play *The Crucible,* a dramatization of the 1692 witch trials in Salem, Massachusetts, is best known as a commentary on the paranoia and mistrust created by McCarthyism in the United States during the 1950s. In the play, suspicion falls on various members of the Salem community, who work to conceal sexual transgressions and to escape blame after Revered Parris's daughter falls ill and witchcraft is suggested as the cause. The central characters are Abigail Williams, a vengeful young woman who begins the accusations; Elizabeth Proctor, who is accused of witchcraft but is spared hanging due to her pregnancy; and Proctor's husband, John, the play's protagonist, who tries to use reason and truth to dispel the townsfolk's growing paranoia. *The Crucible,* which culminates in a courtroom scene and an offstage mass hanging, is an unflinching condemnation of the kind of mass hysteria, social repression, and culture of blame promoted by anticommunists of the 1950s.

As soon as the play debuted on Broadway, critics began to read it in the context of the ongoing investigation of alleged communist activity led by U.S. senator Joseph R. McCarthy. His Senate Permanent Subcommittee on Investigations and its counterpart, the House Un-American Activities Committee (HUAC), encouraged American citizens to spy on and denounce each other even in the absence of concrete evidence of communist involvement. Miller's work resonated strongly with 1950s audiences, who balked at the irrational paranoia created by McCarthy's methods. Although some critics dismissed the play as nothing more than a mouthpiece for anti-McCarthyist sentiments, contemporary scholars have come to interpret *The Crucible* more broadly as a commentary on power and punishment.

HISTORICAL AND LITERARY CONTEXT

In the years before the publication of *The Crucible,* anticommunism had become a prominent feature of American politics. As the Cold War mounted in the years following the Second World War, HUAC made accusations of communist activity in the United States. High-profile hearings created a media firestorm, and trials—such as that of U.S. Department of State employee Alger Hiss, who was accused of espionage—provoked controversy and mass hysteria.

In 1950 McCarthy gave a highly publicized speech in Wheeling, West Virginia, declaring that the State Department was overrun with communists and that he had in his possession a list of their names.

The same year as *The Crucible* debuted, McCarthy became chair of the Senate Permanent Subcommittee on Investigations, setting off a new round of inquiry. Often compared to witch hunts, these investigations targeted academics, artists, filmmakers, and playwrights (Miller himself would testify before HUAC in 1957) and created a national atmosphere of fear, suspicion, and mistrust. Many Hollywood actors, filmmakers, and others involved in the movie industry were blacklisted as suspected or known communists during the decade. *The Crucible* draws parallels between the Salem witch trials and the anticommunist hearings that dominated American politics by highlighting the contagious nature of social panic and the interpersonal complications that can underlie accusations.

Perhaps because of McCarthy's targeting of writers and other artists, Miller was far from alone in using art to comment on the senator's agenda and methods. Notable novels with McCarthy-like figures include William D. Shirer's *Stranger Come Home* (1954) and Ernest Frankel's *Tongue of Fire* (1955). The fearful and suspicious atmosphere created by McCarthyism is evoked in many other works of the period, including Warren Miller's *The Sleep of Reason* (1956), William Wister Haines's *The Hon. Rocky Slade* (1957), Allen Drury's *Advise and Consent* (1959), Richard Condon's *The Manchurian Candidate* (1959), and William L. Reardon's *The Big Smear* (1960). In the theater, *The Crucible* was joined by Maxwell Anderson's *Barefoot in Athens* (1951), Robert Ardrey's *Sing Me No Lullaby* (1954), Jerome Lawrence and Robert E. Lee's *Inherit the Wind* (1955), and William Saroyan's *The Slaughter of the Innocents* (1957), which also address themes of suspicion, censorship, and authority. Scholars often count Miller's 1955 play *A View from the Bridge* (1955) among these works.

As the furor over communism died down and American counterculture grew during the 1960s, *The Crucible* maintained its reputation as a significant work. Although Senator McCarthy's political career effectively ended in 1954, when the Senate condemned his tactics, Miller's play remained significant in light

♦ *Key Facts*

Time Period:
Mid-20th Century

Genre:
Play

Events:
Salem witch trials; McCarthyism

Nationality:
American

THE HOLLYWOOD BLACKLIST

In 1947 HUAC began an investigation into communist activity in Hollywood. The first hearings called on such figures as Walt Disney, Ronald Reagan, Humphrey Bogart, and the socialist playwright Bertolt Brecht—who fled the country rather than testify—to answer the question, "Are you now or have you ever been a member of the Communist Party?" In November of that year, the Hollywood Ten, a group of industry figures who had refused to answer the committee's question, were found in contempt of Congress and barred from working in the American film industry. The same month, the Screen Actors Guild voted to require its members to sign a noncommunist pledge.

The blacklist, which continued to grow and reached its peak between 1952 and 1956, was never made public, though it was widely enforced. The practice of blacklisting suspected communist sympathizers was ended in the late 1950s through the efforts of such groups as the American Federation for Television and Radio Artists. Even in the twenty-first century, the Writers Guild of America has continued to work to restore screen credit to writers such as Dalton Trumbo, the screenwriter for *Roman Holiday* (1953), and other artists whose names were removed from their works as a result of McCarthyist paranoia and anticommunist suspicion.

of the controversy surrounding the Vietnam War and the struggle of truth and reason against superstition and authoritarian abuses of power. Today the play is regarded as one of Miller's most important works, in part because of its universal applicability and its relevance to a variety of social and political contexts.

THEMES AND STYLE

The dominant themes of *The Crucible* are suspicion, its personal causes, and its terrible consequences. In the overture to the first act, Miller posits that suspicion is a persistent and ubiquitous problem: "[The people of Salem] believed, in short, that they held in their steady hands the candle that would light the world. We have inherited this belief, and it has helped and hurt us." *The Crucible* suggests that personal motives are to blame for propagating a culture of fear. Miller demonstrates through his manipulation of perspective how each of the citizens of Salem is motivated by private gain rather than by a professed concern for religious purity. By exposing the characters' personal indiscretions and then illustrating their efforts to conceal their moral failings, he shows how suspicion and accusation can be used to deflect attention from pressing issues and to postpone real social change.

Rhetorically, Miller achieves his goal of portraying the chilling effects of McCarthyist suspicion using the allegory of the Salem witch trials. The metaphoric linkage of McCarthyism and witch hunting allows the author to sidestep the popular debate over how best to

address communism in the United States and instead focus on a portrait of the private treachery of public accusation. Miller grants the audience total access to information, contrasting public courtroom and church scenes with private conversations and exposition of secret grudges. After publicly blaming a slave for Betty Parris's illness, Williams has a panicked, secret interaction with coconspirators Mercy Lewis and Mary Warren to conceal their naked midnight revels. Her admonition, "Let either of you breathe a word, or the edge of a word, about the other things, and I will come to you in the black of some terrible night and I will bring a pointy reckoning that will shudder you," dramatizes the terrifying lengths to which accusers will go to conceal their motives.

The play's style is sparse and fast paced, evoking the hysteria and antipathy toward self-reflection that characterized the witch trials. The characters use antiquated syntax, and their dialogue is formal and melodramatic, especially in public scenes. In private exchanges, however, the sentences are often incomplete, as characters interrupt or silence one another in an effort to effect their personal agenda. The power of Miller's prose owes less to his word choice than to his management of pace and the acceleration produced by his characters' increasingly fragmentary and frenetic speech as they aim to defend themselves by accusing others.

CRITICAL DISCUSSION

The initial reception of *The Crucible* was mixed. Some critics respected the play's intensity, while others were frustrated by its obvious sociopolitical message. Although the Broadway production earned a Tony Award for Best Play in 1953, many critics felt it lacked the formal innovation of Miller's previous works, such as *Death of a Salesman* (1949), an intense psychological portrait of a middle-class family. In a 1953 *Theatre Arts* review, George Jean Nathan writes that the play is "all theme and no character. [Miller's] people are spokesmen for him, not for themselves. They possess humanity, when they possess it at all, only in the distant sense that a phonograph recording of it does. They speak and act at an obvious turning of his crank." However, Richard Hayes, in a 1953 *Commonweal* review, calls the play a powerful and moving piece of drama, though it has a patently obvious message.

As new appraisals of the play appeared in the 1960s and emphasized the great success not of the play's characters but of its form, *The Crucible* became a keystone of American antiauthoritarian literature. In his 1967 essay in *Modern Drama*, Philip G. Hill writes, "A whole generation of theater-goers has grown up in these intervening years to whom the name McCarthy is one vaguely remembered from newspaper accounts of the last decade, and who nevertheless find in *The Crucible* a powerful indictment of bigotry, narrow-mindedness, hypocrisy, and violation of due process of law, from whatever source these evils may

In this scene from the 1996 film adaptation of Arthur Miller's 1953 play *The Crucible*, Abigail Williams (played by Winona Ryder) and townspeople react to a hanging. 20TH CENTURY FOX/THE KOBAL COLLECTION/ART RESOURCE, NY.

spring." Scholars have since applied the play's themes of suppression and blame to a variety of sociopolitical contexts. For example, in an October 1996 interview with the *Detroit News,* Miller describes how a Chinese woman in the late 1980s told him she was surprised that the play had not been written about Maoist China, because it resonates so strongly with that context.

Contemporary critics continue to apply *The Crucible* to a variety of contexts, often in terms of the prevailing social and political climate. Whereas the interplay between religion, society, and free thought in *The Crucible* received great attention from critics in the 1960s and 1970s, the rise of New Historicism in the 1980s and 1990s brought critical attention, notably in the works of E. Miller Budick and Edmund S. Morgan, to the relationship between various historical moments and the play's social commentary. Today, criticism of *The Crucible* ranges widely, to include feminist readings of the work in a larger tradition of literature about gender, witchcraft, and sexual repression.

BIBLIOGRAPHY

Sources

Budick, E. Miller. "History and Other Specters in *The Crucible.*" *Modern Drama* 28.4 (1985): 535–52. Print.

Hayes, Richard. Rev. of *The Crucible,* by Arthur Miller. *Commonweal* 20 Feb. 1953: 498. Web. 4 June 2012.

Hill, Philip G. "*The Crucible:* A Structural View." *Modern Drama* 10.3 (1967): 312–17. Print.

"Interview with Arthur Miller." *Detroit News* 26 Oct. 1996: lC. Print.

"McCarthyism and Literature." *Twentieth-Century Literary Criticism.* Ed. Thomas J. Shoenberg. Vol. 190. Detroit: Gale, 2007. Web. 4 June 2012.

Nathan, George Jean. "*The Crucible.*" *Theatre Arts* 37 (1953): 24–26. Print.

Further Reading

Bonnet, Jean-Marie. "Society vs. the Individual in Arthur Miller's *The Crucible.*" *English Studies* 63.1 (1982): 32–36. Print.

Bredella, Lothar. "Understanding a Foreign Culture through Assimilation and Accommodation: Arthur Miller's *The Crucible* and Its Dual Historical Context." *Text, Culture, Reception: Cross-Cultural Aspects of English Studies.* Ed. Rüdiger Ahrens and Heinz Antor. Heidelberg: C. Winter, 1992. 475–521. Print.

Dukore, Bernard. Death of a Salesman *and* The Crucible: *Text and Performance.* Atlantic Highlands: Humanities Press International, 1989. Print.

Martin, Robert A. "Arthur Miller's *The Crucible:* Background and Sources." *Critical Essays on Arthur Miller.* Ed. James J. Martin. Boston: Hall, 1979. 93–102. Print.

Martine, James J. The Crucible: *Politics, Property and Pretense.* New York: Twayne, 1993. Print.

Morgan, Edmund S. "Arthur Miller's *The Crucible* and the Salem Witch Trials: A Historian's View." *The Golden and the Brazen World: Papers in Literature and History 1650–1800.* Ed. John M. Wallace. Berkeley: U of California P, 1985. 171–86. Print.

Schissel, Wendy. "Re(dis)covering the Witches in Arthur Miller's *The Crucible*: A Feminist Reading." *Modern Drama* 37.3 (1994): 461. Print.

Warshow, Robert. "The Liberal Conscience in *The Crucible*." *Arthur Miller: A Collection of Critical Essays.* Ed. Robert W. Corrigan. Englewood Cliffs: Prentice, 1969. Print.

Media Adaptations

The Crucible. Dir. Raymond Rouleau. Perf. Simone Signoret, Yves Montand, and Mylène Demongeot. Pathé Consortium Cinéma, 1957. Film.

The Crucible. Dir. Nicholas Hytner. Perf. Daniel Day-Lewis, Winona Ryder, and Paul Scofield. Beverly Hills, CA: Twentieth Century Fox Home Entertainment, 1996. Film.

Carina Saxon

FAHRENHEIT 451

Ray Bradbury

OVERVIEW

Written in the wake of World War II and published in the midst of the escalating Cold War between the United States and the Soviet Union, Ray Bradbury's *Fahrenheit 451* (1953) ranks among the most enduring dystopian novels of the twentieth century. Titled after the temperature at which paper catches fire, the book tells the story of Guy Montag, a "fireman" responsible for burning books in an unspecified twenty-fourth-century American city. As the world careens toward its third nuclear war since the 1990s, a totalitarian government and a passive, TV-addicted populace deem literature dangerous. Firemen punish those found in possession of books by incinerating their homes, sometimes with the offending party still inside. The novel is thus often read as a dual commentary on government censorship and propaganda and the decline of literacy in the emerging information age. Montag's gradual disillusionment with his role and his eventual escape to a clandestine society of bibliophiles in the wilderness, however, suggests that resistance to mass culture and government censorship is possible.

Fahrenheit 451 first appeared in *Galaxy Science Fiction* in 1951 as a short story titled "The Fireman." The revised and expanded novel, which tapped into Cold War-era fears, received positive reviews and earned Bradbury a National Institute of Arts and Letters Award in 1954. Its subsequent serialization in the monthly magazine *Playboy* (1954) and the English film adaptation by French director François Truffaut (1966) helped to introduce Bradbury to audiences outside the science-fiction community. Many credit the novel, which quickly became a staple in high school classrooms, with elevating the status of the science fiction genre. The book's legacy was cemented in the 1980s and 1990s, when its message about the dangers of a population forfeiting its right to read freely in the face of mesmerizing new technologies was brought to the forefront by technological advancements that made reading literature an obsolete pastime for some.

HISTORICAL AND LITERARY CONTEXT

Fahrenheit 451 responds to terrifying new forms of cultural and physical annihilation that emerged from World War II, from Nazi book burnings to atomic bombings, as well as to the Cold War and the conformity of postwar American suburbia. While World War II provided Americans with a seemingly clear-cut narrative of good versus evil, the subsequent ideological battle between American capitalism and Soviet communism was not so easily delineated. As the U.S. government sought to counter the spread of communism in Europe and Asia through propaganda efforts such as Radio Free Europe, it also turned its attention to potential subversives at home. In the late 1940s, the House Un-American Activities Committee investigated the alleged communist affiliations of Americans, which, in addition to decimating the lives and careers of those accused, prompted rampant suspicion and surveillance among neighbors. When conservative senator Joseph McCarthy claimed in 1950 to have a list of communist State Department employees, the so-called Red Scare escalated to a full-blown panic.

Bradbury published *Fahrenheit 451* in an era when Americans sought to project a sense of solidarity in the face of a communist threat that was both real and imagined. Anyone who questioned the tenets of unfettered capitalism, the escalating arms race, the numerous proxy wars that the United States and the Soviets entered into, or the wholesome image of the United States promulgated by artists such as Norman Rockwell risked being labeled dangerous and un-American. One method of drowning out dissent was to cloak enforced conformity in the garb of free will. Rampant consumerism in the 1950s, aided by the rise of mass marketing on the radio and the newly affordable television, gave Americans a sense of unlimited choice and personal freedom, but it also encouraged conformity. Bradbury rejected the idea that predictability and conformity are synonymous with personal freedom, making the issue central to Montag's transformation and, as Brian Baker points out, asserting that "the 'high culture' of the literary canon is the means by which mass culture, television, and state control can be opposed." It is no coincidence that the American Library Association and the Association of American Publishers released the *Freedom to Read Statement*, which decried a "pressure toward conformity" and declared that "the suppression of ideas is fatal to a democratic society," in 1953, the year that *Fahrenheit 451* was published.

Fahrenheit 451 is part of a tradition of dystopian novels challenging repressive governments and the

✥ Key Facts

Time Period:
Mid-20th century

Genre:
Novel

Events:
Cold War; nuclear arms race

Nationality:
American

DIGITIZING DYSTOPIA

Given the apparent anti-technology stance of *Fahrenheit 451*, Bradbury came to be seen as something of a Luddite. In a 1960 interview with fellow writer Kingsley Amis, he described being "stunned" to see a couple walking their dog, the woman holding "a small cigarette-package-sized radio" with "a dainty cone plugged into her right ear," which closely resembled the in-ear "seashell" radios that the citizens of Bradbury's future city wear to drown out their thoughts. Bradbury would later clarify in a 1976 interview with *Writer's Digest* that "I'm not afraid of machines, I'm not afraid of the computer, I don't think the robots are taking over. I think the men who play with toys have taken over."

Bradbury was highly skeptical of electronic devices that claimed to replicate or replace real-life experiences, particularly the act of reading a book. Nevertheless, as the popularity of e-books grew exponentially in the twenty-first century, his publishers pleaded to release his works in digital format. At first, as Bradbury said in a 2009 interview with the *New York Times,* he told the publishers, "To hell with you and to hell with the Internet. It's distracting." Yet, in 2011 publisher Simon & Schuster released an e-book of *Fahrenheit 451*—but on Bradbury's terms: the novel would only be digitized if it could be freely downloaded in libraries.

passive populations that enable them. Aldous Huxley's *Brave New World* (1932) and George Orwell's *1984* (1949) are often cited among the novel's important forerunners. Prior to writing *Fahrenheit 451,* Bradbury had begun exploring the relationship of the individual to society and the alienation and isolation that are the inevitable by-products of state-approved culture. In 1950 he published *The Martian Chronicles,* a collection of short stories about the colonization of Mars that featured several book burnings. His decision to serialize *Fahrenheit 451* in *Playboy,* one of the few publications to defy the imposed morality of the McCarthy era, underscored the message that the tradition of ideological freedom in the United States was threatened by the emergent culture of conformity.

As the United States gradually abandoned the paranoid anxieties of the McCarthy era and moved toward a more libertarian worldview in the 1960s, *Fahrenheit 451* was recognized as one of the most prophetic and influential works of dystopian fiction ever written. Bradbury capitalized on the novel's success in building a long and distinguished career as a short story writer, screenwriter, and consultant, but none of his works ever matched the cultural impact of *Fahrenheit 451.* Celebrations of the work have been held on almost every major anniversary of its publication, and the book has been published in more than thirty-three different languages. Bradbury's death in 2012 served

to reinvigorate interest in the novel and to highlight the enduring relevance of its themes.

THEMES AND STYLE

While the central concern of *Fahrenheit 451* is the correlation between censorship and an increasingly violent world, the novel does not blame these problems on power-hungry governments and bloated bureaucracies alone. Instead, it is the tendency of the masses to choose comfort and familiarity over the challenge of critical thought that allows the government to burn books, murder citizens, and engage in cataclysmic warfare without objection. As Captain Beatty, the head of the firemen, explains, "There was no dictum, no declaration, no censorship, to start with, no! Technology, mass exploitation, and minority pressure carried the trick, thank God." It is society's desire to avoid the work of critical thought in the face of controversial ideas, a hallmark of American culture in the McCarthy era and beyond, that leads to the mechanical, utilitarian society of *Fahrenheit 451.* Captain Beatty continues, "Colored people don't like *Little Black Sambo.* Burn it. White people don't feel good about *Uncle Tom's Cabin.* Burn it. Someone's written a book on tobacco and cancer of the lungs? The cigarette people are weeping? Burn the book. Serenity, Montag. Peace, Montag."

Bradbury highlights the consequences of such willful ignorance by setting up several contrasting personalities among the novel's characters. Beatty—who uses his own secret knowledge of literature to portray reading as "an attempt to slide-rule, measure, and equate the universe, which just won't be measured or equated without making man feel bestial and lonely"—finds a foil in Faber. Faber is the former English teacher who argues that books "stitch the patches of the universe together into one garment for us" and helps Montag to escape. Montag's wife, Mildred, who spends all her time in front of the three-walled television and claims to be perfectly content despite having previously attempted suicide, represents the relentless pursuit of the status quo, whereas Montag's unconventional neighbor, sixteen-year-old Clarisse, shakes Montag out of his stupor by asking the simple question, "Are you happy?" Finally, Montag, whose perspective dominates most of the novel, is contrasted with the only other figure whose perspective is described in any detail, a deadly Mechanical Hound that is the literal and metaphorical embodiment of a soulless, ruthlessly automated society.

Though the novel has its share of action—particularly the climactic scene in which Montag turns his flamethrower against Beatty and the subsequent spectacle of Montag being chased through the streets as an entire city watches on television—its major themes unfold through Bradbury's terse dialogue and pointed use of literary references. Beatty, for example, spins a dizzying web of quotes from classic works of literature to prove "what traitors books can be," but his very knowledge of their power and apparent terror at the thought of such power landing in the hands of the masses, making them "ready to blow up the world, chop off heads, knock down women and children, destroy authority," belies the notion that books are inconsequential. In addition, it suggests that, when knowledge is forbidden to the many, it can be used by the few as an instrument of manipulation.

CRITICAL DISCUSSION

Early reviewers of the novel, while sometimes critical of what they saw as undeveloped characters and Bradbury's heavy-handedness with his themes, frequently identified the parallels between Bradbury's dystopian future and the United States in the 1950s. Writing in the *New York Times,* J. Francis McComas notes the author's "virulent hatred for many aspects of present-day culture," and Orville Prescott marvels at the novel's "insane world, which bears many alarming resemblances to our own." Likewise, August Derleth observes in the *Chicago Daily Tribune* that "*Fahrenheit 451* was conceived out of Hitler's burning of the books, and is all the more timely now because of the fortunately ill-fated American venture on a similar path."

As the century progressed, critics broadened their views of the novel's significance, finding in it a commentary on the social and psychological conditions of the modern world, and Bradbury himself reinforced this trend by penning several new forewords and afterwords to accommodate the novel's numerous editions and the changing conditions of the world. The most famous of these commentaries appeared in 1979 and noted the "exquisite irony" of publisher Ballantine Books having "censored some 75 separate sections of the book" for a 1967 edition intended for a high school audience; this observation was punctuated by Bradbury's pithy remark that "there is more than one way to burn a book." Despite its status as one of the most beloved works of science fiction ever written—as evidenced by the numerous adaptations in plays, television and radio programs, graphic novels, and video games—the work continues to spark debate over censorship and the influence of mass culture. In 1999, for example, the novel was removed from a Mississippi high school's required reading list because of its "objectionable content."

Fahrenheit 451 has been the subject of an extensive body of criticism. While many critics focus on the work's admirable confrontation of censorship and nuanced depiction of the individual's place in modern society, some, including Jack Zipes, argue that the work is in fact an elitist argument for the superiority of intellectuals. Others focus on Bradbury's (admittedly sparse) depictions of women in the work or the role that intertextual references play in shaping the novel's themes. The seemingly endless proliferation of critical perspectives on *Fahrenheit 451* only serves to support

Cyril Cusack and Oskar Werner in the film *Fahrenheit 451* (1966). MARY EVANS/ RONALD GRANT/EVERETT COLLECTION.

the novel's insistence that literature promotes critical thinking and fosters a type of freedom that is so essential to human nature that no amount of apathy or oppression can extinguish it.

BIBLIOGRAPHY

Sources

Baker, Brian. "Ray Bradbury: *Fahrenheit 451.*" *A Companion to Science Fiction.* Ed. David Seed. Malden: Blackwell, 2005. 489–99. Print.

Derleth, August. "Vivid Prophecy of Book Burning." Rev. of *Fahrenheit 451,* by Ray Bradbury. *Chicago Daily Tribune* 25 Oct. 1953: H6. Print.

Eller, Jonathan R., and William F. Touponce. *Ray Bradbury: The Life of Fiction.* Kent : Kent State UP, 2004. Print.

McComas, J. Francis. "Nothing but TV." Rev. of *Fahrenheit 451,* by Ray Bradbury. *New York Times* 8 Nov. 1953: BR43. Print.

Prescott, Orville. "Books of the Times." Rev. of *Fahrenheit 451,* by Ray Bradbury and *One,* by David Karp. *New York Times* 21 Oct. 1953: 27. Print.

Zipes, Jack. "Mass Degradation of Humanity and Massive Contradictions in Bradbury's Vision of America in *Fahrenheit 451.*" *No Place Else: Explorations in Utopian and Dystopian Fiction.* Ed. Eric S. Rabkin, Martin H. Greenberg, and Joseph D. Olander. Carbondale: Southern Illinois UP, 1983. 182–98. Print.

Further Reading

Brier, Evan. "'The Incalculable Value of Reading': *Fahrenheit 451* and the Paperback Assault on Mass Culture." *A Novel Marketplace: Mass Culture, the Book Trade, and Postwar American Fiction.* Philadelphia: U of Pennsylvania P, 2010. 45–73. Print.

Brown, Joseph F. "'As the Constitution Says': Distinguishing Documents in Ray Bradbury's *Fahrenheit 451.*" *Explicator* 67.1 (2008): 55–58. Print.

De Koster, Katie, ed. *Readings on Fahrenheit 451.* San Diego: Greenhaven, 2000. Print.

Gottlieb, Erika. "Dictatorship without a Mask: Bradbury's *Fahrenheit 451,* Vonnegut's *Player Piano,* and Atwood's *The Handmaid's Tale.*" *Dystopian Fiction East and West: Universe of Terror and Trial.* Montreal: McGill-Queen's UP, 2001. 88–114. Print.

Watt, Donald. "Burning Bright: *Fahrenheit 451* as Symbolic Dystopia." *Ray Bradbury.* Ed. Martin Harry and Joseph D. Olander. New York: Taplinger, 1980. 195–213. Print.

Media Adaptation

Fahrenheit 451. Dir. François Truffaut. Perf. Oskar Werner, Julie Christie, and Cyril Cusack. Vineyard Film Ltd, 1966. Film.

Jacob Schmitt

First Blast of the Trumpet against the Monstrous Regiment of Women

John Knox

OVERVIEW

Penned in 1558 by religious agitator John Knox (c. 1505–1572), *First Blast of the Trumpet against the Monstrous Regiment of Women* is a sharply worded treatise against women in positions of power. Knox's target throughout the piece is female sovereigns, especially Mary Tudor (1516–1558), the Catholic queen of England, and he hints darkly that the English nobility should take steps to depose her. The piece was intended to further the resistance to Mary, drawing on Scripture and classical texts to argue that allowing a female, Catholic leader to remain in power went against the laws of nature and God. It was also written to protest the persecution of English Protestants under Mary's rule. Knox crafted the text to encourage a rebellion in England that would result in Mary's deposition.

First Blast of the Trumpet is one of the first political tracts that Knox published while living in Geneva. Although it was criticized for not focusing solely on Mary Tudor, the piece reinforced Knox's status as a militant, Protestant reformer who worked tirelessly to rid England and Scotland of Catholicism. Most of Knox's writing deals with the relationship between religion and government, but *First Blast of the Trumpet* is unique in its call for a specific sovereign to be deposed while applying the broad generalization that no woman is fit to occupy a position of power. Even though he published the tract anonymously, it was soon well known that he had authored it. The text also highlights the Protestant movement's growing frustration with Mary Tudor, who had reversed the religious reforms of her father and half-brother (King Henry VIII and Edward VI, respectively) and reestablished Catholic rule in England. *First Blast of the Trumpet* represents Knox's ongoing struggle against Catholicism and women rulers in particular.

HISTORICAL AND LITERARY CONTEXT

By 1558 the Protestant Reformation was well under way. Sparked by Martin Luther's Ninety-five Theses (1517) and the preaching of crusaders such as John Wycliffe and John Calvin, the movement argued against the teachings of the Catholic Church and decried its role in government. During this turbulent time, the Scottish-born Knox converted from Catholicism to Calvinism, which teaches the doctrine of predestination, a belief that God is completely sovereign and has foreordained the salvation of certain souls and the eternal damnation of others. Calvinism gained many followers in France among the Huguenots and also in Switzerland and Germany. A century later, Calvin's teachings would influence the Puritans in England and the British colonies.

In *First Blast of the Trumpet,* Knox argues that women who occupy positions of power, whether in public or private, are an abomination and flout the law of God. At the time, Mary Tudor ruled England, and Mary of Guise ruled as the regent of Scotland, pending the coming of age of her daughter, Mary Stuart. The three Catholic Marys concerned Knox and other reformers, who worried that all the progress of the Protestant movement would be undone by these queens. Their fears were realized when Mary Tudor reenacted England's heresy laws and began ordering nonconformists to be burned at the stake. Knox and his colleagues felt that something must be done to halt the expansion of the Catholic Church and the killing of Protestants, and so he, John Ponet, and others began writing pamphlets, advising their followers throughout Europe of the continuing threat against their faith. *First Blast of the Trumpet,* Knox's warning to the English people that Mary's rule was unlawful, described ways to stop her.

Much of the writing at that time focused on the issue of religion in government. Ponet, a former bishop of Winchester, who had been forced to flee England upon Mary Tudor's ascension to the throne, wrote the *A Shorte Treatise of Politike Power, and of the true obedience which subjectes owe to kynges and other civile governours* in 1556. The text encourages the English nobility and common citizens to revolt and argues that, according to the Old Testament, it was legal to kill a tyrannical ruler. Ponet mainly targets the English bishops and church officials, while *First Blast of the Trumpet* focuses on Mary Tudor and her roles as a woman, a queen, and a Catholic. Critics of the tract charged Knox with misogyny; in response, he produced a summary of a *Second Blast of the Trumpet* to answer the accusations. Despite this reply, Knox was still seen as a religious figure who opposed any woman occupying a position of power.

✣ *Key Facts*

Time Period:
Mid-16th Century

Genre:
Treatise

Events:
Protestant Reformation; rise of female Catholic monarchs

Nationality:
Scottish

Scottish religious reformer John Knox meeting with England's Queen Mary I in a painting by J. R. Skelton. Knox voices his disapproval of female rulers in *First Blast of the Trumpet against the Monstrous Regiment of Women* (1558). © ART DIRECTORS & TRIP/ALAMY.

Most of Knox's political work was published during his life. Although Mary Tudor died in 1558, after *First Blast of the Trumpet* was published, the text had long-lasting consequences for Knox and his followers. Mary's successor, Elizabeth I (1533–1603), found the tract offensive due to its misogynist language, which she and many others felt targeted women rulers in general. Knox was no longer welcome in Britain, and, when he returned to Edinburgh from Geneva in 1559, he did so under threat of arrest. Despite the threat, he worked feverishly to lead the Protestant resistance in Scotland, and by 1560 the country repudiated Catholicism in favor of the Knox-led Presbyterian church. *First Blast of the Trumpet* describes the concerns of Protestants regarding Mary Tudor. Knox's writings also influenced Scotland's reception of Mary Stuart, who ascended the Scottish throne in 1561. Seven years later, she fled the country, with Knox leading the charge against her.

THEMES AND STYLE

Central to *First Blast of the Trumpet* is the argument against women sovereigns, specifically Mary Tudor. Knox immediately targets her in the first sentence when he states, "how abominable before God is the empire or rule of a wicked woman (yea, of a traitress and bastard)." Any reader during that time understood immediately to whom Knox was referring. Although the 1534 Act of Succession, declaring Mary illegitimate, had been revoked before her father's death, many English citizens, especially Protestants, considered her to have usurped the throne. In the statement directly following the opening, Knox assures his readers that the text will address the question of "what may a people or nation, left destitute of a lawful head, do by the authority of God's word in electing and appointing common rulers and magistrates."

Knox's tone throughout the piece is direct and authoritative. He develops three points to address the counterarguments he anticipated from Mary's supporters. Offering proof from the classical texts of Aristotle and others, he first contends that "the empire of a woman" is "a thing repugnant to nature." He then employs a biblical argument to justify his position, quoting the apostle Paul. "As St. Paul does reason in these words: 'Man is not of the woman, but the woman of the man. And man was not created for the cause of the woman, but the woman for the cause of man; and therefore ought the woman to have a power upon her head' [1 Cor. 11:8–10]." Finally, Knox writes "that the empire of a woman is a thing repugnant to justice, and the destruction of every commonwealth where it is received," stating that women in power disrupt the order and equity that organically occurs within a society. Knox's well-crafted claims provided the Protestant opposition with even more reasons for opposing Mary's rule.

Stylistically, *First Blast of the Trumpet* reads like a call to arms, an attempt to rouse a dissatisfied population into taking action against Mary. Knox advises the nobility of England "to retreat [retract] that which unadvisedly and by ignorance they have pronounced; and ought, without further delay, to remove from authority all such persons as by usurpation, violence, or tyranny, do possess the same." Knox employs phrases such as "that cruel monster Mary" and "cursed Jezebel of England, with the pestilent and detestable generation of Papists" to convey emotion and incite the reader's anger against Mary. By the end of the piece, Knox claims that "God shall declare himself to be her enemy, when he shall pour forth contempt upon her according to her cruelty, and shall kindle the hearts of such as sometimes did favour her with deadly hatred against her, that they may execute his judgments," prophesying that Mary would soon be forced to abdicate the throne.

CRITICAL DISCUSSION

After the publication of *First Blast of the Trumpet*, reception of the piece was mixed. Many Protestants exiled from England and Scotland were concerned that they would never be able to return home after Knox's statements. John Aylmer, who had fled England during Mary Tudor's reign but later returned and was appointed bishop of London, stated that the pamphlet focused too much on the rule of women in general. In 1559, Aylmer wrote *An Harborowe for faithfull and trewe subjects* in response to Knox's tract. Aylmer states that, "if he [Knox] had kept him in that particular person [Mary] he could have said nothing to(o) muche, nor in suche wyse, as could have offended any indifferent man." The tract also offended Elizabeth I and Mary Stuart, and Knox was forced to defend his argument to both queens. In a letter to Elizabeth in 1559, he wrote, "My conscience beareth me record, that maliciouslie nor of purpose I never offended your Grace nor your realme." When Mary Stuart arrived in Scotland in 1561, Knox was forced to explain, "for in very deed, Madam, that book was written most especially against that wicked Jezebel of England," referring to Mary Tudor. Neither Elizabeth nor Mary Stuart was convinced, and both remained suspicious of the reformer.

First Blast of the Trumpet matches the fervor and tenor of many of Knox's other political works. Because Mary Tudor died a few months after its publication, the text failed to galvanize the protest movement against her. It did, however, represent the feelings many Protestants had for Mary. More than 300 years later, Robert Louis Stevenson applauded Knox's bravery in his 1882 essay *John Knox and Women*. He writes, "We find in the works of Knox, as in the *Epistles of Paul,* the man himself standing nakedly forward, courting and anticipating criticism, putting his character, as it were, in pledge for the sincerity of his doctrine." Like Stevenson, other scholars have noted Knox's sincerity and enthusiasm for his faith, which he was not afraid to write about.

First Blast of the Trumpet is most often discussed in relation to Knox's other early political writings. In her 1991 essay *The Two John Knoxes: England, Scotland, and the 1558 Tracts,* Jane Dawson argues that many scholars try to lump the tract with the other texts he produced that year, a practice that furthers the common misconception that he was arguing against all women rulers rather than just Mary Tudor. She states, "In his writings to the Scottish nobility Knox never assumed that because Scotland also possessed a female ruler she should automatically be deposed. In the July tracts he had a very different message for the Scottish people. Despite its wide-ranging arguments the *First Blast* was directed solely towards the English." Robert Kingdon also agrees that the majority of Knox's argument is directed at Mary Tudor but states in *Calvinism and Resistance Theory* that the tract's

generalization to all women rulers makes it "a real classic of misogyny, elegantly organised and developed with a relentless scholastic logic."

BIBLIOGRAPHY

Sources

Aylmer, John. *An Harborowe for faithfull and trewe subjects.* Amsterdam: Da Capo, 1972. Print.

Dawson, Jane E. A. "The Two John Knoxes: England, Scotland and the 1558 Tracts." *Journal of Ecclesiastical History* 42.4 (1991): 555–76. Rpt. in *Literature Criticism from 1400 to 1800.* Vol. 37. Ed. Jelena O. Krstovic. Detroit: Gale Research, 1997. *Literature Resource Center.* Web. 16 Aug. 2012.

Kingdon, Robert M. "Calvinism and Resistance Theory, 1550–1580." *The Cambridge History of Political Thought: 1450–1700.* Ed. J. H. Burns and Mark Goldie. Cambridge: Cambridge UP, 1991. 194–218. Rpt. in *Literature Criticism from 1400 to 1800.* Vol. 37. Ed. Jelena O. Krstovic. Detroit: Gale Research, 1997. *Literature Resource Center.* Web. 16 Aug. 2012.

Knox, John. *John Knox's History of the Reformation in Scotland.* Ed. W. C. Dickinson. 2 vols. London: Nelson, 1949. Print.

———. *The Works of John Knox.* Ed. David Laing. 6 vols. Burlington: TannerRitchie, 2010. Print.

Stevenson, Robert Louis. "John Knox and Women." *Familiar Studies of Men & Books.* London: Chatto, 1882. 295–356. Rpt. in *Literature Criticism from 1400 to 1800.* Vol. 37. Ed. Jelena O. Krstovic. Detroit: Gale Research, 1997. *Literature Resource Center.* Web. 16 Aug. 2012.

Further Reading

Greaves, Richard L. "Calvinism, Democracy, and Knox's, Political Thought." *Theology and Revolution in the Scottish Reformation: Studies in the Thought of John Knox.* Grand Rapids: Christian UP, 1980. 169–82. Print.

Jansen, Sharon L. *The Monstrous Regiment of Women: Female Rulers in Early Modern Europe.* New York: Palgrave, 2002. Print.

Lorimer, Peter. *John Knox and the Church of England: His Work in Her Pulpit and His Influence Upon Her Liturgy Articles and Parties.* Whitefish: Kessinger, 2004. Print.

Ryrie, Alec. *The Origins of the Scottish Reformation (Politics, Culture and Society in Early Modern Britain).* Manchester: Manchester UP, 2010. Print.

Todd, Margo. *The Culture of Protestantism in Early Modern Scotland.* New Haven: Yale UP, 2002. Print.

Media Adapations

The Monstrous Regiment of Women. Dir. Colin Gunn. Perf. Sharon Adams, Jennie Chancey, and Carol Everett. Gunn Productions, 2007. Film.

Hannah Soukup

MADMEN AND SPECIALISTS

Wole Soyinka

OVERVIEW

Wole Soyinka's play *Madmen and Specialists* was first performed in August 1970 at the Eugene O'Neill Theater Center in Waterford, Connecticut, during a playwrights' workshop conference. It was edited and published in England the following year and subsequently premiered in Ibadan, Nigeria, in March 1971. A prime example of Soyinka's more abrasive, politically motivated works following his imprisonment during the Nigerian-Biafran Civil War, *Madmen and Specialists* employs absurd characters and nonsensical language as symbols of the oppression and brutality of the Nigerian government against its people. The play serves as a harsh critique of the new postcolonial Nigerian ruling force and is a prime example of post-civil war propaganda.

Madmen and Specialists was Soyinka's first play in more than six years due to his imprisonment for supporting the Biafran secessionists. Upon his release from prison in 1969, he immigrated to France and later the United States to avoid further persecution for his political beliefs. The play criticizes postcolonial Nigerian rulers for destroying African cultural traditions and family values through acts of terrorism and espionage. Although Soyinka's work was met with criticism from the Nigerian government it rebuked, others considered it Soyinka's strongest, most biting social critique to date.

HISTORICAL AND LITERARY CONTEXT

Nigeria gained its independence from colonial rule in 1960, which led to a series of power struggles among the three different regions of the country: the North (Hausa), West (Yoruba), and East (Igbo). In 1964 the results of national elections were suspended, giving the northern region unfair advantage with regard to political power, land rights, and national resources. Soyinka was arrested and detained for several months after responding to the election fraud by posing as the false victor, recording his own victory speech, and airing it over a local radio station. In 1966 the eastern Igbo people staged a coup and seized power of the government, but the victory was short-lived. The North staged a countercoup later that year and instituted a series of massacres of the Igbo living in the North; millions of refugees fled the area. Citing these injustices, the eastern region of Nigeria seceded from the rest of

the country on May 30, 1967, to form its own sovereign nation called the Republic of Biafra.

In August 1967 Soyinka had a secret meeting with Biafran secessionist leader Chukwuemeka Odumegwu Ojukwu and general Olusegun Obasanjo, the leader of the western forces, in an attempt to avoid a civil war. When these talks failed, Soyinka went into hiding, but he was detained and imprisoned later that same year as a Biafran sympathizer. He spent the remainder of the war in prison, and the majority of his twenty-two-month sentence was spent in solitary confinement with no visitation, correspondence, or writing privileges. Despite these conditions, he still managed to improvise writing materials to produce an abundance of works, and the rough draft for *Madmen and Specialists* came out of this period. Although the message of the play is veiled behind its absurd characters and rustic setting, it serves as Soyinka's most prominent propagandistic work for its critique of the brutal tactics used by military police against Biafran secessionists.

Madmen and Specialists is written in the absurdist tradition of Samuel Beckett, though the work's themes are more akin to Jonathan Swift's "A Modest Proposal" with Soyinka's suggestion of cannibalism as a convenient way to save on meat and get rid of the bodies that accumulated during the bloody Nigerian-Biafran Civil War. Soyinka is also often compared to Alexander Solzhenitsyn because both artists' works are politically motivated, both wrote while being held as political prisoners, and both used their writings as propaganda to facilitate change in their respective countries. Soyinka's work is also reminiscent of his political and artistic contemporary Christopher Okigbo, who wrote poetry related to the Nigerian struggle for independence and died fighting the same cause for which Soyinka was imprisoned: the Nigerian-Biafran Civil War.

After his imprisonment and release, Soyinka retreated to Europe, where he finished *Madmen and Specialists*; the play debuted in August 1970 at the Waterford playwrights' conference. It was performed in his homeland of Nigeria in March 1971 with mixed results. Soyinka was seen as a dissident in his own country, maligned by the ruling faction and championed by revolutionaries. At one point, Nigerian officials sentenced Soyinka to death for his beliefs, a verdict that was overturned with the next regime change. As a result, he remains a voluntary refugee from the country of his birth, living between Ghana, England, and the United States. *Madmen and Specialists* is his most famous work of propaganda, and his legacy as a playwright, author, poet, and teacher has inspired future writers to speak out against injustices in their own environments.

THEMES AND STYLE

Madmen and Specialists has two main themes: the effects of civil war on Nigerian society and the breakdown of traditional African culture and the family unit. Soyinka experienced these themes firsthand through his arrest and imprisonment during the Nigerian-Biafran Civil War. Although the play's action takes place in the realm of the absurd, its characters represent archetypes of humanity much like those found in early Greek drama and the Bible, both topics of study for Soyinka. For example, the character of Dr. Bero, who became a specialist in torture during the war, plies these skills against his father, who is referred to as the Old Man. The Old Man has tricked Bero and his compatriots into eating human flesh during the war; however, rather than causing shame, the act has left them bloodthirsty and unforgiving.

The Old Man's grotesque entourage of mendicants serve as a Greek chorus, describing the action of the play and chanting the old man's teachings in search of a mysterious deity named As. Bero seeks to discover what this mysterious "As" represents, leading him to detain and torture his father. When Bero asks "What is As?" the Old Man answers "As Was, Is, Now, As Ever Shall be … As doesn't change." In *Wole Soyinka and Modern Tragedy*, Ketu Katrak (1986) describes this scenario: "Old Man's three simple words, 'As doesn't change,' convey the despairing message that given the lessons of previous history, there is no hope that people will change in their cruelties toward each other. In fact, people excel themselves at inventing newer, more deadly weapons whereby they can control and threaten other people."

Madmen and Specialists uses word play to convey its absurdist message: war is an attempt to make sense of the irrational. Soyinka uses the Old Man's dialogue to express the theme of madness throughout the second act of the play. In the last few pages, Bero attempts to create truth out of his father's nonsense, but the Old Man continues unabated: "Practise, Practise, Practise … on the cyst in the system … you cyst, you cyst, you splint in the arrow of arrogance, the dog in dogma, the tick of a heretic, the tick in politics, the mock of democracy, the mar of marxism, a tic of the fanatic." Failing in his attempt, Bero shoots the Old Man dead, thus joining him in one final act of madness. The play ends with Bero's sister and her compatriots burning the doctor's clinic with him still in it.

CRITICAL DISCUSSION

Soyinka's play was met with criticism and censure by his country's government for its harsh critique

THE LIFE OF WOLE SOYINKA

Akinwande Oluwole Soyinka was born on July 13, 1934, in Abeokuta, Nigeria. Although he was raised Christian, his writings celebrate the traditions of his native Yoruba people, often linking Greek myths with those of his own culture. In 1960 he was commissioned by Nigerian leaders to write the play *A Dance of the Forests* to celebrate his country's independence. Soyinka's criticism of the new ruling elite was met with government opposition, and after the 1966 military coup, he was accused of siding with Biafran secessionists and was imprisoned for twenty-two months before finally receiving amnesty in 1969. He wrote several books while in prison including a memoir titled *The Man Died* (1972).

Soyinka has always been an outspoken author, critical of the Nigerian government and other dictatorships in his native Africa. Although his books have been banned in his own country, he garnered critical acclaim abroad, winning the Nobel Prize for Literature in 1986. In 1994 he was appointed a goodwill ambassador by the United Nations Education, Scientific, and Cultural Organization. However, in 1997 he was charged with treason by African authorities after writing *The Open Sore of a Continent* (1997), but the charges were later dropped. Soyinka has written more than twenty plays, as well as a number of memoirs, books, and volumes of poetry. He has lived in the United States since the late 1990s, teaching at several universities including Emory and the University of Nevada.

of its political ideologies. It was, however, lauded in the United States and Europe as a fine example of antiwar propaganda. In a 1972 *Books Abroad* review, Richard Priebe comments on Soyinka's work: "The Nigerian war, his own imprisonment and his concern for the way Nigeria would emerge from its political crises have made this perhaps the most turbulent period in his life … He has transformed those years into a masterpiece which may prove to be his finest play." Literary critics of the post-Nigerian-Biafran Civil War era acknowledge Soyinka's evolution as an artist in direct correlation to his war experience.

In a 1991 article for *African Languages and Cultures*, Frances Harding describes the timeless message of Soyinka's work and its critique of power gone awry, suggesting that *Madmen and Specialists* is a departure from Soyinka's other pieces perhaps because of the author's experiences in prison. She writes, "The language and imagery of the play, stressing self-focused power, is contrasted with an episodic and open-ended form which compels an audience into an uneasy, judgmental role … The theme of the play is the disruption brought about by the uncontrolled exercise of power by the individual acting without external restraint, and within a system whose only authority is itself. It is self-interested power." The play's critique of government exercising

A scene from a 2005 London production of Wole Soyinka's play *The Lion and the Jewel*. Soyinka's other plays include *Madmen and Specialists* (1971). © MARILYN KINGWILL/ ARENAPAL/THE IMAGE WORKS.

propaganda to express the tragedy of civil war in any time or setting, historical or contemporary.

BIBLIOGRAPHY

Sources

Harding, Frances. "Soyinka and Power: Language and Imagery in *Madmen and Specialists.*" *African Languages and Cultures* 4.1 (1991): 87–98. Print.

Katrak, Ketu H. *Wole Soyinka and Modern Tragedy: A Study of Dramatic Theory and Practice.* New York: Greenwood, 1986. Print.

Msiska, Mpalive-Hangson. *Wole Soyinka.* Plymouth: Northcote House, 1998. Print.

Priebe, Richard. Rev. of *Madmen and Specialists,* by Wole Soyinka. *Books Abroad* 46.3 (1972): 533. *JSTOR.* Web. 15 Sept. 2012.

Soyinka, Wole. *Madmen and Specialists.* New York: Hill and Wang, 1971. Print.

Wright, Derek. *Wole Soyinka Revisited.* New York: Twayne, 1993. Print.

Further Reading

Gibbs, James. *Critical Perspectives on Wole Soyinka.* Washington DC: Three Continents Press, 1980. Print.

Jeyifo, Biodun, ed. *Perspectives on Wole Soyinka: Freedom and Complexity.* Mississippi: U of Mississippi P, 2001. Print.

———. *Wole Soyinka: Politics, Poetics, and Postcolonialism.* Cambridge: Cambridge UP, 2004. Print.

Maja-Pearce, Adewale, ed. *Wole Soyinka: An Appraisal.* Oxford: Heinemann Educational, 1994. Print.

Soyinka, Wole. "Culture, Democracy and Renewal." *Trends in Organized Crime* 5.3 (2000): 110–17. *Academic Search Complete.* Web. 15 Sept. 2012.

———. *Myth, Literature, and the African World.* Cambridge: Cambridge UP, 1990. Print.

———. *The Open Sore of a Continent: A Personal Narrative of the Nigerian Crisis.* New York: Oxford UP, 1996. Print.

Media Adaptations

Madmen and Specialists. Minneapolis Theatre Garage, 2006. Theater Adaptation.

Madmen and Specialists. Dir. Mbala Nkanga. Perf. Jonathan Christopher, Corey Dorris, and Laura Lapidus. Arthur Miller Theatre, 2008. Theater Adaptation.

Ron Horton

unmitigated control over its population continues to serve as a prime example of antiwar propaganda.

At its core, Soyinka's *Madmen and Specialists* is both comedy and tragedy, which is the nature of many absurdist works throughout literary history. In his book *Wole Soyinka* (1998), Mpalive-Hangson Msiska describes the timeless tragic-comic nature of *Madmen and Specialists*: "The acceptance of the human condition without an accompanying desire for its transformation is shown to lead to misanthropy and cannibalism in Soyinka's *Madmen and Specialists* … the play exhibits Soyinka's trained eye for the comic potential of even the most tragic situation." Soyinka uses archetypal characters, absurdist language, and comic situations as

THE ORPHAN MASTER'S SON

Adam Johnson

OVERVIEW

The Orphan Master's Son, a novel by Adam Johnson released in January 2012, imagines life in modern-day North Korea. The story is divided into two parts. The first, told in the third person, traces the life of Pak Jun Do, an orphan whose adventurous, tragic existence overflows with horror and surprise. The second half alternates between the first-person account of a nameless interrogator in Pyongyang, who becomes involved with Jun Do, and "The Best Korean Short Story of the Year," serialized over the nation's loudspeakers with a focus on the famous actress Sun Moon; the disappeared Commander Ga (who Jun Do comes to impersonate); and, most pointedly, leader Kim Jong-Il. Johnson's novel critically examines the dangerous, fear-inducing effect of propaganda in North Korea and serves as its own form of propaganda in opposition to corrupt leadership that threatens, among other things, expressive freedom.

Upon its release less than one month following the death of Kim Jong-Il, *The Orphan Master's Son* reached an audience freshly reminded of the complexity and secrecy shrouding life in North Korea. The book received extensive acclaim. Johnson's attempt to simultaneously recreate the challenging personal lives of North Koreans, while providing readers a page-turning drama laced with love and intrigue, created a stir. Though most responses were positive, some authorities found this medley inappropriate, given the topic. Still, even its critics nearly unanimously regarded the book as a triumph of innovation, a milestone in narratives about a country whose citizens have no freedom to tell personal stories themselves.

HISTORICAL AND LITERARY CONTEXT

Since its establishment in 1945 as a result of the country's division into north and south by the Soviet Union and United States at the end of World War II, the Democratic People's Republic of Korea (DPRK) has been ruled as a hereditary dictatorship. The country is renowned for its totalitarian regime (with stringent controls regulating everything from food rations to lipstick color), an extreme insistence on privacy in the international realm, and strict government management of all media. According to Johnson, his initial interest in the novel's setting and story came from a fascination with North Korean propaganda. As he told the audience during a reading in New York, "The notion that there is an official narrative for a nation … that conscripts every citizen into being an unwilling character of someone else's story was really compelling to me."

Although the novel was published at the beginning of 2012, after Kim Jong-Il's son Kim Jong-Un had assumed leadership of the country, Johnson began his research in 2004. He studied the stories of defectors, investigated prisons (gulags) and disappearances, and read the Pyongyang newspaper. Even still, as the author observed in a discussion with David Ebershoff reprinted in the novel's paperback edition, "Few things about North Korea are verifiable." After several attempts Johnson received a visa to visit the country for just under a week in 2007. Though he was able to view certain sites that appear in the book, such as the Revolutionary Martyrs' Cemetery, he was accompanied during his entire trip by trained "minders" and did not speak to anyone outside the tour, as contact with foreigners is illegal for North Korean citizens. Johnson asserts that this lack of genuine communication furthered his desire to attempt to chronicle this particular population.

A handful of nonfiction books, such as *Nothing to Envy: Ordinary Lives in North Korea* by Barbara Demick, aim to capture life in the DPRK, and books of powerful memoir exist, penned by the defectors Kang Chol-hwan, Kim Yong, and Hyok Kang, but few fictional attempts have previously been deemed valuable by critics. An examination of Johnson's earlier work indicates a writerly interest in darkness, manipulation, and how cultures sway truth. His story collection *Emporium* depicts a violent, cinematic future where, in one story, tech employees who will not relinquish code are tortured or killed by snipers. Johnson's novel *Parasites Like Us* (2004) focuses on an anthropologist who accidently releases a virus from an ancient civilization that was destroyed by excess and was similar to that which the author perceives in contemporary America.

Although a new literary work, *The Orphan Master's Son* certainly has offered a highly imaginative and emotional portrayal of individuals whose stories are barely known, the effect of which has been powerful for readers and critics alike. The work's examination of dictatorial propaganda, and its more covert argument

✥ Key Facts

Time Period:
Early 21st Century

Genre:
Novel

Events:
Extreme economic hardship; human rights abuses; repression under the dictatorship of Kim Jong-Il

Nationality:
American

THE WRITER REGARDS
HIS PROCESS

Best-selling novels such as *The Orphan Master's Son* are necessarily the product of hard work and extensive research. In interviews with Adam Johnson following the book's publication, the author revealed important elements of his practice. "I am a big believer in labor over talent, he told the *Writer*'s Jason Kennedy in 2012. "I think talent is something you can create." Johnson practices what he preaches: he completes one portion of a meticulous spreadsheet each day to chart his progress and learn more about when, where, and how he is most productive.

For Johnson the writing process always begins with research, "a tremendous amount of research." However, the author also endeavors to give a human touch, a lightness, to his stories. "I hate exposition," he also told Kennedy. The substance of what his research on North Korea revealed required significant revision to avoid weighing "too heavy" on the book, resulting in the author's discarding of 270,000 words. His first interview was with a North Korean orphan, who became the perfect lead character for his story since in that country, as he told David Ebershoff in an interview featured in the paperback version of the novel, "your loyalties must lie with the regime first and your family second, which makes an orphan of everyone to some degree, and the Kim regime the true orphan master."

for the necessity of awareness and change, will likely influence future writing on this region and perhaps on any setting worldwide where justice and freedom are lacking.

THEMES AND STYLE

Central to the novel are examinations of freedom and truth. Jun Do, along with fellow orphans, is first sent to the army, where he works in tunnels along the demilitarized zone between North Korea and South Korea, and then is enlisted to participate in clandestine kidnappings of Japanese citizens. After this he is trained in English and sent to assist with a special diplomatic mission in Texas. He befriends an American, Wanda, who asks him if he knows what it means to feel free. He responds by inquiring about whether the United States has labor camps or loudspeakers. Without them, Jun Do says, "I'm not sure I could ever feel free…. When you're in my country, everything makes simple, clear sense." Propaganda is portrayed as a source of guidance and order. Further, Jun Do is often forced to lie in order to protect others, and he becomes skilled in the art. This fascinates the nameless main character, an interrogator, in the book's second half; he examines how knowledge is deadly in a system bolstered by informants. When one character reveals anything personal to another, the latter's life may be at stake should he or she be required to testify against the

other. In the story, people are often held accountable for the choices of their family members, friends, and acquaintances.

Johnson investigates these themes through character development and setting. Throughout his life Jun Do must learn to negotiate darkness and pain. He comes to find his own freedom by going to a place inside himself where no one can reach him. Each of the book's characters comes to accommodate the stringency of their culture in different ways—some exist in silent denial, some hurt others for a living, others notify authorities for their own gain. The story's action occurs in an orphanage, underground (in mine shafts and at Kim Jong-Il's lair below the city), at sea, in prisons, in torture chambers, and briefly in a beautiful house overlooking the capital. In each of these settings characters are forced up against the disparity between what the loudspeakers tell them—that they live "in a worker's paradise where citizens want for nothing"—and the hunger-, fear-, and lie-filled nature of their true existence.

At the book's opening and through its second half, Johnson intersperses chapters of supposed announcements from the propaganda loudspeakers. The tone of these addresses is satirical and exaggerated, opening each time with "Citizens" and an invitation to come closer to the speakers "in your kitchens, in your offices, on your factory floors." What follows is a nearly absurdist medley of "positive" reports ("shipments of sorghum have been arriving from the countryside") interspersed with reminders of proper behavior ("the ban on stargazing is still in effect") and fear tactics ("naked aggression continues from America") and then the "story" of Commander Ga, Sun Moon, and the "Dear Leader." The absurdist tenor of these announcements, with their seemingly random organization, allows Johnson to create propaganda of his own: transmissions like these serve only to brainwash and distract.

CRITICAL DISCUSSION

The Orphan Master's Son was met with considerable attention from the time of its publication. The *Washington Post* stated that Johnson had "taken the papier-mâché creation that is North Korea and turned it into a real and riveting place readers will find unforgettable." According to Michiko Kakutani of the *New York Times,* "Mr. Johnson has written a daring and remarkable novel … that not only opens a frightening window on the mysterious kingdom of North Korea, but one that excavates the very meaning of love and sacrifice." Critics marveled at the ambitious fearlessness of the novel and the manner in which it renders the previously unimaginable lives of DPRK citizens with a realism tinged by terror and valor.

The novel serves as an important example of activist literature. As Ruth Franklin of the *New Republic* observes, the book belongs to the class of "exceptional novels that also serve a humanitarian purpose."

Johnson set his sights high in several senses—the story is complex, brave, informative, and timely. According to Anne Morris, the novel is "many things at once—literary thriller, love story, social history and more.... In the end, we see how humanity survives in spite of a system that would have them surrender their private lives to a story already written for them." Johnson was quoted by *Publishers Weekly* as having felt a "duty to get to that darkness"—the darkness his research and observations associated with life for many in North Korea, a place where no one "is allowed to write [his or her] own story." This sense of responsibility led to the creation of a novel providing, in Johnson's view, a voice for the voiceless.

Most response to the novel can be deemed positive, with the majority of reviews focused on the masterful creation of setting, the courageous content and scope, as well as the levity, hope, and passion Johnson was able to impart. Still, the book was not free from criticism. Although Wyatt Mason's review in the *New Yorker* gives the novel several nods, it discounts the cartoonish portrayal of Kim Jong-Il and the insertion of false propaganda: "the real denouement is no more believable than the false one, and neither seems congruent with the novel." Mason also asserts that the story becomes too complex and at times convoluted. Writing in the *New York Times,* Christopher R. Beha critiques Johnson's portrayal of the North Korean leader and further questions Johnson's moral responsibility and the role of "fun" in any "novel about one of the worst places on earth."

Kim Jong-Il the late leader of North Korea, in a 2010 photograph. Adam Johnson's novel *The Orphan Master's Son* is set in North Korea during the reign of Kim Jong-Il. AP PHOTO/VINCENT YU, FILE.

BIBLIOGRAPHY

Sources

Beha, Christopher R. "North Korean Noir." *New York Times.* The New York Times Company, 15 Jan. 2012. Web. 5 Oct. 2012.

Franklin, Ruth. "The True Lies of Totalitarian North Korea." *TNR.com. The New Republic,* 25 Jan. 2012. Web. 26 Jan. 2013.

Ignatius, David. "'Orphan Master's Son' as Audacious, Believable Tale." *The Washington Post.* The Washington Post, 9 Jan. 2012. Web. 9 Feb. 2013.

Johnson, Adam. *The Orphan Master's Son: A Novel.* New York: Random House, 2012. Print.

Kakutani, Michiko. "A North Korean's 'Casablanca.'" *New York Times.* The New York Times Company, 13 Jan. 2012. Web. 5 Oct. 2012.

Mason, Wyatt. "Dear Leader." *New Yorker* 6 Feb. 2012: 71. *Literature Resource Center.* Web. 2 Oct. 2012.

Morris, Anne. Rev. of *The Orphan Master's Son,* by Adam Johnson. *Dallas Morning News,* 27 Jan. 2012. *GuideLIVE.* Web. 26 Jan. 2013.

Schwabe, Liesl. "Nothing Is Illuminated: Adam Johnson." *Publishers Weekly* 14 Nov. 2011: 26+. *Literature Resource Center.* Web. 6 Oct. 2012.

Further Reading

"Adam Johnson on 'The Orphan Master's Son.'" *Minnesota Public Radio.* Minnesota Public Radio, 6 Sept. 2012. Web. 7 Oct. 2012.

Haven, Cynthia. "Stanford Author Adam Johnson on Truth and Totalitarianism in North Korea." *Stanford University News.* Stanford University, 4 Apr. 2012. Web. 6 Oct. 2012.

Johnson, Adam. *Emporium: Stories.* New York: Viking, 2002. Print.

———. *Parasites Like Us.* New York: Viking, 2003. Print.

Kirkpatrick, Melanie. "Incarceration Nation." *Commentary* 133.3 (2012): 59+. *Literature Resource Center.* Web. 7 Oct. 2012.

Lee, Stephan. "Read This Book! 'The Orphan Master's Son' Author Adam Johnson Talks North Korea." *EW.com.* Entertainment Weekly, 22 Aug. 2012. Web. 6 Oct. 2012.

Mahajan, Karan. "Adam Johnson on 'The Orphan Master's Son.'" *Paris Review Daily.* The Paris Review, 24 Jan. 2012. Web. 23 Oct. 2012.

Rachel Mindell

The Protocols of the Elders of Zion

❖ *Key Facts*

Time Period:
Early 20th Century

Genre:
False document

Events:
Russo-Japanese War;
democratic reform in
Russia

Nationality:
Russian

OVERVIEW

First published in 1903 and widely disseminated in the early twentieth century, *The Protocols of the Elders of Zion* purports to be the minutes from a nineteenth-century meeting of Jewish rabbis elaborating a secret plot to take over the world. The document is composed of twenty-four "protocols" that treat basic philosophy, methods of conquest, and the ultimate aims of "the Jewish Ruler." While widely debunked as a fabrication, the text, which is also known as *The Protocols of the Meetings of Learned/Sage Elders,* is still presented as a legitimate document in print and online and has been used to promote anti-Semitism and to justify crimes against Jews.

The *Protocols* first appeared in September of 1903 in the far right-wing St. Petersburg daily *Znamja* (Banner) under the headline "The Jewish Program for the Conquest of the World." The paper had been founded earlier that year by the anti-Semitic journalist Pavel Krushevan, who in 1903 had instigated the pogrom of Kishinev (in Moldavia). Several versions of the document were published in Russia in the years following its initial appearance, largely as a way of explaining Russia's defeat in the Russo-Japanese War as well as the Russian Revolution of 1905. The Union of the Russian Nation, one of the antirevolutionary Black Hundreds organizations, sought to further scapegoat Jews for fostering the movement that led to the establishment of a constitution and of the Duma (elected legislature) in 1906—actions the monarchists radically opposed. The *Protocols* remained relatively unknown outside of Russia until its export to Europe with "white Russians" fleeing the Bolshevik Revolution of 1917. Within Russia, the *Protocols* had been used to enact widespread slaughter of Jews in the civil wars following the revolution. Abroad, anticommunist Russians emigrating to the West used the document to denounce the Bolsheviks as Jews beginning to enact the plan set forth in the *Protocols.* This allegation would be used to demonize European Jews throughout the twentieth century.

HISTORICAL AND LITERARY CONTEXT

By the beginning of the twentieth century, Jews in the Russian Empire had suffered more than a hundred years of restriction and persecution. With the establishment of the Pale of Settlement in the late eighteenth century, Jews were largely confined to areas of European Russia and lived in communities governed theocratically by a local council of elders. Throughout the nineteenth century, Jewish communities were periodically subjected to pogroms, officially condoned riots resulting in deaths and destruction of Jewish homes, businesses, and religious centers. A particularly virulent wave of attacks occurred after the assassination of Alexander II. Widespread poverty and resentments that had not been sufficiently addressed by the emancipation of the serfs in 1861 are thought to have contributed to these riots, with Jews, a relatively powerless minority, being blamed for a range of unpleasant conditions in the empire.

Starting with the 1905 publication of the *Protocols* by self-proclaimed mystic priest Serge Nilus (as a chapter in a book of his own), the text was used in earnest as an instrument of propaganda aimed at inciting violence against Jews. In the Nilus publication the *Protocols* was attributed to the First Zionist Congress held in Basel, Switzerland, in 1897. Nilus later contradicted this tale, attributing the work variously to a meeting of elders sometime in 1902–1903 and then to a meeting of freemasons in France at an undisclosed date. The existence of contradictory accounts did not, however, appear to weaken paranoia about the conspiracy Nilus purported to uncover.

The actual origin of the *Protocols* is not known definitively, although some scholars trace the document to agents of the Okharana in France in the 1890s and speculate that it was translated into Russian sometime before 1901. French satirist Maurice Joly's 1864 pamphlet *The Dialogue in Hell Between Machiavelli and Montesquieu* is often cited as a key text used to develop the work, though Joly's work, which describes a diabolical plot hatched in hell, is read as a satire poking fun at the ambitions of the emperor Napoleon. While Joly made no mention of the Jews, the pamphlet was subsequently plagiarized by a German anti-Semite, Hermann Goedsche, who included it in his 1868 serial novel *Biarritz.* In a chapter titled "The Jewish Cemetery in Prague and the Council of Representatives of the Twelve Tribes of Israel," Goedsche (writing as Sir John Retcliffe) details a secret Jewish council convening at midnight to review its works of the past century and make plans for operations in the next.

Although an artifact of the declining Russian Empire, the *Protocols* went on to have a lasting impact in the West, most significantly as employed by Adolf Hitler's propaganda machine in Nazi Germany. After its export from Russia, the *Protocols* was widely translated and disseminated across the globe. In the United States the document was initially treated as a Bolshevik manifesto, with all references to Jews removed. Later, sponsored by auto magnate Henry Ford, it was reprinted as a series of pamphlets titled *The International Jew: The World's Foremost Problem*. Ford was later obliged to retract the publications when it came to light that the text was fabricated. The *Protocols* was famously discredited in trials in Bern, Switzerland, in 1935. While the *Protocols* had been debunked a number of times during Hitler's rise to power, he referred to the document in speeches from 1921 on and cited it in *Mein Kampf*. The *Protocols* became required reading for some schoolchildren in Nazi Germany and was used to explain the misfortunes that had befallen the country in the first part of the twentieth century.

THEMES AND STYLE

Written as the minutes of an unnamed Zionist group, the *Protocols* outlines the general steps to be taken in service of a projected Jewish rise to power across the globe. The *Protocols* begins with the idea that force is necessary to gain power and that, because politics has little to do with morality, the ends justify the means to establish Jewish rule. Jewish leaders will seek to control the presses and world economies, destabilizing civilization by corrupting Gentile morals with pornography, alcohol, and materialism, among other things. Instability can then be exploited through widespread warfare, which can be ended by a Jewish savior regime that will appear as a stabilizing force and hence be granted absolute power.

The *Protocols* exploits fears about powerful subterranean forces at work in society. The document as such begins without preamble, necessitating an inclusion of prefatory remarks upon publication. This device underlines the document's status as secret and allows editors to set the framework through which the reader views the text. The document is divided into twenty-four protocols, each beginning with a shorthand list of the themes to be developed, creating a sense of note-taking, as at a meeting, followed by elaboration. The first protocol begins "Right lies in Might. Freedom—an idea only. Liberalism. Gold. Faith. Self-Government. Despotism of Capital. The internal foe. The Mob. Anarchy …" These ideas are then developed, although the elaboration of each protocol is kept rather vague, presumably to make it more readily adaptable when used to scapegoat Jews for enacting the plan.

The *Protocols* develops a sense of institutionalized hatred of and condescension toward "goyim," or gentiles, by combining the language of an official decree with inflammatory descriptions of Gentile stupidity. Non-Jews, referred to in such terms as "alcoholized animals," "goy mobs," and "a pack of sheep," will easily fall victim to the elders' plans. Indeed, many of

WILL EISNER AND *THE PLOT*

Will Eisner was born in Brooklyn to Jewish immigrants. He spent much of the early part of his career producing syndicated comics, as well as educational material for the U.S. Army. In the 1970s he began producing work addressing Jewish experiences and concerns. *A Contract with God and Other Tenement Stories,* which is widely considered the first graphic novel, was inspired by Eisner's early life. *Fagin the Jew,* published several years later, is a book-length refutation of the stereotypes embodied by the character Fagin in Charles Dickens's *Oliver Twist*.

Eisner's final graphic novel, *The Plot: The Secret Story of the Protocols of the Elders of Zion* (2005), imagines a conspiracy story surrounding the production of the phony document. In an interview with the *New York Times,* Eisner explained that the impetus for *The Plot* came from the proliferation of websites treating the *Protocols* as fact, especially in the Arab world. "I wanted to create a work that would be understood by the widest possible audience," he said. *The Plot* provides evidence against the *Protocols* and illustrates the Nazis' use of the document as propaganda.

these plans are described in terms of inevitability, also lending the document an air of prophecy. Further, "while the peoples of the world are still stunned by the accomplished fact of the revolution" they should "recognize once and for all that we are so strong [that] … in no case we shall take any account of them."

CRITICAL DISCUSSION

From the time of its publication, the *Protocols* has been treated both as a legitimate document justifying the persecution of Jews and as a dangerous hoax. In 1905 Pyotr Arkadyevich Stolypin, Russian prime minister and leader of the third Duma, concluded that the *Protocols* was a fraudulent document emerging from anti-Semitic circles in Paris around 1898. Nicolaus II ordered the document confiscated as a result of Stolypin's investigation, although it would be routinely used by other forces in Russia during the decade that followed. In 1921 the *Times* (London) published a multipart article by journalist Philip Graves calling the *Protocols* a "literary forgery" plagiarized from Maurice Joly and Hermann Goedsche (as Sir John Retcliffe). The *New York Times* reprinted the article, and a widely read book debunking the *Protocols* was published in the United States later that year.

The *Protocols,* while not originating the myth of an international Jewish conspiracy, is often cited as the vehicle that perpetuated the idea in the twentieth century. Further, many commentators see in it the beginnings of modern conspiracy-theory literature. While the *Protocols* is generally treated as a hoax in much of Western discourse, it is still treated as a valid source

and circulated by neo-Nazis and Holocaust deniers in the United States and Europe. In the Arab world the text is still regularly taught in schools as fact and has been used by Hamas and other political movements to justify violence against Israel.

Since its publication the *Protocols* has generated a large body of work, particularly by scholars from the Jewish community. Much early work sought to trace the document to its source as well as to discredit it as propaganda. Recent scholarship continues these projects. Cesare De Michelis does a close reading of the language used in the *Protocols* as well as the relationship between the earliest appearances of the document, concluding that the text may have originated as a sort of "parlor game" played by several of its earliest publishers, Georgy Butmi de Katzman, Pavel Krushevan, and Mikhail Menshikov, who were confirmed anti-Semites. Ultimately, however, De Michelis endorses Norman Cohn's view that the work's true importance as a subject of study "lies in the great influence it has exercised on the history of the 20th century." Steven Jacobs and Mark Weitzmen unpack each of the twenty-four protocols, analyzing and then presenting evidence against the "thematic lies of the *Protocols.*" Other recent work has been less focused on the text and more concerned with its political uses, analyzing the *Protocols* as it functions, for instance, in extreme right-wing political groups in the United States and abroad.

BIBLIOGRAPHY

Sources

Cohn, Norman. *Warrant for Genocide: The Myth of the Jewish Conspiracy and the Protocols of the Elders of Zion.* London: Serif, 1996. Print.

De Michelis, Cesare. *The Non-Existent Manuscript: A Study of the Protocols of the Sages of Zion.* Lincoln: U of Nebraska P, 2004. Print.

Graves, Philip. "The Truth about the Protocols: A Literary Forgery." *The Times* [London] 16–18 Aug. 1921. *University of California Digital Library.* Web.19 June 2012.

Jacobs, Steven, and Mark Weitzmen. *Dismantling the Big Lie: The Protocols of the Elders of Zion.* Jersey City: KTVA Publishing House, 2003. Print.

Landes, Richard Allen. *The Paranoid Apocalypse: A Hundred-Year Retrospective of the Protocols of the Elders of Zion.* New York: New York UP, 2012. Print.

Marsden, Victor, trans. "The Protocols of the Meetings of the Learned Elders of Zion." *The Protocols of the Elders of Zion.* David M. Dickerson. Web. 18 June 2012.

Medoff, Rafael. "Will Eisner: A Cartoonist Who Fought Antisemitism." *Midstream* 52.1 (2006): 10–12. *Literature Resource Center.* Web. 19 June 2012.

Further Reading

Boym, Svetlana. "Conspiracy Theories and Literary Ethics: Umberto Eco, Danilo Kiš and the Protocols of Zion." *Comparative Literature* 51.2 (Spring 1999). Print.

Bronner, Stephen E. *A Rumor About the Jews: Reflections on Antisemitism and The Protocols of the Learned Elders of Zion.* New York: St. Martin's Press, 2000. Print.

Gerits, Andre. *The Myth of Jewish Communism: A Historical Interpretation.* Brussels: Peter Lang, 2009. Print.

Kellogg, Michael. *The Russian Roots of Nazism: White Émigrés and the Making of National Socialism, 1917–1945.* Cambridge: Cambridge UP, 2005. Print.

Segel, Binjamin W. *A Lie and a Libel: The History of the Protocols of the Elders of Zion.* Lincoln: U of Nebraska P, 1995. Print.

Daisy Gard

Opposite page:

The Jewish Danger: The Protocols of the Learned Elders of Zion, book cover, 1940. Despite strong evidence that the Protocols were a forgery, they were widely used as a justification for anti-Semitism. COVER OF AN EDITION OF 'THE JEWISH DANGER. THE PROTOCOLS OF THE LEARNED ELDERS OF ZION,' C. 1940 (COLOUR LITHO), FRENCH SCHOOL, (20TH CENTURY)/ PRIVATE COLLECTION/ ARCHIVES CHARMET/THE BRIDGEMAN ART LIBRARY.

RED CAVALRY

Isaac Babel

⁘ *Key Facts*

Time Period:
Early 20th Century

Genre:
Short Story

Events:
Polish-Soviet War;
end of World War I

Nationality:
Russian

OVERVIEW

Isaac Babel's *Red Cavalry* (1926) depicts the Red Army's forays along the Polish front during the Russo-Polish War of 1919–1920/21. By turns lyrical and grotesquely violent, the thirty-four-story cycle is based on Babel's experiences as a Jewish journalist embedded with Semen Budyonny's First Cavalry. Culled in part from Babel's journals, and blending fact and fiction, the stories follow a small cast of characters, including Budyonny and Kirill Liutov, a Jewish journalist who is confronted with the brutality and anti-Semitism of the Cavalry in much the same way Babel was. *Red Cavalry* is one of the earliest literary works to confront the Soviet people with the grim realities of the war and to frame questions about what an individual can do in the face of a closely knit and brutal collective.

The stories that make up *Red Cavalry* were initially published in magazines and newspapers from 1923 to 1925 and turned Babel into a literary sensation. The 1926 book was reprinted numerous times in the decade following its publication. As an esteemed writer, Babel enjoyed travel privileges and other luxuries that were extremely rare under Joseph Stalin's oppressive regime. However, when the political tides in the Soviet Union began to turn in the mid-1930s, Babel's status shifted. He was arrested on May 15, 1939, and executed the following year. His unpublished manuscripts were destroyed by the Stalinist government in the Great Purge, and his writing fell out of favor for a number of years. Babel's reputation was officially rehabilitated in 1954, and his work, especially *Red Cavalry*, now has a place in classic Russian literature.

HISTORICAL AND LITERARY CONTEXT

The Russian Revolution of 1917 toppled the tsarist government and led to the installment of the Bolshevik regime later that year. Civil war followed between the Red (Bolshevik) and White (anti-Bolshevik) armies. During this period, fighting also broke out along the Polish border, which was in dispute owing to the vagueness of the post-World War I Treaty of Versailles. Poland was keen to carve out its borders, having reestablished its statehood in 1918. Meanwhile, Vladimir Lenin, who believed that communist revolutions were necessary in multiple nations, sought to use Poland as a bridge to

other European countries, particularly Germany, where a socialist uprising seemed, in his view, imminent.

In May 1920, Budyonny's First Cavalry engaged Polish forces in the south and, with repeated attacks, was successful in breaking the Polish-Ukrainian front. By mid-June, the Polish were in retreat, leaving Kiev, then the capital of the Ukrainian People's Republic, to the Red Army. Riding with Budyonny, Babel was close to the combat, as well as to attacks on civilians in towns along the border. The First Cavalry was infamous for its brutality against civilians, including Jews, and deliberately incited terror and destroyed infrastructure to achieve its goals. Budyonny's fortunes changed, however, and by August, his troops had been defeated.

Literature produced in the wake of the Bolshevik Revolution often focused on military themes as well as the human cost of the fighting. Mikhail Bulgakov's *White Guard,* which first appeared in serial form in the Soviet-era literary journal *Rossiya* in 1926, explores the fate of the Turbin family after the fighting over Kiev begins in 1918. Leonid Leonov, like Babel a reporter during the Russian Civil War, began publishing short stories after his release from the Red Army in 1921. His first novel, *The Badger* (1924), deals with the impact of the revolution on the Russian peasantry. It is worth noting that few of the writers of this era identified themselves as both Jewish and Russian, making Babel's position and concerns unique. In his introduction to a 2003 edition of *Red Cavalry*, Michael Dirda suggests a certain cross-cultural symmetry between Babel's work and Ernest Hemingway's *In Our Time* (1925), noting the "affectless description" both writers employ to critique violence in their stories.

Red Cavalry made Babel into an overnight literary sensation, both at home and abroad. Not everyone approved of Babel's portrayal of the First Cavalry, however. The character of Budyonny is depicted in *Red Cavalry* as a brutish oaf, and the military commissar Klim Voroshilov is insubordinate and foolish. Unfortunately for Babel, both of these characters had real-life counterparts who would rise to positions of rank in Stalin's government—Budyonny, for example, becoming first deputy commissar for defense and later proclaimed a Hero of the Soviet Union. Both men publicly disparaged Babel and *Red Cavalry*.

Moreover, the unsuccessful campaigns in Poland were a sore point for the Soviet military, and *Red Cavalry* was an indelible record of those defeats.

THEMES AND STYLE

Starting with a description of the "stench of yesterday's blood" in the story "Crossing the River Zbrucz" and ending with "the wasteland of war" in "The Rabbi's Son," *Red Cavalry* unflinchingly reveals the horrors of war. Unlike many accounts of the First Cavalry, Babel's stories depict cavalrymen who are more likely to be motivated by greed or by a sadistic love of violence than by the ideals of the revolution. They kill Polish soldiers, civilians, and sometimes their own comrades without making distinctions. Their violence toward the Jews they encounter, accounts of which both open and close the original cycle, is especially horrific. Journalist Kirill Liutov—with the cavalrymen but not *of* them, in part because of his half-Jewish parentage—vacillates between disgust over their brutality and admiration for their heroics. For example, in "Squadron Commander Trunov," the title character senselessly slaughters several Polish prisoners but then gallantly goes to his death when, armed only with a rifle, he confronts an American bomber.

Originally published separately, the stories in *Red Cavalry* were shaped into a whole by Babel, and they adhere to common elements of style and plot. The brutality of war is present throughout, although many of the stories do not deal directly with fighting but take place in village streets or occupied homes. These latter pieces utilize a narrative technique called *skaz,* which employs the rhythms and slang of a spoken dialect to establish character. Commentators have noted that the character Liutov serves as a bridge between the cavalry stories and the *skaz* stories, with a foot in each camp. As a Jewish intellectual, he is an outsider in the cavalry and is able to relate to the Jews in the Polish ghettos.

Stylistically, *Red Cavalry* relies on vivid descriptions and sometimes startling imagery to convey the horrific violence of the Red Army campaign. In the opening story, as the cavalry rides into Poland, the sun is described as "rolling across the sky like a severed head." This sets the tone for the book. Throughout his work, Babel employs stirring metaphors to echo the drama of war, as well as short sentences that effectively march forward with the army. Although the prose is often dramatic, the violence is described in matter-of-fact terms, an approach that conveys the cavalry's devaluation of human life.

CRITICAL DISCUSSION

As the Soviet Union solidified in the years following the failed incursions into Poland, *Red Cavalry* enjoyed great popularity. In her preface to a 2003 translation of the book, Babel's daughter, Nathalie Babel, quotes the second edition of the *Small Soviet Encyclopedia* (1937), which praises *Red Cavalry*'s "original combination of heroics and humor." The book's detractors—such as

SKAZ IN BABEL'S *RED CAVALRY*

Skaz, from the Russian *skazat* ("to tell" or "to say"), is a narrative device that attempts to duplicate an oral recounting of a story. Traditionally, *skaz* is connected to Russian folklore, but it has come into the international parlance as a technique used to inscribe the voices of illiterate or semiliterate people, often peasants, into a text while maintaining an authorial distance from the characters being presented.

In "*Skaz* and Oral Usage as Satirical Devices in Isaak Babel's *Red Cavalry,*" Janet Tucker discusses Babel's use of the device in two of the *Red Cavalry* stories, "The Letter" and "Salt." "The Letter" reproduces a message from a son to his mother recounting a family conflict that, as Tucker points out, echoes the Russian Civil War: a father kills his son and then another of his sons kills the father. In "Salt," a woman is killed after cavalrymen discover that the "baby" she has been holding in her arms is actually a swaddled lump of salt she is smuggling for use in weapons smelting. Noting the nonstandard usage of words in the dialog of these two stories, Tucker suggests that Babel "parodies the traditional teller of tales and the tales themselves in order to comment satirically on the wasteful violence of revolution and the Civil War." In this analysis, Babel presents not only a critique of war and revolution through the eyes of the intellectual but also gives the reader his version of a peasant's view.

Budyonny, who complained of its character assassination and counterrevolutionary ideas—tended to focus less on its literary aspects and more on its questionable adherence to facts. But Babel's professed primary objective with his stories was not factual historical representation, as he stated in a 1924 letter to the editor of the literary magazine *October,* where much of this debate raged.

Regardless, *Red Cavalry* provides an enduring portrait of Soviet life in the tumultuous years following the revolution. Charles Rougle writes in *Red Cavalry: A Critical Companion* that even Babel's critics might concede that the stories of *Red Cavalry* "succeeded in capturing the very special atmosphere and rich human interest of this war." Accordingly, while the stories may not be accurate in all the external details, they ring true in the "internal" sense. And this emphasis on "internal" as opposed to factual truth has been of keen interest to scholars.

Babel's output was fairly slight, but it has attracted a great deal of scholarly attention, both for its historical details and the elements of its construction. In "The Jew among the Cossacks: Isaac Babel and the Red Cavalry in the Soviet-Polish War of 1920," Stephen Brown argues that Babel opts to invent a Cossack cavalry, rather than describe the largely peasant cavalry of historical fact, so as to disorient his readers and "to undermine simple Soviet formulas of a class war between rich and poor, of violence in the

ВСТУПАЙТЕ ДО ЧЕРВОНОЇ КІННОТИ!

Червона кіннота знищила Мамонтова, Шкуро, Деникина.
Вона била панів і Петлюру,
зараз потрібно знищити недобитка Врангеля.
Робітники й селяне—вступайте до лав Червоної Кінноти.

Propaganda poster for enlistment into the Red Cavalry during the 1920s. BUYENLARGE/GETTY IMAGES.

service of a just cause." Moreover, Brown contends that Babel's ultimate aim is to convey "how unlikely it was that the revolutionary dream of freedom and equality would be realized." Milton Ehre, in discussing *Red Cavalry* within the epic tradition of Russian literature, notes in *Isaac Babel* that while "Babel is fragmentary, elliptical, elusive, very much a modernist in his tendency to decompose a text into pastiche … *Red Cavalry* yet betrays a Tolstoyan aspiration … to create an epic of a decisive historical moment."

BIBLIOGRAPHY

Sources

Babel, Isaac. *Red Cavalry.* Trans. Peter Constantine. New York: W. W. Norton and Company, 2003. Print.

Brown, Stephen. "The Jew among the Cossacks: Isaac Babel and the Red Cavalry in the Soviet-Polish War of 1920." *Slavonica* 3.1 (1996): 29–43. Rpt. in *Short Story Criticism.* Ed. Joseph Palmisano. Vol. 78. Detroit: Gale, 2005. *Literature Resource Center.* Web. 26 July 2012.

Ehre, Milton. "Chapter 6: Red Cavalry." *Isaac Babel.* Boston: Twayne Publishers, 1986. Twayne's World Authors Series 782. *The Twayne Authors Series.* Web. 27 July 2012.

Rougle, Charles. "Isaac Babel and His Odyssey of War and Revolution." *Red Cavalry: A Critical Companion.* Ed. Charles Rougle. Evanston: Northwestern UP, 1996. Print.

Tucker, Janet. "*Skaz* and Oral Usage as Satirical Devices in Isaak Babel's *Red Cavalry.*" *Canadian-American Slavic Studies* 34.2 (Summer 2000): 201–210. Rpt. in *Short Story Criticism.* Ed. Joseph Palmisano. Vol. 78. Detroit: Gale, 2005. *Literature Resource Center.* Web. 26 July 2012.

Further Reading

Andrew, Joe. "Babel's 'My First Goose'." *The Structural Analysis of Russian Narrative Fiction.* Ed. Joe Andrew. Keele UP, 1984. 64–81. *Literature Resource Center.* Web. 26 July 2012

Avins, Carol J. "Kinship and Concealment in *Red Cavalry* and Babel's *1920 Diary.*" *Slavic Review* 53.3 (Fall 1994): 694–710. *Literature Resource Center.* Web. 26 July 2012.

Gillespie, David. *The Twentieth-Century Russian Novel: An Introduction.* Oxford: Berg, 1996. Print.

Hetenyi, Zsuzsa. "'Up' and 'Down', Madonna and Prostitute: The Role of Ambivalence in *Red Cavalry* by Isaac Babel." *Acta Litteraria Academiae Scientiarum Hungaricae* 32.3–4 (1990): 309–326. *Literature Resource Center.* Web. 26 July 2012.

Peppard, Victor. "The Problem of Revolutionary Violence in Isaac Babel's Stories." *Times of Trouble: Violence in Russian Literature and Culture.* Ed. Marcus C. Levitt and Tatyana Novikov. Madison: U of Wisconsin P, 2007. 163–173. *Literature Resource Center.* Web. 26 July 2012.

Terras, Victor. "Line and Color: The Structure of I. Babel's Short Stories in *Red Cavalry.*" *Studies in Short Fiction* 3.2 (Winter 1966): 141–156. *Literature Resource Center.* Web. 26 July 2012.

Daisy Gard

RED CRAG

Lo Kuang-pin, Yang Yi-yen

OVERVIEW

Lo Kuang-pin and Yang Yi-yen's six-hundred-page novel *Red Crag,* published in 1961, tells an elaborate tale of the communist underground in Szechuan, China, at a time when revolutionaries were being captured, imprisoned, and tortured by nationalist forces. Well developed and suspenseful, *Red Crag* is one of a select group of novels written between 1945 and 1965 that are now identified as "red classics." These books establish a mythology of communist nation building, telling the stories of the war of resistance to Japan, the civil war, and the early years of the People's Republic of China. Although the characters in *Red Crag* are both realistic and complex, the emotional rendering of the cadre's total sacrifice to communism is designed to inspire an ever-greater devotion to the cause among the novel's readers.

The novel was written in the years following the antirightist campaign of 1958, an era when many intellectuals were persecuted for depicting the Communist party's weaknesses in addition to its virtues. *Red Crag* exemplifies the combination of revolutionary realism and romanticism that was enforced by supervisor of culture Zhou Yang and others starting in 1958. As Innes Herdan observes in *The Pen and the Sword: Literature and Revolution in Modern China* (1992), this new formulation demanded that writers emphasize "the positive, the growing, the developing side of reality" in contrast to the critical realist approaches of the past that had emphasized the "dark side" of society and had thereby damaged the people's faith in a bright future. *Red Crag* was well received upon its first publication, particularly by the newly literate class. According to Helmut Martin in *Modern Chinese Writers: Self Portrayals* (1992), it quickly became known as "a textbook for the revolution" and remains one of the most popular examples of social realism in China.

HISTORICAL AND LITERARY CONTEXT

Red Crag expresses the revolutionary spirit that inspired the communist resistance during the third-largest war in world history: the Chinese Civil War, which raged from 1927 to 1950. Although Red Crag was published in 1961, it is set in 1949, the year Mao Zedong led the Communist Party of China (CPC) to victory over the Chinese Nationalist Party (KMT), which was headed by Chang Kai Shek. The Nationalist Party had been weakened during the last years of the war by the withdrawal of foreign support. Internal corruption also played a large role in the failure of the KMT, as emphasized in the novel's depiction of greedy KMT officials' competition for power. The heroic underground communist agents featured in the novel fight in secret under the guidance of Mao's top aide, Zhou Enlai, and are frequently imprisoned and tortured. The novel's authors were themselves former inmates of Zhazidong jail in Szechuan. The book blames the Sino-American Cooperative Organization for much of the imprisonment and torture of communists, although recent scholarship argues that these jailings were orchestrated by the KMT secret service without American involvement.

The publication of *Red Crag* came on the heels of the Great Leap Forward, a time of severe hardship for communist China as the country endeavored to industrialize its agrarian economy and modernize its culture. The questionable tactics employed by the CPC and the millions of deaths during this period, among other factors, sparked a chorus of criticism from intellectuals. Although Mao and Zhou had called for intellectual freedom in 1956, the criticism of the CPC during this period upset the communist leadership and brought on the antirightist campaign, during which critical voices, as expressed in journals such as *The People's Literature,* were silenced. Nevertheless, criticism of the Communist party continued to grow, some of which was even encouraged by U.S. and Taiwanese connections.

In this critical climate, Zhou called for a new "revolutionary realism" that would restore the people's faith in the promise of communism. *Red Crag* was among the tens of thousands of novels that were designed to propagate this vision. Combining realism with romanticism, these novels emphasize the role of the masses, the prior accomplishments of the Communist Party, and the bright future of the people. In its effort to spread inspirational, heroic stories of resistance and progress, *Red Crag* follows the example of epic, complex political novels such as Yang Mo's *The Song of Youth* (1958) and Liang Bin's three-volume *Keep the Red Flag Flying* (1958).

Red Crag outshines most other fiction of the communist underground largely because of its mature political perspective. The revolutionaries featured

Key Facts

Time Period:
Mid-20th Century

Genre:
Novel

Events:
Chinese Civil War; "Great Leap Forward"

Nationality:
Chinese

MAO ZEDONG AND THE CHINESE INTELLECTUALS

During the 1950s, many of the same Chinese intellectuals who had been in favor of China's socialist project began to grow critical of the Communist Party's bureaucratic inefficiency and constant surveillance, both of which violated their expectation of increased economic prosperity and intellectual freedom following the country's civil war. In response to the drop in artistic productivity, Mao Zedong and his top aide, Zhou Enlai, called a conference of the Communist Party's Central Committee to discuss the role of intellectuals. Mao, making a point of rejecting the Stalinist suppression of intellectuals, spoke in favor of improving their material conditions and reducing some of their political commitments as a means of allowing them more freedom to write.

During a Supreme State Conference later the same year, Mao declared magnanimously, "Let a hundred flowers bloom together, let a hundred schools of thought contend." The metaphor was to suggest a new climate in which intellectual freedom and diversity could flourish. However, when writers such as Wang Meng and Liu Binyan dared to articulate critiques of the establishment, they were rapidly silenced. This initiated more criticism, which then precipitated a large-scale *xianfang*, or sending down, of thousands of intellectuals to rural China to abandon their bourgeois leanings and to learn the spirit of revolution from the peasants. Historians suggest that this movement, although well intentioned, did not succeed in bridging the gap between the peasant and intellectual classes.

in the story bear the distinguishing marks of hard-won experience, and their commitment to the cause inspires even the most cynical readers. The novel sets new standards for characterization and structure, offering several heroic characters to emphasize the collectivity of the movement without marring their individuality.

THEMES AND STYLE

The primary theme of *Red Crag* is that true revolutionary heroism comes from a total devotion to the collective future. Zheng Gang—a man "broad of shoulder, square-faced and of medium build ... and honest eyes"—fits the heroic mold. He works tirelessly for the Communist party with no regard for himself; yet he modestly claims, "I have done so little for the Party!" He resists developing his personal or romantic life, channeling his desires into his work for the party because he has seen too many people fall in love, get married, and soon "abandon ... the revolution and its ideals for the sake of a few paltry 'comforts' and happiness.'" Maturity and strength of mind characterize older heroes, such as Hsu Yun-fong, who are treated with a special reverence. Sister Jiang, the most inspiring female figure, has entrusted her child to the care of others in order to play her

part in the revolutionary struggle. She attests that "my only worry is that the comrades may pamper the child, and spoil him!" When she sees her husband's decapitated head hanging in a cage as a warning to other revolutionaries, she responds, "Beng Soung-dao! Why aren't you leading your men against the enemy? Didn't we pledge to fight together'til the dawn of a new day?" Like the other heroes depicted in the novel, she focuses only on the future and is willing to sacrifice herself for the collective dream.

The narrative does much interpretive work for the reader, conveying that violence is a necessary part of the struggle and that hope never dies. Whenever the nationalists kill a comrade in a grotesque or cruel way, the audience is reassured through the voices of the heroic characters that "[e]very drop of blood they had shed would sow seeds of revenge!" or that "blood debts must be paid in blood, and the revolution will go on, even if only orphans and widows are left." Gruesome images appear infrequently but bear considerable weight. In the blood-soaked final passage, for example, a violent, individual death is imagistically forged to a future, collective life: "Before Ji Xiao-hsuan's glazing eyes rose a vision of countless golden starred red flags swirling and dancing in the breeze, and merging into a sea of crimson. His lips moved in a last smile."

At times, the text possesses a nearly manic energy that expresses the powerful sense of possibility in the early years of the People's Republic of China. Almost every paragraph ends in an exclamation point, particularly when the promise of a bright future is described: "Some day we'll sink oil wells in the Huaying mountains! A great steel bridge will span the Jialing River!. ...We'll also set up a monument to the martyrs who gave their lives for the revolution!" The text boils with emotion, such as in Sister Jiang's reaction to reading the courageous words of past revolutionaries: "Her eyes watered as she responded with her whole being to the militant call of the staunch fighters of yesterday."

CRITICAL DISCUSSION

Red Crag was positively received in China, even during the years of the Cultural Revolution (1966–76) when many other earlier revolutionary works were censured by communist critics. After it was first published, *Red Crag* enjoyed widespread public exposure. It was frequently quoted at literary events and on the radio, and went on to be adapted to television and film (*Eternal Life in Flames* [1965] and *Sister Jiang* [2003]). In addition, the jail where the story's heroes are imprisoned is now one of China's main "red tourism" sites. Today the book remains a best seller in China, a testament to how art can be an eloquent servant to politics.

Many early Western critics tended to scoff at novels of the social realist genre because, according to Herdan, they are "too predictable, too impersonal ... too lacking in complexity and altogether too much in one mould." However, Herdan acknowledges that these books "nevertheless have a certain charm. They speak with the confident voice of new China." The failure of Western audiences to appreciate these texts can be partially attributed to cultural differences. The books' idealism seems strange to contemporary readers, though the sincerity of the writing is rarely questioned as the novels were written for, by, and about people at the dawn of a new period of great promise.

Today *Red Crag* is primarily valued for what it adds to critical understandings of Chinese history and culture on the eve of liberation (when the novel is set) and during the post-Great Leap Forward period (when the novel was published). In *Heroes and Villains in Communist China: The Contemporary Chinese Novel as a Reflection of Life* (1973), Joe C. Huang argues that "it is possible to reconstruct life in China by focusing on the conduct of characters depicted by the novelists." Huang contends that novels such as *Red Crag* tell far more about Chinese life during this period than nonfiction documents such as newspapers and journals, which are generally awash in "Communist jargon."

BIBLIOGRAPHY

Sources

Herdan, Innes. *The Pen and the Sword: Literature and Revolution in Modern China.* London: Zed Books, 1992. Print.

Huang, Joe C. *Heroes and Villains in Communist China: The Contemporary Chinese Novel as a Reflection of Life.* New York: Pica, 1973. Print.

Lo, Kuang-pin, and Yang Yi-yen. *Red Crag.* Peking: Foreign Languages Press, 1978. Print.

Martin, Helmut. *Modern Chinese Writers: Self Portrayals.* Armonk: Sharpe, 1992. Print.

Paper, Jordan D. *Guide to Chinese Prose.* 2nd ed. Boston: Hall, 1984. Print.

Further Reading

Chao, Yang. "The Red Crag: A Modern Epic." *Chinese Literature* 5 (1965): 89–97. Print.

Fokkema, D. W. *Literary Doctrine in China and the Soviet Influence, 1956–1960.* The Hague: Mouton, 1965. Print.

Goldman, Merle. *Literary Dissent in Communist China.* Cambridge: Harvard UP, 1967. Print.

Hsia, C. T. *A History of Modern Chinese Fiction.* 3rd ed. Bloomington: Indiana UP, 1999. Print.

Terrell, Ross. *The China Difference.* New York: Harper & Row, 1979. Print.

Yang, Winston L. Y., and Nathan K. Mao, eds. *Modern Chinese Fiction: A Guide to Its Study and Appreciation: Essays and Bibliographies.* Boston: Hall, 1989. Print.

Media Adaptation

Eternal Life in the Flames (Red Crag). Dir. Shui Hua. Beijing Film Studio, 1965. Film.

Sarah Gardam

A 1928 drawing commenting on the Chinese Civil War. This war is the setting of *Red Crag,* a novel by the Chinese authors Lo Kuang-pin and Yang Yi-yen. SNARK/ART RESOURCE, NY.

RIDERS OF THE PURPLE SAGE

Zane Grey

OVERVIEW

Zane Grey's *Riders of the Purple Sage* (1912) is an iconic Western novel that demonizes Mormons as criminals and barbarians, and romanticizes the culture of the American West. Set in 1871, the novel follows wealthy ranch owner Jane Withersteen, who has incurred the displeasure of the leaders of her Mormon church because she befriends Gentiles (non-Mormons) and refuses to marry a church elder. She meets a man known only as Lassiter, an archetypal Western hero and a mysterious, purposeful, and deadly gunslinger with streaks of nobility and gentleness. Lassiter helps rescue Withersteen and her cohort from the Mormon leadership, and they ultimately escape to a secluded valley where they can live in peace, away from their persecutors. Throughout the novel, Grey characterizes Mormon church leaders as demonic specters moving silently in the night to kidnap and torture locals.

Grey's first major success, *Riders of the Purple Sage* was popular with readers as a pioneering work in the Western genre and because of its anti-Mormon sentiments. Over the preceding decades, the Mormon Church had been subject to pressure from the U.S. government to cease its illegal practice of performing polygamous marriages. Many Americans decried the practice of polygamy as both anti-Christian and anti-American. Despite the book's popularity with American readers, however, critics panned the work, calling Grey's prose an embarrassment. Nevertheless, the author continued to write, and readers, unconcerned about his lack of critical acclaim, devoured his novels. Many of his more than eighty books became best sellers, and his novels were frequently serialized in popular magazines between 1912 and 1940. Today, despite his famous anti-Mormon novel, Grey is best known as one of the first writers of the modern Western.

HISTORICAL AND LITERARY CONTEXT

Between 1890 and 1907, the Mormon Church came under fire for making allowances for polygamist practices. The Supreme Court decision in *Late Corporation of the Church of Jesus Christ of Latter-Day Saints v. United States* (1890) upheld the Edmunds-Tucker Act of May 19, 1890, which disincorporated the Church of Jesus Christ of Latter-day Saints, citing its polygamist practices as a leading reason. Facing continued scrutiny from government and public alike, in 1904

church president Joseph F. Smith released the "Second Manifesto," a declaration in which he insisted that the church was no longer sanctioning marriages that violated U.S. laws—and in which he announced a doctrine by which Mormons entering into or officiating polygamous marriages would be excommunicated.

Riders of the Purple Sage was inspired by Grey's personal interactions with Mormons living in southern Utah. In 1907, while on a journey with conservationist Buffalo Jones, Grey encountered isolated communities of Mormons living in the northern portions of the Grand Canyon. Grey claimed to have witnessed not only the ongoing practice of polygamy but also violent intolerance of Gentiles and any Mormons who befriended them. The structured, institutional malevolence he observed provided the foundation for the villains against which the novel pits the hero Lassiter, the gunslinging loner who would become an archetype in the mythology of the American West.

Although Grey is often credited as a pioneer of the Western genre, he was neither the first to write Western novels nor the first to vilify Mormons in popular fiction. Most scholars consider Owen Wister's most famous novel, *The Virginian* (1902), the first Western novel. Set against a highly mythologized version of the Johnson County War (a battle between Wyoming ranchers that took place in 1892), *The Virginian* tells the story of an eastern aristocrat who becomes the foreman of the Shiloh Ranch. Sir Arthur Conan Doyle's *A Study in Scarlet* (1889), the novel in which the famous fictional detective Sherlock Holmes makes his first appearance, set the precedent for anti-Mormon sentiments in popular fiction. Doyle's novel presents a biased depiction of the westward Mormon migration and the foundation of Salt Lake City, portraying Mormons as violent and intolerant zealots who systematically terrorized their neighbors and forced polygamous marriages on non-Mormon girls.

The publication of *Riders of the Purple Sage* was notable for the novel's marriage of two genres: Western and anti-Mormon literature. By meeting the demands of two reading audiences, Grey broadened his novel's appeal and expanded readership for the fledgling Western genre. His ornate prose and situational melodrama became hallmarks of the Western novel, providing a formula for later authors like Louis L'Amour, whose novels would sell more than 300 million copies worldwide

Mormon family with two wives and nine children about 1875. *Riders of the Purple Sage* details the struggles of one woman trying to overcome her persecution by members of the Mormon church. © BETTMANN/CORBIS.

and inspire nearly fifty film adaptations. *Riders of the Purple Sage* was adapted for the screen five times during the century following its publication, in 1918, 1925, 1931, 1941, and 1996.

THEMES AND STYLE

Although *Riders of the Purple Sage* explores standard Western themes, it also is dominated by anti-Mormon messages. Lassiter describes the Mormons who persecute Jane Withersteen as "blacker than hell" and "as far from Christlike as the universe is wide." Far worse than criminals, they behave like demons. The atrocities they commit are carried out by an "invisible hand," and, according to Lassiter, "they can think of things an' do things that are really hell-bent." Among many other misdeeds, they kidnap Lassiter's sister, Milly, and a child named Fay, and they horsewhip Lassiter as he attempts to rescue Bern Venters, one of Withersteen's friends. The Mormons' relentlessness and unequivocal malevolence marks them as unredeemable enemies of God.

Ironically, the novel's greatest rhetorical strength is the trait that critics most often cite in denouncing Grey's work: its "purple," or overly ornate, melodramatic prose. Elder Tull, a member of the Mormon council, is described as having "something … in him, barely hidden, a something personal and sinister, a deep of himself, an engulfing abyss." Later Tull exposes his inner evil, his violent zealotry, just prior to whipping Bern Venters: "As his religious mood was fanatical and inexorable, so would his physical hate be merciless." Grey's melodramatic prose, which was

especially appealing to the average serial novel reader of the early twentieth century, stamped on the popular imagination the image of the Mormon church as a cold and ruthless institution similar to an organized crime syndicate.

The tone of the novel is romantic and overwrought, as characters both rejoice and brood over a highly stylized Western landscape. Grey describes how Withersteen's "strained gaze sought the sage-slopes. In times of sorrow it had been her strength, in happiness its beauty was her continual delight." A lengthy description of the proverbial calm before the storm precedes each violent encounter. Only pages before Lassiter is shot, Venters and Bess, a young woman who is revealed to be the daughter of Lassiter's kidnapped sister, stroll through a knell that "bloomed into a paradise," swimming "in thick, transparent haze, golden at dawn, warm and white at noon, purple in the twilight." Even violent moments are romanticized: during a horse chase, amid heavy gunfire, Venters perceives on each side of him "the sage merged into a sailing, colorless wall … its purple breadth split by the white trail." Grey's overindulgent prose paints a pure and ethereal backdrop against which the Mormon villains appear all the more abominable and depraved.

CRITICAL DISCUSSION

During Grey's lifetime, most critics panned his novels, even as their popularity soared. In a 2001 article for *Smithsonian*, Jake Page recalls newspaper columnist and critic Heywood Broun's reaction to Grey's oeuvre: "the plots of any two of Zane Grey's books could be written

PRIMARY SOURCE

EXCERPT FROM *RIDERS OF THE PURPLE SAGE*

"Lassiter, I needn't tell you the rest."

"Well, it'd be no news to me. I know Mormons. I've seen their women's strange love en' patience en' sacrifice an' silence en' whet I call madness for their idea of God. An' over against that I've seen the tricks of men. They work hand in hand, all together, an' in the dark. No man can hold out against them, unless he takes to packin' guns. For Mormons are slow to kill. That's the only good I ever seen in their religion. Venters, take this from me, these Mormons ain't just right in their minds. Else could a Mormon marry one woman when he already has a wife, an' call it duty?"

"Lassiter, you think as I think," returned Venters.

"How'd it come then that you never throwed a gun on Tull or some of them?" inquired the rider, curiously.

"Jane pleaded with me, begged me to be patient, to overlook. She even took my guns from me. I lost all before I knew it," replied Venters, with the red color in his face. "But, Lassiter, listen. Out of the wreck I saved a Winchester, two Colts, and plenty of shells. I packed these down into Deception Pass. There, almost every day for six months, I have practiced with my rifle till the barrel burnt my hands. Practised the draw—the firing of a Colt, hour after hour!"

"Now that's interestin' to me," said Lassiter, with a quick uplift of his head and a concentration of his gray gaze on Venters. "Could you throw a gun before you began that practisin'?"

"Yes. And now..." Venters made a lightning-swift movement.

Lassiter smiled, and then his bronzed eyelids narrowed till his eyes seemed mere gray slits. "You'll kill Tull!" He did not question; he affirmed.

"I promised Jane Withersteen I'd try to avoid Tull. I'll keep my word. But sooner or later Tull and I will meet. As I feel now, if he even looks at me I'll draw!"

on the back of a postage stamp." Page describes how another critic likened the ranchmen in *Riders of the Purple Sage* to purple cows, adding that he didn't "believe in them—or the book." Publishers shared some critics' hesitation regarding the novel's anti-Mormon themes and initially rejected the book. Only a 1912 *New York Times* review seemed to give *Riders of the Purple Sage* a favorable reading, calling it a "thrilling, well-constructed, and well-told story … better balanced in its component elements, [and] deeper and more poignant in its emotional qualities" than other Westerns.

Riders of the Purple Sage stands out among Grey's works as one of only two to offer overt political or social commentary. The other, titled *The Vanishing American* (1925), harshly criticized both the federal government and Christian missionaries for their treatment of the Navajo Nation in the late nineteenth century. Although Grey was criticized for his heavy-handed moralizing in both works, between 1917 and 1925 nine of his titles sold more than one hundred thousand copies each, and each made a Top Ten bestseller list. Thus, for all of Grey's commentary on the evils of the Mormon Church, it appears that it has been his embellished prose that has garnered the most attention from critics and readers.

Contemporary scholarship tends to eschew political and social concerns in favor of placing *Riders of the Purple Sage* in the tradition of the Western genre. In a 2006 article for *Criticism,* Alan Bourassa draws a direct line from Grey's novel to *The Crossing* (1994), by contemporary Western writer Cormac McCarthy, elucidating the ways in which each novelist relies on, and complicates, the relationships of the characters and the story to the landscape. Bourassa argues, "We can see in *The Crossing* the embryonic *Purple Sage* carried along in McCarthy's reckless creative momentum." For Bourassa, *The Crossing* illustrates a "conventional tale of ownership unfold[ing] into a tale of the very impossibility of" ownership. By placing Grey's novel in the context of the evolving Western genre, critics generally overlook the book's anti-Mormon themes, instead focusing on Grey's profound influence on later Western writers.

BIBLIOGRAPHY

Sources

Bourassa, Alan. "Riders of the Virtual Sage: Zane Grey, Cormac McCarthy, and the Transformation of the Popular Western." *Criticism* 48.4 (2006): 433–52. *Academic Search Complete.* Web. 25 July 2012.

"A Good Western Novel." Rev. of *Riders of the Purple Sage,* by Zane Grey. *New York Times* 18 Feb. 1912: 82. *ProQuest Historical Newspapers.* Web. 25 July 2012.

Grey, Zane. *Riders of the Purple Sage.* Roslyn: W. J. Black, 1940. Print.

Gruber, Frank. *Zane Grey: A Biography.* Mattituck: Aeonian, 1969. Print.

"I reckon so. There'll be hell down there, presently." He paused a moment and flicked a sage-brush with his quirt. "Venters, seein' as you're considerable worked up, tell me Milly Erne's story."

Venters's agitation stilled to the trace of suppressed eagerness in Lassiter's query.

"Milly Erne's story? Well, Lassiter, I'll tell you what I know. Milly Erne had been in Cottonwoods years when I first arrived there, and most of what I tell you happened before my arrival. I got to know her pretty well. She was a slip of a woman, and crazy on religion. I conceived an idea that I never mentioned—I thought she was at heart more Gentile than Mormon. But she passed as a Mormon, and certainly she had the Mormon woman's locked lips. You know, in every Mormon village there are women who seem mysterious to us, but about Milly there was more than the ordinary mystery. When she came to Cottonwoods she had a beautiful little girl whom she loved passionately. Milly was not known openly in Cottonwoods as a Mormon wife. That she really was a Mormon wife I have no doubt. Perhaps the Mormon's other wife or wives would not acknowledge Milly. Such things happen in these villages. Mormon wives wear yokes, but they get jealous. Well, whatever had brought Milly to this country—love or madness of religion—she repented of it. She gave up teaching the village school. She quit the church. And she began to fight Mormon upbringing for her baby girl. Then the Mormons put on the screws—slowly, as is their way. At last the child disappeared. 'Lost' was the report. The child was stolen, I know that. So do you. That wrecked Milly Erne. But she lived on in hope. She became a slave. She worked her heart and soul and life out to get back her child. She never heard of it again. Then she sank.... I can see her now, a frail thing, so transparent you could almost look through her—white like ashes—and her eyes!... Her eyes have always haunted me. She had one real friend—Jane Withersteen. But Jane couldn't mend a broken heart, and Milly died."

For moments Lassiter did not speak, or turn his head.

May, Stephen J. *Zane Grey: Romancing the West.* Athens: Ohio UP, 1997. Print.

Page, Jake. "Writer of the Purple Prose." *Smithsonian* 32.9 (2001): 84. *Academic Search Complete.* Web. 25 July 2012.

Further Reading

Cervo, Nathan A. Rev. of *Riders of the Purple Sage,* by Zane Grey. *Explicator* 55.4 (1997): 214–15. *Academic OneFile.* Web. 25 July 2012.

Corbett, Christopher. *Orphans Preferred: The Twisted Truth and Lasting Legend of the Pony Express.* New York: Broadway, 2003. Print.

Lyon, Thomas J. *The Literary West: An Anthology of Western American Literature.* New York: Oxford UP, 1999. Print.

Manley, Will. "The Manley Arts: Game-Changing Westerns." *Booklist* 106.22 (2010): 13. *Academic Search Complete.* Web. 25 July 2012.

"The New Books: *Riders of the Purple Sage.*" Rev. of *Riders of the Purple Sage,* by Zane Grey. *Outlook* 3 Feb. 1912: 289. Print.

Powell, Lawrence C. *Southwest Classics: The Creative Literature of the Arid Lands: Essays on the Books and Their Writers.* Los Angeles: Ritchie, 1974. Print.

Media Adaptations

Riders of the Purple Sage. Dir. Frank Lloyd. Perf. William Farnum, William Scott, and Marc Robbins. Fox Film Corporation, 1918. Film.

Riders of the Purple Sage. Dir. James Tinling. Ed. Nick De Maggio. Cast George Montgomery, Mary Howard, Robert Barrat, et al. Twentieth Century-Fox, 1941. Film.

Riders of the Purple Sage. Dir. Lynn Reynolds. Cast Tom Mix, Marion Nixon, Warner Oland, et al. Phot. Daniel Clark. Grapevine Video, © 1995. VHS.

Clint Garner

THIS SIDE OF INNOCENCE

Rashid al-Daif

OVERVIEW

This Side of Innocence (1997), a novel by Lebanese writer Rashid al-Daif, focuses on an unnamed narrator who is accused of ripping a poster and then must endure a series of interrogations in which he attempts to prove his innocence. Written in unadorned prose, the novel blends the narrator's scattered thoughts and detailed recitation of events with his nightmares and hallucinations, making it difficult for the reader to determine the truth of what occurred. Although it is unclear where and when the story takes place, the novel is most often read in the context of the Lebanese Civil War (1975–90), which proved to be the most devastating conflict in the country's history. Through an exploration of the institutional anxiety and scapegoating that accompany life in a war-torn nation, *This Side of Innocence* exposes the effects of suppression and dissent on the psychology of the individual.

Published seven years after the official end of the Lebanese Civil War, the novel contributes to the sizable corpus of war and postwar literature. The extreme violence and sectarianism of the war, which pitted religious and political factions against each other and left more than 100,000 dead, led to a wave of literary experimentation as old narrative forms and styles proved incapable of representing contemporary society and authors therefore sought new methods of expression. The stripped-down language, interior monologue, and fragmented narrative of *This Side of Innocence,* coupled with an intense focus on the threat and use of violence, identifies the novel as an important and powerful work of postwar Lebanese literature.

HISTORICAL AND LITERARY CONTEXT

The trauma of the Lebanese Civil War, which lasted for fifteen years, continued to haunt the people of Lebanon, especially the residents of Beirut, even after an official cease fire brought an end to the most brutal violence. During the war, the capital had been divided into West Beirut, which was primarily Muslim, and East Beirut, which was mostly Christian. These zones were further fragmented into heavily policed, autonomous political areas under the control of individual militias. Both the economy and the state collapsed, and an entire generation of Lebanese grew up in a war zone. The divisions that had driven so much of the fighting were not erased during peace negotiations

but rather became the framework for institutionalized power-sharing arrangements in the aftermath of the war. Disarmament proceeded slowly and was never completed, and the threat of civil and foreign violence persisted.

In the postwar period, politicians espousing interconfessional reconciliation often adopted the "No Victor, No Vanquished" approach to compromise that had been utilized in the wake of earlier episodes of civil strife in Lebanon. The politics of calculated forgetting was accompanied by efforts to forge a national Lebanese identity, but postwar elections revealed the importance of sect and the continued centrality of formal power-sharing arrangements, which in turn sustained the country's fragmentation. Disloyalty to one's own sect was often seen as a betrayal, making dissension dangerous and an individual's communal or religious identity enough to warrant the label of enemy.

Lebanese authors writing during the civil war and its aftermath discovered that traditional modes of expression failed to adequately capture their contemporary experiences. As a result, writers such as Elias Khoury, Hanan al-Shaykh, Ghada Samman, and Hoda Barakat began to experiment with new narrative forms and styles and in the process created a significant corpus of literature centered on the Lebanese Civil War. Al-Daif was also involved in this movement from early on, publishing several works throughout the 1980s, including *Passage to Dusk* (1986), which focuses on the effects of war and violence on the narrator's interiority.

Upon its translation into English, *This Side of Innocence* received positive reviews praising al-Daif's ability to blur the inner landscape of his narrator with external reality through the manipulation of style and form. However, the text's subtle exploration of the impact of tyranny on the psychology of the individual has largely been overshadowed by al-Daif's more direct treatment of the Lebanese Civil War in *Passage to Dusk* and *Dear Mr. Kawabata* (1995)—although these other texts employ many of the same narrative techniques.

THEMES AND STYLE

This Side of Innocence is centrally concerned with the question, what does it mean to be innocent and who has the right to determine guilt? The contents of the ripped poster and its significance are never described, although the poster likely bears a picture of a politician or a martyr. The narrator knows that defacement of the poster is dangerous because "at the very least, such an act meant defiance." However, despite his protestations of innocence, he becomes increasingly convinced of his own guilt since he had always wanted to rip the poster and had taken steps in the past to prevent himself from doing so. He behaves in a manner that suggests he is guilty of something, such as when he suddenly decides to eat his address book while waiting for his interrogators. The narrator even repeatedly expresses sympathy for his interrogators and their point of view. Essentially, he has so internalized the external mechanisms of oppression that he begins to suspect himself and aid in the suppression of his own disobedience.

Al-Daif explores the damaging effects of suppression of dissent on the psyche through the use of interior monologue. The narrator's internal fantasies and hallucinations blur with external reality until it is no longer clear to what extent his suffering and fear are purely psychological. There are no chapter headings or section breaks to interrupt the narrative, which unfolds without ever providing release from the building tension. As a result, the unstable, fractured narrative invites the reader to sanction the narrator's psychological and physical torture as a means of organizing it and finally revealing the truth. As the tension escalates, the reader, like the interrogators, begins to focus on uncovering the source of the narrator's guilt in order to effect resolution.

Stylistically, *This Side of Innocence* is written in simple, straightforward prose, which distinguishes it from traditional Arabic lyricism and underscores the extent to which horrors have become commonplace. When the narrator decides he must eat his address book to conceal the names he has written in it, he does so with cool logic: "Oh, if only I could swallow it up. … So, why not eat it? It was small enough, and lightweight; the only difficult part would be the cover." Finally, at the end of novel, he decides to stand up to his interrogators, but this determination, rather than bringing the narrative under his control, causes it to completely unravel. Stream of consciousness and hallucinations replace any semblance of structure as the tension between the narrator's certainty of his own guilt and suspicion of his own innocence fractures his psyche.

CRITICAL DISCUSSION

When *This Side of Innocence* was first translated into English in 2001, it was enthusiastically received as a nonlocalized critique of oppression and its effect on the individual. Critic Issa J. Boullata, writing in 2001 for *World Literature Today*, praises al-Daif's attempt "to describe a human being's predicament and mangled life under tyranny." Writing in the *Middle East Studies Association Bulletin* in 2001, Alexander E. Elinson echoes Boullata, asserting that al-Daif "has effectively

AUTOBIOGRAPHY IN THE FICTION OF RASHID AL-DAIF

Rashid al-Daif was born in 1945 in a Maronite Christian village in northern Lebanon. After studying in Beirut, he traveled to France, where he earned his doctorate. He then returned to teach at the Lebanese University in Beirut. During the Civil War, he lived in Ras-Beirut, a neighborhood located in West Beirut, where a majority of Muslims lived. The climate was such that many who had chosen to live apart from their own sect had to adopt false identities to avoid being kidnapped or killed.

Several of al-Daif's narrators are also named Rashid and frequently share identifying details with the author, blurring the line between fiction and autobiography. For example, one day while crossing into East Beirut, al-Daif was severely wounded by a bomb, and he spent two months in the hospital, almost losing his arm. The narrator in *Passage to Dusk* (1986) undergoes a similar ordeal, demonstrating how the author's own intimate encounter with violence informs his treatment of trauma and fear in his fiction.

communicated the feeling of a political and social system in which the arbiters of truth and justice use intimidation and torture to extract, or create, the truth." In an afterward to the 2001 English translation, Adnan Haydar and Michael Beard focus on the text's universality, comparing the form of *This Side of Innocence* to George Orwell's *1984* and Sonallah Ibrahim's *The Committee*. However, they argue that al-Daif manipulates these familiar structures by providing no more than a rough sketch of the society in which it is set.

Although *This Side of Innocence* takes place in an unnamed place and time, scholars have recognized the text as part of a broader trend in postwar Lebanese literature focused on the prolonged effects of violence and sectarianism. In his 2005 essay in *Geomodernisms: Race, Modernism, Modernity*, Ken Seigneurie explores the "continuities between the war and postwar periods" evident in the novel. Arguing that the narrator "embodies an idealized Enlightenment rationality," Seigneurie asserts, "the novel thematizes not the perpetuation of violence, which is all but assumed as normative, but rather the blindnesses and self-deceptions of reason faced with violence." Thus, the novel investigates the rationalization of violence of the civil war and how this became a coping method during the conflict and its aftermath, without directly addressing the event itself.

This Side of Innocence has received little scholarly attention in its own right, although it contains many of the same stylistic features that scholars have noted in their broader study of al-Daif's work. For example, in a 1996 essay for *International Journal of Middle East Studies*, Mona Takieddine Amyuni

A jail cell is featured at the Stasi Museum in Leipzig, Germany, that is dedicated to educating the public about the Stasi, the notorious, disbanded East German secret police force. The secret police force of an unnamed country questions the protagonist of *This Side of Innocence,* a novel by Rashid al-Daif. © IAIN MASTERTON/ ALAMY.

explores the implications of the author's innovative style in several of his other texts, in which he employs the same kind of "language stripped to its bare essentials." According to Amyuni, his writing reveals his "will to regenerate [language] from within, bringing a revolution not only to style but to the frame of thinking itself."

Sources

Amyuni, Mona Takieddine. "Style as Politics in the Poems and Novels of Rashid al-Daif." *International Journal of Middle East Studies* 28.2 (1996): 177–92. Print.

Boullata, Issa J. Rev. of *This Side of Innocence,* by Rashid al-Daif. *World Literature Today* 75.3–4 (2001): 229. Print.

Elinson, Alexander E. Rev. of *This Side of Innocence,* by Rashid al-Daif. *Middle East Studies Association Bulletin* 35 (2001): 217. Print.

Seigneurie, Ken. "Ongoing War and Arab Humanism." *Geomodernisms: Race, Modernism, Modernity.* Ed. Laura Doyle and Laura A. Winkiel. Bloomington: Indiana UP, 2005. 96–113. Print.

Further Reading

Al-Daif, Rashid. *Passage to Dusk.* Trans. Nirvana Tanoukhi. Austin: U of Texas P, 2001. Print.

Fisk, Robert. *Pity the Nation: The Abduction of Lebanon.* New York: Thunder's Mouth, 2003. Print.

Ibrahim, Sonallah. *The Committee.* Trans. Mary St. Germain and Charlene Constable. Syracuse: Syracuse UP, 2001. Print.

Khoury, Elias. *Little Mountain.* Trans. Maia Tabet. Minneapolis: U of Minnesota P, 1989. Print.

Traboulsi, Fawwaz. *A History of Modern Lebanon.* 2nd ed. London: Pluto, 2012. Print.

Allison Blecker

THE TURNER DIARIES

William Luther Pierce III

OVERVIEW

Published under the pseudonym Andrew Macdonald, William Luther Pierce III's futuristic novel *The Turner Diaries* (1978) valorizes violent revolution as a means of achieving Aryan supremacy. The novel is set in a post-apocalyptic twenty-first-century society, where the diary of Earl Turner, leader of the late-twentieth-century "Great Revolution," has been discovered. Framed by an introduction and epilogue from an editor named Andrew Macdonald, Turner's diary outlines his participation in an underground society known as the Organization. It chronicles the Organization's rebellion against the repressive policies and Zionism of the U.S. government and ends with Turner poised for a suicide mission against the Pentagon. Macdonald's epilogue traces the ensuing global nuclear war and wholesale slaughter of non-Aryans.

Written at a time when the United States was undergoing rapid social change, *The Turner Diaries* rejects attempts at racial integration and social equality for racial and religious minorities. The work was initially serialized in Pierce's propagandistic white nationalist periodical *Attack!* with the first installment appearing in January 1975. Its distribution was largely limited to the far-right-wing extremist circles in which its author was a prominent figure. The novel was subsequently published in book form in 1978 and continued to circulate in white supremacist circles throughout the 1980s and early 1990s. It would not reach mainstream audiences in any significant way until 1995, when it was cited as an influence on Timothy McVeigh's bombing of the Alfred P. Murrah Federal Building in Oklahoma City. Following the bombing, the work has received increased scrutiny from both scholars and readers and is considered among the most prominent and influential works of extremist fiction ever published.

HISTORICAL AND LITERARY CONTEXT

The Turner Diaries reacts against the social changes of the 1960s and 1970s, most notably the civil rights and anti-Vietnam War movements. Pierce vehemently opposed legislation outlawing the separation of people based on race and the growing acceptance of romantic relationships between people of different races. He saw the anti-war movement as a reflection of the growing power of Jewish communists around the world. Prior

to writing the novel, Pierce, a former physics professor alarmed by the progressive changes he witnessed on the campus of Oregon State University, established himself as a leading voice of white nationalism. In 1974 he founded the National Alliance, a white supremacist organization, as a means of advocating white separatism and eugenics.

When *The Turner Diaries* began to circulate in the mid-1970s, it helped to galvanize America's white nationalists. Though his ideas were clearly on the fringes, Pierce had many followers and supporters. In the decades following its publication, the work has been associated with numerous hate crimes and acts of domestic terrorism. In addition to the Oklahoma City bombing, which killed 168 people and wounded more than 800 others, the work has been linked to the 1980s crime spree of "The Order," a white supremacist organization that took its name from Pierce's novel; the racially motivated dragging death of James Byrd (1998); and the murders committed by British neo-Nazi David Copeland in London in 1999.

The Turner Diaries is part of a tradition of militaristic hate literature associated with white nationalism and anti-Semitism. In writing the novel, Pierce is believed to have been influenced by Eugene Methvin's *The Riot Makers* (1970) and *The John Franklin Letters* (1959), a work of propagandistic fiction produced by the John Birch Society. He apparently borrowed heavily from both the plot and structure of the latter, which offers a retrospective account of a revolution carried out by Aryan patriots against the forces of global communism. Pierce's novel has also drawn critical comparison to Adolf Hitler's *Mein Kampf,* which in many ways has served as a foundational work for writers and thinkers such as Pierce. The propagandistic appeals for action that are central to Hitler's autobiography find parallel in Pierce's novel, in which Hitler is referred to as "The Great One" and his birth date celebrated as a holiday.

More than three decades after its initial publication, *The Turner Diaries* remains popular among far right extremists. It has served as a model for contemporary extremist works of fiction and nonfiction such as *Patriots: Surviving the Coming Collapse* (1999) by James Wesley Rawles and *Enemies Foreign and Domestic* (2003) by Matthew Bracken. Writing for the *Intelligence Report,* the journal of the Southern Poverty Law

✦ Key Facts

Time Period:
Late 20th Century

Genre:
Novel

Events:
Civil rights movement; desegregation; rise of white nationalism

Nationality:
American

William Luther Pierce III outside his home in West Virginia in 2001. Behind him is a Nordic rune meant to symbolize white power. © SCOTT HOUSTON/SYGMA/CORBIS.

As a piece of propaganda, *The Turner Diaries* works by encouraging its readers to identify with and admire the members of the Organization, particularly its leadership, an elite circle called the Order. Turner's diary describes the members of the Order as "real men, White men … the best my race has produced … combin[ing] fiery passion and icy discipline, deep intelligence and instant readiness for action." Pierce goes to great lengths to differentiate the white supremacists of the Order from the more typical or simpleminded whites. One method he employs to achieve this rhetorical goal is the fervent denunciation of unintelligent and easily manipulated members of the white race. Readers are invited to view themselves as superior to these unsophisticated tools of the government and to identify with members of the Order, who are romanticized as noble rebels—guerrilla soldiers fighting for rights that have been taken away from them by an oppressive government that is controlled by and serves the inferior races. Pierce's strategy is effective as propaganda because, like the movement led by Hitler and the Nazi Party, it establishes those who would commit horrendous crimes against humanity as the victims of overwhelming oppression and bias. It also exhorts its readers to emulate such figures rather than prove themselves to be among the easily manipulated.

Stylistically, *The Turner Diaries* is marked by its accessible prose, overt didacticism, and graphic violence, all of which contribute to its strength as propaganda. In a 2009 article in the *Journal of American Culture*, Rob McAlear examines the target of the work, suggesting that Pierce "has in mind an audience of gun enthusiasts and those that identify with right supremacist groups" and traces how the narrative exploits the perceived vulnerability of this group to specific tactics of propaganda. For readers drawn in by the author's rhetoric, the novel offers descriptions of bomb making and other subversive activities in such detail that numerous critics have referred to the book as a "how-to manual" for terrorists. The novel is also graphically violent and detailed in its descriptions of war, especially the mass hangings that occur on "the Day of the Rope," which Turner's diary labels as "a grim and bloody day, but an unavoidable one." Outlining the events of the day, he describes a scene in which "tens of thousands of lampposts, power poles, and trees throughout this vast metropolitan area the grisly forms hang … each with an identical placard around its neck bearing the printed legend, 'I betrayed my race.'" The novel maintains a similarly emotionally charged tone throughout as Turner adamantly praises his comrades, decries his enemies, or rants about the philosophical underpinnings of the movement in ways that invite sympathy from the reader.

Center, Camille Jackson notes that the copycat works spawned by Pierce's novel "span every category of extremism—neo-Nazi, neo-Confederate, radical environmentalist, anti-immigration, antigovernment—but most stick to Pierce's formula: a white male hero, learning of a massive conspiracy against law-abiding whites, undertakes violent revenge." Pierce would go on to write a second novel, *Hunter* (1984), which extends the themes and ideas of *The Turner Diaries*. The novel tells the story of Oscar Yeager, a veteran of the Vietnam War who murders mixed-raced couples in an attempt to establish white supremacy.

THEMES AND STYLE

The central theme of *The Turner Diaries* is that the white race is inherently superior to all others and that lesser races, as well as inferior members of the white race, must be eliminated if an ideal society is to emerge. Pierce also insists that governments that protect the rights of non-Aryans and limit the freedoms of Aryans are repressive and unjust. Turner's rebellion is set off by an act of government suppression—the Cohen Act, which terminates the right to gun ownership and allows the government to confiscate weapons from civilians. Following the act's passage, Turner's subversive society, the Organization, is forced underground and begins its battle against the Zionist-Occupied Government (ZOG) and its economic and media collaborators, collectively known as the System.

CRITICAL DISCUSSION

When *The Turner Diaries* was first serialized in *Attack!* it developed a following among extremist groups on the far right, its popularity fueled by word of mouth. Mail-order sales were brisk for a self-published work. Enthusiastic fans of the work, among them Timothy McVeigh, were known to distribute the novel at events such as gun shows that attracted fellow extremists. Although Pierce bragged in the book's introduction that he had already sold 200,000 copies, the novel was not widely available outside of extremist circles and was not broadly reviewed in the mainstream press.

The Turner Diaries fell under increased media and scholarly scrutiny after it was revealed to be one of McVeigh's inspirations for the Oklahoma City bombing. It was frequently discussed in articles addressing the attack. Journalists took notice of the book's overtly racist propaganda, and it drew protest from groups such as the Anti-Defamation League, which saw it as an attempt at race baiting and inciting violence. As some scholars have pointed out, however, post-Oklahoma City bombing scrutiny of the text has tended toward superficiality and sensationalism. Writing in *Nova Religio* in 1998, Brad Whitsel asserts, for example, that "as a consequence of the shallow treatment of the novel and its author by the media, the religious vision of *The Turner Diaries* remains underexplored by academic and law enforcement groups." What literary scholarship of the text exists has tended to focus on the work as a piece of propaganda or to consider it within the context of Pierce's political activism and other writings.

Contemporary scholarship typically concentrates on *The Turner Diaries* as a work of explicit propaganda and its potential to incite extremists. Political science scholars Terence Ball and Richard Dagger neatly summarize the propagandist impact of the novel in their 1997 article "Inside *The Turner Diaries*: Neo-Nazi Scripture," in which they note that "here, in a nutshell, is the essence of Nazi, and now neo-nazi, ideology: racial differences are innate and indelible; they lie at the root of all social and political problems; races being unequal and incompatible, people of different races cannot live together in peace or harmony." McAlear examines how Pierce shapes his narrative to his propagandistic purposes, using a relatable "rank and file" Turner as an object of sympathy and the objective narrator as a voice of authority who offers commentary on the future brought about through Turner's sacrifice.

BIBLIOGRAPHY

Sources

Applebome, Peter. "Terror in Oklahoma: The Background; A Bombing Foretold in Extreme-Right 'Bible.'" *New York Times.* New York Times, 26 Apr. 1995. Web. 28 June 2012.

Ball, Terence, and Richard Dagger. "Inside *The Turner Diaries*: Neo-Nazi Scripture." *PS: Political Science & Politics* Dec. 1997. *General OneFile.* Web. 28 June 2012.

Jackson, Camille. "The Turner Diaries, Other Racist Novels, Inspire Extremist Violence." *Intelligence Report.* Southern Poverty Law Center, Fall 2004. Web. 28 June 2012.

McAlear, Rob. "Hate, Narrative, and Propaganda in *The Turner Diaries*." *Journal of American Culture* 32.3 (2009): 192–202. Print.

Macdonald, Andrew. *The Turner Diaries.* Hillsboro: National Vanguard, 1978. Print.

Whitsel, Brad. "*The Turner Diaries* and Cosmotheism: William Pierce's Theology." *Nova Religio: The Journal of Alternative and Emergent Religions* 1.2 (1998): 183–97. Print.

Further Reading

Brodie, Renee. "The Aryan New Era: Apocalyptic Realizations in *The Turner Diaries*." *Journal of American Culture* 12:3 (1998): 13–22. Print.

Griffin, Robert S. *The Fame of A Dead Man's Deeds: An Up-Close Portrait of White Nationalist William Pierce.* Fairfield: 1st Book, 2001. Print.

Lockard, Joe. "Reading *The Turner Diaries*: Jewish Blackness, Judaized Blacks and Head-Body Race Paradigms." *Complicating Constructions: Race, Ethnicity, and Hybridity in American Texts.* Ed. Davis S. Goldstein and Audrey B. Thacker. Seattle: U of Washington P, 2007. 121–39. Print.

Macdonald, Andrew. *Hunter.* Hillsboro: National Vanguard, 1989. Print.

Mirabello, Mark. *Handbook for Rebels and Outlaws.* Oxford: Mandrake, 2009. Print.

Perkinson, Jim. "The Color of the Enemy in the New Millennium." *Cross Currents: The Journal of the Association for Religion and Intellectual Life* 50.3 (2000): 349–68. Print.

Swain, Carol M., and Russ Nieli. *Contemporary Voices of White Nationalism in America.* Cambridge: Cambridge UP, 2003. Print.

Colby Cuppernull

VILLAGE POLITICS

Hannah More

OVERVIEW

Published in 1792, Hannah More's *Village Politics* is a short dialogue between two working-class men that defends the socio-economic hierarchies of late-eighteenth-century England and explodes the republican principles of equality and liberty that motivated the French Revolution and that gained widespread currency in Britain. *Village Politics* is in part a response to the controversial influence of Thomas Paine's *Rights of Man* (1791–1792) among the working classes—the "mechanics, journeyman, and day labourers" to whom it is addressed. In the work itself, Tom Hod, the mason, consults his copy of Paine's work and uncritically parrots the radical ideas expressed therein, only to have them refuted and exposed by Jack Anvil, a blacksmith aware of, and content with, his position in the world. The conversation between the two was More's propagandistic attempt to dissuade a restless populace from overthrowing what More claimed, through Jack Anvil, was a peaceful and well-ordered society.

More went to some lengths to conceal her authorship, using both a pseudonym (Will Chip, a "country carpenter") and a publisher different from her own to distance herself from a work that embarrassed her because it was addressed to the "ignorant" and not to the "polished" elites to whom she usually catered. *Village Politics* was remarkably successful and circulated widely, partly on account of its affordability (2 pence) and the assistance of the Association for Preserving Liberty and Property, which distributed a large number of free copies. Powerful religious figures (such as the bishop of London), celebrated literati (including Horace Walpole), and even the royal family expressed admiration for the work. The dialogue format and simple language of *Village Politics* made it a powerful physic against the radical ideas of Thomas Paine and a convincing vindication of the status quo.

HISTORICAL AND LITERARY CONTEXT

The outbreak of the French Revolution in 1789 inaugurated an era of intense debate, fear, and concern in Great Britain. The reformist energies unleashed in Paris motivated British radicals to press for change at home, and in the early 1790s a healthy body of radical literature appeared whose circulation was aided by the establishment of a vast network of revolutionary societies across Britain. The violence of the French Revolution, coupled with the ascendancy of radicalism among all segments of the British population, soon generated a counterrevolution, an attempt by more conservative thinkers such as Edmund Burke to counter the propaganda of the radical press with their own canon of loyalist literature. The increase in counterrevolutionary publications was complemented by the British government's attempts to discourage revolution and reassert its primacy, initially by prosecuting radical writers and publishers for sedition and later by instituting increasingly repressive measures.

The popularity of radical literature among the working classes was particularly disconcerting to many conservatives, including More, given the widespread belief that their dearth of intellectual ability and education made them more likely to translate radical literature into precipitous, mob violence. It was in 1792 that the bishop of London visited More and encouraged her to "write some little thing, tending to open their [the working class] eyes under their present wild impressions of liberty and equality." More's long experience as an educator among the "lower" orders made her acutely aware of the danger their ingestion and adoption of Painite propaganda could have for the nation as a whole, a danger reflected in Jack Anvil's account of the potentially destructive consequences of his wife's desire to "do everything like the French."

In many ways *Village Politics* was a conservative rejoinder to Paine's *Rights of Man*, a work that had also appealed to the working classes, albeit less aggressively. More's immediate literary antecedents include other popular loyalist tracts and dialogues, such as William Jones's John Bull letters (1792), a series of epistolary exchanges between the Bull brothers, and, less directly, the vast body of cheap, instructive literature of the later eighteenth century designed for the poor, such as Sarah Trimmer's "Village Dialogues" (1789).

More's successful deployment of the dialogue form in the loyalist crusade influenced future endeavors in the same cause, including William Paley's *Equality* (1793), a dialogue between a "Master-Manufacturer and one of His Workmen," and the anonymous *Dialogue between a Labourer and a Gentleman* (1793), in which the laborer's reading of Paine's *Rights of Man* generates a corrective maneuver by the gentleman. More's work in a popular format invigorated her commitment to educating the working classes, and *Village Politics* is often seen as the precursor to her more widely recognized *Cheap Repository Tracts* (1795–1798), a series of less overtly political narratives, dialogues, and ballads devoted to educating and forming the lower orders into a subordinate, god-fearing populace. *Village Politics* is today recognized as both an important document of British loyalism and an instrumental text in the development of working-class reading audiences.

THEMES AND STYLE

The central theme of *Village Politics* is that French notions of equality and liberty, mediated through the work of Thomas Paine, represent a vile threat to what is a peaceful, charitable, and virtuous British socio-political order. The end results of French "levelling," Jack tells Tom, are ominous: "there will be no'firmaries, no hospitals, no charity-schools, no Sunday-schools." Inequalities certainly exist, Jack concedes, but a complete overthrow of the fabric of British social life through "riot and murder" is not the answer. Class hierarchies, in addition to the harmonious division of labor they necessarily ensure, are part of the divine order of the universe ("Providence"). Obedience to the laws of government is merely an extension of one's obedience to God. "The powers that be are ordained of God," Jack tells Tom in one of several scriptural passages that pepper *Village Politics*. Like much political writing in the early 1790s, *Village Politics* takes an extreme position, one that ignores the very real inequalities exposed by British radicals and instead encourages readers to adopt the complacent response of Tom Hod toward the end: "I begin to think we're better off as we are."

The conversational structure of *Village Politics* allows More to stage a hypothetical refutation of French revolutionary principles; the work proceeds with Tom espousing the tenets of British radicalism, only to have them debunked by Jack as thinly veiled justifications for violence. Thus, toward the end of the dialogue, Jack explains that "French Liberty" is really an attempt to "murder more men in one night than ever their poor king did in his whole life," whereas equality is "for every man to pull down every one that is above him, till they're all as low as the lowest." Alongside these more straightforward redefinitions, Jack also borrows metaphors from scripture and classical literature to buttress his claim that the upper and lower classes are both essential components in a project of mutual beneficence. The nation is like a body, with a "Belly and Limbs," Jack says. The limbs (the lower orders) carry the belly (the upper classes), and the belly nourishes the limbs.

Because its interlocutors are two laboring men, *Village Politics* makes use of a palpably "colloquial" language, a style that was designed for and appealed to the work's semiliterate audience. Typical lower-class elisions, such as "had'st," "cou'd," and "ar'n't" abound, as does a measure of syntactic simplicity:

HANNAH MORE AND THE LITERATI

Although best known today for the wealth of popular literature, including *Village Politics* and the *Cheap Repository Tracts,* that she produced in the second half of her life, More spent the earlier part of her career writing for, and navigating among, Britain's literary elite. Her friends and associates at one point included Samuel Johnson (he called her the "most skilled versifacatrix in the English language"), Joshua Reynolds, Edmund Burke, Horace Walpole, and David Garrick, who, according to Anne Stott, thought her the "embodiment of all the nine Muses." She was more popular than both Jane Austen and Mary Wollstonecraft, two writers whose fame has eclipsed More's.

For one accustomed to writing poetry and plays for polite society, the shift to the more "vulgar" aesthetic of *Village Politics* was attended with nervousness and embarrassment. In a letter to Garrick's wife after completing the work, More writes, "I did not send it to any of my friends … I tell you fairly you won't like … for it is not written for the polished but the ignorant." Something of More's frustration is also evident in a letter to Walpole, in which she describes the perusal of cheap literature in preparation for more "vulgar" publications as "harassing to the nerves."

"'Tis all a lie, Tom. Sir John's Butler says, his master gets letters which say'tis all a lie.'Tis all murder, and nakedness, and hunger." The popular, "vulgar" language that predominates is often juxtaposed with what Kevin Gilmartin calls French "cosmopolitan abstractions," evident in Tom's claim that he is "for a *Constitution,* and *Organization,* and *Equalization.*" This rhetorical strategy makes the radical position seem like a foreign entity or "alien language" that has no place in the British provincial world that emerges from *Village Politics* with a more homely, appealing, and peaceful cast.

CRITICAL DISCUSSION

Although there is little "firsthand evidence" describing how the working classes received *Village Politics,* More's friends and other loyalist writers were enthusiastic. Elizabeth Montagu, for example, remarked in a letter to More that the work was "the most generally approved and universally useful of anything that has been published on the present exigency of the times." Fanny Burney, unaware of More's authorship, noted how the nation as a whole could be "reformed" by following the example of the work: "Let every one mend one, as Will Chip says, & then States, as well as families may be safely reformed." The bishop of London gave a copy to the attorney general and referred to the work as a "supremely excellent" dialogue sure to "immortalize" its author. The responses to, and wide distribution of, *Village Politics* indicated that, as Anne Stott suggests in *Hannah More: the First Victorian,* More had "resoundingly trumped most of her male fellow pamphleteers."

Wood engraving depicting Hannah More being introduced to society by the Duchess of Gloucester. © THE PRINT COLLECTOR/ALAMY.

women within the private sphere of the home." Those interested in print culture and mass literacy have long looked to Hannah More as a pivotal figure in the emergence of these phenomena. Richard Altick, for example, once remarked that "Tom Paine and Hannah More between them … opened the book to the common English reader."

BIBLIOGRAPHY

Sources

Altick, Richard. *The English Common Reader: A Social History of the Mass Reading Public, 1800–1900.* Columbus: Ohio State UP, 1957. Print.

Elliott, Dorice. "'The Care of the Poor Is Her Profession': Hannah More and Women's Philanthropic Work." *Nineteenth-Century Contexts* 19.2 (1995): 179–204. *University of Montana Library System.* Web. 17 July 2012.

Gilmartin, Kevin. *Writing against Revolution: Literary Conservatism in Britain, 1790–1832.* New York: Cambridge UP, 2007. Print.

More, Hannah. *Village Politics 1793; with the Shepherd of Salisbury Plain.* Revolution and Romanticism, 1789–1834. Ed. Jonathan Wordsworth. New York: Woodstock, 1995. Print.

Scheuermann, Mona. *In Praise of Poverty: Hannah More Counters Thomas Paine and the Radical Threat.* Lexington: UP of Kentucky, 2002. Print.

Stott, Anne. *Hannah More: the First Victorian.* New York: Oxford UP, 2003. Print.

Further Reading

Guest, Harriet. "The Dream of a Common Language: Hannah More and Mary Wollstonecraft." *Textual Practice* 9.2 (1995): 303–23. *University of Montana Library System.* Web. 19 July 2012.

Hole, Robert. *Pulpits, Politics, and Public Order in England, 1760–1832.* New York: Cambridge UP, 1989. Print.

Kowaleski-Wallace, Elizabeth. *Their Father's Daughters: Hannah More, Maria Edgeworth, and Patriarchal Complicity.* New York: Oxford UP, 1991. Print.

Krueger, Christine L. "Social Prophet: Hannah More as Political Writer." *The Reader's Repentance: Woman Preachers, Women Writers, and Nineteenth-Century Social Discourse.* Chicago: U of Chicago P, 1992. Print.

Pedersen, Susan. "Hannah More Meets Simple Simon: Tracts, Chapbooks, and Popular Culture in Late Eighteenth Century England." *Journal of British Studies* 25.1 (1986): 84–113. *JSTOR.* Web. 15 July 2012.

Philp, Mark. "Vulgar Conservatism, 1792–3." *English Historical Review* 110 (1995): 42–69. *JSTOR.* Web. 15 July 2012.

Sutherland, Kathryn. "Hannah More's Counter-Revolutionary Feminism." *Revolution in Writing: British Literary Responses to the French Revolution.* Ed. Kelvin Everest. Milton Keynes: Open UP, 1991. 53–61. Print.

More's exploration of the role of religious faith and morality in the enforcement of social order proved adaptable to later writers, even after the threat of revolution waned. Kevin Gilmartin asserts that in the early decades of the nineteenth century, for example, a similarly nuanced fusion of the moral, the religious, and the political is palpably evident in works attempting to quell popular unrest fomented by the Napoleonic Wars and by radical writers such as William Cobbett. More's revision of the work in 1819 to make it more germane to present crises is a testament to the work's portability, an aspect that has made it the source of an equally varied set of critical foci.

Village Politics has become a central text for critics with an interest in the oft-neglected conservative side of the Revolution Debates. Gilmartin, for example, enlists More in order to counteract attempts to "flatten out the range and complexity of conservative positions in an age of revolution." Critics interested in female literary voices also found Hannah More an exceptional object of study, a figure whose works, according to Dorice Elliott, "posed an inherent challenge" to ideologies that stressed "the confinement of

Alex Covalciuc

WOMAN FROM SHANGHAI

Tales of Survival from a Chinese Labor Camp

Xianhui Yang

OVERVIEW

Published in 2009, Xianhui Yang's *Woman from Shanghai: Tales of Survival from a Chinese Labor Camp* fictionalizes the true stories of survivors of Mao Zedong's labor camps. To compose the thirteen stories in the collection, Yang interviewed a group of survivors and fictionalized their firsthand experiences to protect the identities of those involved. The stories describe a period of Chinese history known as the antirightist movement, which lasted from 1957 to 1960, by detailing the forceful relocation of three thousand Chinese to the brutal, remote Jiabiangou labor camps in Gansu Province for the purpose of reeducation. The hard labor endured at these camps was so ruthless that only five hundred of the original three thousand workers survived. Taken as a whole, Yang's stories make a compelling argument against China's communist regime, focusing on the cruelty and punishment to which the workers at Jiabiangou were subjected.

Already a top writer in China, Yang gained international renown after *Woman from Shanghai* was translated into English. The short story collection garnered praise both for Yang's talents as a wordsmith and for his frank and honest portrayal of a part of history that political and social interests in China were trying to suppress. Critics have remarked primarily on Yang's unflinching depiction of humanity in the face of adversity. Written in simple, straightforward language that does little to disguise the atrocities of the camp, the book is noteworthy as an honest portrayal of the men and women who intellectually and politically opposed Chairman Mao and as a result suffered at his hands.

HISTORICAL AND LITERARY CONTEXT

Following decades of war, the communist People's Republic of China formed in 1949 under the leadership of Mao Zedong. Almost immediately, Mao made sweeping changes, including widespread land reforms and redistribution of wealth. Throughout the 1950s and 1960s, the Communist Party, under orders from Mao, forcefully took land from wealthy Chinese citizens and redistributed it to their poorer countrymen. Businessmen and intellectuals became targeted as potential traitors, and hundreds of thousands lost their lives in public executions or in labor camps.

As described in *Woman from Shanghai,* Mao's rise to power was marked by a climate of terror that quickly spread throughout China. Anyone who could be considered a threat to Mao's communist reign—from former government officials to successful capitalists and intellectuals—was in danger of being sent to one of Mao's reeducation camps. In 1956 the Hundred Flowers Campaign, based on Mao's ideas, encouraged self-expression in the Chinese community, including the airing of opinions about the communist government. By the next year, Mao had reversed his policies on free speech, ushering in a period of extreme censorship and the antirightist movement.

Following Mao's death in 1976 and the end of his Great Proletarian Cultural Revolution, which censored noncommunist literature, writers and artists felt greater freedom to publish literature that reflected the suffering under Mao's regime. Many novels, such as Yu Hua's *To Live* (1993) and *Chronicle of a Blood Merchant* (1995), use the revolution and the years of Mao's rule as a backdrop. The characters in these works depict the struggles of the common person in China during Mao's reign. Other writers chose not to fictionalize their accounts of the period, only to find their memoirs once again censored. Anchee Min's *Red Azalea* (1994) tells the story of Min's childhood and young adulthood spent in Mao's China and details the abuses of power that she witnessed growing up in the communist system. Perhaps fearing a ban like the one on Min's novels, Yang published his accounts of labor camps as fiction.

Although Yang's work has garnered much critical attention in his home country, *Woman from Shanghai* was his first work to be translated into English and to appeal to an international audience. The book's editors were painstaking in their efforts to ensure the novel's publication, particularly in China, which has a record of suppressing parts of its history that are deemed undesirable. Therefore, to avoid entanglements with the Department of Propaganda, Yang's editors decided to market the book as fiction—despite the fact that Yang's reputation is more closely linked to journalism than to novel writing.

THEMES AND STYLE

The central theme of *Woman from Shanghai* is survival under the most extreme circumstances. Yang

◆ *Key Facts*

Time Period:
Early 21st Century

Genre:
Short Story

Events:
Rise of Mao Zedong; antirightist movement; Chinese labor camps

Nationality:
Chinese

MAO'S CULTURAL REVOLUTION

From 1966 to 1976, Mao Zedong, leader of the People's Republic of China, enacted the Great Proletarian Cultural Revolution in order to strengthen communism in his country. Beginning in May 1966, he endeavored to remove from China anything related to capitalism, believing that its influence was dangerous to his communist vision. Books and art that were seen as promoting capitalism were destroyed, while government officials and businessmen accused of capitalist thought were ousted from their positions in society and often submitted to imprisonment, harassment, and torture. Even religion was not safe from Mao's attack: a propaganda poster featured one of Mao's men crushing a crucifix and a statue of Buddha, proclaiming that the new world was here.

By 1976 violent revolts against Mao's revolution had mostly died out, and in September the communist leader died, closing an era in China's history. Although communist China would persist after his death, the Cultural Revolution ended. Authors who had been afraid to publish during the revolution slowly began to write again, ushering in a new era of post-Maoist literature in China. Literary experimentation marked the 1980s and 1990s, although the Chinese government still kept close reign on the country's literature.

presents readers with bleak images, painting the reeducation camp in raw, severe detail. In the title story, Li Wenham tells of the starvation that the prisoners face. Their hunger drives them to eat anything, including "weeds, rats, or worms." Yet, in spite of the degradation they are faced with, they tell each other that "survival is what's most important." The notion of survival at all costs is amplified when one of the prisoner's wives arrives at the camp a week after her husband has died, and Li is unable to give her the body because it has been dug up, his clothes stolen and his corpse cannibalized by starving men. Prisoner Chao laments, "The human beings here have turned into animals. Even a tiger won't eat his own cub. Men eating other men—how can we call ourselves human beings?"

Although Yang maintains a journalistic distance from his subject, introducing each story with the necessary background information, he uses first-person narration to provide vivid details that make China's forgotten reeducation camps a reality in the minds of readers. Readers understand the dire situation of the men and women at Jiabiangou through the prisoners' personal accounts of "the roaring wind [that] lashed your body like ice water or cut your face like a knife." In one story, Gao Jiyi recounts his "violent vomiting" and "piercing stomach pain" after consuming a big meal of potatoes following two years of starvation. In another story, years after Jiabiangou has closed, a man tells Li Wenham, "time messes up people's memo-

ries"; therefore, Yang aims to keep fresh in the minds of readers the cruelties that the Chinese government would erase.

The tone of *Woman from Shanghai* is candid and austere. Yang unflinchingly describes the horrors faced by the prisoners at Jiabiangou despite the Chinese government's attempts to downplay the camps' atrocities by calling them places for "reeducation" or rehabilitation. Prisoners, sick and dying, are presented to readers in graphic detail reminiscent of depictions of the Holocaust. The workers are described as "thin wooden sticks" with "eyes sunk deep in their sockets"; they have gone so long without food that "their faces stuck like parched paper to their skulls." Such language confronts the reader with the terrors of the labor camps and makes the truth of the atrocities at Jiabiangou impossible to ignore.

CRITICAL DISCUSSION

After *Woman from Shanghai* was translated into English, Yang enjoyed broad international attention. Howard W. French in a 2009 review for the *New York Times* describes Yang's book as an "utterly convincing portrait of a society driven far off the rails" and praises the stories for their "moving" portrayals of the human experience. In addition, French draws comparisons between Yang and Colombian writer Gabriel García Márquez. Sarah Halzack, in a 2009 review for the *Washington Post,* calls Yang's book a collection of "stories of selflessness and fortitude" rendered in "wrenching detail." Halzack notes that although "the stories have been partly fictionalized … these tales remain intense and heartbreaking."

The rave reviews that Yang initially received indicate *Woman from Shanghai*'s legacy as a reminder of the atrocities committed by Mao's communist regime and the triumph of the human spirit in the face of such horrors. David Chau writes in a 2009 review for *Straight.com,* "Despite the inescapable suffering here, there are moments of humanity," such as in "The Love Story of Li Xiangnian," which describes a couple who seeks out each other after many years, or in "Jia Nong," about a group of women who bond over a fellow prisoner who gives birth to a son while in the camp. Such depictions of the endurance of the human spirit have secured Yang's popularity among readers, who return to his stories not for their historical merit but for their commentary on the human condition.

Despite widespread critical attention, *Woman from Shanghai* has been the subject of limited scholarship. Paul Foster in a 2010 review for *MCLC Resource Center* reads Yang's novel as a treatise on "human kindness" rather than as a "criticism of the deterministic politics of the Anti-Rightist movement." However, Foster notes, "kernels of criticism" are present in *Woman from Shanghai.* Like other reviewers, Foster finds "pebbles of humanity" that persist throughout the book despite the "viscerally disgusting acts of self-survival" and the

A Chinese Communist Party propaganda poster portraying chairman Mao Zedong. Xianhui Yang's *Woman from Shanghai* focuses on the suffering caused by political repression during Mao's regime. © PETER PROBST/ ALAMY.

"matter-of-fact tone." Joel Martinsen's appraisal, published in *Danwei* in 2009, is similar to Foster's, though Martinsen questions the marketing of the book to English audiences, particularly the use of a red-lipped "woman in a *qipao*," or traditional dress, on the cover of the hardcover edition. The woman, whose face cannot be clearly seen, does not seem to reflect the novel's intense subject matter and to Martinsen is a marketing ploy to attract American readers interested in women's memoirs.

BIBLIOGRAPHY

Sources

Chau, David. "*Woman from Shanghai*'s Stories Survey Mao's Prison System." Rev. of *Woman from Shanghai,* by Xianhui Yang. *Straight.com.* Vancouver Free. 27 Aug. 2009. Web. 4 Sept. 2012.

Foster, Paul. Rev. of *Woman from Shanghai,* by Xianhui Yang. *MCLC Resource Center.* Ohio State U. Jan. 2010. Web. 4 Sept. 2012.

French, Howard W. "Survivors' Stories from China." Rev. of *Woman from Shanghai,* by Xianhui Yang. *New York Times* 24 Aug. 2009. Web. 4 Sept. 2012.

Halzack, Sarah. Rev. of *Woman from Shanghai,* by Xianhui Yang. *Washington Post.* 23 Aug. 2009. Web. 4 Sept. 2012.

Martinsen, Joel. "*Woman from Shanghai* and the Marketing of Chinese Literature in Translation." *Danwei* 18 Sept. 2009. Web. 4 Sept. 2012.

Yang, Xianhui. *The Woman from Shanghai: Tales of Survival from a Chinese Labor Camp.* Trans. Wen Huang. New York: Pantheon, 2009.

Further Reading

Lau, Joseph S. M., and Howard Goldblatt. *The Columbia Anthology of Modern Chinese Literature.* New York: Columbia U P, 1995. Print.

Min, Anchee. *Red Azalea.* New York: Pantheon, 1994. Print.

Veg, Sebastian. "The Limits of Representation: Wang Bing's Labour Camp Films." *Journal of Chinese Cinemas* 6.2 (2012): 173–87. Print.

Yu, Hua. *Chronicle of a Blood Merchant.* Trans. Andrew F. Jones. New York: Pantheon, 2003. Print.

———. *To Live: A Novel.* Trans. Michael Berry. New York: Anchor, 2003. Print.

Rebecca Rustin

SUBJECT INDEX

Bold volume and page numbers (e.g., **3:269–272**) refer to the main entry on the subject. Page numbers in italics refer to photographs and illustrations.

A

Aaron, Daniel, **1:**199

Abacha, Sani, **2:**102

Abbey, Edward, **1:**285–287, *287*

Abbott's Monthly Review, **2:**29

The ABC of Influence: Ezra Pound and the Remaking of American Poetic Tradition (Beach), **2:**248

Abd El-Fattah, Alaa, **2:**67

Abdel-Latif, Omayma, **2:**67–68

Abolitionist movement

    American Slavery As It Is (Weld), **1:**154–156, *156*

    "An Address to the Slaves of the United States," **1:**3–6, *4*

    Appeal, in Four Articles (Walker), **2:**85–87, *87*

    Blake, or The Huts of America (Delany), **2:**92–94, *94*

    Declaration of Sentiments (Stanton), **3:**160, 162

    The Impending Crisis of the South (Helper), **3:**288–290, *290*

    "Liberty or Death" (Dessalines and Boisrond-Tonnerre), **1:**30–33, *32*

    members of, **2:**124

    "The Negro's Complaint" (Cowper), **1:**37–40, *39*

    "Paul Revere's Ride" (Longfellow), **3:**236–240, *240*

    "A Plea for Captain John Brown" (Thoreau), **2:**123–126, *125*

    Uncle Tom's Cabin (Stowe), **3:**169–172, *171*

    See also Slave rebellions; Slavery

Aborigines' Rights Protection Society (ARPS), **2:**144, 145

Abrahams, Peter, **2:**17, 36

Abrash, Merritt, **1:**298

Absalom and Achitophe (Dryden), **2:**296

Absurdist literature, **3:**194, 336, 337, 338, 340

Abu Ghraib prison, **1:**131–132

Abu-Jamal, **3:**247

Academic Questions (journal), **1:**335

Academic style

    Manufacturing Consent (Herman and Chomsky), **1:**324

    Pale Fire (Nabokov), **1:**177, 178

    Three Guineas (Woolf), **2:**69, 70

Ação Libertadora Nacional (ALN), **1:**283, 284

An Account, Much Abbreviated, of the Destruction of the Indies (Brevísima relación de la destrucción de las Indias) (Las Casas), **1:**95–98, *97*

Acharnians (Aristophanes), **2:**108

Achebe, Chinnua

    Anthills of the Savannah, **3:**299

    Chi in Igbo Cosmology, **1:**89

    The Role of the Writer in the New Nation, **1:**89

    Things Fall Apart, **1:**88–91, *90,* **2:**59, **3:**298

Achilles, **2:**134, **3:**186

Acropolis, **1:**45

ACS (American Colonization Society), **2:**85

Act of Succession (England, 1534), **3:**134, 334

The Actes and Deidis of the Illustre and Valyeant Campioun Schir William Wallace (Henry the Minstrel), **3:**185–188, *187*

Acting the Right Part: Political Theater and Popular Drama in Contemporary China (Chen), **3:**260

Acton, Harold, **3:**243

Acts and Monuments (Foxe), **1:**77

Acts of Union (Great Britain, 1800), **1:**17, 268, 330

Ad status sermons, **1:**10–12, *12*

Adam and Eve, **3:**232–235, *234,* 317

Adam Mickiewicz in World Literature (Lednicki), **3:**223

Adams, Abigail, **3:**160

Adams, Gerry, **1:**268, 270

Adams, Henry, **3:**220

Adams, Hussein M., **1:**370

Adams, John

    The Cantos (Pound), **2:**247, 248

    Declaration of Independence, **2:**162

    Declaration of Sentiments (Stanton), **3:**160

    federalism, **3:**190, 218

    The Group (Warren), **3:**285, 286

Adams, Lorraine, **3:**111

Adams, Robert M., **3:**47

The Adams Cantos (Pound), **2:**248

F

K

Political literature

An Address to the People on the Death of the Princess Charlotte ess Charlotte (Shelley), **2:**81–84, *83*

"An Address to the Slaves of the United States" (Garnet), **1:**5

Animal Farm (Orwell), **2:**241

The Cantos (Pound), **2:**247–249, *249*

Common Sense (Paine), **2:**159–161, *161*

In the Country of Men (Matar), **3:**109–111, *110*

Declaration of Independence (U.S), 2:162–165, *164*

The Dispossessed (Le Guin), **3:**72

"El matadero" (Echevarría), **2:**253–256, *255*

The Federalist (Hamilton, Madison and Jay), **2:**178–180, *180*

The Group (Warren), **3:**285–287, *287*

How to Win (Willard), **1:**64

In Salvador, Death (Neruda), **1:**116–118, *118*

The Influence of Sea Power upon History: 1660–1783 1783 (Mahan), **1:**236

"Johannesburg Mines" (Hughes), **2:**329–332, *331*

John Hopkins's Notions of Political Economy (Marcet), **1:**67–70, *69*

"Liberty or Death" (Dessalines and Boisrond-Tonnerre), **1:**35

The Manchurian Candidate (Condon), **3:**28–30, *30*

"Mario and the Magician" (Mann), **3:**31–34, *33*

"The New Year's Sacrifice" (Lu Xun), **2:**45

"The Paranoid Style in American Politics" (Hofstadter), **1:**333–336, *335*

"Politics and the English Language" (Orwell), **1:**337–339, *339*

The Port Huron Statement (Hayden), **1:**288–290, *290*

The Prince (Machiavelli), **1:**340–343, *342*

The Public and Its Problems (Dewey), **1:**351–354, *353*

Public Opinion (Lippman), **1:**355–358, *357*

The Ragged-Trousered Philanthropists (Tressell), **2:**365–368, *368*

The Secret Agent (Conrad), **1:**297–298

testimonios, **1:**112

Utopia (More), **3:**133–135, *135*

Venice Preserv'd, or, a Plot Discovered (Otway), **2:**296–299, *298*

We (Zamyatin), **3:**136–139, *138*

See also Government corruption; Government role

Political Parties in the Province of New York from 1766–75 (Becker), **1:**213

Political Science Fiction (Hassler and Wilcox), **3:**129

The Political Showman-At Home! (Hone and Cruikshank), **1:**190

Politics (Aristotle), **3:**133

"Politics and the English Language" (Orwell), **1:337–339,** *339*

The Politics of Vision (Favretti), **3:**279

Pollution, **1:**137–140, *139*

Polybius, **1:**46

Polygamy, **3:**352–355, *353*

Pompey, **1:**221

Ponca tribe, **3:**166, 167

Ponce de León, Juan, **2:**188

Ponet, John, **3:**333

Pontin, Jason, **1:**147

Poor Law Amendment Act (England, 1834), **3:**145–147, 163–165, *165*

Poor Laws and Paupers Illustrated (Martineau), **3:**145, **163–165,** *165*

Poor Old Woman (Sean Bhean Bhocht), **3:**197

Pope, Alexander, **1:**178, **3:**89, 153

Popery, **1:**14, **2:**160

Popish Plot (1678), **1:**77, **2:**160, 296, 297

Popper, Karl, **1:**178

Poppy imagery, **1:**23, 24

Popular Movement for the Liberation of Angola (MPLA), **2:**115–118

Popular novels, **2:**320

Popular print culture, **1:**190

Popular Propaganda: Art and Culture in Revolutionary China (Mittler), **1:**81

Population growth, **1:**285–287, **3:**163

Population Registration Act (South Africa, 1950), **2:**36, 105, 112

Populism, **2:**342, **3:**179–182, *181*

Porgy (Heyward), **2:**264

Porgy and Bess (opera), **2:**263–265, *265*

The Port Huron Statement (Hayden), **1:288–290,** *290*

The Portable Bunyan: A Transnational History of The, **1:**79

Porter, Jeffrey L., **3:**266

Portrait of Alexander Hamilton (Trumbull), **2:** *180*

Portrait of Pope Gregory XV (Reni), **1:** *322*

Portrait of Thomas Paine (Easton), **2:** *161*

Portuguese colonialism, **1:**249–251, *251,* **2:**115

Positions: East Asia Cultures Critique (journal), **2:**315

The Positive Hero in Russian Literature (Mathewson), **2:**344

Posner, Richard, **1:**136

Post-Bellum, Pre-Harlem (Mitchell), **2:**56

Post-Express (newspaper), **2:**55

Post-Revolutionary War period, **1:**57–60, *60,* 61–63, *63*

Post-World War II era

Animal Farm (Orwell), **2:**239–242, *241*

The Cantos (Pound), **2:**248

The Feminine Mystique (Friedan), **1:**102–104, *104*

"Iron Curtain" *Speech* (Churchill), **1:**26–29, *28*

Japanese, **2:**155–158, *157*

"National Song" (Petőfi), **2:**206

Propaganda (Ellul), **1:**347–348

See also Cold War

Postbellum period, **1:**64

Postcolonial Contraventions: Cultural Readings of Race, Imperialism, and Transnationalism (Chrisman), **1:**252

Postcolonialism

"Bangladesh I, II and III" (Faiz), **2:**7–9, *9*

Sweet and Sour Milk (Farah), **2:**292–295, *293*

Things Fall Apart (Achebe), **1:**88–91, *90*

The Japan That Can Say No (Ishihara and Morita), **3:**291

Manufacturing Consent (Herman and Chomsky), **1:**323

market deregulation, **3:**273

Nicaraguan Revolution, **2:**98

presidency, **3:**93

"Throw Your Bodies upon the Gears" speech (Savio), **1:**50

The Real Facts of Life (Jackson), **2:**20

Real Folks: Race and Genre in the Great Depression (Retman), **3:**65

The Real World (television series), **3:**3

Realism

"Life in the Iron-Mills" (Davis), **2:**335–337, *336*

Mother (Gorky), **2:**342–345

revolutionary, **3:**349

socialist, **3:**137

See also Social realism

Realism and Allegory in the Early Fiction of Mao Tun (Chen), **2:**290

Reality television, **3:**3, 101

The Rebel Passion (Burdekin), **3:**130

The Reception of Silent Spring (Waddell), **1:**139

Recinos, Adrian, **1:**203

Recio, Leticia Álvarez, **1:**163

Reconstruction (1865–1877), **2:**93, 250–252, *252*

Red Army Faction (Baader-Meinhof gang), **1:**279–281, *281, 282*

Red Azalea (Min), **3:**365

Red Cavalry: A Critical Companion (Rougle), **3:**347

Red Cavalry (Babel), **3:** *346*, **346–348**

Red classics, **3:**349

Red Crag (Lo and Yang), **3:**349–351, *351*

The Red Detachment of Women (ballet), **3:**258, *260*

The Red Man's Greeting. See The Red Man's Rebuke (Pokagon)

The Red Man's Rebuke (Pokagon), **2:127–129**, *129*

Red Scare. *See* McCarthyism

Redburn (Melville), **3:**176

Redemption narratives, **1:**85

The Reduction of Ireland (Borlase), **1:**239

Reed, David, **2:** *168*

Reed, Harry, **1:**6

Reed, Ishmael, **3:**170

Reed, Kenneth T., **2:**264

Reed, T. V., **1:**171

Reeducation camps, **3:**365–367, *367*

Reference Guide to American Literature, **1:**104

Reflections on the Revolution in France (Burke), **2:273–276**, *275*

Reflections on Violence (Sorel), **2:**281

Reformation, **1:**268, **2:**174–177, *176*, 243, **3:**225–227

Reforming Empire: Protestant Colonialism and Conscience in British Literature (Hodgkins), **1:**36

Regarding Our America (Respeto a Nuestra América) (Martí), **3:**295

Rege, Josna, **2:**182

Regency Crisis (1788), **2:**274

A Regency Prophecy and the End of Anna Barbauld's Career (Keach), **3:**280

Reiss, Rom, **1:**298

Reiss, Winold, **1:** *305*

Relaciones, **2:**188

Religious literature

"An Address to the Slaves of the United States" (Garnet), **1:**5

An Almond for a Parrat (Nashe), **1:**7–9, *9*

"Art or Propaganda?" (Locke), **1:**304

A Canticle for Leibowitz (Miller), **3:**67–69, *69*

Charlotte Temple (Rowson), **1:**62

Common Sense (Paine), **2:**160

Crusade Sermons (James of Vitry), **1:**10–12, *12*

General Plan of the Constitution of a Protestant Congregation or Society for Propagating Christian Knowledge (Bray), **1:**314–316, *316*

The Handmaid's Tale (Atwood), **3:**93–96, *95*

The Image, the Icon, and the Covenant (Khalifeh), **2:**25, 26

King John (Bale), **3:**225–227, *227*

"Liberty or Death" (Dessalines and Boisrond-Tonnerre), **1:**35

Marprelate controversy, **1:**13–16

Mein Kampf (Hitler), **2:**196

Paradise Lost (Milton), **3:**232–235, *234*

The Pilgrim's Progress from This World to That Which Is to Come (Bunyan), **1:**77–79, *79*

The Purgatory of Suicides (Cooper), **2:**361–364, *363*

"The War Prayer" (Twain), **2:**230–233, *232*

See also Biblical references; Christianity

Relyea, Sarah, **2:**52

Reminiscences of the Cuban Revolutionary War (Guevara), **2:**99

A Remonstrance of Grievances, **1:**239

Renaissance, **1:**173–176, **3:**133, 317

The Renaissance Englishwoman in Print: Counterbalancing the Canon (Jones), **3:**317

Renaissance Self-Fashioning: From More to Shakespeare (Greenblatt), **2:**177

Reni, Guido, **1:** *322*

Rennick, Andrew, **2:**322

The Reply of the Illustrious Cardinal Perron (Cary), **2:**76

Replye (Cartwright), **1:**13

Report of the Niger Valley Exploring Party: A Treaty Made, Granted, and Assigned at Abbeokuta, Nigeria (Delany), **2:**93

Reportage literature, **2:**290

Representations (journal), **2:**190

Reproduction, **3:**97, 98

Republic (Plato), **3:**133

Republic of Ireland, **1:**17, 18

Republic Revolution (China, 1911), **2:**44

Republicanism, **2:**235, 250

Rereading Aristotle's Rhetoric (Gross and Walzer), **1:**361

Research in African Literatures (journal), **2:**317–318, **3:**13

Reservation Blues (Alexie), **2:**34

Resistance movements

"An Address to the Slaves of the United States" (Garnet), **1:**4, 5

French, **3:**193–195, *195*

The Moon Is Down (Steinbeck), **2:**199–202, *201*

nonviolent, **1:**286

Selected Works (Ho Chi Minh), **2:**211–213, *213*

W

Author Index

The author index includes author names represented in *The Literature of Propaganda*. Numbers in **Bold** indicate volume, with page numbers following after colons.

TITLE INDEX

The title index includes works that are represented in *The Literature of Propaganda*. Numbers in **Bold** indicate volume, with page numbers following after colons.